LUDWIG DERR'S MILL—1772.

ANNALS
of
BUFFALO VALLEY
PENNSYLVANIA

1755-1855

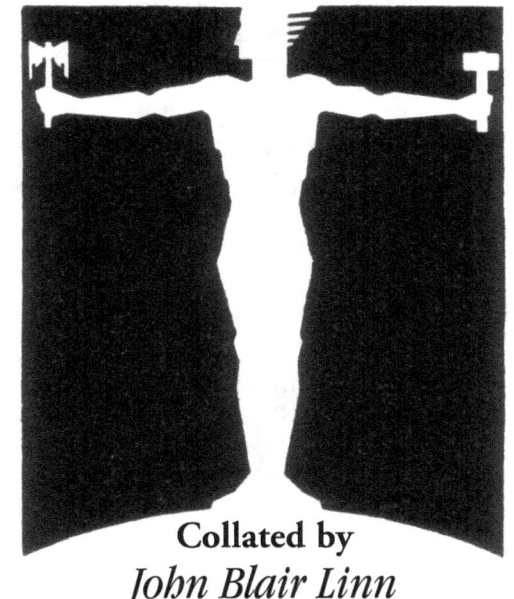

Collated by
John Blair Linn

HERITAGE BOOKS
2008

HERITAGE BOOKS
AN IMPRINT OF HERITAGE BOOKS, INC.

Books, CDs, and more—Worldwide

For our listing of thousands of titles see our website
at
www.HeritageBooks.com

A Facsimile Reprint
Published 2008 by
HERITAGE BOOKS, INC.
Publishing Division
100 Railroad Ave. #104
Westminster, Maryland 21157

Entered according to act of Congress, in the year 1877, by
John Blair Linn,
In the office of the Librarian of Congress, at Washington, D.C.

Originally published:
Lane S. Hart, Printer and Binder
Harrisburg, Pennsylvania
1877

— Publisher's Notice —
In reprints such as this, it is often not possible to remove blemishes from the original. We feel the contents of this book warrant its reissue despite these blemishes and hope you will agree and read it with pleasure.

International Standard Book Numbers
Paperbound: 978-1-55613-206-3
Clothbound: 978-0-7884-7592-4

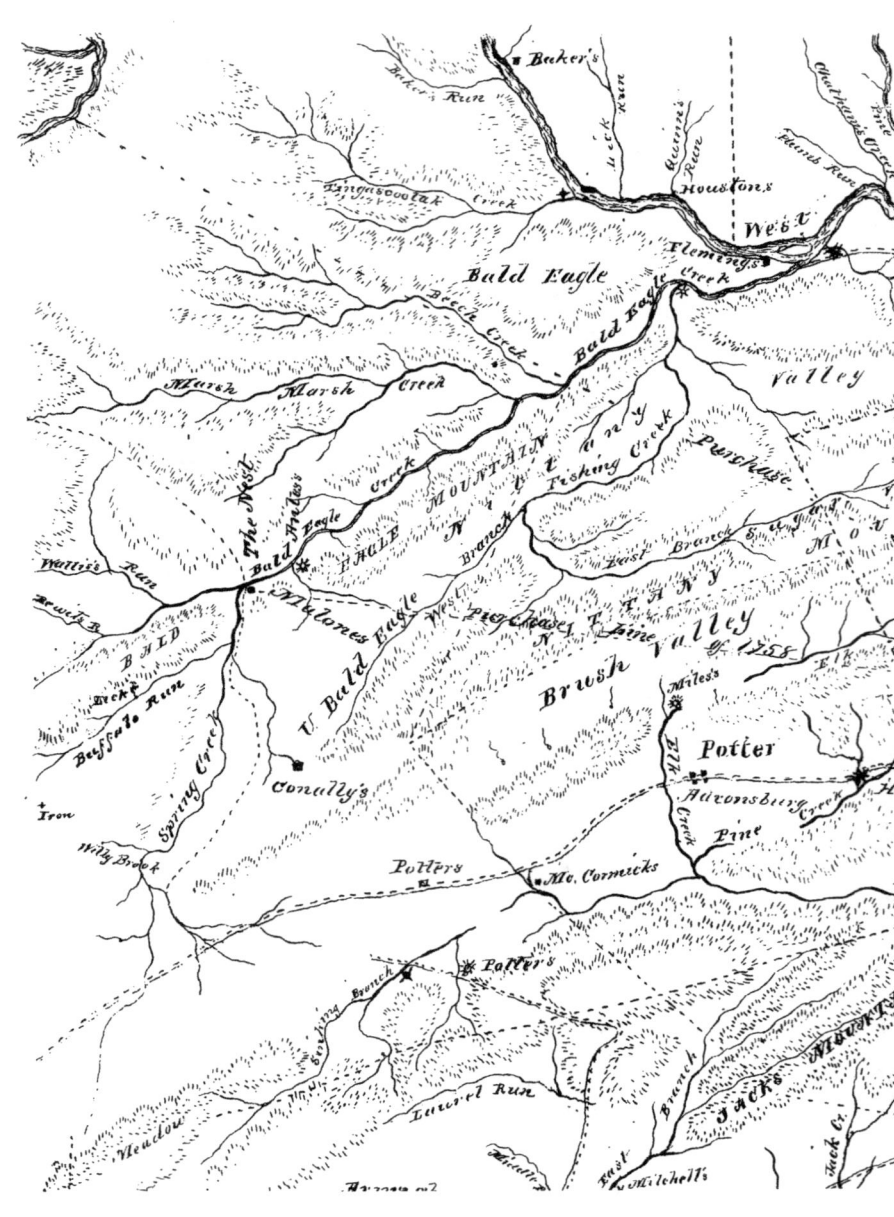

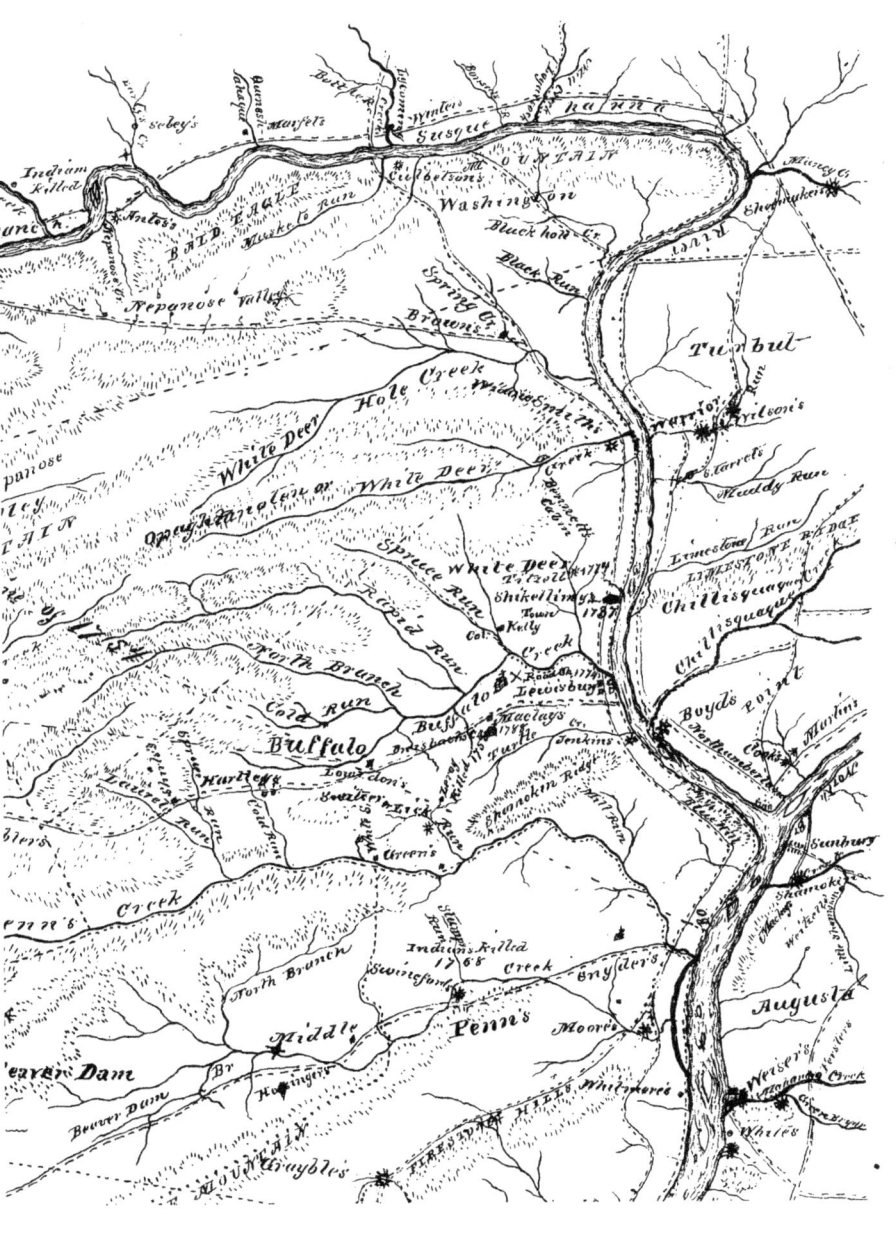

- Notice -

The foxing, or discoloration with age, characteristic of old books, sometimes shows through to some extent in reprints such as this, especially when the foxing is very severe in the original book. We feel that the contents of this book warrant its reissue despite these blemishes, and hope you will agree and read it with pleasure.

INTRODUCTION.

INDIAN TRIBES—SHIKELLIMY—LOGAN—ABORIGINES OF THE VALLEY, THE
VILLAGES AND PATHS—PURCHASE OF 1754—PENN'S CREEK MASSACRE
SOURCES OF EMIGRATION TO THE VALLEY—PURCHASE OF 1758.

N the year 1868, when I proposed to myself the labor collating these Annals, I supposed their commencement would, in point of time, be with the date of the purchase made at Fort Stanwix, November 5, 1768. I thought too, the first sounds breaking the stillness of the Valley were the cheerful ring of the surveyor's axe, and the merry shouts of advancing settlers, let loose upon the "New Purchase," by the land office advertisement of February 23, 1769. But when I came to trace the southern line of that purchase, I found it skirting the deserted clearings and blackened hearth-stones of earlier white settlers, of whose sad fate I had never heard.

These annals, therefore, would not be complete, without an account of the Penn's Creek massacre of 1755, although it makes the history of the early settlement of Buffalo Valley unpleasantly like that of nearly all others in America, in the injustice of the settlers toward the Indians, and the bloody retribution that followed; and I have further concluded to add all the reliable information I could obtain of the Valley prior to its settlement by the whites.

The localities of the Indian tribes prior to William Penn's arrival (October 24, 1682,) have been identified as follows: "The Five Nations," as they were then called, (after 1714, "The Six Nations," occupied the territory north of the sources of the Susquehanna and Delaware rivers. After the partial settlement of the country, these confederate tribes, were known among themselves by the name *Aquanoschioni*, united people; by the English they were called the Six Nations; by the French, the Northern Iroquois; settlers called them sometimes Mingoes and Maquais. This will explain the reason Shikellimy, the first noted inhabitant of Buffalo Valley, is called, in letters from Conrad Weiser and others, indifferently, an Iroquois chief, a Mingo chief, and a chief of the Six Nations.

South of the mouth of the Hudson lived the Delewares; otherwise called Lenni-Lenape, or original people. They occupied the country to the Potomac, and were divided into three tribes: 1, the Turkeys; 2, the Turtles; 3, the Wolfs or Muncys. The Muncys occupied Pennsylvania, from the Kittatinny or Blue mountains to the source of the Susquehanna, and were the most active and warlike. At the time of Penn's arrival, the Five Nations had brought under their dominion the whole country of the Delawares. About the year 1700, the Shawanese, who came originally from Florida and Georgia, by permission of Penn's government, settled in Cumberland valley, having their council fire near Carlisle, and extending northerly into what is now the territory of Snyder county, and as far as Chillisquaque creek, subject, of course, to the authority of the Five Nations.

In 1714, the Five Nations became the Six Nations, by adopting the Tuscarora tribe which had been expelled from North Carolina and Virginia; and subsequently Shikellimy, who was a chief of the Oneida tribe, was sent down upon the Susquehanna as the governing chief of the conquered Delawares and their allies, the Shawanese. In a letter of instruction to Smith and Pettys, written in 1728, Governor Patrick Gordon speaks of Shikellimy as being placed over the Shawanese; adding "he is a good man, and I hope will give a good account of them." Shikellimy fixed his residence at the old Muncy town, in Buffalo Valley, and here he was visited by the first white man who, as far as we know, ever set foot within it.

(1737.) 27th February, 1737, Conrad Weiser records in his journal: "Left home for Onondaga. 1st March, left Tolheo,[1] which is the last place in the inhabited part of Pennsylvania. On the 4th we reached Shamokin[2] but did not find a living soul at home who could assist us in crossing the Susquehanna river. On the 5th we lay still;

[1] At the gap in the Blue mountains, where the Big Swatara breaks through into Lebanon county. [2] Now Sunbury.

we had now made about eighty miles. 6th, we observed a smoke on the other side of the river, and an Indian trader came over and took us across. We again lay still to-day. On the 7th we started along one branch of the river, going to the north-west. An old Shawano, by name Jenoniawana, took us in his canoe across the creek at Zilly Squachne.[1] On the 8th we reached the village where Shikelimo lives, who was appointed to be my companion and guide on the journey. He was, however, far from home on a hunt. Weather became bad and the waters high, and no Indian could be induced to seek Shikelimo until the 12th, when two young Indians agreed to go out in search of him. On the 16th, they returned with word that Shikelimo would be back next day, which so happened. The Indians were out of provisions at this place. I saw a new blanket given for about one third of a bushel of Indian corn."

The site of this village is, beyond doubt, on the farm of Hon. George F. Miller, at the mouth of Sinking run, or Shikellimy's run, as it was called formerly, at the old ferry, one half mile below Milton, on the Union county side. It is a beautiful spot for a village; protected on the north by a range of hills, with the river much narrowed in front, giving easy access to the Northumberland side.

When the land office was open for "the new purchase," on the 3d of April, 1769, there were very many applications made for this location. In all of them it is called either old Muncy town, Shikellimy's town, or Shikellimy's old town. It is referred to as a locality in hundreds of applications for land in the Valley. I will only quote one: "Samuel Huling applies for three hundred acres on the West Branch of the Susquehanna, about one mile above Shikellimy's old town, including a small run that empties into the river opposite an island." The Huling location was secured by John Fisher, one of the oldest of our settlers, and West Milton is now built upon it. Shikellimy's town was on the "Joseph Hutchinson" and "Michael Weyland," warrantee tracts, from whom the title can be readily traced to the present owner. Colonel James Moore, who lived there many years, told me that thousands of Indian darts were plowed up there, and once, when blasting at the quarry, they uncovered a grave hollowed in the solid rock, in which they found the skeleton of an Indian.

Shikellimy, sometime after Weiser's visit, removed to Shamokin,

[1] Chillisquaque.

now Sunbury, as a more convenient point for intercourse with the Proprietary Governors. On the 9th of October, 1747, Conrad Weiser says he was at Shamokin, and that "Shikellimy was very sick with fever. He was hardly able to stretch forth his hand. His wife, three sons, one daughter, and two or three grandchildren were all bad with the fever. There were three buried out of the family a few days before, one of whom was Cajadis, who had been married to his daughter above fifteen years, and was reckoned the best hunter among all the Indians." He recovered, however, from this sickness, and, in March, 1748, we find him at Weiser's, in Tulpehocken, with his eldest son, Tagheneghdourus. He died in April 1749, at Sunbury, and the latter succeeded him as chief and representative of the Six Nations.[1]

Loskiel thus notices this celebrated inhabitant of our Valley: "Being the first magistrate and head chief of all the Iroquois living on the banks of the Susquehanna as far as Onondaga, [now Syracuse, New York,] he thought it incumbent upon him to be very circumspect in his dealings with the white people. He mistrusted the brethren [Moravians] at first, but upon discovering their sincerity, became their firm and real friend. Being much engaged in political affairs, he had learned the art of concealing his sentiments; and, therefore, never contradicted those who endeavored to prejudice his mind against the missionaries, though he always suspected their motives. In the last years of his life he became less reserved, and received those brethren that came to Shamokin into his house. He assisted them in building and defended them against the insults of drunken Indians, being himself never addicted to drinking, because, as he expressed it, he never wished to make a fool of himself. He had built his house upon pillars for safety, in which he always shut himself up when any drunken frolic was going on in the village. In this house, Bishop Johannes Von Watteville, and his company, visited and preached the Gospel to him. It was then the Lord opened his heart. He listened with great attention, and at last, with tears, respected the doctrine of a crucified Jesus, and received it with faith. During his visit to Bethlehem, a remarkable change took place in his heart, which he could not conceal. He found comfort, peace, and joy by faith in his Redeemer, and the brethren considered him a candidate for baptism. But hearing that he had been already baptized by a Roman Catholic priest

[1] As such, signing the deed for the Indian purchase of 22d August, 1749.

in Canada, they only endeavored to impress his mind with a proper idea of the sacramental ordinance, upon which he destroyed a small idol which he wore about his neck. After his return to Shamokin, the grace of God bestowed upon him was truly manifest. In this state of mind, he was taken ill, was attended by brother David Zeisberger, and in his presence fell asleep, happy in the Lord, in full assurance of obtaining eternal life through the merits of Jesus Christ."

The most celebrated of his sons was Logan, the Mingo chief. By the journal of Mack and Grube, Moravian missionaries, it appears he lived at the mouth of the Chillisquaque creek, August 26, 1753. In 1765 he lived in Raccoon valley, at the foot of the Tuscarora mountain. Loudon, in his "collections," says he could speak tolerable English, was a remarkably tall man—over six feet high— and well proportioned; of brave, open, and manly countenance, as straight as an arrow, and apparently afraid of no one. In 1768 and 1769 he resided near Reedsville, in Mifflin county, and has given his name to the spring near that place, to Logan's branch of Spring creek, in Centre county, Logan's path, &c. See a notice of an interview with him in the memoir of Samuel Maclay, postea, year 1811. Heckewelder says he was introduced to Logan in 1772. "I thought him a man of superior talents. He then intended settling on the Ohio, below Big Beaver. In April, 1773, I called at his settlement, and was received with great civility." In 1774 occurred Lord Dunmore's expedition against the Shawanese towns, now Point Pleasant, West Virginia, which was the occasion of Logan's celebrated speech, commencing "I appeal to any white man to say if he ever entered Logan's cabin hungry, and he gave him not meat;" which will go down to all time, whether properly or not, as a splendid outburst of Indian eloquence.

Heckewelder says he afterwards became addicted to drinking, and was murdered, between Detroit and his own home, in October, 1781, and he was shown the place. "He was, at the time, sitting with his blanket over his head, before a camp-fire, his elbows resting on his knees, when an Indian, who had taken some offense, stole behind him, and buried his tomahawk in his brains." Howe's Ohio Collections, page 409, who quotes as his authority Good Hunter, an aged Mingo chief.

Aborigines of the Valley.

Of the Indians who occupied Buffalo Valley, nothing can be positively ascertained, except that they belonged to the Muncy-Minsi (or Wolf) tribe of the Lenni-Lenape, or original people. The Valley was more a hunting ground than a residence. Some remains have been found at prominent points along the river, as, for instance, at Colonel Slifer's house, on the river, above the mouth of Buffalo creek. some skeletons, evidently of one family only, were uncovered. The large mounds were on the other side of the river, on Joseph Nesbit's place; and the principal towns or villages, Chillisquaque, at the mouth of that creek, south side, and Shamokin, on the island and mainland, where Sunbury now stands.

In quite a number of applications of 1769 mention is, however, made of an old Indian town and fort, on the Dietrick Rees tract, just above New Columbia; an Indian improvement at Laird Howard's spring, in Kelly; one on the Craig tract, on the river, near Winfield; one below that yet, on the Andrew Culbertson, afterwards known as the Merrill place; on the "Richard Edward's," now Stoltzfus' place, in Kelly, was an Indian field and plum orchard; and there was an improvement at Strohecker's landing, south of Lewisburg.

Indian Paths.

The great Indian path through the Valley left the river at the first ravine, a few rods below the Northumberland bridge, passed up it, following the main road, as it now is, for a few miles, then turning towards the river, it came down the hill upon the Merrill place; thence followed the bank of the river, up through the old Macpherson place, to Lees, Winfield; thence passing up the present road, it crossed directly through the fields from the Gundy road to Fourth street, Lewisburg; thence to Buffalo creek, where the iron bridge now is, a very old fording place; thence it curved towards the river, passed up through Shikellimy's town, and along the river road, around the rocks, into White Deer Hole valley. A. H. McHenry, the noted surveyor, told me it could be distinctly traced by the calls of surveys; but as all traces of it are now obliterated within the Valley, further identification is unnecessary.

The paths through the Valley westward are obliterated, historically and topographically, except the small portion of the one passing into Brush valley, which may still be traced in the woods west of Solomon Heberling's.

Early Notices of Names of Creeks, &c.

Buffalo creek is mentioned by its name in the Indian deed of October 23, 1758. Penn's is called John Penn's creek in the same deed. In the deed of July 6, 1754, it is called Kaarondinhah. It was called by the settlers, between 1754 and 1769, and marked on Scull's map of 1759, Big Mahany, and is so recited in deeds as late as 1772. Thus the "Henry Christ" warrantee, (now in Monroe township, Snyder county,) afterwards Herbster's place, is described as in "Buffalo township, formerly of the name of Shamokin, and bounded by Big Mahany creek, lands of George Gabriel, Abraham Herr, and others."—Deed of Herbster to George Haines, 26th May, 1772. In a deed from John Turner to John Harris, June, 1755, for an improvement, (now in Hartley township, owned by R. V. B. Lincoln, Esquire,) the creek is called "Mahanoy."

Turtle creek was so called before 1769, and in the latter year I found the stream below it, traversing Dry valley, called Lee's run, after John Lee, the first settler of the site of Winfield.

Switzer run had an *alias* in 1769—Lick run, probably after Peter Lick, who was carried off by the Indians in 1755; but the interest felt in the mournful tragedy hereafter related substituted the name of Switzer for the name given it by the surveyors in 1769.

White Deer creek is marked on Scull's map of 1759 with the Indian name of Opaghtanoten, or White Flint creek. The run entering the river on the late Samuel Henderson's place, in White Deer township, was called by William Blythe, the first settler there, Red-Bank run; and the bottom above, between it and White Deer creek, had, before 1769, the name Turkey bottom, from the immense number of wild turkeys haunting it.

Dog run came in by the old Indian fort, which stood near New Columbia. Beaver run, in Buffalo township, had that name before 1769, from a large beaver dam near its mouth. Wilson's run, entering at Lewisburg, had the name of Limestone run. White Springs (at Barber's, in Limestone township) is so called in the return of a survey made by Colonel John Armstrong, in 1755. Laurel run had that name prior to 1773; and Spruce run is so called on Colonel Kelly's application for land upon it, dated 11th June, 1769.

The hills bounding the Valley on the south were called Shamokin, from the earliest times I find them mentioned; of late years they have had the name of Chestnut Ridge. Nittany mountain had its name as early as 1768. Buffalo and White Deer mountains took their names from the respective creeks. Jack's mountain, extending from Centreville, Snyder county, to Scottsville, Huntingdon county, was so called from Jack Armstrong, an Indian trader, who was murdered in the narrows, in 1744, near Mt. Union. Pennsylvania Archives, second volume, 136.

(1755.) *The Mahany or Penn's Creek Massacre.*

Cumberland county was erected out of Lancaster, on the 27th of January, 1750, and was to embrace all the lands within the Province of Pennsylvania westward of the Susquehanna and north and westward of York county. The country was then purchased from the Indians as far north as the present southern line of Perry county. Nevertheless, settlers pushed on north of the boundary—the Kittatinny or Blue mountains. As early as 1753, at a council held at Carlisle, the Indians protested against the occupation of the country north of the line by the white settlers, and "wished the people called back from the 'Juniata' lands until matters were settled between them and the French, lest damage should be done, and then the English would think ill of them." Then came the treaty of the 6th of July, 1754, at Albany, between the chiefs of the Mohawks, Oneidas, Onondagos, Cayugas, Senecas, and Tuscaroras, known as the Six Nations, and Thomas and Richard Penn, conveying that part of the Province west and south of a line commencing at the "Kittochtinny" or Blue hills, on the Susquehanna river, (a little south of where the southern line of Perry county now strikes the river;) thence, by said river, to a point one mile above the mouth of a certain creek, called Kaarondinhah; thence north-west and by west as far as the Province of Pennsylvania extends, to its western line or boundary, &c. On an old map I have, printed in 1771, this line is marked running from a mile above Penn's creek, N. 45° W., crossing the river a little above the mouth of Sinnemahoning, and striking Lake Erie a few miles north of Presqu'Isle, (now Erie.) Within the Valley, it crossed Penn's creek, near New Berlin, the turnpike, near Ray's church, thence over Buffalo creek and mountain.

The Indians alleged afterwards (see Weiser's journal of the conference at Aughwick, September, 1754) that they did not understand the points of the compass, and that if the line was so run as to include the West Branch of the Susquehanna, they would never agree to it.

Settlers, nevertheless, pushed their way up along Penn's creek. George Gabriel had a house where Selinsgrove now stands as early as 1754, and Godfrey Fryer, John Young, George Linn, George Schnable, and others were in his immediate neighborhood. The Proprietaries, with their understanding of the line, made surveys along Penn's creek, in Buffalo Valley, as early as the 13th of February, 1755; and William Doran had an improvement where Jacob Shively now lives before that date. I have a copy of a survey General John Armstrong, then deputy under Nicholas Scull, made for Henry Nufer, adjoining Doran's, dated 13th February, 1755.

The inhabitants along the creek in the Valley proper numbered twenty-five. Their names and their places of residence, for the most part, were obliterated with them. One John Turner had improved Esquire Lincoln's place. It appears by John Harris' ledger, published among "The Dauphin County Historical Contributions," that Turner sold his improvement to Harris, June 17, 1755. There was a settlement near Kaufman's grist-mill. A man by the name of Andrew Smith lived at White springs. Jacob LeRoy, or King, as he was called by the settlers, lived at the spring on the late Hon. Isaac Slenker's place, in Limestone township. There was a settlement on the New Berlin road, called for many years afterwards Breylinger's improvement, after the German killed there. The late Philip Pontius told me his grandfather had made an improvement at Cedar spring, his late residence, in 1755.

(1755.) Braddock's defeat (July 9) emboldened the Indians, and they determined to clear out all these settlements; and they did it so effectually, that although, by the treaty of 1758, the western part of the Valley became the Proprietaries, no settlers ventured upon the bloody ground until after the surveys of 1768.

In October, 1755, the Indians came down upon the settlers. Two men were murdered within five miles of George Gabriel's, and four women carried off. The following cotemporary record tells the whole story. It is a petition, addressed to Robert Hunter Morris, then Governor under the Proprietaries:

"We, the subscribers, living near the mouth of Penn's creek, on the west side of the Susquehanna, humbly show that, on or about the 16th October, the enemy came down upon said creek, killed, scalped, and carried away all the men, women, and children, amounting to twenty-five in number, and wounded one man, who, fortunately, made his escape, and brought us the news. Whereupon the subscribers went out and buried the dead. We found thirteen, who were men and elderly women, and one child, two weeks old; the rest being young women and children, we suppose to be carried away. The house (where we suppose they finished their murder,) we found burned up, the man of it, named Jacob King, a Swisser, lying just by it. He lay on his back, barbarously burned, and two tomahawks sticking in his forehead; one of them newly marked W. D. We have sent them to your Honor. The terror of which has drove away all the inhabitants except us. We are willing to stay, and defend the land, but need arms, ammunition, and assistance. Without them, we must flee, and leave the country to the mercy of the enemy.

George Glidwell,
George Auchmudy,
John McCahan,
Abraham Sowerkill,
Edmund Matthews,
Mark Curry,
William Doran,
Dennis Mucklehenny,
John Young,

Jacob Simmons,
Conrad Craymer,
George Fry,
George Schnable,
George Aberhart,
Daniel Braugh,
George Linn,
Godfrey Fryer.

Jacob King, *alias* John Jacob LeRoy, was killed at the spring on the late Mr. Slenker's farm. He came over, in the ship Phœnix, from Rotterdam, arriving at Philadelphia, November 22, 1752, in the same vessel which brought over John Thomas Beck, grandfather of Doctor S. L. Beck, of Lewisburg. Rupp's Collection, page 225.

In the third volume of the Pennsylvania Archives, on page 633, will be found the "Examination of Barbara Liningaree and Mary Roy, 1759. They say they were both inhabitants of this Province, and lived on John Penn's creek, near George Gabriel's; that on the 16th October, 1755, a party of fourteen Indians fell upon the inhabitants at that creek by surprise, and killed fifteen, and took and carried off prisoners examinants and eight more, viz; Jacob Roy, brother of Mary Roy; Rachel Liningaree, sister of Barbara; Marian Wheeler; Hannah, wife of Jacob Breylinger, and two of her children, (one of which died at Kittanin' of hunger;) Peter Lick and two of his sons, named John and William.

"The names of the Indians were Kech Kinnyperlin, Joseph Compass and young James Compass, young Thomas Hickman, one Kalasquay, Souchy, Machynego, Katoochquay. These examinants were carried to the Indian town Kittanning, where they staid until September, 1756, and were in ye fort opposite thereto when Colonel Armstrong burned it. Thence they were carried to Fort Duquesne, and many other women and children, they think an hundred, who were carried away from the several Provinces of Pennsylvania, Maryland and Virginia. They staid two months, and were carried to Saucang, twenty-five miles below, at the mouth of Big Beaver creek. In the spring of 1757 they were carried to the Kuskusky, up Beaver creek twenty-five miles, where they staid until they heard the English were marching against Duquesne, and then the Indians quitted Kuskusky, and took these examinants with them to Muskingham, as they think, one hundred and fifty miles, On the 16th March made their escape, and got to Pittsburgh on the 31st." The date of this deposition is about May 6, 1759.

There was a Catharine Smith among the prisoners re-captured by General Armstrong, September 8, 1756, at Kittanning, and brought back, said to have been taken from Shamokin; but as her name is not mentioned above, it may be doubtful whether she was of the family of Andrew Smith, who lived at White springs. As the others were captives over four years, possibly they had forgotten her. Barbara Leininger was the name of the girl called Liningaree. The next place west of David Oldt, and about two miles below New

Berlin, is called, in the old survey, "Breylinger's improvement," and was where Jacob Breylinger lived. Peter Lick, no doubt, lived on Lick run, or Switzer run, a short distance above New Berlin. A full narrative of Anne M. LeRoy and Barbara Leininger's adventures was published by Peter Miller, at Philadelphia, in 1759. I have had diligent search made for it, but without success.

Anne M. LeRoy was living in Lancaster in 1764, when she made affidavit again in regard to her capture and the visits of the Conestoga Indians to Kittanning. The only further trace of the LeRoy family that I can find is a recital in a deed, that on the 19th of October, 1772, John James LeRoy, the son, of Prince George county, Maryland, sold the LeRoy tract in Buffalo Valley to Andrew Pontius, of Tulpehocken. The latter was an uncle of the late Philip Pontius, of Buffalo, to whom I am indebted for several reminiscences. He said, years afterward, when clearing up John Hoy's place, adjoining, they found several gold eagles, dropped, no doubt, by the Indians or their captives. This gave rise to rumors that money had been buried on the place. Many expeditions were made by night to dig for the treasure; but, except a few sleeve buttons, nothing was ever found. From conversation with people of the neighborhood, I find the witch cloud still lingers about that fateful spring, although the wintry winds of more than a century have swept above it. Switzer run preserves the nationality of the first settler. It empties into Penn's creek, a short distance above New Berlin.

Among the settlers on Middle creek, then called Christunn, I. D. Rupp informed me, was John Zehring, a relative of the Rupp family, who was driven off by this massacre. He is corroborated by a recital I find upon Zehring's warrant, dated November 12, 1765, "for two hundred acres, including his improvement made in 1755, from which he was driven off by the Indians, adjoining Christunn or Middle creek." The Zehrings have still descendants there. Old Peter Decker married a Zehring, and Michael S. Decker, of Paxtonville, Snyder county, is of the family.

(1756.) A sequence of the Penn's creek massacre was the building of Fort Augusta, (Sunbury,) at the then Indian town of Shamokin, in July, 1756. This was done with the consent and at the request of the Indians, from a well-grounded fear that the French meant to take possession of the place, and build a fort there. Among the officers of Colonel Clapham's regiment, by whom the fort was built, I note the names of John Hambright and William Plunket, afterwards prominent in the political affairs of Northumberland county. George Gabriel and Joseph Greenwood, as appears by their autographs to an affidavit before James Burd, Esquire, dated 2d June, 1756, were sworn as guides to Colonel Clapham's regiment.

Ensign Miles, afterward Colonel Samuel Miles, of the Revolution, and proprietor of Milesburg, in Centre county, who belonged to Colonel Clapham's regiment, in his manuscript journal says, "we marched up the west side of the Susquehanna, until we came opposite where the town of Sunbury now stands, where we crossed in batteaux, and I had the honor of being the first man who put his foot on shore at landing, In building the fort, Captain Levi Trump and myself, had charge of the workmen; and after it was finished, our battalion remained there in garrison until the year 1758. In the summer of 1757, I was nearly taken prisoner by the Indians. At about one-half mile distance from the fort stood a large tree that bore excellent plums, on an open piece of ground, near what is now called the Bloody spring. Lieutenant Samuel Atlee and myself one day took a walk to this tree, to gather plums. While we were there, a party of Indians lay a short distance from us, concealed in the thicket, and had nearly got between us and the fort, when a soldier, belonging to the bullock guard not far from us, came to the spring to drink. The Indians were thereby in danger of being discovered; and, in consequence, fired at and killed the soldier, by which means we got off, and returned to the fort in much less time than we were in coming out." See Burd's journal, Pennsylvania Archives, second series, 745, for an interesting account of difficulties encountered in completing the fort.

As it will be of interest to many to trace their ancestry as far backward in the history of the settlement of the Province as possible, I have collated from I. D. Rupp's histories and other sources all I could find in reference to the emigration and former settlement of the families of the Valley.

(1723.) Among those who came from Albany, New York, with Conrad Weiser, and settled in Tulpehocken, now in Berks county, in the year 1723, occur the names of Henry Boyer, Philip Brown, Simon Bogenreif, George Christ, John A. Diffenbach, Jacob Fisher,

Jacob Follmer, Jacob Huffman, Peter Kephart, John Pontius, Leonard Rees, Henry Reidenbaugh, Adam Ream, John Spyker, Ulrich Schwartz, Adam Stein, Peter Sarvey, Mathias Shafer, Christopher Weiser.

In the same year, there were already settled in Donegal township, Lancaster county, the Andersons, Campbells, Clarks, Cooks, Carothers, Ewings, Fosters, Howards, Kerrs, Kellys, Lowreys, Littles, Moores, McClellans, Pattersons, Semples, Scotts, Smiths, and Walkers.

(1729, August.) Robert Barber, Esquire, ancestor of the Barber family, was the first sheriff of Lancaster county. The Wrights came from Lancastershire, England, in 1714. Settled at Columbia in 1726, and John Wright named Lancaster county from his old residence.

As early as 1735, the following families had settled in Lancaster county: the Allisons, Adams's, Alexanders, Bishops, Buchanans, Barretts, Bears, Blythes, Blacks, Douglass's, Daughertys, Greenes, Hustons, Hennings, Hendersons, Irwins, Ketlers, Keysers, Klings, Lowdons, Lynks, McClenahans, Murrays, Mitchells, Meixells, McPhersons, McClures, Phillips's, Royers, Ramsays, Robinsons, Ranks, Ross's, Steeles, Saunders's, Thomas's, Wolf's, Wise's, Webbs, Watsons, Walters, and Walls.

(1749, September 27.) Wendell Baker, ancestor of the Baker family, landed at Philadelphia. On the same vessel came John George Schnable, John Henry Beck, John Simon Shreiner, and R. Fries.

(1750.) Among the dwellers in West Derry, Lancaster county, (now Dauphin,) were the Candors, Clarks, Chambers, Caldwells, Lairds, Morrisons, Ramseys, Shaws, and Thompsons. In East Derry, the Boyds, James Duncan, James Foster, John Foster, Hugh and Patrick Hayes, William Huston, John Moore, Orrs, William Wilson. In Paxton, West—Robert Correy, George Gabriel, George Gillespie, James Harris, Samuel Hunter, Thomas McCormick, James McKnight, James Reed. South end—John Gray, John Johnston, Richard McClure, John Morrison, John Wilson. Of the Narrows—the Armstrongs, Robert Clark, George Clark, William Foster, Thomas McKee. In Hanover—John Brown, James Finney, William Irwin, William Laird, Thomas McGuire, Robert Martin, George Miller,

INTRODUCTION. 15

Andrew Wallace, Samuel Young. In Hanover, East—John Crawford, John Graham, Robert Haslett, Adam Harper, Jacob Musser, Edward McMurray, and James Young.

In Middleton township, Cumberland county, we find the names of William Armstrong, William Blythe, James Chambers, James Dunlap, William Fleming, Andrew Gregg, James Henderson, Jonathan Holmes, William Jordan, John Kinkaid, Hugh Laird, John Robb, John Reed, Robert Reed, George Templeton. In Hopewell, Cumberland also, were John Beatty, Robert Chambers, John Nesbit, Robert Simonton, William Thompson. In Logan township, now in Franklin county, were Isaac Grier, William Greenlee, Samuel Jordan, Samuel Laird, William Linn, senior, William Linn, junior. In Peters township, same county, John Potter, (father of the General) and Samuel Templeton.

(1754.) In Bethel, the most remote north-west township in Berks county, we find, in 1754, George Boeshor, George Emerick, Michael Grove, George Grove, Nicholas Pontius, George Reninger, Jacob Leininger, Jacob Seirer, Ulrich Seltzer, Baltzer Smith,. Michael Weyland.

(1756.) In Cumru township, occur the names of George Englehart, George Ream, Andrew Wolf, &c. In Exeter, the same year, the names of John Aurand, William Boone, Peter Boechtel, Leonard High, Fredrick Kunkle, Mordecai Lincoln, Michael. Ludwig, Peter Noll, Peter Smith, Jacob Yoder. In Greenwich, same year, John C. Baum, Henry Faust, Michael Gotshall, Peter Leonard, Michael Leiby, Michael Lesher, Michael Smith. In Heidelberg, same year, George Aumiller, Peter Betz, Peter Bolender, Philip Bower, Henry Christ, Ludwig Derr, Andrew Ruhl, George Rorabaugh, Frederick Stump, Jacob Wetzel. In the docket of Peter Spyker, Esquire, Tulpehocken, 1756, we find, among the names of referees, John George Anspach, Henry Bogenreif, George Christ, Peter Gebhart, John Heberling, Henry Hetzel, Peter Kaufman, Jacob Lutz, Jacob Miller, Nicholas Pontius, Nicholas Reed, William Spotts, Adam Smith, Martin Trester, Nicholas Wolf, Peter Winkleplecht, Jacob Zerbe. He records that Adam Guyer was bound to learn the shoemaker's trade, (a trade the same family, to my knowledge, followed a hundred years.) John George Wolfe also bound to Jacob Follmer, for thirteen years, &c.

(1757.) In Maiden Creek township, occur the names of the Dunkels and Hoys. In Maxatawney, John Bear, Andrew Boalich, John Frederick, Joseph Gross, Samuel Guilden, Samuel High, Jacob Kaufman, Henry Lutz. In Oley, John Yoder. In Rockland, John Albright, George Angstadt, Lewis Bitting, Peter Keiffer, John Moll, Henry Mertz. Windsor—Mathias Alspach, Killian Dunkel, Jacob Hummel, John Hess, Conrad Heiser, Wendell Keiffer, Jacob Roush Michael Rentchler, Leonard Reber. October 16, 1768, came over in the same vessel Michael Beeber, Valentine Beeber, (grandfather of John Beeber, late of Lewisburg, deceased, to whose accurate memory I am indebted for many dates and incidents,) Andrew Hauck, and John Peter Frick. More than a century has elapsed, and their descendants are still within an hour's ride of each other.

(1758.) The south-western portion of Buffalo Valley was included in the purchase from the Six Nations, made at Easton, Pennsylvania, on the 23d of October, 1758, with the bounds of which they declared themselves perfectly satisfied. I copy the boundary line from the original deed in the Executive Chamber, at Harrisburg: "Beginning at the Kittachtinny or Blue hills, on the west bank of the river Susquehannah, and running thence up the said river, binding therewith, to a mile above the mouth of a creek called Kaarondinhah, (or John Penn's creek;) thence north-west and by west to a creek called Buffalo creek; thence west to the east side of the Allegany or Appalachian hills; thence, along the east side of the said hills, binding therewith, to the south line or boundary of the said Province; thence, by the said south line or boundary, to the south side of the Kittachtinny hills; thence, by the south side of the said hills, to the place of beginning."

The change of boundary from that of the deed of 1754, it will be observed, excluded all the territory subsequently included in the purchases of 1768 and 1784, or more than one half of the State as now constituted. To localize and modernize the change and new boundary, it excluded more than the one half of the territory of Union county as at present constituted. The boundary, instead of running north-west to Lake Erie, stopped at Buffalo creek, near where Orwig's mill now stands, in Lewis township, and thence ran directly west, or nearly so, to the junction of Spring creek with Bald Eagle, now Milesburg; thence south-westerly to what is now the

SITE OF SHIKELLIMY'S TOWN—1737.

INTRODUCTION.

north-east corner of Cambria; thence along the west side of Blair and Bedford, terminating at the Maryland line, between the boundaries of Bedford and Somerset counties.

This line was never run, nor were there any official surveys made quite near it until six years afterwards. So cautious were the Proprietaries at this period of offending the Indians by making surveys beyond the lines, that the most positive instructions were given on this head, and the west end of Nittany mountains, Lamont now, appeared to have been assumed as the most northerly and westerly station. Its assumed locality, however, marked the boundary between Cumberland and Berks counties, which can still be identified upon the ground. As, for instance, a little distance north of Ray's church, on the turnpike, on or near the boundary line of Benjamin and Abraham Mench's, stood, and probably stands yet, a black oak, common corner of the Little, Templeton, Mackamiss, and David Johnston's surveys of 1769. The course of the south-western line of the latter survey being N. 57° W., that of the county or Indian line N. 45° W., left a little corner of the David Johnston, a Berks county survey, in Cumberland county, and it was not cleared for many years, under the supposition that it could not be held by the David Johnston warrant, not being in Berks county.

The north-east corner of this purchase was, no doubt, made one mile above the mouth of Penn's creek, in order to include Gabriel's improvement, on the spot where Selinsgrove now stands. Otherwise, what more natural course than to stop opposite the mouth of Mahanoy creek, the north-western corner of the purchase of 1749, now Port Trevorton.

A line of marked trees was made by George Gabriel and the Indians, from a Spanish oak standing on the river bank, which, in 1766, when William Maclay ran the John Cox survey, stood two hundred and ninety-two perches above the mouth of Penn's creek, to a black oak on Penn's creek, about one mile up Penn's creek, near App's grist-mill, (corner of Henry Christ and Adam Ewig surveys.) Their line, being made without a compass, ran west, instead of N. 45° W., or rather N. 49° W., as Mr. Maclay made the boundary line between the two purchases in 1768. Gabriel settled on the site of Selinsgrove in 1754. His location was surveyed to John Cox, by Mr. Maclay, on the 15th of May, 1766; but Mr. Maclay notes on his return to the Cox warrant that Gabriel had made a settlement and improvement upon it *at least ten years ago*, and that he then lived on and claimed the property, and his pretensions must be satisfied by Mr. Cox before the return could be accepted. In quite a number of surveys this line of marked trees is alluded to; and its western *terminus*, on Penn's creek, was identified, on the 25th of October, 1765, by William Maclay, when he surveyed the "Henry Christ" tract, (lately owned by Leonard App,) at the black oak, which, he says, "was made a corner of the purchased lands by Gabriel and the Indians, say both Weiser and Gabriel."

The line of this purchase of 1758 was the line between Cumberland and Berks counties, within Buffalo Valley, until the erection of Northumberland county, out of Berks and other counties, in 1772, (when Mahantango creek became the north line of Cumberland.) This line, as stated, ran from a black oak that stood on the bank of the West Branch of the Susquehanna river, one mile above the mouth of Penn's creek, N. 45° W., to Buffalo creek, near what is now Orwig's mill, in Lewis township; thence directly west. The settlers north of this line were assessed in Berks county, and repaired to Reading to attend court; those south of that line were assessed in Penn township, Cumberland county, and attended the sessions at Carlisle. From 1772, Sunbury attracts attention as the seat of justice for the people of the Valley, until the erection of Union county, March 22, 1813—a period of forty-one years, to a day—when New Berlin became the county seat, holding it for forty-two years; when, (March 2, 1855,) by the erection of Snyder county out of Union, Lewisburg became the political center of the territory within the immediate scope of these Annals.

(1760.) A letter from Governor James Hamilton, dated November 15, 1760, to Richard Peters, Esquire, incloses a rough draft, showing the mountains north of the Valley, Buffalo creek, Penn's creek, the North and West Branches, and main river down to Gabriel's, (whose place is marked at the mouth of Penn's creek,) Shamokin creek, Shamokin marked between it and the North Branch and Chillisquaque creek. The space included within a dotted line running from the mouth of Buffalo creek down to a point opposite the mouth of the Chillisquaque, thence in a semi-circle to a point on Buffalo creek, six or eight miles above its mouth, is marked "Manor."

The letter states: "Abel James and two others of the Friendly Association have been with me, and delivered me the inclosed plot of lands about Shamokin, and particularly of the Manor, which, by Job Chillaway's information and description, they suppose John Armstrong to have lately surveyed, and at which they are in fear the Indians will take offense. I told them I was entirely ignorant of it, as I supposed you to be, from what you said to me yesterday, but that I would order an inquiry to be made. I, therefore, desire that you will immediately write to Mr. Armstrong, and know from him what truth there is in all this, what it is he has actually been doing in that part of the country, and by what authority, and require his answer as soon as possible.

"I think it also advisable that you should see Teedyuscung before he leaves town, apprise him of this report, and satisfy him that nothing is intended to the prejudice of the Indians with respect to lands, lest, hearing it from other hands on his return, it may make impressions on him and other Indians to our disadvantage."

Mr. Peters wrote Mr. Armstrong, Philadelphia, 17th November, 1760:

"SIR: Inclosed is a letter I received from the Governor, with a draught of a pretended survey delivered to him by the clerk of the Association of Friends for Indian Affairs, who said that John Chillaway, the Indian, who was with you, complained that the lines run into the land not yet granted by the Indians.

"Be pleased to send to the Governor a letter fully explaining this affair, in order to obviate any complaints that may be made, and make no delay.

"It is proposed that the west line, which is the boundary in the proprietary release executed at Easton, shall be run by the surveyors on behalf of the Proprietaries, and by a deputation of Indians, to be appointed at the next public Indian treaty, to be held in this city, in the spring."

The above allusion to Teedyuscung will be understood from the following information, taken from "The Memorials of the Moravian Church," edited by the late Reverend William C. Reichel, a thorough investigator and the best authority upon the history of the Indians who resided within our state:[1]

[1] Reverend William C. Reichel born at Salem, North Carolina, died at Bethlehem,

The Lenape or Delawares, although under the power of the Six Nations, had their own king. Allummapees held this position as early as 1718, and as the purchases of the Proprietaries forced the withdrawal of the tribes from the Delaware, he removed, in 1728, from on the Delaware to Shamokin, "which is eighty miles from Tulpehocken, and the residence of the king (Allummapees) of the Delawares, and of the Oneida (Shikellimy) viceroy. The latter virtually maintains the balance of power between the different tribes and between the Indians and the whites, acting as agent for the Iroquois confederacy in all affairs of state and war."—Zinzendorf's Narrative, dated at Shamokin, September 29, 1742, Reichel, page 67. (The year 1728 is, no doubt, the date of the withdrawal of the Muncys, "who were proverbially impatient of the white man's presence in the Indian country," from Buffalo Valley, and their removal to the head waters of the Allegheny, succeeded by the straggling Shawanese.) In July, 1739, Richard Penn treated with deputies of "the Shawanese, scattered far abroad from the Great Island to the Allegheny."

In June, 1746, Weiser writes that Allummapees has no successor of his relatives, and will hear of none as long as he is alive. Shikellimy advises that the Government should name a successor, and set him up by their authority; that he has lost his senses, and is incapable of doing anything. Allummapees is dead, writes Weiser to Peters, in 1747. Lapappiton is allowed to be the fittest to succeed him, but he declines. Finally, Teedyuscung was made king of the Delawares, in the spring of 1756. He had his headquarters in 1757-8, at Teedyuscung's town, (a little below the site of Wilkes-Barre,) marked Wioming on Scull's map of 1759. Here he was burned in his lodge, on the night of the 19th of April, 1763, and hence the Delawares fled, in October of the same year, after having struck the last blow for the possession of the "Great Plains," on the 15th of the month, when they fell upon the Connecticut settlers.

Reichel differs from Loskiel as to the date, before quoted, of Shikellimy's death, and places it on the 17th of December, 1748, and adds, that his son Logan, returned home from a far off journey sev-

Pennsylvania, Wednesday, October 25, 1876, *Atnt* 53. "Murmuring of the Rock of Ages, he passed away quietly as an infant falls asleep." He was professor in the Moravian Theological Seminary, a ripe scholar, an indefatigable student, and, in the language of John Jordan, junior, Esquire, his decease an irreparable loss.

eral days after his decease, to weep over the lifeless body of a parent he so much esteemed. The brethren, Zeisberger and Henry Fry, made him a coffin, and the Indians having painted the corpse in gay colors, and decked it with the choicest ornaments, carried the remains of their honored chieftain to the burial place of his fathers, on the banks of the "winding river." He was succeeded in his vicegerency by his eldest son, Tachnachdoarus, "a spreading oak," *alias* John Shikellimy. His second son was James Logan, named for Secretary Logan, of Germantown. Logan was lame. John Petty was the youngest of the three brothers, and bore the name of an Indian trader.

ANNALS OF BUFFALO VALLEY.

1768.

PENN TOWNSHIP SETTLERS—WILLIAM GILL—MURDER OF WHITE MINGO—WILLIAM BLYTHE—PURCHASE OF 1768.

HE following list of inhabitants of Penn township, Cumberland county, is taken from the original assessments at Carlisle, Penn township then embracing nearly all of what is now Snyder county: John Aumiller, Philip Aumiller, William Blythe, Jacob Carpenter, George Drowner, Adam Ewig, George Gabriel, Jacob Hammersly, John Lee, Arthur Moody, Michael Regar, George Rine, John Reighbough, junior and senior, Michael Rodman, Casper Reed, Frederick Stump, (who is taxed with one negro,) Peter Straub, Adam Stephen, and Andrew Shafer. The freemen are John McCormick, William Gill, Edward Lee, and Joseph Reynolds.

Of these early settlers I can fix the locality of but few. William Blythe lived at the mouth of Middle creek; Adam Ewig on the creek just above App's mill; George Gabriel on the site of Selinsgrove; Frederick Stump where Middleburg now stands; Peter Straub at Straubstown; William Gill on Tuscarora creek, not far from New Berlin. The latter came originally from Bucks county. Belonging to a regiment in Forbes' campaign, he was wounded in the leg in Grant's defeat, September 14, 1758, or in the attack on

Bouquet's camp, at Loyalhanna, and made for home, through the woods, with a bullet in his leg. He lived mostly on wild grass on the way. Reaching Penn's creek, he stopped, married a German woman there, and settled. He served in Captain Clarke's company the winter of 1776-7, and when, during the war of 1812, one of his sons was drafted, and for some reason could not go, the old man went with him to Sunbury, and asked to be substituted for his son. The board rewarded his patriotism by discharging his son. He died in Beaver township, about the year 1820, leaving a large family of boys. His grandson Jacob was a member of Captain Middleswarth's company, in 1814, and now resides about two miles from Bellefonte, (1877.) I am indebted for these facts to William Gill, nephew of William, senior, who at the advanced age of ninety years, had a remarkable recollection of dates and events, which I have frequently verified by old papers and assessments. He died at Bellefonte, November 21, 1876.

Murder of White Mingo.

Sunday, 10th of January, occurred the murder of White Mingo and five other Indians, by Frederick Stump. The information of William Blythe, made at Philadelphia, on the 19th of January, is in substance, that, hearing of the murder, he went to George Gabriel's, where he met Stump and several others, on the 12th, and was then told by Stump himself that six Indians, White Mingo, Cornelius, John Campbell, Jones, and two women, came to his house, near the mouth of Middle creek. Being drunk and disorderly, he endeavored to get them to leave, which they would not do. Fearing injury to himself, he killed them all, dragged them to the creek, and making a hole in the ice, threw in their bodies. Then fearing the news might be carried to the other Indians, he went the next day to two cabins, fourteen miles up the creek, where he found one woman and two girls, with one child. These he killed, and putting their bodies into the cabin, he burned it. That he (Blythe) sent four men up the creek, who reported that they had found the cabins burned, and the remains of the limbs of the Indians in the ashes. The scene of the latter deed was on the run that enters the creek at Middleburg, which goes by the name of Stump's run to this day. Stump and his companion, Iron-Cutter, were arrested at Gabriel's, and taken to Carlisle jail. They were forcibly rescued on the 29th, were concealed about Fort Augusta a few days, and then fled the country. Tradition has it, that Stump died in Virginia, many years afterwards.

For William Blythe's services in this matter, he received the two tracts of land which were surveyed on applications in the names of his daughters, Margaret and Elizabeth, containing, together, six hundred and forty acres, lying immediately south of White Deer creek, whither he removed during the year, and was, therefore, one of the first settlers of Buffalo Valley after the purchase. He was an Indian trader at Shippensburg in 1748, and a lieutenant in the French war, 1758.

His cabin stood on Red-Bank run, near the river, on the Elizabeth Blythe tract, below the late Samuel Henderson's house. Her application of 3d April, 1769, describes it as including an old Indian fort and a settlement begun by her. William Blythe lived to be a very old man. Roley McCorley informed me he knew him well, and that he was a tall, raw-boned man, and, in latter years, quite blind.

His daughter Margaret married Captain John Reed, who had commanded the "Paxton Boys." Her tract was patented to Captain Reed in 1774. Her children by Captain Reed were William, (father of James Reed, who still resides near Hartleton, and grandfather of Doctor Uriah Reed, of Jersey Shore, and of Robert Reed, now of Clearfield, Pennsylvania,) James, who moved west, and Elizabeth, who married John Armstrong. Captain Reed died before 1778, and, with "the Runaway" of that year, the Reeds went to Cumberland county. William Reed's family remained there until some years after, when he came up and settled in Hartley township. Captain Reed's widow married Captain Charles Gillespie, an officer of the Revolution, and raised a second family—Edward Gillespie, Susanna, (married to Arthur Thomas,) Eleanor, Charles, junior, Thomas, and John. By a division of the place, the lower half, one hundred and seventy-six acres, fell to Charles Gillespie and wife, the upper to the Reeds, who conveyed it, on the 6th of May, 1796, to Gillespie and wife. The Gillespies all went west, except Edward, who hung himself, many years ago, at the old homestead, which passed into the hands of the late Daniel Ludwig, Esquire. Margaret Blythe survived the fortunes of her second family, and took refuge with her first husband's children. She died at her son's, William Reed, in Hartley township, and her remains were interred in the graveyard at Kester's school-house.

Elizabeth Blythe married Doctor Joseph Eakers, who had been a surgeon in the revolutionary army.[1] In October, 1798, they sold the place to James Hepburn, and went West, where she died. The Doctor returned, resumed practice, and was drowned in Muddy run, above Milton, many years ago.

5th November. Thomas and Richard Penn purchased from the Six Nations, at Fort Stanwix, (now Rome, New York,) the remainder of the Valley whose annals we are writing. As one of the incentives to this purchase, I may state that, as early as the year 1764, the officers of the first and second battalions who served under Colonel Bouquet, made an agreement with each other, in writing, at Bedford, "that they would apply to the Proprietaries for a tract of land sufficiently extensive and conveniently situated, whereon to erect a compact and defensible town; and, also, to accommodate each of us with a reasonable and commodious plantation; which land and lots of ground, if obtained, we do agree shall be proportionably divided, according to our several ranks and subscriptions," &c. Signed by Lieutenant Colonels Turbutt Francis and Asher Clayton, Major John P. deHaas, Captains Jacob Kern, John Procter, James Hendricks, John Brady, William Piper, Timothy Green, Samuel Hunter; Henry Watson, adjutant first battalion; Conrad Bucher, adjutant second battalion; William Plunket and James Irvine, captains; Lieutenant Daniel Hunsicker; Ensigns McMeen and Piper, *et al.* They appointed Colonel Francis, Captain Irvine, &c., commissioners to act for all the officers. These commissioners made an application to the Proprietaries on the 30th of April, 1765, in which they proposed to embody themselves in a compact settlement, on some good land, at some distance from the inhabited part of the Province, where, by their industry, they might procure a comfortable subsistence for themselves, and by their arms, union, and increase, become a powerful barrier to the Province. They

---

[1] In a petition to the Executive Council, dated February 15, 1779, he states that he had been a long time surgeon's mate in the hospital department.

further represented that the land already purchased did not afford any situation convenient for their purpose; but the confluence of the two branches of the Susquehanna at Shamokin did, and they, therefore, prayed the Proprietaries to make the purchase, and make them a grant of forty thousand acres of arable land on the West Branch of the Susquehanna. Lieutenant Thomas Wiggins and Ensign J. Foster, who were absent from Bedford when the agreement was signed, were subsequently admitted into the association. The minutes of the association are published in full in the first volume of the Collections of the Historical Society of Pennsylvania.

1769.

OFFICIALS—FIRST SURVEYS IN THE VALLEY—JOHN EWING, *et al.*—OFFICERS' SURVEYS—ORIGINAL SETTLERS.

OVERNOR, JOHN PENN. Representative of Berks, Edward Biddle; Sheriff, Jacob Shoemaker.

Representatives of Cumberland, William Allen and John Montgomery; Sheriff, David Hoge; Prothonotary, Hermanus Alricks.

On the 3d of February, the commissioners of the officers of the first and second battalions met at the Governor's, and obtained an order allowing them to take up twenty-four thousand acres, to be divided among them in distinct surveys, on the waters of the West Branch of the Susquehanna, each three hundred acres to be seated with a family within two years from the time of survey, paying £5 sterling per hundred, and one penny per acre, &c. The names of the officers in whose favor the order of survey issued were Colonel Francis, Major deHaas, Captains Irvine, Plunket, Hunter, Kern, Green, Houssegger, Sems, Hendricks, Brady, Piper, Bucher, Lieutenants, Stewart, Wiggins, Hays, Nice, Hunsicker, Askey, McAllister, Ensigns Piper, McMeen, Morrow, Steine, and Foster; and the order signed by John Lukens, surveyor general, and directed to William Scull and William Maclay.

By advertisement, dated the 23d of February, the land office was to open to receive applications for lands in the "New Purchase," on the 3d of April. "So long a day was fixed to give the back inhabitants time to repair to the office." Meanwhile surveys were made on special orders for the Proprietaries or their friends.

On the 18th of February, William Maclay made the first survey in person on the west side of the river. His field notes are yet preserved among the records of the deputy surveyor's office of Union county. He began at a black oak on the river, afterwards the southeast corner of the Richard Manning tract, and ran S. 60° W. 70, W. 212, S. 45° W. 755, S. 49° E. 295, to the black oak or Spanish oak on the river, on the line of the purchase or Gabriel's land; thence up the river N. 36° E. 51, N. 45° E. 233½, N. 39° E. 462, and N. 26½° E. 220, to the place of beginning. He says this survey is of land above George Gabriel's, for which Andrew Allen has a warrant, and on which Charles Willing intends an old right of five hundred acres, "neither of which are in my hands yet." The next day, Sunday, the 19th, he says he received from Colonel Francis the Charles Willing location. The *caveat*, Willing *vs.* Allen, was determined on the 21st of December, 1772, by the board of property. Present, Mr. Tilghman, Hockley, Physick, and Lukens. "That the location on the warrant of Charles Willing (which bore date the 24th December, 1768) is such an appropriation of five hundred acres and allowance, that it was not liable to the Proprietaries' warrant," and they directed the surveyor general to divide the land by a line N. 49° W. from the river, so as to leave five hundred acres of the lower end to be returned for Willing. This division line is about where the present road running west from Hettrick's store, in Monroe township, Snyder county, is laid.

The distance of the river line of the John Cox survey, (which included Gabriel's settlement,) from the mouth of Penn's creek to the Indian line, was two hundred and ninty-two perches; of the Richard Willing, from the black oak or Spanish oak, marked by Gabriel and the Indians, to a white oak, which stood on the river bank near Hettrick's store, was two hundred and ninty-five and one half perches.

The Andrew Allen reached thence six hundred and seventy-one perches, to a black oak which stood below the Sunbury ferry, nearly opposite the old tavern. The Richard Manning survey (made in 1770) extended up one hundred and fifty perches to a maple, where began the John Galloway, which ran up three hundred and forty-eight perches, to the confluence of the West Branch. I will here add, as having interest upon the question of the location of Fort Augusta, that a topographical survey found among the same papers of this date, has a station on the mouth of the little stream that enters the river below the present bridge. The course to the main point is N. 27° E. and S. 53½° E. to the "redoubt at Fort Augusta."

The survey next above the "Galloway," is the Daniel Hoffman, (1814,) extending one hundred and eighteen perches; then comes the Joshua McAfee, (the John Mason place,) surveyed in 1771, extending up sixty-eight perches, and we are in Buffalo Valley.

22d February, the Reverend John Ewing's survey was made; the first in the Valley. It extends from the mouth of Buffalo creek, six hundred and seventy-five perches, to a walnut that formerly stood on Doctor Dougal's line. Mr. Maclay's starting point for this survey was sixty or seventy rods above the present site of the iron bridge across Buffalo creek. This survey contained eleven hundred and fifty acres.

24th February, Mr. Maclay surveyed the Bremmer tract for John Penn. He notes in his field-book the fine spring at late Andrew Wolfe's, the one on the Cameron farm, and the one at Ellis Brown's, and leaves out "the pine barrens," as he calls the present Linn place. This tract contained one thousand four hundred and thirty-four acres, and was called the "fiddler's tract," tradition said, because given a fiddler for one night's performance on the violin. Bremmer was a music dealer in the Strand, London, and was, perhaps, a fiddler by occupation.

28th February, the site of Lewisburg was surveyed for the Proprietaries, by Mr. Maclay, commencing at a white oak, at the present Strohecker's landing. At sixty-eight perches he notes the spring now belonging to the University grounds. This line he makes one mile long, to the mouth of Buffalo creek; he then ran up the creek to a hickory that stood where the present road reaches the creek at the iron bridge; thence he ran due south, two hundred and eight perches, to a pine, the stump of which was dug up when the railroad excavation was made north of the Eighth Street school-building; (it stood some eight feet inside of Jacob Derr's fence;) thence he ran S. 50° E., two hundred and ninety-eight perches, to the river. Several of the latter line trees stand near the cemetery. These lines now mark the limits of the borough, with the exception of the Jacob Spidler place, which was taken out of the borough many years ago by act of the Legislature.

In the latter part of February many of the officers of the first and second battalions met at Fort Augusta, and agreed to take the land upon the terms proposed by the Proprietaries, and that one of the tracts should be surveyed on the West Branch, adjoining Montour's place, (Chillisquaque creek,) and one in Buffalo Valley. In order to expedite business, it was agreed that Captains Plunket, Brady, Piper, and Lieutenant Askey, should go along with Mr. Maclay to Buffalo Valley, and Captains Hunter and Irvine with Mr. Scull, to direct the survey in the Forks.

On the 1st, 2d, and 3d of March, Samuel Maclay, for William, ran out the officers' survey. He commenced at a white oak on now William Spotts' land, at the east of the Limestone ridge, and ran west and south-west to the east line of what is now William Young's land, in Lewis township. The western line he ran N. 318 to Buffalo creek; thence he ran north of the present turnpike, until he crossed its site a little east of Vicksburg, and came back to a white oak, yet standing, one hundred and twenty-five rods east of where Salem church is now; thence he ran south to an elm on Turtle creek, and west and south-west to the place of beginning. This survey embraced the heart of Buffalo Valley, and, as their minutes say, "was made without opposition;" and the officers returned to Fort Augusta, held a meeting, and determined that the third tract of eight thousand acres should be surveyed on Bald Eagle creek. Captains Hunter, Brady, and Piper were appointed to over-see that survey, to be made by Charles Lukens. The record says that Colonel Francis, Doctor Plunket, and Major deHaas, furnished the stores on the present occasion.

16th May, The officers met at Harris' Ferry. Messrs. Maclay, Scull, and Lukens laid before them the drafts of their respective surveys. Mr. Maclay reported the tract surveyed by him in Buffalo

Valley contained eight thousand acres; Mr. Scull that in the Forks, six thousand and ninety-six, which left nine thousand nine hundred and four for Bald Eagle creek, and Mr. Lukens' survey was several thousand acres short of the quantity. They agreed then that Colonel Francis should receive his share, two thousand seven hundred and seventy-five acres, surveyed to him in one tract, adjoining the tract purchased by him of Montour. Colonel Francis' tract accordingly extended from Chillisquaque creek down to and included Northumberland point. Boyd and Wilson purchased of him, and erected the mill at the mouth of Chillisquaque creek, in 1791, and John Lowdon bought the site of Northumberland town from Colonel Francis, and it was patented to his wife, Sarah Lowdon, 7th July, 1770. Same day, 16th of May, lots were drawn for the choice of lands. Captain Hendricks, having won the first choice, took the eastern end of Buffalo Valley survey, now the Zellers, Aurands, &c., farms. Captain William Plunket then chose the Dreisbach place, site of the church, &c. Captain Brady the Maclay place afterwards, now Joseph Green's, William Cameron, Esquire's, &c. Captain Kern next took the site of Vicksburg. Lieutenant Doctor Thomas Wiggins got three hundred and thirty-nine acres. Doctor Wiggins resided in Lower Paxton township, now Dauphin county. By his will, proved August 31, 1798, he devised to his brother, John Wiggins, his land in Northumberland county; and by the will of John Wiggins, second, proved November 30, he devises it to John and James Wiggins Simonton, each one hundred and ten acres. Honorable John W. Simonton many years associate judge of Union county, still owns this military fief. Reverend Captain Conrad Bucher secured the tract now owned by the Pontius's; Captain Timothy Green the site of the Rockey mill; Lieutenant Askey the site of Mifflinburg; Captain Irvine the place so long owned by the Kleckners; Lieutenant Stewart the old Foster place; and Lieutenant McAllister the old John Hayes place. Captains Plunket and Brady superintended the running of the division lines, which was accomplished by Samuel Maclay, on the 25th, 26th, 27th, and 28th of May.

The John Ewing survey was made on the 3d of March, extending from the east line of the officers' survey, down Turtle creek, to the Gundy farm. These are the leading surveys, run with astonishing accuracy, and well marked all around.

The John Harris surveys, from Jacob M. Shively's, near White spring, up to and including Esquire Lincoln's farm, were also upon special warrants, before the opening of the land office. They were made on the 23d of February. The walnut, the beginning point, stood on Penn's creek, below the mouth of White Spring run. John Harris had bought, as stated before, the improvement made by Turner in 1755. He also owned the Edward Lee, the White Spring tract, the improvement title of which also dated back to 1755; both re-surveyed, however, by Mr. Maclay, in February, 1769. He was the father-in-law of William Maclay, and was favored by the Proprietaries in consequence of his services with the Indians.

On the 3d of April the land office was opened, and a great crowd attended. Numerous applications or *locations*, as they were called, were received for the same spots of land, from different persons, under various or similar descriptions. The method taken to decide the preference was to put them all into a trunk, and after mixing them well together, an indifferent person drew them out, and they were numbered in the order of drawing, priority thus being determined by lottery. To illustrate by example: there were numerous applications for the old Muncy town or Shikellimy's town tract. Michael Weyland's was the thirty-second application drawn, and so numbered, and put down on the list. Any subsequent application descriptive of the same locality was, when opened and read, laid aside. Jacob Weyland's application for land, "on a run of water adjoining Michael Weyland's at Shikellimy's town," was the sixth drawn. John Grove now owns part of that warrantee tract. Dietrick Rees' application for land, "on a run below Dog run, adjoining land of Ludwig Derr, in Walnut bottom," came out the eighth. It embraces New Columbia, and the land north and west of it. Derr seems to have marked out a claim for himself, near New Columbia, before the drawing, which he failed to get.

In August, the greater part of the surveys on the north side of Buffalo creek were made, from Colonel Slifer's place up to Farmersville, together with most of the surveys in Buffalo and the Lowdon surveys in West Buffalo. Those along the river, down to Turtle creek, also in August. From thence to the county line below, in October.

The surveys from Doctor Dougal's place up to the mouth of White Deer creek, along the river, were made by Charles Lukens, in October. He speaks in his field notes of Ludwig Derr being with him. Along Penn's creek, above and including the mouth of Switzer run, the surveys were made in August. In November, William Maclay made surveys of some of the best land in the Valley, including Ray's church, John and Isaac Reish's land, in which he was interested. Colonel Kelly's tracts were also surveyed in August. In December, Samuel Maclay surveyed the lands in Dry valley, now owned by Isaac Eyer, David Gross, &c.

The settlers this year, as far as I can ascertain them, were John Lee, at the spring near the stone barn at Winfield; John Beatty, at the spring near New Berlin; Jacob Grozean, near Hoffa's mill; Barney Parson, at the old Iddings place; John Wilson,[1] at Jenkin's mill; Adam Haines, on the McCorley place, White Deer. William Blythe's cabin is marked on a survey made 24th October, as standing twenty-five rods from the river, on the little run above the Ard place. Joseph McLaughlin had an improvement on White Deer creek, west of Blythe's, and one Bennett had a cabin on White Deer creek, about one mile above the cotton factory. John Fisher took up the place now known as Datesman's, West Milton, and settled upon it. Michael Weyland the George F. Miller place. William Armstrong lived where the road comes out to the old ferry, below New Columbia. James Pair commenced an improvement on the same tract, a little above, and they agreed to divide the land, Armstrong to fill up his application by taking more land in the rear. In doing so, he encroached on the Earnest Burke, a tract belonging to Hawkins Boone. Hence a law suit reported in 2 Binn., 55.

[1] John Wilson died in 1774. He was the father of Thomas Wilson, afterwards a prominent citizen of Erie county, and of Mrs. David Mead, (of Meadville.) Sanford's Erie, page 220.

1770.

Early Surveys—Settlers from Paxton—Scull's Map.

OHN PENN, Governor. Officials the same as in 1769. May 21, Turbutt Francis, Esquire, appointed Prothonotary of Cumberland county, *vice* H. Alricks, resigned.

The following notices of settlers are derived from old conveyances and notes of surveyors:

As early as the 28th of March, John Buchanan and his father resided on the Richard Edwards tract, where Stoltzfus now lives. By a lease, dated that day, he agreed with Thomas Lemmon and Sarah, his wife, to build a log house, eighteen by twenty, thereon, clear and fence ten acres of field, two of meadow, plant ten apple and twenty cherry trees, &c.

Jacob Fought bought of Captain Timothy Green two hundred and sixteen acres at the mouth of Cedar run, including the forks of Buffalo creek, the Rockey mill site, and moved there. 23d March, James Wilson surveyed the George Palmer tract, embracing Winfield, for John Lee. He speaks of commencing at Lee's spring, and running S. 40°, E. 53, to an ash at the river, and thence, by the back side of Lee's fields, N. 40° W. This explains the corner left out of the Craig survey below, and shows that Lee had cleared the fields where Thomas Pursel now lives as early as the 4th of October, 1769, when Craig's survey was made. The first regular clearing, perhaps, in the Valley, and its exact locality is thus identified. In May, Wilson surveyed the addition to David Moore, along Buffalo creek, now A. J. Rishel's, and speaks of Hans Fleming living in there. On the 12th of May, he surveyed the Thomas Sutherland place in Dry valley, where Emerick's family was afterwards captured. He says " this land Robert King has bought," indicating the residence of the first constable of Buffalo township. 17th May he surveyed the John Umstead tract, on Stony run, which empties into Buffalo creek, east of the mouth of Rapid run. On the 18th, the Peter Horning, where Esquire Sheckler now lives. This land was afterwards in litigation between Christopher Johnston and Matthew Irwin for over thirty years. His field notes explain the origin of the trouble. He commenced at an ash, (which stood in the road afterwards laid out, nearly in front of Esquire Sheckler's house,) in the line of the eight hundred tract made for Foster and Rees; thence ran north 168, to a black oak of same, (this distance was found by subsequent surveys to be one hundred and eighty-two perches;) and thence, by an old Indian cabin, W. 74 to a maple; and thence, by a ridge, crossing a run at seventy-two perches, N. 78 to a hickory, west 122 to a chestnut oak, and by a ridge S. 138 to a Spanish oak, E. 80 to a white oak, and by a ridge S. 122 to a white oak, (subsequent surveys made this distance 135.) " I had set the course east from this white oak, and at 54 I intersected a line of Doctor Plunket's, made by Samuel Maclay, which I found ran north and south. The distance between two black oak corners was between sixty and seventy perches, where, I made a halt, and left open the line between white oak and ash beginning." Leaving this line open, made the difficulty, the white oak having disappeared.

On 25th of September, he surveyed for John Lee the small thirty-eight acre tract, at Strohecker's landing. He says he began at the white oak of the survey Ludwig Derr *lives on*; thence ran N. 50°, W. 56, &c., showing that Derr then lived on the site of Lewisburg. I found Lee's receipt for the purchase money among Youngman and Walters' papers, who lately owned the place where Lee was killed by the Indians.

Michael Pfoutz was Wilson's chain-carrier.

Colonel John Kelly at this time lived on the place where he died, as appears by Mr. Wilson's notes.

In an assessment for the year 1770, of Paxton township, now Dauphin county, occur the names of Robert Clark, Walter Clark, Robert Fruit, William Maclay, Matthew Smith, William Plunket, George

Overmeier, Michael Troy, William Clark, the four last named marked inmates, indicating either a widower or unmarried man; and in Middletown we find the name of Albright Swineford, all prominent in the subsequent annals.

William Scull's map of date April 4, 1770, has Mahantango creek, Middle creek, Penn's creek, Turtle, Buffalo, and White Deer creeks laid down, with their respective names. Reed's residence is marked half-way between Mahantango and Penn's. Gabriel's, now Selinsgrove, is marked "Cox's borough." Nittany and Jack's mountains are on, with these respective names, but he has a range of mountains running up the river from the mouth of Buffalo creek.

1771.

GREAT FLOOD — PENN TOWNSHIP SETTLERS — GEORGE GABRIEL — FIRST MILLS BUILT — DREISBACH'S CHURCH — MICHAEL WEYLAND.

RICHARD PENN, Lieutenant Governor from October 16. Edward Biddle and Henry Christ, Representatives of Berks county; Sheriff, George Nagle. William Allen and John Montgomery, Representatives of Cumberland; Sheriff, Ephraim Blaine.

9th March, the Susquehanna river, Bald Eagle creek up to Spring creek, and Penn's creek, for twenty miles above its mouth, were declared public highways. John Lowdon was appointed one of the commissioners for making them navigable. 1 Smith's Laws, 324.

On the same day, the officers of the first and second battalions held another meeting. Charles Lukens reported that the whole tract surveyed by him on Bald Eagle creek contained only eight thousand three hundred and eighty acres, which is fifteen hundred and twenty-four acres less than the quantity allowed them. He divided the Bald Eagle tract into twenty shares, the last of which

Lieutenant Askey got; so that Lieutenant McAllister, Ensign Piper, Captain Sems, and Captain Kern yet lacked their shares. Colonel Francis then said that a grant might be obtained for the tract of land in Buffalo Valley formerly intended to be located by Captain Plunket, and since surveyed for the Proprietaries, containing one thousand and five acres. Piper was, therefore, given lot No. 6, on Bald Eagle, surveyed for Ensign Morrow, who was excluded from the grant by the Penns, because he was of the party that rescued Stump and Iron-Cutter, the murderers of the Indians on Middle creek; Captain Kern, two hundred and eighty-seven acres, late the Chamberlain mill tract, in Kelly, now Hoffa's; Lieutenant McAllister, two hundred and ninety acres, late Howard farm, adjoining the above; and Colonel Francis, for Captain Sems, five hundred and twenty-seven and one half acres, adjoining. Colonel Francis sold the latter tract to William Linn, of Lurgan township, Franklin county, who divided it among his children. His grandson, W. T. Linn, still owns his father's share.

Loskiel mentions that in the spring of this year there was a great flood in the Susquehanna, which compelled the Indians at Wyoming to leave their houses, and take to the hills, where they remained four days.

The assessment of Penn's township contains this year the names of the following additional settlers: Frederick Albright, Thomas Allen, Tobias Bickle, Henry Bower, Robert Boyd, Tobias Bickle, junior, Michael Beidenbaugh, William Burchard, Abraham Billman, George Bowerman, Peter Druckenmiller, Widow Dowd, Michael Egulph, John Foutz, George Herrold, Joseph Jacobs, Michael Kerstetter, Bostian Kerstetter, Andrew Moor, Jacob Myer, Robert Moody, Edward McConnell, William Nees, John Regenbach, junior, Michael Stoke, Michael Swingle, Harman Snyder, Michael Weaver, George Miller, Andrew Ulsh. Freemen: Casper Snyder, Conrad Hayslick, and Michael Foutz.

George Gabriel, no doubt, died this year, as his name disappears from the assessment list. His obituary, or the only one I can find, at least, is not very complimentary. On the 13th November, 1772, at a meeting of "the officers," Mr. Lukens and Little had a claim, they said, for a location of three hundred acres, presented to them by Colonel John Armstrong, which was included in the officers' survey, insisting that the place now called Cedar springs, Pontius's now, was the same to which Colonel Armstrong gave the name of Snake spring, in 1755; and Mr. Ewing read a paper, said to be a copy of George Gabriel's deposition, who was with Colonel Armstrong when the name was given. "We told them that their location was extremely vague, being for land near John Penn's creek, twelve miles southward of Fort Augusta, which did not affect our claim in the least. As to Gabriel's deposition, it is but *ex parte* testimony. The man is since dead, but is well known to have been a man of infamous character. That Colonel Armstrong, the gentleman who gave the location, is still living, and has declared that he cannot fix upon the spot." This claim was, no doubt, founded upon the Manor survey of 1760.

Jacob Fought built the first mill in West Buffalo township, and, perhaps, the first in the Valley, unless, we except Derr's, at Lewisburg, the exact date of the building of which I cannot ascertain, though, probably, in 1770. The date of Fought's is fixed by an agreement, yet on record, with George Rote, dated 14th November, 1776. It recites that Fought built the mill in 1771, and a dam on the south branch of the creek. Finding that insufficient, he dug a water-course, and erected a dam to take the water from the north branch of Buffalo creek. George Rote had purchased the adjoining tract of Colonel deHaas, who had purchased of Ensign Foster. By this agreement, the yearly damage to Rote's land was fixed at £1 5*s*, and Fought bound himself, his heirs, and successors to pay said sum yearly; but if the mill-dam became "extink" or the water ceased to do damage, the agreement was to be void. Marks were to be made on a big rock, on an iron-wood, and on a white oak. When the water reached these marks, it was to be run over the dam. The dam on the north branch was to be three feet, and no higher. At Fought's mill the first elections in the Valley were held.

James Wilson made numerous surveys this year: 31st May, the William Kelly tract, on Black's run, on which Stahl, the noted wagon-maker, lived so long; 22d June, Peter Herrold and John Flackinger, on White Deer creek; 16th August, the Thomas Mackemiss, beginning at a black oak, he says, where Samuel Maclay stopped with the officers' line, on the west line of Cumberland county, (north of Ray's church;) 17th September, the Joseph Updegraff, the leading survey on the north branch of Buffalo creek, (Kelly's mills.) Thomas McGuire, the elder, was then a resident of the Valley. Hawkins Boone made this year the John Musser surveys, in White Deer Hole valley, four miles from the river.

From a short sketch of the Dreisbach church, compiled by the late John Schrack, Esquire, it appears there were Lutheran and German Reformed churches organized in the Valley at this date. He speaks of a record of baptisms, extending from 1771 to 1775. The church was not built, however, and worship was held in private houses. Among the names of parents, occur those of Henry Bolender, Henry Pontius, Christian Storms, Simon Himrod. (The latter lived in Turbutt township. Was afterwards member of Assembly. The family removed to near Waterford, Erie county, in 1798.) Leonard Welker, Philip Stover, Christian Biehl, Yost Derr, Christian Ewig, Stephen Duchman, and Henry Bickel, afterwards killed by the Indians.

During this year, Daniel Nargong made an improvement on Dog run, near the site of New Columbia. He afterwards took up a tract higher up the run. His daughters married Nicholas and Jacob Welch, whose family owned the place within a few years back, and, perhaps, do still.

In November, 1771, Walter Clark, of Paxton township, bought the one thousand one hundred and fifty acres, surveyed to Reverend John Ewing, in trust for himself, Robert Fruit, William Gray, Robert Clark, and William Clark, all of the same township. They divided it into six tracts, agreed each to take one sixth, and sell the remaining tract, which they did to Ludwig Derr, 31st July, 1773. Walter Clark settled on the place now owned by Honorable Eli Slifer, William Gray where Major Paul Geddes now lives, Robert Fruit on the Heinly place, William Clark on the place now owned by M. H. Taggart, and Robert on what is now Judge Hummel's farm. Walter Clark sold to Joseph Musser in 1802, and moved to Mercer county, where his family became prominent. His son John was a member of the Legislature from that county. Captain Gray, afterwards an officer in the Revolution, lived and died on his place. He was ancestor of Dunlaps's, Hayes, Hutchinsons, Hudsons, Wallaces, W. G. Williams, (of Bellefonte,) &c. Richard Fruit sold out to Henry Hursh in 1812, and moved to Derry, Northumberland county. Robert and William Clark died on their respective places. Among the deaths this year occurred that of Michael Weyland, leaving a widow, Magdalena, and nine children, Michael, junior, Jacob, George, John, Samuel, Mary, (married to Peter Swartz, junior,) Margaret, (to Christian Moyer,) Catherine, and Magdalena. He was buried on the place, in an old grave-yard there. Colonel James Moore told me it was still in existence when his father lived there, a little piece up the road running from the river.

1772.

NORTHUMBERLAND COUNTY ERECTED—OFFICIALS—BOUNDARIES OF TOWN-
SHIPS—SUNBURY LAID OUT—FIRST ROADS—CONNECTICUT CLAIM—
WILLIAM SPEDDY—LUDWIG DERR—DEATHS.

RICHARD PENN, Lieutenant Governor. Representative in Assembly, Samuel Hunter. George Nagel, Sheriff of Berks and Northumberland.

Additional residents in Penn's township: Abraham Clements, Michael Hawn, Henry Miser, George Miller, John Swartz, Melchior Stock, Adam Steffy, Simon Scouden, widow of Andrew Moore, Benjamin Ewig, Conrad Hafflich, John Reber. The first assessments of Penn's and Buffalo, from the organization of the county down to 1775, seem to have been lost when the records were forwarded to Paxton, during the great runaway. List of settlers cannot, therefore, be given for the three years intervening.

21st March, Northumberland county was erected out of parts of Berks, Bedford, Lancaster, Cumberland, and Northampton, by the following bounds: Beginning at the mouth of Mahantango creek, up the south side, to the head of Robert Meteer's spring, (in West Perry, near Mr. Winey's, sometimes miscalled Montour's spring;) thence west by north, to the top of Tussey's mountain; thence along the summit to the little Juniata; thence up the east side of the main branch, to the head thereof; thence north to the line of Berks county; thence north-west, along the same line, to the extremity of the Province; thence east, along the north boundary, to a point due north of the most northern part of Great swamp, (the numerous ponds in the upper end of Luzerne county are here referred to;) thence south to the most southern point of said swamp; thence, with a straight line, to the head of Lehigh; thence down the creek so far that a line run west south-west will strike the forks of Mahantango creek, where Pine creek falls into the same, at the place called Spread Eagle, (now Klingerstown,) on the east side of the Susquehanna; thence down the south side of the creek to the river; thence across the river to the beginning.

The county, therefore, extended as far west as Lake Erie, the head of Lehigh on the east, (Pike county,) New York State on the north, and the mouth of Mahantango creek on the south. Fort Augusta was fixed as the place of election, and the county to be entitled to one Representative. The Governor was to nominate a competent number of justices, any three of whom could hold the several courts on the fourth Tuesday of February, May, August, and November, at Fort Augusta, until a court-house should be built. William Maclay, John Lowdon, Samuel Hunter, Joseph Wallis, and Robert Moodie were appointed trustees to purchase a piece of ground on which the court-house was to be erected, subject to the Governor's approval. Thomas Lemmon was made collector of excise. Joshua Elder, James Potter, Jesse Lukens, and William Scull were appointed to run the boundary line.

Officials.

William Plunket, Turbutt Francis, Samuel Hunter, James Potter, William Maclay, John Lowdon, Thomas Lemmon, Ellis Hughes, and Benjamin Weiser confirmed as justices in Council, and William Maclay, prothonotary and clerk of the several courts, March 24.

The first county commissioners were William Gray, Thomas Hewitt, and John Weitzel. November 23, Casper Reed, of Penn's, was sworn in as county commissioner; Alexander Hunter, county treasurer; Walter Clark, Jonathan Lodge, Peter Hosterman, James

Harrison, Nicholas Miller, Jacob Heverling, and Samuel Weiser, assessors.

9th April, the first court, which was a private sessions of the peace, William Plunket presiding, James Potter and John Lowdon assisting, was held. The county was divided into seven townships: Penn's, Augusta, Turbutt, Buffalo, Bald Eagle, Muncy, and Wyoming. Our annals relate only to Buffalo and Penn's.

The boundary of Buffalo commenced at the mouth of Penn's creek, at the head of the Isle of Que; thence up the same to the forks, (a few miles south of Millheim, Centre county;) thence by a north line to the West Branch, (this struck the river at the mouth of Bald Eagle creek, a mile below Lock Haven;) thence down the river to the place of beginning. Thus embracing all of Union, a large part of Snyder and Centre, and a great part of Lycoming counties, as now constituted. Robert King was the first constable.

The boundary of Penn's, before that in Cumberland county, began at the mouth of Mahantango creek; thence, by the county line, to Meteer's spring; thence, with the same line, to the top of Tussey's mountain; thence, along the top thereof, easterly, to Penn's creek; thence down the creek to its mouth; thence down the river to the place of beginning. This boundary ran along the present line of Snyder county; thence to the north line of Mifflin county, at the corner of the present townships of Jackson and Brown, and embraced part of Brown, nearly all of Armagh and Decatur townships, in Mifflin, the southern portions of Hartley and Lewis, and all the present county of Snyder, except Monroe township.

The first court of common pleas was held on the fourth Tuesday of May, before Justices William Plunket, Samuel Hunter, Caleb Grayson, Thomas Lemmon, and Robert Moodie. The commission of William Maclay, prothonotary, was read, and the following members of the bar sworn in: James Wilson, of York, (a signer of the Declaration of Independence and Associate Justice of the Supreme Court of the United States,) then residing at York; Robert Magaw, of Carlisle, (afterwards colonel of the Sixth Pennsylvania and defender of Fort Washington;) Edward Burd, district attorney; Christian Hucks[1] and George North. After examination, James Potts, Charles

---

[1] Afterwards the Tory, Captain Hucks, of Tarleton's dragoons, killed in South Carolina, in 1780-81.—Graydon Memoirs, page 270.

Stedman, and Andrew Robinson. Tavern keepers applying for license were George Wolf, (below the Northumberland bridge,) Martin Trester of Buffalo, and Martin Cost. The number of suits brought to August term was thirty-three. No. 1 was James Patton *vs.* James Garley—Magaw for plaintiff, Wilson for defendant. Of the first grand jurors were Captain John Brady, foreman, George Overmeier, John Rearick, Peter Leonard, William Gray, Ludwig Derr, Andrew Hafer, Hawkins Boone, James Park, and John Walker, all of Buffalo Valley.

Sunbury.

In a letter, dated June 2, 1772, Mr. Tilghman, Secretary of the Land Office, writes to William Maclay : "Mr. Lukens goes to lay out the town, agreeably to instructions. You are joined with him in the work. You are to treat with Mr. Lowdon, and if his title be good, and he will take a sum named in the instructions, (£200,) the town is to be laid out in the Forks; otherwise on the fort side. Wallis and Haines have said they had a right, and they must relinquish it. As Lowdon's application was in his wife's name, she must convey. As putting the town in the forks is a concession against the interest of the Proprietaries to accommodate the people, if the place cannot be clear of claims, the town must be on the other side."

Some of the difficulties were insuperable, for the instructions to treat with Lowdon for three hundred and thirty acres, or thereabouts, situated near the point of the Forks, are stricken out of the rough draft, and on the 16th of June, the Governor and his Council issued an order to the Surveyor General, John Lukens, to repair to Fort Augusta, and, with the assistance of William Maclay, lay out a town for the county of Northumberland, to be called by the name of Sunbury, at the most commodious place between the forks of the river and the mouth of Shamokin creek. Main street to be eighty feet wide, the others sixty, the lanes and alleys twenty, &c. The town was accordingly laid out in June, 1772. On the 31st of August, William Maclay writes, that the noise about the point town is already greatly quieted, and the people begin to think Sunbury the best situation.

The Ferry.

August 14th, Thomas Penn and Richard Penn, by letters patent, granted to Robert King, his executors and assigns, the privilege of keeping a ferry, over the main branch of the Susquehanna at Sunbury. (King conveyed his right to Adam Heverling, November 30, 1773; Heverling to Christopher Gettig, April 17, 1775; Gettig to Abraham Dewitt, October 8, 1779; Eleanor Dewitt, *alias* Coldern, administratrix of Dewitt, to John Lyon, October 25, 1787; and on the 2d of November, 1787, John Lyon presented a petition to the Assembly for the privilege for a term of years, which was granted.)

The first criminal case was tried at August sessions, King *vs.* John Williams, for larceny—Robert Fruit and Robert Clark were on the jury. He was found guilty, and sentenced to pay a fine of £5, to receive twenty-one lashes on his bare back, and to be committed to the magazine of the fort until the sentence was complied with.

Thomas Hartley, (lieutenant colonel of Eleventh Pennsylvania regiment,) Casper Weitzel, Andrew Ross, and James Whitehead were sworn in as attorneys, at August term. Hawkins Boone and Thomas Sutherland had suits at this term—Weitzel for Boone, Stedman for Sutherland; also, Michael Regor *vs.* William Blythe. The latter suit referred to Samuel Maclay, John Brady, and George Wolfe, to settle. George Nagel, sheriff of Berks, acted as sheriff until Colonel William Cooke was commissioned, in October, the first sheriff of Northumberland county.

The first road up the river from Fort Augusta was reported by the viewers, Richard Malone, Marcus Huling, John Robb, and Alexander Stephens, in October:

"To begin at the end of the road lately laid out from the head of the Schuylkill to Fort Augusta; thence north-east, one hundred and sixty perches, to the fording; thence across the North Branch, to a marked hickory, near the bank on the main point; at two miles eighty-six perches, they came to John Alexander's; at one and a half miles further, they crossed Chillisquaque creek; at nearly one mile further, they came to William Plunket's; at three miles further, John Dougherty's; at two miles further, Marcus Huling's; at ten miles, the gap in the Muncy hills; at four miles, Muncy creek; at two hundred and seven rods, Wolfe's run; four hundred and forty-two rods, crossed the run above Samuel Wallis' house; three hundred and twenty-two rods, crossed next run above; at four and a half miles, Loyalsock creek; at five and a half miles, Lycoming creek." Total, thirty-seven miles from Northumberland point to now Newberry, in the city of Williamsport. This road was confirmed, and ordered to be opened, thirty-three feet in width. The line of the Indian purchase was then assumed to be at Lycoming creek, afterwards, admitted by the Indians to be at Pine creek. The order specified the "Indian line," as the *terminus* of the road.

Of the Connecticut Claim.

It will be recollected that the Connecticut people, or Yankees, as they were called by the Pennamites, claimed under their charter the land as far south as the forty-first degree of latitude, which passes through the county a mile or more north of Lewisburg. By the following *memorandum*, furnished me by O. N. Worden, Esquire, which he found among the records of the Susquehanna Land Company, at Hartford, Connecticut, it appears that William Speddy (the elder) was their authorized agent to take and hold possession of land claimed by them in the Valley. "1771, William Speddy voted one 'selling right' in Wyoming, for previous efforts in holding possession in June, and for further intended efforts."

The following affidavit, in the handwriting of William Maclay, which I found among the papers of the deputy surveyor's office of Union county, is the first notice I have of his appearance in Buffalo Valley. It is worthy of note in this connection, that, in deeds of this year (1772) for lands in our Valley, special warrants were common "against the claim of the inhabitants of New England." It appears (Votes of Assembly, 1773, page 492) that in June a large band of armed men from Connecticut appeared upon the West Branch, to dispossess the inhabitants, and were prevented. Speddy was the mere advanced skirmisher or picket:

"*Northumberland County, ss:*

" John Scott, of Northampton county, being duly sworn on the Holy Evangelists of Almighty God, deposeth that the night before last, this deponent and his son and another man from Bucks county, lay in the woods near Buffaloe creek, and in the morning a certain William Speddy came to them and told them he supposed they were travelers and looking for lands to buy; this deponent and company answered in the affirmative. He then desired them to take care how they purchased of Penn, unless they had likewise New England rights; this deponent answered that he would not give a copper for New England rights. He said this deponent might be mistaken in being too sure in depending on Penn's rights. That the New England people had more right than we thought for; he owned that he stood by and saw Stuart shoot Ogden, and justified the action. Much more was said to nearly the same purpose by the said Speddy, who spoke with great violence, and would not bear any contradiction to what he asserted. Sworn and subscribed the 17 of June, 1772."

William Speddy's name first appears in "a list of rioters in the fort at Wyoming, 21st January, 1771, when Nathan Ogden was murdered," to use the language of Governor John Penn. (John Penn's proclamation offering a reward of £50 for the arrest of William Speddy, 9th February, 1771.) In Hugh Gaines' *New York Gazette* of November 14, 1771, there is a paragraph of Philadelphia news, dated November 4, 1771, as follows: "At the Supreme Court, held here on Tuesday last, William Speddy was arraigned and tried for the murder of Lieutenant Nathan Ogden, who was shot from the block-house at Wyoming, whilst it was in the possession of Lazarus Stewart and company. After a long and impartial hearing, the jury soon gave in their verdict 'not guilty.'" Doctor Peck, in his history of Wyoming, notices him thus: "Another of these rioters, as they were called, was William Speddy. He was somewhat in years, and was called 'Old Speddy,' but his age could not abate the rigor of the Pennsylvania authorities, for they kept him in close confinement in Philadelphia for more than two years. How, where, or precisely when Speddy was captured we are not able to say, but his final examination must have taken place some time in the year 1771. Mrs. Myers says when her sister Polly was two years old, and she was twelve, her mother was desired to go to Philadelphia, as a witness in favor of Speddy, who was to be tried for the murder of Nathan Ogden. This journey Mrs. Bennett performed alone on horseback, a distance of one hundred and twenty miles, most of the way through the wilderness.

When she reached Philadelphia, she found that the court had adjourned, and she then made a journey to Goshen, and attended to some business. When the trial came on she was present, and her testimony cleared Speddy. He was wasted away to a mere skeleton. When he was discharged his joy and gratitude overleaped all bounds. He fell upon his knees before Mrs. Bennett, and almost worshiped her. 'Get up, Speddy,' said she, 'I have done no more than any one ought to do for a fellow-creature.' He kissed her hand and bathed it with tears." This story of "Pennsylvania rigor" is reduced in dimensions from two years to probably eight months, as no man was ever tried twice for the same murder in Pennsylvania; and he was acquitted on the 4th of November, 1771. Long enough, however, for this old war hawk of New England rights, to be caged, to render him very grateful to Mrs. Bennett.

As it is said the honey bee precedes about fifty miles and heralds the advance of the white man into the wilderness, Speddy was the honey bee of New England civilization in Buffalo Valley.

He chose for his residence the prettiest little dale in Buffalo Valley. It is on Turtle creek, near what is now Supplee's (formerly Treaster's) mill. Jacob Brown now owns the place. In December, 1776, he volunteered in Captain John Clarke's company of Northumberland county, and served during the campaign of Trenton and Princeton. In 1778 he resided upon the same tract, which was known as the George Gall tract of two hundred and sixty-two acres. In 1780 he is taxed with the same tract, one horse, and three cows. In 1782, in connection with John Lee and William Storms, he was assessor of Buffalo township. His signature to the assessment is in a full, round, beautiful hand. In 1785, his name is dropped from the assessment books, and he disappears from our local history. He had a son, William Speddy, junior.

J. W. Speddy, of Mifflintown, Pennsylvania, wrote me in 1870 that William Speddy, senior, was his great-grandfather, and that the latter removed to Lost creek valley, Juniata county, and died at a place called Speddy's Gap, near McAllisterville. H. Swartzell, Esquire, deputy surveyor of Mifflin county, allowed me to copy a draft of the Speddy tract. It is the border one of the Valley surveys, and the finger-board to the Shade mountain surveys, and, therefore, though dead, he yet speaks, and his name will, no doubt, be called over in court and out of court for hundreds of years yet to come.

In April, James Wilson made a number of surveys for John Lowdon, in what is now the territory of West Buffalo. On the 15th of May he made the leading survey in the lower end of what is now Union township, for Daniel Rees, so many years owned by Joseph Fearon, and now owned and occupied, in part, by Joseph Shannon. In consequence of the suit between Bonham and William Gibbons, referred to hereafter in connection with the capture of the Emerick family, the Rees lines were often run and found well marked. On his original field notes, Wilson says: "This land is situated about two miles from John Lee's, on both sides of the path that leads to Treaster's." Trester's was at the mouth of Tuscarora creek, on Penn's, one mile above New Berlin, now in Jackson township, Snyder county.

Ludwig Derr bought the tract on which Lewisburg now stands, during the summer of this year, from the Reverend Richard Peters. His mill, which is still standing, being the front portion of Smith & Fry's, so many years John Brown's mill, was in existence in the fall of this year. How long previous I cannot ascertain. Derr bought the "Joseph Hudnot tract," (still owned, except the part belonging to Joseph W. Shriner, by his grand and great-grandchildren,) in June, 1772, of John Coxe, merchant, of Philadelphia, for £175.

On the 3d of October, John Aurand bought the "Jenkin's mill" property, on Turtle creek, and it went by the name of "Aurand's mill," when he sold it to Morgan Jenkin. It is still owned by the Jenkin's family. Doctor Harbaugh, in his "Fathers of the German Reformed Church," states, upon the authority of John Aurand, of Yellow Springs, Blair county, a grandson of John Aurand, that the latter built both flour and saw-mill at Turtle creek. Wilson, however, had some sort of a mill there as early as 1771. John Wilson died during the year 1772, according to my researches—Miss Sandford, *ante*, says in 1774.

In the fall Robert Barber, Esquire, built the first house on the White Springs tract of which we have any knowledge, as he recites in a lease dated 9th August, 1773, to John Scott, that he leases him the house he had built last fall at the head of White springs for seven years. It was on the Edward Lee warrantee, which Barber had purchased, in August, from Reuben Haines.

Christian Diehl (written Dale) lived on part of the Ewing tract, (now Colonel Slifer's upper farm, near the iron bridge.) The late John Beeber told me that his father's term of service was purchased by Mr. Diehl from the captain whose ship he came over in, and he helped Mr. Diehl clear that place in 1772, owned then by Ludwig Derr. Adam Beeber then returned to Philadelphia, served five years in the army, after which he came up to Muncy, where he settled and died. Christian Diehl's grandson, Captain Christian Dale, of Harris township, Centre county, aged sixty-six, confirms the story, as a tradition of the family, in regard to Adam Beeber's service with his grandfather.

William Wilson bought of James Wilson, his father, the John Moore warrantee. Settled there during this year. He was then unmarried. Boarded at a house near Mortonville, whence he walked over every day to clear his place, on which he died in 1824. His mansion residence is now owned by Reverend Jacob Rodenbaugh.

Wendell Baker bought of Samuel Maclay the George Calhoun tract, still owned by his descendants, in August, and moved into the Valley from York county. Mrs. David H. Kelly and J. T. Baker Esquire, are of his descendants.

John Lowdon settled on the Levi Shoemaker place, near Mifflinburg, which he called "Silver Spring," removing there from Northumberland point, where he subsequently laid out the present town of Northumberland.

John McClung settled on the place known as "Hard Scrabble," in East Buffalo. In 1807 Matthias Macpherson bought that portion of the McClung place, and sold off the lots.

In December occurred the first wedding in the Valley I find any record of. Magdalena, widow of Michael Weyland, to Peter Swartz, senior. The latter then moved upon the place described as containing three hundred acres at Sinking spring—Shikellimy's old town. On the 18th of December, Mrs. Swartz took out letters of administration upon her former husband's estate, the first ever issued in Northumberland county. Her account was filed 8th September, 1774, in which Peter Swartz joins. It has an item on the debtor side of deer skins, accepted for a debt due the estate from Captain John Brady.

Peter Smith, who lived at White Deer Mills, (part of his old stone house still stands, now occupied by Doctor Donowsky,) died this fall. Jesse Lukens had the rightful title, and brought a suit, in 1772, against Peter, marked abated by the death of Smith, in 1773, February. His widow held on the possession, (postea 1785.)

Thomas McKee, the Indian trader, from whom McKees' Half-Falls gets its name, died in April, 1772.

1773

SETTLERS—ROADS—BUFFALO CROSS-ROADS CHURCH—EJECTMENT CASES.

RICHARD PENN, acting Lieutenant Governor until July 19. After August 30, John Penn, who was confirmed Lieutenant Governor by the King, June 30, was awarded the title of Governor by the Provincial Council.

Member of Assembly, Samuel Hunter; Presiding Justice, William Plunket; Prothonotary, William Maclay; Sheriff, William Cooke; Coroner, James Murray; County Commissioner, Casper Reed.

Officers of Buffalo: Constable, James Boveard; Supervisors, Joseph Green and Martin Trester; Overseers of the Poor, William Irwin, late of Carlisle, and John Lee.

Settlers during this year: Abel Reese, on the place now owned by John Gundy's heirs, in East Buffalo; Joseph Sips, on the David Henning place, in Buffalo; Philip Hoy purchased the place in Limestone township, still owned by his descendants; James Fleming settled on Dale's place, opposite late Thomas Clingan's, erected a cabin, and cleared four or five acres. He sold out to Samuel Dale. See Gray *vs.* Dale, 4 Yeates, 494, for an account of their dispute about the dividing line.

On the grand jury for May occur the names of William Irwin, John Foster, Peter Swartz, Abel Reese, John Gillespie, William Foster, William Leech, and John Thompson. Leonard Groninger and James Buchanan had a battle, which came before them. Joseph Green became Buchanan's bail.

Christian Van Gundy recommended for license. He kept a tavern at the Strohecker landing, his house standing on Derr's land. Its remains were removed by excavation for the railroad in 1854.

William Irwin, John Kelly, Robert King, Jacob Grozean, (called French Jacob,) and Ludwig Derr were appointed viewers to lay out a road "from the fording between Ludwig Derr's and John Aurand's mill through Buffalo Valley to the Narrows." They never reported, and at May sessions, 1774, Samuel Maclay, William Irwin, Henry Pontius, Christian Storms, and William Gray were appointed in their stead. They reported in February, 1775. William Foster and John Lee (first tavern at Winfield) were recommended for license. Among the viewers to lay out the road from Great Plains to Sunbury were James Potter, John Thompson, Joseph Green, *et al.* Among the jurors were Thomas Sutherland, William Thompson, Philip Cole, the first inhabitant of Hartleton. He was colonel of the militia regiment of the Valley in 1776, went on a tour of duty to Reading and Philadelphia; he left the Valley with the "great runaway," 1778, and never returned. Peter Kester succeeded Cole as tenant of Colonel Hartley, who purchased of Cole in 1784. It went by the name of Kester's until Colonel Hartley laid out the town. An indictment was found against Martin and Michael Trester for assault and battery; they were found guilty, and that was all the sessions business of this year.

Buffalo Cross-Roads Presbyterian Church.

According to Mr. Hood's account, this church was organized this year, and James McClenachan and Samuel Allen were its first ruling elders, the former ordained at Derry, now in Dauphin county, the latter at Silver Spring, Cumberland county. Mr. McClenachan was from Hanover township, Dauphin county, and came into the Valley in April, 1773. These gentlemen continued to act as elders to receive supplies until 1781, when the church was broken up in consequence of the country being overrun by the Indians. In 1783 the people returned, and in the same year Mr. McClenachan died, and as Mr. Allen had died while the people were away, it appears the congregation were without elders until the year 1785, when Matthew Laird, who had been an elder at Big Spring, came to reside in the congregation. (Doctor Grier's manuscript sermon.)

Ejectment.

At May term, Adam Christ brought ejectment against William Speddy, tenant in possession of the George Gall tract, now Supplee's mill, in East Buffalo. Speddy's possession under his Connecticut title did not avail, and he was ousted. Hartley and Burd for Christ; Stedman and Wilson for Speddy.

Japhet Morton also brought suit *vs.* Christian Storms, tenant in possession of Captain John Brady's land, now Frederick's, adjoining Mortonsville. Brady held it, and it was in possession of his widow until 1783. The family lost it after her death, and Morton became owner.

I copy, as a curiosity, a deed for a tract of land now owned by David Heinly, in White Deer township, near New Columbia:

"I promise to deliver to Valentine Lees, his heirs or assigns, a convience for fifty aciers of land adjoining Rees' grief and John Cox, and to agine when surveyed to land belonging to Valentine Lees, which warent was entered some time last Spring in My own name, and for the performance I bind myself, my heirs, in the sum of one hundred pounds, if in consequence of the said Lees pein me 5 pound 10 shillings of cash and one pair of lether britches to the valy of one pound 11 shillings. Witness my hand this 26th day of August, 1773.

HAWKINS BOONE.

Witness present: SAMUEL YOUNG.

William McMurray, of Sunbury, made many surveys in the Valley this year. The Leonard Welker, East Buffalo, 11th May; Frederick Deel, on Penn's creek, near Centreville bridge; James Watson, east of Wehr's tavern, on 13th; Thomas Procter, on Penn's creek, Robert Jewel, Joseph Alston, Samuel Breck, James Barnes, ditto; Philip Cole tract, McMurray and Grant, &c., in Hartley township.

William Black settled on Black's run, in Kelly township, and was a juror this year.

Extract from a manuscript journal of Richard Miles, (who died in Centre county many years ago,) April 20, 1773 : "Started for Shamokin, in company with James and Enos Miles, Abel Thomas, and John Lewis," (from Radnor, Chester county.) They passed up the river, stopping at Malone's, Huling's, Muncy Hill, Wallis's, Loyalsock, Lycoming, Pine creek, Great Island, and returned, by way of the Narrows, down through Buffalo Valley, to Tarr's Mill, where they got a horse shod ; thence they went to Huling's, (Milton now ;) thence down the river to the Fort, (Augusta.)

In June a large body of armed men from Connecticut attempted to dispossess the inhabitants of the West Branch. This attempt was successfully resisted by the *posse* of the neighborhood, only to be renewed in 1774.

1774.

POTTER TOWNSHIP ERECTED—POLITICAL DOCUMENTS—CROSS-ROADS CHURCH TITZELL'S MILL—ENNION WILLIAMS' JOURNAL.

OHN PENN, Governor. Samuel Hunter, Member of Assembly. 4th April, Robert Fruit and Thomas Hewitt sworn as County Commissioners. William Gray elected in October.

Officers of Buffalo : James Young, Constable ; James Park and Michael Hessler, Supervisors, the latter lived where Crotzerville now stands ; Hawkins Boone and John Foster, Overseers. In February, William Wilson, (grandfather of Doctor T. H.,) and Samuel Dale, appear as jurors. Colonel Kelly was foreman in May. John Clarke, William Hutchinson, grand jurors.

At May sessions Potter township was erected out of Penn's, Buffalo, and Bald Eagle. Bounded eastward by a north north-west line from the top of Jack's mountain, by the four-mile tree on Reuben Haines' road, in the Narrows, to the top of Nittany mountain ; thence along the top to the end thereof, at Spring creek, on the old path ; thence south south-east to the top of Tussey's mountain ; thence along the county line, to the top of Jack's mountain, and along the same to the beginning.

To August term one hundred and forty suits were brought. The ninety-ninth was Slough *vs.* Blythe. Margaret Blythe's title was confirmed. There was also an ejectment brought by Christian Van Gundy *vs.* Ludwig Derr for the site of Lewisburg.

In May Daniel Christ settled and made the first clearing on the place where C. Sheckler, Esquire, now resides, in West Buffalo. James Anderson was then his neighbor, and had an improvement on the Matthew Irwin place. Anderson left before the runaway of 1778. Irwin took possession after the war. George Books also cleared a part of the Sheckler place.

Political.

The following letter, found among the papers of Captain John Lowdon, discloses the means taken to organize an opposition to the encroachments of the mother country upon the liberties of the American people, which culminated in the Revolution and the Declaration of Independence, on the 4th of July, 1776 :

PHILADELPHIA, *June* 28, 1774.

"*To William Maclay, William Plunket, and Samuel Hunter, Esquires, Northumberland :*

" GENTLEMEN ; The committee of correspondence for this city beg leave to inclose you printed copies of the resolves passed by a very large and respectable meeting of the freeholders and freemen, in the State House square, on Saturday, the 18th instant ; and by the fourth of these resolves, you will observe that it was left for the committee to determine on the most proper mode of collecting the sense of this Province in the present critical situation of our affairs, and appointing Deputies to attend the proposed Congress. In pursuance of this trust, we have, upon the maturest deliberation, determined upon the mode contained in the following propositions, which we hope may meet with the approbation and concurrence of your respectable county, viz :

" 1st. That the Speaker of the House of Representatives be desired to write to the several members of Assembly, requesting them to meet in this city as soon as possible, but not later than the 1st of August next, to take into consideration our very alarming situation.

" 2d. That letters be written to proper persons in each county, recommending it to them to get committees appointed for their respective counties, and that the said committees or such number of them as may be thought proper, may meet at Philadelphia at the time the Representatives are convened, in order to consult and advise on the most expedient mode of appointing Deputies for the General Congress, and to give their weight to such as may be appointed.

"The Speaker of the Assembly, in a very obliging and ready manner, has agreed to comply with the request in the former of these propositions; but we are now informed that, on account of the Indian disturbances, the Governor has found it necessary to call the Assembly to meet in their legislative capacity, on Monday, July 18, being about the same time the Speaker would probably have invited them to a conference or convention in their private capacity.

"What we have, therefore, to request is that, if you approve of the mode expressed in the second proposition, the whole or a part of the committee appointed, or to be appointed, for your county, will meet the committees from the other counties at Philadelphia, on Friday, the 15th day of July, in order to assist in framing instructions, and preparing such matters as may be proper to recommend to our Representatives at their meeting the Monday following.

" We would not offer such an affront to the well-known public spirit of Pennsylvania, as to question your zeal on the present occasion. Our very existence in the rank of freemen, and the security of all that ought to be dear to us, evidently depend upon our conducting this great cause to its proper issue with firmness, wisdom, and unanimity. We cannot, therefore, doubt your ready concurrence in every measure that may be conducive to the public good ; and it is with pleasure that we can assure you that all the Colonies, from South Carolina to New Hampshire, seem animated with one spirit in the common cause, and consider this as the proper crisis for having our difference with the mother country brought to some certain issue, and our liberties fixed upon a permanent foundation. This desirable end can only be accomplished by a free communion of sentiments and a sincere, fervent regard to the interests of our common country.

"We beg to be favored with an answer to this, and whether the committee from your county can attend at Philadelphia, at the time proposed.

THOMAS WILLING, *Chairman*."

On this letter is indorsed, in Joseph Green's handwriting, the following: "At a meeting of a number of the principal inhabitants of the township of Buffalo, at Loudowick Derr's, of Saturday, the ninth of July, John Lowdon, Esquire, and Samuel Maclay were chosen as committee-men to meet the other committee-men from the other townships, on Monday, the 11th instant, at Richard Malone's, in order to choose proper persons out of the township committees to go to Philadelphia to the general meeting of the committees chosen by the respective counties of this Province; and likewise to fix upon some proper way and means to correspond with the other committees of this Province.

"By order of the meeting.

JOSEPH GREEN, *Clark*."

The committees that met on the 11th, at Richard Malone's, selected William Scull and Samuel Hunter to represent Northumberland county, at the Provincial meeting, at Philadelphia. This meeting convened in Carpenter's Hall, at Philadelphia, on Friday, the 15th day of July: Thomas Willing, chairman, and Charles Thompson, secretary. William Scull was of the committee to draft instructions to the Assembly. The resolutions were as follows, (Some passed unanimously, indicated by "U;" in case of difference of sentiment, the question being determined by the Deputies voting by counties:)

"U. 1. That we acknowledge ourselves and the inhabitants of this Province liege subjects of His Majesty King George III, to whom they and we owe and will bear true and faithful allegiance.

"U. 2. That as the idea of an unconstitutional independence of the parent state is utterly abhorrent to our principles, we view the unhappy differences between Great Britain and the Colonies with the deepest distress and anxiety of mind, as fruitless to her, grievous to us, and destructive of the best interests of both.

"U. 3. That it is, therefore, our ardent desire that our ancient harmony with the mother country should be restored, and a perpetual love and union subsist between us, on the principles of the constitution and an interchange of good offices, without the least infraction of our mutual rights.

"U. 4. That the inhabitants of these Colonies are entitled to the same rights and liberties within these Colonies that the subjects born in England are entitled to within that realm.

"U. 5. That the power assumed by the Parliament of Great Britain, to bind the people of these Colonies, 'by statutes in all cases whatsoever,' is unconstitutional, and, therefore, the source of these unhappy differences.

"U. 6. That the act of Parliament for shutting up the port of Boston is unconstitutional; oppressive to the inhabitants of that town; dangerous to the liberties of the British Colonies; and, therefore, that we consider our brethren at Boston as suffering in the common cause of these Colonies.

"U. 7. That the bill for altering the administration of justice, in certain criminal cases, within the Province of Massachusetts Bay, if passed into an act of Parliament, will be as unconstitutional, oppressive, and dangerous as the act above mentioned.

"U. 8. That the bill for changing the constitution of the Province of Massachusetts Bay, established by charter, and enjoyed since the grant of that charter, if passed into an act of Parliament, will be unconstitutional, and dangerous in its consequences to the American Colonies.

"U. 9. That there is an absolute necessity that a Congress of deputies from the several colonies be immediately assembled, to consult together and form a general plan of conduct to be observed by all the Colonies, for the purpose of procuring relief for our suffering brethren, obtaining redress of our grievances, preventing future dissensions, firmly establishing our rights, and restoring harmony between Great Britain and her Colonies on a constitutional foundation.

"U. 10. That although a suspension of the commerce of this large trading Province with Great Britain would greatly distress multitudes of our industrious inhabitants, yet that sacrifice, and a much greater, we are ready to offer for the preservation of our liberties. But in tenderness to the people of Great Britain, as well as of this country, and in hopes that our just remonstrances will at length reach the ears of our gracious Sovereign, and be no longer treated with contempt by any of our fellow-subjects in England, it is our earnest desire that the Congress should first try the gentler mode of stating our grievances, and making a firm and decent claim of redress.

" 11. *Resolved by a great majority*, That yet, notwithstanding, as an unanimity of counsels and measures is indispensably necessary for the common welfare, if the Congress shall judge agreements of non-importation and non-exportation expedient, the people of this Province will join with the other principal and neighboring Colonies in such an association of non-importation from and non-exportation to Great Britain, as shall be agreed on at the Congress.

" 12. *Resolved by a majority*, That if any proceedings of the Parliament, of which notice shall be received on this continent, before or at the General Congress, shall render it necessary, in the opinion of that Congress, for the Colonies to take further steps than are mentioned in the eleventh resolve, in such case the inhabitants of this Province shall adopt such further steps and do all in their power to carry them into execution.

"U. 13. That the venders of merchandise of every kind within the Province, ought not to take advantage of the resolves relating to non-importation in this Province or elsewhere, but they ought to sell their merchandise which they now have, or may hereafter import, at the same rates they have been accustomed to do within three months last past.

" U. 14. That the people of this Province will break off all trade, commerce, and dealing, and will have no trade, commerce, or dealing of any kind with any Colony on this continent, or with any city or town in such Colony, or with any individual in any such Colony, city, or town, which shall refuse, decline, or neglect to adopt and carry into execution such general plan as shall be agreed to in Congress.

"U. 15. That it is the duty of every member of this committee to promote as much as he can the subscription set on foot in the several counties of this Province for the relief of the distressed inhabitants of Boston.

"U. 16. That this committee give instructions on the present situation of public affairs to their Representatives who are to meet next week in Assembly, and request them to appoint a proper number of persons to attend a congress of Deputies from the several Colonies, at such time and place as may be agreed upon, to effect one general plan of conduct, for attaining the great and important ends mentioned in the ninth resolve."

The instructions are too long to be copied. They commence, however, with a recital that the dissensions between Great Britain and her Colonies commenced some ten years since, and arose from the power claimed by Parliament to bind the people of the Colonies by statutes, *in all cases whatsoever*, when from local circumstances they could not be represented in it. The object of the convention of Deputies is stated to be to obtain a renunciation on the part of Great Britain of all powers under the statute of 35 Henry 8th, cap. 2—of all powers of internal legislation, of imposing taxes or duties, internal or external, and of regulating trade, except with respect to any new articles of commerce, such as silk, wine, &c., which the Colonies may hereafter raise, reserving the right to carry these from one Colony to another; to obtain a repeal of all statutes for quartering troops in the Colonies, or subjecting them to any expense on account of such troops; of all statutes imposing duties to be paid in the Colonies, that were passed at the accession of his present Majesty, or before this time, which-ever period shall be judged most advisable ; of the statutes giving courts of admiralty in the Colonies greater power that the courts of admiralty have in England; of the statutes shutting up the port of Boston and affecting the Province of Massachusetts Bay. Offering, in case this was agreed to, to settle a certain annual revenue on His Majesty, his heirs and successors, and to satisfy all damages done to the East India Company—the executive powers of the crown to retain their present full force and operation, and we to receive all manufactures from Great Britain, and in case of war, to contribute all aid in our power. In the event of a refusal of these terms, agreements of non-importation and non-exportation were recommended, "and a continual claim and assertion of our rights."

These proceedings being communicated to the General Assembly, it took up and promptly (22d July) passed a resolution "that there is an absolute necessity that a Congress of Deputies from the several Colonies be held as soon as conveniently may be, to consult upon the unhappy state of the Colonies, and to form a plan for the purpose of obtaining redress of American grievances, &c., and for establishing that union and harmony between Great Britain and the Colonies which is indispensably necessary to the welfare and happiness of both."

During this year Catherine Smith, widow of Peter Smith, commenced building a grist and saw-mill near the mouth of White Deer creek, which she completed in 1775. See her statement, year 1785.

5th July, Robert Fruit and Thomas Hewitt, county commissioners, at the request of Ludwig Derr, who desired to borrow money from the loan office, valued the land, three hundred and twenty acres, (now the site of Lewisburg,) "on which said Derr now lives, having a grist and saw-mill, dwelling-house and barn, clear upland and meadow, at £1,000, Pennsylvania currency." On 7th, their sworn valuation of Robert Clark's, now Judge Hummel's, two hundred and fourteen acres, *et al.*, dwelling-house, and barn, was £428; Walter Clark's, (Slifer place,) one hundred and eighty-eight acres, dwelling-house, and barn, £564; Aurand mill tract, (now Jenkins,) grist-mill, two pair stones, saw-mill, dwelling-house, and barn, two hundred and twenty-eight acres, at £700.

Buffalo Cross-Roads Presbyterian Church.

We come now to the first record evidence in regard to Buffalo Cross-Roads church. December 17, Edward Shippen and Joseph, his brother, by a written agreement, on the application of some of the inhabitants of Buffalo Valley, agreed to give a lot of five acres, to be laid off at the north-east corner of the Edward Bonsall tract, including a spring, for the purpose of erecting a meeting-house thereon for the Presbyterian congregation. The building was probably erected the ensuing year. The only clew I can find is a receipt among my grandfather's papers dated December 23, 1778, to William Rodman for ten pounds, being in full of a subscription lodged in his hands for building a meeting-house in Buffalo Valley, signed William Clark, Thomas Hutchinson, who were probably the building committee. In 1797 the Shippens made a deed to Samuel Dale and David Watson, trustees appointed by the congregation for that purpose. The courses and distances are important, as the land has been encroached upon. Beginning at a white oak; thence by land then vacant, now (1797) said to belong to Francis Zellers, N. 51° E. 20 perches, to white oak; thence S. 39° E. 40; thence S. 51° W. 20; thence N. 39° W. 40; "for the use of such person or persons who now are, and from time to time hereafter shall be, inhabitants of said Valley, members of and forming together a Presbyterian congregation, to have a meeting-house for worship and a place of burial thereon, and for *no other purpose.*" Deed book "C," page 81, Union county.

It seems from Doctor Greer's statement that the church received an additional grant of five acres adjoining, of the "Isaiah Althouse" tract, either of Henry Vandyke or Francis Zeller, former owners. The old church was accordingly built on both tracts and the one half on land now claimed by Daniel Reugler, as an inspection of the old foundation will show, and many persons were buried in Mr. Reugler's field. The Althouse tract was patented to Henry Vandyke, 14th of December, 1774. On the same day he sold off to Captain John Foster nineteen acres and ninety-four perches, adjoining Foster's. Henry Vandyke's will, dated 18th October, 1782, wills his mansion, farm and tan-yard to John. John and Martha, his wife, sell to Francis Zeller two hundred and eighty-nine acres. This would, therefore, include the alleged five acres given to the church. It is probable, therefore, that Francis Zeller was the donor, and the addition made in 1789 to the building was put on that part.

Flavel Clingan says ",the old church had three doors and nine windows, one immediately behind the pulpit and two on each of the ends and sides. Part of the church covered where the present pulpit is, and extended out into the fields behind the present church, that it was put on the line of the two grants of five acres each, and the careless trustees lost five acres when Mr. Reugler bought."

Surveys, &c.

Among the surveys made this year in "Upper Moreland," as Hartley township territory was then called, William McMurray, on the 31st of May, surveyed the Jacob Young and Conrad Weiser tracts; also Anthony Fricker and Daniel Levan; June 2, Philip Cole tract, adjoining Jacob Landis.

In this year William McCandlish, senior, and Samuel Martin came from North Britain, and settled on the Billmyer place, afterwards Gebhart's, and the place now owned by Joseph Meixell's heirs; which Martin sold to George May, who sold it to Thomas Wilson, (grandfather of Francis Wilson,) 30th July, 1793.

James Young settled on the place now owned by David Gross, in Union township. Isaac Hanna, a gunsmith, from Lancaster, bought it in 1780 for £600. Three hundred and nine acres, *et al.*

The Weyland place, (now George F. Miller, Esquire,) in Kelly, was valued at 40*s*. per acre by witnesses.

Titzell's Mill.

1st of December is the date of the deed from William Robb and Olive, his wife, to Henry Titzell, for fifty acres on Little Buffalo creek, the mill tract now owned by Jonas Rauch, in White Deer township. The mills were built during this winter, as he is assessed in 1775 with grist and saw mill. Titzell's mill was a rendezvous during the Revolution, and a station of the defenders of the frontiers.

Titzell never returned from Cumberland county after the great runaway of 1778, and we find Nagel Gray, of Northampton county, in possession in 1783, and a conveyance from Titzell to Gray on the 5th of May, 1786. Gray died the same year, and his son John took the tract, who, with Jane his wife, sold to George Reniger on the 18th of April, 1796. Reniger failed, and it went by the name of Kelly's mills for a long time after, until Mr. Rauch's purchase.

Deaths.

Joseph Rotten, of Buffalo, died this year. His will is the first one recorded at Sunbury, on 4th August. He left a widow, Mary, children, Thomas, Roger, and Elizabeth, He lived up Penn's creek, near White springs. Samuel Mathers and James McCoy witnessed it.

Thomas McGuire also died in June. He left a son, Francis.

Major Ennion Williams' Journal.

Ennion Williams, afterwards major of Colonel Miles' rifle regiment, kept a journal of a trip to the frontiers. The original is in possession of Captain A. H. McHenry, the noted surveyor of Jersey Shore, from which I extract:

"October 19, at Fort Augusta, Messrs. Scull, Maclay, Hunter, Troy, &c., entertained me in a very kind and friendly manner. October 25, started for Kishacoquillas valley, with William Foster; forded the river, and arrived at Wolfe's tavern, two miles from Sunbury, (this must have been at Shamokin dam,) where I took suddenly sick. A person in the next room played so pleasantly on a violin, and with such an effect, I was soon able to get up. We then passed through a level country to Michael Swingle's, eight miles; thence to Is. Dalton's, on Middle creek. The land here is good. We lately sold it for £100 per hundred acres. We passed through Potter's tract, which is very fine land, and John Swift's land, which is very good. Several friends settled above this. The land is well timbered—walnut, black oak, and maple—and a very pretty valley, called Beaver Dam valley. 27th, slept at Nathaniel Hazen's on a chaff bed on the floor; breakfast—elegant milk, butter, pumpkin butter, Indian corn, and venison. (Snyder county fare in the olden time.) Then rode nine miles through a valley between Jack's mountain and Limestone ridge.

"We crossed the run on which is our one hundred and fifty-nine acres, with a mill seat. The stream is now pretty large. The land is stony, but very well timbered. October 27, Hazen tells me that Reed has got (within this twelve months) a warrant for the hundred and fifty-nine acres, and that he intends to build a mill there, in spite of any person. They say that he is a scheming fellow, and that he has taken out warrants for other person's lands, as well as ours. We dined in the shade of a tree, screened from the remarkable heat of the sun, and fed our horses on a blanket near a run, and eat heartily of our hard cakes and solid venison. We continued up this valley, and passed by some good bottoms, with poplar, walnut, and shelbark, &c.; but there are no large bodies together. The road is very stony for several miles, yet level, and the land well timbered.

"Foster's, and the land near it, is very good wheat land, and but little meadow. We passed in sight of our two hundred acres on a branch of Jack's creek, in the name of D. Beveridge, and the land near is very good meadow ground." The D. Beveridge tract he describes as situate on Mitchel Springs, which empties into Jack's creek about two miles from Kishacoquillas, (probably now in Decatur township, Mifflin county.)

On the 19th of July a petition was presented to the Assembly from the inhabitants of Northumberland county, stating that the county was but thinly inhabited, and had within the limits of its jurisdiction a great body of intruders from the Colony of Connecticut, who refused subjection to the government, and that they found themselves unable to enforce the laws, through the want of a proper goal; whereupon an act was promptly passed, on the 23d, granting £800 out of the treasury to build a goal.

1775.

PENNSYLVANIA CONVENTION—ASSESSMENT LIST OF BUFFALO—REVOLUTIONARY STRUGGLE INAUGURATED—ROLL OF CAPTAIN JOHN LOWDON'S AND CAPTAIN JAMES PARR'S COMPANIES.

OHN PENN, Governor. Samuel Hunter, member of Assembly. On the 20th of May, James Potter was returned, and took his seat as additional member of Assembly. Samuel Hunter and William Plunket presided in turn over the courts. 29th July, Samuel Maclay, Robert Robb, John Weitzel, and Henry Antis, Justices of the Quarter Sessions, &c. March 17, Alexander Hunter was appointed Collector of Excise, *vice* Thomas Lemmon. 12th October, William Scull was commissioned Sheriff; Samuel Harris, Coroner. County Commissioners, Casper Reed, William Gray, Esquire; County Assessors, Paul Geddes, George Wolfe, Joseph Green, James McClure, John Weitzel,

and James McClenachan. Officers of Buffalo: Constable, Henry Vandyke; Overseers, John Thompson and John Aurand; Supervisors, Robert Clark and Henry Pontius.

On the 23d of January the convention for the Province of Pennsylvania assembled at Philadelphia, and continued until the 28th. William Plunket, Esquire, and Casper Weitzel, Esquire, representing the county of Northumberland.

This convention approved of the proceedings of the Continental Congress, recommended a law prohibiting the future importation of slaves into the Province; resolved to afford all necessary assistance and relief in case the trade of the city of Philadelphia should be suspended in consequence of the struggle; that it was the earnest wish to see harmony restored between Great Britain and the Colonies, but in the event the former should determine to effect a submission by force to the late arbitrary acts of Parliament, it was our indispensable duty to resist such force, and at every hazard to defend the rights and liberties of America.

It was resolved to kill no sheep under four years old, or sell such to the butchers, and the setting up of woolen manufactures, especially for coating, flannel, blankets, rugs, &c., was recommended; also, the raising of madder and dye stuffs, flax and hemp, making of salt and saltpeter, gunpowder, nails and wire, making of steel, paper, setting up manufactures of glass, wool, combs, cards, copper in sheets, bottoms and kettles. It was further recommended to the inhabitants to use the manufactures of their own and neighboring Colonies, in preference to all others; and that a manufacturer or vender of goods who should take advantage of the necessities of the country to raise prices should be considered an enemy to his country.

At February sessions, Samuel Maclay, Henry Pontius, William Irwin, and William Gray reported the first public road ever laid out by order of court through the Valley. Haines' road ran from Northumberland, by way of Dry valley, crossing into Limestone township now, and along Penn's creek, and by way of the Narrows, into Penn's valley, where he owned large tracts of land about Aaronsburg; but this was a private enterprise. His four mile tree is referred to as a landmark ever since his day, standing in the center of the Narrows. The road we now speak of commenced on Ludwig Derr's land, about fifteen perches above where Christian Het-rick* now lives, at a hickory on the West Branch of the Susquehanna, and ran the following courses and distances: S. 85° W. 742, to white oak, W. 156 post; N. 85° W. 80, pine; S. 85° W. 300; S. 70° W. 550, pine; S. 82° W. 224, black oak; S. 67° W. 174, white oak; S. 74° W. 138, pine; S. 49° W. 138; S. 62° W. 419; S. 75° W. 168; S. 85° W. 158, white oak; N. 87° W. 98; S. 71° W. 136; S. 85° W. 266; S. 75° W. 116, white oak: twelve miles twenty-eight perches. After protracting, I found the course to correspond with the site of the road as described by old citizens, viz: Leaving the river at Strohecker's landing, it passed up his lane and by an old house that formerly stood in the southwest corner of Adam Gundy's field; thence along the line between John G. Brown and J. M. Linn, or near it, to and through Mortonsville, through or by the site of Ellis Brown's new house, to a white oak about one hundred rods west of his house. Thus far one course. Thence it curved about the hill, and ran in front of Frederick's, where stood the pine; and thence by Schrack's it ran straight, crossing the present turnpike beyond Biehl's tavern. It then ran north of the turnpike a little distance; thence along its site to another pine which stood near where the Great Western hotel now stands; thence it followed the turnpike site until it reached its terminus, where the Orwig mill road now comes out upon the turnpike, east line of Jane Little warrantee, one hundred and twenty rods west of the officers' survey. It was ordered to be opened thirty-three feet.

Inhabitants in 1775.

It appears, from a memorandum made by Daniel Montgomery, in 1781, that the county assessments were carried off to Paxton (Harrisburg) in 1778, and those of 1773, 1774, and 1776 lost.

The following list is copied from that of 1775, which is in the handwriting of Joseph Green, grandfather of Joseph Green, of Lewisburg. I copy it in full. Matter in brackets I have added. It enumerates the acres of *cultivated* land, of horses, cows, sheep, slaves, and servants belonging to each settler:

* His name is sometimes written Espig. Hetrick resided near the site of John Strohecker's present residence. He was afterwards killed by the Indians. (See postea, 1781.)

ANNALS OF BUFFALO VALLEY. [1775.]

	Acres.	Horses.	Cows.	Sheep.	Slaves.	Servants.	
Allen, Samuel.....	45	2	2				
Aurand, Henry....	15	1	2				
Albright, Jacob ...	6	1	2				
Aurand, Jacob	4	1	1				
Aurand, Daniel....	10	1	1				
Armstrong, William	18	1	2				
Aurand, John.....	40	2	3	....	.....	...	Also grist and saw-mill.
Books, George	12	2	3				
Buchanan, James..	30	2	2	3	.....	...	[Late A.McClure's, now Stolzfus.]
Burn, Peter......	10	2	1	1			
Beatty, Alexander..	30	2	2	....	.....	...	A new settler.
Bolender, John...	20						
Beatty, Hugh.....	....	....	....	....	.....	...	Inmate to Thomas Sutherland.
Bickel, Henry.....	10	1	2	....	.....	...	[Now Henry Mertz's.]
Brunner, Jacob....	4	2	2				
Barnett, Matthew..	....	....	....	....	.....	...	Tenant on James Bremmer's land.
Bolender, Henry..	15	....	....	....	.....	...	Tenant of James Bremmer.
Baker, Wendell....	20	2	2	1	.....	...	[D. H. Kelly's.]
Bashor, John......	4	1	1	....	.....	...	[N. W. of New Columbia.]
Baker, Jacob......	30	2	2	....	.....	...	[Hoffman's, above Datisman's.]
Brundage, Joseph..	50	2	2				
Black, Thomas....	6	1	2	....	.....	...	Stahl's saw-mill, [n'r Union ch.]
[1] Boveard, James ..	50	2	2	....	.....	...	[Isaac Eyre, sr.]
Boveard, William,	....	....	....	....	.....	...	Inmate to James Boveard.
Bower, Casper	10	2	2				
Brosius, John	10	2	2	6			
Boone, Hawkins...	20	...	1	7			
Bennett, William..	3	1	1	....	.....	...	And grist-mill on land belonging to Wm. Blythe.
Blythe, William...	12						
Bennett, William,jr.	17	1	...	3	.....	...	On Wm. Blythe's land.
Blue, Frederick....	10	1	1				
Brown, Matthew...	60	1	2				

[1] Boveard is marked a *free man*, which, under Markham's charter, indicated an elector's qualification. "No person shall be capable of being an elector, or of being elected, unless of the age of twenty-one, and have fifty acres of land, ten whereof being seated or cleared, or be otherwise worth £50, clear estate, and have been resident within the government two years before such election."

Name	Acres.	Horses.	Cows.	Sheep.	Slaves.	Servants.	
Cornell, Abraham,	....	...	...	....	...	...	[Coryell?]
Clark, William....	15	2	2				
Cole, Philip.......	25	2	3	....	...	...	[Hartleton.]
Clarke, John......	50	2	3	6	1	1	[He lived on the first farm above Mifflinburg; the name of his slave was "Mel."]
Crawford, Edward,	5	1	1				
Clark, Walter.....	60	2	4	10	...	1	
Clark, William....	50	2	3	2	...	1	
Cupples, David....	10	2	2				
Cooper, Robert ...	....	1	2	....	...	...	Lives with William Bennett & crops on the shares.
Cook, Henry.....	7	1	2				
Caldwell, Hugh...	35	2	2				
Clark, Robert ...	60	2	3				
Carson, James....	2						
Correy, Robert....	....	1	1	....	...	...	Inmate to John Kelly.
Carter, William....	15	1	2				
Coon, Nicholas....	10	2	3				
Ditelman, Peter ...	2	...	...	....	...	...	Poor; [lived where late Jno. Schrack, Esquire, lived.]
Duchman, Stephen,	10	1	...	....	...	...	Lives on Derr's land.
Doudrick, John....	3	1	1	....	...	...	[Adam Young's.]
Derr, Ludwig.....	30	5	4	2	...	...	Grist and saw-mill.
Dale, Samuel.....	20	1	2				
Doty, Levi.......	15	1	1				
Davis, John.......	....	...	...	....	...	...	Is a mason; lives at Abel Reese's.
Deats, Morris.....	5	1	1				
Deats, David.	36	...	1				
Dale, Christian....	2	2	1	....	...	...	Lives on Peter Wilson's place, [now Jas. Lawson, Esquire's.]
Derr, Yost........	15	1	1				
Duncan, David....	....	2	4	....	...	...	Lives on L. Derr's.
Daniel, Adam.....	3	...	...	....	...	...	Tenant on Colonel Francis', below Grove's, [now W. T. Linn's.]
Emerick, David ...	3	...	...	....	...	...	[Widow Brown's tavern in Union township.]
Evey, Adam......	30	...	2	....	...	...	On Simon Snithers' land.
Etsweiler, George..	15	2	2	3			

	Acres.	Horses.	Cows.	Sheep.	Slaves.	Servants.	
Eaken, John	....	1	1				On Rob. Clark's.
Elder, Thomas	....	1	1				Living on James Fleming's, (late James Dale's.)
Eyer, Abraham	4	2	2				
Evey, Christian	12	2	1				
Farren, James	5						
Fought, Jonas	20	2	3	4			[South Chap. Hollow.]
Fought, Michael	....	....	....	....	....	....	Lives with Jonas.
Frederick, George	13	1	3	1			} [These two lived at Cross Roads on McCreight's.]
Frederick, Peter	13	2	2				
Foster, John, senior,	20	2	3	3			
Fought, Jacob	40	2	4				
Foster, William	....	....	1				
Foster, John, junior,	60	....	1	2	....	1	
Fleming, James	10						
Fruit, Robert	3	3	5	1	....	1	
Fisher, John	10	2	1				[Datisman's.]
Fisher, Christian	....	1	2				[White Deer mills.]
Fought, Conrad	5	1	1				
Fisher, Samuel	3	2	2				Ferry.
Fulton, John	15	1	2				
Fleming, Hans	15	1	2				Up Black's run.
Filey, John	35	3	1				
Green, Joseph	30	2	2				
Glen, Andrew	10	....	1				[Afterwards Emerick's.]
Greenlee, William	10	1	2				
Grochang, Jacob	49	1	3				[Heberling's.]
Gundy, Christ., Van	10	....	2				
Gray, William	60	2	3	7			[Paul Geddes.]
Gibson, Andrew	100	1	2				Ferry.
Green, Ebenezer	10	1	3				
Graham, Edward	100	1	2				
Graham, Thomas	4	....	2				
Groninger, Leonard	10	2	2				
Grove, Michael	20	1	2	2			Ferry.
Huston, John	8	1	1				
Haines, George	30	2	3	3			Grist and saw mill.
Hessler, Michael	6	2	1			1	
Hessler, John	5	....	1				
Hunter, Samuel	10	5	2	1	1	1	
Hamilton, Robert	28	1	1	3			
Hoy, Philip	12	2	2	1			

	Acres.	Horses.	Cows.	Sheep.	Slaves.	Servants.	
Hiney, Hieronimus	7	1	1				Capt Irwin's place.
Hiltman, John....	6	2	2				[John Beeber's, on Buffalo.]
Heckel, Andrew...	2	1	1				[Doctor Dougal's.]
Hammond, David..	3	1	1				
Hammond, James...	10	1	1				
Hunter, James.....	40	1	1				
Hutchinson, Thos..	50	2	2				[Little Buffalo creek.]
Hood, Elizabeth...	50						
Harbster, David..	20	2	2				
Huling, Marcus...	5	1	1				
Irwin, William....	24	2	3	5		1	
Iterburn, Jacob....	5	2	2				
Johnston, Alex....	20	1	1				Lives on George Cribble's land.
Jordan, William...	20	2	1				[William Stadden's White Deer.]
Klinesmith, Baltzer,	15	2	1				Lives on George Shultz's land.
Kilday, John......	10	1					On John Reed's, [mouth of White Deer creek.]
Keen, Jacob......	5		1				
Kelly, Lawrence...		1	1				
Leonard Peter,....	15	2	1				On Dr. Wiggins' land, [now Major Simonton's.]
Lee, John........	20	1	1	10		1	
Leech, William....	35	1	1				
Lewis, Daniel.....	9	1	1				
Laughlin, Samuel..	30	1	1				Freeman.
Links, Jacob......	25	4	3				Adjoining William Clark's.
Low, Cornelius....	40	3	3				
Leas, Nicholas.....		3					On John Boal's land, on White Deer creek.
Low, William.....	7	1	2				
Luckens, Thomas..	25	2	2				New settler.
Lowdon, John.....	50	6	6		1	2	
Miller, Benjamin...							Lives on James Thom's land.
McKelvey, James..	4	1	1				
Moore, James.....	25	1	1				On Joseph Green's land.
McCashon, John...	7						Lives on Abram Cribble's land, [de Haas' large tract.]
Miller, Frederick..	5						
Miller, Jacob......	2						

	Acres.	Horses.	Cows.	Sheep.	Slaves.	Servants.	
Maclay, Samuel...	25	2	2	....	1	1	Slave aged 20.
Moor, William.....	13	1	2				
Myers, Henry.....	6	2	1				
McCoy, James....	15	1	2				
Mathers, Samuel...	15	2	2				
Mitchell, John....	12	1	1				
McCandlish, Wm..	16	2	3	....	....	....	[John Lesher lives on site of McCandlish's residence.]
Martin, Samuel...	15	2	3	....	....	....	[Now farm-house of Joseph Meixell's heirs.]
McClure, Thomas..	....	....	....	....	....	....	On William Armstrong's land, [south of New Columbia.]
Moore, Thomas...	12	2	....	....	1		
Moore, Henry....	....	....	....	.	....	....	At Thos. Moore's.
Martin, Robert...	6	1	1	....	....	....	New settler.
McLaughlin, James,	10	2	1				
McGinnet, Charles.	9	2	2				
McMahan, Patrick.	9	2	2				
Mackey, William..	....	1	1.	..	....	....	New settler.
McClenachan, Jas..	80	...	1				
Mason, William...	....	2	3	....	....	....	On Thos. Hutchinson's.
McComb, John....	10	1	2				
McGrady, Alex....	20	2	2				
McClung, John....	20	1	3				
Martin, George....	10	1	1				
McCloud, William.	....	....	1				
McDonald, Randall	....	....	....	....	....	....	Lives with John Hiltman.
Nees, John........	..·.	2	1				
Norcross, John.....	....	....	....	....	....	....	Lives on Robt. McCorley's land.
Nobel, Robert.....	....	....	....	....	....	....	On J. Thompson's.
Norconk, Daniel...	3	2	2.	.,...	. . ...	....	[Near New Columbia.]
Overmeier, George	40	2	2	2			
Poak, James	40	2	4				
Patton, Hugh.....	10	2	2				
Pearson, Benjamin..	25	1	2	6			
Pontius, John.....	20	4	4	1			
Pontius, Henry....	15	2	2				

	Acres.	Horses.	Cows.	Sheep.	Slaves.	Servants.	
Pontius, Andrew...	15	2	1				
Reed, William.....	20	1	1				
Reese, Abel.......	40	3	1				
Rearick, John.....	15	2	3				
Rinehard, George..	15	1	1				
Reed, John........	3						
Rote, George......	30	2	5	9	....	1	
Reasoner, John....	3	2	2	....	....	....	New settler.
Rorbaugh, George..	....	....	1	....	....	....	Living at Ludwig Derr's.
Redmond, John...	2	....	1				
Sutherland, Thomas	20	1	2				
Storms, Christian..	30	2	2	2			
Sierer, John.......	60	1	2				
Smith, Adam	10	1	1	....	....	..	[In Limestone, his gr'd children still occupy the old place, near White springs.]
Snyder, Michael...	15	2	2	2			
Scott, John.......	15	1	2	....	....	..	On Rob't. Barber's land.
Shively, Christian..	8	....	1				
Smith, David.....	7	1	1	....	....	....	[The first miller, at Barber's little mill, called Smith's mill, for many years.]
Shively, John.....	9	2	2	....	....	....	[Afterwards captured by the Indians, on Esquire Lincoln's place. He never came back.]
Seller, Peter.......	18	1					
Sips, Joseph.......	10	1	1	....	..:	...	[Lived on late farm of D. Henning.]
Swartz, Peter.....	20	1	3	3	....	....	[Hon. George F. Miller's place.]
Stover, Philip.....	20	2	3				
Smith, Catherine...	10	3	2	....	....	....	[White Deer Mills.]
Sutherland, Daniel..	3	....	1				
Smith, John.......	50	2	1	2	....	....	New settler.
Steen, Alexander...	4	1					
Speddy, William...	25	1	2				
Shoemaker, Peter..	....	1	4				
Shaw, Hamilton...	....	2	1				

Name	Acres	Horses	Cows	Sheep	Slaves	Servants	Notes
Sample, John	23	1	2				
Sample, Robert		1	3				Living on Jas Mc-Clenachan's.
Dreisbach, Martin	30	3	6				
Dreisbach, Jacob							
Dreisbach, Henry							
Townson, C	16	1					
Templeton, Ann	5	1	2				
Thompson, John	60	2	1			1	
Thomas, James							On John Foster's land.
Thornbury, Thomas			1				On Ludwig Derr's.
Tate, John			1				William Clark's.
Tate, Joseph	50	6	1	1			
Titzell, Henry	50	2	2	2			Grist and saw-mill.
Thom, James	4						
Thompson, Robert	10	1	2				
Tavler, Joseph	12	2	3				Freeman on John Lowdon's.
Varner, Daniel	1	1	1				New settler.
Vandyke, Henry	30	2	3				[Now Jackson Rishel's.]
Wilson, John		1	1				
Wilson, Matthew	6	1	2				
Wilson, Peter	30	2	2				
Wolfe, George	40	3	2	4			
Welker, Leonard	15	1	2				
Wise, Jacob	20	2	2				
Watson, Patrick	7						On Robert Barber's land.
Wierbaugh, John	8	2	3				
Williams, George	20	2	2				
Watson, Hugh	20	2	2				
Wolfe, Andrew			1				LudwigDerr's land.
Weyland, George	8	1					
Weeks, Joseph	20		5				
Wertz, Dietrich	3	1	1				New settler.
Wilson, William	25	2	1				[Now Rev. J. Rodenbaugh's.]
Young, Matthew	8	1	3				
Young, James	50	2	2				
Young, Samuel	15	2	2				[Dry valley.]
Kennedy, Samuel	10	2	3				On Wm. Blythe's.
Kennedy, John		1	1				
Anderson, Thomas	12	1	1				
Rodman, William	60	2	3				

	Acres.	Horses.	Cows.	Sheep.	Slaves.	Servants.
Row, Joseph	30	1	1			
Johnston, John	8	1	1			
Wildgoose, Michael	4	1	1			
Glover, John	5	2	2			

Whole number of acres cultivated in the Valley, four thousand three hundred and eighty-three; total horses, three hundred and forty; cows, four hundred and fourteen; sheep, one hundred and forty-one; taxable inhabitants, two hundred and sixty; six grist and saw-mills, and five slaves.

In the summer of 1873, John Lesher tore down the old house, known many years as Billmyer's tavern, and afterwards as "Gebhart's." On taking off the more modern weather-boards, a log building, about forty-four feet square, was disclosed. In the logs were marks of arrows, and many bullet holes. Between the flooring he found a shingle, on which was written, "James Taler; built, 1775," the name, no doubt, of the carpenter, as William McCandlish was the owner. William McCandlish died in the fall of 1783, and it was sold, in 1784, to Andrew Billmyer, (grandfather of Philip Billmyer, of Lewisburg,) who sold it on the 21st of May, 1812, to Philip Gebhart. It was the place of rendezvous for the people in the lower end of the Valley during the subsequent Indian troubles, 1776–1783.

In 1815, Michael Shirtz's deposition was taken, in a suit between John Hoy and John Stees. He said he came to live in the neighborhood in 1775. That the land in dispute between them was then occupied by Michael Snyder, (east end of Peter Wolfe's warrantee.) He had cleared eight or nine acres and had grain in. It adjoined what was called the "Switzer tract," surveyed in the warrantee name of John James LeRoy, and between it and the Limestone ridge. Snyder occupied it until the country was drove by the Indian, 1778 and 1779. After that, Martin Rinehart bought the land, and sold part to Andrew Pontius and part to Christopher Boohave, (Bogenreif.) That the first year the settlers returned after the war, he saw Andrew Pontius in possession of it, inclosed in fence and grain growing upon it. The latter sold to John Stees. The deponent moved to the territory of Ohio in 1800.

In the spring of 1775, Yost Hoffman, of Lancaster county, blacksmith, bought of Jacob Baker, the place next above Datisman's. His descendants still occupy it. John Forsyth, a deputy for William Maclay, made quite a number of surveys this year. These and other surveys are noted, because they show what lands were yet unsettled. The Richard Manning for John Lee, on the river next above the Proprietaries, in Monroe township now. 25th March, the addition to John Foster's order, in the name of John Umstead, near Farmersville. 29th, Jacob Long's, a little north-east of Hartleton. 31st March, 1775, took Daniel Long's note for surveying fee, £2 10s. The William Kelly, on Buffalo mountain, 1st April. Jacob Haines, in Union, lately owned by Major Gibson, 6th May. Aaron Levy on Buffalo mountain. "North line open," he says. No wonder subsequent surveyors could not find it.

12th July, Nehemiah Breese, of Sunbury, surveyed the John Sneagon tract, now Chappel's Hollow, then called Haverly's gap. Whoever tabled his notes, (he died not long after,) and made the return of survey, made the N. 20° W. line from the pine one hundred perches, instead of sixty, to chestnut, which produced a great dispute afterwards between Abraham Eyer and John Brown.

12th August, Breese surveyed the Thomas Smith tract for Joseph Green, on which the latter built his mill, latterly known as Bellas', on Penn's creek, below White spring. He says, not finding the adjoining surveyed line on the west of Craig's survey, to extend by the supposed adjoining lands, to include the above quantity to post, thence an open line by vacant land, to make the beginning. One Nees lived on the west of this open line. When Green's land was sold at sheriff's sale, in August, 1784, it was supposed to include Nees' improvement, and so sold by Mr. Awl, who bought at the sheriff's sale, to Badger, so that twenty acres now owned by Miller, Smith, and others, near White spring, has been occupied, bought and sold over and over again for a century, without any title from the Commonwealth.

27th August, he surveyed a small island for Martin Trester, nearly opposite his house, and another one half mile below his house.

24th, the Joseph Green, south of Captain T. Green. 8th September, Robert Martin, on north branch of Buffalo creek. 8th September, the Thomas Graham, adjoining McClenachan, in White Deer, west of George Leiser's.

Philip Seebold informed me (1872) that George Overmeier, senior, John Rearick, Christian Shively, and Michael Focht were brothers-in-law. Overmeier settled near where Mr. Seebold still lives; Shively, at the mouth of White Spring run; Rearick, near Wehr's tavern; Focht, in Dry valley; and added the singular fact, that he, Seebold, owned at one time the Overmeier, Rearick, and Focht homesteads. He is a grandson of George Overmeier. Conrad Sharp settled upon his tract, in Union township, west of Joseph Shannon.—See case reported, 4 Yeates, 266.

The Revolutionary Struggle Inaugurated.

SUNBURY, 20*th April*, 1775.

GENTLEMEN: The time is at hand when the spirit of Americans that love liberty and constitutional principles will be put to the trial. What has been by them in their different resolves avowed must, perhaps, at last be put in execution. The late alarming news just received from England (which we may depend upon) informs that the British Parliament are determined by force to put in execution every of their supreme edicts, as they style them, together with their late oppressive acts, which we have so long, and with so little or no effect, hitherto complained of. We consider it absolutely necessary to have a general meeting of the whole county, in order to form some regular plan, in conjunction with our countrymen, to give every opposition to impending tyranny and oppression, either by force or otherwise. The time of meeting, we think, will be best on the first day of May next, at ten o'clock in the forenoon, and the place most convenient, at Vandyke's, near Beaver run, in Buffalo Valley. We do, therefore, earnestly request that you will immediately, on the receipt hereof, in the most expeditious manner, notify the inhabitants of your township of this matter, and insist on their attendance without fail there on that day. The place of meeting is such where we cannot expect much accommodation. It will be,

therefore, necessary that every man should provide for himself. We are your humble servants.
<blockquote>Signed by order of the committee.
CAS. WEITZEL. </blockquote>

Directed to John Lowdon, Esquire, and Mr. Samuel Maclay, in Buffalo Valley.

PHILADELPHIA, *June* 15, 1775.

GENTLEMEN: Inclosed are resolves of Congress which we have transmitted to you, and request you will use your utmost diligence to have as many of the best marksmen procured to enlist as fast as possible. They are wanting for immediate service at Boston, and we have not the least doubt but the spirit of our people of this Province will induce them without delay to enter into so glorious a service. You will please to consult with gentlemen of knowledge and interest, as you can, (though not of your committee,) for the more speedy raising of the men, and let us know your sentiments relative to such gentlemen as may be proper for officers, and such as may be agreeable to the men. We hope the counties will advance any moneys necessary, as they shall shortly be repaid by Congress. The honor of Pennsylvania is at stake, and we have not the least doubt but that every nerve will be exerted, not only collectively but individually, to carry this matter into instant execution. You will see by the attestation to be signed by the men, they are to serve one year, unless sooner discharged. This may seem inconvenient, as the enlistments will be in one day. The intention is to discharge on the first day of July, 1776, unless their service may not be wanting so long, according to the attestation, which may possibly happen to be the case, and they may be discharged this fall. Let the committees or officers give certificates for any moneys necessary for the service which the Congress will discharge. It is expected that Cumberland will raise two companies, York one, Lancaster one, Northampton one, and Northumberland and Bedford one.

You will keep the resolves of Congress as secret as the nature of the case will admit, that the arrival of the men at Boston may be the first notice General Gage has of this matter.

The pay of the officers is on the establishment of the whole army; but we beg leave to assure the officers that our interest will be exerted with our Assembly to the utmost to have an addition to their pay, so as to be equal to the pay of officers of the same rank in the Pennsylvania service last war.

We are, with esteem, gentlemen, your most humble servants,

THOMAS WILLING,   JOHN DICKINSON,
JAMES WILSON,   THOMAS MIFFLIN,
CHARLES HUMPHREYS,   GEORGE ROSS.
JOHN MORTON,

IN CONGRESS, *June* 14, 1775.

Resolved, That six companies of expert riflemen be immediately raised in Pennsylvania, two in Maryland, and two in Virginia. That each company, as soon as conpleted, shall march and join the army near Boston, to be there employed as light infantry under the command of the chief officer in that army. That the pay of the officers and privates be as follows:

A captain, at 20 dollars per M.
A lieutenant, at 13⅓ dollars per M.
A sergeant, at 8 dollars per M.
A corporal, at 7⅓ dollars per M.
A drummer, at 7⅓ dollars per M.
A private, at 6⅔ dollars per M.
To find their own arms and clothes.

That the form of enlistment be in the following words:

I have this day voluntarily enlisted myself as a soldier in the American Continental army for one year, unless sooner discharged, and do bind myself to conform in all instances to such rules and regulations as are or shall be established for the government of the said army.

CHARLES THOMPSON, *Secretary.*

True copy: CAS. WEITZEL, *Secretary.*

On this paper is indorsed the following: "July 1, 1775, Cornelius Daugherty enlisted, this day, Robert Tuft, Edward Masters, James Garson, George Saltsman, Robert Rickey, Thomas Gilston, Robert Liney, Robert Carothers, John Hamberton, Michael Hare," in Joseph Green's handwriting.

I have a copy of Captain Lowdon's commission, which is still in possession of Samuel Wright, at Columbia, furnished by the kindness of Mr. Thomas Barber's son, who was at school there. It reads:

IN CONGRESS: The Delegates of the United Colonies of New Hampshire, Massachusetts Bay, Rhode Island, Connecticut, New York, New Jersey, Pennsylvania, the counties of New Castle, Kent, and Sussex, in Delaware, Maryland, Virginia, North Carolina, and South Carolina:

To John Lowdon, Esquire:

We, reposing especial trust and confidence in your patriotism, valor, conduct, and fidelity, do, by these present, constitute and appoint you to be captain of a company of riflemen in the battalion commanded by Colonel William Thompson, in the army of the United Colonies, raised for the defense of American liberty, and for repelling any hostile invasion thereof. You are, therefore, carefully and diligently to discharge the duty of captain, by doing and performing all manner of things thereunto belonging. And we do strictly charge and require all officers and soldiers under your command to be obedient to your orders as captain; and you are to observe and follow such orders and directions, from time to time, as you shall receive from this or a future Congress of the United Colonies, or committee of Congress for that purpose appointed, or commander-in-chief for the time being of the army of the United Colonies, or any other superior officer, according to the rules and discipline of war, in pursuance of the trust reposed in you. This commission to continue in force until revoked by this or a future Congress.

By order of Congress.

JOHN HANCOCK, *President.*

Attest: CHARLES THOMPSON, *Secretary.*

PHILADELPHIA, *June* 25, 1775.

Roll of Captain John Lowdon's Company, First Rifle Regiment, Commanded by Colonel William Thompson.

Captain—Lowdon, John.
First Lieutenant—Parr, James.
Second Lieutenant—Wilson, James.

Third Lieutenant—Wilson, William; promoted second lieutenant January 4, 1776.

Third Lieutenant—Dougherty, John; appointed January 4, 1776.

Sergeants—Hammond, David; McCormick, Alexander; McMurray, William; Dougherty, Cornelius.

Corporals—Henry, Thomas; Edwards, William; Dougherty, Cornelius; White, John, died January, 8, 1776; Carson, James; Cochran, Charles.

Drummer—Grosvenor, Richard.

Privates—Adkins, William; All, Joseph, discharged July 31, 1775; Bernickle, John, afterwards sergeant in the German regiment; Brady, Samuel, afterwards captain lieutenant Eighth Pennsylvania; Briggs, William; Butler, John, discharged January 25, 1776; Calhoun, William; Carothers, Robert; Carson, James, advanced to corporal, January 4; Casaday, John; Cealy, Samuel; Clements, David; Cochran, Charles, advanced to corporal January 8, discharged July 1, 1776, living in Crawford county in 1819; Condon, Peter; Davis, David; Dean, John; Eicholtz, John, residing in Lancaster in 1813; Evans, John; Finkboner, Jacob; Ford, Charles; Garson, James; Ginter, Philip; Gilston, Thomas; Hamilton, John; Harris, David; Hare, Michael; Hempington, Thomas; Henning, Christopher; Humber, William; Jamison, William; Johns, Samuel; Johnston, James; Jones, Lewis; Kilday, Thomas; Kline, Nicholas; Ladley, John; Lowdon, Samuel; Leek, William; Lines, Robert; Lobden, Thomas; Masseker, Reuben, deserted July 31, 1775; Madock, Moses; Malone, John; Maloy, Charles; McMullen, Alexander; McGonigal, Patrick; McConnell, Cornelius; McCoy, Martin; McCleary, James; McMasters, Edward, residing in Lycoming county in 1823; Morgan, William; Murray, William; Murphy, Timothy; Murphy, John; Neely, John, he was captured at Fort Freeland, July, 28, 1779, and taken to Canada; Oakes, Daniel; Oliver, John; Parker, Michael; Peltson, Thomas, re-inlisted in the First Pennsylvania, and was killed by Joseph Blackburn in 1777; Pence, Peter; Ray, John; Richie, Robert; Roach, Bartholomew; Robinson, John; Sands, George; Saltzman, George; Segar, George; Silverthorn, Henry; Shawnee, John, (was a Shawanese Indian, died at Milesburg—see Jones' Juniata Valley, page 352;) Smith, John, (son of Widow Smith, of White Deer Mills;

he never came back from the army;) Speddy, James, (lived and died at New Berlin;) Sutton, Arad, (lived on Lycoming creek; the first Methodist society in northern Pennsylvania was formed at his house, in 1791;) Sweeney, James, discharged July 20, 1775; Teel, John; Tuft, Robert, discharged October 25, 1775; Valentine, Philip, discharged July 20, 1775; Ward, Peter; Ward, John; West, Charles, died January 4, 1776; Whiteneck, Joseph; Wright, Aaron, (residing in Reading in 1840;) Youse, John; Young, Robert, (died in Walker township, Centre county, in 1824.)

Quite a large number of this company re-enlisted for three years, or during the war, in Captain James Parr's company, first regiment, commanded by Colonel Edward Hand, who became colonel when Colonel Thompson was made brigadier.

Of the company, Lieutenant Parr rose to the rank of major, served brilliantly in command of riflemen under Morgan, at Saratoga and Stillwater, and under Sullivan, in 1779. Second Lieutenant William Wilson was promoted captain, March 2, 1777, and continued in the army until the close of the war in 1783. He died at Chillisquaque mills in 1813, while an associate judge of Northumberland county. David Hammond rose to the rank of lieutenant. He was severely wounded in Wayne's attack upon the block-house at Bergen Point, now Jersey City. He died April 22, 1801, from the effects of his wound, and is buried in the Chillisquaque graveyard. He was the father of the late General R. H. Hammond, of Milton. Peter Pence was celebrated in border warfare, and figures conspicuously in Van Campen's narrative. Captain McHenry informs me he died in Crawford township, Clinton county, in 1827. He left a son, John, living in that neighborhood.

Captain Lowdon's company rendezvoused at Sunbury; marched thence to Reading and Easton; thence through northern part of New Jersey, crossed the Hudson at New Windsor, a few miles north-west of West Point; thence, through Hartford, to Cambridge, where it arrived about the 8th of August. McCabe, in his sketches of Captain Samuel Brady, has preserved some few incidents of this service. He says, on one occasion, Brady was sitting on a fence, with the captain, when a cannon ball from a British battery struck the fence, and leveled them both. Brady was the first up, saying "we are not hurt, Captain." I found in a contemporary newspaper an account of the island fight, to which McCabe alludes, when he says: "Lowdon's company was ordered to drive the British from an island on which they had landed to forage. Brady was considered too young to go along, and left behind; but, to the astonishment of the captain, he followed after, and was the second man on the island."

November 9, the British landed at Lechmere Point, one and a half miles from Cambridge, under cover of a fire from their batteries on Bunker, Breed, and Copp's hills, as also from a frigate, which lay three hundred yards off the point on which they landed. The high tide prevented our people crossing the causeway for nearly an hour. This time they employed in shooting cows and horses. The battalion of Colonel Thompson took to the water, although up to their armpits, for a quarter of a mile, and, notwithstanding the regular fire, reached the island. Although the enemy were lodged behind stone walls and under cover, on Colonel Thompson's approach they fled, and although the riflemen followed them to their boats with all speed, they could not bring them to an engagement. Our loss was one killed and three wounded; English loss seventeen killed and one wounded.—*Philadelphia Evening Post*, 1775.

In "The Letters of Mrs. Adams," wife of John Adams, page 61, under date 12th November, 1775, is also a notice of this incident: "A number of cattle were kept at Lechmere Point, where two sentinels were placed. In a high tide it is an island. About four hundred men were sent to take the cattle off. As soon as they were perceived, the cannon on Prospect hill were fired on them and sunk one of their boats. A Colonel Thompson, of the riflemen, marched instantly with his men, and though a very stormy day, they regarded not the tide nor waited for boats, but marched over neck-high in water, when the regulars ran without waiting to get off their stock, and made the best of their way to the opposite shore. The general sent his thanks in a public manner to the brave officer and his men."

Colonel Thompson's men are thus described in Thacher's Military Journal: "Several companies of riflemen have arrived here from Pennsylvania and Maryland, a distance of from five hundred to seven hundred miles. They are remarkably stout and hardy men, many of them exceeding six feet in height. They are dressed in rifle shirts and round hats. These men are remarkable for the accuracy of their aim, striking a mark with great certainty at two hundred yards distance. At a review, a company of them, while on a quick advance, fired their balls into objects of seven inch diameter, at a distance of two hundred and fifty yards. They are now stationed on our lines, and their shot have frequently proved fatal to British officers and soldiers." Journal, pages 37 and 38.

PHILADELPHIA, *August* 13, 1775.

DEAR SIR:—We hope this letter will find you safe at the head of your company, acting in support and defense of American liberty; a glorious cause, which must stimulate the breast of every honest and virtuous American, and force him, with undaunted courage and unabated vigor, to oppose those ministerial robbers. We hope the contest will be ended where it began, and that the effusion of blood may be providentially prevented, but, at the same time, we hope to see American liberty permanently established, to have the honor, ere long, to serve in her righteous cause; and we are well convinced that these sentiments prevail throughout this Province. You can't conceive what a martial spirit prevails here, and in what order we are. Two battalions, with the light infantry companies, are very expert in all the manoeuvres, and are generally well furnished with arms. Several companies of riflemen are formed in this city and the adjacent counties, who are become expert in shooting; besides we have sixteen row galleys, with latteen sails, now building. Some of them are already rigged and manned. These galleys are rowed with from twenty-four to thirty oars, and carry each one gun, from eighteen to thirty-two pounds, besides swivel guns, fore and aft. We are told by experienced men that these galleys will prevent any ship of war from coming up this river. All the coast to Georgia is alarmed—prepared to oppose our ministerial enemies. Where, then, can these British bastards, those servile engines of ministerial power, go to steal a few sheep. God and nature has prescribed their bounds. They can't deluge our lands, nor float their wooden batteries beyond the bounds prescribed, nor dare they to penetrate so as from afar to view those high-topped mountains which separate the lower plains from our Canaan, and from whence, should their folly or madness prompt them to attempt it, would come forth our thousands and tens of thousands, with gigantic strides, to wash the plains with the blood of those degenerate invaders of the liberties of mankind.

We, in conjunction with many others, presented a memorial to the Congress, representing the threatened encroachments of the Connecticut invaders of our Province. It was well received, and the Connecticut Delegates and those of this Province were desired to write to their people respectively, and inclosed I send you a copy of the Connecticut letter to Wyoming. Stansbury has in it charge, and it seems to be all that honorable body could do in the affair.

Our partiality for the rifle battalion is so great that we are very anxious to hear of their having distinguished themselves in some great enterprise. This partiality is natural and allowable, when, from one's personal acquaintance with many of their commanders, we can and do with martial pride celebrate their distinguished abilities as riflemen and soldiers.

We are, with great esteem, dear sir, your most humble servants,
ROBERT LETTIS HOOPER, junior,
REUBEN HAINES.

Captain JOHN LOWDON.

P. S.—Present our compliments to Mr. Lukens and Mr. North. Mr. Musser desires his compliments to you and them.

P. S.—August 17. Since the date of this letter Hawkins Boone has been down, and says that the Connecticut people have not attempted any encroachments lately, and, from circumstances, have little reason to think they will.

Major Ennion Williams (journal before referred to) gives the the details of a trip to the camp at Cambridge, under date October 17. He says: guns of one of our batteries, two miles from Boston, firing. One bursted, and killed one man and wounded six. I returned thence to the riflemen's camp, and stopped with Captain Lowdon over night. At daybreak I awoke, and a few minutes after the morning gun fired. All aroused directly; the men repaired with arms and accouterments to the forts and lines, and in about ten minutes the captains, with their companies, were in the fort, drawn along the sides of the fort, and in two or three minutes they began their firing.

The captain stepped on the banket or step, inside at foot of breastwork, and gave the word, "Make ready!" The front rank step on the banket, and second step forward. "Present!" He does not give the word "Fire!" but makes a pause. Then they recover, and face to right about, and march through the files. At the word "Make ready!" again the next rank steps on the banket, and so on continually. Every man is to be sure of his object before he fires, as he rests his piece on the parapet. In about a half an hour the flag was hoisted. They ceased, and retired by regiments to their quarters, and the orderly sergeant read the orders of the day and trials by court martial, &c.

There are numerous notices of this company in the Hand papers in the possession of Mrs. S. B. Rogers, of Lancaster, the granddaughter of General Edward Hand, who was lieutenant colonel, and afterwards colonel of the First Rifle Regiment. On the 24th of October he says: "This morning at dawn Parr, from Northumberland, with thirty men from us, marched for Portsmouth, New Hampshire, to defend that place." On the 8th of March: "I am stationed on Cobble Hill, with four companies of our regiment. Two companies, Cluggages' and Chambers', were ordered to Dorchester on Monday; Ross' and Lowdon's relieved them yesterday. Every regiment is to have a standard and colors. Our standard is to be a deep green ground, the device a tiger, partly inclosed by toils, attempting the pass, defended by a hunter, armed with a spear, (in white,) on crimson field. The motto, *Domari Nolo*."[1]

On the 14th of March, 1776, the company left Cambridge with the battalion which was detached by General Washington, with five other regiments, under General Sullivan, to prevent a landing of the British at New York, when they evacuated Boston. Arrived at Hartford on the 21st, and at New York on the 28th. The company was stationed on Long Island during May and until June 30th, when it was mustered out of service.

[1] This standard is still in possession of Thomas Robinson, Esquire, grandson of Lieutenant Colonel Thomas Robinson, of the First Pennsylvania, and was on exhibition at the Centennial, 1876. I identified it by this description, found among the Hand papers.

Roll of Captains James Parr's company, enlisted for three years or during the war, from July 1, 1776.

Captain—Parr, James, promoted major October 9, 1778.
First Lieutenant—Wilson, James.
Second Lieutenant—Wilson, William, promoted captain March 2, 1777.
Third Lieutenant—Dougherty, John.
Sergeants—Hammond, David, (promoted second lieutenent, September 14, 1777; first lieutenant, May 12, 1779,) McCormick, Alexander; McMurray, William; Dougherty, Cornelius.
Privates—Allen, David; Bacher, Michael; Bradley, John; Callahan, Daniel; Campbell, Daniel; Condon, Peter; Conner, James; Coons, Mansfield; Davis, David; Dubois, Richard; Delling, Cornelius; Donahue, Patrick; Edwards, William; Griffin, John; Hagerty, William; Hammond, John; Henry, Philip; Hinson, Aquila; Hutchinson, John; Jones, Lewis; Leech, William; Lochry, Michael; Loughrey, James; McCleary, James; McConnell, Cornelius; McCormick, Henry; McGaughey, Hugh; Malone, John; Meloy, Charles; Moore, James; Moore, William; Morgan, William; Murphy, John; Murray, Patrick; Noishen, John; Norton, George; Oliver, John; Paine, Thomas; Peltson, Thomas; Peter, Philip; Rankin, John; Ray, John; Ryan, William; Saltman, George; Scott, Samuel; Scott, William; Sprigg, James; Speddy, James; Stewart, Thomas; Sullivan, Maurice; Thompson, Alexander; Toner, John; Warren, George; Washburn, Jonathan; Wilson, Matthew; Willson, Samuel; Whiteneck, Joseph; Youse, John.

Road from Bald Eagle to Sunbury.

The viewers reported this road at November sessions. I copy so much as relates to our Valley, as it indicates the names and residence of early settlers:

"From a white oak in the Narrows, between White Deer and Buffalo Valleys, two miles ninety-nine perches, to Smith's mills, (now Candor's;) thence to white oak, west side of Blythe's mill (which was probably nearer the mouth of the creek;) thence to McClures, (who lived on Blythe's land;) thence to a white oak opposite the lower end of Marcus Huling's island, (Milton bridge island;) thence to a plumb at Peter Swartz's, (Miller's place;) thence to a stone at Clark's, (late John Kling's ;) thence to a post at Robert Fruit's, (Hinely's;) thence to a post at William Gray's, (now Paul Geddes' ;) thence to Buffalo creek, (where the iron bridge now spans the creek;) thence to a pine near the head of Derr's dam ; thence to a pine, corner of Abel Reese's, (*i. e.* through the University grounds, to Adam Gundy and William Brown's corner;) thence to a post at Aurand's barn, (Jenkins' ;) thence to John Lee's, (Winfield ;) thence to Andrew Gibson's ; thence to the gum near Reuben Haines' road ; thence down the same to the black oak on the west bank of the river, opposite Sunbury."

At the same sessions, the great road up the Valley was extended, through the Narrows, to the Great Plains, now in Centre county.

25th December occurred Plunket's expedition to Wyoming. Colonel Kelly and some others from the Valley were along. Jesse Lukens, Surveyor General Lukens' son, was killed. The history of this expedition, taken from the records at Harrisburg, I will give in brief :

On the 23d of November, the Speaker laid before the Assembly a letter from Samuel Hunter, and others, stating that two of the magistrates and the sheriff of the county had an interview with Zebulon Butler and some others of the principal men among the Connecticut settlers at Wyoming, and read the resolves of the Assembly to them, and inquired whether they would peaceably submit to the laws of Pennsylvania. They answered that they despised the laws of Pennsylvania, and never would submit to them unless compelled by force. The magistrates received a great deal of abuse, and returned a different road from that in which they had gone, on account of the risk of their lives.

The Assembly, on the 25th, requested the Governor to issue orders for a due execution of the laws of the Province in Northumberland county, which the Governor did in a letter of that date to the justices and sheriff. The report of the latter to the Governor is dated Sunbury, 30th December, 1775, and states that pursuant to his orders, a number of warrants for the apprehension of a number of persons residing at Wyoming, charged on oath with illegal practices and crimes, were placed in the Sheriff's hands. He judged it prudent to raise the *posse* of the county, and a body of near five hundred men accompanied him to the neighborhood of Wyoming. They were met by some of the people; one of whom was said to be an officer. The intentions of the sheriff and his *posse* were explained, and that no violence or molestation would be offered any one submitting to the laws. The sheriff had proceeded but a little further when he was fired upon, and Hugh McWilliams was killed and three others dangerously wounded. It was found impossible to force a passage on that side of the river, as the Narrows had been fortified with great care, and were lined with numbers of men, to which ours bore no reasonable proportion. An attempt was then made to cross the river in the night, for greater secrecy, to reach the settlements of the persons against whom the process had issued. When the boats had nearly reached the opposite shore, and were entangled in a margin of ice, too thin to bear the weight of a man, they were, without previous challenge, repeatedly fired upon by a party on top of the bank. Jesse Lukens received a mortal wound, of which he is since dead. As a landing could not be effected, the boats returned. Baffled in the second attempt, and the weather being intolerably severe, and receiving information that the parties he desired to arrest were chief in command in the breastworks, it was deemed advisable to desist from any further attempt. A constant fire was kept upon our men from the opposite side, while they retreated through a long narrows. One man only, however, was wounded in the arm, &c.

This report is signed by William Scull, sheriff; Samuel Harris, coroner; and the justices, William Plunket, Samuel Hunter, Michael Troy, and John Weitzel.

1776

White Deer Township Erected—Associators—Second Battalion—
Colonel Potter—Inhabitants of Penn's—Churches of the Valley—
Constitutional Convention—Incident at Derr's Trading-House—
Minutes of the County Committee—Roll of Captain Weitzel's
Company—Fourth Battalion of Associators—Roll of Captain John
Clarke's Company—Roster of Twelfth Pennsylvania.

OHN PENN, Governor, until September 28, when the New Constitution went into effect. The surveys, made under John Penn's warrants, until December of this year, were afterwards legalized. James Potter, additional Member of Assembly. Colonel Samuel Hunter, member of the Committee of Safety, at Philadelphia. William Maclay, Prothonotary; William Scull, Sheriff; County Commissioners, Thomas Hewitt, William Gray. 22d January, John Weitzel sworn in as County Commissioner. Attorneys admitted, William Price Gibbs, and William Lawrence Blair.

Officers of Buffalo township: Constable, Christian Storms; Overseers, John Clarke and John Pontius; Supervisors, Joseph Green and Jacob Fought.

At February sessions, White Deer township was set off from Buffalo, by a line beginning at the upper side of Buffalo creek, at its mouth; thence up the same to the mouth of Spruce run; thence up the same to the forks thereof; thence up the north-east branch to the head thereof; thence by a straight line to the four-mile tree, on Reuben Haines' road, on the line of Potter township. Its first officers were: Peter Swartz, constable; Walter Clark and Matthew

Brown, overseers; Hugh Caldwell and Robert Fruit, supervisors. Henry Iddings bought the Parsons' place, adjoining Colonel Kelly's, and moved into the Valley. During the summer of this year Widow Smith added a boring-mill to her other mills, near the mouth of White Deer creek. Here a great number of gun-barrels were bored for the Continental army.

NORTHUMBERLAND, *January* 24, 1776.

I do hereby certify that at an election for field officers, held at Ludwig Derr's, on the West Branch of the Susquehanna, on Tuesday, the 12th day of September last, the following gentlemen were regularly chosen for the upper division, of the county of Northumberland, viz: James Potter, Esquire, colonel; Robert Moodie, Esquire, lieutenant colonel; Mr. John Kelly, first major; Mr. John Brady, second major.

WILLIAM SCULL,
Chairman of the Committee.

A Return of the Names of the Captains and other Officers of the several Companies, in the Upper Division of the County of Northumberland, with the Ranks of said Companies and number of Men.

Arthur Taggart, first captain,
Cornelius Atkinson, first lieutenant,
James McClung, second lieutenant,
James Wilson, ensign.
} 85 privates.

William Gray, second captain,
William Clark, first lieutenant,
James Murdoch, second lieutenant,
William Thompson, ensign.
} 90 privates.

David Berry, third captain,
William Hammond, first lieutenant,
Israel Parsels, second lieutenant,
Benjamin Burt, ensign.
} 45 privates.

Samuel Dale, fourth captain,
William Bennet, first lieutenant,
Hawkins Boone, second lieutenant,
Jesse Weeks, ensign.
} 67 privates.

Cookson Long, fifth captain,
William Mucklehatton, first lieutenant,
Robert Fleming, second lieutenant, } 59 privates.
Robert Fleming, junior, ensign.
Samuel Wallis, sixth captain,
John Scudder, first lieutenant,
Peter Jones, second lieutenant, } 91 privates.
James Hampton, ensign.
James Murray, seventh captain,
William Murray, first lieutenant,
Thomas Plunket, second lieutenant, } 60 privates.
Andrew Robinson, ensign.
Henry Antes, eighth captain,
Thomas Brandon, first lieutenant,
Alexander Hamilton, second lieutenant, } 58 privates.
Simon Cole, ensign.
John McMillan, ninth captain,
John McConnol, first lieutenant,
John McCormick, second lieutenant, } 43 privates.
Charles Wilson, ensign.
David Hayes, tenth captain,
Charles Clark, first lieutenant, } 41 privates.
Thomas Gray, ensign.
Philip Davis, eleventh captain,
James Aspey, first lieutenant,
John Nelson, second lieutenant, } 74 privates.
Jacob Fulmore, ensign.

NORTHUMBELRAND, 24*th January*, 1776.

I do hereby certify the above to be a true return, of the several companies, which, form the battalion in the upper division of the county of Northumberland, as delivered in to me.

WILLIAM SCULL,
Chairman of the Committee.

To the COMMITTEE OF SAFETY OF THE PROVINCE OF PENNSYLVANIA.

The following imperfect list of the inhabitants of Penn's township is taken from the duplicate of Christian Seecrist, collector for this year, duplicate being mutilated: Adams, George; Albright,

Jacob; Albright, Frederick; Arnold, Casper; Arnold, Lawrence;
Augustine, Hieronimus; Ault, Michael; Balt, Adam; Bander,
Adam; Baker, William; Berst, Peter; Bear, Jacob; Bickel, Tobias;
Bomberger, John; Bower, Peter; Bower, Henry; Bright, John;
Bressler, Nicholas; Brouse, John; Brau, Martin; Bombach, George;
Crean, John; Hassinger, Jacob; Hosterman, Peter; Hosterman,
Jacob, junior; Jacobs, Joseph; Jorday, Peter; Jordan, Philip;
Jost, Casper; Kerstetter, Michael; Kerstetter, Bastian; Keller,
Michael; Kebler, John; Kline, Andrew; Kline, Jacob; Kline,
George; Kline, Stophel; Kroo, Godfrey; Kremer, Peter; Kremer,
Daniel; Graybill, (Krebill,) John; Kreger, Henry; Krail, Michael;
Laudenslager, George; Seiver, Adam, inmate; Lewis, John, inmate;
Lepley, Michael; Leist, David; Lemley, Leonard; Livingood,
Jacob; Lively, John; Livengood, F.; Livey, Peter; Lowrey,
George; Long, Christian; Livengood, George; Maurer, Lawrence;
Maurer, Peter; Manning Richard; Markley, Peter; Markley,
Simeon; Martin, Frederick; Mensch, Charles; Menich,
Simeon; Meiser, Michael; Meiser, John; Meiser, John; Meese,
Thomas; Miser, Henry; Miller, Henry; Miller, Christian; Miller,
Frederick; Miller, Dewalt; Miller, George; Moon, William; Moon,
Casper, junior; Motz, George, inmate; Motz, John; Moore, Andrew;
Moon, Casper, senior; Motz, Michael; Mull, Anthony; Murray,
Alexander; Myer, Charles; Myer, Jacob, junior; Myer, Jacob,
senior; Myer, Alexander; Myer, Stophel; McQueen, John; McKean,
William; Newcomer, Francis; Nees, William; Newman,
Jacob; Neff, Jacob; O'Brien, Patrick; Puff, Dewall; Pyle, Peter;
Reger, Michael; Reed, John; Reager, Adam, junior; Reichenbach,
John, senior; Reichenbach, John, junior; Reed, Casper;
Ream, John; Riddle, Yost; Richart, Henry; Righter, Christian;
Right, Ellis; Row, George; Row, George, junior; Row, John;
Row, Martin; Roush, Casper; Roush, George; Robert, John;
Rush, John; Ryne, Henry; Sense, Frederick; Seecrist, Christian;
Schrock, John; Schrock, George; Shaffer, Peter; Shaffer, Andrew;
Shaffer, Ludwig; Sharrett, Jacob; Sherrick, John; Shedderly,
Andrew; Shallenberger, Lawrence; Shock, Mathias; Simeon,
Joseph; Smith, John; Smith, Nicholas; Snyder, Harman; Snyder,
Simon; Snyder, Anthony; Snider, John; Snevely, Abraham;
Swift, John; Spayd, Jacob; Spees, Jacob; Stees, Jacob; Steel,

John; Stephen, Adam; Stinley, Daniel; Stigleman, Jacob; Straup, Peter; Strayer, Mathias; Strump, Casper; Stroam, Christian; Stock, Melchior; Summerouser, Henry; Sutton, Stephen; Swengle, Michael; Swartz, John; Swift, John; Swoab, George; Trester, Martin, junior; Trester, Michael; Truckenmiller, Peter; Troutner, George; Ulrich, George; Wales, John; Wallace, Samuel; Walter, Ludwig; Walter, Jacob; Warfel, Henry; Weaver, Michael; Weiser, Peter, senior; Weiser, Benjamin, Esquire; Weirich, Peter; Weirich, William; Whitmer, Peter; Whitmore, Michael; Wittenmyer, Andrew; Wittenmyer, Ludwig; Wing, Hugh; Wise, George; Worrah, or Woodrow, Ludwig; Zellar, John; Zerbach, Bartel; Zimmerman, Stophel; Zanzinger, Adam.   Single men—Bickle, Simon; Dellman, Andrew; Dill, Leonard; Dunkle, Charles; Garret, Henry; Havelock, Jacob; Isenhower, Frederick; Kremer, Daniel; Kerstetter, Martin; List, Andrew; Maxwell, James; Meshall, Daniel; Miller, Conrad; Myst, John; Rickert, John; Stroup, John; Snider, Stophel; Stock, Peter; Weaver, John; Zeller, Henry.

The churches in what was called in general Shamokin, on both sides of the Susquehanna, about the junction of the North and West Branches, namely, Mahony, Sunbury, Middle Creek and Buffalo Valley, were in existence as early as 1776. In the minutes of *Cœtus*, held in Lancaster, May 1, is a minute " that different congregations in Shamokin having asked for such an arrangement as to have ministers visit them, it was resolved that ministers should visit them occasionally during this year, and preach to them," &c. Harbaugh's Fathers of the German Reformed Church, 3d vol., 34th page. The German Reformed Church was under the supervision of the church in Holland until about the year 1791, and only such ministers were received by the church as were either sent over by the Fathers in Holland, or had their indorsement. *Ibid.*, 2d vol.

Convention of 1776.

In consequence of a circular letter from the Committee of the City and Liberties of Philadelphia, inclosing the resolution of the Continental Congress of the 15th of May, recommending the adoption of the State Government in each of the Colonies, a provincial conference was held at Philadelphia, on Tuesday, June 18. For the committee of Northumberland county appeared Colonel William Cooke, Alexander Hunter, Esquire, John Weitzel, Robert Martin and Matthew Brown. This conference met at Carpenters' Hall, and chose Colonel Thomas McKean, President. It was resolved unanimously that a convention should be called to form a new Government. Qualifications of an elector were fixed as follows: He must be twenty-one years of age, have lived one year in the Province, and paid either a provincial or county tax, and further, swear that he would no longer bear allegiance to George III. To be a member of the convention required like qualifications, and further, that he must swear that he would oppose any measure that would interfere with or obstruct the religious principles or practices of any of the good people of the Province; and still further, sign a declaration of faith in the Trinity and in the Divine inspiration of the Old and New Testament.

It was determined that each county should have eight Representatives or members, the election for whom should be held on Monday, the 8th of July, and it passed resolutions to raise four thousand five hundred militia, to join a flying camp to consist of ten thousand men in the middle Colonies, &c.

The election for Northumberland county was held at George McCandlish's,[1] (Turbutt.) Thomas Hewitt, William Shaw and Joseph Green were the judges. The members elected were: William Cooke, James Potter, Robert Martin, Matthew Brown, Walter Clark, John Kelly, James Crawford, John Weitzel. The convention met on Monday, the 15th of July, in Philadelphia, and Doctor Franklin was chosen President. It continued, by adjournments, until the 28th of September, when the Constitution was adopted and signed.

A short statement of its salient points will be of interest, and serve to explain the political statistics of these Annals. The law-making power was vested in a House of Representatives, the members of which were to be chosen annually, by ballot, on the second Tuesday of October, to meet on the fourth Monday of the same month. No member could serve more than four years. It was to choose the

[1] McCandlish lived in a log house just back of Milton, on the late Samuel Hepburn, Esquire's, farm. In July, 1779, Marcus Hulings sold him his tavern stand on the river, at the end of Broadway street, Milton, Hulings returning to his old home, Duncan's Island.—J. F. Wolfinger, Esquire.

State Treasurer and Delegates to Congress annually, of which no one could be a member more than two years successively, nor be capable of re-election for three years afterward. Each county was to be entitled to six members until a proper apportionment could be made. There was also a provision for the election of a council of censors in 1783, and every seven years thereafter, two persons from each city and county, whose duty it was to inquire whether the Constitution had been violated.

The execution of the laws devolved upon the President and Supreme Executive Council. This consisted of twelve persons, one for the city of Philadelphia, and one from each of the eleven counties into which the Province was then divided. They were, however, chosen by districts. Northampton, Bedford, Northumberland and Westmoreland constituting one district, the embryo of the present senatorial representation. Every member of Council was a justice of the peace for the whole State. The President and Vice President of the State were chosen of members of the Council in joint convention of the Assembly and Council. The President had the power of appointing and commissioning judges, &c., and of sitting as judge in impeachment cases, and could grant pardons, &c. The judges of the Supreme Court held office for seven years. Two or more persons were chosen in each township as justices, and the Council commissioned one or more of them for seven years. These justices held the several courts. It did not follow, as remarked by Judge Duncan, in Albright's case, who was both associate and justice in 1813, the legality of holding both offices at the same time being then tested and affirmed, that the Council should appoint the justices of the sessions from the justices elect, though they generally did. Two persons were to be voted for for sheriff, one of whom was commissioned by the Council. The county commissioners and assessors of taxes were to be elected by the people, thus embodying in the Constitution the principles for which the Revolution was inaugurated, the right of the people to tax themselves.

The convention, by an ordinance dated September 3, created a new Council of Safety, of which Samuel Hunter and John Weitzel were the members for Northumberland county. It also appointed the following justices: Samuel Hunter, James Potter, William Maclay, Robert Moodie, John Lowdon, Benjamin Weiser, Henry Antes, and John Simpson.

John Lowdon, of Silver Spring, near Mifflinburg, became member of the Supreme Executive Council by choice of the Delegates from the district of Northampton, Bedford, Westmoreland, and Northumberland counties.

Buffalo, White Deer, and Potter were in the third election district; and the first election under the constitution was held at Fought's mill, (near Mifflinburg,) on 3d of November. The Assembly met in Philadelphia on the 28th of November, when Thomas Wharton, junior, was elected President of the Council and State; John Jacobs Speaker of the House.

Copy of Certificate on file in the office of the Secretary of the Commonwealth.

NORTHUMBERLAND COUNTY, *November* 7, 1776.

Agreable to an ordinance in Convention for the State or Commonwealth of Pennsylvania, this is to certify that the following persons were duly elected for the respective offices annexed to their names for the county aforesaid:

Council, John Lowdon; Assembly, Thomas Hewitt, Samuel Dale, Jacob Fulmer, Robert Fruit, David Robb, and Samuel Wallis; Sheriff, Jonathan Lodge and James Murray; Coroner, James McMahan, John Murray; Commissioners, William Gray, Philip Cole, Joseph Wallis; Assessors, David Mead, Andrew Moore, James Thompson, James McClure, William Watson, and William Shaw.

(Signed)   JOHN BRADY,
JAMES MCCLENACHAN,
JOHN GRAY,
THOMAS ROBINSON,
Judges of the Different Districts.

Incident at Derr's Trading-House.

It is singular, after a careful search of contemporary documents, I can find no allusion to the treaty, said to have been held at Fort Augusta, at the time this incident occurred. It appears by contemporary evidence, that the Indians cut down their corn, and moved off their families and effects, on the 1st of July. Two Seneca Indians came to the Great Island, (just below Lock Haven,) the day before, and the whole party moved off suddenly, to join the Six Nations in the war. That is the last we know of them as *residents* of the West Branch valley, and our troubles with them then began.

In a letter, dated Paxton, August 27, 1776, John Harris says: "The Indians, to the northward, southward, and westward, are for war against us, as I am informed by a letter from Northumberland county, by their post, two days ago. The Susquehanna Indians are only for peace with us. About twenty Indians, (enemies,) men, women, and children, have been many days past at Sunbury, and make said report." In all probability this was the party that stopped at Derr's trading-house, and the date of the incident, therefore, August, 1776.

Christian Van Gundy (father of Captain Jacob Gundy, who is my authority,) often related the incident. He said, his father, Christian Van Gundy, senior, lived between John Strohecker's and the late Jacob Spidler's, and kept the ferry there. He thought he was about thirteen years old at the time; but it appears, by his tombstone, that he was born about the 1st of March, 1766, and if thirteen, it would throw the date beyond that of the death of Captain John Brady, (11th April, 1779.) He could, therefore, have been only ten years of age. To resume his story: he said he saw the Indians come up the river, until they arrived opposite where they lived. They stopped, carried some things ashore, and left the women there, then crossed over to Derr's trading-house. He asked his father for permission to go up to see the Indians. He said he saw Derr knock in the head of a whisky barrel, and give the Indians tin-cups to drink with. They drank and danced, and showed how they scalped by gestures. Most of them got beastly drunk; but one would not drink any. He then saw Brady approach, and kick over the barrel, which put an end to the frolic. He said they would seize each other by the hair, and go through the form of scalping, tearing off the scalp with the teeth. (Derr's house stood by the cherry tree in the present garden, and the barrel was just in front. So John Brown, senior, said, who owned the mill property many years.)

R. B. McCabe, Esquire, of Blairsville, Indiana county, (whither William P. Brady removed,) published, some forty years ago, in the

Blairsville Record, some sketches of the life of Captain Samuel Brady, written upon the dictation of one of the Brady family, (so the late Jasper E. Brady informed me,) in which this incident is alluded to. He says Captain John Brady lived on the West Branch, opposite the site of Lewisburg, on the place owned by Honorable George Kremer's heirs. Derr had a small mill on the run that empties into the river below the town, where he supplied the Indians with powder, lead, rum, &c. Brady discovered that the Indians were likely to be tampered with by the British, and proposed making a treaty with the Seneca and Muncy tribes, who were up the West Branch, and were at variance with the Delawares, who were on the North Branch. Captain Brady and two others were selected by the people at Fort Augusta to go after the Senecas and Muncys. The Indians met them in a very friendly manner, and promised to attend at Fort Augusta on the day appointed.

They came down about one hundred strong, and dressed in war costume. The people at the Fort were too poor to give them anything of value, and they did not succeed in making a treaty. They left the fort, however, in a good humor, and taking their canoes, proceeded homeward.

Late in the day, Brady thought of Derr's trading-house, and mounting a small mare he had, crossed the North Branch, rode home with all speed. He saw the canoes of the Indians on the bank of the river, near Derr's, and, when near enough, saw the squaws working the canoes over to his side of the river, and when they landed they made for the thickets of sumac which grew on his land. They were conveying the rifles, tomahawks, and knives into the thickets, and hiding them. Brady jumped into a canoe and crossed to Derr's trading-house, where he found the Indians drunk, and a barrel of rum standing on end before Derr's door, with the head out. He instantly overset it and spilled the rum, saying to Derr, "My God, Ludwig, what have you done?" Derr replied, "Dey dells me you gif um no dreet down on de fort, so I dinks as I give um one here, als he go home in bease." One of the Indians told Brady he would one day rue the spilling of that barrel; and Brady, being well acquainted with the Indian character, was constantly on his guard for several years.

On the 4th of July, there was a convention of the associators, at

Lancaster, to elect two brigadiers general. Colonel Hunter's battalion was represented by Captain Charles Gillespie, Lieutenant George Calhoun, privates. Frederick Stone and Laughlin McCartney. Colonel Plunket's, by Major John Brady, Lieutenant Mordecai McKinney, privates Paul Geddes and Andrew Culbertson. Colonel Weiser's, by the colonel, Lieutenant Colonel Samuel Maclay, privates Seth Matlock and Jonas Yocum. Colonel Potter's, by Lieutenant Colonel Robert Moodie, Captain William Gray, privates James McClenachan and Benjamin Starret. Daniel Roberdeau and James Ewing were elected, Colonel Potter receiving a very respectable vote.

July 29, Walter Clark and John Kelly, in attendance upon the convention at Philadelphia, petition the Council of Safety that they had just grounds to believe that the county would be disturbed by the Indians, and stated that there was not sufficient ammunition in the county for the four battalions already raised.

The original of the following minutes were given to the late Joseph G. Wallace, of Lewisburg, by his grandfather, Captain William Gray, of Buffalo Valley, and loaned by him to Sherman Day, who never returned them. I am indebted to John Jordan, junior, Esquire, of Philadelphia, for a printed copy of them, published by the Historical Society among their proceedings in 1846:

Minutes of the Committee of Safety of Northumberland county, Pennsylvania,

From February 8th, 1776, to April 17th, 1777.

[From the original MS. lately presented to the Historical Society of Pennsylvania.]

On the 8th of February, 1776,

The following gentlemen, being previously nominated by the respective townships to serve in this committee, for the county of Northumberland, for the space of six months, met at the house of Richard Malone, viz.:

Augusta township.
John Weitzel, Esquire,
Alexander Hunter, Esquire,
Thomond Ball.

Mahoning township.
William Cook, Esquire,
Benjamin Allison, Esquire,
Mr. Thomas Hewet.

Turbut township.
Captain John Hambright,
William McKnight,
William Shaw.

Bald Eagle township.
Mr. William Dunn,
Thomas Hughes,
Alexander Hamilton.

Wioming township.
Mr. James Maclure,
Mr. Thomas Clayton,
Mr. Peter Melick.

Moughonoy township.

Muncey township.
Robert Robb, Esquire,
William Watson,
John Buckalow.

Buffaloe township.
Mr. Walter Clark, removed to White Deer,
William Irwin,
Joseph Green.

Penn's township.

Potter township.
John Livingston,
Maurice Davis,
John Hall.

White Deer township.
Walter Clark,
Matthew Brown,
Marcus Huling.

The committee proceeded to elect a chairman and clerk, when Captain John Hambright was unanimously appointed chairman during the continuance of this committee, and Thomond Ball clerk.

A return was presented to this committee, signed by William Scull, Esquire, chairman of a meeting of the officers and committeemen of the lower division of this county, held at Northumberland, the 7th instant, certifying that the following gentlemen were duly elected field officers for the battalion of said division, viz :

Samuel Hunter, Esquire, colonel.
William Cook, Esquire, lieutenant colonel.
Casper Weitzel, Esquire, first major.
Mr. John Lee, second major.

Resolved, That we accept of the same as a true return, and that the gentlemen therein mentioned be recommended to the Honorable Assembly or Committee of Safety to be commissioned accordingly.

Complaint being made that the battalion of the upper division of this county have not yet met, so as to have a fair election for field officers,

Resolved, That it be recommended to the officers, with three committeemen from each township in said division, to meet at the house of John Scudder, on Saturday, 24th instant, to elect their field officers, and return them to this committee on Monday, 26th instant, in order to be recommended to the Committee of Safety.

Resolved, That the absence of several gentlemen chosen captains of companies in this county, (upon their several occasions,) and such as did appear (from the short notices they have had) not being provided with as regular returns of their officers and companies as we think can authorize our recommendation of said captains or their subalterns to the Assembly or Committee of Safety of this Province, to remedy this inconvenience it is recommended to the committeemen of each township to advertise a meeting of the several companies on Wednesday, 21st instant, at such places as the majority of the committeemen shall think most convenient, where, under the inspection of two or more committeemen, each company shall establish their present, or elect other officers, as they shall think proper, and the captains so established or elected shall make returns of their subalterns and companies to this committee on Monday, 26th instant. It is expected that no gentlemen will offer to return a company that does not consist of forty privates with the officers and non-commissioned officers, agreeable to the regulations of our Honorable House of Assembly.

Resolved, That if a committeeman or committeemen be elected officers, one or more magistrate or magistrates present may certify for them; and if no magistrate be present, then two or more reputable men certifying for the justness of the election will be accepted of.

Resolved, That it is the opinion of this committee that a petition be presented to the Honorable Assembly of this Province, setting forth the late murder of two of the sheriff's *posse*, near Wioming, for attempting to act in conformity to the laws.

Resolved, That John Weitzel, Esquire, Alexander Hunter, Esquire, and Mr. Thomond Ball, be a committee to frame said petition and present it to this committee at their next meeting.

The committee then adjourned to Monday, 26th instant, at the house of Laughlin McCartney, in Northumberland town.

Monday, February 26th, 1776.

The committee met, according to adjournment, at the house of Laughlin McCartney, in Northumberland town, Captain John Hambright in the chair.

Messrs. Weitzel, Hunter and Ball presented the form of a petition to the Honorable Assembly, relative to the Connecticut intruders, which was approved of and ordered to be copied fair.

The following gentlemen appeared and produced certificates of their being regularly chosen captains of companies in Colonel Hunter's battalion, and produced lists of their subalterns, companies, &c., viz:

  Captain, Nicholas Miller,
  First Lieutenant, Christopher Gettig,
  Second Lieutenant, Nehemiah Breese,
  First Ensign, Gustavus Ross,
  Second Ensign, William Sims.

  Captain, Hugh White,
  First Lieutenant, John Forster,
  Second Lieutenant, Andrew Gibson,
  Ensign, Samuel Young.

  Captain, James McMahon,
  First Lieutenant, John Murray,
  Second Lieutenant, William Fisher,
  Ensign, William Baily.

  Captain, Charles Gillespie,
  First Lieutenant, Robert King,
  Second Lieutenant, Samuel Fulton,
  First Ensign, William Boyd,
  Second Ensign, John Woodside.

  Captain, William Scull,
  First Lieutenant, Jonathan Lodge,
  Second Lieutenant, George Colhoun,

First Ensign, William Sawyers,
Second Ensign, George Grant.

Captain, William Clarke,
First Lieutenant, John Teitson,
Second Lieutenant, William McDonald,
First Ensign, John Moll.

Resolved, That the above six companies appear to be full and regularly officered, and that they, with the field officers of that battalion, be recommended to the Committee of Safety to receive their respective commissions; which was done in a letter, of which the following is an abstract:

NORTHUMBERLAND, *February* 26, 1776.

GENTLEMEN: At a meeting of the committee for this county, held this day, the following gentlemen were returned as duly elected field officers, captains, and subalterns of a battalion raised in this county, viz: the officers mentioned above. The above returns of six companies belonging to the battalion expected to be commanded by Samuel Hunter, Esquire, appear to be well and regularly certified as complete companies. There are two or three companies more intend to belong to said battalion, but their captains being at present out of the county, we have received no returns of them. We further have the pleasure to inform you there is another complete battalion formed in this county, intended to be under the command of William Plunket, Esquire; but he with his other field officers being so lately promoted, their companies have not had sufficient time to elect captains in their room, we, therefore, think we cannot at present, with propriety recommend them, but hope in a few days to have the honor of transmitting to you a proper return of said battalion. In the meantime take the liberty to recommend the above named gentlemen to be commissioned in the several stations annexed to their names.

And are, gentlemen, with due esteem, your very humble servants.
By order of the committee,

JOHN HAMBRIGHT, *Chairman.*

To the COMMITTEE OF SAFETY, *Philadelphia.*

Resolved, That as several companies belonging to battalions in this county have not yet brought in their returns, and it may be inconvenient to call the whole committee together to receive their returns, that the chairman, with four others of the committee, be sufficient to receive such returns, and recommend the officers to the Committee of Safety.

Resolved, That this committee be adjourned to Wednesday, 13th of March next, then to meet at the house of Frederick Stone, in Northumberland town.

Wednesday, March 13, 1776.

The committee met at the house of Frederick Stone, in Northumberland town, agreeable to adjournment, Captain John Hambright in the chair, when the following gentlemen made returns of their officers, captains, subalterns, &c., properly certified, viz:

William Plunket, Esquire, Colonel,
James Murray, Esquire, Lieutenant Colonel,
Mr. John Brady, First Major,
Mr. Cookson Long, Second Major.

Captain, Henry Antis, Esquire,
First Lieutenant, Thomas Brandon,
Second Lieutenant, Alexander Hamilton,
First Ensign, John Morison,
Second Ensign, James Alexander.

Captain, Samuel Wallis,
First Lieutenant, John Scudder,
Second Lieutenant, Peter Jones,
Ensign, James Hampton.

Captain, John Robb,
First Lieutenant, William Watson,
Second Lieutenant, Robert Wilson,
Ensign, James White.

Captain, William McElhatton,
First Lieutenant, Andrew Boggs,
Second Lieutenant, Thomas Wilson,
Ensign, John McCormick.

Captain, William Murray,
First Lieutenant, Richard Irwin,

Second Lieutenant, Thomas Plunkett,
First Ensign, Andrew Robinson,
Second Ensign, Benjamin Jordon.

Captain, Simon Cool,
First Lieutenant, Thomas Camplen,
Second Lieutenant, James Brandon,
First Ensign, William King,
Second Ensign, James Hewes.

Captain, David Berry,
First Lieutenant, William Hammond,
Second Lieutenant, Joseph Bonser,
Ensign, Israel Pershel.

Resolved, That the returns made of the above mentioned field officers and seven companies appear to be regular and well certified as full companies, and that [the] officers be recommended to the Committee of Safety; which [was] done by letter, of which the following is a copy:

NORTHUMBERLAND, *March* 13, 1776.

GENTLEMEN: Agreeable to the promise of our last of 26th ultimo, we now inform that at a meeting of the committee for this county, held this day, the following gentlemen were returned as fairly elected field officers, captains, and subalterns of a battalion raised in this county, viz:

William Plunket, Esquire, Colonel, and the rest as above.

The above returns of officers for a battalion, consisting of seven companies, appear to us to be regular and well certified to be complete companies; we, therefore, take the liberty of recommending said gentlemen to the respectable Committee of Safety, appointed for the Province of Pennsylvania to receive commissions in the several stations annexed to their names. Being unwilling to trouble the committee, who, we apprehend, are already overburthened with business, we have transmitted an enumeration of grievances, under which we think this county labors, to Samuel Hunter, Esquire, our Representative, and one of your respectable body, who is well acquainted with the circumstances of this county, requesting he may, if necessary, lay the same before you, and should be glad of your opinion how to act in the different cases therein mentioned.

We are, gentlemen, &c.

Signed by order of the committee,

JOHN HAMBRIGHT, *Chairman.*

To the COMMITTEE OF SAFETY, *Philadelphia.*

[Copy of Letter referred to in the above.]

NORTHUMBERLAND, *March* 13*th*, 1776.

SIR: We have this day wrote to the Committee of Safety, recommending officers of another battalion, to wit: Colonel Plunket's. We had it in contemplation to write to the Committee of Safety concerning the recruiting parties that have lately been amongst us and taken away some good men, when both officers and men could be sent from this, if any ought to be sent out of the county. It is unnecessary for us to inform you of our situation, as you are so well acquainted with it. There have been different applications to us for recommendations as officers of companies to be raised in this county, to go into immediate service. We are somewhat at a loss what to do; but would be desirous, if men are to be taken for the continental service out of this county, officers should go with them. We, not considering it proper to trouble the Committee of Safety with our sentiments on this occasion, have taken the liberty to write to you, with an intention to get your advice upon the matter, as we cannot prevent recruiting parties from coming amongst us, or stop men from going into the army out of this county. If more battalions should be raised, or more men wanted, would it not be proper, from our situation as a frontier county, to have two or three companies raised, officered, and disciplined, and put into immediate pay; and if not wanted nearer home, to be always in readiness to go upon any service on which the continent may have occasion for them. We have sufficient information that Hawkins Boone has enlisted several men in this county, and has declared his having received his authority and money from the Congress for that purpose, and that he is to be a guard to the Congress. By this conduct he has drawn off some men from the different companies of military associators. We have, as a committee of the county, taken liberty to cite him to appear before some of us, and show by what authority he has undertaken so to do; but he has not appeared. We think when men are enlisted in this county, we have a right to know for what service they are enlisted. It is from our zeal for the good cause now carrying on that we are desirous to know the reason of such procedure. This, if you think proper, you may communicate to the Committee of Safety, and are requesting your advice how to act.

With due respect, your very humble servants.

Signed on behalf of the committee,

JOHN HAMBRIGHT, *Chairman.*

To SAMUEL HUNTER, Esquire, *Philadelphia.*

Information being given to the committee that a certain Hawkins Boone is now enlisting men in this county, without giving any satisfactory account for what purpose or service the said men are enlisted,

Resolved, That the chairman of this committee call upon the said Hawkins Boone, by letter or otherwise, to appear before him and two or more of said committee, as he, the chairman, shall think expedient, on such day and at such place as he shall appoint, to show cause why he, the said Boone, enlists men as aforesaid.

Resolved, That this committee be adjourned to Monday, 25th of March, instant, then to meet at the house of Thomond Ball, in Sunbury.

MONDAY, *March 25th*, 1776.

The committee met pursuant to adjournment at the house of Thomond Ball, in Sunbury, Captain John Hambright in the chair.

Resolved, That it appears to this committee that several recruiting officers belonging to the battalions of different counties in this Province, have lately come to this infant frontier county and drained it of a number of useful men, to the prejudice of the same.

Resolved, That for the future no officer or non-commissioned officer be allowed to recruit men in this county, except the officers who are or may be appointed therein.

John Simpson, Esquire, presented a return, wherein appears the following list of officers, the company belonging to Colonel Hunter's battalion, viz:

Captain, John Simpson, Esquire.
First Lieutenant, Robert Curry.
Second Lieutenant, John Ewart.
First Ensign, Thomas Gaskins.
Second Ensign, David Mead.

Resolved, That the same appears a full company, and that the gentlemen therein mentioned as officers, be recommended to the Committee of Safety to receive their several commissions; which was done accordingly, by a letter, of which the following is a copy:

SUNBURY, *27th March*, 1776.

GENTLEMEN: Our last to you was of 13th instant, recommending William Plunket, Esquire, colonel, with other officers of a battalion commanded by said colonel. At this meeting, John Simpson, Esquire, presents a return in which it appears that he is captain, Robert Curry, first, and John Ewart, second lieutenants, Thomas Gaskins, first, and David Mead second ensign, which is well certified to be a full company, belonging to Col. Hunter's battalion; we, therefore, take the liberty of recommending said gentlemen to receive commissions agreeable to the ranks to which the people have appointed them. We are now, gentlemen, to inform you of what we think a grievance to this young and thinly inhabited county, viz: a constant succession of recruiting officers from different counties in this Province. Our zeal for the cause of American liberty has hitherto prevented our taking any steps to hinder the raising of men for its service, but finding the evil increasing so fast upon us as almost to threaten the depopulation of the county, we cannot help appealing to the wisdom and justice of your committee to know whether the quota of men that may be demanded from this county under their own officers is not as much as can reasonably be expected from it. Whether, at a time when we are uncertain of peace with the Indians, (well knowing that our enemies are tampering with them,) and a claim is set up to the greatest part of this Province by a neighboring Colony who have their hostile abettors at our very breasts, as well as their emissaries amongst us, is it prudent to drain an infant frontier county of its strength of men? and whether the safety of the interior parts of the Province would not be better secured by adding strength to the frontiers?

Whether our Hon. Assembly, by disposing of commissions to gentlemen in different counties to raise companies which are to form the number of battalions thought necessary for the defense of the Province, did not intend that the respective captains should raise their companies where they [were] appointed; and not distress our county by taking from it all the men necessary for the business of agriculture, as well as the defense of the same? From our knowledge of the state of this county, we make free to give our opinion of what would be most for its advantage, as well as that of the Province, (between which we hope there never will be a difference,) and first are to inform you [of] the poverty of the people, many of whom came bare and naked here, being plundered by a banditti who call themselves Yankees, and those who brought some property with them, from the necessary delay of cultivating a wilderness before they could have any produce to live upon, together with the necessity of still continuing the closest application to labor and industry for their support, renders it morally improbable that a well disciplined militia can be established here, as the distance which some men are obliged to go to muster is the loss of two days to them, which, not being paid for, they will not, nor indeed can they, so often attend as is necessary to complete them even in the manual exercise. We would recommend that two or more companies be raised and put in pay for the use of the Province, to be ready to march when and where the service may require them, and when not wanted for the service of the public at any particular place, to be stationed in this county in order to be near and defend our frontier, should they be attacked by our enemies of any denomination, the good effect of which, we imagine, would be considerable, as though they may be too few to repel, they may stop the progress of an enemy until the militia could be raised to assist them. Should this proposal appear eligible, please to inform us thereof, and we will recommend such gentlemen for officers as we think will be most suitable for the service and agreeable to the people.

We are, gentlemen, with due respect, your very humble servants,
Signed for and in behalf of the committee,
JOHN HAMBRIGHT, *Chairman.*
To the COMMITTEE OF SAFFTY, *Philadelphia.*

August ye 13, 1776.

The following gentlemen being unanimously chosen by their respective townships to serve in the committee for the county of Northumberland, for the space of six months, met at school-house in the town of Northumberland, viz:

For Augusta township.
Mr. William McClay,
Mr. David McKinney,
Mr. John McClay.

Mahoning township.
Laughlan McCartney,
Thomas Robinson,
John Boyd.

Turbit township.
George McCandish,
Wm. Shaw,
Paul Geddis.

Muncy township.
Mordecai McKinney,
James Giles,
Andrew Culbertson.

Bald Eagle township.
Robert Fleming,
Thomas Campling,
John Section.

Buffaloe township.
Martin Treaster,
William Speedy,
Philip Coal.

Wyoming township.
Samuel McClure,
Peter Meelick,
John Clingman.

Penn's township.
Simeon Woodrow,
Adam Bolinger,
Paul Gemberling.

Moughonoy township.
Bastian Brossius,
George Reitz,
Peter Almang.

Potter township.

White Deer township.
James McClanachan,
Robert Fruit,
Wm. Gray.

The committee proceeded to elect a chairman and clerk, when Mr. Robert Fruit was unanimously appointed chairman during the time of six months, and John Boyd, clerk.

1st. *Resolved*, That no complaint be received by this committee that arises in any township and does not respect the county at large, except upon an appeal from the township committee, and that such appeal be delivered in writing, as well as all complaints that are received, and that all complaints be signed by the persons aggrieved or complaining.

2d. *Resolved*, That Andrew Culbertson, Mordecai McKinney, and James Giles, call upon Colonel Wm. Plunket for the dividend of ammunition belonging to the six companies of his battalion that lie above Muncy, and in case it is inconvenient for him to make the dividend, Laughlan McCartney, at whose house the ammunition is lodged, is hereby desired to do it and deliver the quotas allotted for the aforesaid six companies to the aforesaid Andrew Culbertson, Mordecai McKinney, and James Giles, who are to deliver the same to the respective captains, and by them kept in some convenient dry place, ready to be delivered out when occasion requires.

3d. *Resolved*, That the committee, or any two of them, belonging to the other three battalions of this county, call upon Laughlan McCartney for their equal dividend of what ammunition is in hand, and deliver to the respective captains in each battalion an equal dividend of said ammunition according to their number of men, and by them kept secure in some convenient dry place, ready to be delivered out when occasion requires.

4th. *Resolved*, That each colonel recommend to their respective captains to use all possible exertions to have any arms that are out of repair put in as good order as soon as possible.

As this committee is informed of a quantity powder and lead at Mr. John Harris's ferry, which belongs to the associators of this county, we do recommend Major John Lee and Captain Charles Gillespy as two suitable persons for to bring up the same, and we do appoint Laughlan McCartney and John Boyd for to agree with them for the bringing up of the said ammunition.

5th. *Resolved*, That this committee be adjourned to Tuesday, the 10th of September next, to meet in the town of Northumberland.

Tuesday ye 10 of September, 1776.

The committee met according to adjournment, in the town of Northumberland, Mr. Robert Fruit in the chair.

Complaint being made to this committee against Mr. Aaron Levy and John Bullion, setting forth that the aforesaid Levy and Bullion have a quantity of salt on hand, which they refuse to sell for cash, by a former resolve of the committee,

Resolved, That the aforesaid salt that is in the hands of the aforesaid Levy and Bullion, (as they have refused the same for sale,) be put into the hands of Mr. William Sayers, and by him sold at the rate of fifteen shillings per bushel, and not to sell unto any family above half a bushel for the time that the said salt is selling, and that the said Sayers shall keep a particular account of every bushel that he sells, and when sold, he shall return the money arising from said salt to this committee, first deducting one shilling out of the pound for his trouble of selling said salt, and six shillings and four pence for porterage.

A complaint being made to this committee against two certain men, namely, William Chattim and James Parker, of not behaving themselves as friends to our country in general, and had armed themselves with two pistols ; therefore, it was

Resolved, That the aforesaid Chattim and Parker should be sent for and examined.

Being brought before the committee and examined, they confessed themselves to be two of his His Britannic Majesty's soldiers, and both prisoners. Therefore, this committee thought it most proper to convey the two aforesaid men into the care of Lancaster committee, where we understand there is a number of their fellow prisoners, and that the aforesaid arms should be sold at public sale, and the money arising from the sale of said arms, should, as far as it would admit of, be put to discharge of such expenses as would arise for the trouble of said prisoners.

And as there was a bill of expenses produced to this committee by John Chattim, against the two aforesaid prisoners, and he refusing to approve the same, it was *Resolved*, that the aforesaid bill shall not be accepted of by this committee unless the aforesaid John Chattim do prove the same.

September 12th, 1776.

On examination of the two different quantities of ammunition heretofore forwarded to the care of the committee of this county, and on a careful examination of the number of associators in this county, it appears that the quota of each associator is half a pound of powder and one pound of lead.

AND WHEREAS, the greater part of Col. Plunket's battalion are situated on the frontier, and the most exposed parts of this county; therefore, *Resolved*, that the further quantity of eighty-nine pounds of powder and one hundred and seventy-eight pounds of lead be delivered into the hands of Mr. Fleming, Mr. Jackson, Mr. Kempling, Mr. Culbertson, and Mr. Giles, and that the same be by them delivered among the different captains of the said battalion, with the strictest charge that the same be preserved for the purposes of the defense of this county. The same division to be made with a proper regard to the different number in each company.

And it is further *Resolved*, that the further quantity of eighty-six pounds and three quarters of powder and the quantity of one hundred and seventy-three pounds and one half of lead, be delivered to Mr. Fruit, Mr. Gray, Mr. McClenachan, Mr. Shaw, Mr. Mc-Candles and Mr. Geddis, to be by them distributed among the captains of Col. Potter's battalion, in such sort, that each private have one quarter of powder, and half a pound of lead, Captain McMillan's company excepted, who are to have each half a pound of powder and one pound of lead.

And it is further *Resolved*, that the further quantity of fifty pounds of powder and one hundred pounds of lead be delivered to Mr. Coal, Mr. Treaster, Mr. Bolander, Mr. Brousers and Mr. Ritz, by them to be divided among the captains of Col. Wiser's battalion in the same proportions as the former fifty weight of powder was directed to be divided.

It is likewise further *Resolved*, that the additional quantity of fifty pounds of powder and one hundred weight of lead be delivered to John Maclay, Laughlin McCartney, and James McClure, to be by them divided among the captains of Col. Hunter's battalion, in due proportion to the number of privates in their respective companies.

WHEREAS, This committee being informed by one of our members of convention, that there is a dividend of salt in Philadelphia, which is allotted for this county, by a late resolve of convention, wherefore, this committee thought proper to appoint two suitable persons to go to Philadelphia and take charge of said salt, and [to] be by them conveyed to this county and delivered to the care of this committee. Therefore, William Maclay and Mordecai McKinney were unanimously appointed by this committee for the purpose above mentioned.

Resolved, That the salt belonging to this county is to be sold at fifteen shillings per bushel.

A complaint being laid unto this committee by Samuel Dail against Col. William Plunket, the same being read, was postponed until our next meeting.

A record of Mr. Robert Fruit's letter to this committee, respecting salt, &c.:

PHILADELPHIA, *November* 23, 1776.

GENTLEMEN: I have received from the Council of Safety, in this city, seventy-seven bushels of salt for the use of the inhabitants of the county of Northumberland, which I have delivered to Marcus Hulings to forward up.

It is delivered to me on the express condition of being divided amongst those of the inhabitants who did not get any part of the former quantity; therefore, you will please to take notice to inform the county of this exception, when you advertise for the distribution of it. Mr. Hulings has advanced all the money for the salt, together with all costs, &c.

I am, gentlemen, your very humble servant,

ROBERT FRUIT.

To the COMMITTEE OF NORTHUMBERLAND COUNTY.

The Committee of the County of Northumberland,

To MARCUS HULINGS, Dr.

For cash paid the Council of Safety, in Philadelphia,
    for seventy seven-bushels of salt, at 15*s* per bushel, £ 57 15
For cash paid for casks, to pack said salt . . 3
Porterage and cooperage, ... 18

Cash paid Hugh Cook for carriage of seventy-seven bushels of salt, from Philadelphia to Middletown,	£13	9	6
Storage at Middletown, ...		8	6
Carriage from Middletown to Northumberland, .		11	11
	£ 87	2	0

December 14, 1776.

The committee met, by express from Captain John Brady, upon sundry charges, produced by said Brady, against a certain Robert Robb. Sundry evidences were referred to, to prove the several charges against said Robb, which are as follows:

The evidence of Thomas Newman against Robert Robb.

This deponent, being duly sworn, deposeth and saith that said Robb had a paper, at a certain house, where they were erecting a chimney, which paper was supposed to be from Lord Howe, concerning conditions of peace, of which said Robb said this is the very thing I would be at; says further, Mr. Frankling was a rogue, he well knew, and that he has led the Government into two or three scrapes already known to him. Also, it was thought Frankling had a pension from home; likewise that it was thought the convention was bribed. Also, said Robb says that Lord Howe used the members of Congress politely that were sent to treat with him, but that they used him ill.

And that, as this deponent was one of the township committee, he, the said Robb, thought it was proper he should call a few of the township together, to consult concerning these things. And further saith not.

his
THOMAS ✕ NEWMAN.
mark.

Joseph Newman's evidence against said Robb.

That Robert Robb read, at the aforesaid place, a paper, [which] (as the deponent supposeth,) was a declaration of peace from Lord Howe, and asked this deponent's father if he would call a few of the neighbors to consult concerning it, and that his father refused to do it. And concerning the members of Congress, Mr. Robb said Lord Howe used them politely, and they used him ill. And as for Mr. Frankling, there were very hard thoughts of him, and that it was thought he had a pension from home; also that it was thought there was bribery in the convention.

And further saith not.

JOSEPH NEWMAN.

The substance of John Morris' evidence against Robert Robb.

This deponent saith he heard Robert Robb read a paper concerning terms of peace from Lord Howe. Said Robb was asked why this paper was not made public sooner. Robb said, because it was kept back by the Congress and committees below. Said Robb said, also, it is well known what Writtenhouse and Frankling was. Mr. Newman asked said Robb what was the reason there was such men in Congress. Robb said it was thought there was bribery in the convention; also said, it was a minority that held this new form of government, and that the majority would not be ruled by the minority.

And further saith not.

JOHN MORRIS.

The substance of James Giles' evidence.

This deponent saith, that he saw Mr. Robb pull out a paper at the aforesaid building, read it, which he said was printed in New York near three months ago. Mr. Newman asked said Robb how it came to be kept back. This deponent saith, he understood Mr. Robb said it was our rulers kept it back, and that the substance of the above paper was terms of peace from Lord Howe.

And further saith not.

JAMES GILES.

The evidence of George Silverthorn for Robert Robb, viz:

This deponent, being at Mr. Robb's house, and from there went together to a chimney raising in the neighborhood. After a while said Robb pulled out a handbill which gave an account of General Washington's army being in need of a reinforcement, and Mr. Robb said in public, that it was necessary for every one to turn out that would go. However, after a while, Mr. Robb pulled out another paper, which he said was a declaration of peace, from Lord Howe, and read it in public. After reading the said paper, Mr. Robb said he came on purpose to see Mr. Newman, and whether or not he thought proper to call some of the neighbors together, in order to see whether or not the said declaration was of any effect or not, as he was one of the town committee, or how they would take it, as he would not depend upon his own judgment on such an occasion, as being but one person. And this deponent saith, that after the papers came out which gave an account of what passed between General Howe and them at Staten Island, this deponent was telling said Robb that he had heard them read at Mr. McKinney's, and that Mr. Robb said that he thought it would not be proper to lay down their arms till peace would be concluded on better terms than these for the benefit of the country.

And further saith not.

GEORGE SILVERTHORN.

Lieutenant John Scudder, being duly sworn, saith that Robert Robb said that the King's troops are able to learn us to beat themselves, as Peter the Great said of Charles, King of Sweden, and that the said Robb never did anything against the cause of America, but always encouraged the same, to the best of his knowledge; and further saith, that Mr. Newman charged Robert Robb with discouraging people going into the service, and that George Silverthorn and his family were the people.

And further saith not.

JOHN SCUDDER.

December 17th, 1776.

NORTHUMBERLAND COUNTY.—The committee of this county, taking the proofs and allegations for and against Robert Robb under their serious consideration, do judge that the said Robb hath behaved in such manner as gives just grounds for this committee to suspect him of being not only unfriendly, but inimical, to our common cause; therefore,

Resolved, That said Robert Robb shall either take his gun and march immediately with the militia of this county into actual service, for the defense of the United States, in order to wipe off the present evil suspicions, or otherwise to be committed to the care of

Lieut. Col. James Murray, of the second battalion, to be by him sent to some proper place of confinement, until released by further authority. Signed by order of the committee.

PAUL GEDDIS, *Chairman.*

December 18th, 1776.

The above Robert Robb desires to appeal to the Council of Safety of this State:

Resolved, That said Robb may appeal to said council, under the care of the said Col. Murray.

PAUL GEDDIS, *Chairman.*

Muster Roll of Captain Casper Weitzel's Company, in the first Battalion of Pennsylvania Regiment of Rifiemen commanded by Colonel Samuel Miles. Camp near Kingsbridge, September 1, 1776.

Captain—Casper Weitzel, Esquire, of Sunbury appointed March 9, 1776.

First Lieutenant—William Gray, appointed March 15; captured August 27; exchanged December 8, 1776, for Lieutenant Thompson.

Second Lieutenant—John Robb, appointed March 16, 1776, promoted captain 18th April, 1777.

Third Lieutenant—George Grant, appointed March 19, 1776, captain in the 9th P. C. L. Died 10th October, 1779.

Sergeant Major—John Gordon.

Sergeants—Jacob Snider, Thomas Price, William Orr, Thomas Shanks.

Drummer—John Everard. September 1, sick at New York.

Privates—[1]Allison, William; Arthur, John; Aumiller, John; Barr, William; [1]Brady, Peter; Brinson, Stout; Burke, John; Carson, Samuel; Carson, William, junior; Carson, William, senior; [1]Carter, Andrew; Carter, Charles; [1]Caruthers, Robert; Chisnell, James; Clark, William; Clayton, James; Connell, Jeffry; Cribs, John; Curry, David; Davis, Peter; Doran, Edward; Durell, David; Durell, Stephen; Elder, James; Ewig, Christian; [1]Gass, Henry; Gerhart, Henry; Glover, James; Hardy, John; Harper, William; Hissom, Thomas; [1]Huggins, Dennis; Hunt, Elijah; Irvine, James; [1]Kerstetter, Martin; Little, Thomas; McCleane, Charles; [1]McCor-

[1] Missing after the battle of Long Island, August 27.

mick, William ; McDonald, John ; McInnis, Patrick ; McManus, Patrick ; McMath, William ; ¹McVey, Patrick ; Madden, Joseph ; Miller, Henry ; ¹Morehead, Robert: Newman, Richard ; Noland, Michael ; Ralston, Andrew ; Randolph, James ; ¹Rice, John ; Sands, John ; Shaffer, John ; ¹Spiess, Jacob ; Staples, Samuel ; Turner, David ; ¹Watt, James ; Wilson, Robert ; Winters, Christian ; Wolcot, Silas.

Lieutenant William Gray, afterwards Captain Gray, died at Sunbury, July 18, 1804, aged fifty-four.

Sergeant Price ended his days in a small log house on Water street, in Selinsgrove. It seems he was carried to Halifax, in Nova Scotia. Made his escape traveling through the vast forests intervening between that country and the nearest American settlements. See History of West Branch, page 109. In a letter to Honorable Samuel Maclay, member of Congress at Philadelphia, dated Penn's township, December 4, 1798, written in a very good hand, he complains that he had been three times elected colonel, beating Charles Drum twice and Frederick Evans once, and yet had not been commissioned, because, as he says, it was alleged that he was too poor for such a post. He says, "I settled in these parts before the war, and have resided here ever since, except while I was out in the army. I enlisted in Captain Weitzel's company, and was wounded and taken prisoner at the battle of Long Island. I underwent many hardships, but at last found means to escape, returned to the army, and served my time out ; was honorably discharged, and never received my pay. Soon after my return home I was elected adjutant, and continued in that post many years. Afterwards was elected major."

Associators.

On the 31st of August the field officers for the battalion in Buffalo and Penn's townships were chosen, and the 8th of October commissions were issued to them as fourth battalion of Northumberland county associators and to the company officers :

        Colonel—Cole, Philip.
        Lieutenant Colonel—Sutherland, Thomas.
        First Major—Foster, Thomas.

Second Major—Yost, Casper.
Standard Bearer—Miller, Dewalt.
Adjutant—McCoy, James.

Company No. 1.

Captain—Clarke, John.
First Lieutenant—Pontius, Henry.
Second Lieutenant—Moore, James.
Ensign—Watson, Patrick.

Four sergeants, four corporals, one drummer, one fifer, and forty-six privates, certified by me, this 26th day of September, 1776. John Clarke, captain.

Second Company.

Captain—Weaver, Michael.

Third Company.

Captain—Links, Jacob.

Fourth Company.

Captain—Weirick, William.
First Lieutenant—Sherred, Jacob.
Second Lieutenant—Gill, William.
Ensign—Moon, Nicholas.

Four sergeants, four corporals, one drummer, one fifer, forty privates. The whole of the above as associators testified by me, this 26th day of September, 1776. William Weirick, Captain.

Fifth Company.

Captain—Wolff, George.
First Lieutenant—Conrad, George.
Second Lieutenant—Wildgoose, Michael.
Ensign—Hessler, John.

Four sergeants, four corporals, one drummer, one fifer, forty-one privates.

Sixth Company.

Captain—Overmeier, George.
First Lieutenant—McCelvey, James.
Second Lieutenant—Weirick, Peter.
Ensign—Snyder, Michael.

Four sergeants, four corporals, one drummer, one fifer, forty privates. The whole of the above as associators testified by me, this 26th day of September, 1776. Captain George Overmeier.

This battalion, or rather drafts from it, went into service in December, when Colonel Cole was with part of it at Reading. Colonel Brodhead writes that he made use of a company from Buffalo Valley to apprehend some of the disaffected and to compel some of the militia of Berks to march.

It is probable that when the danger to Philadelphia became imminent, officers and men volunteered to fill up Captain Clarke's company, as we find their names on the following roll. I am indebted to John C. Watson, of West Buffalo township, a grandson of Captain Clarke, for an old account book which contained the names. The company left the Valley on the 5th of December, and served three months and eighteen days.

It appears from some memorandums in this book, that the company did not leave Reading until the 3d of January, 1777, and consequently did not participate at Trenton and Princeton, but was in the subsequent skirmishes. It was attached to Colonel Potter's second battalion, Lieutenant Colonel James Murray, Majors John Kelly and Thomas Robinson. Joseph Green assigned as surgeon's mate to Doctor Benjamin Allison. Four companies, Clarke's, Lee's, Taggart's, Cookson Long's, had casualties during the campaign:

Roll of Captain John Clarke's Company.

Allen, Robert; Augustine, Hieronimus; Barnett, Joseph; Beatty, John; Bower, George; Cery, Thomas; Clark, George; Cogh, Daniel; Colpetzer, Adam; Commer, Daniel; Conner, Jacob; Conrad, George; Conrad, Henry; Cousins, William; Esterly, Jacob; Etzweiler, George; Ewig, Philip; Fought, Michael; Foster, Thomas; Fry, John; Gill, William; Gilman, Henry; Green, Joseph; Greenlee, William; Groninger, Joseph; Grove, Wendell; Hain, John;

Harpster, Jacob; Heny, Stophel; Hessler, William; Hessler, John; Hessler, Michael; Kellahan, Patrick; Keeny, Jacob; Kishler, Francis; Kneedler, Frederick; Kneedler, Conrad; Lamb, Michael; Links, Jacob; Long, Jacob; Long, William; Lowdon, Richard; McCashon, John; McCelvey, James; McClung, Matthew; McDonneld, Randal; Macklin, Valentine; Miller, Benjamin; Moor, William; Morrow, Andrew; Nees, Henry; Nees, Peter; Overmeier, George; Pontius, Nicholas; Pontius, George; Rinehart, Frederick; Rinehart, George; Rith or Ritle, Yost; Rote, Michael; Row, Ludwig; Sierer, George; Schneider, Michael; Schock, John; Schock, Michael; Schock, George; Scott, Robert; Smith, Michael; Speddy, William; Speese, Jacob; Stevenson, James; Storm, David; Thompson, Robert; Ulrich, George; Weaver, John; Weaver, David; Wenderbach, Henry; Wilson, Robert; Wolfe, George.

Captain Clarke lived on the first farm above Mifflinburg, south of the turnpike; died February 22, 1809, aged seventy-three; buried in the Lewis graveyard. Lieutenant Thomas Foster, grandfather of Mrs. Mark Halfpenny, died June 4, 1804; buried in Lewis graveyard. Augustine was a weaver; lived near Selinsgrove as late as 1800. George Bower lived in Union township. Joseph Barnett became the patriarch of Jefferson county, Pennsylvania. See a full notice of him in Day's Historical Collections. Honorable I. G. Gordon, of Brookville, writes me, 1871, that some of his grandchildren live near that place. John Beatty lived near New Berlin. George Clark was a prominent surveyor in the Valley until 1800, and then removed West. He lived in a house near Judge Hummel's, now torn down. He was an exceedingly tall man, and took delight in making his axe marks as surveyor beyond the reach of other men. He once made a narrow escape from the Indians by leaping Little Buffalo creek, from the high bank, near late Jacob Moyer's. It was attributed to Brady, but Brady's leap was in the western part of the State, in Armstrong county. Jacob Conner lived in Buffalo. Adam Colpetzer, in West Buffalo; married a daughter of George Rote, of Mifflinburg. George Etzweiler was killed by the Indians in 1780, at Heberling's mill, then French Jacob Grochong's. Michael Fought, in Union, on Seebold's farm, near Chappel Hollow, east of it. William Gill, in Penn's. Wendell Grove, in Derrstown. Henry Gilman, in White Deer. Joseph

Groninger, in Kelly, on Clingan's place. Joseph Green near Philip Pontius'; he was grandfather of Joseph Green, of Lewisburg. Jacob Harpster, in Beaver township. John Hain, in Penn's. The Hesslers, near Crotzerville. The church there bears their name. Christopher Heny, on General James Irvine's, now, or lately, Kleckner's, west of Mifflinburg. Patrick Kellahan, north-west of Mifflinburg. Jacob Keeny, on John Aurand's place, Turtle creek. Richard Lowdon was a brother of Captain John, and lived with him. Andrew Morrow was a tenant on Samuel Maclay's place. Benjamin Miller, afterwards owned James Biehl's place. Matthew McClung, late George Gundy's heirs, near Turtle creek. Randal McDonneld, on S. Maclay's, just north of the Great Western, now Mrs. Shoemaker's. Peter Nees died of wounds· received February 1, 1777. George Overmeier lived near Seebold's, in Limestone. Nicholas Pontius was the father of the late J. F. Pontius. George was his brother, sons of John, who owned the Captain Bucher tract, where his descendants still reside, or a few of them, as the name is *legion* now. David Storm, where B. Lahr lives, on Esquire Cameron's farm. Robert Scott, on Barber's place, White Springs. Jacob Speese lived, within our memory, in White Deer. William Speddy, *see* 1772. The Schock's, about Mifflinburg. Michael Smith, in East Buffalo, above Henry Mertz's. George Wolfe was the grandfather of Jonathan, of Lewisburg.

Colonel William Cooke's regiment was directed to be raised in the counties of Northampton and Northumberland. Among the last acts of the convention, on the 28th of September, was the election of field officers of this regiment. Four companies, Miller's, Boone's, Brady's, and Harris', were from Northumberland county. These companies were nearly full on the 11th of December, and left Sunbury about a week thereafter, as Marcus Huling claimed for loss of a boat in taking them down the river at that time.

The regiment went immediately into active service. Being composed mainly of good riflemen, large drafts were made upon it for picket and skirmish duty. A portion, under Boone, was sent into the northern army, and assisted in the capture of Burgoyne. At Brandywine the regiment lost heavily in officers and men, and at Germantown; so that, after wintering at Valley Forge, the field officers were mustered out, the supernumerary line officers discharged, and what remained of officers and companies distributed into the third and sixth regiments.

Roster of Colonel William Cooke's Twelfth Pennsylvania Regiment of the Continental Line.

Colonel—Cooke, William, of Northumberland, commissioned October 2, 1776.

Lieutenant Colonel—Gray, Neigal, of Northampton county. He moved to Buffalo Valley after the war.

Major—Crawford, James, commissioned October 8, 1776. Afterwards justice of the peace in Lycoming county, where he died.

Adjutant—Hanson, Thomas.

Paymasters—Levers, Robert; Dungan, Thomas; appointed April 29, 1777.

Quartermaster—Vaughan, George.

Surgeon—Ledlie, Doctor Andrew, of Easton.

Surgeon's Mate—Woodruff, Aaron.

Captains—Withington, Peter, commissioned October 1, 1776; took sick, in Philadelphia, in December, 1776; sent home, to Reading, where he died May 11, 1777; his widow, Eve, survived him over fifty years, and died in Mifflinburg; Miller, Nicholas, appointed October 4, 1776, from Northumberland county; died, in 179–, in Northampton county; Boone, Hawkins, appointed October 4, 1776; killed, at Fort Freeland, July 28, 1779; Brady, John, appointed October 14, 1776; killed, by the Indians, April 11, 1779; Harris, John, appointed October 14, 1776; McKinley, Reverend Henry, of Carlisle, appointed October 16, 1776; Patterson, Alexander, of Northampton county; Work, William, appointed October 16, 1776.

Lieutenants—Brandon, Thomas, appointed October 4, 1776; Lincoln, Hananiah, appointed October 4, 1776; he was a sergeant in Captain George Nagel's company, Colonel William Thompson's regiment, 1775–1776; resigned, after battle of Brandywine, and went to Daniel Boone's settlement, in Kentucky; he followed Boone to Missouri, where he died; Gettig, Christopher, appointed October 14, 1776, from Sunbury; wounded at Piscataway, New Jersey, May 11, 1777; taken prisoner, and had his leg amputated; justice of the peace many years afterward at Sunbury; his descendants reside near

Bellefonte; Reily, John, appointed October 16, 1776; promoted Captain, May 20, 1777; mustered out of service November 3, 1783; Chambers, Stephen, Esquire, appointed October 16, 1776; promoted captain; one of the council of censors, in 1783; Delegate to the Federal Convention, December 12, 1787; wounded in a duel with Doctor Jacob Rieger, on Monday, 11th May, 1789; died on Saturday, 16th, at his house, in Lancaster; McElhatton, William, appointed October 16, 1776; wounded, at Bonhamtown, New Jersey, in right shoulder; disabled, and transferred to the invalid corps July 1, 1779; died April 26, 1807; Henderson, John, appointed October 16, 1776; Sayre, William, appointed October 16, 1776.

Second Lieutenants—King, Robert, October 4, 1776; promoted lieutenant, third Pennsylvania, May 20, 1777; left out of service June 23, 1779; Williamson, James, October 4, 1776; McCabe, Edward, October 16, 1776; Hays, John, October 16, 1776; Quinn, Samuel, October 16, 1776; Boyd, John, of Northumberland, promoted lieutenant in third Pennsylvania, June 18, 1779; died February 13, 1832; Bard, William, October 1, 1776; Carothers, John, October 16, 1776; killed, at Germantown, October 4, 1777; Falconer, Robert.

Ensigns—Lodge, Benjamin, junior, October 16, 1776; promoted lieutenant sixth Pennsylvania, October 11, 1777; Hamilton, Thomas, October 16, 1776; Blackall, William Ball, October 16, 1776; promoted lieutenant third Pennsylvania, 11th September, 1778; mustered out November 3, 1783; Boyd, William, appointed October 16, 1776; killed at Brandywine, September 11, 1777; Stone, John, October 16, 1776; resigned January 8, 1777; died March, 1792; Herbert, Stewart, October 16, 1776; promoted lieutenant sixth Pennsylvania, January 9, 1778; Engle, Andrew, October 16, 1776; promoted lieutenant of third Pennsylvania, December 20, 1778; retired January 1, 1781; Stricker, Henry, October 16, 1776; Seeley, John, February 3, 1777; Armstrong, John, formerly sergeant; served until the end of the war, and promoted lieutenant in Captain James Moore's corps.

PHILADELPHIA, *December*, 1776.

I am commanded by the House to request your attendance in this city, in order to take your seat in Council, that we may immediately carry all the powers of government into execution. As this must appear absolutely necessary to every good man, we can have no doubt, from your general character, but you are so well disposed to the public, and so desirous of order and good government, that you will not neglect to take your seat in that important body. Compliance will much oblige the State in general, and in particular thy real, though unknown, friend.

JOHN JACOBS, *Speaker.*

JOHN LOWDON, Esquire, *Northumberland county.*

24th December, Colonel Hunter writes that a company out of his battalion had volunteered; chosen Major John Lee, captain; Hugh White, first lieutenant; Thomas Gaskins, second lieutenant, and marched that day; and he had impressed guns and blankets for them, and had them appraised.

1777.

OFFICIALS—MINUTES OF THE COMMITTEE OF SAFETY, CONTINUED—MAJOR KELLY AT PRINCETON—ROLL OF CAPTAIN B. WEISER'S COMPANY—MATTHEW BROWN—PAOLI—GENERAL POTTER'S LETTERS.

THOMAS WHARTON, President of the State. John Lowdon member of Council until October, when he was succeeded by Captain John Hambright, of Turbut township. Members of Assembly elected in October: Samuel Dale, Robert Fruit, James Murray, William Irwin, Simon Himrod, and Robert Fleming.

On the 9th of June the following justices were appointed under the new constitution: Samuel Hunter, Thomas Hewitt, Robert Crawford, John Weitzel, Robert Martin, Michael Troy, Samuel Allen, John Aurand, William Shaw, and John Livingston. William Maclay, Prothonotary until September 11, when he was succeeded by David Harris; Jonathan Lodge, Sheriff, elected in October; John

Simpson, the first Register and Recorder of the county, appointed March 14.

March 21, Samuel Hunter appointed lieutenant, and Walter Clark, William Murray, George Wolfe, and William Wilson, sub-lieutenants of Northumberland county.

Constable of Buffalo : Martin Trester ; White Deer, Henry Derr.

Elias Younkman's name appears on the grand jury. He resided in Turbut before moving into Buffalo, in 1783.

Minutes of the Committee of Safety—Continued.

January 1st, 1777.

The complaint of Peter Smith against Robert Robb.

To the Honorable Committee of Northumberland County :

That on the 20th of last month, at the house of Captain John Brady, said Robb did violently beat and very much abuse said Smith, and further produceth James Brady and Jean Kennan as evidence of said charge, and also Patrick Murdock as evidence afterwards to the wounds alleged to be received by said Smith from said Robb.

his
PETER X SMITH.
mark.

The above named Peter Smith maketh oath that he received the above-mentioned abuse, by the above-named Robert Robb, at the time and place above-mentioned, and that he, this deponent, has not been able, ever since receiving the above-mentioned abuse, to follow his usual vocation, as formerly.

his
PETER X SMITH.
mark.

James Brady's Evidence between Peter Smith, complainant, and Robert Robb, defendant.

This deponent saith, that on Friday, the 20th day of December last, Robert Robb did, at the house of this deponent's father, and in his presence, violently beat and abuse the above-said Smith, and continued so to do until he, this deponent, rescued him out of his hands. This deponent further saith, that Robert Robb said he believed the committee got very little satisfaction of him, and that they were a set of rascals, some of them were robbers, some were horse-thieves, and some of them were murderers.

And further saith not.

JAMES BRADY.

Jean Cannon's Evidence.

This deponent saith, that she saw Peter Smith immediately after difference with Robert Robb, and that said Smith seemed to her to have been very much abused. as she understood, by said Robert Robb. This deponent further saith, that said Robb said the committee was a set of rascals, some of them were horse-thieves, some robbers, and some of them were murderers.

And further saith not.

her
JEAN X CANNON.
mark.

January 4th, 1777.

Resolved, That this committee be adjourned until the 14th day of this instant, to meet at the house of George McCandlish.

January 14.

The committee met, by adjournment, at the house of Mr. George McCandlish, and proceeded to hear the evidence of James Patton, in behalf of Robert Robb.

James Patton, being duly sworn, deposeth and said, that he, this deponent, with Peter Smith and some others, were drinking together at the house of Captain John Brady, when said Smith asked Mr. Robb what news. Mr. Robb answered that he desired none of his discourse, and asked James Brady if there was any fire in the new house. Brady said there was. Mr. Robb then got up and asked this deponent if he would go into the said house and drink share of half a pint. This deponent said he would. After sitting down, the aforesaid Smith came in. Says Mr. Robb, you have followed me here again, Peter. Mr. Robb further said, if you choose to sit here, I will go into the other house, and if you follow me, I will flog you, or turn you out. Mr. Robb then got up, and asked this deponent to go with him to the other house. This deponent further saith, that Mr. Robb said that once in his day he never thought to be tried by such men as some of the committee. Some of them had been tried for murder and some for horse stealing.

And further saith not.

JAMES PATTON.

WHEREAS, A certain Robert Robb was brought before the committee of this county, on account of sundry charges proven against him, and a resolve of this committee entered thereon, bearing date December 17th, 1776, by virtue whereof he was committed to the custody of Colonel James Murray, to be by him sent to some proper place of confinement until released by a superior authority:

AND WHEREAS, The said Colonel Murray, out of lenity to said Robb's family, saw fit to appoint the mansion-house of the said Robb as a prison for him, on a promise of his good behavior for the future, but as said Robb hath since (as appears by sufficient testimony given before this committee) very ungratefully abused the lenity shown him by said Colonel Murray, by barbarously beating and much abusing a certain Peter Smith, of this county, so as to render him unable, for a considerable time, to support himself and his small family by his industry, as usual, as appears by the testimony of said Smith, and other evidences produced before this committee:

AND WHEREAS, He did, at the same time, not only despise all authority of this committee, but also charge them with horse stealing, robbery, and murder, as appears by the testimony of said evidences: therefore,

Resolved, Notified to take, or order to be taken, the aforesaid Robert Robb before the Council of Safety, of this State, to whom he hath appealed, in order to answer the several charges proven against him before this committee, which we have inclosed in a letter directed to the said Council of Safety, which you are desired to deliver with said prisoner.

Signed by order of committee.

PAUL GEDDIS, *Chairman*.

January 15, 1777.

Resolved, That notice be sent to Captain Murray, requesting his attendance to-morrow morning, which was accordingly sent by Mr. Johnson.

January 16.

Upon Captain Murray's not appearing according to notice,

Resolved, That Thomas Combs be hired and sent with a second notice to Captain Murray, requesting his attendance immediately.

Upon Captain Murray's non-appearance upon second notice,

Resolved, That the aforesaid Thomas Combs be again sent with a third notice to Captain Murray, and paid five shillings for his trouble.

January 17.

Thomas Combs returned from Captain Murray's, and brought a letter of which the following is a copy:

January 17, 1777.

GENTLEMEN: I sent you word by Mr. McKnight and Mr. Johnson that I would not act any longer as an officer; and since you wont take my word, I now send you my commission, and I hope you will believe me now.

WILLIAM MURRAY.

To the committee.

Upon Captain Murray's non-compliance with the resolve of this committee,

Resolved, That Simon Himrod and Buchanan Smith be appointed to conduct Robert Robb to the Council of Safety of this State, and that they be paid two pounds five shillings for their trouble.

Resolved, That the sum of one pound ten shillings be paid to Captain John Hambright, for this book found by him for the use of this committee.

Resolved, That Mordecai McKinney be paid by the chairman one pound two shillings and six pence, out of the balance received by Mr. Clay, on account of expresses to the different officers of Colonel Murray's battalion.

Job Jolloway applied to this committee for a letter to Thomas Ferguson, to go with him to the Six Nations.

Resolved, That a letter be sent accordingly.

NORTHUMBERLAND, *February* 13, 1777.

The following gentlemen being unanimously chosen by their respective townships to serve in the committee of this county for the ensuing six months, met at the house of Laughlan McCartney, in Northumberland, and gave in the following returns of their election, viz :

Augusta township.

Potter's township.
John Livingstone,
John McMillan.

Turbutt township.
Thomas Jordan,
John Nelson,
Josiah Espy.

Buffalo Township.
John Aurand,
Thomas Sutherland,
George Overmire.

Bald Eagle township.
John Fleming,
James Hughs,
John Walker.

Mochonoy township.
George Yeakle,
Henry Zartman,
Henry Krebs.

Penn's township.
Andrew Moore,
David Miller,
Jacob Hosterman.

White Deer township.
William Blyth,
James McCormick,
William Reed,

Muncy township.
John Coates,
James Hampton,
William Hammond.

Mahoning township.

Wyoming township.
James McClure,
Peter Milleck,
John Clingman.

The committee, according to order, proceeded to elect their chairman and clerk, when Thomas Jordan was unanimously chosen chairman, and John Coates, clerk.

Resolved, That this committee be adjourned till Tuesday, the 11th day of March next, when they are to meet at the house of George McCandlish; and as sundry of the townships have neglected to send out their members at this meeting, the committee have ordered the chairman to give notice to the said townships by public advertisement to attend at next meeting.

March 11th, 1777.

The committee met according to adjournment, Mr. Thomas Jordan in the chair.

Upon complaints being made by a certain Allis Read, of Wyoming township, that he, the said Read, had a horse strayed or stolen from him some time ago, and was found in the custody of a certain John Drake, when said Read replevied the horse and got him and kept him in his possession for about six months, and then the widow of said Drake came and took him forcibly out of said Read's stable, he not being at home himself, and now keeps the horse, and absolutely refuses to give him up again to the said Read.

Resolved, That Messrs. James McClure, Peter Milleck, and John Clingman, with the assistance of the committee of Wyoming township be a joint committee to meet at the house of James McClure, in said township, on Saturday, the 22d day of this instant, March, to hear the complaint and defense of both parties concerning the said horse, and that the chairman of this committee issue summons for the evidences of the complainer to attend at said meeting, which summons are to be served by the complainer himself, as also a summons for the said Widow Drake to attend with the horse and her evidences or reasons, if any she have, why the complainer should not have his horse upon proper proofs being made of his being his property, and the aforesaid persons are hereby authorized to judge and determine betwixt both parties, and upon proper proofs being made, give their final judgment in the matter.

A certain Captain Jacob Links, of Buffalo township, appealed to this committee in consequence of a resolve of the committee of said township, a copy of which is as follows, viz:

"*Resolved,* That Jacob Links does return several sums of money, which a number of the inhabitants of this township did deliver to him for the use of purchasing salt, he, said Links, acknowledging he could have had salt, but it being troublesome times, he was afraid he should suffer loss if he would purchase the salt, and a certain evidence did declare that he said he was going on his own business to Philadelphia, and he, said Links, did not bring salt.

December 21, 1776, by the committee of Buffalo township.

(Signed,) WILL. IRWIN, *Chairman*."

In consequence of said appeal, Mr. Links was called in before this committee and asked if he had evidence to produce. He said he had, but that he had them not then ready.

Resolved, That Mr. Links appeal be referred till the next meeting of committee, and that his evidence be summoned to attend.

WHEREAS, Colonel or Captain Benjamin Weiser has made complaint to this committee that a number of persons who had been out under his command in the militia of this county, in order to join the continental army, in New Jersey, and that the said persons were deserted from him and returned home to this county, as the same is more fully expressed in a letter to this committee, bearing date ———, craving their assistance.

Resolved, That a day of muster be assigned for the said persons to meet and march off to camp, and serve out their time, allowing them to elect new officers, if they had any objections to the old ones, certifying them also, that if they neglect to obey this resolve, they are to be taken up and committed as deserters.

WHEREAS, This committee have received a letter from the committee of the township of Bald Eagle, together with a resolve of their committee anent the selling of grain, &c., in their township, craving advice before they should carry their resolve into execution, of which the following is a copy :

February 26th, 1776. We, the committee of the township of Bald Eagle met, and as a complaint was made to us by a number of the inhabitants that there is a quantity of rye that is going to be carried out of the township, for stilling, and that there are some of the inhabitants, which have not sold their grain as yet, nor will not sell without they get eighteen pence or two shillings per bushel above the highest market price that grain is giving in the county, but will keep it up and carry it off ; and as it appears to us that a great number of the inhabitants of the township will suffer if such a practice is allowed to go on ; therefore, we

Resolve, That no stiller in this township shall buy any more grain this season for to still, or still any more than what he hath already by him. And further, we resolve, that no grain be carried out of this township till the necessity of the poor is supplied, or till the first day of May next; and any person having grain of any kind to dispose of, and will not take the market price at Sunbury, reducting a reasonable carriage or the highest price that it will be there when the grain is wanted, we allow to seize on it and take it by force, and pay them their money. Given under our hands the day and year above mentioned.

      (Signed,) JOHN DICKSON,
           ROBERT LOVE,
           JAMES ERWIN.

Resolved, That the committee of Bald Eagle is the most competent judges of the circumstances of the people in that township; that, therefore, the affair be referred back to them to act as they shall see just cause, but, in the meantime, that they be cautioned against using too much rigor in their measures, and that they keep by moderation as much as possible, and study a sort of medium between seizing of property and supplying the wants of the poor.

Whereas, Report has been made to this committee of a certain Henry Sterratt profaning the Sabbath in an unchristian and scandalous manner, causing his servants to maul rails, &c., on that day, and beating and abusing them if they offered to disobey such his unlawful commands.

Resolved, That the committee of Bald Eagle township, where he now resides, be recommended to suppress such like practices to the utmost of their power.

Resolved, That this committee be adjourned till Tuesday, the 15th of April next, when it is again to meet at the house of George McCandlish.

April 15*th,* 1777.

The committee met according to adjournment, Mr. Thomas Jordan in the chair.

WHEREAS, A certain Jacob Dreisbach having disobeyed a summons issued by this committee at their last sitting, for him to have compeared at this meeting of committee as evidence in the affair of Jacob Links,

Resolved, That a special warrant be now granted for bringing him before this committee to-morrow, at nine o'clock.

April 17th.

Jacob Dreisbach was brought before the committee, and being duly sworn, he saith that he asked Captain Links if he was the man that was to go to Philadelphia for salt, and the said Links answered that he was, and said that he had a sister in Philadelphia, and wanted to see her, and said it would suit him better to go than another who had no errand of their own ; but says, for his own part, he was willing to allow Captain Links whatever came to his share of the expenses, at the same rate that the rest of his employers allowed him, and further saith not.

JACOB DREISBACH.

Mr. George Overmire, a member of this committee, declareth that he was present when Captain Links agreed with his employers, and says that he was to have his expenses allowed him, whether he got salt or not.

Captain Links compeared and produced his account for traveling expenses, which amounted to £5 15, acknowledging the receipt of £39 from his employers, part of which he had yet in his hands, and says he could have got salt, but it being salt that had been already purchased or allotted for the use of this county, and was to be distributed over the county at large, it was not answering his purpose to bring it, and there was no other salt he could get to purchase.

Resolved, That Captain Links be authorized to keep the sum of two shillings and eleven pence half penny out of every pound of his employer's money for payment of his expenses, as his account appears to this committee to be very moderate.

WHEREAS, A certain William Read, of Bald Eagle township, has been taken into custody and carried before this committee to answer for his conduct in refusing to associate and bear arms in behalf of the States ; and being asked his reasons for so refusing, his answers were as follows, viz :

That he was once concerned in a riot that happened in Ireland, commonly known by the name of the Hearts of Steel, and was taken prisoner, tried, and acquitted, upon his taking an oath of allegiance to the King, and coming [under] solemn obligations never to lift arms against him for the future ; he, therefore, looked upon it as a breach of his oath to muster or bear arms in behalf of the States, as the arms of the States were now employed against the King to whom he had sworn allegiance.

Being further asked if he had any objections to the cause the United States were now engaged in, he said he had not any, and would be as forward and willing as any to join in it, could he do it without breach of his oath. Being asked if he would take an oath of allegiance to the United States, he said he would if it did not oblige him to take up arms.

Accordingly an oath was tendered to him, and he swore as follows :

I do swear to be true to the United States of America, and do renounce and disclaim all allegiance to the King of Great Britain, and promise that I will not, either directly or indirectly, speak or act any thing in prejudice to the cause or safety of the States, or lift arms against them, or be any way assistant to their declared enemies in any case whatsoever.

WILLIAM READ.

Whereupon, the committee resolved to dismiss him, upon his paying the sum of seventeen shillings and one penny half penny, being the costs of bringing him before the committee.

In consequence of sundry accounts, from different parts of the county, of a dangerous plot being on foot by some of our enemies to bring on an Indian war, and in particular by an intercepted letter, wrote by a certain Nicholas Pickard, directed to a certain John Pickard, at the house of Caspar Read, in Penn's township, with all speed, a copy of which was transmitted to us by Nathaniel Landon, of Wyoming, and is now before this committee, and is as follows:

WYOMING, *March 7th*, 1777.

WORTHY FRIEND : I cannot omit but write you a few lines, that I am in a good state of health, and, further, I let you know that, as soon as the river is clear of ice, we shall march from every part ; therefore, I would advise you, as a friend, to go out of the way, for we then, as soon as the river is clear of ice, intend to cut all off ; therefore, I think it is better for you to go out of the way with the rest, for against May it will go as you heard it should go. Perhaps against Easter I will be with you; then I shall tell you further, and give you a better account of it. No more at present, but I remain your trusty friend. Give my compliments to them all a thousand times; tell them all that I intend to see them soon. I have wrote to you as much as I durst.

(Signed.) NICHOLAS PICKARD.

In consequence of which letter, Colonel James Murray and Captain James Espy were sent out, by order of this committee, in search of the said Nicholas and John Pickard.

April 17*th.*

Captain Espy returned, and brought the body of John Pickard before this committee; and being legally sworn, upon the Holy Evangelist of Almighty God,

He saith, that he went up the river, some time about last Christmas, from Middletown to Wyoming, in a boat, and at Wyoming he met with the aforesaid Nicholas Pickard, his own cousin, and that they two went by land about twenty miles further up the river, to a place called Tankhannock, to see some friends, and being in the house of a certain Nicholas Phillips, he, the said Phillips, told his cousin and him that the Indians had told him they would come down, and cut off all against this spring, or as soon as they got their orders; and that they would in particular strike upon the Mohawk river and the waters of the Susquehannough; and that when he parted with the said Nicholas, at that time, he promised to write to the deponent as soon as he thought there was immediate danger, so that he might go out of the way; withal telling him that the Indians did not want to kill any that did not take up arms against them, so that if he would go out of the way, or lie still on one side, there would be no danger of him. And further told him, about a fortnight ago, that there were five hundred Indians at Shamung, waiting for their orders from Niagara. Likewise, that he, the deponent, asked the said Nicholas what his reason was for coming down to Caspar Read's at that time, (being about a fortnight ago,) and he told him that the Yankees were going to apprehend him for a Tory, and that a certain Dennis Clark came to him about midnight, and gave him notice of it, and accordingly he made his escape down the river to Caspar Read's, or that neighborhood. And he has told the deponent, that he has wrote him two letters, one of which was sent by a man of the name of Clark, which the deponent thinks is the same Clark that gave him notice to go off; and that Clark took sick upon the way, and when he could not proceed forward with the letter, by reason of his illness, he threw the letter in the fire and burnt it; and that the contents of the letter was, that the Indians were coming down, and for the deponent to go out of the way, and further saith not.

JOHN PICKARD.

An oath of allegiance to the United States being proposed to John Pickard, and bail for his good behavior, he complied with both. and produced Caspar Read as his bail, who bound himself in a bond of an hundred pounds for the good and orderly behavior of John Pickard, for a year and a day next to come after this date. Then the oath of allegiance was tendered to him, and he swore as follows :

'I do swear to be true to the United States of America, and do renounce and disclaim all allegiance to the King of Great Britain, and promise that I will not, either directly or indirectly, speak or act anything in prejudice to the cause or safety of the States, or lift arms against them, or be any way assistant to their declared enemies, in any case whatsover. So help me God.

JOHN PICKARD.

Upon the satisfaction given to the committee by the said John Pickard, it was unanimously agreed that he be dismissed.

April 17*th.*

Colonel Murray returned, and brought the body of Nicholas Pickard before this committee, and being [questioned] anent the aforesaid letter, confesseth that he wrote it, and a copy of the letter being read unto him, he ackowledged the same in every particular; and further confesseth, that he is in connection with the ministerial troops at Niagara, and that he has taken an oath of allegiance to the King of Britain, but says he was forced to it; and further, concerning the letter, he says that he wrote it in a kind of mysterious manner, by reversing the letters, so that it might not be understood, in case it should be intercepted; and that he sent it by a person of the name of Dennis Clark, and that he has seen said Clark since that time, who told him that he took sick upon the way, and, seeing that he could not get the letter forwarded, he had burnt it.

He likewise says that one Nicholas Philips, at Tankhannock, notified him and several others thereabouts to move away with their families and connections to a place called Tiogo, in the Indian country, as the English were coming down to cut off the inhabitants upon the waters of the Mohawk river and the Susquehannough. That there were fifteen thousand of the ministerial troops at Niagara, which were to be divided; four thousand of them were to come down the North Branch and four thousand down the West Branch of Susquehannough, and seven thousand down the Mohawk river, and a number of Indians were to be along with them, and that the person who informed this Philips of it was one John DePeu, who is gone off and joined the English at Niagara, and that he sent him this piece of information by an Indian, after he went off.

Upon due deliberation upon the examination of Nicholas Pickard, the committee are unanimously of opinion that he is an enemy to the States: therefore,

Resolved, That he be immediately sent from before this committee to the Supreme Executive Council of this State, to be dealt with as their superior judgments shall direct them in the case, and that John Coates be the person who shall carry him thither, and that he call as many to his assistance as may be needful.

Resolved, That this committee be adjourned till the 10th day of June next, when they are to meet at the house of Mr. Laughlan McCartney, in Northumberland.

January 3, was fought the battle at Princeton, in which Colonel Potter's battalion took part. Washington, it will be recollected, slipped away from Cornwallis at Trenton, made a forced march on Princeton, and had already won the battle there, when Cornwallis, having made a forced march, arrived near Stony Brook. Washington sent an order to Colonel Potter to destroy the bridge at Worth's Mills, on Stony Brook, in sight of the advancing British. Colonel Potter ordered Major Kelly to make a detail for that purpose. Kelly said he would not order another to do what some might say he was afraid to do himself. He took a detail and went to work. The British opened upon him a heavy fire of round shot. Before all the logs were cut off, several balls struck the log on which he stood, and it broke down sooner than he expected, and he fell into the stream. His party moved off, not expecting him to escape.

By great exertions he reached the shore through the high water and floating timbers, and followed the troops. Incumbered, as he was, with his wet and frozen clothes, he made prisoner of an armed British scout, and took him into camp. (Lossing, in his Field Book of the Revolution, says he was taken prisoner. This is a mistake.) Colonel Kelly used to tell that during this tour, for three days at one time there was no service of provisions, and during the march before and after the battle, they were thirty-six hours under arms without sleep.

Muster roll of Captain Benjamin Weiser's company, at Philadelphia January 30, 1777.

Captain—Weiser, B.
First Lieutenant—Snider, Christopher.
Second Lieutenant—Shaffer, Adam.
Third Lieutenant—Van Gundy, Joseph.
First Sergeant—Hain, Matthew.
Second Sergeant—Markle, George.
First Corporal—Moyer, Philip.
Second Corporal—Eisenhauer, Frederick, enlisted in the service of the United States.

Privates—Brosius, George; Brosius, Nicholas; Faust, John; Furst, Christian, sick at present, (discharged at Reading, by Doctor Potts;) Furst, Conrad; Groninger, Henry; Hauser, John; Heim, John; Herter, John; Herrold, George; Hosterman, Peter; Kaufman, Henry; Kerstetter, Adam; Kerstetter, Martin; Kerstetter, Leonard; Kitch, Thomas; Leffler, Adam; Livengood, John; Meiser, John; Moyer, George; Neitz, Philip; Newman, Michael; Peifer, George; Pickel, Tobias; Reitz, Andrew; Shafer, Christian; Shafer, Nicholas; Snider, Jacob; Spengle, Zacharias; Stroub, John; Troutner, George, (enlisted in the United States service;) Weis, Peter; Witmer, Mathias.

28th January, the Assembly passed an act reviving all laws in force on the 14th of May, 1776, and such of the common and statute laws of England as had been in force previously, except the act of allegiance, or those that acknowledged the authority of the heirs and devisees of William Penn, or were repugnant to the lately formed constitution. The courts were directed to be held at the times and places of old, and the President and Council should designate the presiding justice; in his absence, the justices to chose one. The election for justices was fixed for the 25th of April, two persons from each township to be elected, one commissioned. Licenses for taverns to be granted by the Executive Council, on recommendation of the justices. 14th March, register and recorder's offices established in every county; and on the 14th of June, the county was districted; Buffalo, White Deer, and Potter placed in the third district. The elections to be held at Fought's mill.

February 1, occurred the skirmish at Piscataway, New Jersey. Patrick Kellahan, of Captain Clarke's company, was wounded by a musket ball in the right thigh. He lay a long while under the doctor's hands. The ball, however, was never extracted, at least in 1786, when Colonel James Murray certified to the facts, in order to his drawing a pension. Peter Nees was wounded in the privates, and died from want of proper care. He left a widow, Mary Nees, and three children. Henry Dougherty and John Fitzsimmons, of Northumberland county, were wounded. Lieutenant Gustavus Ross, of Lee's company, was killed. Captain Thomas Robinson, who was second in command that day, said he was wounded in the bowels, and died that night, at Ash Swamp, east New Jersey. Robert Wilson, who became ensign of Cookson Long's company, and John Norcross, were wounded. Wilson in the left foot, Norcross in the left shoulder.

The following receipt is a curiosity in its way. It bears date 27th May: "Received of Captain John Clarke the sum of five pounds and twelve shillings and nine pence, together with three pounds seven shillings and three pence, together with four pounds, seven shillings bounty and subsistence, being the full pay for a private for three months and eighteen days. I say received by me.

"Jos. Green."

During the summer Colonel Kelly was commanding on the frontier. Van Campen, in his narrative, says he served a tour of three months with him at this time. Colonel Kelly's guide was Job Chilloway, a friendly Indian. They were stationed at the Big Island, near Lock Haven.

Job Chilloway, says Jones, in his history of Juniata valley, page 351, spent his latter days on Spruce creek, Huntingdon county, where he was found dead in his cabin, by some hunters, about the close of the last century. He was a tall, muscular man, with his ears cut so as to hang pendant, like a pair of ear-rings; so said the late E. Bell, Esquire. He was of the Delaware tribe, and his name occurs frequently in the Archives, from 1759 on, as a spy, and always friendly to the whites.

April 5th, General James Potter appointed third brigadier general.

April 22. "Matthew Brown, whose remains lie buried in White Deer Hole valley, was quite a prominent man in our history. He was one of the first overseers of the poor for White Deer township; in February, 1776, one of the committee of safety for Northumberland county; in June 1776, a member of the Provincial Council that met in Philadelphia to dissolve our political connection with Great Britain, and in July, 1776, a member of the State Convention that formed our State Constitution of 1776, which he signed on the 28th day of September, in that year. In the autumn of 1776 he entered our provincial or United States army as a soldier, and while serving thus contracted what was called 'the camp fever,' which compelled him to return home, and finally carried him to his grave. He lies buried here in a field, about half a mile south of my residence. His grave is surrounded with a rude unmortared stone wall, put there by his wife, Eleanor Brown, the widow named in our above list of names. After surviving him for a period of thirty-seven years, she also died, and now lies buried at his side. The inclosure is about ten or twelve feet square in the clear, inside, and contains two upright, plain white marble tombstones, now much discolored and blackened by time, leaving the following inscriptions and nothing more, to wit:

'MATTHEW BROWN,
Died April 22d, 1777.'

'ELEANOR BROWN,
Wife of Matthew Brown,
Died August 9, 1814.'

"And inside of this stone inclosure there stands four living trees, viz: a straight and handsome hickory tree of about sixteen inches in diameter near the ground, and three other crooked and scraggy trees, a wild cherry tree, and two elm trees of some seven or eight inches in diameter near the ground. Mr. Brown seems to have been well off, and doubtless owned this land and lived somewhere near where he now lies buried."—*J. F. Wolfinger.*

10th May, occurred the action at Piscataway, New Jersey. Christopher Gettig, afterwards many years a justice at Sunbury, was acting first lieutenant that day in Colonel Cooke's regiment. He was wounded in the leg and taken prisoner. His leg had to be amputated. Some of his descendants live near Bellefonte, Centre county, (1877.)

11th September, battle of Brandywine. Captain John Brady was badly wounded. William Boyd,[1] his lieutenant was killed. Adam Christ, of Buffalo Valley, was wounded in the breast, a musket ball passing clear through his body. Samuel Brady was also in this battle. The twelfth was under General Wayne, at Chadd's Ford. General Potter was with General Armstrong at Pyles' Ford. Christ was in Lieutenant Colonel James Murray's battalion, under Potter.

20th, occurred the Paoli massacre. Samuel Brady was on guard, and laid down with his blanket buckled around him. The British were nearly on them before the sentinel fired. Brady ran; and as he jumped a fence, a soldier struck at him with a musket and pinned his blanket to a rail. He tore the blanket, and dashed on. A horseman overtook him, and ordered him to stop. He wheeled and shot the horseman dead, and got into a small swamp, supposing no one in but himself. In the morning he found fifty-five men in it, of whom he took command and conducted to camp.

1st November, Colonel Hunter writes that he had orders for the third and fourth classes of militia to march, but he had neither arms or blankets for them; that the first and second classes were on the frontiers, and had all the good arms that could be collected; that the people were in a bad way; had not got in any crops. For the state of the country, he referred President Wharton to Captain John Hambright, who had been chosen of the Council. That the

---

[1] William Boyd was the son of Sarah Boyd, a widow, who resided at Northumberland, and a brother of Thomas, who shared in all the dangers and fatigues of the Canada campaign, (see Judge Henry's Memoirs of Arnold's Expedition,) and fell a sacrifice to Indian barbarity in Sullivan's expedition. Another brother, Captain Boyd, lived at Northumberland many years afterwards. See Meginness, page 286, for his adventures.

county was the worst off of any in the State for salt. His next letter, 11th November, Fort Augusta, is as follows:

SIR: This day the third and fourth classes of the third battalion march to join the army of General Washington, under the command of Colonel James Murray. The two classes of Colonel Cookson Long's battalion I have ordered to duty on the frontiers, as the first class, that was commanded by Colonel John Kelly, has come off from thence, after serving two months, to encourage the poor, scattered inhabitants to return back to their habitations, which I hope will be approved by the Council. The militia that now marches is badly off for blankets, and several go without any, and but thinly clothed, which shows their attachment to the American cause; though poor, yet brave, and can be depended upon for their integrity. The first class that did duty up the Bald Eagle looks to me for pay. It has come home with the loss of two men, drowned in the river.

Your obedient servant,
SAMUEL HUNTER.

By way of appendix to the year 1777, I insert a letter to General James Potter. His correspondence, embracing letters from all the principal characters in the Revolution, from General Washington to Lady Harriet Ackland, after being many years carefully preserved on his garret, were scattered to the four winds, in the misfortune of some of his descendants, some twenty years ago. His dark lantern is still in the possession of Colonel William P. Wilson, of Trenton, New Jersey, one of his descendants.

General Potter's positions are indicated as follows: July 22, in command at Billingsport; 29th August, in command of the first brigade, Pennsylvania militia, at Chester; September 1, at Wilmington; 2d and 5th moved up to Newport.

HEAD QUARTERS, 31st October, 1777.

SIR: As soon as the Schuylkill is fordable, I shall send over a large body of militia to you, for the purpose of executing some particular matters. The principal one, to endeavor to break up the road by which the enemy have a communication with their shipping over the islands, if it is practicable; and to remove the running stones from the mills in the neighborhood of Chester and Wilmington. This last I would have you undertake immediately, with your present force, as I have information that the enemy are about making a detachment to Wilmington, probably with an intent to take post there, and secure the use of the mills. To execute this matter at once, you should impress a sufficient number of wagons for the purpose, without letting any person know what they are for, and send them under good officers, with sufficient parties, to the following mills :

Lloyd's, about two miles on this side of Chester; Robinson's, on Naaman's creek; Shaw's, about one mile back of Chester, and the Brandywine mills. If there are any other that I have not mentioned, contiguous to the river, they are also to be dismounted. The stones should be marked with tar and grease, or in some other manner, that it may be known to what mills they belong, that they may be returned, and made use of in the future, and they should be moved to such distance that the enemy cannot easily recover them. If there is any flour in the mills, it should be removed, if possible, after the stones are secured. I am informed that there is considerable quantity in Shaw's mill, particularly, which there is reason to believe is intended for the enemy. It is very convenient to the navigation of Chester creek, and should be first taken care of. I beg you may instantly set about this work, for the reason above mentioned. That no previous alarm may be given, let a certain day and a certain hour be fixed upon for the execution of the whole at one time, and even the officers who are to do the business should not know their destination till just before they set out, lest it should take wind.

I have yours of yesterday afternoon, and am glad to hear that the flood has done so much damage to the meadows. Endeavor by all means to keep the breakers open. When the party that I mentioned in the former part of my letter gets down, I hope you will be able to break up the dyke effectually.

I am sir, your most obedient servant,

GEORGE WASHINGTON.

P. S. I have desired Captain Lee, of the light horse, to give you any assistance that you may want.

GENERAL POTTER.

From the camp at Mr. Lewes', November 12, 1777, after recommending Thomas Jordan for paymaster, General Potter writes:

"As for news, I have not much. Yesterday came up the river thirty-eight sail of the enemy. What number of troops were on board is a secret to me. I went to Chester in the evening, but could not learn. There has been very heavy firing for three days past. The first day they did no damage to the works or the men. I have intelligence almost every day from the city. Howe is the best Whig-maker in the United States. He has converted many from the evil of their ways, and turned them unto the country. Distress and want is likely to abound in the city. I am told the poor would have suffered before this time, if General Washington had not allowed them to get flour at the Frankfort mills. Friend Howe is not a partial man. He uses Whig and Tory alike, which is the best thing I can say of him. The friends to the Government lent friend Howe £100,000. I believe by this time they would not refuse security, if offered. The enemy have made two floating batteries, but they are constructed so badly and sunk so deep in the water, they will do us little damage. My men brought in to-day five British soldiers prisoners. We catch them napping, sometimes. Firing has been heavy to-day, but we stand it as yet. I have tried to get a man to go to Red Bank to-day, and to-morrow I hope I will get an account from there. I have just received a letter from George Read, Esquire, President of Delaware State, informing that their militia had seized a number of people, who were supplying the enemy's shipping with fresh provisions, and destroyed six of their vessels in Duck creek. Three weeks ago I advised the taking and keeping of Province and Carpenter's Islands. If this had been done, friend Howe would have been hungry by this time. We have it reported that on Wednesday last our people sank a sixty-four gun ship. On Monday our people took twelve light horse and some foot prisoners. The soldiers in the city say often that they look upon themselves as our prisoners. One day one of the sentinels told Major Taylor so.

"With esteem, your Excellency's obedient, humble servant,

"JAMES POTTER."

Directed, on public service, His Excellency, Thomas Wharton, Esquire, Lancaster, favor of Mr. Thomas Jordan.

11th December occurred the action, at Guelph's mills, (near Philadelphia,) in which the enemy endeavored to surprise General Potter. The second battalion, under Colonel Murray, was engaged.

Timothy Lennington, of Northumberland county, was wounded; Robert McQuilliams was also wounded, and cut to pieces by the light horse, the same evening; Charles Clark, first lieutenant of Captain Taggart's company, was wounded in the left arm; had his skull fractured; he remained in captivity three years.

December 15, General Potter writes home, that in an action a few days previous his people behaved well, particularly the regiments of Colonel Chambers and Colonel Murray.

December 31, the Council request General Potter to stay in the field during the winter, or for some time yet at least. The year closes gloomily enough, with the army encamped at Valley Forge.

A return, dated Camp, in Montgomery, Philadelphia county, December 22, shows that Colonel Murray's regiment, of Northumberland county militia, was then in Major General John Armstrong's division, and numbered two hundred and twenty-six men on the rolls.

1778

List of Inhabitants—Indian Troubles—Great Runaway of 1778—Covenhoven's Narrative—John Bashor Killed—Incident of Quinn Family—Monmouth Battle—James Brady's Death—Colonel Hartley's Expedition.

THOMAS WHARTON, President of the State until his death at Lancaster, 23d May. Members of Congress, Clingan, William; Morris, Robert; Roberdeau, Daniel; Reed, Joseph; Smith, James; and Smith, Jonathan B. Samuel Hunter, Lieutenant of the county. John Hambright, member of Council. Members of Assembly elected, October 2, Chambers, Stephen; Dale, Samuel; Himrod, Simon; McKnight, James; Martin, Robert; and White, John. The candidates voted for, having, according to the returns of the judges of the election, received the following number of votes each: Samuel Dale, 251;

Simon Himrod, 250; James McKnight, 247; Robert Martin, 246; John White, 211; Stephen Chambers, 201; Robert Fruit; 173; James Crawford, 170. Another return, signed by John Kelly, Walter Clark, and Jacob Fulmer, judges, declared Robert Fruit and James Crawford elected, instead of White and Chambers; but the House declared, November 7, that the return of John Clingman, William Fisher, and Michael Hessler, was the legal one. David Harris, Prothonotary. Jonathan Lodge, Sheriff. January 1, Benjamin Weiser of Penn's, appointed a justice. County Commissioners, William Gray, John Nelson, and Thomas Sutherland; John Lytle elected in October. Officers of Buffalo: Constable, Martin Trester; Supervisors, John Pontius and George Williams; Overseers, William Speddy and Martin Dreisbach. White Deer: Constable, Henry Derr; Supervisors, James Hammond and William Rodman; Overseers, Charles McGenet and William Wilson.

Inhabitants of Buffalo who came in after 1775. Books, Henry; Barnhart, Martin; Colpetzer, Adam; Chambers, Robert; Cox, Samuel; Divler, Joseph; Dempsey, Cornelius; Dugan, William; Frederick, Thomas; Ferguson, John; Gilliland, John; Haughawaut, Liffard, tenant of Samuel McClay's place; Irvin, William, (miller,) Mensch, Abraham, (who owned and lived on Abraham Wolfe's place, in East Buffalo. His wife died in the Valley, and was buried at Jenkins mill. He left with the runaway of 1779, taking with him his boys, Christian and John, and one horse. He never returned. He married again, and the late Reverend J. Nicholas Mensch, was a son by the second wife. Christian went to Ohio, John to New York; the latter died, about the same time the Reverend J. Nicholas died, at Lewisburg, in 1854. The father of Abraham and Benjamin, of Lewis township, was a nephew of the one here spoken of.) Mizener, Henry and Conrad; Prinkler, Charles; Shirtz, Michael; Struble, Richard; Stroh, Nicholas, on now Samuel Dunkel's place. (Mathias Allspach made crocks there. The latter killed, with a potter's stick, a wolf following the sheep into the yard;) Henry Winkert.

List of Inhabitants of White Deer.

Allen, Samuel; Ammon, George; Armstrong, William; Baker, Jacob; Blue, Frederick; Blue, William; Blythe, William; Boone, Hawkins; Brown, Eleanor ; Brundage, Joseph ; Buchanan, James ; Caldwell, James ; Carnachan, William ; Campbell, John ; Charters, William ; Clark, Robert; Clark, Walter; Clark, William; Cook, Henry ; Cooper, Robert ; Correy, Robert ; Couples, David ; Crasher, William ; Croninger, Leonard ; Dale, Samuel ; Deal, Christian ; Dean, Benjamin ; Derr, Joseph ; Derr, Henry ; Diffenderfer, Michael ; Diermand, Thomas ; Dilce, David ; Dunbar, Samuel ; Earl, Michael ; Elder, Thomas ; Ellis, Richard ; Etterburn, Jacob ; Ewing, Alexander ; Fisher, Christian ; Fisher, John ; Fisher, Samuel, saw-mill ; Fleming, Hans ; Fockler, George ; Foutz, Conrad ; Fruit, Robert ; Fulton, John ; Gibson, Robert ; Graham, Edward ; Graham, John ; Graham, Thomas ; Gray, William ; Green, Ebenezer ; Hammond, David ; Hammond, James ; Hays, James ; Hazlett, John ; Heckle, Andrew; Heckman, Andrew ; Hill, James ; Hood, Elizabeth ; Houston, Doctor John ; Huling, Marcus, saw-mill ; Hunter, James ; Hutchinson, Thomas ; Iddings, Henry ; Irwin, George ; Irwin, Richard ; James, Thomas ; Johnson, John ; Johnson, William ; Jordan, William ; Kelly, John ; Kilday, George ; Kirkwood, John ; Lafferty, Isaac ; Laird, Nicholas ; Leacock, John ; Linn, John ; Lobden, Thomas ; Low, Cornelius ; Low, Cornelius, junior ; Low, William ; Lykens, Thomas ; McCard, James ; McClenachan, James ; McCollum, John ; McComb, Daniel ; McClure, Thomas ; McCord, Samuel ; McCormick, James ; McCormick, Thomas ; McGinnes, Samuel ; McLaughlin, James ; McJannet, Charles ; Mackey, William ; Maffit, Joseph ; Martin, Robert ; Mason, William ; Mitcheltree, John ; Moodie, Robert ; Moore, Henry ; Moore, John ; Moore, Thomas ; Nicholson, William ; Noraconk, Daniel ; Norcross, John ; Orr, William ; Pearson, Widow ; Poak, James, saw-mill : Poak, Joseph ; Reed, William ; Reed, Widow ; Reese, George ; Robb, William ; Rodman, William ; Row, James ; Row, Joseph ; Ridehower, Peter ; Semple, John ; Semple, Robert ; Shaw, Hamilton ; Shearer, Samuel ; Shields, Archibald ; Smith, John, senior ; Smith, John, junior ; Smith, Widow ; Stephen, Alexander ; Stephen, Philip ; Story, John ; Stover, Philip ; Sunderland, Daniel ; Swartz, Peter ; Tate, John ; Tate, Joseph ; Titzell, Henry, grist and saw-mill, (Rauch's now ;) Townsend, Codder ; Turner, Thomas ; Weeks, Jesse ; Weeks, Joseph ; Weitzell, John ; Wertz, Deidrich ; Wheeland,

George; White, Joseph; Wilson, Peter; Wilson, Peter, junior; Wilson, William; Yarnall, Jesse.

Doctor John Houston was the earliest physician in White Deer township, that I have any knowledge of. He is said to have resided at or near the present village of Hightown.

Additional List of Inhabitants, Penn's Township.

Aumiller, Philip; Bader, George; Bartges, Christopher; Bearsh, Peter; Begel, Thomas; Benford, George; Billman, Abraham; Bickel, John; Bornson, Catharine; Bowerman, George; Bowerman, John; Borald, Adam; Bowersox, Paul; Boreminginan, Peter; Bollinger, Adam; Braucht, Daniel; Brenard, Francis; Buchtel, John; Bumbach, George, senior; Byerly, Anthony; Carrol, Hugh; Clemens, Abraham; Conrad, George; Dauberman, Christian; Deininger, Frederick; Eberhart, Frederick; Eckart, Jacob; Fannery, Benjamin; Fisher, Jacob; Fisher, Adam; Fiddler, Stephen; Foulke, Jacob; Fry, John; Gast, Christian; Gay, Frederick; Gemberling, Paul; Gemberling, Jacob; Gill, William; Giltner, Jacob; Gillan, Moses; Gift, Adam; Glass, George; Gundy, Peter; Hafer, Andrew; Hains, John; Hampshire, John; Harmin, Henry; Hassinger, Herman; Havelock, Conrad; Hawn, Michael; Hendershot, Casper; Herrold, Simon; Herrold, George, a grist mill; Hess, Mathias; Hosterman, Jacob; Houser, Mathias; Kern, Yost; Kiester, Martin; Knippenberger, Paul; Kline, David; Krain, Hugh; Laudenslager, Ferdy; Lepley, Jacob; Lever, Adam; Lower, Peter; McAteer, Robert; McCabe, Edward; Magill, Valentine; Manning, Simeon, senior and junior; Maris, William; Miller, Conrad; Miller, Dewalt, saw-mill; Miller, Sigamund; Mitchell, Daniel; Mockell, Nicholas; Molly, Anthony; Moon, John, one grist mill; Moon, Casper, junior; Moore, Andrew, two mills; Moyer, Jacob; Moyer, Charles; Mower, Michael; Musser, John; Nees, Thomas; Netz, Ludwig; Oatly, Edward; Paul, Dewalt; Phillips, Benjamin; Reed, John; Reger, John; Reiber, John; Richter, Christena; Rine, Henry; Rorabaugh, Simon; Roush, Jacob; Roush, John; Seecrist, Christian, saw-mill; Sherk, John; Shirtz, Jacob; Shock, Jacob; Shoop, George; Snyder, Christopher; Spangler, Andrew; Spengle, Zachariah; Stock, John; Stock, Peter; Stock, Michael; Stoke, George; Stum, Abraham, junior; Swineford, Albright, one grist and saw-mill; Thomas, John; Trester, George; Trester, Martin; Trester, Jacob; Weirich, William; Weiser, Philip; Weiser, John; Welsh, John; Willis, John; Wittenmyer, Andrew; Woodrow, Simeon; Yost, Casper; Zimmerman, Christopher.

January 1st, (from minutes of Council,) Joseph Green presented his claim for supplying the militia with provisions while on their expedition up the West Branch, and an order was issued for £1,600 to Colonel Hunter for the same.

January 9th, General Potter gets leave of absence, in consequence of sickness of Mrs. Potter, and Brigadier General John Lacey appointed to his command.

February 17th, General Wayne detached Captain William Wilson, Lieutenant John Boyd, and Captain George Grant to recruit for the Pennsylvania regiments in Northumberland county. At February sessions, Samuel Maclay presented a petition, stating that his servant had enlisted in the Twelfth Pennsylvania regiment, and John Thompson and William Irvine (Irish) were appointed to appraise the time of said servant. February 20th, Samuel Dale, member elect, took his seat in the Assembly, at Lancaster. March 9th, James Murray appeared. Nothwithstanding the Indian troubles, courts were held in February and in May. At the latter, John Clark, John Crider, George Overmeier, Martin Dreisbach, and William Irwin were appointed viewers on a petition to divide Buffalo township, by a line commencing at the mouth of Beaver run, thence a south-west course to Switzer run. This was never acted upon.

At August term, Stephen Chambers was admitted to the bar. On the grand jury, were Albright Swineford, Elias Younkman, Henry Richard, and Thomas Sutherland. At November term, Collinson Read and John Vannost, were admitted to the bar. Abraham Mensch, Peter Wicoff, and William Clark, were jurors.

As early as Dececember, 1777, the Indians re-appeared up the West Branch, and Colonel Hunter ordered out Colonel Cookson Long's battalion, as he says he is an excellent good woodsman; but for all that, on the 1st of January, one of the inhabitants was killed and scalped, two miles above the Great Island, and eleven Indians seen, who were pursued, and two killed. In consequence, the order for the fifth class of militia to march to join the army was countermanded on the 19th. It will be recollected that the main army was in camp at Valley Forge, at this time. On the 1st of May, General Lacey's militia command was surrounded at Crooked Billet. General Lacey says, the alarm was so sudden that I had scarcely time to mount my horse, before the enemy were within musket shot of my quarters. He escaped, with the loss of his baggage, and thirty killed and wounded. Some were butchered in a manner the most brutal savages could not equal. Even while living, some were thrown into the buckwheat straw, and the straw set on fire. The clothes were burned on others, and scarcely one without a dozen of wounds.

From the diary of James F. Linn under date, December 2, 1845, I extract the following : " Uncle David Linn told me some anecdotes of Abraham Smith, who was married to his sister Jane, and who died in Ohio some years since. He was at Crooked Billet, and was taken prisoner with some others. They lost four or five men by shots. They knew not where they came from. At last Morrow (grandfather of my brother William's widow) got sight of the man, who was shooting from behind a tree. He told them to keep still, and he would fix him. When the man stepped from behind the tree to load, Morrow fired, and one of them saw him drop his hands upon his belly, and fall forward. They lossed no more men in that way. After they were taken, they were ordered to be shot as rebels. The reason for shooting the prisoners was, that they were short of provisions. They shot Maclay and Conner, and burned their bodies in a pile of buckwheat straw. It was Smith's turn next. He stood up, and kept his eye on the man who was to shoot him, until he thought he was about to draw the trigger, when he dodged forward, and the bullet took the depth of itself out of his back, opposite his breast. An officer then interfered, and stopped the shooting." Crooked Billet is now called Hatborough, in Montgomery county, Pennsylvania.

John Dietrich Aurand (afterward Reverend) enlisted in Colonel Stewart's Regiment, General Wayne's brigade. He had been learning milling at his father's mill, on Turtle creek. His father sold the mill this year, and, possibly, going down the country in search of employment, he fell in with the recruiting officer. Before his term expired his father went to the army, and made an effort to secure his release, on the ground of minority ; but he declined returning, and served until the year 1781, when occurred the revolt of General Wayne's troops, when he was honorably discharged, and returned to his father's home on Turtle creek.

May 4, Colonel Cooke, twelfth regiment, under General Wayne, in camp at Mount Joy. 5th May, Colonel John Kelly, with part of his battalion, on duty in Penn's valley. May 8, Jacob Standford killed at his own house, in Penn's valley, with his wife and daughter, and his son, ten or eleven years old, missing.[1]

May 17, General Potter writes from upper Fort, Penn's valley, that he was informed by Colonel Long that a few families coming to Lycoming, escorted by a party under the command of Colonel Hosterman, were attacked by twelve Indians, who killed six of them, and six were missing. Three men were killed, at the same time, on Loyal Sock; twenty persons killed on the North Branch. One who was taken prisoner made his escape, and says the Indians are determined to clear the two branches of the Susquehanna this moon. He says we have two forts in the Valley, and are determined to stand as long as we are supported. The people were poor, and bread very high. May 30. Jacob Morgan writes, that he had just returned from camp at Valley Forge. He saw fifteen regiments under arms, as well disciplined as any of the British troops can be. They performed several maneuvers, with the greatest exactness and dispatch, under the direction of Baron Steuben. General Washington afterwards reviewed them. The British were about evacuating Philadelphia, and our army would follow. One regiment, under Arnold, was to go into Philadelphia for civil service, until the Executive Council could get there.

31st May, Colonel Hunter writes, "we are in a melancholy condition. The back inhabitants have left their homes. All above Muncy are at Samuel Wallis's. The people of Muncy are at Captain Brady's. All above Lycoming are at Antes' mill and the mouth of Bald Eagle. The people of Penn's valley are at one place in Potter township. The inhabitants of White Deer are assembled at three different places. The back settlers of Buffalo have come down to the river. Penn's township people have, likewise, moved to the river. All from Muncy hill to Chillisquaque have assembled at three different places. Fishing creek and Mahoning settlements

[1] Their graves are on Ephraim Keller's farm, west of Potter's Fort, (1872.)

have come to the river side. It is really distressing to see the people flying away, and leaving their all, especially the Jersey people, who came up here last winter and spring. Not one stays, but sets off to Jersey again." 2d June, he writes that the people have drawn up a petition to Congress for relief, and Robert Fruit and Thomas Jordan were set off to lay it before the Executive Council, for their approval, before presenting it to Congress.

May 6, Colonel Kelly and Thomas Hewitt were appointed agents of forfeited estates within the county.

June 13, Michael Campbell, of Colonel Hosterman's battalion, killed by the Indians.

June 14, Colonel Hunter writes that communication between Antes' mill and Big Island was cut off.

June 17, General Potter writes that Captain Pealer's company, in Nittany valley, had discovered a number of tracks, leading down Logan's Gap, quite fresh; thirty in number.

July 1, army moved toward New York. The twelfth Pennsylvania, in Wayne's brigade, left wing, under General Stirling.

The "Great Runaway."

July 3d occurred the massacre at Wyoming, the news of which, received on the 5th, caused the general stampede of the settlers of our Valley, called the "Great Runaway."

On the 9th, Colonel Hunter writes that both branches are nearly evacuated, and Northumberland and Sunbury will be the frontier in less than twenty-four hours. His letter evinces the agony of a strong man, who, with all supports taken away, was determined to fall, if need be, in defense of the charge committed to him. He says:

"Nothing but a firm reliance upon Divine Providence, and the virtue of our neighbors, induces the few to stand that remain in the two towns; and if they are not speedily reinforced they must give way; but will have this consolation, that they have stood in defence of their liberty and country as long as they could. In justice to this county, I must bear testimony that the States never applied to it for men in vain. I am sure the State must know that we have reduced ourselves to our present feeble condition by our readiness to turn out, upon all occasions, when called for in defence of the common cause. Should we now fall, for want of assistance, let the neighboring counties reconcile to themselves, if they can, the breach of brotherly love, charity, and every other virtue which adorns and advances the human species above the brute creation. I will not attempt to point out the particular cruelties or barbarities that have been practised on our unhappy inhabitants, but assure you that, for the number, history affords no instance of more heathenish cruelty or savage barbarity than has been exhibited in this county."

July 12, Matthew Smith writes from Paxton, (Harrisburg,) that he had "just arrived at Harris' Ferry, and beheld the greatest scenes of distress I ever saw. It was crowded with people who had come down the river, leaving everything."

Same day, Peter DeHaven writes, from Hummelstown: "This day there were twenty or thirty passed through this town from Buffalo Valley and Sunbury, and the people inform me that there are two hundred wagons on the road coming down. I was at Mr. Elder's meeting to-day, and Colonel Clark and Colonel Rodgers made an appeal to the inhabitants to turn out one hundred volunteers," &c.

A letter written by William Maclay, from Paxton, on the 12th, gives a very graphic picture of the distress. "I left Sunbury, and almost my whole property, on Wednesday last. I will not trouble you with a recital of the inconveniences I suffered while I brought my family, by water, to this place. I never in my life saw such scenes of distress. The river and the roads leading down it were covered with men, women, and children, flying for their lives. In short, Northumberland county is broken up. Colonel Hunter only remained, using his utmost endeavors to rally the inhabitants to make a stand. I left him with few. I cannot speak confidently as to numbers, but he had not a hundred men on whom he could depend. Mrs. Hunter came down with me. As he is now disencumbered of his family, I am convinced that he will do everything that can be expected from a brave and determined man. It was to no purpose, Colonel Hunter issued orders for the assembling of the militia. The whole county broke loose. Something, in the way of charity, ought to be done for the many miserable objects that crowd the banks of this river, especially those who fled from Wyoming. You know I did not use to love them, but I now pity their distress."

(Plunket and Maclay were the leading land proprietors who were affected by the Connecticut claim.)

Colonel Hunter, in another letter, dated later in the day of the 12th, says: "The towns of Sunbury and Northumberland are the frontiers, where a few virtuous inhabitants and fugitives seem determined to stand, though doubtful whether to-morrow's sun shall rise on them freemen, captives, or in eternity!"

A letter dated Lancaster, 14th July, from Bertram Galbraith, says: " On Sunday morning last, the banks of the Susquehanna, from Middletown up to the Blue mountain, were entirely clad with the inhabitants of Northumberland county, who had moved off, as well as many in the river in boats, canoes, and on rafts. This I had from Captain Abraham Scott, a man of veracity, who was up at Garber's mills for his sister, the wife of Colonel Samuel Hunter, and spake with a lieutenant, who was in the action at Wyoming. He also seen six of the wounded men brought down."

Robert Covenhoven, (Crownover,) describing the scene nearer home, says: " I took my own family safely to Sunbury, and came back in a keel-boat to secure my furniture. Just as I rounded a point above Derrstown, now Lewisburg, I met the whole convoy from all the forts above. Such a sight I never saw in my life. Boats, canoes, hog-troughs, rafts hastily made of dry sticks, every sort of floating article, had been put in requisition, and were crowded with women, children, and plunder. There were several hundred people in all. Whenever any obstruction occurred at any shoal or ripple, the women would leap out into the water and put their shoulders to the boat or raft and launch it again into deep water. The men of the settlement came down in single file, on each side of the river, to guard the women and children. The whole convoy arrived safely at Sunbury, leaving the entire range of farms along the West Branch to the ravages of the Indians."

At this time occurred the death of John Michael Bashor. Michael Weyland, who survived many years afterwards, often related the story to my informant. He said it was at the time of the Great Runaway; and as Bashor's name is dropped from the assessment of 1778, it, no doubt, occurred in the first week in July, 1778. I can find no allusion in the Archives, or in any other written record, to the event, which is to be accounted for from the confusion occurring at that time. Bashor came to the Valley in 1774, and in June of that year purchased a part of the "Jacob Rees'" tract, near

New Columbia, of Hawkins Boone. In April, 1777, he sold it again to Richard Irwin, and moved down upon the place of his father-in-law, Peter Swartz, senior, who owned the land from Doctor Dougal's nearly up to John Datisman's. Weyland said, himself and another person pushed a boat over from the east side and took up Bashor's goods, and then pushed out into the river. Bashor went to the stable and got a horse, and attempted to drive some cattle down along the shore. When he got down to the bluff that comes out to the river, at the present limekiln of Honorable George F. Miller, just by a red oak, that was still standing a few years since, he was fired upon by some Indians in ambush and killed. Weyland and his comrade, who were lying down in the boat, rose to fire, and Weyland was struck on the lip with a spent ball, the mark of which he carried to his grave. He said Bashor was buried on the river bank. I. D. Rupp, who is a descendant of the Bashor family, wrote me that the bloody clothes of John Bashor were still preserved in the garret of his grandfather's house, in Bethel township, Berks county, as late as 1820; and that he talked with a brother of John Bashor, who said he recollected of his brother's corpse being brought home. He said, also, his uncle, Martin Bashor, who used to live near McKee's Half-Falls, told him that John was killed near Georgetown, and a man named Reedy was in company with him. This is certainly a mistake. It shows how uncertain, as to dates and places, tradition is.

John Bashor's daughter, Catherine, married Jacob Wolfe, son of George Wolfe, one of the first settlers of our Valley. Her children were Samuel Wolfe, late of Lewisburg, Michael, Jacob, and Jonathan, still living at Lewisburg.

Albert Pohlhemus and wife, driven off from Muncy, both died at Northumberland. They left seven small children, who became charges upon the public. One of them was bound to Elias Younkman; some to William Thompson. Court ordered them to be brought up in the Presbyterian form of worship.

Paul Fisher (of Slifer) tells me that at the time Bashor was killed, his grandfather, John Fisher, lived at Esquire Datisman's. The Indians burned Peter Swartz's house, and killed a man named Ayres, near White Deer creek. His grandfather, with his two sisters, concealed themselves in the straw in their barn, and expected every moment to be burned up in it; but the Indians went into Hoffman's house, just above, and carried out a good many articles, among the rest a clock. They seated themselves to examine the clock, when Aaron Norcross, John Fisher, junior, and others who had gathered, hallooed and startled them off, leaving their plunder. This old clock is still in the possession of Jacob Hoffman, living up near the Muncy hills.

David Quinn, Esquire, of Chicago, grandson of Terrence Quinn, has furnished me with an interesting incident of this attack of the Indians in Dry valley. He says, "my great grandfather Corinnius Michael, an old soldier of the days of Frederick the Great, emigrated to America, prior to the Revolution, and brought with him two daughters. What became of the youngest, after her arrival, for some time, is now unknown; but the oldest, Mary, was sold for a term of years, as was the custom in those days, to pay her passage over. While residing with the family that purchased her in Lancaster, Pennsylvania, my grandfather, Terrence Quinn, formed her acquaintance, purchased her unexpired time, and married her. In 1778, they had four little children, and the other sister, unmarried, was living with them. The night the Indians entered the Valley, the news was spread through a system of alarms previously arranged; and those who received warning, fled precipitately. My grandfather and family ran in one direction, and my grandaunt in another.

"They were thus separated, and continued separated for fifty-two years, each one supposing the other had been tomahawked. At the end of this long period, one of my grandmother's neighbors, whose name I have forgotten, was traveling in the Mahanoy valley, at a time when the stream was so swollen that she was compelled to stop at a farm house for shelter. While here, she fell into conversation about friends and relatives with an old woman, who proved to be the grandmother of the house full of children, and the mother of John Lechman, the proprietor of the premises. The old lady related the story of her kindred, and among other things remarked, that she once had a sister, but she had been killed by the Indians, in a place called Dry valley, more than fifty years ago. A little more conversation developed who she was, and the joyful information, that her visitor was a neighbor of her sister, and she was still alive, and lived on Turtle creek, near Lewisburg. The traveler returned, and told her story. Before the sun had risen over Montour's ridge the next morning, Mary Quinn, though in her ninetieth year, was on her way to see her long lost sister. They met, but not as they parted. Each frame, now bent with the weight of years, embraced its kindred, long mourned as dead. Such a meeting, who can describe? The sacred pensman of the history of Joseph, alone. It was their final meeting, too; but they are now where there are no partings."

(1872.) Philip Seebold told me he often heard old Mrs. Fought tell of this raid. She said, they were threshing flax on their place, where the road through Chappel's Hollow comes out into Dry valley, when the Indians came upon them suddenly. Her baby was near her, and she picked it up and ran. Another child, that could just run about, was back of their little barn. She heard it call, "O mother, take me along, too." She looked around, and the Indians were close upon her. She ran the whole way, two miles, to Penn's creek, to a house where the neighbors had gathered. She never heard of her child again; but as there was no indication that it was killed, she hoped for its return some day. At night and in the quiet hours of the day, the last words of her child, "O mother, take me along, too," she said, rang in her ears, long years after.

She said the house they took refuge in, was surrounded by the Indians. They suffered from thirst, and a man named Peter ——— said he would have water, if he died for it. They allowed him to go out, and as he turned the corner of the house, a rifle cracked, and he fell dead. The next day the Indians withdrew, and they embarked in canoes, and went down Penn's creek. On the Isle of Que, she said, she went into a house, and found no one about. A baby sat propped up in a cradle. On close inspection, she found it was dead, and the marks of the tomahawk.

Incidents of the Battle of Monmouth.

Captain William Wilson Potter, of Bellefonte, has the flag of the Royal Grenadiers, captured on the field of Monmouth, by his (maternal) grandfather, the late Judge William Wilson, of Chillisquaque Mills, Northumberland county, Pennsylvania.

The ground or main surface is lemon, or light yellow, heavy corded silk; five feet four inches by four feet eight; corresponding, in proportions, with the flag of the seventh regiment, surrendered, among others, by Cornwallis, at Yorktown, and presented, by order of Congress, to General Washington, lately in the museum at Alexandria, Virginia, but eight inches less in size; the latter being six feet long, and five feet four inches wide.

The device at the upper right corner is twenty inches square, and is that of the English Union, which distinguishes the *Royal* standard of Great Britain. It is composed of the Cross of Saint George, to denote England, and Saint Andrew's Cross, in the form of an X, to denote Scotland. This device was placed in the corner of the Royal flag, after the accession of James the Sixth of Scotland to the throne of England, as James the First. The field of the device is blue, the central stripes (Cross of Saint George) red, the marginal ones white. It wants the Crown and Garter, and full blown rose in the centre, of the Alexandria flag.

The flag has the appearance of having been wrenched from the staff, and has a few old dust marks on the device; otherwise it looks as bright and new as if it had just come from the gentle fingers that made it, although ninety-nine years have rolled away since its golden folds drooped in the sultry air of that June-day battle.

The battle of Monmouth occurred on the 28th of June, 1778; a fearfully hot day, evinced by the fact that fifty-nine of the British soldiers died of heat, without receiving a wound. This flag was captured near the old parsonage of the Freehold, New Jersey, church, where the hottest of the fighting was. A short description of that portion of the engagement will interest many:

After General Lee's retreat was checked by General Washington, in person, the latter formed a new line for his advanced troops, and put Lee again in command. General Washington then rode back to the main body, and formed it on an eminence, with a road in the rear and a morass in the front. The left was commanded by Lord Stirling, with a detachment of artillery; Lafayette, with Wayne, was posted in the center, partly in an orchard, and partly sheltered by a barn; General Greene was on the right, with his artillery, under General Knox, posted on commanding ground. General Lee maintained his advanced position as long as he could, himself coming off with his rear across a road, which traversed the morass in front of Stirling's troops. The British followed sharp, and, meeting with a warm reception, endeavored to turn the left flank, but were driven back. They then tried the right, but were met by General Greene's forces, and heavy discharges from Knox's artillery, which not only checked them, but raked the whole length of the columns in front of the left wing. Then came a determined effort to break the center, maintained by General Wayne and the Pennsylvania regiments, and the Royal Grenadiers, the flower of the British army, were ordered to do it. They advanced several times, crossing a hedge row in front of the morass, and were driven back. Colonel Monckton, their commander, then made a speech to his men, (the troops at the parsonage and those in the orchard heard his ringing voice above the storm of the battle,) and, forming the Grenadiers in solid column, advanced to the charge like troops on parade, the men marching with such precision that a ball from Comb's hill, enfilading a platoon, disarmed every man.

Wayne ordered his men to reserve their fire, and the British came on in silence within a few rods, when Monckton waived his sword above his head, and ordered his Grenadiers to charge; simultaneously, Wayne ordered his men to fire, and a terrible volley laid low the front ranks, and most of the officers. The colors were in advance, to the right, with the colonel, and they went down with him. Captain Wilson and his company, who were on the right of the first Pennsylvania, made a rush for the colors and the body of the colonel. The Grenadiers fought desperately, and a hand to hand struggle ensued, but the Pennsylvanians secured his body and the colors. The Grenadiers gave way, the whole British army fell back to Lee's position in the morning, and decamped so quietly in the night that General Poor, who laid near them, with orders to recommence the battle in the morning, was not aware of their departure.

Colonel Monckton was a gallant officer. He had been lieuenant colonel in the battle of Long Island, where he was shot through the body, but recovered. He was buried, the day after the battle, in the Freehold church-yard, about six feet from the west end of the building. The only monument that marks his grave is a plain board, painted red, upon which is painted in black letters, "Hic Jacet, Col. Monckton, killed 28th June, 1778. W. R. W." By a note-worthy coincidence in name, this board was prepared and set up by a Scotch school-master, named Wilson, who taught the young people in the school-house near the old meeting-house.

Chappel's painting of this battle represents the scene as Monckton fell, and the fearful hand to hand fight over his body; and the little old-fashioned sword looks as if it might have been painted from the original, now in the possession of Mrs. Abram S. Wilson, of Lewistown, Pennsylvania. On the left is the old parsonage. Beyond it the morass, (now, 1872, good meadow land with a fine stream of water running through it,) extending right and left. On the right is the rising ground from which the Grenadiers made their charge.

The sword had many adventures, and never got back to its captor in his life time. (Judge Wilson died in 1813, and is buried in the Presbyterian church-yard, in Northumberland. He was associate judge of Northumberland, from 1792 until his death, when he was succeeded by the late Honorable Andrew Albright.) Captain Wilson gave it to General Wayne, who presented it to General Lafayette, who took it with him to Europe, retained it all through the upheavals and riots of the French revolution, his captivity in a dungeon at Olmutz, and brought it with him to America in 1824, when he visited America, upon the invitation of the United States Government. It is a remarkable instance of his thoughfulness that, after the lapse of nearly half a century, he desired to restore it in person to Captain Wilson. He made inquiries in Philadelphia for him, and not being able to hear anything of him, he left it with old Captain Hunter, with express directions to restore it to Captain Wilson, or if dead, to some of his family. After some years Captain Hunter, found out through Mrs. Billington, of Sunbury, that Judge A. S. Wilson was a son of Captain Wilson, and had the pleasure of delivering the sword to the judge, the next time he went to Philadelphia.

The flag was always in the possession of Judge Wilson, senior, and his family. I can recollect well, at least thirty-five years ago, when his son William used to display it on the 4th of July, at Lewisburg and Milton, make a speech about it, and then have a salute fired from sheriff Brady's cannon, brought from Fort Freeland.

Mrs. John B. Linn, of Bellefonte, has a very fine oil portrait of her grandfather, Captain William Wilson, taken sixty or seventy years ago, pronounced by aged people about Northumberland an excellent likeness.

On the 16th of July, Colonel Brodhead's regiment, on its way to Fort Pitt, was ordered to the West Branch; part of Colonel Hartley's regiment was on its way to Sunbury, and the militia were ordered up from Lancaster and Berks, and the people came back to reap their crops. July 24th, Colonel Brodhead, then at Muncy, detached a captain and twenty-four men into Penn's valley to protect the reapers at General Potter's place. General Potter writes from Penn's valley, on the 25th, that "the inhabitants of the valley are returned, and were cutting their grain. He left Sunbury last Sunday afternoon, and the people were returning to all parts of the county. Yesterday, two men of Captain Finley's company, of Colonel Brodhead's regiment, went out from this place on the plains a little below my fields, and met a party of Indians, five in number, whom they engaged. One of the soldiers, Thomas Van Doran, was shot dead; the other, Jacob Shedacre, ran about four hundred yards, and was pursued by one of the Indians. They attacked each other with their knives, and our excellent soldier killed his antagonist. His fate was hard, for another Indian came up and shot him. He and the Indian lay within a perch of each other. These two soldiers served with Colonel Morgan in the last campaign." James Alexander, who, in after years, farmed the Old Fort farms, near Centre Hall, casually kicked up a hunting knife, so rusted as to indicate that it might have belonged either to the Indian or the soldier killed. Two stones were put up to mark the spot on William Henning's place, near Old Fort.

August 1, Colonel Hartley was in command at Sunbury, with his regulars and two hundred militia. On the 8th he was at Muncy, Colonel Brodhead's regiment having resumed its march to Fort Pitt. Lieutenant Samuel Brady belonged to this regiment—the eighth—in which he was appointed Captain July 28, 1780.

Sunbury, August 1, General Potter writes: "I came here last week to station the militia. I found General deHaas here, who said he commanded all the troops. The next day Colonel Hartley came and showed me his orders to command the troops, and politely requested me to take the command, which I declined, as I never was very fond of command, and this is a disagreeable one.

I rather chose to act as a private gentleman, and do all the good in my power; but people will make observations."

August 8, James Brady was killed above Loyal Sock. Colonel Hartley relates the circumstance as follows: A corporal and four men of his regiment, with three militia, were ordered to guard fourteen reapers and cradlers who went to cut the grain of Peter Smith, who had his wife[1] and four children killed by the Indians. On Friday they cut the greater part, and intended to complete the work next morning. Four of the reapers improperly moved off that night. The rest went to work—the cradlers, four in number, by themselves, near the house; the reapers somewhat distant. The reapers, except Brady, placed their guns around a tree. Brady thought this wrong, and put his at some distance from the rest. The morning was very foggy, and an hour after sunrise the sentry and reapers were surprised by a number of Indians, under cover of the fog. The sentry retired towards the reapers, and they in turn fell back. Brady ran towards his rifle, and was pursued by three Indians, and, within a few rods of it, was wounded. He ran for some distance, and then fell. He received another wound with a spear, and was tomahawked and scalped in an instant. The sentry fired, but was shot down, as also a militia-man. Young Brady, who is an exceeding fine young fellow, soon after, rose and came to the house. Jerome Vanness ventured to remain with him; the others fled. There were thirty Indians, supposed to be Mingoes. Brady wanted Vanness to leave him, but he would not do it. He assisted him to the river, where he drank a great deal of water. Captain Walker and a party came up from the fort at Muncy. When they approached, Brady, supposing them to be Indians, sprang to his feet and cocked his gun. They made a bier and carried him to Sunbury, where his mother then was. Robert Covenhoven was one of the party. On the way he became delirious, and drank large quantities of water. It was late at night when they got there, and they did not intend to arouse his mother. But she had fears that something had happened, and met them at the river. He was a fearful looking object, and the meeting with his mother was heart-rending. He lived five days, the first four being delirious; but on the fifth his reason returned, and he related the whole cir-

[1] Peter Smith's farm was on Turkey run, across the river from Williamsport.

cumstance distinctly. He said Bald Eagle belonged to the party, who was afterwards killed by Captain Samuel Brady, on the Allegheny. James Brady was buried at Fort Augusta, but his grave has, with that of many others, been long since plowed over.

August 8, the justices of the court, through Thomond Ball, deputy prothonotary, notify the president of the State Council that business is much impeded for want of an attorney to prosecute for the Commonwealth; that it was the second court at which no State attorney had appeared, and many persons had to be admitted to bail; that the long suspension of justice, from February, 1776, to November, 1777, had rendered the people licentious enough, and a further delay of executing the laws must lead them to lengths too difficult to be recalled; tippling-house keepers, the notorious promoters of vice and immorality, remained unpunished, though frequently returned, for want of an indictment; that there were two prisoners for murder, one was admitted to bail and the other in close confinement, who should be brought to trial. In August, bill found against Isaac Webb for misprision of treason.

September 1, Captain John Brady returned to the army.

21st September. As some of our settlers took a very prominent part in Colonel Hartley's expedition, it is worthy of a short sketch. It left Muncy on the 21st, two hundred rank and file strong, at four, A. M., with twelve days provisions. Great rains, swamps, mountains, and defiles impeded the march. They waded or swam the Lycoming creek twenty times. On the morning of the 26th, the advance party of nineteen men met an equal number of Indians. Our people had the first fire, and an important Indian chief was killed and scalped; the rest fled. A few miles further, they came upon a camp where seventy Indians lay the night before. These also fled. They then pressed on to Tioga, now Athens, Bradford county. They burned Tioga, Queen Esther's palace and town. On the 28th, they crossed the river and marched towards Wyalusing, where they arrived at eleven o'clock that night. Here seventy of the men took to the canoes and the rest marched by land. Lieut. Sweeney commanded the rear guard of thirty men, besides five scouts under Captain Campleton. The advance guard consisted of an officer and fifteen men. At two o'clock, a heavy attack was made on the rear, which gave way. At this critical moment Captains Boone and Brady, and Lieutenant King, with a few brave fellows, landed from the canoes, joined Sweeney, and renewed the action. They advanced on the enemy on all sides, with great noise and shouting, when the Indians fled, leaving their dead, (ten.) The expedition arrived at Sunbury on the 5th of October, having performed a circuit of three hundred miles, and brought off fifty head of cattle, twenty-eight canoes, &c.

November 9, Colonel Hartley writes from Sunbury that the enemy had come down and invested Wyoming, and destroyed the settlements on the North Branch as far as Nescopeck. About seventy Indians were seen twenty-two miles from here yesterday, advancing towards the forks of the Chillisquaque creek. They took some prisoners yesterday.

14th, he writes from Fort Jenkins that he is advancing towards Wyoming.

December 4, John Macpherson bought the Andrew Gibson place and ferry, now Cauley's, Winfield.

In the fall of 1778, as a party of settlers were leaving Fort Freeland, they were fired at, and Mrs. Durham's infant was killed in her arms. They scalped her, and when the men came there, she raised up and asked for a drink of water. Elias Williams ran to the river and brought his hat full. They put her in a canoe and took her to Northumberland, where Dr. Plunket dressed her wounds, and she lived for fifty years afterwards. She is buried in the Warrior Run grave-yard.

The mill of Samuel Fisher, who resided on what is now Kaufman furnace tract, was burned this fall, it was said, by some settlers, to get nails, the place having been abandoned. In a letter, in December, Colonel Hunter expresses great regret at Colonel Hartley's departure. He says he made the very best possible use of his troops. He complains of the forestallers of grain, whom he looks upon as worse than savages, for raising the price of grain upon the people.

December 1, Joseph Reed elected President of the State, Chambers, Dale, and Himrod voting for him.

1779.

DEATH OF CAPTAIN JOHN BRADY—INDIAN OUTRAGES IN THE VALLEY—JOHN SAMPLE AND WIFE KILLED—CAPTURE OF FORT FREELAND—DEATH OF CAPTAIN HAWKINS BOONE.

RESIDENT of the State, Joseph Reed. Councillor, John Hambright. Members of Assembly, Samuel Dale, Robert Martin, and William Montgomery. Presiding Justice, Thomas Hewitt. Prothonotary, David Harris. Officers elected in October: Sheriff, Major James Crawford; Coroner, John Foster; County Commissioners, Walter Clark and William Mackey; Assessors, Albright Swineford, Peter Kester, William Clark, etc.

Buffalo: Constable, Joseph Taveler; Supervisors, Casper Bower and Alexander McGrady; Overseers, Ludwig Derr and James McCelvey.

White Deer: Constable, James Pollock; Supervisors, Thomas Leckey and James McClenachan; Overseers, Thomas Hutchinson and Philip Stover.

At February sessions, Jacob Links was licensed, the first tavern in Derrstown.

25th March, Joseph McHarge made affidavit before the court, that he, with others of Colonel Cooke's twelfth Pennsylvania regiment, was taken prisoner at Piscataway, (10th May, 1777;) that he was carried to New York, compelled to take the oath of allegiance, and sent on board the vessel that carried General Howe's baggage to Philadelphia, whence he made his escape in disguise; that his sight had failed him, and, on account of bodily infirmity, he could not go

back into service. The court discharged him. Some companies of
the twelfth were now in General St. Clair's division, first brigade.
St. Clair complained to the Council, which ordered Justice Hewitt
to deliver him over to the military authorities.

 11th April, Captain John Brady was killed. He was born in the
State of Delaware, in 1733. His father, Hugh, an emigrant from
Ireland, first settled in Delaware, and then removed to within five
miles of Shippensburg, Pennsylvania. John Brady married Mary
Quigley, and their eldest son, Samuel, was born in Shippensburg, in
1758. He was a surveyor and pioneer in the settlements, and lived
at Standing Stone, now Huntingdon, in 1768, when his son, General Hugh, and twin sister, Jennie, were born. In 1769 he came
over on the West Branch, and settled on what is still the property of
Honorable George Kremer's heirs, opposite Strohecker's landing,
below Lewisburg, where he resided until the fall of 1776, when he
removed to a place a little above Muncy, and built upon it. October 14, 1776, he was appointed captain in the twelfth Pennsylvania,
and was wounded severely in the battle of Brandywine.

 I copy McCabe's account, published many years ago in the Blairsville (Indiana county) *Record*. For General Hugh Brady's account,
see 1783. McCabe, no doubt, received his version from William P.
Brady, senior:

 "It became necessary to go up the river some distance to procure
supplies for the fort, and Captain John Brady, taking with him a
wagon team and guard, went himself, and procured what could be
had. On his return in the afternoon, riding a fine mare, and within
a short distance of the fort, where the road forked, and being some
distance behind the team and guard, and in conversation with a man
named Peter Smith, he recommended Smith not to take the road the
wagon had, but the other, as it was shorter. They traveled on together, until they came near a run where the same road joined.
Brady observed, 'This would be a good place for Indians to secrete
themselves.' Smith said, 'Yes.' That instant three rifles cracked,
and Brady fell. The mare ran past Smith, who threw himself on
her, and was carried in a few seconds to the fort. The people in the
fort heard the rifles, and, seeing Smith on the mare, coming at full
speed, all ran to ask for Captain Brady, his wife along, or rather
before the rest. Smith replied, 'In heaven or hell, or on his way

to Tioga;' meaning he was either dead or a prisoner to the Indians. Those in the fort ran to the spot. They found the Captain lying in the road, his scalp taken off, his rifle gone, but the Indians were in such haste that they had not taken either his watch or his shot pouch."

Jasper E. Brady, Esquire, told me, in 1870, that some thirty years before, when General Hugh Brady visited him at Chambersburg, some old citizen, in conversation with him, asked him whether he ever knew John Montour. He became very much excited, and said, "Yes, he is the damned scoundrel that killed my father." I am unable to reconcile this with the fact that General Brady, in his account of his father's death, (postea, 1783,) says nothing about it. Besides, Heckewelder's letter, the proper date of which is April 28, (see Pennsylvania Archives, Appendix, 1790, page 111,) from Conshocking, which was in the lower part of Ohio, says that John Montour had come there from the Wyandotte town, (now Sandusky, Ohio,) and from a council near Detroit, where the English commander had ordered his arrest as a spy, and the men had followed him nine days. The whole letter shows that he must have been about Detroit, four hundred miles, as the crow flies, from where Captain Brady was killed, on the 11th of April. Further, on the first of July, as appears by Colonel Brodhead's letter, *ibid.*, page 134, Captain Samuel Brady and John Montour had left Fort Pitt with a party to capture Simon Girty and seven Mingoes, who were on a raid. He would hardly have consorted with the murderer of his father. Heckewelder, in a letter of 30th of June, to Colonel Brodhead, says, "John Montour is to be looked upon as without deceit." Captain Brady's death is not mentioned in any contemporary written record that I have been able to find. It is possible it was the result of revenge, but most likely it was an attack by one of the marauding parties that preceded McDonald and his rangers.

Mishael Lincoln (grandfather of R. V. B. Lincoln, Esquire) said he was in the fort when Captain Brady was killed, and assisted in carrying in his body. Captain Brady made surveys in Buffalo and White Deer valleys. I have, perhaps, the only autograph of him in existence, attached to an old survey of date 1770.

The accounts of John Montour are conflicting. Meginness says he was wounded at Fort Freeland, 29th July, and died and was buried at Painted Post a few days after. Nevertheless, he was alive on the 12th of December, 1779. See Colonel Brodhead's letter, *ibid.*, 197.

Colonel Kelly used to relate that one of the Montours released two American prisoners and conducted them safely to within a few miles of Northumberland, and the ungrateful scoundrels killed him there; and he pointed out where he was buried, near a clump of trees that stood to the left of the road, a short distance below what is now known as "Molly Bullion's spring."

26th April, Michael Lepley, of Penn's township, aged 41, killed at Fort Freeland. Jacob Speese, in a certificate dated the 26th of June, 1786, states that he was stationed there with a party of militia. He was a lieutenant in command, and on the request of Mr. McKnight, he sent a guard of six men to go with him to his plantation, a short distance from the fort.

Aaron K. Gift, Esquire, of Middleburg, furnished me with the following narrative of this occurrence, as related by his grandfather, Jeremiah Gift, who died at an advanced age, in 1843. The Gift, Herrold, and Lepley families came to Middle Creek valley in the year 1771. John Adam Gift, (great-grandfather of A. K.,) settled on the left bank of Middle creek, three miles west of where Middleburg now stands; owned and occupied the farm now owned by John H. Walter. His three sons were Jacob, Anthony, and Jeremiah. The militia were then drawn in classes. Jacob had been drawn, and served a tour in the eastern part of the State. The lot in 1779 fell upon John Adam, the father. Jacob insisted on serving in his stead. Michael Lepley and —— Herrold were drawn at the same time. They were stationed at Fort Freeland, near which lived a family named McKnight, father and son. They secured a guard consisting of fourteen persons, among whom were Jacob Gift, Michael Lepley, and Herrold, to go to milk their cows. The cows were driven into a pen, and while milking, they were surprised by a party of thirty Indians, who fired upon them. They were so completely surprised, they could make very little resistance. Lepley, with others, and old Mr. McKnight, were killed. Herrold ran for the fort. As he ran along a field which sloped towards the fort, the soldiers in the fort heard the report of a rifle, and saw him fall, and an Indian scalp him. Jacob Gift also tried to make his escape, but was overtaken. When the pursuing soldiers came up, they found evidence of a hard fight; the ground was bloody, his rifle broken in pieces, and himself tomahawked and scalped. He had sold his life as dear as possible. Young McKnight was the only one who escaped. He jumped Warrior run, and a tomahawk struck the top rail of the fence just after he cleared it. He was the only one left to tell the tale. Upon Jacob Gift's father the stroke fell heavy. He said, "It was my lot to go, but my son went and gave his life for mine." Michael Lepley left a widow, Mary A., and some children. She drew a pension for many years afterwards.

In May, John Sample and wife were killed. The inhabitants had mostly left the Valley. The militia were out, under Colonel Kelly.— *William Lyon's letter, May* 13. This marauding party consisted of from fifteen to seventeen Indians. Christian Van Gundy, senior, was one of a party, with Henry Vandyke, who went up to bring these old people away. (They lived on a farm lately owned by Abram Leib, near Ramsay's school-house, in White Deer, where their graves may still be seen.) Van Gundy was a sergeant, and had six men in his party. Six more were to follow them the next day. After Van Gundy got there, he had slabs put up against the door, and water carried upon the loft. After dark an Indian came around the house, barking like a dog, and rubbing against the door. They paid no attention, but lay down, and slept until about three, A. M., when Van Gundy got up, and lighted a fire. The Indians then surrounded the house, and, mounting a log on their shoulders, tried to beat in the door. Those inside then fired, wounding two, whom they saw carried off. An Indian then came around behind the house, and set it on fire. Van Gundy mounted the loft, knocked off some of the roof, and put out the fire. In this encounter he was struck on the leg by a spent ball, which marked him for some time. Another of the party had his side whiskers shot off. When daylight came they put it to vote, whether they should remain in the house or try to get off. Two voted to stay, four to go. On opening the door they found an Indian chief lying dead in front of it. Van Gundy took the Indian's rifle, Vandyke his powder horn, (which was still in the possession of John Vandyke, in Illinois, some years ago.) The Indians came on suddenly, with loud yells, and the men separated. Van Gundy, with his two guns, took into a ravine, and tried to get the old people to follow him. They refused, and followed the young folks, one of whom, Adam Ranck used to say, was their son. Van Gundy said he soon heard several shots. These killed the old people, who were scalped, and left lie.

The Indians followed them several miles. Van Gundy said he never expected to get out alive, but with his two guns he thought he could kill two at least. He made a circuit of seven miles, and came out at Derr's mill. Colonel Kelly pursued this party; he had a dog that could follow an Indian trail, and, coming pretty close, would immediately drop. On this occurring, Colonel Kelly separated his party, and they made a circuit. As Kelly glided very quietly through the wood, he suddenly stepped into a hole, made by an up-rooted tree. Glancing along it, to his surprise, he saw five Indians sitting like turkeys on the trunk. He made a hole through the root, and leveled his rifle. Simultaneously there was the crack of rifles from the opposite side. Four Indians fell, and, notwithstanding their utmost exertions, the fifth escaped. This dog was of great service to the colonel. During this summer, most of the inhabitants of the Valley, or at least their families, had abandoned it. The men left usually occupied their homes, had signals of alarm, upon which they assembled at some point agreed upon. Colonel Kelly's cabin stood in front of the present building, near the spring, at the present road. He was awakened one night by the growls of this dog. He had a hole cut in the door for observation, and, as it was then getting daylight, he could see something moving among the bushes, at the end of an oak log, that laid across Spruce run. On closer inspection, he discovered an Indian. He took aim at a spot above the log, and, when the Indian raised his head, fired. The ball passed clear through his head, killing him instantly. He buried him himself in the little lot by the spring, marking the grave by a large stone, and kept the secret many years, not telling even his nearest neighbor or friend, knowing that there was no city of refuge to protect him from the vengeance of the next of kin, an Indian law that proves our common origin. No time or distance overcame it. There occurred one case in the Valley of the killing of an Indian, which was avenged many years after, when the settler had removed to Kentucky. The Indian was apprehended, and confessed that he had often sought the opportunity to kill the man here, but was as often foiled, and he followed him to Kentucky, and dogged him many years before it came. Colonel

Kelly's secret only leaked out a few years before his death, in 1832. The little patch by the spring he preserved undisturbed, but took a notion about this time to have it cleared up. He had a boy, Isaac Bower, living with him at the time, to whom he promised a half dollar to plow it. He superintended it, and when Isaac proposed taking out a large stone with the grub hoe, he told him to let it alone, and plow around it. This aroused Isaac's curiosity, and the next time they had big meeting at Buffalo, and the colonel and all his family were gone, Isaac got to work with a shovel, and had not proceeded far until he reached a huge skeleton. The skull was very large, and had the marks of the bullet in holes on the opposite sides. He carefully covered up the place, and hid the skull under the porch. Some days after old Doctor Vanvalzah came along, and stopped to talk with the colonel on the porch. Something was said about large heads, and Isaac, who became interested, hauled the skull out from under the porch, to show it to them. Doctor Vanvalzah was astonished at its size, and Colonel Kelly then asked Isaac where he got it, and when he heard, became very angry, and would have whaled Isaac but for the doctor's presence. He then told the doctor the story as I have related it.

1st November, 1872, I visited William Allison, of Potter's Mills, Centre county, confined to his house by a paralytic stroke, (he died on 11th February, 1877, aged eighty-five,) who told me that his father, Archibald Allison, was one of the party that had gone to bring the Samples off. He related the story substantially as I have given it, as related to me by Captain Jacob Gundy. He added some particulars: that after they got there, they heard the peculiar gobble of wild turkeys, and Gundy said he would go out and shoot one. Vandyke said: "You'll catch turkey, if you go out there." (Surmising a common trick of the Indians to imitate turkey calls; two soldiers at Potter's Fort were enticed out in that way and killed.) That the man wounded through the thumb cried and howled so they had to threaten him to keep him quiet. That they drew the old chief inside the house and scalped him, and divided his accouterments. His father got the string of wampum, which was about the house for a long time. On leaving the house, the two wounded men, with the old people, were placed in the center. They had left the house about sixty rods in the rear, when the Indians sallied out from behind the barn, about thirty in number, according to Mr. Allison's account. Gundy and party held a hurried consultation and agreed to separate, Gundy taking the left, with the old people, the rest of the party the right. Allison concealed one of the wounded men under a log, and the Indians crossed it without discovering him. In the race, Allison lost his moccasins, and when he arrived at the fort, (as the rendezvous was called, on John Lesher's place, formerly Billmyer's,) his feet were bleeding so that he could have been tracked by the blood. Archibald Allison was then only eighteen years of age. He was at John Lee's shortly after the massacre there, in 1782, and saw the bodies of the murdered, and was one of the party that pursued the Indians. He left the Valley in 1783 or 1784, and pushed on into Penn's valley, where he married a daughter of George McCormick, one of the first settlers near Spring Mills, where he remained, and died in 1844, aged eighty-four years. William Kelly, son of Colonel John, married one of Archibald Allison's daughters.

19th May, General Potter, from Penn's valley, writes that the greater number of the people of Buffalo Valley had left.

26th May, Colonel Hunter writes that he had come poor speed raising the company of rangers, owing to the number of people that had got appointments to recruit for the boat service, (convoying General Sullivan's commissary up the North Branch;) that he had appointed Thomas Campleton captain; that the few people remaining above were assembled in small bodies at the forts, and very little farming going on; that on the 25th, twelve large boats, loaded with provisions, left for Wyoming.

June 7, General Sullivan writes from Easton that he has so great desire for the services of General Potter, and so high an opinion of him, that he will give him a command equal to his wishes if he will go along.

June 21, Lieutenant Colonel Adam Hubley, with part of his regiment, occupied Fort Muncy, Fort Jenkins, and Sunbury.

26th, Colonel Hunter says Captain Campleton's company is at Bosley's mill, Chillisquaque creek, and the country was quite drained of men for the boat service. The few spirited men that remained were guarding the women and children at the different posts they were assembled at, while the army marches from Wyoming. He had only thirty men, exclusive of those at Fort Freeland, and with General Potter, whom he would keep at Sunbury until the return of the army to Wyoming. Colonel Hartley's regiment marches immediately to join General Sullivan, which leaves Fort Muncy and Fort Jenkins vacant.

June 24, Captain Samuel Brady killed Bald Eagle, a notorious warrior, of the Muncy tribe, near Kittanning. July 4, he, with John Montour, went out with two or three other Indians to capture Simon Girty. 9th, reports Simon at Conshocking. (Colonel Brodhead's letter.)

July 8, Widow Smith's mills burned, and one man killed, in White Deer township.

July 16, General Wayne captures Stony Point.

July 17, Starrett's mill and all the principal houses in Muncy township burned. July 20, three men killed at Fort Freeland. 21, General Sullivan at Wyoming.

The depreciation of continental money was excessive at this time, Vattel's Law of Nations brought $400; one volume of Gibbon, $40. 23 March, 1779, a ream of paper, £75. George Read's Life, page, 350.

Capture of Fort Freeland.

July 26, William Maclay writes from Paxton (Harrisburg) that he had just returned from Sunbury. That the whole of the troops had moved from Sunbury, a week before, to join General Sullivan. "Northumberland county is in a deplorable situation, without a single man, except the militia of the county, and Captain Kamplen, with fourteen men. Almost every young man on the frontier engaged in the boat service. Everything above Muncy Hill is abandoned. Forty savages had penetrated as far as Freeland's mills. Freeland and sundry others had fallen victims. The stores at Sunbury are in my dwelling-house, which is large and conveniently situated for defense. The back part of it was stockaded last year, by Colonel Hartley."

28th July, Colonel Hunter writes: "This day, about twelve o'clock, an express arrived from Captain Boone's mill, informing us that Freeland's fort was surrounded; and, immediately after, another express came, informing us that it was burned, and all the garrison either killed or taken prisoners; the party that went from Boone's saw a number of Indians and some red-coats walking around the fort, or where it had been. After that, firing was heard off towards Chillisquaque. Parties are going off from this town, and from Northumberland, for the relief of the garrison. General Sullivan would send us no assistance, and our neighboring counties have lost the virtue they were once possessed of, otherwise we should have some relief before this. I write in a confused manner. I am just marching off, up the West Branch, with a party I have collected." A few days before the capture Robert Covenhoven went up as far as Ralston, (now,) where he discovered Colonel McDonald's party in camp. He returned to Fort Muncy, (Port Penn,) and gave the alarm. The women and children then were put in boats and sent down, under his charge, to Fort Augusta. He took with him the families at Fort Meminger, at the mouth of Warrior run; but Freeland's fort being four and a half miles distant, they had no time to wait for the families there, but sent a messenger to alarm them. Covenhoven (spelled Crownover,) is buried in the Presbyterian grave-yard, in Northumberland. Born December 7, 1758; died October 29, 1846.

Mrs. Mary V. Derrickson (born 10th February, 1779,) a daughter of Cornelius Vincent, in a letter, dated Delaware run, December 17, 1855, gives the following account of the early settlers, and of Fort Freeland : In 1772, Jacob Freeland, Samuel Gould, Peter Vincent, and his son Cornelius cut their way through the wilderness and settled within two miles of where the fort was afterwards built. In the summer of 1778, the year of the Great Runaway, they had to leave the country. They returned and picketed a large two-story house, which had been built by Jacob Freeland. During the winter all the families lived in the fort. In the spring of 1779 the men planted corn, and were occasionally surprised by the Indians; but nothing serious occurred until the 21st of July, when a party at work in the corn-field were attacked by Indians, about nine A. M. Isaac Vincent, Elias Freeland, and Jacob Freeland, junior, were killed. Benjamin Vincent and Michael Freeland taken prisoners. Daniel Vincent outran the Indians, and leaping a high log fence, escaped. Benjamin Vincent, then only ten years old, hid himself in a furrow; he left it to climb a tree, and was seen and captured. He knew nothing about the fate of the others until in the afternoon, when an Indian thrust the bloody scalp of his brother Isaac into his face. At daybreak, on the 28th Jacob Freeland, senior, was shot as he was going out of the gate, and fell inside. The fort was surrounded. There were twenty-one men in it, and very little ammunition. Mary Kirk and Phoebe Vincent commenced immediately and ran all their spoons and plates into bullets. About nine a flag was raised, and John Lytle and John Vincent went out to capitulate, but could not agree, and one half hour was given to consult those within. It was finally agreed that all who could bear arms should go as prisoners, the old men with the women and children to be set free, and the fort given to plunder. The latter left the fort at twelve. Not one eat a bite that day, and not a child was heard to cry or ask for bread. They reached Northumberland, eighteen miles distant, that night. Mrs. Kirk put girl's clothes on her son William, a lad of sixteen, and he escaped with the women. Elizabeth Vincent was a cripple, and could not walk. Her husband, John Vincent, went to Captain McDonald and told him her situation, and asked for the horse the Indians had taken from his son Peter a week before. He carried his wife to the lower end of the meadow, where they lay and saw the fort burned. It rained hard that night, and she lay partly in the water. In the morning the horse came to them. Vincent plaited a halter out of the bark of a hickory tree, set his wife on, and led it to Northumberland, where wagons were pressed to take the people down the country. Colonel Hunter's account says: "That the firing at Freeland's was heard at Boone's mill, about seven miles off. (This mill was on Muddy Run, six hundred yards from its mouth, the site of what is now Kemmerer's Mill, two miles above Milton.) Captains Hawkins Boone, Kemplen, and Daugherty marched with thirty-four men, but were met before they reached the fort. Captain Kemplen, who observed the first Indian, shot him dead. Our men behaved with great bravery, but were overpowered, and fifteen were killed and two wounded. Among the dead, Captain Boone and Captain Samuel Daugherty, two very good men."

This engagement took place at McClung's place, above Milton. William Miles, who was taken prisoner at the fort, and afterwards resided in Erie county, said that, in Canada, Captain McDonald spoke in the highest terms of the desperate bravery of Hawkins

Boone. His scalp, with that of Daugherty, was brought into fort Freeland.

Boone came originally from Exeter, Berks county, and was a cousin of the celebrated Daniel Boone, of Kentucky. His grandfather, George Boone, had a large family of sons : William, Joseph, James, Benjamin, John, Hezekiah, Squire, and Josiah Boone. Hawkins was a son of Squire, who moved to North Carolina in 1752. Hawkins was a surveyor, and lived on the place just above New Columbia now owned by Samuel Gemberling. He owned, also, the Jacob Rees' place, north-west of the latter place, the Earnest Book tract, &c. He was commissioned a captain in the twelfth Pennsylvania regiment, and selected to accompany a detachment of riflemen from the regiment, sent under Morgan to Saratoga. In a return of Morgan's command, dated at Lowdon's ferry, on the Mohawk, September 3, 1777, he is marked absent; wounded. In February, 1779, the State Council allowed him clothes out of the State stores, "in consideration of his situation and spirited intrepidity of his conduct in the campaign under Colonel Hartley, when his situation might have justified him in remaining at home." He left a widow, Jane, and two daughters. Some years after his death, his widow married a Mr. Fortenbaugh, and moved to Halifax, Dauphin county, where she resided many years.

Of Boone's party, Samuel Brady, (uncle of Captain Samuel,) James Dougherty, and James Hammond made their escape. Daniel Vincent, father of late Mr. Vincent, of McEwensville, had been recently married, and after the capture, his wife returned to New Jersey. For four years she heard nothing of him. One evening, when she was out with a sleighing party, a roughly dressed man stopped at the tavern where they were, and inquired if a Mrs. Vincent lived near there. She was pointed out to him, and he told her he had met her husband in Canada. He rode home in the same sleigh, and was disposed to take her upon his lap. She declined the favor until she discovered the impertinent stranger was her husband.—*Day's Collections*, 1843. [See Meginness' West Branch Valley, page 257, &c., for an interesting notice of the return of the captives.]

In a letter from Sunbury, dated January 27, 1783, to General James Potter, member of the Executive Council, Colonel Hunter incloses a roll of the men taken prisoners at Fort Freeland, the 28th July, 1779. "Captain's company, John Neely, sergeant; George Bailey, George Armitage, Aaron Martin, (died at Fort Chambly, January 8, 1780,) Thomas Smith, Isaac Wilson, and John Forney. The following persons, being those of the militia that enrolled themselves for the defense of the garrison : John Lytle, adjutant; Cornelius Vincent, quartermaster; sergeant, Samuel Gould; Henry Townley, Peter Williams, Isaac Williams, Elias Williams, Henry Gilfillan, James Durham, Daniel Vincent, John Watts, William Miles, John Dough, Thomas Taggart, (died 16th January, 1780;) Francis Watts, made his escape on the same day he was taken; Peter Vincent, likewise made his escape the same day." Colonel Hunter adds: "I appointed Captain Thomas Kemplen to recruit a company under a resolve of Congress authorizing the Council to raise a company for each frontier county, and to appoint the officers thereof, in place of Captain John McElhatten, who was not in the county, or expected soon. Kemplen engaged on the 7th of May, and was of as much service as any man could be with the small company of men he had during the time. A number of his men who were taken prisoners at Fort Freeland, have come home poor and naked."

Colonel Kelly went over with a party from Buffalo Valley, and buried the dead at Fort Freeland.

November 27, the German regiment arrived at Sunbury, and Colonel Hunter proposes to station a sergeant's guard at Titzell's mill, in Buffalo Valley. Among the deaths this year are Samuel Allen, of White Deer, in May. In July, William McLaughlin, of the same township. Samuel Allen left a widow, Lavinia; children, Ruth Reynolds, Agnes, Mary Rippey, Elphina, Samuel, Joseph, James, John, and Robert.

Joseph Weeks, (of now Gregg township,) left a widow, Rachel; children, Jesse, Hannah, Frances, Jemima, Sutherland, Hyllothem, Nacum, and Fronk.

John Foster, Esquire, who died at Buffalo Cross-Roads some years since, and who was a son of Captain John Foster, was wont to relate an incident occurring at this time. One night the family were alarmed by Indians, and fled to a rye patch adjoining the house, where they passed the night. A small dog that was usually very noisy at night stayed with them and made no noise. The family always considered it a special act of Providence, as the next morning plenty of Indian tracks were found around the house.

1780.

INHABITANTS OF BUFFALO, WHITE DEER, AND PENN'S—INDIAN TROUBLES— DAVID COUPLES KILLED—ATTACK AT FRENCH JACOB'S MILL—GEORGE ETZWEILER AND OTHERS KILLED—ROLL OF CAPTAIN THOMPSON'S COMPANY—PATRICK WATSON AND BALTZER KLINESMITH KILLED—PETER GROVE'S PURSUIT OF THE INDIANS—BARBER'S MILL BUILT.

OUNCILLOR, General James Potter. Representatives in the Assembly, William Montgomery, David McKinney, and Major John Kelly. Prothonotary, Captain Matthew Smith, appointed February 4. County Commissioners, Daniel Montgomery, William Clark, and John White. Collector of Excise, Daniel Montgomery.

Names of the Inhabitants of Buffalo Township, in the beginning of April, 1780.

Allison, Archibald; Auld, George; Aurand, Henry; Aurand, Jacob; Baker, Wendel; Beatty, Hugh; Beatty, Alexander; Bernhard, Mathias; Bickle, Henry; Bickle, Christopher; Bilby, John; Black, Thomas; Brady, Mary; Braton, Caldwell; Brindle, John; Bolender, Henry; Book, Conrad; Book, John; Book, George; Boveard, James; Bower, Casper; Burn, Peter; Burger, Martin; Chambers, Robert; Charters, William; Clarke, John; Crawford, Edward; Crider, John; Conner, Jacob; Coon, Nicholas; Cox, Tunis; Cox, Widow; Davis, John; Derr, Ludwig; Doudrick, John; Dreisbach, Jacob; Duncan, David; Elder, Thomas; Emerick, David; Etzweiler, George; Ewig, Adam; Eyer, Abraham; Fiddler, Stephen; Filey, John; Fleming, Robert; Fleming, James; Frederick, Peter; Frederick, George; Foster, John; Foster, William; Foster, Captain John; Gibson, Andrew; Gibson, James; Gilman, Henry, senior; Gilman, Henry, junior; Glen, Andrew; Green, Joseph; Greenlee, William; Groshong, Jacob, grist-mill; Grove, Michael; he was taxed with a ferry, which was at the old Judge McPherson place, near Winfield; Gothard, John; Hains, George; Hains, George, junior; Hains, John; Huntsman, James; Hamilton, Robert; Harbster, David; Harbster, Jacob; Hiltman, John; Henry, Christopher, distillery; Hessler, John; Hessler, Michael; Holman, Charles; Hone, Henry; Hoy, Philip; Hub, Daniel; Hunter, Samuel; taxed with servants, negro, horses, cows, spoons, &c.; he resided on Penn's creek, on the tract he took up, now owned by the Messrs. Oldts, in Union township; Irvine, William, (Irish;) Irwin, James, distillery; Jenkins, James; Jermony, Thomas; Johnston, William; Johnston, John; Kester, Peter; King, Samuel; Kishler, Francis; Klinesmith, Baltzer; Links, Jacob; Laughlin, Samuel; Lee, John, two stills; Leech, William; Leonard, Peter; Lewis, Daniel; Lowdon, John; McCaley, Alexander; McCandlish, William, senior; McCandlish, William, junior; McClung, John; McCoy, James; McDonald, Randall; McGee, James; McGrady, Alexander; McKelvey, James; Metzgar, Jacob; Miller, Benjamin; Milligan, John; Mitchell, John; Mizener, Henry; Mizener, Conrad; Mook, John; Moore, William, saw mill; Morrow, Andrew; Nees, John, grist mill; afterwards Green's and Bellas'; Noble, Robert; Overmeier, George, senior; Overmeier, George, junior; Parkinson, Daniel; Price, Thomas; Pontius, Andrew; Pontius, John, senior; Pontius, John, junior; Pontius, Nicholas; Pontius, George; Pontius, Henry; Quinn, Terrence; Ray, John; Rees, Abel; Richard, Henry; Rinehard, Frederick; Rinehart, George; Rosabaugh, George; Rote, George; Scott, John; Sharp, Daniel; Shirley, Charles; Shively, John; Shively, Christian; Sierer, John; Sips, Joseph; Shaw, William; Slack, Henry; Smith, Adam; Smith, Ludwig; Smith, David; Snyder, Peter; Snyder, Michael; Speddy, William; Storms, Christian; Storms, David; Stroh, Nicholas; Sutherland, William; Tate, Edward; Taveler, Joseph; Templeton, Samuel; Thom, James; Thornburg, Thomas; Thompson, John; Trester, Martin, senior; Trester, Martin, junior; Trinkle, Charles; Vandyke, Henry, tanyard; Vought, Michael; Walker, John; Watson, Hugh; Watson,

Patrick; Watson, David; Welker, Leonard, grist and saw-mill; Weyland, Henry; Williams, William; Williams, James; Wilson, Robert; Wise, Jacob; Wise, Frederick; Wolfe, Andrew; Wolfe, George; Young, Samuel, distillery; Young, Matthew; Zeller, Peter.

Of these the following returned money for taxation only: Bickle, Christopher, £100; Chambers, Robert, £60; Frederick, George, £500; Green, Joseph, £140; McCandlish, William, £40; Storms, Christian, £450.

Additional Residents or Taxables of White Deer in 1780.

Allen, Joseph; Allen, John; Auman, Philip; Barber, John; Caldwell, John; Campbell, Charles; Cherry, John; Clendenin, John; Collins, Daniel; Couples, Sarah, widow; Crawford, Robert; Daraugh, Ephraim; Derr, Widow; Eakins, John; Heckle, Andrew, distillery; Gibson, James; Glen, Joseph; Gray, Robert; Hammel, Charles; Hayes, David; Hill, Elizabeth; Hill, Jacob; Hoffman, Joseph; Huling, Marcus, of the Island; Hood, Moses; Huston, Samuel; Iddings, Jonathan; Kelly, Lawrence; King, William; Love, Robert; McClenachan, William; McCracken, John; McCord, Robert; McCord, James; McGowan, John; McKinney, James; McLaughlin, John; Marshall, William; Miller, Archibald; Millwright, Mathias; Montgomery, Samuel; Murray, William; Poak, John; Randels, Joseph; Randels, Hugh; Row, James; Shields, Widow; Shearer, Widow; Turner, Thomas, distillery; Swartz, Peter, junior; Tanahill, John; Vandyke, Lambert. Improvements, saw-mill at William Blythe's, Red Bank run.

Among the Residents of Penn's Township in 1780.

Barnard, France; Bart, Jacob; Bartges, Stophel; Beard, William; Berts, Benjamin; Bickard, John; Bickle, Thomas; Bickle, Simon, distillery; Bickle, Tobias, distillery; Bickle, Jacob; Borald, Adam; Bolender, Adam, senior; Bolender, Adam, junior; Bombaugh, widow, still; Borer, Peter; Bower, Peter; Bunker, Abraham; Carstetter, Martin; Cline, Jacob; Cline, Andrew; Coleman, John; Collins, Moses; Copenberger, Paul; Crow, Godfrey; Deaner, George; Deininger, Jacob; Dowdle, widow, (widow of Captain Dowdle;) Dreese, Joseph; Eberhart, Bernard; Egeh, William;

Evans, John; Faucy, Benjamin; Fisher, Abraham; Freyburg, Ludwig; Gan, Frederick; Gaws, Christian; Ginney, (weaver;) Graybill, Christian; Green, John; Graybill, John; Guyer, Valentine; Hains, John; Harman, John; Heffling, Jacob; Heffling, Conrad; Hermon, Henry; Hoan, Michael, senior; Hornberger, Charles; Hooks, Stephen; Horn, Samuel; Kemerer, Peter; Kemerer, Daniel; Kerstetter, Leonard; Kerstetter, widow; Kerel, Hugh; Kettleman, David; Kreek, Philip; Kreek, Jacob; Koch, Daniel; Label, Jacob; Leist, David; Liber, Adam; McTaget, Billy; Manning, John; Manning, Richard; Mateer, Robert; Meikle, Simeon; Mattig, Daniel; Merkley, George; Motz, Michael; Meyer, John; Meyer, Charles, distillery; Mogel, Valentine; Moon, Thomas; Moon, James; Moore, Andrew, four hundred and seventy-nine acres of land, oil-mill, two distilleries, one grist and one saw-mill; Morton, Jacob; Mull, Anthony; Neyman, Jacob; Newcomer, Peter; Nitz, Philip; Nitz, John; Ogden, Joseph; Oudly, Edward; Peters, Michael; Reybert, John, senior; Reger, Elias; Reger, Michael; Reichenbaugh, Jacob; Reed, Casper, saw-mill; Reihm, Henry; Retzel, Youst; Reit, John; Ritchie, Robert; Rodgers, John; Roush, Jacob; Row, Martin, junior; Row, Ludwig; Ryhart, John; Schock, George; Schock, John; Shaffer, George; Sharrer, Michael; Shoemaker, Peter; Smith, Stephen; Snyder, Thomas; Stees, Jacob, grist and sawmill; Steffy, Adam; Straub, John; Styer, Henry; Styers, Jacob; Sutton, Zachariah; Swineford, John; Swineford, Albright, six hundred and eighty acres, and grist-mill; Tremgel, Peter; Trenkle, Matthias; Truckenmiller, Frederick; Ulrich, George, junior; Woodward, Simon; Zellner, John.

2d April, William Maclay writes to President Reed, from Sunbury:

"SIR: I will not trouble you with the distress of this county. It will, no doubt, be painted to the Council in lively colors, and, indeed, the picture cannot be overcharged; nor should I, at this time, write to you, but for a strong belief and persuasion that a body of Indians are lodged about the head of Fishing and Muncy creek. They were with us to the very beginning of the deep snow last year; they are with us now before that snow is quite gone. Many of our hunters, who went up late last fall into that country, (which is a fine one for hunting,) were so alarmed with the constant reports of guns, which they could not believe to be those of white men, that they returned suddenly back. We are not strong enough to spare men to examine this country, and dislodge them. The German regiment are under their own officers, and, for my part, I expect no service from them. I cannot help uttering a wish that what troops we have might be all Pennsylvanians. There is a certain love of country that really has weight. This is a strange divided quarter. Whig, Tory, Yankee, Pennamite, Dutch, Irish, and English influence are strangely blended. I must confess I begin to be national, too, and most sincerely believe every public interest of America will be safer in the hands of Americans than with any others. But I will not trouble you with any more of my opinions. Help us if you can, and much oblige a distressed country."

Colonel Samuel Hunter writes, on the same day: "The savages have made their appearance on the frontiers in a hostile manner. Day before yesterday they took seven or eight prisoners about two miles above Fort Jenkins, and two days before they carried off several people from about Wyoming. The German regiment that is stationed here is no ways adequate to grant us the necessary relief. The case is quite altered from this time twelve months ago. We then had a pretty good garrison at Muncy, Brady's fort, Freeland's, with our own inhabitants. Now we have but forty or fifty at Montgomery's, and thirty at Fort Jenkins. The latter was not able to spare men enough to pursue the enemy, that carried off the prisoners, though there were but thirty Tories and Indians, and a pretty deep snow had fallen the night before, by which they could be tracked. I have seen the time within three years that we could turn out some hundred of good woodsmen, but the country is quite drained of our best men."

The rapid depreciation of money may be noted through an item in the State Treasurer's account: May 17, order to Samuel Dale, additional pay as Member, in consequence of the price of wheat raised from £15 to £20 per bushel. 11th March, cassimere was $300 per yard; jean and habit cloth, $60 per yard.

April 8, a party of Indians made a descent on White Deer creek. At Redbank, one and one-half miles south of White Deer Mills, a little below where Charley Bly's blacksmith shop used to be, toward the river, lived David Couples, with his wife and two children. They killed and scalped Couples and two of the children, and took his wife prisoner. They camped for the night on the hills above the mills, where she made her escape, although one of them had lain himself down upon her clothes, so that her moving would alarm him. The next day, when the people came to the house, they found the children had crawled under the bed, but their eyes were rent with intensity of suffering. One daughter survived, Margaret Couples. She married a man named William Armstrong, a wagoner on Doctor Eaker's place, and they moved to Centre county. The widow married a man named Elliot, of Chillisquaque. Some of the family live about Northumberland. Captain John M. Huff, of Milton, is a grandson.

In Doctor Harbaugh's Fathers of the German Reformed Church, we find the following notice of the first stated Reformed minister nearest to the region of our annals: As early as the 18th of May, the Reverend Samuel Dubbendorff labored as a minister at Lykens valley. A letter of that date says: "like John the Baptist, he at present preaches to three congregations, bordering upon the Indians. The people greatly love and honor him, yet owing to their poverty, can give him only the most necessary articles of food, but not a cent of money as salary." Mr. Dubbendorff, no doubt, preached as a supply for the churches on Penn's creek, and, perhaps, in Buffalo Valley, as we find that when he beame too feeble, from age, to labor any longer in the ministry, he removed to a friend's, near Selinsgrove, where he died. He is buried in Selinsgrove, but no memorial, we believe, marks his grave.

Attack on French Jacob's Mill.

NORTHUMBERLAND TOWN, *May* 18, 1780.

I am unhappy enough to inform you the savage enemy have, on the 16th inst., made a stroke on the inhabitants of this much distressed county, at Buffalo Valley. At French Jacob Grozong's mills four men killed, viz: Jno. Forster, jr., —— Eytzwiller, James Chambers, and Samuel McLaughlen. The enemy got only one of the scalps. The neighboring inhabitants, on hearing the firing, briskly turned out, and pursued the enemy very brave, but was not able to overtake them. The inhabitants have stood here, indeed, longer than could been expected, were it not desperation. But, sir, unless some support can be instantly afforded, the State must shortly count one county less than formerly—which God forbid. I refer you, D'r sir, to the bearer, Gen. Potter, for further information, as he waits on horseback, whilst I write this imperfect, distress'd acc't. Provisions none, cash none, nor can it be had in this place. Gen. Potter's acc'ts from this place to the Hon'ble the Assembly, which I doubt not you will see, will fully satisfy you of the state of this place.

I am, D'r sir, your most obt. humble serv't,

MATTHEW SMITH.

Gen. Jos. REED.

Sometime between 1776 and 1779, Jacob Groshong, familiarly known as French Jacob, built a little log mill, the site of which is now familiarly known as Solomon Heberling's, on what he supposed was his own location. He was defeated in a suit at Sunbury, rode home the same night, dismantled the mill, moved the wheels, &c., down to the site of what is now Dater & Reish's mill. Here he re-built his mill in 1782 and 1783, and added a saw-mill in 1785. In 1793, Enoch Thomas got the property, and Groshong moved up to the end of the Nittany mountain, in Centre county, and thence West. From Thomas, it passed into the hands of Christopher Johnson, in 1797, and into the hands of John Hofferd, in 1808, and finally into the Reish's.

The old mill building, where this fight occurred, Mr. Philip Pontius told me he took down when he owned the property, and that he carefully preserved the timbers that had the bullet marks in them, and placed them in another building there, where they could still be seen.

This will explain the impression on the minds of some old people I have talked with, who alleged the site of French Jacob's mill, where the fight occurred, was at the old Hofferd or Reish mill ; whereas, in truth, it occurred at the little old mill, the site of which is on Solomon Heberling's place.

Groshong's name, or rather his nick-name, is still preserved in connection with the large spring a little above the tavern, on the Brush Valley road. I find in 1787 he was assessed by his nickname, "Jacob, French." He is the hero of all the wild tales of Indian troubles in that part of the Valley. The place where he hid from the Indians, beside this spring, is still pointed out.

The place became more noted in after years as the residence of Captain John Bergstresser, who, as early as 1811, had an oil, fulling-mill, saw-mill, and kept store upon the premises. Bergstresser came in after Henry Snyder, who had some sort of mills there as early as 1802.

Christian Shively told my informant, John Beeber, that he heard the signal firing at this time. He was threshing some grain at the time. He had a hard, smooth place tramped on the ground, and was throwing the wheat up in the air to allow the wind to blow the chaff away. He immediately hid his wife and two children near the mouth of White Spring run. He slipped silently about, rolled some logs into Penn's creek, tied them with hickory withes into a raft, put his wife and children on, and floated down to Beatty's, where New Berlin now stands.

Philip Pontius told me his father also heard the signal. He unhitched his horses, and made a circuit through the woods, gun in hand, and came to the mill. He said William Fisher made a narrow escape. He was running into the mill, when his foot slipped on a board, and he fell into the door. The bullet intended for him struck the building on a line where his head would have been had he not fallen.

One tradition of the neighborhood is that this was a patrol of five men which passed every day between Titzell's, late Kelly's, mill and French Jacob's, and they were attacked by the Indians in sight of the mills. Another has it that the soldiers were out washing when they were fired on.

John Forster was an uncle of the late Captain John Forster, of Mifflinburg, and a brother of the old Major Thomas Forster. James Chambers was the son of Robert Chambers.

George Etzweiler, junior, left a widow named Mary. George Etzweiler, a son of the one killed, kept hotel at McKee's Half-Falls, as late as 1812. William Fisher was the grandfather of James Crossgrove and Sheriff John Crossgrove, and resided in Limestone, where James Crossgrove lately resided. William Gill told me he heard old Mrs. Overmeier say that the people who were killed, were brought over to the place adjoining Philip Seebold's residence, above New Berlin, and were buried in the old grave-yard on the bluff at the creek, where Dry run comes in, nearly opposite where

Tuscarora run enters Penn's, on the Snyder county side.[1] Here old John Trester and the first settlers were buried. This grave-yard, probably the oldest in the county, was not used after 1791, when the people commenced burying in New Berlin. It belonged to Thomas Barber, who was killed in 1792, by the timbers of an old barn falling upon him. Some time during this year, one of the Mizener's, who resided where Daniel Pontius now resides, near Reish's distillery, was captured, and carried off from that place by the Indians. Esquire Sheckler informs me it was Adam Mizener, who moved to Ohio, and died there some years ago. He remained in captivity about eighteen months.

On the 14th of July, the Archives state that a man and three children were killed, near the mouth of Buffalo creek. According to the statement of William Wilson, (Doctor T. H's. grandfather,) this occurred at the old house where Thomas Ream now lives. The woman escaped across the creek and, looking back, saw an Indian dash the brains out of the small child against a tree. The name of the family was Allen.

Copy of Roll found among Colonel John Kelly's papers.

A pay-roll of my company of the first battalion, Northumberland county militia, commencing 16th of July, 1780. Enrolled, July 16, 1780. Discharged, August 15.

Colonel—Kelly, John.
Captain—Thompson, James.
Lieutenant—Poak, Joseph.
Ensign—Ewing, Alexander.

Black, William; Black, Thomas; Brindage, Joseph; Fleming, Hance; Green, Joseph; Hamersley, James; Iddings, Jonathan; Poak, John; Poak, Thomas; Poak, James Smith; Rodman, Hugh; Wilson, Peter; Wilson, John; Young, John.

Letters of administration on Patrick Watson's estate, were granted on the 23d of July, of this year; and his death, perhaps, occurred during May, when the stroke on the Valley, spoken of in Captain Matthew Smith's letter, was made. His cabin was on a slight elevation, a little east of the new school-house (1877) at White Springs,

[1] Philip Seebold said, in 1872, that George Etzweiler was buried on John Cook's place, now Peter Slear's, in Limestone township.

Limestone township. The site was pointed out to me, by Jacob M. Shively, whose grandfather, Christian Shively, showed him the spot, and told the story. He said he heard the firing, and went to Watson's cabin, and found Mrs. Watson, Patrick's mother, lying on the floor, shot, and a dog licking her scalped head. She could only make motions in reply to his inquiry, intimating that Patrick had gone down the run. He went out after him, and found him near the White spring. Watson did not know he was shot until, stooping down by the spring to drink, the water ran out of his wound. He died within two hours. He and his mother were among the first buried in the Lewis grave-yard. He was an uncle of David, William, and John C. Watson.

Friday, 14th July, Baltzer Klinesmith, who resided then on George Sholtz's land, lately owned by John Byler, on the second road south of Dreisbach's church leading to Jenkins' mills, and had a small clearing upon it, was killed. The versions of this story are quite numerous. The one in the "History of the West Branch," was furnished by George A. Snyder, Esquire, deceased. The dates I get from the widow's pension papers, and an old certificate, in which it is further stated that he was a private in Captain Joseph Green's company, Lieutenant John Cryder, in Colonel Kelly's battalion. My version is from one who often heard Mrs. Chambers tell it herself. She, with her father and sister, went out in the field to work. He, seeing some squirrels, sent Baltzer, junior, back for his gun. Meanwhile, the Indians came along and captured the old man and the two girls, Elizabeth and Catherine.

Just where the road winds around the hill, above Heimbach's blacksmith shop, on the road to New Berlin, they killed Klinesmith. Mrs. Dreisbach, the Judge's mother, pointed out the place. She helped carry his body down, and they buried it in the Dreisbach church-yard.

The Indians then made their way to the spring, north of New Berlin, where they left the girls in charge of an old man of their party, and went down Dry valley. After a little while it began to rain, and the Indian motioned the girls to gather brush to cover the flour bag. He laid down under a tree, with the tomahawk under his head. The girls, in passing with brush, worked it gradually from under him as he dozed. Elizabeth picked up the tomahawk, and made a motion to her sister to run. She then sank it into the old man's head. The old man yelled fearfully, and the girls ran. By this time the Indians were on their return, and heard the old man yell. They pursued the girls and fired on Catherine, just as she was springing over a fallen tree. The ball entered below the right shoulder-blade and came out at her side. She had the scars until her dying day, as large as a half dollar. She rolled herself under the tree, and the Indians passed over her, in pursuit of the sister. Elizabeth, being active, reached Beatty's harvest field. The men ran to their rifles and pursued the Indians. When they came pretty near Catherine, one of the men, supposing an Indian in ambush, was about firing, when she pulled off her apron and waved it. They found her much weakened from loss of blood, but she soon recovered. Philip Pontius, still living, told me that the Indians were going to Beatty's, and George Rote, who was a lame man, but great on a halloo, frightened them back, by hallooing to an imaginary company to surround the black rebels. Klinesmith's widow drew a pension as late as 1819, at New Berlin. "Elizabeth married John Boal, moved to French creek, near Meadville first, and, in 1843, was still living in Ohio or Indiana, her husband, being one of those restless spirits, who fancy that the land is over-crowded, when the population exceeds one to every ten square miles, and she, from her courage and energy, being an excellent second to a man always exposed to the perils of frontier life."—*Manuscript of G. H. Snyder*.

Katy, as she was called, first married Daniel Campbell, a revolutionary soldier, and had, by him, two children, John, who died near Mifflinburg, and Ann, who married Robert Barber. They removed West, and are now both dead. Katy married next Robert Chambers, by whom she had one child, the first wife of John A. Vanvalzah, deceased. Notwithstanding her wound, she survived two husbands. My informant, William M. Vanvalzah, tells me that when a boy, many a night he heard her and old Captain Thompson talk over the events of their early life. Klinesmith's land, in Lewis township, was valued in 1810, Robert Chambers taking one portion, and Baltzer Klinesmith, junior, the other. Baltzer, junior, sold his land, some thirty years since, to Christian Mensch, and moved to a lot owned by his wife, near Hartleton, where he died, and is buried in the Laurelton grave-yard. His wife was a daughter of Melchior

Smith, their children, David, Samuel, John Melchior, daughters Mary Ann and Margaret, who married Messrs. Stover, in Centre county. Catherine married —— Miller. Martin Trester, a few years after, found a rifle near the spring, supposed to belong to the old Indian.

Traditions of the Valley have always connected the following incident with the pursuit of the murderers of Klinesmith; and the date mentioned in the note below probably confirms that belief:

Van Campen, in his narrative, see Meginness, page 277, says that "in the summer of 1781[1], a man was taken prisoner, in Buffalo Valley, and made his escape. He reported there were about three hundred Indians on the Sinnemahoning. I was then a lieutenant in Captain Robinson's company. Colonel Hunter selected a company of five to reconnoitre, Captain Campbell, Peter and Michael Grove, Lieutenant Cramer, and myself. We took with us three days' provision, and went up the West Branch, with much caution and care. We reached the Sinnemahoning, but found no tracks. A little below it we discovered a smoke, and that there was a large party of them.

"As soon as it was dark we new primed our rifles, sharpened our flints, and examined our tomahawk handles; and, all being ready, we waited with great impatience until they all lay down. The night was warm, and as we advanced upon them in the utmost silence, rifle in one hand, tomahawk in the other, we found some of them rolled in their blankets, a rod or two from the fire. Having got among them, we first handled our tomahawks. They arose like a dark cloud. We now fired on them and raised the war-yell. They took to ɩ ight in the utmost confusion. We remained masters of the ground and of all their plunder. It was a party of twenty-five or thirty, which had been down as low as Penn's creek, and had killed and scalped two or three families. We found several scalps of different ages, and a large quantity of domestic cloth, which we took to Northumberland, and distributed among the distressed who had escaped the tomahawk."

[1] Van Campen made a mistake in the year, no doubt, and his description would lead one to believe more than two Indians were killed. Grove speaks only of two, and the following item, in the State Treasurer's account, September 30, 1780, indicates that Grove was correct: Cash paid Robert Martin, for Jacob Creamer, Peter Grove, William Campbell, and Michael Grove, for two Indian scalps, £1,875. The same account September 29, ten head of cattle for the Commissioners of Purchases, £10,400, shows the immense depreciation of currency at this time.

There were four of the Grove brothers, Wendell, Adam, who lived where George Wolfe now lives, in Mortonsville, Michael, who lived on the back road to Mifflinburg, and Peter. Peter disappears very early from our Valley. The only notices I can find of him are the mixture of truth and fiction, in the Appendix to Meginness' History. Michael lived within the recollection of many of my readers. He died in Nippenose, south of Jersey Shore, in September, 1827, aged seventy, and was brought home, and buried in the Dreisbach graveyard. Meginness says he was attended by Doctor Davidson in his last illness, and gave a vivid account of the engagement above spoken of. Before they commenced the attack, an old Indian annoyed them very much. He was troubled with a severe cough, and frequently rose up, and looked carefully around, seeming to anticipate danger. At length the old man fell asleep, and they commenced creeping up, intending to use their tomahawks first. One of them, unexpectedly, crawled over an Indian, who lay some distance from the rest, and the old man rose up at this moment. Michael, with a powerful blow with his hatchet, clove the old man's skull, and, striking it into the back of another, could not withdraw it, when the Indian drew him over the bank into the creek, where, however, he succeeded in killing him. Some of the Indians got on to the other side of the creek, and commenced firing, and they had to retire. They waded down the creek, taking to the hills, and, thence over to the Bald Eagle ridge. John Beeber describes Michael as having an eye like a hawk, and being able to travel at night, even in his old age, nearly as well as in day time. He told Beeber that Joseph Groninger, of White Deer, was along, and going up, they stopped at James Ellis', uncle of William Cox Ellis, and took their dinner with their rifles on their knees.

Michael left three children, John, Sarah, married to Samuel Lutz, and ──── to Jacob Smith. To the two girls he gave farms in Nippenose, and he was there visiting when he died. His son John is now dead. He left a son, Michael, and daughter, Esther. Michael also died on the old farm, where his grandfather lived. Esther married Enoch Kauffman. Michael's son, Peter, still lives in West Buffalo, and other descendants are in the same township.

Adam lived on the Nesbit property, which he sold to Thomas Nesbit, in 1822. His son, Samuel, married a sister of the late Joseph Glass, and is the father of Simon, Joseph, William, Mrs. Jacob Parks, and Wesley, (who was starved to death in one of the rebel prisons.) Samuel moved West, where his family has become wealthy, and influential at the bar and other pursuits.

In July, George Row, of Penn's township, was wounded in the breast, at Fought's mill, (near Mifflinburg,) and died in eight hours. He left a widow, Mary M., who drew a pension for many years afterward.

The original Barber's mill, on Penn's creek, was built this year by Adam Smith. It was long known as David Smith's mill. The latter sold to Barber and Heise, who built the present structure.

8th September, General Potter marched a body of one hundred and seventy men to Fort Swartz, and then went up to Colonel Kelly, who lay at the mouth of White Deer creek. Fort Swartz was most likely Peter Swartz's, who lived on the farm now owned by Honorable George F. Miller. Day's Historical Collections says this fort was a mile above Milton; but as General Potter says nothing of crossing the river, it was no doubt the block-house at Peter Swartz's.

24th September, Henry McCracken, private in Captain William Clark's company, killed. He left a widow, Mary, and five children.

1781.

NARRATIVE OF CAPTAIN JAMES THOMPSON—CAPTAIN CAMPLETON KILLED—LETTER FROM GENERAL POTTER—STORY OF THE EMERICK FAMILY—ROLL OF PETER GROVE'S AND MCGRADY'S COMPANIES—CHRISTIAN HETRICK AND DAVID STORM KILLED.

MEMBER of Council, General James Potter. Assembly, William Maclay, William Montgomery, and Colonel William Cooke. Presiding Justice, Frederick Antes. Sheriff, James Crawford. Treasurer, William Gray. County Commissioners, William Antes, James Espy, and Daniel Montgomery.

On the 11th of April, David Kennedy was appointed Secretary of the Land Office, Colonel Francis Johnston, Receiver General, and John Lukens, Surveyor General.

Buffalo: Constable, Henry Gilman; Supervisors, Abel Rees and John Reighard; Overseers, Michael Hessler and John Clark.

10th March, Saturday, at ten, A. M., Black Ann, for larceny from Eleanor Green, was whipped at the public whipping-post, in Sunbury—twenty lashes on her bare back, well laid on.

March 31, Peter Grove, of Buffalo, commissioned lieutenant of the rangers; Samuel Quinn, ensign. In 1788, the latter was deputy surveyor, and Quinn's run, in Clinton county, was called from his camping there during that year.

May 3, fast day, by order of Congress.

June 26, William Gray, Esquire, appointed paymaster of the militia.

Penn's Township Residents, &c.: Anderson, William, tan-yard; Arnold, Casper; Arnold, Widow; Campbell, Clary, (tenant on Charles Gemberling's place,) he was from Bald Eagle settlement; Cripps, John; Dillman, Andrew; Espert, Widow; Graybill, John, non-juror; Gast, Christian; Grow, Godfrey; Gillen, William; Hafflich, Jacob; Heiner, Frederick; Hauser, John; Hessler, William; Hassinger, Frederick; Jordan, Benjamin; Jost, Widow; Kester, Peter; Kerk, Michael; Kinney, Jacob; Kohler, Andrew; Lepley, Jacob; Miller, Adam; Miller, Simon; Maddox, Richard; Merkel, Peter; Meraby, Edward; Pickard, John; Potter, James, two slaves; Repass, Jacob; Showers, Michael, tenant of Jacob Stees; Stephen, Adam; Shaw, William; Shetterly, John; Witmer, Peter; Woods, Joseph.

In Buffalo: Antes, Philip; Baker, John; Bickle, Widow; Blair, Samuel; Boatman, Claudius; Coon, John; Dean, David; Ferguson, James; Green, Joseph, two grist and one saw-mill; Holman, Eli; Houghton, John, tenant of Samuel Maclay; Keen, Jacob, tenant of John Aurand; Knipper, Paul; Klinesmith, Widow; Laughlin, Widow; McAdam, William; McDonald, Widow; Reem, Nicholas; Rezner, John; Templeton, Widow; Trester, William; Vandyke, John; Watson, James, saw-mill, at Seebold's now.

White Deer—Single men: Ammon, Philip; Caldwell, James; Clendenning, John; Collins, Daniel; Crawford, Robert; Gamble,

Charles; Gibson, James; Hamel, Charles; Hayes, David; Hood, Moses; Huston, Samuel; McCartney, Robert; McKinney, James; McLaughlin, John; Montgomery, Samuel; Murray, William; Poak, John; Tannehill, John.

The ejectment for White Deer mills property was resumed. The suit is brought by Vannost, and has this distorted title: "Timothy Macabees, lessee of James Claypoole, *vs.* Judias Iscariot, with notice to Catherine Smith, widow in possession." To November term we have the commencement of a series of suits between Ludwig Derr and Christian Van Gundy, which, after many years, ended in the pecuniary ruin of the latter. It was brought to November term, lessee of Christian Van Gundy *vs.* Thomas Troublesome, lessee of Ludwig Derr, with notice to Christian Hettrick, tenant in possession· It astonishes a lawyer of the present how our predecessors managed to keep cases so long in court. Van Gundy's application had not the shadow of chance against Derr's title; yet the contest went on for years, until Van Gundy's money gave out. This suit was for the present site of Lewisburg.

Captain James Thompson's Narrative.

In the manuscript journal of the late James F. Linn, Esquire, under date of June 14, 1832, is the following entry: "Old Captain James Thompson was with us last night. He told us a good part of his adventures when with the Indians. He appeared not to wish to tell the story. I got it out of him, only in answers to questions." The narrative was entered in my father's journal. I have supplemented by the article of Elizabeth Gundaker, now Dale, niece of Captain Thompson, in the *Lancaster Intelligencer*, 1842.

"In March, 1781, I was going from this town (Lewisburg) up to my home, on Spruce run, preparatory to following my wife and family down to Penn's creek, whither, I had taken them for safety. On the road, between John Linn's old place and Colonel Kelly's, I was captured by four Indians. When we came to the hollow, which is now cleared by Thomas Iddings, they discovered a fresh track in the mud, and one of them hallooed 'squaw.' Two of them set off on a run, the remaining two staid with me, one walking before and the other behind. I soon heard the scream of a woman, whereupon, the one behind me gave me a punch in the back with the butt of his gun, and said 'waugh'—run. We all started off on a run, and when we got to the top of the hill, I saw the father of the girl fall, and the Indians seize her. She had lost a shoe in the race. She was Mary Young, the daughter of Mathew Young, who lived on Spruce run. William Hayes now owns the place ; he bought it as James Black's property, a few years ago, (now, 1877, Gabriel Huntingdon's.) We crossed the White Deer mountains, north of the Valley, and camped the second night on Lycoming creek. They tied me, with my arms behind me, to two grubs. I managed to get the cords off, after they got to sleep ; two of them laid on one side of the fire, near me, and two on the other, with the girl. I tried to get one of the tomahawks, but they were lying upon them. I then got a stone, they had been using to pound corn with, got on my knees near one of them, and prepared to give him a mortal stroke. I intended striking him on the temple, but he had a blanket wrapped around his head, and I struck too high. The Indian gave a yell and awoke the rest. I started to run, but the cord stretched between the two grubs, caught me about the middle, and in trying to get around it, one of the Indians caught me by the coat collar, and in the struggle, tore it clear down to the middle. He drew his tomahawk to strike me, but stopped, and addressed the wounded one in their language. Drew it the second and third time, when I was sure I would get it; but I had made up my mind, to try to catch it, and wrest it from him. They then got a gourd, put shot in it, and tied it to my waist. This was my death warrant. I could have readily escaped myself, but I was anxious to rescue Mary. After that, they tied me so tight, I lossed all feeling in my arms and hands. Before we got to Towanda, one of the Indians shot a turkey, took out the entrails, and roasted them on a stick, and gave them to us. It was very delicious, as we had but a few grains of corn a day to eat. One of them shot a dipper-duck, and skinning it, after making an opening at the belly, slipped it over the hurt man's head for a night-cap.

"When we got to Towanda, the Indians became careless, supposing there was no danger of my running away. They made me gather wood for the fire, and as I returned each time I slipped a few grains of corn out of the kettle, and every load I wandered further from camp. At last, seeing no one looking my way, I started with twenty-two grains of corn for a provision for a journey of nearly two hundred miles. I could have escaped before, but I could not bear the idea of leaving the girl with them. Her hardships were fearful. Often her clothes were frozen solid after wading the creeks. We had encamped that night at the foot of a hill by a stream of water. She urged me to leave her, and finally I followed her advice. I carried two loads, I think, still going further up the hill. I took a different direction from home at first. I stepped upon a rotten stick, which made a noise, and then, mistaking the sound of two trees rubbed together by the wind, for the Indians, I ran with all my might, and reached a pond, in which I buried myself up to the head. Finding the Indians did not come that way, I proceeded, keeping upon the tops of the mountains. One night I spent in a hollow tree. At another time I came very near getting into an Indian encampment before I was aware of it. I saw the Indians pass between me and the fire. At another time, coming upon a camp, the Indians hallooed. I felt certain I was discovered, but squatted down among the bushes, and when they began to cut wood I made off. At one place I found two walnuts, at another the bone of a deer, which I cracked, and sucked the marrow. This, with the corn, was all the provision I had, and, in crossing Lycoming creek, I nearly drowned from excessive weakness. I struck the West Branch a few rods above where we crossed going up, and found one of the canoes lying on the bank, as the river had fallen. I was so weak I could not lift it in, but, by means of a handspike and some rollers, I managed to get it in. After I got it in, I discovered the other canoe sunk, which I ladled out, and lashed to the other. When I got opposite Watsontown, I was so weak I could only lay in the bottom of the canoe, and wave my hands. Fortunately I was here noticed, and the people came to my relief. They considerately fed me with sweet milk only, until I got stronger, but it was some time before I could tell them about my adventures."

Mary Young they carried with them to their town. They set her to hoeing corn. An old negro, who was also a prisoner, told her to dig up the beans planted with the corn, and they would sell her to the English. She did as she was advised, and they thought her too stupid to learn to work, and sold her. She said two of the Indians pursued Captain Thompson part of two days. The wounded Indian left them shortly after they got out. She supposed he died, as he was very much hurt. Mary was sent to Montreal, and sold. Her purchaser's name was Young, and, on tracing the relationship, they found they were cousins. She remained there until after the war, and then returned to her friends in Buffalo Valley. Tradition says her health was very much undermined, and she died soon after. She was still living in 1787, when her father died; but I can trace her no further. But for the entry in my father's journal, her history would have been as evanescent as her foot-prints, which revealed her presence to the Indians.

Captain Thompson removed his family to Chester county, where they remained until after the Indian troubles were all over. They then returned, and he purchased of the widow Dempsey the place now owned by Jacob Ziebach, on Spruce run, in Buffalo, and resided there until the year 1832, when he went to reside with his son-in-law, Boyd Smith, (son of Gideon Smith, who lived at the mouth of Little Buffalo,) near Jersey Shore, where he died, February 9, 1837, aged ninety-three years nine months and nine days. When ten years of age, he was with his father at Braddock's defeat. He was a remarkable man in old age, often walking from Jersey Shore down into Bufalo Valley, a welcome guest in every house from Pine to Penn's creek. His son William married Susan Linn, in 1804, and removed to Sugar Creek, Venango county. Their son James died from an explosion, which took place in his store, in 1833. He was carrying out ashes in an empty keg, as he supposed, but which had several pounds of powder in it. Ann married John B. McCalmont, Esquire, nephew of old Judge McCalmont. She died in 1849. John Linn Thompson died in Venango, leaving a family. William resides in New Brighton, Beaver county.

In a letter to General Potter, Colonel Hunter states that Captain Thomas Kempling, as he writes it, and his eldest son, were killed by the Indians, at the mouth of Muncy creek, in March, 1781. In the petition of his widow, who writes her name Mary Campleton, presented to the Assembly, September 23, 1784, she says: "My husband and son, with others, went on a tour of duty up the West Branch, early in the spring of 1781, and lying one night at the mouth of Muncy creek, in the morning the savages came on them, when my unfortunate husband and son, with one William Campble, fell a sacrifice to all the cruelties and barbarities that savages could inflict, leaving your petitioner and six children. We were driven from house and home, and so reduced that I am unable to return to the place we had improved upon."

About this time, John Shively who lived on the place now owned by R. V. B. Lincoln, Esquire, was captured by the Indians, in the meadow, in the rear of Esquire Lincoln's house. He was never heard of afterwards. He left a widow and sons, Christian and Frederick, who owned the place until the year 1804. His widow married Philip Mann, who lived in the Valley up to 1805.

George Rote and his sister Rody, aged about twelve and fourteen, were taken at Mifflinburg, where their father, George Rote (or Rhodes) lived. They were separated and carried into the Cornplanter's country. When peace was proclaimed they were liberated, and met at a furnace, near Clarion, Pennsylvania, and came back together. Rody married James Ben, and they moved to Centre county. They were uncle and aunt to the late Captain John Rote, who never could hear of an Indian in latter times without getting into a passion. Jacob and Conrad Caderman were captured at the same time. The former told my informant that Limestone hill seemed full of Indians; that he had a gun and fired into the ground, to indicate that they surrendered. He said he liked Indian life so well that he would have remained among them, but for his wife and children. Conrad played stupid, and did all the mischief he could. They soon got tired of him, and sold him to the English for a five gallon keg of whisky. They both returned and lived long in the Valley. James Ben lived on a place adjoining Philip Fishburn, now in Spring Creek, Centre county. His wife died many years ago, and he subsequently married a widow Murphy.

In the life of Rev. John Dietrich Aurand, Harbaugh's "Fathers," mention is made of his return from the army early this year; that his mother, Mrs. John Aurand, had died but a short time before his return, and amid the tenderest longings to see her son once more before her departure. A deep sadness took possession of the young soldier's spirit when he found his mother no more among the living. He often went to her grave to weep and pray. She was buried on a gentle knoll on the west side of the present road, and on the south side of Turtle creek, near the mouth of the stream, under an aged yellow pine, in the midst of a clump of white pines of smaller growth.

Tradition has it that a number of people were buried here before and during the Revolution. Bickle, who was killed at Henry Mertz's place, is said to have been buried here. In my earliest recollection it went by the name of the old Indian burying-ground. It is now, however, a cleared field, (1872,) and all marks of its former use probably obliterated.

SUNBERY, *April* 12, 1781.

SIR: I arrived at my house on Sunday last, and on Monday I came to this pleace, and since, I have maid a visite to difrent parts of the frunteers, who I find in great disstress, numbers of them flying for their lives. At this early season of the year, the enemy has maid five different strookes on our frunteers, since the 22d of March. On the sixth instant, they fiered on an old man, his son, and daughter. The boy was shott ded, and the Indians imedatly maid a prisoner of the young woman. The old man had a stick in his hand, with which he nobley defended himself against one of the Indians, who had a tomhack and maid the fellow drope his wapon. Col. Kelly, with a few of his neighbours, was in a house at a little distance. On hearing the enemy guns go off, run to the pleace, and obleged the enemy to retreat, leving the young woman there prisner, and our brave old Irishman, and his stick behind them, and all there blankets. They out run Col. Kelly and his party, and got off as usile.

On Sabath day last, the eight instant, in the evening, they came to the house of one Durmes, about five miles from this pleace. Immedatly on there entring they house, they shot Dunn and tooke one Capt. Solomons a prisoner. There was four weemen and a number of children in the house. They plundered the house of every thing that was vallibel. But what is surprising, they went off with Captd. Solomon and there plunder, leving behind the weeman and children. This hapened leat in the evening. The next day they were persued but not come up with.

Capt. Robinson has got forty men enlisted for the war, but many of them are so naked, for want of all kinds of clothing, that the can not do duty. They have not a blanket among them all. I know it is not in the power of Council to provide for them at present, but I hope they will as soon as posable.

I most sincerely wished for our Assembly to have been with me in my disagreeable visit along the much disstressed fruntiers. I have not language to express their distresses.

With great esteem, your humble serv't,

JAS. POTTER.

JOS. REED, *Pres't.*

The Story of the Emerick Family.

On the farm now owned by Jacob Seebold, to the right of the road going to New Berlin, after passing the road through Chappel's Hollow, lived David Emerick, with his wife and four children, his other daughter being down the country at that time. Emerick had first settled upon the tract where the Widow Brown's tavern is, or near it, before the revolutionary war, in 1773, where he built a house, cleared ten acres of land, planted apple trees, &c. He sold this place, by deed dated 21st June, 1780, to Daniel Rees. On the 15th of November, 1779, he had purchased of Andrew Glen and wife the tract of two hundred and eighty acres, (on which he subsequently removed, and was captured.) for £2,925. Here he cleared a piece and built a cabin, and was residing in April, 1781.

Here Henry Bickel, (who lived where Henry Mertz now does,) was shot. He had come there to help roll logs. His family was not disturbed. They plundered Emerick's house of everything, and loaded him down with baggage. After proceeding a little way, they pulled down a sapling, sharpened the end of it, impaled the babe, and let it fly in the air. Emerick became so exhausted with his load that he sat down upon a log, and refused to go any further. One of the Indians sank his tomahawk into his head, and killed him. One of the daughters died from excessive bleeding at the nose, on the journey through the wilderness. They were taken to Niagara,[1] and the wife and daughters married Indians, their captors; and many years ago

[1] Heckewelder says, that the Muncys took refuge during the Revolution in Canada, and remained there. It is reasonable, to conclude, that the party making this descent upon the Valley were of its aboriginal inhabitants, familiar with its localities, and, therefore, able to enter and withdraw with comparative safety.

Mrs. Emerick and her Indian husband came to Henry Myer's, near Harrisburg, in order to draw some money coming to her from her grandfather's estate. Thus far I had the story from Benjamin Shell, (court crier,) of New Berlin. Emerick was an uncle of Mr. Shell's mother, and the Emericks came from what is now Dauphin county, and settled, as he heard the story, in the "Shamokin country."

My own researches among the records developed the dates and the rest of the narrative. There is on record, in Sunbury, a letter of attorney, dated the 12th of January, 1805, recorded in deed book M, page 516, the parties to which are Archibald Thompson, of Stamford, in the district of Niagara, province of Upper Canada, and Catherine, his wife, formerly the widow of David Emerick, to James Thompson, of the same place, authorizing him to collect their interest in the rents, issues, and profits of lands, and all the goods and chattels, late of David Emerick; and also from the heirs and executors of Conrad Sharp, of Berks county, their interest in his estate. It is dated at Willoughby, and acknowledged before Archibald Stewart. It is recorded on the 4th of March, 1805. It is followed by a letter of attorney from James Thompson to George Schoch, to sell and convey their interest in a tract of land, in Buffalo township, adjoining lands of Hessler, Hugh Beatty, George Olds, and James Jenkins, containing one hundred and seventy-one acres, "which they hold as tenants, in common with John Bickle," recited to be conveyed by Andrew Glen and wife. On referring to deed book C, page 378, it will appear that Andrew Glen and Sarah, his wife, on the 16th of November, 1779, deeded to David Emerick, a warrant of the 15th of December, 1772, for two hundred and eighty acres, consideration, £2,925. It describes the land as adjoining Thomas Sutherland, James Hunter, and George Olds.

9th August, 1786, John Aurand appointed guardian of Margaret and Catherine Emerick, children of David Emerick, deceased. Finally there is a release recorded at Lewisburg, dated the 26th of September, 1816, from James Thompson to George Schoch, which recites that David Emerick left a widow, named Catherine, and two daughters, Margaret, intermarried with James Thompson, and the other intermarried with George Bauder, and he, Thompson, releases his wife's share of David Emerick's estate, amounting to $516 75. So it seems that the wife, and at least one of the daughters, married their captors, who, many years after, came back and received their share of the estate of the man they murdered. Mr. Shell said Mrs. Emerick was infatuated with the Indian style of life, and endeavored to persuade some of her female relatives to go off with them when here. The recollection of one of the old inhabitants of the Valley was, that they came here in grand style, on horseback, Mrs. Emerick decorated with all the tinsel of Indian dress.

In 1825, Bonham's heirs brought an ejectment against William Gibbons, for a tract of land, in the warrantee name of David Emerick, and, to sustain their title, gave in evidence a deed, dated the 21st of June, 1780, from David Emerick to Daniel Rees, under whom Bonham claimed. The evidence on the trial is all lost, but from some manuscript notes taken by the late James F. Linn, it appears that the defense, who had no real defense, subpœnaed all the old settlers in the country to prove that David Emerick was killed in 1778 or 1779, from which the lawyers argued the deed a forgery, though it purported to be acknowledged before Christopher Gettig, Esquire. We are unable to say exactly, but think this was a dodge of the lawyers, taken upon the second trial, the other side, Mr. Bellas and Hepburn never dreaming of parol testimony thus affecting their title. Among others called to prove that Emerick was killed prior to the date of the deed, was Michael Smith, grandfather of A. W. Smith, Esquire. He said "I was living in the place where I am now living (1830[1]) during the revolutionary war. There was a massacre by the Indians in Dry valley. Henry Bickle was killed; the only one, as far as we know. David Emerick and his family were taken prisoners on the same day. His woman came in afterward, and said Emerick was killed on the road. David Emerick never appeared again. It was three years afterward when his wife returned. She was afterward married to Thompson, in York State. I was eight or nine years of age at the time of the massacre. Bickle's wife had a son, about four months after his murder. He is now in court, and his name is Henry Bickle. I was born in 1769. I saw Henry Bickle after he was murdered. My father lived about two miles from Bickle at that time. My wife's mother and Emerick's wife's mother were sisters. I saw Thompson after he was married to Mrs. Emerick. They were married about the last of the war, or in it."

Smith lived on Kunkle's place, west of Henry Mertz.

"*Lee's massacre* was about a year after Emerick's. It was in Dry Valley, and about the time of the general runaway. I saw Lee's family all lying scalped. Emerick has some children. I never saw any of them. There was one of the girls down below at the time, and was at my house about a year ago. Emerick lived near the hill, not far from Hummel's tavern, in Dry Valley. Emerick's children were all taken, except the one below. I saw Lees' killed in the house where they were killed. They had their heads all scalped, and were laid on a bundle of straw." Jacob Bower, of Union township, whose deposition was read, stated that knew David Emerick, and, three years after he became acquainted with him, he was taken by the Indians. "They killed him on the hill, and we fled to Lee's, and lived there until after hay-making. Lee was after the Indians when Trinkle and Faught were killed. Lee was killed by the Indians afterwards. Emerick was not taken prisoner the same summer Lee was killed, but the year we lived at Lee's."

Henry Bickle, sworn: "I am fifty-one or fifty-two years of age, and was born in 1778 or 1779, one of the two. I have been always told I was born about four months after my father was killed. I saw Emerick's wife when she was in. My mother lives twenty miles from here. Mrs. Emerick gave me a pen-knife when she was in. I cannot recollect how long since. My mother is eighty-five the 7th of next September. I was born in July, and my father was killed in April, as I have always been told by my mother and others. Emerick's wife and my mother were sisters. My mother was married to old George Schoch, who is since dead. She has lost her mind, and would not do any good if she were here."

The plaintiffs then gave in evidence the records of an ejectment, No. 138, May Term, 1834. James Thompson and Margaret, his wife, late Margaret Emerick, in right of said Margaret, George Bauder and Catherine, his wife, late Catherine Emerick, *vs.* David Zeluff and Robert Hilands, and called the late James Merrill, Esquire, who said that he had brought "this suit at the instance of David Thorburn, who showed me a power of attorney, which he took away with him again. I never knew the man before. He said he lived in Canada."

They also offered letters from Thorburn from Canada, post-marked Lewistown, which were rejected. This ejectment was non-prossed under the rules.

Defendants called Philip Hoyens, who swore he knew David Emerick and Henry Bickle. "Emerick first lived on the Gibbons place. He made an improvement, built a house, and cleared about ten acres. Bickle and Emerick were killed by the Indians. I think they took Emerick away a piece. Emerick moved to this place of Gibbons' before the war. It was two miles from Northumberland."

Instead of contending stoutly that such evidence could not contradict a deed as to date, and could raise no presumption of death as against a written document, Mr. Hepburn, for the plaintiff, seemed to yield to the force of the old men's testimony, and said that Emerick's name might be a fictitious one, which Bonham had used; it was the practice of the day to use fictitious names to obtain a warrant of survey, and argued further, that there was no evidence that the David Emerick killed by the Indians was the one who owned this land.

The jury, in the former trial, had found for the defendants. It was taken to the Supreme Court, and the case is reported in 2 Rawle, 45, reversed on error of the judge. At this, the second trial, they came in with a sealed verdict, finding for defendant again. On being polled, one dissented, and they were sent out, and, not being able to agree, they were discharged.

At May Term, 1830, the cause was called again, and after the jury were in the box, the parties settled by an agreement that Gibbons should hold the interference during life, after which it was to revert to Bonham's heirs. Lashells and Greenough were for the defense, as could be guessed by any one reading the trial, and knowing their peculiar ability in ejectment cases.

An examination of the assessment books in the commissioners' office, would have shown that John Lee was assessor on the 27th of March, 1782, wherefore, according to the testimony of all the witnesses, the Bickle and Emerick massacre must have been in 1781. The deed from Glen and wife to Emerick, showed that Emerick was alive on the 15th of November, 1779, while Smith and Bickle's testimony would make out that he was killed in 1778 or 1779. The assessment books show that Emerick and Bickle were both alive on 1st of November, 1780, and in the one made by John Lee himself, in March, 1782, for the year 1781, Bickle's property is assessed to his widow, and the name and family of Emerick disappear forever from the assessment lists after 1781.

Hummel's tavern, in Dry valley, was at the intersection of the roads at Adam Miller's, beyond Samuel Guise's.

The Fought and Trinkle murders I can get no trace of, except the allusion in this evidence. They both lived in Dry valley.

Henry Bickle, who was killed when Emerick's family was captured, left the following family: Christopher, the eldest, who took the farm in 1792, at 40 shillings per acre; Maria C., married to Benjamin Stroh; Elizabeth afterwards married Jacob Kamerlin. Henry, as stated. The widow, Esther Regina, married George Schoch. Christopher sold it to John Meyer in 1806, who sold to Daniel Nyhart, who sold, 4th May, 1822, to Jacob Mertz, whose son, Henry, resides at the old place.

John Wierbach's daughter, (sister of Nicholas and John,) of Buffalo, was carried off by the Indians. She married among them, and after the war her father went West, and found her, but could never induce her to return, though he offered every inducement he could. She preferred the wild life of the savages.

Pay-roll of Peter Grove's Detachment for Services on the Frontier, June 1.

Lieutenant—Grove, Peter.
Sergeants—Clark, William; Wilson, Matthew.
Privates—Trester, John; Lamberscn, Nicholas; Rough, John; Barber, Uriah; Trester, Jacob; Shock, John; Fisher, Paul; Bower, George; Bradley, Matthew; Bower, Daniel; Houser, Jacob; Harriott, William; Grove, Michael.

Pay-roll of Lieutenant Samuel McGrady's Detachment.

Lieutenant—McGrady, Samuel.
Sergeants—Montgomery, Samuel; Armstrong, Daniel.
Privates—Love, Robert; Daraugh, Ephraim; Fleming,[1] Hans; Fulton, Samuel; Marshall, William; Lykens, Joseph; Misener, John; Clark, George; Rees, Daniel; Speddy, William; Pollock,

---

[1] His proper name was Archibald Fleming. He lived at Shippensburg in August, 1799, as appears by his receipt.

William ; Dougherty, William ; McClung, Charles ; English, William ; Allen, Robert ; Parsons, Barnabas ; McGrady, Alexander.

In 1781, the first battalion of Northumberland county militia, commanded by Colonel John Kelly, was composed of the following companies:

Captain John Foster, numbering, officers and privates, 55 men.
" James Thompson, " " " 44 "
" George Overmeier, " " " 51 "
" Samuel Fisher, " " " 55 "
" Samuel Young, " " " 51 "
" Abraham Piatt, " " " 53 "
" William Irvine, " " " 53 "
" William Gray, " " " 44 "

Among the rangers commanded by Captain Thomas Robinson, June 1, occur the following from Buffalo Valley: Claudius Boatman, fifer, William Armstrong, Ludwig Rough, Conrad Katherman, Jacob Links.

The names of Thomas Perry, Hugh Rodman, John Linn, William Black, James Rodman, James Boyd, Thomas Black, John Rhea, William Black, James Hamersly, appear among those who received pay for seven months' services.

Indian Outrages in the Valley.

July 18, Colonel Hunter writes that the Indians have again made their appearance, and that there were no stores of any kind, and meat very scarce in the county.

August 3, Walter Clark and William Antes write: "With pain and with the utmost truth we are obliged to declare that we cannot comply with the law passed for supplies. The whole personal property of the county, even if removed to a place where cash could be paid for it, would not pay the tax. The improvements are grown up, burned, or destroyed, and the most of the personal property moved into the lower counties."

September, Captain Robinson writes : " The savages have been quiet for some time. They made their appearance in harvest, but did no damage. Lieutenant Van Campen and six men have gone up into the Indian country, to discover their moves." He recommends Doctor Eaker, who was then in the county, and intended to settle there, for surgeon of his company, and refers to Doctor Shippen, who knew him.

October 26, William Antes, James Espy, and Daniel Montgomery, the county commissioners, write: "That the county books and papers are yet in Paxton; that it appeared by the treasurer's books that the residents paid their taxes, while the non-residents did not; that they would now proceed with the tax business with dispatch."

6th October, Christian Hetrick, a private in Captain Samuel McGrady's seven-months men, was killed. He lived at Derr's, and his party was called out upon the appearance of some Indians on Buffalo creek. They did not come up with them, and on Hetrick's return home, a mile and a half above Gundy's mill, he was shot. When found he had a bullet wound, and was scalped and tomahawked. His widow, whose name was Agnes, married Ephraim Morrison, in 1787, and from an affidavit made to get a pension for Hetrick's children, I got the facts. Her children were Andrew, born May 1, 1775; Catherine, 15th March, 1777; Elizabeth, 15th June, 1779; Polly, 16th October, 1781. He was one of the first residents upon the site of Lewisburg, and is buried just above Andrew Wolfe's, where the rocks jut out upon the road, in the corner of the woods. My father often pointed out the place, but he did not know the man's name.

During this year David Storms was killed, on the place now owned by Esquire Cameron, in Buffalo, (Benjamin Lahr tenant.) David Storms, a son, married Elizabeth Baker, aunt of Mrs. John Beeber, from whom I received the story. David Storms, the son, lived awhile in Centre county, and laid out Stormstown, called after him. David Storms, senior, was outside the house at work, and his two daughters were engaged spinning. He saw the Indians, and ran into the house. They knocked the door in, killed and scalped him. The girls ran up stairs into different rooms. The one closed the door; the other got behind the open door. They killed the one, and an Indian looked in the other room; seeing no one, went down stairs. She watched them from the window, and, thinking they noticed her, she sank down in a fainting fit; but they did not return.

19th October, Jane, widow of William McClung, killed at Fort Freeland, was married by the Rev. Hugh Magill, to David Martin. She had three children, the youngest not born when their father was killed.

Among those deceased this year occur Casper Yost, of Penn's; William Rodman, of White Deer; (his widow, Martha, afterwards married James Fleming.) Children: James, Thomas, Alexander, John, Samuel, Benjamin, and William.

1782.

INDIAN INCURSIONS—REZNER KILLED—MAJOR JOHN LEE KILLED—HISTORY OF LEE'S FAMILY, AND WALKER'S—DEATH OF CAPTAIN CASPER WEITZEL.

ILLIAM MOORE, President of the State. James Potter, Vice President. Frederick Antes, Presiding Judge. At the general election held in October, William Montgomery, William Cooke, and William Maclay were elected members of the General Assembly. Thomas Grant received the highest number of votes for Sheriff, but Henry Antes, the next highest in number of votes, received the commission; John Chattam, Coroner; and David Mead was elected County Commissioner. The officers of Buffalo were: Constable, Peter Burns; Supervisor, Nicholas Reem; Overseers, Michael Hessler and George Hains.

In Penn's township, George Herrold is assessed with two mills and a ferry; Tobias Bickle, senior, with a tan-yard; William Anderson, tan-yard. Additional residents: Frederick Bubb, Frederick Guy, (non-juror,) Andrew Gift, John Rush.

Captain Matthew Smith was a better warrior, no doubt, than prothonotary, but answered for war times, when there was little to do. I copy a specimen of his orphans' court records:

"At an orphans' court held at Sunbury, January 11, 1782, the court are of opinion, from information given, that Benj. Elliot and Jean Irwin (*alias* Elliot) be and appear at Sunbury, on Monday, the 14th inst., to answer said court on some complaint of misdemeanour. Fail not under the penalty of £100. Note: the complaint is that the estate of Richard Irwin is embezzling, and that the above Benjamin and Jean is to be provided with security to cloath, maintain, and educate the minor children ; otherwise, other security will be given, that no expense will accrue to the said minor children.

MATTHEW SMITH."

The Indian outrages commenced early this year, and on the 1st of May Captain Joseph Green had a party out in defense of the frontier.

May 6, Edward Tate, a private in Captain George Overmeier's company, was wounded by a ball through his foot, in an engagement with the Indians, which ocurred on a place then occupied by Frederick Wise, (now in Limestone township, somewhere between Mifflinburg and Wehr's tavern.) A number of the company were on a scout, and were talking, at the time, of the merits of their respective guns. One said he could shoot the drop from an Indian's nose. Just at that moment the Indians, who were in ambush, fired upon them, and several fell. Tate, who was wounded, ran and concealed himself. An Indian, in pursuit, came near to where he lay, and looked over the fence, but did not discover him. Philip Seebold, whose authority was old Mrs. Overmeier, said the names of the two men killed were Lee and Rezner ; that their bodies were brought to Captain Overmeier's, and she washed them, and they were buried in the grave-yard at Dry run, near late Philip Seebold's residence.

Major Lee and others Killed by the Indians.

The attack on John Lee's (now Winfield) was made in August. A letter directed to Colonel Magaw, at Carlisle, found among his papers, from Colonel Butler, dated 25th August, says, a party of Indians, supposed to be sixty or seventy in number, killed Mr. Lee and family, a few miles above Sunbury. Letters of administration were issued to Captain John Lowdon and Thomas Grant on the 31st of August. Lee was assessor in April of this year.

I copy from Meginness his narration of the occurrence, as I can find no contemporaneous account of it. Meginness, however, confounds Major John Lee with Sergeant Lee, killed at Fort Rice, on the 24th of October, and relates an incident occurring at Sergeant Lee's funeral as happening at Major Lee's funeral:

"It was a summer evening, and his family were at supper. A young woman named Katy Stoner escaped up stairs, and concealed herself behind the chimney. Lee was tomahawked and scalped, and a man named John Walker shared the same fate. A Mrs. Boatman and daughter were also killed. Mrs. Lee, with a small child and a boy named Thomas, were led away captives. They took the path up the Valley, crossing White Deer mountain, and then the river. One of Lee's sons, Robert, returning about the time, saw the Indians leaving. He fled to Northumberland, and gave the alarm. A party was organized by Colonel Hunter, and started in pursuit. Henry McHenry, father of A. H. McHenry, of Jersey Shore, was in this party, and gave an account of it to his son. In crossing the mountains, Mrs. Lee was bitten by a rattlesnake, and her leg became so much swollen, she traveled with great difficulty. The Indians finding themselves pursued, urged her on as rapidly as possible, but her strength failed her. When near the mouth of Pine run, four miles below Jersey Shore, she gave out and sat down. An Indian slipped up behind her, placed the muzzle of his rifle to her ear, and blew off the whole upper portion of her head. One of them seized her little child by the heel and dashed it against a tree. They then fled, crossing the river at Smith's fording, and ran up Nippenose bottom. When Colonel Hunter came up with his men, the body of Mrs. Lee was yet warm, and the child, but little injured, was moaning piteously. Near Antes' Gap the Indians separated, and ran up both sides of the mountain, and the party gave up the chase, as they were nearly exhausted. They came back and buried Mrs. Lee where she died, and brought the child back. They dug a hole alongside of Walker's body and rolled him in. Mrs. Boatman's daughter survived and lived many years afterwards. Young Thomas Lee was not recovered for many years afterwards. His brother made arrangements with the Indians to bring him to Tioga Point, (Athens now,) where he was delivered to his friends. Such was his love of Indian life that they were obliged to tie him and place him into a canoe to bring him home. When near Wilkesbarre they untied him, but as soon as the canoe touched the shore, he was out and off like a deer. They caught him, however, and, on arriving at Northumberland, he evinced all the sullenness of a captive. Boys and girls played about him for several days before he showed any disposition to join them. At last he began to inquire the names of things. By degrees he became civilized, and obtained a good education."—*Meginness, page* 276.

John Van Buskirk told me when he came to the Valley, in 1816, the old people thereabouts showed him the spot where Lee was killed, by what is now (1877) a blasted pine, some little distance in a westerly course from the furnace stone stable; and he said Lee was buried, with his family, near their residence, which Isaac Eyer, senior, tells me, stood just where the furnace railroad crosses the road to the river, and that his father lived in it until he built the new house, within his own recollection.

I once had occasion to examine the title papers of Youngman's and Walter's place. Among them is the release of Thomas Lee, the eldest son, his signature, excellent hand-writing, dated 1st April, 1797, to Robert Lee, of Point township. Release of Sarah, married to William Beard, of Lycoming county, 24th April, 1797, to Robert. Rebecca, married to Robert Hursh, of Lycoming county, of same date; and Eliza Lee. She was probably the infant spoken of in the narrative. Robert Lee then sold to Abraham Eyerly, (now Eyer,) 2d May, 1797.

The sequel to John Walker's murder, Mr. Meginness relates, as follows: "In the year 1790 his sons Benjamin, Joseph, and Henry Walker were living on a farm not far from the mouth of Pine creek, a few miles above Jersey Shore, when two Indians, one a youth and the other a middle-aged, well-proportioned man, came into the neighborhood. At Stephenson's tavern, near the mouth of the creek, some people, and among them the Walkers, had gathered. The Indians got drunk, and performed many antics; and the old Indian, putting on the most horrid grimaces, and twisting his face into all sorts of shapes, said, 'this is the way old Walker looked when I killed and scalped him.' That evening the brothers persuaded one Samuel Doyle to accompany them, and murdered the Indians, placing their bodies in the creek near where Phelps' mill stands. The bodies were washed out by a freshet, and suspicion pointed to the Walkers, who fled the country."

The county records show that letters upon the estate of John alker were granted to his widow, Jane, and eldest son, Benjamin, in ugust 1782, and the rest of his family consisted of William, who ed before 1790, (leaving a son, John,) Henry, Joseph, John, muel, and Sarah, married to William Morrison.

During this year, a boy sent to Van Gundy's mill (now J. W. iriner's, near Lewisburg,) was shot from his horse. This occurred the Meixell place, a short distance above Francis Wilson's. He as only fourteen years of age, and his name has not been preserved, it the spot, a marsh by the present road, was haunted, people said, y his ghost riding a white horse.

Deaths.

Casper Weitzel, Esquire, was a lawyer, practicing at Sunbury, hen the war broke out, in 1775, and as secretary of the county ommittee, took a very active part in favor of independence. In 776 he raised a company in and around Sunbury, which was at-.ched to Colonel Miles' regiment, and participated in the disastrous attle of the 27th of August, on Long Island. He fought through e British ranks, and made his way into camp, with Lieutenant olonel Brodhead, with a loss of twenty, officers and men, of his ompany. His rolls, written in his own neat hand, are in the office : the Secretary of the Commonwealth. He was a granduncle of . R. Weitzel, Esquire, of Scranton, Pennsylvania.

John Smith, of Buffalo township; his children were Mrs. Cath- ine Norgang and Mrs. Christian Storms. Martin Trester and dam Smith, of Buffalo. James Poak, of White Deer, leaving a idow, Mary; Sarah, married to Colonel John Kelly; Deborah, to phraim Darrough,—James, Thomas, William, and David were his ildren. He lived at the mouth of Little Buffalo creek, Fort Horn, Cameron's.)

1783.

STATE OFFICIALS—ELECTION RETURNS—CONTESTED ELECTION—REVEREND CYRIACUS SPANGENBERG—THE BRADY FAMILY.

TATE OFFICIALS: His Excellency, John Dickinson, President. Judges of the High Court of Errors and Appeals, John Dickinson, Samuel Miles, and Henry Wyncoop. Edward Burd, Prothonotary.

Councillor, John Boyd. Members of Assembly, William Maclay, James McClenachan, and William Cooke. President Justice, William Montgomery. Prothonotary, Major Lawrence Keene, appointed September 25, *vice* Matthew Smith. (Among the applicants for this appointment were Colonel Atlee and Daniel Montgomery.) County Commissioner, John Clarke. County Treasurer, Frederick Antes, appointed October 20. Collector of Excise, William Wilson, appointed October 20.

Officers of Buffalo: Constable, Ludwig Derr; Supervisors, Jacob Dreisbach and John Dabellon; Overseers, George Overmeier and Alexander McGrady. Additional residents: Foster, Andrew; Foster, Thomas; Frederick, Thomas; Garret, John; Greenhoe, Andrew; Gibson, James; Gray, John; Grosvenor, Richard; Gunner, Jacob; Hart, John; Harman, Samuel; Hanna, Isaac; Kennedy, Alexander; Knox, George; Lincoln, Mishael; May, George; Macpherson, John; Spangler, Christian; Thompson, John, junior; Troxell, George. Improvement, Andrew Morrow, grist and saw-mill.

Residents of White Deer: Iddings, Samuel; Potter, James, Esquire.

Penn's: Boop, George; Moore, George; Pyle, George; Sherk, John; Weaver, Michael. Widow Stees is taxed with grist and saw-mill.

ANNALS OF BUFFALO VALLEY.

ELECTION RETURNS—October 14 and 15, 1783.

	COM'R		CORONER			SHERIFF			ASSEMBLY						COUN'R		COUN. OF CENS'RS			
	John Clarke.	John Byers.	John Scott.	Charles Gillespie.	Christopher Gettig.	John Lytle.	Thomas Grant.	Henry Antes.	James McClenachan.	Daniel Montgomery.	Frederick Antes.	John Weitzel.	William Cooke.	William Maclay.	Robert Martin.	John Boyd.	James Potter.	William Montgomery.	William Gray, (Buffalo.)	Samuel Hunter, junior.
Augusta, October 15,	14	191	32	63	192	61	141	121	21	21	27	187	191	193	35	171	22	31	182	189
Buffalo, October 14,	73	....	54	14	16	52	22	61	52	50	32	8	22	23	18	22	16	53	23	24
Northumberland, Oct. 14,	217	16	214	40	....	167	71	209	171	169	176	....	69	59	168	66	167	173	64	69
Muncy,	56	3	58	....	6	54	12	56	60	60	60	6	6	6	58	7	60	60	5	6
	360	210	358	117	214	334	246	447	304	300	295	201	288	281	279	266	265	317	274	288

Two returns were made of this election, one signed by Elias Youngman, Anthony Geiger, and John Tschops, judges of the Augusta or Sunbury district, and Jacob Dreisbach, for the Buffalo district, certifying to the election of Samuel Hunter, junior, and William Gray, of Buffalo, as members of the Council of Censors; John Boyd, as member of the Supreme Executive Council; William Maclay, William Cooke, and John Weitzel, as members of Assembly; John Byers, Commissioner; Henry Antes, Sheriff, &c.; the other return, signed by James Murray, James Espy, and Simon Spaulding, of the Northumberland district, and Richard Manning, of the Muncy district, certified to the election of William Montgomery and Samuel Hunter as Censors, Robert Martin as Councillor, James McClenachan, Daniel Montgomery, and Frederick Antes as members of Assembly; Henry Antes, Sheriff; John Clarke, Commissioner, &c.

The former judges arrived at their result by throwing out the Northumberland and Muncy boxes. They did this because intruders from Wyoming were allowed to vote at Northumberland, and residents upon the Indian lands were allowed to vote at Muncy.

On the 25th of November, the House of Representatives arrived at a little different result, by rejecting the Muncy box alone, thus admitting William Maclay, William Cooke and James McClenachan as members; Samuel Hunter and William Montgomery became members of the Council of Censors, on November 13, by counting all the votes; John Boyd, Councillor, and John Clarke, (Buffalo,) County Commissioner.

The deposition of Thomas Hamilton proved that, at the Muncy election, Richard Manning, who lived on Long Island, supposed to be Indian land, acted as judge, and David McKinney, who lived opposite the Great Island, on Indian land, acted as inspector; that John Price, John Hamilton, Britton Caldwell, one Thorp, and others, who resided upon Indian land had voted at the Muncy district election, held at Amariah Sutton's. The Muncy district was composed of Bald Eagle and Muncy. Robert Fleming was the only one from Bald Eagle who voted. Manning testified that he acted as judge; lived on Long Island; that Daugherty, who acted as inspector of the election, lived fifteen miles from the district, in Turbut township, which was in the Northumberland district; that the Indian land men voted generally in favor of Montgomery, Antes, and McClenachan for Assembly, &c.

William Sims' testimony, with that of others, in regard to the Northumberland box, was that he had been up at Wyoming, and saw William Bonham there, in company with Colonel Zebulon Butler, and Bonham acknowledged to him that it was his business there to get the Wyoming people to go down to Northumberland and vote; that Bonham was exceedingly busy in inviting and persuading the New England people to go down and vote; that Colonel Butler told Captain Gaskins that there would be over one hundred down; that many of them were in Northumberland and had voted, and Bonham kept an open house for them; heard Bonham tell Schott to go up to his house and get his dinner; and further said the election had cost him $20. Captain Spaulding, one of the New England men, acted as judge, and Lord Butler, son of Colonel Zebulon, acted as clerk.

Simon Spaulding testified that he lived at Stoke; had been seven years captain in the army, &c.; that the principle on which the people came down to vote was to show their design of conforming to the laws of Pennsylvania, and that they took that as the first opportunity of doing it, &c.

A petition to the Assembly remonstrating against receiving the returns from Muncy and Northumberland was numerously signed by the inhabitants along Penn's creek, and of Buffalo Valley, and other parts of the county. Among the names of the Hesslers, Ulrichs, Jacob Welker, &c., occurs that of Cyriacus Spangenberg, V. D. M. The autograph is that of an elegant penman, and fixes the date of his residence on Penn's creek two years earlier than Doctor Harbaugh supposed when he wrote the following notice of him: "In the latter part of the year, one Rev. Cyriacus Spangenberg, who had come over with the Hessian mercenaries, and had secured, irregularly, ordination by a frivolous preacher named Philip J. Michael, thus, not by the door, but 'climbing up some other way,' was this wolf admitted into the fold; located near Selinsgrove and began to preach there, at Row's Church, Mahantango, Middle Creek, and other places.

"Such characters often found their way into the quiet and rural settlements of Pennsylvania, as the serpent did into Eden, insinuate themselves into the favor of the needy and unsuspecting, before their old sins could follow them, or new ones could disclose their true character. Hungry souls, who had been for years without the ministry, would hope the best, even amid doubts and fears, and thus were in a favorable position to be deceived. Like all others, the German Reformed Church has not escaped these painful afflictions.

"Spangenberg was not long here before his true character appeared. He had represented himself as a single man, drew upon himself the affections of a young female, obtained her promise of marriage, and the day was fixed for the wedding. But on the day previous, a letter was discovered from his wife, still living in Europe. This at once arrested the whole business, and set the son of perdition bare before the community. He now left Selinsgrove, to the great relief of the people. There are still (1857) aged persons along Penn's creek, who in youth heard the story of this vagabond's doings, and much of it still floats, in half uncertain tradition, among those of the present generation.

"His fate will interest our readers. In 1795 he had succeeded in introducing himself to congregations in (then) Bedford county, including Berlin, now Somerset county, Pennsylvania. A division had for some time been growing wider in the congregation at Berlin—some anxious to be relieved of him, others as desirous of retaining him. On a day appointed for a vote, the people assembled in the church, Spangenberg being also present. Just before voting, a pious and influential elder, named Jacob Glassmore, who sat in the altar with Spangenberg, made some remarks favoring a change of ministers, and expressed a hope that the result of the vote would show that the congregation were inclined in that way. Whereupon Spangenberg sprang to his feet in wrath, drew a dirk from his pocket and plunged it into the elder's heart. In a moment Elder Glassmore lay in blood and death in the altar before the whole congregation.

"Spangenberg was seized immediately and placed in Bedford jail. His trial ended on the 27th of April, and he was found guilty of murder in the first degree. Efforts were made with the Governor for a pardon, or to have the sentenced commuted. The Governor submitted the records to the chief justice. The reply was unfavorable, and on the 10th of October, 1795, between ten A. M. and two P. M., Spangenberg was hanged at Bedford."

Reminiscences of the Brady Family.

October 20, died Mrs. Mary Brady, widow of Captain John Brady. Her remains rest in the Lewisburg cemetery. She died on the Japhet Morton place, a long tract, which extends from (and gives the name to) Mortonsville, (better known as Smoketown,) up to the place lately owned by John Schrack, Esquire. She was born in 1735, and her maiden name was Quigley. She died at the early age of forty-eight years, and left the following family :

Captain Samuel Brady, born 1758, at Shippensburg. James Brady, killed in 1778. John Brady, born 1761, and known as Sheriff. Mary (married to Captain William Gray, of Sunbury,) died December 13, 1850. William P. Brady, who removed to Indiana county, Pennsylvania. He was deputy surveyor in Northumberland county many years. His son, Hugh, was a noted attorney in the western counties of the State. The latter married a daughter of Evan Rice Evans, Esquire, and their son, the first Brady that ever was killed in battle, fell at Antietam, in 1862. General Hugh Brady, who died in Detroit, in 1851. Jennie Brady, a twin sister, born 29th July, 1768. Robert, married afterwards to a daughter of Colonel William Cooke. Hannah. Liberty, born August 9, 1778, so called as she was the first child born to them after the Declaration of Independence. She married William Dewart, and died without issue, July 25, 1851.

I copy here, in full, General Hugh Brady's account of the family, taken from an appendix to his funeral sermon by Reverend George Duffield, loaned me by Mrs. Nancy Eckert, of Lewisburg, granddaughter of Captain John Brady :

"I was born on the 29th day of July, 1768, at the Standing Stone, in Huntingdon county, Pennsylvania, and was the fifth son (they had six sons and four daughters) of John and Mary Brady. My brothers all lived to be men, in every sense of the term, and at a period when the qualities of men were put to the most severe and enduring tests. While I was yet a child, my father moved on to the West Branch of the Susquehanna river, and pitched his tent about eight miles above the town of Northumberland. At this time, (as well as in later periods,) titles to wild lands could be obtained by erecting a log-house, and by girdling a few trees, by way of improvement or cultivation. In this way, my father, John Brady, took up a vast quantity of land; and, had he not fallen in the war of 1776, would have been one of the greatest land-holders in the State. But, owing to the dishonesty and mismanagement of those connected with him, his family received but little benefit from his exertions. Soon after the commencement of the war of 1776, he was appointed a captain in the twelfth Pennsylvania regiment; and, in a few weeks having recruited his company, he joined the army, with which he remained until after the battle of Brandywine.

"At this time the Indians had become very troublesome in the settlements on the Susquehanna; so much so, that application was made to General Washington for regular troops to protect the frontier. Not being in a condition to spare any troops at that moment, he ordered home Captain John Brady, Captain Boone, and Lieutenants John and Samuel Dougherty, to use their influence in inducing the people to sustain themselves, until he could afford them other relief. And nobly did they execute his design. All that brave and experienced men could do, was done by them, even to sacrificing their lives in the defense of their country; for, in less than two years from that date, Captains Brady and Boone, and Lieutenant Samuel Dougherty, had fallen by the hands of the savages. Ten months before the death of Captain John Brady, his son James had fallen (in 1778) by the Indians. Another son, Samuel, was then an officer in the United States army. John was then at home, in charge of the family, and in his sixteenth year.

" After the fall of Captain Brady, my mother removed, with her family, to her father's place in Cumberland county, Pennsylvania, where she arrived in May, 1779, and where she remained till October of that year. She then removed to Buffalo Valley, about twenty miles below our former residence, and settled on one of our own farms. We found the tenant had left our portion of the hay and grain, which was a most fortunate circumstance. The winter following (1779 and 1780) was a very severe one, and the depth of the snow interdicted all traveling. Neighbors were few, and the settlement scattered, so that the winter was solitary and dreary to a most painful degree. But, while the depth of the snow kept us confined at home, it had also the effect to protect us from the inroads of the savages. But, with the opening of the spring, the Indians returned, and killed some people not very remote from our residence. This induced Mrs. Brady to take shelter, with some ten or twelve families, on the West Branch, about three miles from our home.[1] Pickets were placed around the houses, and the old men, women, and children, remained within during the day; while all who could work and carry arms, returned to their farms, for the purpose of raising something to subsist upon. Many a day have I walked by the side of my brother John, while he was plowing, and carried my rifle in one hand, and a forked stick in the other, to clear the ploughshare.

"Sometimes my mother would go with us to prepare our dinner. This was contrary to our wishes; but she said that, while she shared the dangers that surrounded us, she was more contented than when left at the fort. Thus we continued till the end of the war, when peace—happy peace—again invited the people to return to their homes.

"In 1783, our mother was taken from us. In 1784, my brother John married, and, soon after, my eldest sister followed his example. All the children younger than myself lived with them. I went to the western country with my brother Captain Samuel Brady. He had been recently disbanded, and had married a Miss Swearingen, in Washington county, Pennsylvania. He took me to his house at that place, and I made it my home until 1792, when I was appointed an ensign in General Wayne's army. Previous to this, my brother had moved into Ohio county, Virginia, and settled a short distance above Charlestown. At that day, the Indians were continually committing depredations along the frontier. West of the Ohio the settlements were very sparse, and the people from the east side went frequently in pursuit of parties of marauding Indians who visited the neighborhood.

"I joined with several parties in pursuit of Indians, but only met them once in action. This was, I think, on the 22d of May, 1791. Our spies in front had discovered a trail of Indians, about eight miles up Indian Cross-cut, making for the settlements. The next morning, ten citizens were met by Lieutenant Buskirk, with twelve State rangers, at the old Mingo town, and from there we went in pursuit. After following their trail till near sunset, we were fired on by the enemy, who lay concealed in a thicket. Lieutenant Bus-

[1] At Jenkins' mill in East Buffalo.

kirk was killed, and three men wounded. After a fight of about ten minutes, the Indians retreated, leaving one gun on the ground and much blood on the bushes. We pursued the party then till dark, but did not overtake them. The next day, we returned to the field with a large party; and, about one hundred yards up the stream which had divided the combatants, we found twenty-two Indian packs, showing that our party of twenty-two men had fought the same number of Indians. It was afterwards ascertained that eight of them died of wounds received before they reached their towns. I had a fair shot at the bare back of one of them. I do not know whether I hit him or not. He did not fall, and I think I was somewhat excited.

"On the 5th of March following, 1792, I was appointed an ensign in a rifle company, commanded by Captain John Crawford, a soldier of '76. William Clarke, of Kentucky, was the first lieutenant. I reported to my captain, and was put on the recruiting service. But, as the pay of a soldier was only $3 per month, I met with little success. Our clothing was also indifferent, and the feelings of the people generally averse to enlisting. They did not consider regular soldiers the thing, exactly, to fight Indians. I then joined the headquarters of the army, at Legionville, the spot where Harmony now stands, twenty miles below Pittsburgh. The first duty I performed was on Christmas day, 1792, when I commanded a picket guard. The officer of the day, Major Mills, saw, at guard-mounting, that I was very green, and when he visited my guard, at twelve o'clock, he took much pains to instruct me. He also let me know at what hour at night the grand rounds would visit me. I had Baron Steuben's Tactics, and a good old sergeant, and was pretty well prepared to receive the rounds when they approached.

"The major complimented me, and remained with me for some time. His treatment had the effect to inspire me with that confidence which is indispensable in a young officer, to enable him to perform any duty in a suitable manner. I then thought Steuben had nothing with which I was not familiar, and the confidence it gave me has unquestionably been of service to me up to the present day. The history and movements of that army are before the world; but its sufferings and privations are only known to those who shared them, of which I had my full proportion. Our campaign in Canada, during the war of 1812, was by no means interesting, and its privations, &c., were the subject of much discussion. Compared with the campaign of General Wayne, it was all sunshine. At its close, I was left under the command of Colonel Hamtramck, at Fort Wayne. The force consisted of Captain Porter's company of artillery, Captains Kingsbury's, Grattan's, and Reed's companies of infantry, and Captain Preston's company of riflemen, to which I was attached.

"During that winter, 1794-5, we lived very poorly. Our beef came to us on the hoof, and poor, and we had little or nothing to fatten them with. Having no salt to cure it, it was slaughtered, and hung up under a shed, where, by exposure, it became perfectly weather-beaten, and as tough as an old hide. Of course, it made a miserable soup. At the same time, our men received but half rations of flour, and were working like beavers to complete our quarters. Thus we lived until about the middle of February, when a brigade of pack-horses arrived, loaded with flour and salt, and with them came a drove of hogs. From this time forward we considered ourselves as living on the 'fat of the land.' An early spring followed, and with it came ducks, geese, and trout, to improve our living; and the Indians, soon after, came in with their flags to sue for peace; and our time passed away pleasantly. The treaty was opened at Greenville on the 4th of July, 1795, on which day I arrived at that place. I had been ordered there as a witness in the case of Captain Preston, who was tried for disobeying the orders of Colonel Hamtramck. The court sentenced him to be reprimanded, and the General laid it on pretty heavy.

"I remained at headquarters till the treaty was concluded, and then returned to Fort Wayne. While at Fort Wayne, I received many letters from my brothers, urging me to resign. I had not seen them for ten years. Those letters held out the idea that they would *make my fortune.* That, (and a desire to return to the land of my early habits, and to see my brothers and sisters, who had grown from children to be men and women, and most of them married,) decided me to leave the service. I resigned my commission and left Fort Wayne on the 20th of November, 1795, and passed the next winter in Lexington, Kentucky. About the 1st of March following, I rode through to Limestone, (Maysville.) I there got into a quartermaster's boat, and, in about three weeks, landed at Wheeling, Virginia. I spent a few days with the widow of my brother Samuel, who had died on the Christmas previous. I then purchased a horse, and reached home about the 20th of July. I went first to Captain William Gray's, my brother-in-law. My sister, Mrs. Gray, came to the door, and, as I inquired for Mr. Gray, she put on rather an important look, and replied: 'I presume you will find him at the store,' and turned into the parlor. I was about turning on my heel, when I heard steps in the entry, and, turning round, I saw my sister Hannah. She immediately raised her hands and exclaimed: 'My brother Hugh!' and flew into my arms. This was not a little surprising, as when she saw me last she could not have been more than eight years old. She knew me by my resemblance to my twin sister, Jane. I found my connections all living happily, and moving at the head of society. I passed a happy three or four months with them, when I became weary of an idle life, and began to look for my *promised fortune;* but, up to this day, have never been able to find it. I remained out of business till the winter of 1798 and 1799, when I was appointed a captain in Adams' army, and, in less than two years, was disbanded. My brother William, who had been most urgent for me to resign, now requested me to assist him to improve some wild lands he owned on the Mahoning river, about fifty miles from Pittsburgh. We commenced this settlement in the spring of 1802, and, that summer, built a gristmill and a saw-mill. All our breadstuff had to be carried about thirty miles on horseback. Meat I procured with my rifle, deer being plenty, and I could kill them without much loss of time from other business.

"I married in 1805, and took my wife to our place in 1806, where Sarah and Preston were born. During the time we were there, we were happy, and had a plenty of such things as the country afforded. All being on an equality, as regarded our resources, were not annoyed by the insolence of wealth. Still, I saw that *my fortune* could not be made there, and, in 1810, I returned, with my family, to Northumberland, and got along as well as I could, until 1812, when the war again called me into service; since which time the Government has provided for me. I have rendered her some service, and, with my brother officers, have kept my shoulder to the wheel. This was no more than our duty to a country which supports us, and of which we are justly proud.

"Thus, I have given a sketch of my life, containing nothing unusual or strange among those of my day and generation. But what a wonderful generation it has been—the most wonderful of any since the days of our Saviour!

"I have already stated that my brother James fell by the Indians, in 1778. It was in this manner: With ten or twelve others he went to help a neighbor harvest his wheat, about ten miles from the nearest station. On entering the field, they placed a sentinel at the most exposed point, and their arms convenient to their work. They had worked but a short time when the sentinel gave an alarm. They all ran to their arms, but it proved to be a false alarm. After reprimanding the sentinel for his unsoldierly conduct, they returned to their work; but they had not long been reaping when they heard the report of a rifle, and their sentinel was killed. Without noticing the conduct of others, my brother ran to his rifle, and as he stooped to pick it up, he received a shot which broke his arm. This caused him to fall forwards, and before he could recover, a stout Indian was upon him, tomahawked him, scalped him, and left him for dead. After the Indians left the field, my brother recovered and went to the house, where he found the rest of the reapers who had run from the field without their arms, and without making any attempt to defend or rescue him. They sent James to his parents, at Sunbury, forty miles from the spot where he received his wound, which was on Saturday. He lived till the Thursday following, retained his senses, and related what is stated above.

"James Brady was a remarkable man. Nature had done much for him. His person was fine. He lacked but a quarter of an inch of six feet, and his mind was as well finished as his person. I have ever placed him by the side of Jonathan, son of Saul, for beauty of person, and nobleness of soul, and like him, he fell by the hands of the Philistines.

"My father was killed on the 11th of April, 1779, not more than half a mile from his own house. He had left that morning at the head of a party of men, to move in a family that had wintered at their farm, about ten miles from my father's place. Having seen no sign of Indians, my father stopped at Wallis's Fort, and let the party go on with the family. He was the only person mounted, and intended, soon, to overtake the party, but unfortunately for him, his family, and the settlement, he overtook a man who had fallen behind, and remained with him till the Indians shot him dead. The man escaped by mounting my father's horse, after he had fallen. It is a remarkable fact, that this man, *Peter Smith*, was in the field where my brother was killed, and afterwards, his own family was mostly destroyed by Indians, and he again escaped. After the war he settled in the Genesee country, and became a wealthy man. Some men are born to luck.

[NOTE.—It is worthy of notice, that although General Brady frequently sought, he was never successful in finding, the spot where his father was interred. One of his surviving daughters, Mrs. Backus, wife of Major Backus, was providentially made acquainted with the spot, during a visit (1851) to the place of her grandfather's residence. An old revolutionary soldier,[1] who was with the father of General Brady when he fell, and had known and marked the place of his interment, a short time before her visit, had, on his death bed, requested to be buried beside his old captain, and designated the spot. His request was granted, and there lie together in the woods, the captain and the private of his company, in a place where the inhabitants of the neighborhood intend, it is said, to erect an appropriate monument.—*George Duffield, D. D.*]

"My brother John, in his fifteenth year, was in the battle of Brandywine, and was wounded. On the retreat he would have been captured had not his colonel, William Cooke, taken him up behind him.

"John had gone to the army with my father, in order to take home the horses ridden out, and was directed by my father to return. But John heard from Ensign Boyd that a battle was expected to be fought soon. He, therefore, remained to see the fun; and when my father took command of his company, on the morning of the battle, he found John in the ranks, with a big rifle by his side. My father was wounded in the battle, Ensign Boyd was killed, and John received a wound during the retreat.

"As one good turn deserves another, two of my brothers, many years after, married two of the colonel's daughters.

[1] Henry Lebo.

"Captain Samuel Brady entered the army as a volunteer when he was nineteen years of age, and joined General Washington at Boston. A year after, he was appointed a lieutenant, and returned home to recruit. He did not remain long. He belonged to Captain John Doyle's company, Wayne's brigade, and was with him at the surprise of Paoli. In 1779, his regiment, the eighth Pennsylvania, was ordered to Pittsburgh. It was then commanded by Colonel Brodhead. Soon after, my brother heard of his father's death; and he waited, with impatience, for an opportunity to avenge it, on the Indians. Nor was the opportunity long delayed. The Indians had attacked a family and killed all in it, except a boy aged twelve, and his sister, ten. These were taken prisoners, and their father was absent from home at the time it occurred.

"The place was thirty miles east of Pittsburgh, and it so happened Samuel was out in that direction, and, hearing of it, he started in pursuit, having with him a friendly Indian, very useful as a guide. The second evening of the pursuit the party stopped on the top of a high hill, and the Indian guide pointed with his wiping stick to the foot of the hill, and said, 'The Red Bank runs there.' The men sat down, while the captain consulted with the Indian about his future movements. Suddenly, the Indian sprang to his feet, and said he smelt fire; and soon after they saw the smoke curling above the trees, on the opposite side of the Red Bank.

"The Indian said, 'They will sleep by that fire to night.' 'And I will awake them in a voice of thunder in the morning,' replied the captain. The Indian also said, 'After they smoke and eat, and the sun has gone to sleep, they will give the scalp halloo.'

"With breathless impatience, the party watched the setting of the sun, and, as its light disappeared from the tops of the trees in the east, they heard seven distinct scalp halloos, with the usual whoop between each. After it was over, Cole, the Indian, observed, 'There are fourteen warriors, and they have five scalps and two prisoners.' The night being clear and the weather mild, the captain remained in his position till near morning, when he forded the stream above the Indians and posted his men, to await the crack of his rifle as the signal of attack. As day broke an Indian rose up and stirred the fire. The signal was given. The Indian standing pitched into the fire. The attack continued, and resulted in eight of the warriors being deprived of the pleasure of ever again giving the scalp halloo. When the captain got to the fire he found the children much alarmed. After quieting their fears, the boy asked for the captain's tomahawk, and commenced cutting off the head of the Indian that fell in the fire, observing that this was the leader of the party, and the man that killed and scalped his mother. The boy was permitted to finish the job he had commenced.

"Three easy days' march brought the captain back to Pittsburgh. The father of the children was sent for to receive his lost ones. He showed much affection, on meeting his children, and thanked the captain for having restored them; and then asked the captain what had become of his 'big basin.' It appeared the Indians had carried off, or destroyed, a big basin, from which Henry and his numerous family ate their sourkrout. The honest Dutchman thought there could be no impropriety in asking for it, of the man who had the best chance to know.

"In 1804, the writer met Henry (the boy) at a friend's house, in Greensburg, Pennsylvania. Henry had stopped, with a wagon, before the door, and had a barrel of cider for my friend, who, pointing to me, said, 'This gentleman is a brother of Captain Brady, who took you from the Indians.', Henry was assisting to remove the cider, and he gave me a side look for a moment, and then continued his work. I felt hurt at the coldness he showed towards the brother of a man who had risked his life to rescue him from death or bondage, and to avenge the murder of his family. My friend informed me that Henry owned the farm from which he was captured, and was as rich as any farmer in the county. I thought, then, if his circumstances were as easy as his manners, he probably had at home, in the old family chest, as many dollars as would fill his father's big basin.

"At the request of his colonel, Captain Brady visited the Sandusky towns, at the head of four or five men, and lay concealed over ten days, so that he could see all their movements. It was a time for horse racing among the Indians, and men, women, children, and dogs were all in attendance. A gray horse was the winner until the evening of the second day, when they compelled him to carry two riders, (a new way to handicap,) when he was finally beaten. The Indians then retired from the field. That evening

Captain Brady took two squaws prisoners, and started for home. On the second day of their journey they were overtaken by a frightful thunder storm, which destroyed their provisions, and destroyed most of their powder, having but three or four loads of good powder left in a priming horn. The stormy weather continued several days. After it cleared away, the captain, just before night, went ahead of his party, hoping to kill some game, as they were without provisions. The party was then traveling on an Indian trail. He had not gone far when he met a party of Indians returning from the settlements, with a woman and child, prisoners. The captain shot the leader of the party, rescued the woman, and endeavored to obtain the child, that was strapped to the back of the Indian he had shot. But he had not time to do so, as the Indians had ascertained that he was alone, and had returned to their leader. He was, therefore, compelled to fall back, and he took the woman with him. His men, seeing the Indians, and supposing the captain was killed, made their way to the nearest fort, and let the squaw run away. The other squaw had escaped during the great thunder storm. The next day he met a party coming from Fort McIntosh, to bury him, his men having reported him killed. A few days after, he returned with a party to the battle ground, and found the dead Indian.

"In 1835, the writer met, at the town of Detroit, a son of the boy that was strapped to the back of the Indian. He informed me that after Wayne's treaty, his father was delivered up, at Pittsburgh, by the Indians. When the land west of the Ohio came into market, his father bought the lot on which the affair took place, and built his house, as near as he could ascertain, on the spot where the Indian fell, and lived there till eighteen months prior to our conversation, when he was killed by the falling of a tree. His name was Stupps, and he was a fine looking man. I remember his grandmother's name was Jane Stupps, and I have often heard my brother relate the above story.

"On the Beaver river is a place known as Brady's Bend, where he had a hard fight, and killed many of the enemy, with small loss on his own side. His enterprising disposition and his skill in stratagems, in which he equaled any Indian, enabled him to do more towards protecting the frontier than all his regiment besides. Indeed, he was looked upon by the whole country as their surest protector, and all the recompense he ever received was in a reward of $500, being offered by Governor McKean for his person, for having, in 1791, killed a party of Indians on Brady's run, thirty miles below Pittsburgh. He surrendered himself for trial, and was honorably acquitted; he having proved, to the satisfaction of the court and jury, that those Indians had killed a family on the head of Wheeling creek, Ohio county, Virginia. That, on receiving notice of the murder, he suspected those Indians had come out of Pennsylvania. He, therefore, crossed the Ohio at the mouth of the Wheeling, and by steering west, came on the trail, and pursued it to where he attacked them.

"When General Wayne arrived at Pittsburgh, in 1792, he sent for Captain Brady, who lived in Ohio county, Virginia, and gave him command of all the spies then in the employ of the Government, amounting to sixty or seventy men. The captain so disposed of them that not a depredation was committed on the frontier. On the contrary, three or four times the Indians were surprised in their own country, thirty or forty miles in advance of the white settlements. His plan of carrying the war into the Indian country put a stop to all murders on that frontier. He continued in command of these rangers until the period of his death, which occurred on Christmas day, 1795, at his house, about two miles west of West Liberty, Virginia, (in the thirty-ninth year of his age.) His disease was pleurisy. He left a widow and two sons.

"Never was a man more devoted to his country, and few, very few, have rendered more important services, if we consider the nature of the service, and the part performed by him personally. He was five feet eleven and three fourths inches in heighth, with a perfect form. He was rather light; his weight exceeding at no time, one hundred and sixty-eight pounds. As I have said before, there were six brothers, viz: Samuel, James, John, William P., Hugh, and Robert. There was but half an inch difference in our heights. John was six feet and an inch, and I was the shortest of them all. Is it not remarkable that I, who was considered the most feeble of all, should outlive all my brothers, after having been exposed to more dangers and vicissitudes than any, except Samuel? Is it not a proof that there is, from the beginning, 'a day appointed for man to die?' It is said, 'the race is not to the swift, or the battle to the strong, but safety is of the Lord.' That has ever been my belief."

Among the deaths this year, William McCandlish, senior, of Buffalo. (Will dated 11th September. Children: Peter, John, George, Grizzelda, William, junior, Jennette, Alexander, and Martin. Mr. McCandlish lived on the place now owned and occupied by John Lesher, in Buffalo township.) William Greenlee, and in November, Mathias Trinkle, (of Union now.)

In 1783 the people generally returned to the Valley. Mr. Allen having died, Mr. McClenachan became sole elder of the Buffalo Cross-Roads church until his death, in June, 1784, when the congregation was without an elder until 1787, when Matthew Laird, who had been an elder in Big Spring, came to reside within the congregation.—*Doctor Grier's Sermon.*

1784.

Joe Disbury—Bear's Mill (now Hoffa's) Erected—Flood of 1784—Captain Lowdon's Roll—Death of Colonel Samuel Hunter.

OUNCIL of Censors, General James Potter, *vice* Samuel Hunter, deceased. Members of Assembly, elected in October, Frederick Antes, Daniel Montgomery, and Samuel Dale. Henry Spyker, Esquire, was a Representative for Berks county. Presiding Judge, John Buyers. Sheriff, Henry Antes. Lieutenant of the county, William Wilson, *vice* Samuel Hunter, deceased. Collector of Excise, Alexander Hunter, *vice* William Wilson, resigned. County Commissioner, Walter Clark, qualified at November Term.

The celebrated thief, Joe Disbury, was tried. On his jury were Adam Grove, Michael Grove, William Clark and Adam Christ. His sentence was severe: That he should receive thirty-nine lashes, between the hours of eight and nine to-morrow, stand in the pillory one hour, have his ears cut off and nailed to the post, that he be imprisoned three months, and pay a fine of £30 to the President of the State, for the use of the Government. [See his history in Meginness.]

George Herrold this year opened the "Herrold Tavern," on the river below Selinsgrove, and Captain Anthony Selin the first hotel in Selinsgrove. In September, John Bear, of Lancaster, bought the Hoffa Mills, (now) property of William Charters, and erected the first grist-mill there. The saw-mill he added in 1787; and in 1790 he had four mills (grist, clover, oil and saw-mill) there.

Additional Residents in White Deer Township in 1784.

Allison, David; Ant, Jacob; Bennett, Justice; Bennett, Ephraim; Bennett, Thaddeus; Bentley, Green; Brown, John; Brown, Joseph; Brown, widow, Elinor; Buchanan, David; Buchanan, James; Buchanan, James, junior; Buchanan, William; Campbell, Alexander; Carnahan, Robert; Creal, Michael; Daugherty, Daniel; Davis, William; Dodds, Andrew; Dunlap, William; Feager, widow; Fisher, Paul; Fisher, Paul, (single;) Fisher, Henry; Gillespie, Captain Charles; Gilman, Philip; Gray, George; Gray,[1] Neigal, grist-mill, formerly Titzel's; Heany, Hieronymus; Heany, Frederick; Heany, Philip; Huston, Samuel; Iddings. Samuel; Iddings, Samuel, (single;) Jordan, William; Jordan, Andrew; Judge, William; Kerkendale, Herman; Landon, Nathaniel; Lean, Abraham; Lean, Hannah; Low, widow; McComb, John; McCracken, Mary; McLanahan, David; McLanahan, widow; Moore, John; Moore, John, junior; Moore, George; Morrison, Samuel; Montgomery, Samuel; Perry, Thomas; Plants, Jacob; Poak, widow, Mary; Potter, James, Esquire; Ramsey, John; Rodman, widow, Martha; Sheaffer, Nicholas: Tenbrooke, John; Turner, Robert; Vandyke, John; Welsh, Nicholas; Welsh, Ludwig. (William Wilson, William Gray, and William Clark, assessors.)

In a memorial, on file at Harrisburg, signed by Robert Martin and John Franklin, they state "that on the 15th of March, 1784, the Susquehanna rose into a flood, exceeding all degrees ever before known; that its rise was so sudden as to give no time to guard against its mischief; that it swept away about one hundred and fifty houses,

---

[1] Neigal Gray was lieutenant colonel of twelfth Pennsylvania, Continental Line, appointed from Northampton county.

with all the provision, house furniture, and farming tools and cattle of the owners, and gave but just opportunity for the inhabitants to fly for their lives; that, by this dreadful calamity, one thousand persons are left destitute of provisions, clothing, and every means of life."

Muster-Roll of Captain John Lowdon's Company of Northumberland County Volunteers who marched to Suppress the Riot at Wyoming, by Orders of the Supreme Executive Council, August 4, 1784.

Captain—Lowdon, John.
Lieutenant—Vancampen, Moses.
Ensign—Grove, Michael.
Sergeants—Snyder, Frederick; Vancampen, Garret.

Privates—Adams, John; Allen, John; Antes, William; Armstrong, Hamilton; Armstrong, John; Backinstow, John; Baker, William; Boo, George; Busher, John; Calhoon, Matthew; Campble, Andrew; Champ, John; Clark, William; Clingman, Jacob; Crawford, Edward; Crawford, James; Dering, Stophel; Doyle, Samuel; Drake, Samuel; Emmons, Alexander; Eply, Leonard; Ewing, Jasper: Ewing, John; Fowler, Eshel; Fowler, Nathan; Gillespie, Charles; Gibbons, Alexander; Giles, Thomas; Goodheart, Henry; Goodman, Daniel; Gettig, Stophel; Grant, Thomas; Gregg, Andrew; Gregg, John; Gregg, William; Hamilton, Thomas; Hammond, David; Hammond, James; Harris, John; Harris, Samuel; Hepburn, James; Hessler, Michael; Hilman, James; Hunter, Alexander; Jones, John; Keel, John; Keel, Philip; Lamison, Jacob; Lougan, David; Ludwick, John; Lyon, Benjamin; Marshall, John; Martin, Benjamin; Martin, Thomas; McCoy, Neale; McKinney, Abraham; Meads, Ely; Moreland, Thomas; Morrow, James; Ogdon, John; Pearson, George; Rees, Thomas; Robins, Zack; Rope, Michael; Rurer, Frederick; Salomin, John; Shaffer, Adam; Shaffer, Henry; Smith, Jacob; Steuart, William; Stout, John; Teterly, George; Vanderslice, Henry; Volin, Leonard; Webb, William; Weitgur, John; Weitzel, Jacob; Wheeler, John; Wilkeson, Joseph; Wilkeson, William; Wilson, James; Young, John.

One sergeant and twelve men, two days guarding the prisoners at Sunbury.

I do hereby certify the above muster-roll to be just; without fraud to the State of Pennsylvania, or any individual, according to my best knowledge.

JOHN LOWDON, *Captain.*

Mustered the above company as specified in the above roll.

W. WILSON,
Lieutenant Northumberland County.

AUGUST 9, 1784.

Deaths.

April 10, Colonel Samuel Hunter died, aged fifty-two. His grave is near the site of Fort Augusta, which he so heroically defended. His will is dated the 29th of March, and proved the 21st of June. His wife's name was Susanna Scott, sister of Abraham Scott, formerly member from Lancaster. Colonel Hunter was from the county of Donegal, Ireland, and when he died had a mother and two brothers still living there. He left two daughters, Mary and Nancy, minors. 1. *Mary*, married Samuel Scott, who died before her, leaving children, Samuel H. Scott, Sarah, Susanna. Samuel Scott lived on what is now the Cake farm, and was drowned. He was a son of Abraham Scott, who lived on the island which he had purchased of Mungo Reed, the original owner. Abraham Scott died there in August, 1798, leaving a widow, Sarah, and children, Samuel, (above,) Mary, wife of General William Wilson, afterwards of Chillisquaque Mills, Susanna, and Sarah. Susanna married ———— Rose. Their daughter, Isabella, is the widow of Honorable Robert C. Grier, late Justice of the United States Supreme Court. 2. *Nancy*, married her cousin, Alexander Hunter, who died in June, 1810, leaving her also a widow, and children, Mary, Elizabeth, Nancy, and Samuel.

Henry Vandyke, formerly of Hanover township, Lancaster county, leaving a widow, Elizabeth; children, Lambert, John, Sarah, Hannah, Mary, and Elizabeth. He resided on the second farm east of Buffalo Cross-Roads, now Jackson Rishel's.

John Forster, of Buffalo, (will proved 24th October.) He left a widow, Margaret; eldest son, Thomas, grandfather of Mrs. Mark Halfpenny; second son, Andrew; eldest daughter, Christena, married to John Montgomery; Robert Forster was his youngest son;

Jane, second wife of William Irvine; Elizabeth Gray, and Rebecca McFarland. Robert was the father of the late Captain John Forster, of Mifflinburg.

Simon Himrod, elder in the Dreisbach church, and late member of Assembly. He resided in Turbut. His descendants live near Waterford, Erie county, Pennsylvania.

James McClenachan, (in June.) Widow, Sarah; daughters, Margaret, Elizabeth; sons, Robert, David, and Andrew.

1785.

LEWISBURG LAID OUT BY LUDWIG DERR—BOUNDS OF—FALL ELECTION—WASHINGTON TOWNSHIP ERECTED—WIDOW SMITH'S PETITION—MILITIA OFFICERS.

ICE PRESIDENT, Charles Biddle. William Montgomery, Presiding Justice. Justices, 24th January, Simon Snyder, William Irwin; Colonel John Kelly, in August, and William Wilson. Sheriff, Thomas Grant, elected in October. Walter Clark, John Clarke, and William Gray, all of Buffalo, County Commissioners.

Representatives declared elected: Frederick Antes, Samuel Dale, and William Maclay, over Daniel Montgomery, John Weitzel, and Anthony Selin. General Potter, William Maclay, William Montgomery, junior, William Gray, and Joseph J. Wallis, Deputy Surveyors in the "old purchase." Lawyers admitted: John W. Kittera, John Clark, and John Reily, all officers of the war of the Revolution. Vannost, suspended at February term, for treating the justices with contempt, re-admitted at May term.

Of Buffalo officers: Constable, John Thompson; quota of State tax, £194; county, £45.

Among the Buffalo taxables were: Armstrong, William, tan-yard;

Baldy, Christopher; Barber, Robert, Esquire, who moved from near Wrightsville; Billmyer, Andrew; Brown, John; Burd, David, who lived where Sherry now lives, in the same township; Christ, Adam; Colpetzer, Adam, who lived where Jacob Engle now lives, in Limestone; Douglass, William; Evans, Daniel; Everett, Abel; Giles, Isaac; Haughawaut, Leffard; Huston, Robert; Jenkins, Morgan; Knox, George, tan-yard; Laughlin, Adam; Mucklehenny, John; Voneida, Philip, who purchased of John Crider part of the Captain Kern's tract, (late Peter Voneida place.)

Single Men in Buffalo Township, in 1785—Allison, Archibald; Bann, Lewis; Beatty, David; Black, William; Black, Thomas; Books, George; Clark, John; Cosaith, George; Cough, Adam; Cox, Tunis; Dale Henry; Dale, Christian; Derr, George; Dreisbach, Martin; Goodman, John; Gilkeson, a tailor; Iddings, William; Ingram, John; Jenkins, Morgan; Katherman, George; Leonard, Peter; Lewis, Paschall; Lowdon, Richard; McGahey, Neal; McGrady, Captain Samuel; Mook, John; Rearick, John; Reese, John; Rees, Daniel; Scott, William; Shively, Henry; Stewart, Archibald; Taylor, Christopher; Templeton, David; Thompson, John; Vanvalzen, Levi; Waggoner, Christopher; Wilson, Samuel; Youngman, George. Joseph Green, John Aurand, and Thomas Forster, assessors; which list they returned the 4th of January, 1786.

Among the Residents in White Deer were—Allen, Robert; Bear, John; Coulter, Nathaniel; Eaker, Doctor Joseph; Lacock, John; Leckey, John; McAllister, Archibald; McGinnes, James; McCorley, Robert, taxed with negro girl; Marshall, Widow; Potter, General James, negro and one servant; Vandyke, John, junior, (Widow Smith, grist-mill.) In 1785, William Blythe's name disappears from the assessment list, and the two tracts, taken up in his daughters' names, are taxed to his sons-in-law, Captain Charles Gillespie and Doctor Eakers. Daniel Lewis' name disappears, and Paschall Lewis appears in its place. His wife, who was Margaret Paschall, was a relative of Thomas Paschall, a hatter, of Philadelphia, who owned a great amount of wild lands, was married three times; first to a man named Watson, by whom she had Jesse, James, (who built Seebold's mill,) and John Watson, all settlers in the Valley. Second, to Mathers, by whom she had Samuel Mathers and Thomas, also early settlers; and third to Daniel Lewis, father of Paschall. One of the

Mathers once went to Philadelphia to get his share of the fortune. He got as his share—a lot of hats—enough to hat the whole Valley, nearly.

Among the Penn's Taxables were—Arbogast, John ; Dreis, Jacob ; Herrold, Simon, ferry and grist-mill; Miller, Dewalt, saw-mill; Pontius, John ; Pontius, Peter ; Schoolmaster, Abel ; Shipton, Thomas ; Shisley, Jacob, Sinclair, Duncan ; Smith, David ; Selin & Snyder, store, negro slave, and forty acres of land ; Speakman, James ; Stoll, Mathias ; Swineford, John ; Vanhorn, Daniel ; Weiand, Jacob ; Witmer, Peter, with ferry.

In March, 1785, Ludwig Derr laid out the town of Lewisburg. Samuel Weiser, of Mahanoy township, was the surveyor, and for his services received lot No. 5, on which is now erected the store of Walls, Smith & Co., 1870. His first donation of lots was for religious purposes. 26th March, he, with Catherine, his wife, conveyed lots Nos. 42, 44, and 46 to Walter Clark, William Gray, and William Wilson, in trust for the Presbyterian congregation at or near Lewisburg, for a meeting-house and burying-ground.

William Maclay made the survey of the tract the town stands on the 28th of February, 1769. Ludwig Derr lived upon it as early as 1770. It was patented on the 11th of August, 1772, to Reverend Richard Peters, who conveyed, on the 17th of September, 1773, to Ludwig Derr, by the following description, "containing three hundred and twenty acres, situated at the mouth of Spring run, below and adjoining the mouth of Buffalo creek." Weiser's survey was as follows:

The southern boundary commenced at a post at the river, at the the corner of the tract on which the mill is erected ; thence along the land of the said Derr, S. $80\frac{1}{2}°$ W. 121 perches $2\frac{1}{2}$ feet, to a stone ; thence N. about $10\frac{1}{2}°$ W. 164 perches, to a stone ; thence N. about $80\frac{1}{2}°$ E. about 139 perches $2\frac{1}{2}$ feet, to a post or stake, by the north-west side of Buffalo creek ; thence down the creek to its mouth, and thence down the river to the place of beginning, and contained about one hundred and twenty-eight acres, which was divided into three hundred and fifty-five lots.

By the act of the 31st of March, 1812, which incorporated " the president and directors of the streets, lanes, and alleys of the town of Lewisburg," the charter bounds commenced at the south side

of the mouth of Lyman's (formerly called Derr's) run, and ran
thence up the south side of the run, including the said run in its
meanders, to the line of George Derr's land; thence along the same
to the fording of Buffalo creek; thence down the south side thereof
to the river, and down the river to the place of beginning. And by
the act of the 21st of March, 1822, incorporating "the borough
of Lewisburg," the bounds were still further increased southerly, as
they commenced at the river, at a corner of Jacob Zentmeyer and
Margaret Spidler's land, and ran along the same N. 52° W. 62
perches, to a pine; thence, the same course, by land then of William Shaw, James Bennet, James Geddes, George Berryman, and
William Hayes, 236 perches, to a pine on land of George Derr.
From this pine the line ran N. 2° W. 208 perches, to the creek;
thence down the creek and river to the beginning.

Ludwig Derr made a lottery the same year, and disposed of some
of the lots in this way, among the rest, lot No. 21, corner Fourth
and Market, on which (1877) Doctor Howard Wilson is now residing, was drawn by John Brown, and for which he paid three pounds,
as appears by the deposition of John Hennig, taken before Colonel
John Kelly, on the 2d of May, 1791.

The very first lot sold was No. 351, corner of Water and St.
Lewis, to William Wilson, 26th March.

The first residents of Lewisburg were Bolinger, John; Conser,
Henry, (Reverend S. L. M. Conser is a grandson;) Dering, Godfrey, (removed to Selinsgrove; one of his descendants was postmaster there;) Evans, Joseph, cabinet-maker, (descendants still in
Lewisburg;) Leonard, Peter, (descendants still in Lewisburg;)
Long, Edward; Smith, Nicholas; Welker, Jacob, tailor, (moved to
Mifflinburg, and died there.) [See 1788, for a description of Lewisburg at that time.] In September, Ludwig Derr went to Philadelphia to sell lots. The date of his death there is not known. The
last deed he signed is dated October 18. December 9, George Derr,
Walter Clark, and John Weitzel, administered upon his estate. He
left a widow, Catherine, who survived him a very short time, and
only one heir, George Derr. September 13, Northumberland county
divided into four election districts, Buffalo, White Deer, and Potter in
the third, and held their elections at Fought's Mill, (near Mifflinburg.)
August sessions, Washington township, now partly in Lycoming,

erected, the division line commencing a short distance above Widow Smith's mills, thence west, along the south side of White Deer creek, to where Spruce run commences. It was a mere sub-division of White Deer township, calling the northern division Washington. The following is a list of the inhabitants of Washington, as thus erected:

Bennett, Ephraim; Bennett, Justice; Bennett, Thaddeus; Bennett, Abraham; Bennett, William; Bently, Green; Brown, Charles; Brown, Judson; Brown, William; Caldwell, William; Creal, Michael; Coats, widow; Eason, Robert; Emmons, John; Emmons, Jacob; Emmons, Jacob, (single;) Gray, William, junior; Green, Ebenezer; Harley, John; Hendrick, Nathan; Hickendoll, Herman; Hood, Moses; Huling, Marcus; Hunter, widow; Landon, Nathaniel; Layn, Abraham; Layn, Isaac; Low, Cornelius, senior and junior; McCormick, Seth; McCormick, Thomas; Mackey, William; Mitchell, John; Ramsey, John; Reynolds, Joseph; Shaffer, Nicholas; Stephen, Adam; Stricker, John; Sunderland, Daniel; Tenbrooke, John; Towsend, Gradius; Towsend, Gamaliel; Weeks, Jesse. Assessors: William Gray, Joseph Allen, and Thomas McCormick.

The fall election for members of the House was contested. Paul Baldy, John Macpherson, and Samuel Quinn, among others, went to Philadelphia as witnesses. The officer reported Richard Sherer, a witness, absent, and John Gray, another, gone to Fort Pitt. It appears, by the report of the committee, that Frederick Antes had 414 votes, Daniel Montgomery 410, Samuel Dale 414, William Maclay 407, John Weitzel 396, Anthony Selin 297. Daniel Montgomery was ousted, and William Maclay put in, upon a tie vote, the Speaker deciding. Twenty-five members signed a protest against these proceedings, which seem to have been dictated by party rancor, for the protestants say the reason of the contest was, that in one district the names of the electors on the poll-list were ten short of the number of tickets received by the inspectors, and that the testimony accounted for this defect. They contended that the whole election should have been set aside; that the vote of the House was destructive to the rights of the people, and an unwarrantable usurpation, of a very dangerous character.

In a petition to the Assembly of this year by Catherine Smith, indorsed, read December 8, 1785, she sets forth "that she was left a widow, with ten children, with no estate to support this family, except a location for three hundred acres of land, including the mouth of White Deer creek, whereon is a good mill-seat; and a grist and saw-mill being much wanted in this new country, at that time, she *wast* often solicited to erect said mills. At length, in 1774, she borrowed money, and in June, 1775, ·completed the mills, which were of great advantage to the country, and the following summer built a boring-mill, where a great number of gun-barrels were bored for the continent, and a hemp-mill. The Indian war soon after coming on, (one of her sons, her greatest help, went into the army, and, it is believed, was killed, as he never returned,) the said mills soon became a frontier, and in July, 1779, the Indians burned the whole works. She returned to the ruins in 1783, and was again solicited to re-build the grist and saw-mills, which she has, with much difficulty, accomplished, and now ejectments are brought against her by Messrs. Claypool and Morris, and she, being now reduced to such low circumstances as renders her unable to support actions at law, and, therefore, prays relief," &c. The facts set forth in this memorial are certified to by William Blythe, Charles Gillespie, Colonel John Kelly, James Potter, the younger, and many other citizens of Northumberland county.

The Legislature, of course, could grant no relief, under the circumstances, and the petition was dismissed. How long the litigation went on I am unable to determine; but in 1801, Seth Iredell took possession of the premises as tenant of Claypoole and Morris. She is said to have walked to Philadelphia and back thirteen times on this business. Her house was where Doctor Danousky now (1874) lives, on the Henry High place, part of the old stone house being still used as a kitchen. She was buried in the old settlers' grave-yard, which was at the corner of the Dan Caldwell barn. Her bones were disturbed in Mr. Caldwell's time, in erecting a sheep-pen, and were identified by old Mr. Huff, by her peculiar projecting teeth. Some years since, an old man came to the place and desired to look about the old dwelling. He spent several hours about the place. When leaving, said he had come in from Ohio to see it; that he was a son of Catherine Smith, and that if justice had been done her, they would still own the place. Rolly McCorley, who recollects the mill last built by her, said it was a small, round log mill.

Field Officers Elected in April.

First Battalion—Peter Hosterman, lieutenant colonel; Christopher Gettig, major.

Fifth Battalion—John Kelly, lieutenant colonel; Thomas Forster, major.

Company Officers of the Fifth.

Captains—Michael Andrews, William Clark, John Thompson, Joseph Poak, Joseph Green, Samuel McGrady, James Potter, junior, John Macpherson.

Lieutenants—Adam Harper, Joseph Eaker, James Irwin, Samuel Iddings, Henry Pontius, Jacob Dreisbach, John Brown, M. Wildgoose.

Ensigns—Joseph Price, George Clark, George Books, James Moore, J. Hunter, James Templeton.

1786.

SLAVES IN THE VALLEY—PICKERING'S VISIT AT GENERAL POTTER'S—BUFFALO VALLEY SOLDIERS AT SARATOGA—FIRST FULLING-MILL ERECTED.

RESIDENT of the State, Benjamin Franklin. Member of Council, William Maclay. Members of Assembly, Frederick Antes and Samuel Dale. Lawyers admitted: on examination, John Andre Hanna and Charles Smith; on motion, John Joseph Henry and Jacob Hubley.

Buffalo, Officers—Collector, George May; Constable, John Crider; Supervisors, George Rote and Leonard Welker; Overseers, John Aurand and Samuel Mathers.

Among the taxables—Carney, Anthony; Moore, James, tailor;

Ohrendorf, Henry; Piper, Henry; Potts, David; Stephens, William; Straub, Jacob; Swartzcope, Anthony; Pool, William, ferry at Macpherson's. Single Men: Getz, Adam; Grove, Philip; Holmes, Jonathan.

In Lewisburg, additional residents—Armor, Thomas; Hammersly, John; Roan, Flavel; Snodgrass, David; Steele, Alexander; Troxel, George; Williams, William.

White Deer—Bear, Isaac; Coburn, John; High, Rudolph; Sherer, Thomas; Sims, William.

Penn's—Auple, Jonas; Bolender, Adam, junior; Bossler, George; Businger, Conrad; Dauberman, Christian; Devore, Abram; Garmon, John; Gemberling, Jacob; Giltner, Jacob; Gross, Henry; Gruber, Christian; Mertz, Philip; Nerhood, Henry; Winkelpleck, Henry.

In the Valley, Eli Holman, Samuel Hunter, and John Linn are each taxed with female slaves. From the bill of sale, it appears John Linn purchased his slave, called "Judy," of John McBeth, of Chester county, on the 10th of April, 1786. After residing fifty-eight years in the Valley, she removed with John Linn's (second) family to Knox county, Ohio, and died near Mount Vernon, in that county, November 4, 1855, upward of one hundred years old.

In March, George Derr and his mother sold George Langs the ground between the railroad bridge and the site of the old wagon bridge. It is not included in the town plan of Lewisburg, or laid out in lots by number. At the same time, William Williams bought No. 343, in Lewisburg, built a stone house, still standing, (Martin Hahn's,) and a frame store-room, adjoining it on the south, and opened the first regular store in the town.

At May sessions, C. Van Gundy was bound over for forcible entry, &c., renewing the old controversy with George Derr, Ludwig's son.

In the life of Colonel T. Pickering, volume 2, page 251, is a letter from him, dated August 12, 1786, "at Philip Francis', about a mile above the mouth of Muncy creek, and three miles below Mr. Wallis'," in which he states Mr. Wallis was to go with him to make surveys in Wyoming. "As Mr. Wallis was not ready, we spent two nights and one day at General Potter's, where we were kindly entertained." On the 15th he adds: "We were to set off for Tioga, but my horse has wounded himself. I am going down to General Potter's to borrow or purchase another." This proves clearly that General Potter then resided on the Ard farm, just above New Columbia. At August sessions, Andrew Billmyer's tavern was licensed. He kept two miles up the Valley, where his grandson, John Lesher, now lives. Magdalena Pohlhemus, an indentured servant to E. Younkman, presented a petition to court to be allowed her freedom dues; and after giving due notice, the court ordered Mr. Younkman to pay her five dollars down, and three dollars next May, as freedom dues for seven year's service.

23d September, an orphans' court was held at the house of Flavel Roan, (at the mouth of Buffalo creek,) before William Irwin and John Kelly, justices, when the applications of George Martin and Samuel McClurgan for pensions were considered. They belonged to Colonel Cooke's twelfth regiment, but were drafted into Colonel Daniel Morgan's riflemen, sent to resist Burgoyne. They were wounded at Saratoga, in October, 1777.

In September, George Derr sold Flavel Roan and Sankey Dixon the ground between St. John's street and St. Anthony's, along the creek. Sankey and Ann, his wife, sold out to Roan, and went on West. Sankey had been sergeant and ensign all through the war, in sixth Pennsylvania regiment. He died at Nashville, Tennessee, in 1814. Roan then kept the ferry, two years before it had been leased to Henry Conser, who sold to Stephen Duchman, the latter to Roan. Christopher Weiser built the first fulling-mill in the Valley, on Turtle creek, on what is now Peter Wolfe's place, and James Watson built the first grist-mill, erected at Seebold's, above New Berlin.

Deaths.

Catharine, widow of Ludwig Derr.

Captain John Forster, often mentioned in Brady's adventures. His old log house stood to the left of the road to Hoffa's mills, beyond Rishel's stone house. He left a widow, Jane. First son, James, afterwards married to a daughter of William Clark, to whom he willed the old place. James moved to Ohio. His son John, who lived in Brush valley, was the father of Mrs. William C. Duncan, of Lewisburg. Second son, William, a bachelor, said to be the first white child born in the Valley. Third, John Forster, so long a partner of James Duncan, at Aaronsburg. (Descendants: Sarah, married to William Vanvalzah; Emeline, to S. S. Barber; Margaret, to Doctor Charles Wilson; Jane, to R. B. Barber, Esquire.) Fourth, daughters: Agnes, Margaret, and Dorcas.

James Jenkins, aged eighty-two, left widow, Phoebe, and sons William and James.

Cornelius Dimpsey, left widow, and children, Mary, James, and Jonathan. Captain James Thompson bought the place of his widow, in 1796, late Jacob Zeibach's, in Kelly.

Lietenant Colonel Neigal Gray, twelfth Pennsylvania, of White Deer. Children: John; Elizabeth, married John Auld; Isabella, and Robert.

1787.

FAMILIES IN WHITE DEER HOLE VALLEY—ANDREW GREGG'S WEDDING—CALL TO REVEREND HUGH MORRISON—MEMBERS OF HIS CONGREGATION.

MEMBERS of Assembly: Samuel Maclay and John White. Sheriff, Thomas Grant. County Commissioners, John Lytle, Walter Clark, and William Gray.

Buffalo township: Constable, John Clark; Overseers, David Watson and Michael Vought; Supervisors, Thomas Forster and Andrew Billmyer; Assessor, William Irwin, Esquire; Assistants, William Moore and Flavel Roan; Collector, John Sierer.

Among residents—Anderson, William; Barber, Thomas; Barber, Samuel; Baum, Charles; Carothers, William; Dixon, Sankey; Getz, Adam; Irwin, Matthew; Johnson, Christopher; Nevius, Christian; Pickle, Jacob; Wales, Henry.

White Deer, additional residents—Falls, James; Farley, Caleb; Farley, John; Laird, Matthew; Marshall, Richard.

Washington—Grub, Peter; Hagerman, James; Lawson, John; Sips, Joseph; Swan, Samuel.

Penn's, among residents, &c.—Ball, George; Bickle, Simon, distillery; Biegh, Frederick; Burkert, John; Bright, Michael; Ditzler,

John; Grum, Jacob; Herrold, Simon, hemp-mill; Hertz, John; Kremer, Daniel; Lutz, John; Manning, Nathan; Miller, Widow, saw-mill; Motz, John, oil-mill; Mumma, John; Reedy, Peter; Ruch, John; Snyder, John; Stump, William, with distillery; Swineford, Albright, taxed with a slave; Zieber, Adam.

Isle of Que: Weaver, Michael, junior; Wayland, George.

Sketches by John F. Wolfinger, Esquire.

In 1787, White Deer Hole valley had fourteen families of white settlers, whose names and places of residence were as follows:

1. Rachel Weeks, an old English widow woman, occupied a small log hut or cabin, near the mouth of White Deer Hole creek, between the bank of the river and where the fine brick mansion of John S. Smith now stands. Rachel had six children, named Jeth, Job, Hanna, Jemima, Naomi, and Annie.

2. Thomas Weisner, occupied a cabin on the river bank, near where the bridge at Uniontown now crosses the river Susquehanna, about half a mile north of Rachel Weeks'. Thomas, who had a wife and six or seven children, afterwards moved away to parts unknown.

3. John Rumsey, occupied a cabin on the river bank, north of Wiesner's, and had a wife and nine children, and a small farm here. He is supposed to have come here from the State of New York, and soon after returned to that State. He talked English.

4. George Gray, occupied a cabin on the river bank, about three quarters of a mile north of Rumsey's, and had a wife and three children. He talked English, and worked at little jobs around among his neighbors, but moved away about two years afterward to parts unknown.

5. Marcus Huling, occupied a cabin on the river bank, about three hundred yards north of Gray's, and had a wife and five children. He talked English, and worked at his trade, being a blacksmith. He afterwards moved higher up, or west, into the Valley, and from thence to Newberry, and from thence again to Youngmanstown, (Mifflinburg,) and finally into York State. He is supposed to have been a cousin of the Marcus Huling, also a blacksmith, who lived at the town of Milton at that day.

6. Cornelius Vanfleet, a New Jerseyman, occupied a cabin that

stood on the White Deer Hole creek, a little west of the widow Weeks'. He acted as a justice of the peace for many years, and died here on the 7th of December, 1841, in the eighty-fifth year of his age. His remains lie buried in the Presbyterian grave-yard.

7. Peter Dougherty, an Irishman, occupied a cabin on the White Deer Hole creek, about a mile and a quarter above the mouth of the creek. He had a wife and children, and afterwards moved farther west into the Valley, and finally out to the State of Ohio.

8. Eleanor Brown, commonly called "Nellie Brown." She was the widow of Matthew Brown, already noticed, and occupied a cabin on the White Deer Hole creek, about two and a half miles west of its mouth. She died at her son's, William Brown's, cabin, that stood about half a mile west of her own cabin, on the 9th of August, 1814, and her descendants are still found in this Valley and its adjacent parts.

9. Samuel Swan, occupied a cabin that stood about two hundred and thirteen yards due west of Eleanor Brown's. Swan talked English, had a wife and children, and afterwards moved away to parts unknown.

10. Seth McCormick, an Irishman, occupied a cabin on South creek, a branch of White Deer Hole creek, about a mile west of Swan's cabin. Seth died here on the 17th of January, 1835, in the seventy-ninth year of his age. His remains lie buried in the old Presbyterian, (now Lutheran,) grave-yard, at the "stone church," on the south-west side of Penny Hill. He left a wife and nine children, and his descendants are still living here, and occupy a part of their great ancestor's estate.

11. Thomas McCormick, an Irishman, and a brother of Seth's, occupied a cabin on South creek, about half a mile from Seth's. He seems to have acted as a justice of the peace for some years. He died on the 6th of October, 1826, aged seventy-two years, and his remains also lie buried in the old grave-yard, near the above "stone church."

12. Jesse Weeks, a son of the widow Weeks, already noticed, occupied a cabin that stood on the north side of "Spring creek," the northern branch of White Deer Hole creek, and about four miles west of its junction with "South creek." Jesse Weeks died here, but his age and place of burial are unknown.

13. Daniel Sunderland, an Englishman, occupied a cabin that stood about a mile further up on Spring creek, and he died there.

14. John Farley, a New Jerseyman, came here in 1787, from the State of New Jersey, with a wife and seven children, named Jacob, Barbara, Minard, John, David, Naomi, and Fanny. He immediately built himself a log cabin, and occupied it, on White Deer Hole creek, about two hundred feet from where the dwelling house of the late Charles Gudykunst now stands, and being an active and enterprising man, he soon afterwards built himself a log grist-mill here, the *first* one in the Valley, as already stated.

I have obtained all of the above facts relative to these fourteen families, (excepting what relates to their times of death and places of burial,) from Mr. John Farley, a son of the above John Farley, and who is still living in our Valley, a venerable white haired old gentleman, in the eighty-eighth year of his age, whose house I visited for that purpose on Tuesday, the 17th of July, 1870.

He says: "I was born in Tewksbury township, Hunterdon county, State of New Jersey, on the 9th of July, 1783, and came here into this Valley with my father, John Farley, in 1787, when I was four years old. And I have resided here ever since, for the long space of eighty-three years, and knew and remember the names of all the white settlers that lived in this Valley in the spring of 1787, when I came here, and where their log huts or cabins stood, and how their cabins were made. My father built one of the same kind of cabins here in 1787, and four or five years afterwards he also built a small log grist-mill here, with but one pair of grinding stones in it; the first grist-mill erected in this Valley. In the year 1800, my father, after living here thirteen years, moved back to the State of New Jersey. But he died here in this Valley in June, 1822, while he was up here on a visit to me and my family. He was upwards of seventy years of age when he died, and my brothers and sisters are all dead, and I am now the only one left of all my father's family. Very great changes have taken place in the appearance of this Valley, its farms, houses, barns, &c., since I came here; changes far greater than any I ever expected to see here, and all for the better."

John Swineford opened the first hotel at Middleburg, Snyder county. 10th June, George Derr sells George Knox as much water as will run out of an inch hole at the bottom of the race, two poles from Derr's house.

29th January, Andrew Gregg was married by the Reverend John Hoge to Martha Potter, daughter of General James Potter, at the latter's residence, the first farm above Jacob McCorley's, Esquire. Mr. Gregg rode up from Carlisle on horseback, and brought Mr. Hoge with him. There were then no Presbyterian clergymen settled in this part of the country, and some sixteen or seventeen couples took advantage of Mr. Hoge's presence, hurried up their matches, as Mr. Hoge had to return to Carlisle within a limited time.

Andrew Gregg moved to Oldtown, now Lewistown, where his first daughter, Mary, afterward Mrs. McLanahan, of Greencastle, was born, November 3, 1788. In 1789 Mr. Gregg moved to Penn's valley, within two miles of Old Fort. In 1790 he was elected member of Congress, and by seven successive elections for several districts, as they were arranged from time to time, including one by a general vote over the whole State, was continued a member of that body for sixteen successive years, and during the session of 1806–1807 was elected a member of the Senate of the United States. In December, 1820, Governor Hiester appointed him Secretary of the Commonwealth. He died in Bellefonte, on the 20th of May, 1835, aged eighty years. He had removed there some years previous, for the purpose of educating his children. His wife died in 1815. He was born on the Conodoguinet creek, near Carlisle, July 10, 1755, and received a classical education; was tutor for some years in the University of Pennsylvania, and first settled at Middletown, Pennsylvania, where he kept store. He had a fine library, containing all the Greek and Latin classics, most of which are still in the possession of his daughter, Mrs. Margery Tucker, of Lewisburg. His grandchildren, Governor A. G. Curtin, General D. M. Gregg, and General John I. Gregg, have flung far forward into the future the light of their family fame.

In May, 1787, a call was given to the Reverend Hugh Morrison,[1] by the Buffalo Cross-Roads congregation, in connection with the con-

---

[1] The Reverend Hugh Morrison, the first regular pastor of the Presbyterian Church in this Valley, came from Ireland, Presbytery of Root, in 1786. Among the records of the Synod, under date May 18, 1786, "the Presbytery of Donegal reported that they had, since our last meeting, admitted Hugh Morrison, a licensed candidate from the Presbytery of Root, in Ireland," &c.

gregations of Northumberland and Sunbury, and among the records of the Synod, May 22, 1788, is the following: Carlisle Presbytery reports that it has, since our last meeting, ordained to the work of the Gospel ministry Mr. Samuel W. Wilson, in the pastoral charge of "Big Spring" congregation, and Mr. Hugh Morrison, in the pastoral charge of the Sunbury, Northumberland and Buffalo Valley congregations. The following is a copy of the call, for which, with other material in reference to this church, I am indebted to Isaac Grier, D. D., of Mifflinburg:

"Mr. HUGH MORRISON, *Preacher of the Gospel:*

"SIR : We, the subscribers, members of the united congregations of Buffalo, Sunbury, and Northumberland, *having never in these places had the stated administration of the Gospel Ordinances,* yet highly prizing the same, and having a view to the advancement of the Kingdom of Christ, and the spiritual edification of ourselves and families, have set ourselves to obtain that blessing among us. And, therefore, as we have had the opportunity of some of your labors in these places, and are satisfied with your soundness, piety, and ministerial ability to break unto us the bread of life, we do most honestly and sincerely, in the name of the Great Shepherd of the flock, Jesus Christ, call and invite you to come and take the pastoral charge and oversight of us in the Lord. And for your encouragement, we do promise, if God shall dispose your heart to embrace this our call, that we will pay a dutiful attention to the word and ordinances of God by you administered ; that we will be subject to your administrations and reproofs, should our falls and miscarriages expose us thereto ; and will submit to the discipline of the Church, exercised by you agreeably to the word of God. And, also, that we will treat your person with friendship and respect, and behave in all things towards you as becomes a christian society to behave towards their pastor, who labors among them in word and doctrine. Further, we are persuaded that those who serve at the altar, should live by the altar. We do promise, in order that you may be as much as possible freed from worldly incumbrances, to provide for you comfortable and honorable maintenance, in the manner as set forth in our subscription papers attending this our call, during your continuance with us as our regular pastor. In witness of our hearty desire to have you settle among us, we hereunto set our names this 31st day of May, 1787."

Signed by seventeen from Northumberland, eight from Sunbury, and forty-eight from Buffalo. On it is the following deputation:

"We, the undersigned, do nominate, appoint, and intrust the Reverend Mr. Wilson with the annexed call for the Reverend Mr. Morrison, to be by him presented to the moderator of the Carlisle Presbytery, for the purpose mentioned. Signed: William Gray and Abram Scott, for Sunbury; William Cooke and James Hepburn, for Northumberland; and William Clark, for Buffalo."

In October, Reverend Hugh Morrison became pastor of the Buffalo Cross-Roads Presbyterian church. The congregation engaged to pay him £75 per year. From a list of contributing members found in the treasurer's book, I gather the following names: Anderson, John; Allen, Joseph; Baldy, Christopher; Barrett, James; Black, Thomas; ¹Boyd, James; ¹Brady, John; ¹Buchanan, James; ¹Charters, William; Clarke, Captain John; Clark, Robert; ¹Clark, Walter; ¹Clark, William; Cox, Samuel; Cox, Tunis; Davis, David; ¹Davis, John; Derr, George; ¹Douglass, William; Dugan, William; Elder, Thomas; Evans, Joseph; ¹Farley, John, Fleming, William; ¹Forster, Andrew; ¹Forster, James; ¹Fruit, Robert; Graham, Edward; ¹Gray, John; Gray, Captain William; Green, Joseph; Grogan, Charles; Hammersly, George; ¹Holmes, Jonathan; Hudson, Joseph; Huntsman, James; Hutchinson, Thomas; Irvine, William; Irvine, Matthew; ¹Irwin, William, Esquire; Johnston, Christopher; Kennedy, Alexander; ¹Kelly, Colonel John; Knox, George; Laird, Matthew; Lewis, Paschall; Links, George; ¹Linn, John; Lowdon, Captain John; McClenachan, William and Andrew; McDougal, William; McGrady, Alexander; Maclay, Samuel; Magee, James; Marshall, William; ¹Miller, Benjamin; Milligan, John; Montgomery, Samuel; Moore, George; Nichols, William; Poak, Charles; ¹Poak, Joseph; ¹Poak, Thomas; Poak, Widow; Porter, Samuel; ¹Ray, John; Rees, Daniel; Reznor, John; Roan, Flavel; Rodman, Widow; Rorison, Alexander; Scroggs, Allen; Sherer, Richard and Joseph; Sims, William; Snodgrass, David; Steele, Alexander; ¹Thompson, Captain James; ¹Thompson, John; Vanvolsan, Levi; ¹Watson, David; Williams, William; and Wilson, William.

Shortly after Mr. Morrison's arrival, an election for elders resulted in the choice of Walter Clark, John Linn, William Irwin, David Watson, John Reznor, and Joseph Allen. The subscriptions by the more wealthy attendants upon service were Andrew Forster, £2; Samuel Maclay, John Lowdon, and William Irwin, each, £1 10s.; William Irvine £1 6s.; James Forster £1 2s.

Those marked (¹) were signers of Mr. Morrison's call, and as such, in 1803, were sued for back stipends. The principal and interest and costs, when they made the last payment, in December, 1810, was $1,179 30.

September 17, the Constitution of United States was adopted, and on December 12, the State Convention ratified it. The delegates to the latter from Northumberland county were Colonel William Wilson and his partner, John Boyd. They then kept store in the town of Northumberland. In 1791, Colonel Wilson built the Chillisquaque mills, at the mouth of that creek, and moved to that place.

At November sessions, the road commencing at the head of Penn's valley; thence through Aaronsburg to the road at Richard Lowdon's barn; thence down the same to John Davidson's ferry, was laid out.

Deaths.

Alexander Beatty, of New Berlin. Children: Jane, Agnes, Hugh, John, Hannah, Sarah, James, and Alexander. The deceased carried on the first tannery in the Valley, on site of present town of New Berlin.

Matthew Young, of Buffalo. Children: Margaret, (see her capture, related 1781,) still living, in 1787, John, Sarah, and Agnes. One of his daughters married Robert Dixon. Sarah was residing in Westmoreland county, in March, 1796, when she gave Colonel Kelly and Captain Thompson a letter of attorney to draw her share under her father's will.

John Snyder, original owner of Selinsgrove, brother of Simon, subsequently Governor.

John McClung, of Buffalo. Children: John, James, Matthew, Charles, Rebecca, Esther, and Elizabeth.

Sebastian Kerstetter, of Beaver. Children: Martin, Lenhart, Peter, Sebastian, Catharine, and Margaret.

James Thom, of Buffalo.

1788.

Dreisbach Church—Roads—Houses in Lewisburg—Matthew Laird's Family.

EMBER of Council, William Maclay. Members of Assembly, Samuel Maclay and John White. County Commissioners, William Gray, Peter Hosterman, and John Lytle. Treasurer, John Buyers.

By act of 26th of September, the Buffalo election place was changed from Fought's to Andrew Billmyer's tavern, on the road mentioned below.

In August, Christian Van Gundy, William Irvine, John Thompson, David Watson, and Andrew Billmyer reported that they had laid out the road, beginning at Derrstown, on the West Branch; thence to the meeting-house, in Buffalo; thence to Thompson's mill, on Buffalo creek; thence to the east side of George Rote's lane, where it intersects the road leading from Davidson's ferry to the narrows; distance, nine and a half miles. (Thompson's mill became Rockey's in 1789.) This is the road leading past the late Francis Wilson's, (by old Billmyer place,) to Mifflinburg.

In November, John Clarke, John Lowdon, and Philip Voneida reported a road from Michael Shirtz's, at the narrows of Penn's creek, past Peter Kester's, on the Cole place, to a pine tree at the end of Colonel Clarke's lane. This is still the main road down Penn's creek, through Laurelton, Hartleton, and then south of the turnpike to Mifflinburg.

Additional Residents of Buffalo—Betz, Abraham; Bogenreif, Christopher; Caldwell, Samuel; Dobbins, Robert; Miller, Christian; Sims, William, weaver, at Alexander McGrady's; Vanvalzah, Doctor Robert; Yentzer, Christian.

Lewisburg—Eaton, John; Grove, Wendell; Kendig, Jacob, (Isle of Que;) McCracken, Widow; Scroggs, Allen; Wise, Frederick.

Improvements in White Deer—John Bear's saw-mill.

Among Residents—Adams, Joseph; Bennage, Samuel; Denning, Samuel; Derr, Frederick; Henning, Philip, distillery; Hoover, John; Linn, William, on Joseph Brundage's place; McLanahan, Andrew; Perry, Thomas.

Single Men, taxed 10s. *each*—Black, Timothy; Hammersly, James; Iddings, Isaac; Iddings Henry; Laird, Moses; Scott, Thomas; Smith, Ludwig.

Penn's Township—Bickle, Tobias, grist-mill; Brownlee, William; Bowerman, Daniel; Buchtell, John; Carstetter, Bostian; Eberhart, Philip; Howell, Adam; Kay, Frederick; Koons, John; Meiser, Henry, saw-mill; Miller, Widow, saw-mill; Miller, Benjamin; Notestone, John; Neiman, Weiand; Pyle, George, distillery and saw-mill; Quinn, William; Quinn, Thomas; Rush, Daniel; Shipton, Thomas, distillery; Shock, Jacob, grist and saw-mill; Snyder, S.; Spade, David; Spade, Jacob; Swineford, George.

The following memorandum, relative to the Dreisbach church, is derived from the late John Schrack, Esquire:

"In this year the German Reformed and Lutheran congregations united in building a log church, where the Dreisbach Church now stands. John Pontius had set apart some land, on the south end of the Bucher tract, for a church and burying-ground, (the family burying-ground is still there,) but Martin Dreisbach, senior, offering to donate seven and a half acres for that purpose, it was judged best to accept that. On the part of the Reformed, John Aurand and Elias Younkman were trustees; Martin Dreisbach and Jacob Grozean were elders; Peter Frederick and Henry Dreisbach, deacons. On the Lutheran side, Herman J. Shellhart was pastor; Christian Storms and Adam Christ were trustees; Casper Bower and Henry Meizner, elders; Jacob Metzgar and John Sierer, deacons. The names of some of the members of the Reformed Church were: Aurand, George; Aurand, Henry; Barnhart, Matthias; Barnhard, Henry; Brown, John; Dreisbach, John; Dreisbach, Jacob; Frederick, George; Fisher, George;

Mook, Jacob; Michael Vought, and John Pontius. Of the Lutheran, John G. Buch, George Bower, John Hiltman, Stephen Duchman, Jacob Gebhart, John Meizner, Leonard Welker, Mathias Alsbaugh, Adam Kreichbaum, William Rockey, Peter Fisher, Leonard Groninger, George Smith, Christopher Wagner, Adam Meizner, George Buch, Christopher Bickel, Jacob Welker, Christopher Baldy, John Crider. In 1839 the log church was taken down, and a brick building erected. Among the pastors of this church were Dietrick Aurand, Gentzler, Pfriemer, Shellhart, Geisweit, William Ilgen, John C. Walter, and Herbst, but the dates of their service are unknown."

In November, William Gray, Esquire, deputy surveyor, made a re-survey of Lewisburg, and in his plan indicated the roads then existing, and the lots built upon, with their occupiers.

The road from Sunbury to Muncy is marked as along the bank, on the opposite side of the river, and Captain John Brady's house as immediately opposite Strohecker's landing. Thomas Rees is marked as the owner of the house at Strohecker's, and the road to Penn's valley, as running directly west from it. The road from Sunbury to Buffalo and Penn's valley is marked as intersecting the last mentioned road, some distance from the river, and crossing Limestone run, opposite Third street; then entering Fourth street, and running along it out to the creek, it crossed the creek at Colonel Slifer's upper farm, the site of the new iron bridge built there, then the site of High's saw-mill, the remains of which are yet visible, where it intersected a road leading up to Gundy's mill above, and thence up the Valley. From High's mill at the creek it ran over to William Gray's, (there was no road then crossing Buffalo creek at its mouth;) thence by Robert Fruit's, &c. There were no houses west of Fourth street, and the first one on it is where John Griffin built a fine house, (1871.) Alexander Steele had a house where John Beeber resided, and a tan-yard, on that square. Edward Long lived opposite, on the Charles Buyer lot, and next to him, north, was Wendell Grove. John Bolinger had a house on the alley behind William Nogel's present residence. John Hamersly lived on the corner of Third and St. George, where Reverend Job Harvey now lives. There was also a small log house, burned down some thirty-five years ago on the same lot.

On Second, George Troxell lived, and owned the adjoining lot.

Doctor Buyers built the present house, on the corner of St. Catherine's, where Troxell lived. There was a house also on Spyker's corner, opposite James S. Marsh's new residence. Jacob Welker lived on the site of Marsh's new house. David Snodgrass lived on the Chronicle lot, opposite where his widow afterwards kept a cake and beer saloon. Nicholas Smith occupied the only house on Market, now Jonathan Wolfe's lot, west of his residence. The two lots where the depot now stands are marked "Roman Chapel." On Front, Joseph Evans, cabinet-maker, had the only house, on the lot now owned by William Cameron, Esquire. Joseph Sherer lived on the corner of Water street, where Halfpenny's woolen store or warehouse now is.

William Williams had a store where Martin Hahn's stone house is now. Ellenckhuysen's ferry was opposite to it. Henry Conser, probably, lived where Spyker's heirs now live. He was the grandfather of Reverend S. L. M. Conser, so James Kelly tells me. Thomas Armor, probably, lived on the Griffin lot, and the only other inhabitant of Lewisburg, Flavel Roan, lived in Derr's tenant house. Where that was I do not know. Roan owned three lots, James Walls, John Nesbit, and Henry Frick's, lying close together, and had the ferry over Buffalo creek. George Derr, of course, lived at the mill. The old house stood in what is now the garden, just two rods north-east of the place where Hull's tannery water-pipe taps the race. George Knox, father of Mrs. William Armstrong, probably, made his tanyard this year, where E. J. Hull now has his. In July of 1787, George Derr conveyed to Knox, for tan-yard purposes, as much water as will run out of an inch hole, at the bottom of the race, two poles from Derr's house.

October 1, William Maclay and Robert Morris, first United States Senators from Pennsylvania, elected. A paper of the day says: "The landed and commercial interests of the State will be well represented."

The Congressmen were elected on a general ticket, and not from districts.

Matthew Laird, who came to the Valley this year, is the ancestor of a large generation. He came originally from Ireland, where his son James was born. He was a wagoner with General Braddock's army, and was in Colonel Dunbar's camp when the news came back of General Braddock's defeat, 9th July, 1755. [See his statement in the Colonial Records, volume 6, page 482.] He says, "a wounded officer was carried into camp on a sheet; then they beat to arms, on which the wagoners and many common soldiers took to flight, in spite of the sentries, who forced many to return, but many got away, among them, this examinant." His daughter, Isabella Black, was twelve years old when he came to White Deer. Matthew Laird died in August, 1821. His children were James, John, Isabella, married to James Black, Moses, (father of R. H. Laird, Esquire,) who died in Derry, in January, 1816, Margaret, married to John Blakeney, Matthew, who died in Tiffin, Ohio, Elizabeth, and Ann. Moses married Jane Hayes, and their son, Reverend Matthew, married a Miss Myers, and went out as missionary to Africa, dying there, May 4, 1834. Their other children were John, Mrs. McCalmont, Mrs. Joseph Milliken, of Clinton county, ———, married William Caldwell.

Deaths.

Leonard Groninger, leaving widow, Elizabeth. Children: Leonard, Daniel, Jacob, Susanna, Margaret, and Elizabeth.

Jacob Aurand.

John Rearick, senior. Children: Mary and John.

Margaret Green, wife of Joseph.

1789.

Boude Family—Residents of Beaver Township—First German Reformed Pastor—Manufactures, &c.—Deaths of Major Lawrence Keene and General James Potter.

RESIDENT of the State, Thomas Mifflin. William Wilson, member of the Supreme Executive Council. Samuel Maclay and John White, members of Assembly. William Montgomery, President Judge. Abraham Piatt, William Shaw, &c., Associates.

July 28th, Jasper Ewing, Esquire, appointed Prothonotary, *vice* Major Lawrence Keene, deceased. John Simpson, re-appointed Register and Recorder; Frederick Antes, Treasurer; Martin Withington, elected Sheriff. County Commissioners, John Lytle, Peter Hosterman, and William Hepburn. Commissioner's Clerk, H. Douty. Bernard Hubley, Lieutenant of the county.

On the 7th of January, the first election for presidential electors resulted in the choice of General Edward Hand, Colonel George Gibson, John Arndt, Colinson Reed, Lawrence Keene, James Wilson, James O'Hara, Colonel David Grier, Samuel Potts, and Alexander Graydon.

November 19th, Daniel Brodhead, Surveyor General, appointed the following deputy surveyors: Henry Vanderslice, for part of Berks; Joseph J. Wallis, for part of Northumberland; James Harris, for part of Mifflin; William Gray, part east of the Susquehanna.

Officers of Buffalo: Constable, C. Baldy; Overseers, Isaac Hanna and Wendell Baker; Supervisors, William Williams and James Watson; Fence Viewers, John Crider and Benjamin Miller.

Additional Taxables of Buffalo—Mathias Alsbach; Henry Fulton, merchant at Lewisburg; Philip Grove, Jacob Kephart, Joseph Oldts, George Oldts, William Rockey, John Rengler, (grist and saw-mill,) Henry Sassaman, John Shuck.

Officers of White Deer—Constable, Robert Clark; Supervisors, John Lackey and Samuel Dale; Overseers, Thomas Hutchinson and Richard Irwin. Additional resident, Roan McClure, (taxed with a negro.)

Caleb Farley built the grist-mill on White Deer Hole creek, late Charles Gudykunst's.

January 1st, Paschall Lewis married to Elizabeth Boude by Colonel John Kelly, justice. The Boudes were a highly respectable family, from Lancaster county, one of whom, Major Thomas Boude, distinguished himself as an officer in the revolutionary war, and stands connected with some of the largest and most respectable families in our Valley. Thomas Barber's wife, Mary, and Robert Barber, Esquire's wife, Sarah, were Boudes, sisters of Mrs. Lewis.

Names of the Residents of Beaver Township, taken from an Assessment made by Daniel Hassinger, in April, 1789.

Albright, Jacob; Aupel, Peter; Barnes, John; Beak, Frederick; Beard, Jacob; Bell, George; Bopp, Conrad; Boutch, Anthony, distillery; Breiner, Philip; Briesenger, Conrad; Carrel, Hugh; Carrel, Frederick; Christy, James; Clark, James; Deininger, Frederick; Deward, Francis; Dido, Frantz; Diese, Michael; Dries, John; Dries, Jacob; Dries, Peter; Everhart, Barnard; Everhart, Frederick; Gift, Adam; Gooden, Moses; Gothers, Henry; Grim, Jacob; Hall, Matthew; Hartz, John; Hassinger, Jacob; Hassinger, Daniel, saw-mill; Hassinger, Frederick; Herbster, David; Houser, Jacob; Kern, Yost, (Joseph;) Kline, George; Kline, Christopher; Kline, Stophel; Kricks, Jacob; Krose, Henry; Krose, (Gross,) Henry, junior; Krose, Daniel; Laber, John; Lepley, Jacob; Lewis, Thomas; Manning, Nathan; Mattox, Jacob; Maurer, Michael; Maurer, Michael, junior; Meek, Andrew; Meek, Peter; Meyer, John; Meyer, John, (weaver;) Meyer, Mary; Michael, Jacob; Mook, George; Moon, Nathaniel; Moriarty, Francis; Mumma, John; Nerhood, Henry; Newcomer,

Peter; Nyer, Nicholas, grist-mill; Oatley, Edward; Oatley, Asa; Philips, Benjamin; Poe, Jacob; Reger, Adam; Reger, Elias; Reigelderfer, Adam; Roush, Jacob; Royer, Stephen; Royer, Bastian; Sharred, Jacob; Snyther, John; Snyder, Peter; Stock, George; Straub, Andrew, grist-mill and two distilleries; Strayer, Mathias; Stroub, Jacob; Stull, Mathias; Stump, William, distillery; Thomas, John; Thomas, George; Treminer, Paul; Vanhorn, Daniel; Walter, Jacob; Wannemacher, Casper; Watts, John; Weiss, Stophel, grist-mill; Wiant, Jacob; Woods, John; Yost, Widow; Young, Matthew. Single men taxed ten shillings each: Collins, Joseph; Gift, Anthony; Gross, John; Hassinger, John; Hassinger, Henry; Lewis, Stephen; Lewis, Enos; Manning, Elisha; Manning, Nathan; Phillips, Benjamin; Sherrard, George; Strayer, Mathias.

In March or April, the German Reformed Churches of Mahony, Sunbury, Middle Creek, and Buffalo Valley, united in a call to Reverend Jonathan Rahauser, which he accepted, and accompanied by Mr. Jacob Meyer, he arrived in his new field September 22. He only performed such duties as come within the province of a licentiate until the 27th of June, 1791, when he was ordained, at Lancaster, by the coetus of the church. It is well to observe here, that all regular ministers of the German Reformed Church in the United States, although they had a coetus, or assemblage of ministers, of their own, from the year 1748, were under the care, and received their authority from the Church of Holland until about the year 1791. Mr. Rahauser was one of the first ordained without authority from Holland. His application having been transmitted thither, and no reply received. In October, 1792, Mr. Rahauser removed to Hagerstown, Maryland, and took charge of the congregation there. He died there September 25, 1817. He was a very energetic and laborious pastor, and caught his last sickness, in crossing a swollen creek, to fulfill one of his appointments. He was the first regular German Reformed clergyman who performed stated services in our Valley. He died at the early age of fifty-two.—*Harbaugh's "Fathers."*

At May Session, Samuel Mathers, Colonel John Clarke, John Macpherson, Christian Shively, and William Moor make report that they have laid out the road from the second hollow in the Big Blue hill to Hartley's house, where Peter Kester now lives, on the road from Davidson's ferry to Penn's valley.

On the 19th of October, a convention was held at Paxton, to take measures for the improvement of the river. Charles Smith, Anthony Selin, William Wilson, Frederick Antes, Aaron Levy, Andrew Straub, and others, were delegates. They resolved to do it by subscriptions, to be received in money, grain, or produce of any kind. Boyd & Wilson's store, in Northumberland, Yentzer & Derr, at Lewisburg, Selin & Snyder, in Penn's township, &c., were designated depositaries.

Review of manufacturers, &c., in Buffalo Valley, in 1789—Jonathan Holmes, tan-yard; John Dreisbach, gunsmith; James Watson, saw and grist-mill; William Jenkins, grist-mill; Christopher Weiser, fulling-mill; William Rockey, saw and grist-mill, formerly Fought's and John Rengler's grist and saw mill; George Wolfe, saw-mill; Benjamin Miller, merchant; George Knox, tan-yard; George Derr, two grist and two saw-mills; Henry Fulton, merchant; William & Alexander Steele, tan-yard; Joseph Green, grist and saw-mill; Wendell Baker, saw mill; Jacob Groshong, saw-mill; David Smith, saw and grist-mills; Benjamin Herr, merchant; Alexander Beatty, tan-yard.

Distilleries in White Deer—William Gray, Philip Henning, Samuel Huston, Robert Carnahan, Matthew Laird, and Robert McCorley.

The old log church at Buffalo Cross-Roads was repaired and somewhat enlarged in October.

Deaths.

March 10, Dreisbach, Anne Eve, wife of Martin, aged sixty-seven.

In July, Lawrence Keene, prothonotary. He served in the Revolutionary war as captain, in the eleventh Pennsylvania, commissioned February 3, 1777, and as aid-de-camp to General St. Clair; promoted major, and mustered out November 3d, 1783. His wife was Gainor Lukens, a daughter of John Lukens, Surveyor General. He left three children, Samuel L., who died in Philadelphia, May 11, 1866; Lawrence, who married Maria Martin, daughter of the celebrated Luther Martin, and died August 13, 1813; and Jesse L. Keene, who died November 27, 1822.

David McClenachan, of White Deer.

Adam Smith, of Buffalo, whose children were Adam, Mary, George, Catherine and Barbara.

Major General James Potter died in the latter part of November or beginning of December. James Potter, junior's, letter to Chief Justice McKean is dated Penn's valley, December 10, 1789, in which he states, "doubtless before you receive this, you will have heard of the death of my father.—*Pennsylvania Archives*, volume 11, *page* 661.

He was assisting in building the chimney of one of his tenant houses, in Penn's valley, and, in turning about suddenly, injured himself internally. He went to Franklin county, to have the benefit of Doctor McClelland's advice, and died at his daughter's, Mrs. Poe, and is buried in a grave-yard at Brown's Mills, near the present railroad station of Marion, in that county, with no tablet to mark his grave. He was a son of John Potter, the first sheriff of Cumberland county, and in January, 1758, was a lieutenant, with William Blythe, in Colonel John Armstrong's battalion. He next appears in command of a company in pursuit of the Indians, who had murdered, that morning, July 26, 1764, a schoolmaster, named Brown, and ten children, near where the town of Greencastle now stands.

He married a Miss Cathcart, sister of Mrs. George Latimer, of Philadelphia, who died, leaving a son and daughter. He then married Mrs. Chambers, sister of Captain William Patterson. He resided principally on the Ard farm, in White Deer township, just above New Columbia, though, no doubt, he changed his residence on account of the Indian troubles. One year, 1781, he resided in the Middle Creek settlement, now Snyder county, as the assessments show, and family tradition has it, his eldest son, John Potter, died there. In 1786, Pickering visited him at the Ard farm, and in 1787, Mrs. Gregg, his daughter, was married there.

In *personnel* he was short and stout, with a hopeful disposition, which no troubles could conquer. In a letter, dated May 28, 1781, he says, "look where you will, our unfortunate country is disturbed, but the time will come when we shall get rid of all these troubles.

His eldest daughter married Captain James Poe. Mary married George Riddles, who died March 14, 1796, and is buried at Northumberland, in the Presbyterian church-yard. Their daughter, Mary

A., married W. H. Patterson; Eliza, Doctor Joseph B. Ard, whose heirs still own the old place in White Deer; Martha, married Mr. Gregg.

General Potter's son James married Mary Brown, daughter of Judge Brown, of Mifflin county. Of their children: 1, General James Potter, (third,) married Maria, daughter of General William Wilson, of Chillisquaque; 2, William Potter, Esquire, late of Bellefonte, attorney-at-law; 3, Mary P., married Doctor W. I. Wilson, of Potter's Mills; 4, John Potter; 5, Martha G., married to Abraham Valentine; 6, Peggy Crouch, married Doctor Charles Coburn, of Aaronsburg; 7, George L. Potter, Esquire, who practiced awhile at Danville, Pennsylvania. Mrs. Andrew G. Curtin, who is a daughter of Doctor W. I. Wilson, of Potter's Mills, is a great-granddaughter of the revolutionary general, and the Governor is a great-grandson, on the Gregg line of descent.

John Lukens, Surveyor General of the State, died in October, and was succeeded by Colonel Daniel Brodhead, on the 3d of November. John Lukens' estate, at this date, (1877,) is still before an auditor for distribution. Charles Lukens Barnes, an heir, lived and died in Lewisburg, making his living sawing wood, while waiting for his share of this veritable Jarndyce *vs.* Jarndyce.

1790.

OFFICIALS— SURVEY OF THE SUSQUEHANNA FOR INLAND NAVIGATION—NEW CONSTITUTION, AND ELECTIONS UNDER IT.

THE following is a list of the county representatives and officials during the year, under the Constitution of 1776, which was superseded by the Constitution adopted September 2, 1790: William Wilson, Councilor; Samuel Maclay and John White, members of Assembly; William Montgomery, Presiding Justice; Jasper Ewing, Prothonotary; Martin Withington, Sheriff; Peter Hosterman, John Weitzel, and William Hepburn, County Commissioners.

Officers of Buffalo: Constable, C. Baldy; Supervisors, George May and Alexander McCaley; Overseers, Peter Zeller and John Macpherson.

Of White Deer: Constable, Robert Fruit; Supervisors, Joseph Poak and Alexander Stephens; Overseers, William Clark and Robert Martin.

Additional Taxables in Buffalo—Betzer, William; Boveard, William; Cress, Conrad; Carroll, William; Campbell, John; Caldwell, William; Depuy, Hugh; Dunlap, William; Hempstead, Joshua; Jones, Benjamin; Lourey, Samuel; McDaniel, Daniel; Oatley, Isaiah; Porter, Samuel; Shreiner, Nicholas; Sherer, Joseph; Wilson, John; Clarke, Joseph; Mann, Philip: Wilson, Hugh, (father of Francis.)

Additional Taxables in Penn's—Evans, Frederick; Metterling, Baltzer; Reiber, John; Stees, Frederick; Snyder, John S.; Weirick, Peter; Zerber, Peter; Snyder, Simon, (son of Henry.)

At February Sessions of the quarter sessions of Northumberland county, the name of Potter township (now in Centre) was changed to that of "Haines." In May, Josiah Haines and John Thornburg started a store in Lewisburg. Prices of grain at Philadelphia, in July, were, wheat, 9*s*. 6*d*.; rye, 6*s*.; oats, 3*s*. 5*d*.; Indian corn, 3*s*. 9*d*.; buckwheat, at 2*s*.

Survey of the Susquehanna.

On the 6th of April, Timothy Matlack, John Adlum, and Samuel Maclay were appointed commissioners to survey and examine the Swatara, part of the Susquehanna, Sinnemahoning creek, and the Allegheny river, with a view to the promotion of inland navigation. The commissioners started in May, and were engaged most of the summer in their work. Mr. Maclay's journal of this expedition is in the possession of his grandson, Doctor Samuel Maclay, of Mifflin county.

On the 26th of April he started with James McLaughlin's boat, him, Edward Sweney, and Mathew Gray taken into pay. They went first down to the Swatara, which, it appears they were to examine, to see whether it could be made navigable; got to Herrold's on the 27th, where breakfast and a quart of whiskey cost him 5*s*. 2*d*.; then to Harrisburg and Lebanon. The commissioners, however, for some reason, failed to meet him. He, with the rest of the commissioners, came up on the 17th of May, and at Herrold's one of Erwin's boats came up, and they raced from that to Sunbury, McLaughlin's boat coming out ahead. From there they came up to the point at Northumberland, and dined with Colonel Wilson. Mr. Maclay then went over to visit his family, in Buffalo Valley. May 19, he says: Colonel Matlack detained the boat at Northumberland, to carry Josiah Haines' goods up to Derrstown, where he and one Thornburg are erecting a new store. The boat then came up to T. Rees', where Mr. Maclay wanted some things landed. At Derrstown they met with Captain Lowdon, who told Matlack that Rees had sent for Mr. Maclay, but Matlack would not wait. So he had to shoulder his baggage and follow on foot. He trudged through the rain and bad roads, up to James McLaughlin's, opposite the mouth of Warrior run, where he arrived at ten o'clock, and found the boat landed.

Major Adlum was detained at Northumberland until the 23d, when he joined them at Loyal Sock. He speaks of leveling the race-ground at Wallis's Island, (near Muncy, I suppose.)

Sunday, 23d, they reached the mouth of Bald Eagle, at sunset, and stayed there on Monday, baking bread and providing horses. There they breakfasted with Mrs. Dunn. They leveled the Sinnemahoning, and also made canoes there. From "canoe place" Mr. Adlum and part of the men started and run a line to the Allegheny. The object of the expedition was to determine what method of communication the country would admit of, between the eastern and western parts of the State. He speaks of catching beaver, and of the large wolves that frequently crossed their track, in a very indifferent manner. On the 14th, he surveyed the West Branch of the Sinnemahoning, and got a little above Boyd's whetstone quarry. 15th, got to Bennett's cabin, three quarters of a mile above the forks. July 2d, they reached the Ohio, and went down it, having an Indian, named Doctor Thomas, for guide. At the State line, Con-ne-Shangom, the chief, had gone to Venango, but Captain John makes them a speech of welcome, which he inserts in full in the journal. Near this place Mr. Maclay met a Dutchman, who had been taken prisoner by the Indians in the last war, and chose to continue with them, and was living among them. July 7th, they had an interview with Cornplanter, at Jenoshawdego.

The Indians were very jealous of them, until they explained their business. Cornplanter then welcomed them in a speech, which Mr. Maclay inserts. He says, we were addressed by an orator, on behalf of the *women*. The principal points were, that as they, the women, had the hardest part of the labor of making a living, they had a right to speak, and be heard. They welcomed them, because, they were the pioneers of the good roads that were to come, and make intercourse easy and merchandise cheaper, and they hoped good correspondence would make them all one people in the future. Colonel Matlack responded to this speech. They then went down to Captain John O. Beales' town, and "had the honor of his company for supper." July 14, they struck the old French road to Erie. He says the ruts were quite plain yet. He says, Lake Erie is a fresh water sea. "You can see the horizon and water meet." They arrived at Fort Franklin, on the 20th. The commanding officer, Lieutenant Jeffries, was very polite to them. He speaks of killing a cat-fish with Mr. Adlum's Jacob staff, which weighed ten and one half pounds.

2d of September, the new constitution was adopted by a convention, convened at Philadelphia, 24th November, 1789. Simon Snyder and Charles Smith,[1] Esquire, were the delegates from Northumberland county.

The first election under the new constitution took place on the 12th of October. In Northumberland county, for Governor, Thomas Mifflin received 865 votes, to 68 cast for General Arthur St. Clair. William Montgomery, elected State Senator without opposition, having 1,029 votes. Samuel Maclay and John White were elected members of Assembly, over Samuel Wallis and Alexander Hunter; Martin Withington, sheriff, over Charles Gobin, John Boyd, and Flavel Roan; Joseph Lorentz, coroner; and Daniel Montgomery, county commissioner. John Simpson was re-appointed register and recorder.

It having been decided that the powers of the House of Assembly and State officers were superseded by the constitution, on the 2d of September, the house in a paper filed, September 4, declined acting longer. On the 20th of December, the Executive Council ceased acting, and on the 21st, Governor Mifflin was inaugurated.

February 17, by Reverend Hugh Morrison, Hugh Wilson married to Catherine, daughter of Captain William Irvine.

Deaths.

George Troxell, of Lewisburg.

Christopher Haney, of Haines township. He was a private in Captain Clarke's company, in 1776. His children were Hieronimus, Christopher, Adam, John, Eve, Elizabeth, and Frederick.

John Black, of Sunbury, (brother of James, of Lewisburg.)

Ulrich Lotz. His children were John Jacob, Anna Maria, and Catherine. In his will he recommends his children to adhere strictly

---

[1] Charles Smith was the third son of Doctor William Smith, Provost of the College at Philadelphia. He was admitted to the Sunbury bar, in 1786, and married, in 1791, to a daughter of Jasper Yeates, Esquire. He was the compiler of Smith's laws, and afterwards president judge of the Cumberland and Franklin district. He died in Philadelphia, in 1840, aged seventy-five.

to the advice which Tobias, in fourth chapter, gives, "Keep God before your eyes," &c.

Peter Burns, senior, of Buffalo.

Jonas Fought. Children: Michael, Barbara, Ann Elizabeth.

John Wierbach, (who lived upon the place next above Weidensaul's mill, in Hartley now.) He left a widow, Catherine, who died in 1804, of cancer. Sons: John, Nicholas. One daughter, married to Frederick Wise, who moved to Brush valley, Centre county. One married to John Hoover, and moved to Clearfield, and one married Philip Dale. One of his daughters was taken by the Indians. (See 1781.)

Charles Grogan, of Buffalo, was returning home, from a woodchopping, with a yoke of oxen, one cold night this winter, and, becoming bewildered, was frozen to death. He left a widow, sister of James Burney, and two sons, Alexander and James, and two daughters. His widow, after some years, married Henry Van Gundy, and removed to now Clinton county. James and Alexander Grugan, as they now write their names, became the heads of quite large families. Grugan township derives its name from this family. Honorable Coleman Grugan, late associate judge of Clinton county, is a grandson of Charles Grogan.—*Maynard's Clinton County, page* 153.

1791.

LIST OF STATE AND COUNTY OFFICIALS—ADDITIONAL TAXABLES—DEATH OF DOCTOR WILLIAM PLUNKET—MRS. SAMUEL MACLAY'S FAMILY LINEAGE.

OVERNOR, Thomas Mifflin. Judges of the Supreme Court, Thomas McKean, Edward Shippen, Jasper Yeates. Attorney General, Jared Ingersoll. State Treasurer, Christian Febiger. Receiver General, Francis Johnston. Secretary of the Land Office, David Kennedy. Surveyor General, Daniel Brodhead. Secretary of the Commonwealth, A. J. Dallas. Deputy Secretary, James Trimble. The Judges of the several Courts were, Jacob Rush, President; William Montgomery, Joseph Wallis, Thomas Strawbridge, and John Macpherson, Associates, commissioned August 17. Jasper Ewing, Esquire, Prothonotary, August 17. Member of Congress, Andrew Gregg, representing Bedford, Northumberland, Huntingdon, Franklin, and Mifflin. Senator, William Montgomery. Members of Assembly, Samuel Maclay and John White.

September 3, Flavel Roan was commissioned a Notary Public; he was sole notary in the county until his death; John Teitsworth succeeded him, April 26, 1815; Flavel Roan was commissioned Sheriff, October 18; William Hepburn, John Weitzel, and Daniel Montgomery were County Commissioners; Bernard Hubley, Lieutenant of the county; Justices of the Peace commissioned, Colonel Kelly, August 31; Simon Snyder, October 26; William Irwin, August 31; Captain William Gray, December 30; for Penn's and Beaver Dam, John Bishop, August 31.

Frederick Evans was Deputy Surveyor of Peters, in Mifflin county, Haines, Beaver Dam, Penn's, and that part of Buffalo south of the

Indian purchase of 1754; Christopher Dering appointed Collector of Excise, September 1.

Officers of Buffalo: Constable, Henry Pontius; Supervisors, John Crider and Peter Kester; Overseers, John Reznor and William Irwin.

White Deer: Constable, John Bear; Supervisors, Richard Fruit and Thomas Hutchinson; Overseers, Robert McCorley and John Steel.

Martin Withington opened hotel in Mifflinburg.

Additional residents in Lewisburg—Black, James, (ferry;) Ellenhuysen, Joseph; Lewis, Alexander; Metzgar, Jacob, innkeeper; Moore, John, blacksmith; Poak, William; Stroh, Nicholas.

27th May, Andrew Kennedy, senior, commenced the publication of the *Sunbury and Northumberland Gazette*, at Northumberland. This paper was extensively circulated in the Valley, and continued up to 1813.

Among those assessed in Buffalo township—Barnhart, George; Barnhart, Henry; Black, William; Book, George; Bower, Casper; Bower, George; Caldwell, Thomas; Cox, Tunis; Frantz, Lewis; Fox, Andrew; Gettig, Frederick; Getz, Peter; Getz, Andrew; Gibbons, Edward; Glover, John; Gooden, Moses; Graff, (Grove,) Philip; Grimes, Samuel; Hixon, John; Hudson, George; Kelly, Hugh; Kemmerling, Jacob; Leitzell, Anthony; Lowry, Andrew; Lowry, John; Lowry, Robert; Lowry, William; McElrath, Robert; McMurtrie, Hugh; Meizner, Adam; Metzgar, John; Patton, John; Richard, Henry, (name which disappears from the assessment after 1784, re-appears again with the supplement "thief," which is carried all through the assessments afterwards;) Rees, Daniel; Roan, Flavel; Sarvey, Jacob; Struble, Adam; Thornburg, John; Thompson, John, erects a mill to be driven by the water from Thompson's spring; Van Gundy, Christian; Van Gundy, Henry; Van Gundy, John; Weeker, William; Wilson, Hugh; Yentzer, Christian; Zimmerman, Christian; Zimmerman, Jacob.

4th August, 1791, Christopher Baldy, William Irwin, and Christian Yentzer, assessors. Robert Barber erects a saw-mill at White springs.

Penn's—Adam, Widow; Berry, Jacob; Bishop, Jacob; Grove, Adam; Goy, Frederick, distillery; Gwynn, Hugh; Heimbach,

Peter ; Housel, Peter ; Oberdorf, Andrew, grist and saw-mill to
Anthony Selin ; Snyder, John, tan-yard ; Stees, Frederick, grist,
saw, and oil-mill ; Thornton, John ; Witmer, Peter, distillery, ferry,
and saw-mill.

Beaver—Bopp, Conrad, hemp-mill ; Collins, David ; Edmunson,
William ; Hassinger, Jacob, tan-yard ; Johnston, John and James ;
Myer, Henry, grist and saw-mill ; Myer, Jacob, tan-yard ; Knepp,
George ; Sherrard, Jacob, grist and saw-mill ; Wise, John, grist and
saw-mill.

Buffalo Cross-Roads Church.

In October we find the pews in the Presbyterian Church at Buffalo Cross-Roads rated and rented for the first time. There were thirty-six pews or seats. No. 1, probably reserved for the minister's family ; No. 2, rated at £3 5*s*., taken by David Watson, Colonel John Clarke, Alexander Kennedy, and Joseph Clark ; No. 3, Thomas Forster, Andrew Forster, Robert Forster and Robert Chambers ; No. 4, £3, Christopher Johnston ; No. 5, Captain James Thompson, William Thompson, Samuel Porter, and James Boyd ; No. 6, £2 15*s*., Arthur Clellan ; No. 7, Robert Clark, Richard Sherer, and Joseph Allen ; No. 8, Samuel Dale, Esquire, and Joseph Evans ; No. 9, John Reznor and David Tate ; No. 10, Samuel Maclay, (this seat he retained until his death, in 1811 ;) No. 11, John Steel, Joseph Hudson, and William Steele ; No. 12, Joseph Green, £1 9*s*. 6*d*. ; No. 13, James Irwin and Matthew Irwin ; No. 14, William Irwin, Esquire, £2 ; No. 15, John Thompson ; No. 16, Benjamin Miller ; No. 17, John Ray, William and Thomas Black ; No. 17, Roan McClure ; No. 18, Mr. Lincoln ; No. 19, George Knox ; No. 20, Walter Clark ; No. 21, William Irvine ; No. 22, Jonathan Holmes and Joseph Sherer ; No. 23, James Poak, William Poak, Widow Poak, and Thomas Poak ; No. 24, Edward Graham and John Davis ; No. 25, William Wilson and James Black ; No. 26, vacant ; No. 27, John Linn, John Gray, and Joseph Patterson ; No. 28, Robert Fruit and Gideon Smith ; No. 29, William Gray and Thomas Howard ; No. 30, William Clark, James Forster, and Widow Forster ; No. 31, Thomas Elder, David Buchanan, and Robert Elder ; No. 32, Charles Pollock, Thomas Hutchinson, and William Williams ; No. 33, Colonel John Kelly and Captain Joseph Poak ; No.

34, Samuel Demming, James Moore, (Widow Moore,) George Moore, Widow Fleming, Thomas Rodman, James Meginness ; No. 35, Adam Laughlin, Widow McGrady and James Clelland ; No. 36, Matthew Laird and Andrew McClenachan.

With the meeting of Congress, at Philadelphia, on the 14th of October, we note the division of the people into two great parties, the Federalists and Democrats, the funding of the public debt, chartering the United States Bank, and other measures, inflaming the States Rights or Democratic party so much that, at this session, they, for the first time, appeared in open and organized opposition to the administration.—*George Read's Life, page* 536.

Notice of William Plunket.

William Plunket, the first presiding justice of Northumberland county, died in the spring of this year. He resided, as early as 1772, a little above Chillisquaque creek, at his place called "Soldiers' Retreat," now owned by Mr. Solomon Walters. He was the father of Mrs. Samuel Maclay, whose lineage is traceable to John Harris, senior, whose grave is yet to be seen on the bank of the river at Harrisburg, in front of the residence of General Simon Cameron. Near it are the remains of the mulberry to which he was tied by the Indians, to be burned. I will only add to the story, that it was his negro slave, Hercules, who crossed the river, and brought the neighboring Indians to his rescue, while the drunken Indians were about applying the fire to him. For this he gave Hercules his freedom, and directed his burial on the same spot. John Harris, senior, died in 1748. His wife, Esther Say, was a lady of rare endowments, who came from England, in the family of Judge Shippen. Among their children were John, the proprietor of Harrisburg ; Samuel, who settled at the outlet of Cayuga lake, New York, and a daughter, who married Doctor William Plunket.

Doctor Plunket, at the time of his marriage, resided at Carlisle, Pennsylvania, and his daughters, four in number, were born there. His wife dying, he remained a widower, which fact gave rise to Meginness' mistake in stating that he was a bachelor. His daughters were Elizabeth, born in 1755, married to Samuel Maclay ; Isabella, born January, 1760, married to William Bell, Esquire, of Elizabethtown, New

Jersey; Margaret, married to Isaac Richardson, removed to Wayne county, New York, then known as the Genesee country. She left four sons and two daughters. Israel J., in Delaware, Ohio, and David H., of Monroe county, New York, of her sons are still living. Hester Plunket, the youngest, married Colonel Robert Baxter, of the British army, and died about a year after her marriage. Her daughter, Margaret, married Doctor Samuel Maclay, of Mifflin county. John Harris' wife, Elizabeth McClure, said to have been the most lovely woman of her day, died young, from fright and grief, at the report, brought her by a neighbor, of her husband's death. He saw a man shot, and fall off his horse, in attempting to swim the river, and supposed it was Mr. Harris. It proved to be a young physician, whom Mr. Harris had taken up behind him (25th October, 1755.) Her daughter, Mary Harris, who inherited much of her mother's beauty, married Senator William Maclay. A miniature likeness of her is now in the possession of her granddaughter, Mrs. Eleanor M. Brinton, of West Chester, Pennsylvania. Mrs. Samuel Maclay and Mrs. William Maclay were cousins, and married brothers.

The late William C. Plunket, Lord Chancellor of Ireland, was a nephew of Doctor Plunket. A brother of Doctor Plunket came to this country, bringing with him a daughter, Margaret, who married Samuel Simmons, of Pine creek. His name was Robert. Another brother, David Plunket, settled at Baltimore, and was lost at sea on a voyage to the West Indies. Doctor Plunket served in the French war as a lieutenant, and secured for his services six hundred acres of land, part now owned by Judge Dreisbach. He owned large bodies of land, and was one of the leaders in the Pennamite war. He lived afterward and died in the office owned by Ebenezer Greenough, and lately occupied by David Rockefeller, Esquire, at Sunbury. His will is dated January 3, 1791, and proved May 25, 1791, in which he mentions his granddaughter, Margaret Baxter, one of the most beautiful and accomplished ladies of the State, who died at Milroy, Mifflin county, July 6, 1863.

The three sisters, Mrs. Maclay, Mrs. Bell, and Mrs. Richardson, survived to a good old age, and resided together, in Mifflin county. Mrs. Maclay was a Presbyterian, Mrs. Bell an Episcopalian, and Mrs. Richardson a Quaker. They were all three remarkable ladies. Mrs. Bell was a very handsome and highly polished woman. She had a boarding-school at Albany, New York, where Mrs. Catherine Sedgwick, and many of the celebrated ladies of the time, received their education.

1792.

East and West Buffalo Townships Erected—Mifflinburg and New Berlin Laid out—Notice of Reverend J. G. Phreemer—Simon Snyder's Dam Controversy—Death of Captain Anthony Selin and M. J. Ellenkhusen.

MEMBERS of Assembly, Samuel Dale and John White. January 13, General William Wilson appointed Associate Judge, *vice* Joseph Wallis, resigned. February 23, Samuel Maclay appointed Associate, also. Flavel Roan, Sheriff. John Weitzel, Daniel Montgomery, and Robert Fleming, County Commissioners. 18th January, Joseph J. Wallis appointed Deputy Surveyor of Charles Lukens' and William Scull's district, (both of whom are deceased,) and of that part of William Maclay's district north of Penn's creek, and of Upper Bald Eagle, in Mifflin county.

Officers of Buffalo—Constable, C. Baldy; Supervisors, Adam Christ and John Sierer; Overseers, William Irvine and Henry Dreisbach; Fence Viewers, Philip Voneida and George Frederick; Collector, Christian Yentzer; November 29, Robert Barber commissioned Justice of the Peace for Buffalo; School-teachers in Buffalo, Alexander Templeton and George Paget. The latter taught many years at a school-house near Michael Grove's, the former in New Berlin.

Officers of White Deer—Constable, William Robb; Supervisors, Andrew McClenachan and John Gray; Overseers, Robert Finney and Robert Clark.

Additional Taxables of White Deer—Charles Nogel, Gideon Smith.

East and West Buffalo Townships Erected.

At January Sessions, William Irwin, Samuel Dale, John Thompson, Christopher Baldy, Benjamin Miller, and Henry Pontius were appointed viewers to divide Buffalo township. They commenced the line at two gum saplings, on the south bank of Spruce run, at the line of White Deer and Buffalo, a little west of Daniel Rengler's old saw-mill, (Applegate's;) thence south to the head of the spring at Andrew Pontius'; thence down Switzer run to its mouth, at Penn's creek, (Philip Seebold's,) and the townships were called East and West Buffalo.[1] The first officers of this township were, Robert Forster, constable; John Reznor and Thomas Forster, overseers; Elias Younkman, supervisor; Andrew Forster and Robert Chambers, fence viewers.

At January Sessions, the road from Brush valley, by way of French Jacob's old mill, (now Heberling's,) to James Irwin's, was laid out. George Langs, Henry Dreisbach, Matthew Irwin, were of the viewers. It commenced at a black oak, near the gap of Buffalo mountain, by way of said mill to a corner of Wendell Baker's field, where it intersected "the meeting-house road." Distance, six miles fourteen perches, (now road by way of Cowan.)

Improvements of this year—Wendell Baker's saw-mill, (at Cowan;) Alexander Beatty's tan-yard, at New Berlin; Christopher Weiser's fulling-mill, on Turtle creek, now Peter Wolfe's.

Lower ferry, at Lewisburg, kept by James Black.

At November Sessions, the road from Wolfe's tavern (afterwards Lyon's, on the Cumberland road, leading to Sunbury) to Jenkins' mill, thence to Derr's town, at the south end of Second street, along Second to Market, to Front, by way of St. John's, to the mouth of Buffalo creek, laid out. Mifflinburg, laid out by Elias Younkman, in the summer of this year; and New Berlin, laid out by George Long, Frederick Evans, surveyor. The dates of the first deeds for lots in these places I can find on record are 30th Novem-

---

[1] East Buffalo always went by the name of Buffalo among the people; is so called in deeds and elsewhere, except on the assessment books, until the erection of the present Buffalo.

ber, 1792, lot No. 55, in Mifflinburg; 18th January, 1793, George Long to Adam Snyder, for No. 53, in New Berlin.

John Hager built one of the first dams on Penn's creek, about one half mile below App's present mill, according to William Gill's recollection.

Samuel Dale, Esquire, moved from where New Columbia now stands to his place, now in Kelly, owned by his grandchildren.

Reverend John G. Phreemer.

The Reverend John G. Phreemer, who was connected with the religious movement which resulted, at length, in the sect of the United Brethren in Christ, and sometimes professing to be a minister of the German Reformed Church, made frequent and extensive tours through middle Pennsylvania. The aged Mrs. Fulmer says that about this year, 1792, Andrew Straub and Michael Weyland used to push their canoe, containing their families and others, across the river, where Milton now is, in order to worship under a tree on the opposite side. The tree stood at Hoffman's, (1854,) a short distance above the bridge. On such occasions, the preaching and service were conducted by Mr. Phreemer, and afterwards by Mr. Phreemer and Deitrick Aurand. Mrs. Fulmer often crossed herself to attend worship under this tree. Phreemer leute, or "Phreemer people," was a common expression in Buffalo Valley at an early day. He was very fanatical. A very pious old man once told me he had the people act the fool by his preaching. He is said once to have remarked that he could preach the Devil out of hell. Abraham Brown said he saw him in Ohio, in 1814, where Phreemer was on a visit. He was then residing in Kentucky, and associate judge of the court there. He died at his home in Harrison county, Indiana, in 1825.—*Harbaugh's Fathers.*

Selin and Snyder's Mill-Dam.

On the 28th of December, a petition was presented to the Senate on the part of Simon Snyder and Anthony Selin's heirs, to enable them to maintain a dam across Penn's creek of the height of two and one half feet. This aroused the settlers along the creek and produced a remonstrance, read in the Senate, March 4, 1793, which is interesting from some statements it contains. It states "that Simon Snyder, and Anthony Selin, before his death, erected a dam across the main current of Penn's creek; that there were no less than ten mills within nine miles of Snyder's, some of which grind the year round unobstructed by ice, and they subjoin a list of the mills, with their distances from Snyder's: Lauterslager's and Pickle's, within three miles; Moore's, three miles and a half; Shock's, four miles; Rush's, five miles; Hickadron's, six; Maclay's, seven miles, Swineford's, ditto; Weitzel's, eight; and Frederick Stees', nine miles. This being the case, we consider it highly injurious to stop the whole navigation of Penn's creek, in order to promote the individual interest of Simon Snyder, Esquire," &c. This petition is signed by James Beatty, George Long, Christian Miller, Alexander Beatty, Samuel Templeton, William Fisher, Benjamin Griffith, Robert Tait, David Tate, Robert Barber, Thomas Barber, John Green, Paskel Lewis, John McMullen, James Davis, Peter Kester, William Douglass, Adam Laughlin, John Glover, John Thompson, junior and senior, David Burd, Alexander Connel, Andrew Lowery, Joseph Green, Ludwig Schmidt, James McKelvey, Martin Trester, &c.

Notwithstanding this remonstrance, the Legislature, April 10, 1793, passed an act authorizing the dam. [See Dallas' Laws, volume 3, page 364.]

Deaths.

Alexander McGrady, died in May. His children were Alexander, William, Agnes, wife of Eli Holeman, Jane, wife of James Johnston.

Samuel Barber, who lived at the mouth of Switzer run, was killed by the falling timber of an old barn he was taking down. One of his daughters married William McConnell, the other Swinehart. His widow, Martha, lived on the old place (now owned by Philip Seebold) as late as 1812.

Captain Anthony Selin, founder of Selinsgrove. He was commissioned by Congress, December 10, 1776, captain in Ottendorff's corps, afterwards attached to Armand's legion, and was still in service in 1780, at Wyoming. His children were Anthony, Charles, and Agnes. His wife was a sister of Governor Snyder, and Selin purchased the ground on which the town now is, at the death of his brother-in-law, John Snyder. Finding Snyder's plot would not fit, he re-surveyed the ground, laid it out anew, and named it. His son, Anthony Charles, was a major in the war of 1812. The widow of the latter, Mrs. Catherine Selin, died at the residence of her son-in-law, Robert Swineford, in Selinsgrove, November 3, 1868, aged eighty-two, the last of the family name in the United States.

George Hudson, of White Deer.

James Fleming, of Buffalo. He left his property to his wife's children, Samuel, Jane, and Benjamin Rodman.

Abel Rees died, (at Strohecker's now.)

James Thom, of West Buffalo. His children were Robert, Arthur, Annie, married to John Boude, Sarah E., married to James Robb, Elizabeth, and Mary.

At Lewisburg, July 17, 1792, Mathias Joseph Ellenkhusen. He came to Lewisburg in 1790, was the son of Carl Ellenkhusen, who had purchased the principal part of the town, and was sent over by his father from Amsterdam, Holland, to look after his interests, or to found a family in the western world. The principal notice we have of the son and his wife are from the recollections of Mrs. Mary Brady Piatt, taken down by O. N. Worden, Esquire. Mrs. Ellenkhusen was short in stature, considerably pock-marked, very lady-like in manner, spoke the Low Dutch language, and astonished the people by her elegance and passionate fondness for skating. She and Mr. Ellenkhusen took that method of visiting the different towns on the river. She married John Thornburg, who also soon died. She afterward married Mr. Moore, and removed to Erie, Pennsylvania. Ellenkhusen was a man of very genteel address, and fond of society. His father had given him the town site, and a good outfit of clothing and money, hoping, no doubt, he would build up a fortune ; but emigration suddenly declined, and the convivial habits he had acquired, probably before leaving Europe, shortened his days. Personally, he was much esteemed. He was quite an artist, and often drew with pencil striking likenesses of his companions. Sheriff John Brady was a joker. He had found a cannon near Muddy run, and he told Ellenkhusen that he would present it to him if he would take care of it. On cleaning out the mud which covered the muzzle, two large black snakes came out, greatly to the horror of Mr. Ellenkhusen. He told Brady the circumstance afterward. "Why," said Brady, "they were my pets; I would not have lost them for a $100," and Ellenkhusen, no doubt, died in the belief that he had let loose some play-fellows of Brady's. Ellenkhusen and Thornburg were both buried beneath what is now the vestibule of the Presbyterian church. The annalist recollects well the wild cherry tree that stood near, and the brick wall inclosing these graves. The tombstone of Ellenkhusen was preserved by the late James F. Linn, Esquire, and is in the cellar of the church. Its inscription is: "Here lie the body of Mathias Joseph Ellenkhusen, who departed this life July 17, 1792, age thirty-eight years and three months."

> "Since it is so we all must die,
> And death no one doth spare;
> So let us all to Jesus fly,
> And seek for refuge there."

1793.

ADDITIONAL TAXABLES—YELLOW FEVER IN PHILADELPHIA—FALL ELECTIONS—DEATHS IN THE VALLEY.

ANDREW GREGG, Member of Congress. Josiah Haines and James Davidson, members of Assembly. Daniel Montgomery, Robert Fleming, and Richard Sherer, County Commissioners. John Brown was commissioned a Justice of the Peace for Washington township March 13. Number of taxable inhabitants in Northumberland county, three thousand eight hundred and seventy-eight.

Additional Taxables, East Buffalo—Barber, Martha (Widow;) Baily, John; Betz, William; Brown, Christian; Carstetter, Martin; Covert, Luke; Dale, Samuel; Dunkle, Jacob; Doty, Doctor; Gass, George; Gelitzler, William; Getz, Adam; Hayes, John;

Hummel, John ; Miller, Christian, (Berlintown ;) Morton, Thomas ; Myer, George, (Berlintown ;) Ray, John ; Reedy, Conrad ; Seebold, Christian, grist-mill, formerly James Watson's ; Sheckler, Daniel ; Sheckler, Tobias ; Speddy, Jeremiah ; Stahl, Philip ; Wilson, Thomas.

List of Residents in Lewisburg—Black, James ; Caldwell, Thomas ; Deering, Francis ; Delong, Edward ; Donachy, John ; Dunlap, John, (ferry ;) Ellenckhuysen, Clara ; Evans, Joseph ; Groninger, Leonard ; Grove, Adam ; Grove, Wendel ; Heineman, Samuel ; Holdship, George ; Kemble, Lawrence ; Knox, George ; Links, George ; Lewis, Alexander ; Metzgar, Daniel ; Poak, William ; Russell, David ; Sherer, Joseph ; Snodgrass, David ; Swinehart, Lewis ; Thornburg, John ; Troxel, Abraham ; Wells, Benjamin ; Wells, Joseph ; Yentzer, Christian.

Christopher Baldy commenced the tan-yard at Buffalo Cross-Roads.

Doctor Charley Beyer practicing medicine in Lewisburg.

Still-houses—Andrew Billmyer's, Andrew Blair's, John Beatty's, George Gass', on John Aurand's place, Peter Leonard's, Henry Pontius', Daniel Rees', Levi Vanvolsen's.

New Saw-mills—John Hager, Michael Moyer.

Additional Residents in White Deer—Adams, James ; Chamberlin, Colonel William, of Anvil township, Hunterdon county, New Jersey, bought the mill known as Bear's, and moved into the Valley ; Dale, Henry ; Fruit, Richard ; Howard, Thomas, one slave ; Howard, David ; Miller, Samuel ; Marshall, Stephen, lived on George Riddle's place or General Potter's place, late Doctor Ard's ; Rose, Andrew ; Stillwell, Daniel ; Williams, William. Stephen Marshall and James Adams, above, were grandparents of late Honorable James Marshall. Philip Heany moved to Penn's valley.

First Residents in Mifflinburg—Dreisbach, John ; Holmes, Robert ; Holmes, Jonathan ; Longabaugh, Henry ; Longabaugh, Michael ; Reedy, Nicholas ; Sampsel, Nicholas ; Youngman, George ; Waggoner, Christopher.

West Buffalo, State of Improvements, &c.—Thomas Barber, saw-mill ; Jacob Grozean, grist and saw-mill ; Joseph Green, grist and saw-mill ; William Rockey, grist and saw-mill ; Michael Shirtz, grist and saw-mill at Penn's Valley narrows, finished this year ;

Christopher Seebold, grist, saw-mill, and still; David Smith, grist and saw-mill.

Stills—Robert Barber, John Boude, George Rote, Elias Younkman. Slaves: One taxed to Colonel John Clarke, named Mel, and one to David Watson, named Kate.

Additional Residents—McCreight, John; Shriner, Henry; Wilson, Hugh, on General Irvine's land, late Solomon Kleckner's; Zippernock, Frederick.

Penn's Township—App, Mathias; Aurand, Daniel; Bastian, Daniel, Michael, and George; Blasser, ——; Burchfield, Charles; Clements, Peter; Dusing, Nicholas and John; Gable, Frederick; Grogg, Peter, saw-mill; Hager, John, saw-mill; Hershey, John; Highlands, John; Hoffer, Elizabeth; Hummel, George Adam; Jasemsky, Reverend Frederick William; Kern, Mathias; Kendig, Jacob; Krebs, John; McKinney, Abraham; Nyhart, David; Pfiel, Henry, saw-mill on Middle creek; Ram, Nicholas; Rhoads, Francis, junior; Shatzburger, Christopher; Shawber, Christopher, junior; Silverwood, James; Snyder, John, tan-yard; Snyder, Simon, junior; Solt, David; Strausser, John N.; Sutherland and Vanvalzah, grist and saw-mill on Penn's creek; Trester, Michael, saw-mill; Walter, John, Jacob, junior, David, and Philip; Weirick, William, saw-mill; Witmer, Peter, junior, saw-mill; Wolfe, John and George, junior; Young, George; Zering, John.

March 28, petition presented to the House, asking Buffalo creek to be declared a public highway up as far as Rockey's mills.

In September, the yellow fever prevailed so badly, that the Supreme Court held no session in Philadelphia. It broke out early in August, and continued its ravages until November. Over four thousand deaths in that period, out of a population of fifty thousand.

In October, Thomas Mifflin re-elected Governor. Vote in Northumberland county, Mifflin, 1443; Muhlenberg, 514. The candidates for Senate were William Hepburn, Daniel Montgomery, Evan Owen, Samuel Wallace, and Bernard Hubley, and William Hepburn was elected. The candidates for Assembly were Josiah Haines, James Davidson, William Cooke, Samuel Dale, John White, Jacob Fulmer, and John Weitzel. The candidates for County Commissioner were Chistopher Dering, John Buyers, David Ireland, Robert Clarke, John Thornburg, Charles Gobin, and William Bonham.

December 12 was observed in the churches as a day of humiliation and thanksgiving, for removing the plague from Philadelphia.

In December, the court-house and jail at Sunbury were in such ruinous condition, that the president and associate judges threatened the commissioners with prosecution, "unless new buildings are commenced next year."

Deaths.

Nicholas Smith, White Deer.

George Barnhart, East Buffalo.

James Ferguson, Buffalo. His children were Mrs. William Thompson, Mrs. Hugh McConnel, Mrs. Charles Hummel, and a son, John, married to David Hanna's daughter.

In West Buffalo, 22d April, Daniel Campbell, a soldier during the whole war of the Revolution. He married Catherine Klinesmith, who was wounded, as described *ante* page 190, and had by her two children, John and Ann. John died near Mifflinburg. Ann married Samuel B. Barber. Campbell had received a land warrant for one hundred acres, and, in order to locate it, Barber and wife had to make proof of their identity. Catherine Chambers, the widow, and Baltzer Klinesmith, junior's, depositions were taken; on file at Lewisburg.

Robert McCorley, of White Deer, died in the fall. Left widow, Anna, and children, Isabella, wife of William McLaughlin; Mary Seidel, Robert, James, Roley, (still living, 1877,) and Jacob, afterwards member of Assembly.

Levi Vanvolsen lived in Dry valley, and had a distillery. A girl, living with him, took one of his children into the still-house, and placed it upon a barrel, and went to draw some beer. The child fell off into a vessel of boiling mash, and was scalded to death. The girl, Nancy Grimes, afterwards married Jeremiah Speddy.

1794.

FIRST BAPTIST SETTLERS—SAMPLE OF Mr. MORRISON'S SERMONS—REVEREND GEORGE GEISTWEIT—EXCITEMENT INCIDENT TO THE WHISKY INSURRECTION—COUNTY POLITICS—ELECTION RETURNS—FLAVEL ROAN'S POETRY.

HOMAS SMITH appointed Justice of the Supreme Court, *vice* William Bradford, resigned. Senator, William Hepburn. Members of Assembly, Flavel Roan, George Hughes and Jacob Fulmer. Henry Vanderslice, Jailer. County Commissioners, Robert Fleming, Richard Sherer, and Christopher Dering.

On the 8th of January a special election was held for a Senator, in the place of William Montgomery, resigned. William Hepburn was elected by sixty-four majority over Rosewell Wells, for the unexpired term.

Among the Officers of West Buffalo—John Reznor, Adam Laughlin, and William Moore, assessors.

The additional Taxables were—James Barklow, John Barton, John Kleckner, Solomon Kleckner, Benjamin Jones, Conrad Coons. The name of Jacob Groshong disappears from the list, and his mill is assessed to Enoch Thomas.

Additional Residents of Mifflinburg—John Irvin, store-keeper; Henry Neal, Ludwig Gettig, Jacob Welker, William Welker, Israel Ritter, John Earnhart.

Of Lewisburg—Alexander McBeth, Matthias Shaffer, Hugh McLaughlin, William Stedman, Esquire.

First Residents of New Berlin—Hugh Beatty, George Moyer, Christopher Miller, Zeba Smith, Philip Harmony, William Black, John Mitchell, and Martin Carstetter.

Among the names of those who moved into the Valley this year, I note particularly James McClellan, Esquire, and Gabriel Morrison, school-teachers, both from Chester county; widow Mary Harris, grandmother of William Laird Harris, of East Buffalo; John Betz, and Samuel Baum.

Improvements—The bridge across the Buffalo creek, at its mouth, For this, the court of quarter sessions directed an allowance of £50, ($133 33.) It was without a roof. Travel now deserted the road by way of the ferry, where the iron bridge now (1877) stands, for the road on the river bank. Seventy-seven years elapse, and the engines at the boat-yard of Frick, Billmyer & Co. frighten it back again. Stedman and Smith keep store at Lewisburg. The courthouse at Sunbury was commenced. William Gray, of Sunbury, Alexander Hunter, and John Weitzel were the trustees for building it.

O. N. Worden, in a short history of the Baptist churches, published in Meginness' History of the West Branch, quotes from the minutes of the Philadelphia Baptist Association, (1794:) "A letter was received and read from the church in Buffalo Valley, Northumberland county, requesting to be received into the association. Postponed, no messenger appearing to receive the right hand of fellowship." Mr. Worden adds that there were a few Baptists and preaching stations in Buffalo Valley after the Revolution, but there is no knowledge of any Baptist church in Buffalo Valley until the formation of the Lewisburg church, in 1844.

Colonel James Moore informs me that Colonel William Chamberlin was a Baptist; and after his arrival in the Valley, with other New Jersey people of the same persuasion, he probably made an effort to establish a Baptist church, which was abandoned, on account of the distance the people lived from each other.

Additional Taxables, East Buffalo—Beatty, James; Bickle, Christopher; distillery, erected by Conrad Reedy; Elliot, George; Freeman, Doctor; Pfreemer, Reverend George; Gray, Robert; Harris, Widow Mary; Hoy, John; Lytle, Anthony; Lutz, Jacob; McClellan, James; McConnel, William; McLaughlin, John; Schrack,

Benjamin ; Smith, William, store-keeper, Lewisburg ; Steel, David ; Stockman, Nathan ; Thompson, Benjamin.

Additional Taxables, White Deer—Armstrong, Andrew ; Awl, Samuel ; Elder, James and John ; Fisher, Christian ; Goodlander, Christian ; Henderson, William ; Hilliard, Guy ; Hoffman, John ; Jordan, Widow ; Luther, Andrew ; McCorley, Widow ; McGines, Thomas ; Martin, Hugh ; Reninger, George ; Riddle, George ; Woods, John.

Penn's—Drum, Charles, grist and saw-mill ; Forey, Christian ; Hendricks, Samuel ; Landis, George ; Menges, Adam, grist and saw-mill ; Ott, George ; Page, Abraham, still ; Pawling, Joseph ; Reish, Daniel, saw-mill ; Ritter, Simon, still ; Stober, William ; Tryon, Frederick, fiddle ; Wetzel, Philip.

Beaver—Aurand, Henry and George ; Cummings, James ; Ewing, Thomas ; Ewing, John ; Gill, William ; Hendricks, Jacob, mill ; Harman, Samuel ; Hileman, Adam, mill ; Romich, Joseph ; Shipton, Thomas ; Shultz, John ; Troxell, John ; Wilson, Moore.

Dietrich Aurand, who had followed milling at different places down the river, removed, with his family, into the Valley, and settled on a farm on Turtle creek, midway between its source and outlet, about five miles above Jenkins' mill. The farm he was on had a reserved water right, and was given to him by his father, with the design that he should build a merchant mill on it, and he intended so to do ; but the Hessian fly having proved very destructive to the wheat crops for upwards of ten years, he lost severely in purchases of wheat for the French, and lost by bailing, so he could not build the mill, and had to sell and remove to an adjoining farm, in 1801.

Mr. Morrison's Sermons.

The late James McClellan, Esquire, left his father's home, near Fagg's Manor church, Chester county, on the 2d of April. He had been in the habit for years of writing down a skeleton of the sermons of Messrs. Sample, Latta, senior and junior, Smith, senior and junior, Barr, Dayton, Mitchel, Findley, and others, who filled the pulpit there. The last, by Mr. Sample, was March 15. Then his manuscript is destroyed, and the next that can be made out is 18th of May, John xv, from the 16th to the end, by Mr. Morrison.

He says parsed by Mr. Morrison, and nothing but what is clearly contained in the verses offered. From the few skeletons preserved by Esquire McClellan, Mr. Morrison seems to have fallen into the lazy habits, still indulged in by some of our present preachers, of commenting on quite a number of verses, instead of delivering a logical and prepared discourse on one theme. For instance, his fast-day sermon, June 13, on Matthew v, 1st to the 9th, is stenographed thus: "'This is Christ's sermon on the mount. He went up on a mountain, some of the commentators say, because the law was given on a mountain. However, he made choice of this place to deliver his sermon. Verse 2: He opened his mouth, expressive of deliberation, judgment, and authority, and taught. Verse 3: This cannot mean poor in possession, as some allow, as some are poor and wicked; but it means those children of God who are broken under a sense of guilt, whatever their external circumstances may be, but frequently it is that of middle circumstances. Verse 5: The 'meek' does not mean the external, affected polish which prevails; it means a christian behavior, whereby he serves God as becometh Christians," &c., to the end. Perhaps we do injustice to Mr. Morrison's memory by putting on record this "Chatband" style of preaching, but it is the only memorial, perhaps, in existence to throw any light on his pulpit services, not abilities, may be, as he could make a flaming political harangue.

At a meeting of the German Reformed Synod, held at Reading, in May, the Reverend George Geistweit was licensed as a minister, and a call immediately presented him from the Shamokin churches. The congregations in all these regions had been vacant since the Reverend J. Rahauser left them, in 1792. Mr. Geistweit preached statedly at Selinsgrove, Sunbury, &c., and occasionally in Buffalo Valley, in the newly-built town of New Berlin, at Penn's creek, &c. He labored here until the year 1804, when he accepted a call to York, Pennsylvania. He died there, November 11, 1831, aged seventy years, and was buried in the Reformed grave-yard there. There are still (1857) some people living in the Valley who were confirmed and married by him, and speak of him with great affection and gratitude.—*Doctor Harbaugh.*

Mr. Geistweit bears the enviable reputation of having been one of the kindest and most benevolent of men. It is reported of him that, on one occasion, he even took the hat from his own head and gave it to a poor wanderer, whose destitute condition appealed to his charity.—*Reverend D. Y. Heisler, Fathers German Reformed Church, volume* 3, *page* 77.

The Whisky Insurrection.

September 30. The summer and fall of this year are noted for the excitement through the State, culminating in the whisky insurrection. Some of the whisky boys determined to erect a liberty pole, at Northumberland; Judge William Wilson, of Chillisquaque, and Judge Macpherson, of Dry Valley, hearing of it, determined to prevent it. They called upon Daniel Montgomery, also a justice, to assist them. He told them he would pull at the rope if the people required it. He, however, went with them, but rendered them no assistance in suppressing the disturbance. A fight took place; Judge Wilson read the riot act, as he called it, to disperse the crowd, but they paid no attention to it. One of them presented his musket at the judge, but the old revolutionary captain cocked his pistol and made him put down the musket, under the penalty of having his brains blown out. They arrested the judge. He would not give bail, and they were afraid to put him to jail. In the *melee*, Jasper Ewing, the prothonotary, drew his pistol and snapped it at William Cooke. See the case reported in 1 Yeates, 419. *Kennedy's Gazette,* of 3d December, has General Henry Lee's proclamation to the people of western Pennsylvania, dated at camp, at Parkinson's ferry, November 8, in command of the troops of New Jersey, Maryland, and Virginia. Also, an advertisement of Doctor Priestly's works, he was then publishing.

Indictments were found *versus* Robert Irwin, Daniel Montgomery, John Frick, William Bonham, John Mackey, senior, and Samuel McKee. Mr. Meginness says they were tried in Philadelphia, convicted, and sentenced, and that General Washington pardoned them at the end of twenty days. His account of the riot is, that the liberty pole was erected at the corner of Second and Market streets, in Northumberland. The arsenal was under care of Robert Irwin, (grandfather of the Nesbit brothers of Lewisburg.) The rioters took possession of the arsenal, and distributed the arms. The pole was driven full of nails, and guarded day and night. John Brady, junior, was deputy marshal, and a very determined man. A collision was imminent, when Captain Robert Cooke's company, from Lancaster, arrived, and dispersed the rioters at the point of the bayonet. An axe was called for to cut the pole down. Mrs. Bernard Hubley came running with one, her sister, Mrs. Jacob Welker, met her and tried to take the axe. Mrs. Hubley got past her, and the pole came down.

This company passed through Buffalo Valley. At Andrew Billmyer's, a little beyond Lewisburg, a pole had been erected, but the report of the advancing troops got there before they did, and the pole was cut down and hid. The soldiers could not find it, and took their revenge in drinking up all the whisky, eating everything in the house, leaving word that Uncle Sam would pay the bill.

Politics.

By an act of the 2d of April, Dauphin and Northumberland constituted our congressional district, and by the act of the 22d of April, Northumberland, Luzerne and Mifflin our senatorial district, electing two members for the term of four years, and Northumberland became entitled to three members of Assembly.

Slates were at that early day made at Philadelphia, but usually smashed by the people. George Green writes from Philadelphia to Robert Irwin, September 24:

"SON ROBERT: I am at loss to know whether the county of Northumberland or the county of Mifflin, as I understand they are in one district, is entitled to one or two Senators. If two, Mr. Martin, I hear, is to run in your county, and there is a certain Mr. John Culbertson mentioned in the other county. I look upon him as a good man, and if there are two for the district, I could wish the two above-mentioned to run; if but one for the district, you may act as you think proper. I think they are both good men. There are great preparations being made here for an army to go to the Fort Pitt country to subdue the rioters, as they are called. It appears to me to be a serious affair. How it will turn out only time can tell."

The following schedule of election returns is printed in full, so as to show the strength of party in each election district in the county. I found it among Flavel Roan's papers, kindly loaned me by his nephew, Flavel R. Clingan, of Kelly township.

GENERAL ELECTION RETURNS—October 14, 1794.

DISTRICTS.	CONGRESS.			SENATE.				ASSEMBLY.						SHERIFF.						
	Samuel Maclay.	John Andre Hanna.	John Carson.	George Wilson.	William Hepburn.	Samuel Dale.	Rosewell Wells.	Flavel Roan.	George Hughes.	Jacob Fulmer.	James Davidson.	William Cooke.	Abraham Scott.	Robert Irwin.	John Brady.	Henry Shoemaker.	Christopher Baldy.	William Gray.	M. Withington.	Daniel Aurand.
1. Sunbury,	331	68	....	277	131	218	69	296	288	215	72	38	69	130	66	69	83	4	228	39
2. Northumberland,	236	24	....	125	139	45	91	232	148	112	40	144	67	161	135	7	12	12	6	15
3. Buffalo,	464	14	....	373	26	460	36	451	381	418	51	14	1	246	91	16	306	135	20	17
4. Lycoming,	30	245	....	109	230	14	35	190	71	42	143	211	88	137	176	122	2	28	17	....
5. Penn's Valley,	137	17	....	139	47	127	....	66	134	152	52	45	11	2	22	51	80	56	....	63
6. Penn's and Beaver,	118	79	....	103	113	108	28	168	42	49	18	68	5	43	55	25	45	1	20	28
7. Fishing Creek,	364	6	....	45	258	32	28	323	363	103	243	40	....	179	135	168	21	9	13	34
8. Turbut,	220	212	....	267	293	202	48	352	259	294	83	175	18	196	203	134	58	90	2	4
9. Bald Eagle,	39	206	....	163	235	25	2	225	20	1	175	121	115	162	102	27	....	120	45	....
Total,	1979	871	....	1581	1472	1231	337	2303	1706	1386	877	856	324	1196	985	619	607	455	351	200

Samuel Maclay's large majority will be remarked; also, the still greater popularity of Flavel Roan, as he has a majority in every election district. It will be noticed that the Federalists ran three revolutionary officers, Surgeon Davidson, Colonel Cooke, and Major Abraham Scott, for Assembly, yet they were largely defeated by civilians; Republicans, as the opposition called themselves. This must be attributed to the personal influence of William and Samuel Maclay, and the excitement caused by the whisky tax. William Maclay, I infer from his private journal, differed with General Washington very early in the first session of Congress. The Maclays, though aristocratically descended, their ancestor being Baron Fingal, were intensely democratic in sentiment. We notice William Maclay grumbles at the state or ceremony of Washington's intercourse with Congress and the public; his objections to the President's presence while business was transacted, and his boldness in speaking against the President's measures in open Senate, and the President a listener. These are matters more proper for a biography of Mr. Maclay; but their reflex influence upon Northumberland county elections must be noted in these Annals.

It will be noticed that Robert Irwin has the highest vote for sheriff. Nevertheless, Governor Mifflin appoints the next highest, John Brady, a Federalist. The law then gave the Governor the privilege of appointing from the two highest candidates. Henry McAdam was elected coroner over Henry Lebo, Paul Baldy, John Gray, &c. Henry Vanderslice was elected county commissioner over Charles Gobin, Thomas Forster, &c. Joseph Barnett, Hugh Beatty, and Robert Clarke, each, had quite a number of votes for Assembly.

In the case of the sheriff, many depositions were filed by the friends of Irwin and those of Brady. In one by John McGrath, he says, having a store to build for Mr. Irwin, on the 29th of September, when the tree was hauled in to make the "liberty pole," he watched the pole during the night, using the unfinished store-room for that purpose, without Mr. Irwin's knowledge or concurrence; that the night of the watch Mrs. Brady gave him a quart of whisky to treat the watch with; that Lawrence Campbell brought a quart of brandy, and said that Mr. Brady had sent it; that John Brady said his brother had no more sense than Jimmy Logan, and while his brother was cutting the pole down here, he was helping to raise one in Milton, and that if they would raise another, he would put a silk flag on it at his own expense.

John Tietsworth swore, a voter in Buffalo told him that when he proposed the name of Brady for sheriff, in Buffalo, "he liked to have got his head broke for doing it," &c.

A memorial to the Governor, signed by William Wilson, William Hepburn, Jasper Ewing, William Gray, Jonathan Walker, Thaddeus Hamilton, Daniel Smith, John Kidd, Bernard Hubley, Joseph J. Wallis, and B. W. Ball, sets forth, "that since the commencement of the insurrection to the westward, this county has furnished daily proofs of a disposition inimical to the cause of Government, by erecting what they call liberty poles. One attempt has been made by the friends of Government to cut down these poles, which was attended with imminent danger to the lives of some of our best citizens. The arrival of our friends from Luzerne gave great activity to the spirit of the county. They were a standard about which the friends of order might rally, and an object of dread and hatred to the party in opposition. After they had been here a few days, General Wilson and Judge Macpherson issued warrants against a number of persons who had been most active in opposition. The sheriff served them, and reported that they willingly submitted and entered into recognizances. But the moment they had done so, we are informed, that they set out through the country with inflammatory falsehoods against some of our good citizens who were candidates. Of John Brady, a candidate for the sheriff's office, and a sworn friend of Government, they reported that he had rode his horse over a pole before it was raised, and that he or his brother had assisted in cutting down a pole, and if he was elected, he would summon juries friendly to the Government, and that by it they would all be hung."

They allege that, but for these reports, Brady would have been elected. They further represent John Brady to be strongly in favor of the Government; that his father and brother were killed by the Indians, and that he had two brothers in the United States service, and allege that Irwin sympathized with the whisky insurrectionists, and ask Governor Mifflin to appoint Brady, although they admit he was two hundred votes behind Irwin.

David Hammond testified that the report among the people was, that William Perry Brady had cut down the liberty or whisky pole at Northumberland, and that they would not vote for John Brady on that account, "as they believed he was against the pole."

John Hayes (Esquire) testified "that he saw at Derrstown, in Buffalo township, Robert Irwin, as active a person as there was there in helping to put up a pole that was erected there, with a large flag with a motto thereon, 'Liberty;' that the people said Brady was for the Government, and, if he was elected, he would do everything in his power against them, as they had been active in raising the pole."

Samuel Maus testified "that he saw John Brady assist raising the first pole at Northumberland, and had heard him say that he had helped raise a pole in Buffalo, and another in Milton, and that he would purchase a very genteel large flag for the next pole at Northumberland, and that his brother was a damned rascal for cutting down the first pole; that John Brady's girl brought the brandy to the people who were watching the tree for the pole the night before it was raised, and the girl told the people the brandy came from Mr. Brady, upon which the people cried out huzzah! for John Brady's brandy!"

William Spring certified that some time in October last John Mason, of Northumberland town, came to James Tawar & Co.'s store and ordered a sufficient piece of red Persian to make colors for the liberty pole, and directed it to be charged to John Brady's account, or his own, whichever I thought proper.

Henry Lebo testified that when the first pole was set up in Northumberland, the people, on motion of Mr. Eddy, formed a circle, and sat down, said Eddy in the chair; that Robert Brady came into the ring with two case bottles of whisky, and called upon him (Lebo) to tell the people this was John Brady's treat, John Brady being in the company; that this deponent, thinking his neighbor Irwin should not be behind in treating the people, went to Irwin's store, and not finding him at home, asked the clerk for a half gallon of whisky, who refused. Mrs. Irwin was then applied to, and she refused; that he then got a half gallon on his own account, took it out to the people, who, thereupon, drank his health.

James Faulkner testified he heard Irwin say that a friend of Brady's told him, "that at a collection of a number of people in Younkmanstown, (a village in Buffalo,) at the raising of a liberty pole, John Brady came along in his route electioneering, at which place he expressed himself too freely against such unlawful measures, which exasperated the people so much, that it had completely ruined his election in the Buffalo district."

Jonathan Walker (afterwards Judge Walker,) testifies " that John Brady always was, and still is, opposed to liberty poles ; that William Bonham, John Mackey, and Daniel Montgomery, were the principal persons concerned in raising the pole at Northumberland ; that Daniel Montgomery told him that he was determined to run Irwin in his own defense, as a number of them might be indicted for erecting liberty poles, and they had no favors to expect from John Brady if he should succeed ; that Bonham said at first that he would give all his interest to, and make all the Methodists in the county vote for, John Brady, but he had changed around to Irwin, and run a dead ticket for him," &c., &c.

Governor Mifflin, in a note to James Trimble, Deputy Secretary, says that he has "shown the depositions produced by the friends of the Government in favor of Brady, the lowest on the return, to Mr. Ingersoll, (the Attorney General,) and he conceives it proper that Brady should be commissioned. Therefore, let the commission forthwith issue."

A Specimen of Flavel Roan's Poetry, taken from Kennedy's Gazette of May 14, 1794.

Mr. Kennedy,

Please to insert the following advertisement, and oblige yours, &c., Flavel Roan.

I am an old man, my case is quite common,
I want me a wife, a likely young woman.
I late had an old one, but three years ago,
She sickened and died, and left me in woe ;
I whin'd J. B. preached a sermon when she was buried,
Wore my old wig a fort'night, then long'd to be married.
If any one knows where a wife's to be had,
Such as seventy wishes when reason is dead :
A girl that will warm my old bones in the winter,
Let them leave the intelligence with Mr. Printer.

Deaths.

Thomas Taggert, at Northumberland. Children: Robert, David, William, James; Elizabeth, married to William Bonham; Catherine, to John Painter; Christina, to James Semple; Mary, to Benjamin Patterson.

Lambert Vandyke, of White Deer. Children: John, Henry, James, William, Archibald, and Alexander. Lambert's widow afterward married Benjamin Thompson.

George Smith, (of Hartley now.)

John Fisher, of White Deer. Children: Henry, Paul, John, Michael, George, and three daughters. One married Thomas Perry, another Jacob Wertz, and another to Philip Haines. John Fisher was one of the first settlers. Took up the land in his own name, on part of which West Milton now stands. He is buried in the corner of the field above John Datisman, Esquire's, store, where the Valley road strikes the river. He was the grandfather of Paul and Daniel, of Gregg township.

Casper Bower, (East Buffalo.) Children: Henry, Margaret Holler, Susanna Dressler, Catherine Saunders, Maria Flickinger, Barbara Smith, and Maria, unmarried then.

Andrew Fox, (of Hartley now.)

Mathias Barnhart, East Buffalo. Children: William H., Matthias, Lorentz, Magdelena, married to Peter Getz.

Edward Tate, a soldier of the Revolution. His children were, Edward, who moved to Rock Forge, Centre county, around which his descendants reside, and William, who married a daughter of Hugh Beatty, and whose children live in and near Bellefonte.

Kennedy's Gazette says that "Colonel Matthew Smith died at Milton, aged fifty-four. He was captain of the rifle company that went through the wilderness with Arnold to Quebec. A company of light infantry, under Major Piatt and Captain James Boyd, marched about six miles to Warrior Run burying-ground. Many tears were shed over the old patriot's grave, and, after his remains were deposited, three volleys were fired over his grave."

He was prothonotary in 1780. His son, Wilson Smith, was sheriff of Erie county in 1804, and Senator from that district in 1812. Quartermaster General under Governor Snyder, in 1814. His grandson, Matthew Smith, still resides in Waterford, in that county.

1795.

Henry Spyker's House—Politics—Jay's Treaty—George Kester and Anna M. Smith's Bequests for Schools—Death of William Irvine, and Notice of his Family.

EMBERS of Congress, Samuel Maclay, and Andrew Gregg. Senator, Samuel Dale, elected *vice* William Hepburn, who resigned on the 20th of April. Members of the House, Flavel Roan, Hugh White, and Robert Martin. County Commissioners, Richard Sherer, C. Dering, and Henry Vanderslice. John Brady, Sheriff.

In East Buffalo, the additional Taxables are—Joseph Phares, John Hubler, Jacob Lutz, Job Thomas, Doctor Rosewell Doty.

John Pollock opened a store in Mr. Lewis' house, in Lewisburg.

On 5th August, Henry Spyker commenced building the first brick house ever erected in Lewisburg, (still standing,) on the corner of Front and St. Catherine streets, and owned by James S. Marsh. John Meffert, of Tulpehocken, was the contractor. Most of the brick were brought from some point down the river, and a few made on Thomas Wilson's place, now a part of George Wolfe's, near the fair ground. Abraham Troxell did the hauling.

In White Deer: Archibald Hawthorne appears as a taxable.

In West Buffalo: John Wintelbleck, John Wilt, Joseph Wilt, Adam Armor, and John Collins.

In Penn's: George Benfer, Michael Beaver, Peter Hackenberg, Samuel McClintock, Philip Yocum, (Big) John Kerstetter.

Saturday and Sunday, 24th and 25th of January, fell the deepest snow had for many winters—two feet on the level. From April 10th to the 19th, the weather was excessively warm, like in the middle of summer.

Thursday, 19th February, was observed as a day of thanksgiving and prayer, upon a proclamation of President Washington. "Good George, take care you do not fall," writes Republican Henry Spyker, in his diary.

To April Session, 1795, Hugh Wilson, Henry Dreisbach, Leffard Haughawaut, William P. Maclay, C. Baldy, and John Thompson, junior, reported that they had laid out a public road from Dreisbach's church to the Presbyterian church at Buffalo Cross-Roads.

Politics.

Jay's treaty with Great Britain was signed on the 19th of November, 1794. General Washington received a copy on the 7th of March, of the present year. An extra session of the Senate was called on the 6th of June, and it advised the President to ratify it, except one article in relation to the West India trade. While Washington was waiting, a little, the progress of events, one of the Virginia Senators, S. T. Mason, in violation of the obligation of secrecy, sent a copy of it to the *Aurora*, a violent, partisan Democratic (or Republican, as was the party name then) paper, in Philadelphia. It was spread before the people without any of the accompanying documents or letters, necessary for a fair appreciation of it by the people. The treaty was the best that could be obtained at the time, and public policy recommended its ratification. Nevertheless, the warm feeling of our people towards the French gave the opportunity to the politicians to raise a tremendous storm. Meetings were held all over the country, and the treaty denounced violently. Jay was burned in effigy, the British minister insulted, and Hamilton stoned at a public meeting. We can give no idea of the bitterness engendered, except by large quotations from speeches and correspondence of the day. The clergy, at least many of the prominent ones, took part, and some of their vituperations appal us. The upshot of the matter was, General Washington stood firm, and the treaty became a law. Nevertheless, the party feeling it elicited increased until it ended in the overthrow of the Federal party, in the fall of 1800.

William and Samuel Maclay were the influential men of the middle and western portions of Pennsylvania, and were decided Republicans. Buffalo Valley, ever since a hot place about election times, was doubly hot at this time. Samuel Maclay's influence, from his good character and ability, was almost unbounded. Nevertheless, Mr. Morrison led a determined few in opposition to the dominant Republicans. The result was, pew rates ceased in the Buffalo church, and we only find the names of William Sherer, John Allen, Joseph Allen, John Reznor, George Knox, Walter Clark, Joseph Patterson, William Gray, and Thomas Howard, marked as paying up their stipends. In 1797, the foregoing and William Wilson and William Irwin, Esquire, only are marked as having paid up. In 1798, occur the same names only paying up. In 1799 and 1800, the same names. In 1801, only the names of George Knox, William Wilson, William Gray, Esquire, and Walter Clark.

Mr. Morrison commenced preaching at Mr. Maclay from the pulpit, and Mr. Maclay refused to go any longer, and, of course, took the larger body of the congregation with him. Mr. Morrison alleged that the majority had conspired to shut him out of the church, and he and his party went so far as to shut themselves out of the church, one day, and then went over to the school-house to hear Mr. Morrison preach, and endeavored to put the odium of it upon the majority.

Marriage.

December, 16, Tobias Sheckler to Catherine, daughter of George Frederick.

Deaths.

John Thornburg, of Lewisburg. Charles Pollock, White Deer. Henry Bolender. Theobald Miller, of Penn's. His widow married George May, of Buffalo. His children: Benjamin, who went down the Ohio, and was killed by the Indians; Valentine, father of Carpenter John, of Lewisburg; Margaret, married to John Metzgar; Catherine, to John Adam; Mary, to Philip Moore, of Freeburg; Valentine, married a daughter of Joseph Evans, of Lewisburg, served in the war of 1812; father of Reverend Theobald, of Ohio.

George Kester, (Hartley now.) In his will he provided for the erection of a school-house on his place, which was to be furnished with a good stove, at the expense of his estate. This is still known as the Kester school-house. A burying-ground is attached, in which are interred many of the old settlers. Kester's children were Peter, Elizabeth, Christina, and Henry.

Anna M. Smith, of East Buffalo. She left in her will £30, to erect a school-house for poor children on Turtle creek.

William Irvine, died November 18. His place was the "Thomas Wilson" warrantee tract, about a mile above Rengler's mill, adjoining then John Beatty, Wendell Baker, James Magee and John Sierer, two hundred and sixty acres; ninety cleared. It was sold by his executors, on 4th May, 1798, to Peter Dunkle, for $1,500.

William Irvine came into the Valley, probably in the year 1774, when he patented the tract. He is marked on the assessments William Irvine, (Irish,) to distinguish him from William Irwin, Esquire, who is marked as "late of Carlisle." His wife was an Armstrong, connected with the family at Carlisle, and his eldest daughter, Catherine, (afterwards Catherine Wilson,) was born November 16, 1758. He served during the French-Indian war, 1754–1763. I have his powder horn, on which are etched the stations between Philadelphia and Pittsburgh, to Fort Stanwix and Crown Point, the plan of Fort Duquesne, the English insignia "*Honi soit que mal,*" Indians with scalping knives, &c. With the runaway of 1779, he removed his family to Cumberland county. The spring served as a hiding place for many things, and a griddle, now in possession of J. M. Linn, still shows some rust-holes gotten there. His wife died near Carlisle, and he returned to his place in the Valley, accompanied by his daughter Catherine, and from her have come down many incidents of the hardships endured by the early settlers.

When alarmed by incursions of the Indians, they rendezvoused at McCandlish's, (now John Lesher's.) Once, when on a flight, the quick ear of the father caught the report of a bush cracking behind them. He pushed her behind a tree and cocked his rifle, but it was only a deer running by. Once they were pursued so close they had to leave a cow with a calf only a few days old. He pushed down the fence so that she could get into the meadow, and they then fled for their lives.

Later in life, he married Jane Forster, daughter of John. She died in 1824, aged eighty-four, and is buried in the Lewis grave-yard. His children were, 1, Catherine, married to Hugh Wilson, father of Doctor W. I. Wilson, still living; Francis, who died February 15, 1873, Mrs. James F. Linn, Mrs. William Stedman; 2, Elizabeth, married to William Love; 3, Nancy, to William Milford. (The latter took a boat load of produce to New Orleans, in 1809, and was never heard of afterward.) His wife survived him forty-one years; 4, Mary, married to James McClellan, Esquire; 5, Sarah, married to Walter Charters. William Irvine's father's name was Andrew, of the county of Fermanagh, Ireland; and John, Matthew, and Thomas, of Philadelphia, frequently mentioned in the Pennsylvania Archives in connection with the purchase of ships for the navy and powder for the continental army, were William's cousins, as were also General William Irvine, of the Pennsylvania Line, Matthew, the celebrated surgeon of Lee's legion, and Andrew, who survived so many wounds received at Paoli.

1796.

BISHOP NEWCOMER VISITS THE VALLEY—LIST OF INHABITANTS OF EAST BUFFALO, LEWISBURG, NEW BERLIN, WEST BUFFALO, WHITE DEER, AND MAHANTANGO.

SENATOR, Samuel Dale, re-elected in October. Members of Assembly, Hugh White, John White, and Thomas Grant. William Cooke, commissioned Associate Judge January 19th, *vice* Samuel Maclay, resigned December 7, 1795. County Commissioners, Joseph Dering, Henry Vanderslice, and Nathan Stockman. Coroner, William McAdam. Brigadier General, William Wilson. Brigade Inspector, Bernard Hubley. Peter Hosterman, Justice of the Peace, commissioned March 14; George Youngman, March 17; Frederick Stees, June 9.

January 18, George Clark, Lazarus Finney, and Roan McClure made a valuation of the real estate, &c., of White Deer township. Real estate, $37,445 ; personal, $4,438 ; buildings, $6,448.
March 18, Conrad Weiser moved from Tulpehocken to his place on the Isle of Que.—*Spyker's Journal.*
May 6, Bishop Christian Newcomer, of the United Brethren Church, visited the Valley, and held meetings on the 6th, 7th, 8th, and 9th. Many souls confessed their sins, among the rest a woman came forward leading her daughter. Blessed be God ! she, with many others, found mercy.—*Newcomer's Journal.*
James Jenkins sold his slave, Tom, to Colonel John Patton, of Centre county. Tom was thirty years old when the emancipation act of 1780 was passed, but was registered defectively, and lived in the belief that he was still a slave. After living many years with Colonel Patton, he came back to Buffalo Valley, and became a charge. The overseers removed him to Ferguson, in Centre, and that township had to keep him.

List of Inhabitants of East Buffalo.

The occupation, where not mentioned, is that of farmer ; improvements, when not added to the name, are log-house and barn ; c, for cabin : Alsbach, Mathias ; Anderson, William, c ; Aurand, John ; Aurand, Dietrich, c ; Aurand, Peter, c ; Bailey, John ; Baker, Wendell ; Baldy, Christopher ; Barber, Martha, c ; Barnhart, Henry ; Barton, John, on Jasper Ewing's place ; Baum, Charles ; Baum, Samuel ; Beatty, Alexander ; Beatty, John ; Betzer, William ; Betz, Abram ; Betz, Solomon ; Bickel, Christopher ; Bickel, Jacob ; Billmyer, Andrew, tavern-keeper ; Boveard, James, c ; Bower, Casper ; Bower, George ; Bower, Jacob ; Burd, David, c ; Campbell, John, on William Gray's place ; Carothers, Samuel ; Cherry, Charles, on C. Baldy's place ; Christ, Adam ; Croninger, Joseph ; Colpetzer, Adam, c ; Conaly, John, distiller ; Connell, William, c ; Coryell, Abram, joiner ; Coryell, George ; Covert, Luke, c ; Cox, Tunis ; Dale, Samuel, Esquire ; Davis, Robert ; Derr, George ; Dempsey, Widow, c ; Dennis, John ; Dersham, Christian ; Donnell, Andrew, Esquire ; Doughman, Stephen ; Dreisbach, Henry ; Dreisbach, Jacob ; Dreisbach, Martin ; Dunlap, William, c ; Dunkle, Jacob ;

Eaylor, Frederick, c; Emrey, Jacob; Emrey, William, a blacksmith, on John Sierer's place; Eyerly, Abram, stone barn; Farley, John, c; Farley, Michael; Fisher, George; Fisher, William; Foster, James; Fought, Michael; Frantz, Ludwig; Frock, Henry, c; Freeman, Reverend George; Freeman, Nathaniel; Frederick, Peter; Frederick, George; Foster, William; Gass, George; Gass, Peter; Goodman, George, c; Goodman, John; Gray, Robert, c; Greenhoe, John; Grogg, Peter, c; Groninger, Joseph, c; 'Grove, Michael, c; Grunner, Jacob, c; Gundy, Christian, grist and saw-mill at George Derr's; Harris, Widow; Hartley, John; Haughawaut, Leffard, c; Hayes, John, surveyor; Hayes, David; Holdship, Thomas, shoe-maker; Holeman, Martin; Housel, Peter; Hoy, John; Hoy, Philip; Hubler, John; Hummel, John; Hummel, James, house-joiner; Hunter, Samuel; Huntsman, John, junior; Huntsman, James, senior; Irwin, James, c; Jenkins, James, stone gristmill; Kemble, Joseph; Kemberling, Jacob, c; Knight, Isaac, c; Lincoln, Mishael; Long, George; Lowrey, Hugh, c; Lowrey, Widow; Lutz, Jacob; McClellan, James; McConnel, William, c; McGee, James; McLaughlin, John; Maclay, Samuel, Esquire; Macpherson, John; Maize, Michael; Markle, John; May, George; Metzgar, Jacob; Miller, Benjamin; Miller, Christian; Miller, Conrad; Miller, George, c; Mizener, John; Mook, Jacob, c; Morrison, Reverend Hugh; Morrison, Gabriel, c; Morton, Japhet; Moyer, Michael, saw-mill; Nichols, James, fuller; Nickle, Samuel; Overmeier, George, senior; Overmeier, George, junior; Overmeier, Peter; Peters, Henry, c; Peters, Philip; Piper, William; Poak, William; Poak, Thomas, malster; Pollock, John, store-keeper; Pontius, Frederick; Pontius, Nicholas; Pontius, Henry; Porter, Samuel; Ray, John; Reed, Robert, c; Reedy, Conrad; Reedy, Jacob; Rengler, John, saw and grist-mill; Rees, Daniel, c; Rees, Thomas; Richard, Henry; Rote, John; Sailor, Henry, c; Schrack, Benjamin; Scroggs, Allen, c; Seebold, Christopher, grist-mill; Sheaffer, Henry, (ferry;) Sheckler, Tobias; Sheckler, Daniel; Shipman, John, c; Shively, Henry, c; Shuck, John; Sierer, John; Smith, Michael, blacksmith; Stadler, Valentine, c; Stahl, Philip, saw-mill; Steel, David, blacksmith; Sterrett, Thomas; Struble, Conrad; Struble, Adam; Snoddy, James; Templeton, Samuel; Thomas, Job; Thompson, William, c, school-master; Thompson, James; Thomp-

son, Benjamin ; Thompson, John, senior ; Thompson, John, junior ;
Toner, Charles ; Treasonrighter, Conrad ; Ward, Thomas ; Weiser,
Christopher, fulling-mill ; Wilson, Hugh ; Wilson, Thomas ; Wine-
garden, Widow ; Wise, Peter ; Wise, Frederick, blacksmith ; Wise,
Frederick ; Wise, Jacob ; Voneida, Philip.

Lewisburg—Armstrong, William, tailor; Beyer, Doctor Charles,
log house ; Black, James, stone house, store-keeper ; Caldwell,
Thomas, log house, store-keeper ; Dunlap, John, ferry and tavern,
renter to James Black, $120 ; Ensworth, Andrew, log house, peddler ;
Evans, Joseph, log house and shop, cabinet-maker ; Fulton, Henry,
cabin ; Gray, John, tavern ; Grove, Adam, carpenter ; Grove, Wendell, carpenter ; Henning, Frederick, tavern, log ; Hyndman, Samuel ; Kemble, Lawrence, log house, tinner ; Knox, George, tanner ;
Langs, George, cooper ; Lewis, Alexander, stone house and kitchen,
and a frame house ; McLaughlin. Hugh, tailor ; Metzgar, John, two
houses, store-keeper ; Metzger, Daniel, saddler ; Murphy, John ;
Poak, William, log house and kitchen, tavern-keeper ; Poak, Thomas,
log house ; Poak, George ; Roan, Flavel ; Sherer, Richard, log
house ; Stedman, William, stone house ; Shaffer, Matthias, carpenter ; Troxell, John ; Welker, Jacob, log house; Wells, Joseph,
shoe-maker ; Wells, Benjamin, shoe-maker ; .Yentzer, Christian, log
house.

New Berlin—Beatty, William ; Beatty, Hugh ; Black, William ;
Cook, James; Gill, Isaac ; Henderson, James ; Miller, Christian,
shop-keeper ; Mitchell, John ; Moyer, George, tailor ; Overmeier,
John ; Rerich, William, blacksmith ; Seebold, Christian, tavern-
keeper ; Smith, John, tavern-keeper ; Smith, Peter, tailor ; Specht,
Adam, shoemaker ; Trester, Martin.

*A List of all the Inhabitants of West Buffalo Township, with a
Description of their Dwellings and Occupations.*

Anthony, George, wheelwright, round log cabin ; Armstrong,
William, farmer ; Adamson, William, cooper, log cabin ; Ammer-
man, Daniel, jobber, cabin ; Allen, Obediah, farmer, round log
cabin ; Boerhave, Christopher, blacksmith, scutched log house,
stable, and cabin shop, one hundred and thirty-seven acres ; Beeb,
George, cropper; Bruner, Jacob, farmer, cabin, one hundred acres;

Bruner, John, jobber, cabin, one hundred acres; Brown, John, farmer, chip log house and barn, spring-house, shell of a new log house, one hundred and seventy-two acres; Brown, Christian, jobber, hewed log house, not lined; Black, William, school-master, chip log cabin; Beigh, Frederick, cordwainer, round log cabin; Bartges, Michael, nailor, frame nailor shop; Ben, James, living with his father-in-law; Books, George, sawyer, log cabin; Banter, John, farmer; Bole, Henry, farmer, chip log house and barn; Buckalew, Peter, farmer; Bubb, George, farmer, cabin; Boveard, William, jobber, log house and barn; Buyers, John, farmer, log cabin; Barton, Kimber, a school-teacher; Clarke, Joseph, colonel's son, farm occupied by John Conser, one hundred acres; Carmany, John, cordwainer, small hewed log house; Cox, William, jobber, hewed log house and kitchen; Christ, Conrad, cooper, round log cabin; Coon, Conrad, cordwainer, round log cabin; Clay, David, farmer, round log cabin; Conser, John, stiller, log house; Clark, John, farmer, log house; Coderman, George, farmer, hewed log house; Ciark, Joseph, farmer, round log cabin; Carney, Anthony, blacksmith, round log cabin; Crawford, Edward, farmer, log house; Crawford, William, farmer, log house; Coderman, David, farmer, log house and barn; Carnes, William, farmer; Coderman, Jacob, farmer, log cabin; Chambers, Robert, farmer, log cabin; Chambers, Mary, housekeeper, log cabin; Chambers, Benjamin, single man; Dersham, Ludwig, farmer, hewed log house and barn, one hundred acres; Dreisbach, John, gunsmith, hewed log house, stable, brick kitchen and frame shop; Derr, Christian, house carpenter, small chip log house; Duncan, James, weaver; Douglass, William, farmer, log house; Earnhart, John, blacksmith, hewed log house and blacksmith shop; Emery, John, blacksmith, hewed log house and shop on John Kleckner's place; Evans, Nathan, saddler, round log cabin; Emery, Peter, farmer, log cabin; Emery, John, farmer, log cabin; Everet, Abel, miller; Fry, Jacob, farmer, hewed log house, kitchen, barn, and cabin; Forster, Thomas, farmer, chipped log house; Forster, Robert, farmer, hewed log house; Fough, Henry, round log cabin; Ford, Thomas, farmer, chip log cabin; Fisher, Peter, sawyer, cabin and saw-mill; Fiddler, Stephen, blacksmith, log house and shop; Frederick, Thomas, farmer, log house; Getgen, Ludwig, mason, hewed log house; Ghien, Nathan, farmer, chipped log cabin; Gray, Henry, farmer, round log cabin; Getchey, Adam, farmer, chipped log cabin; Gast, Jacob, jobber, chipped log cabin; Glover, John, farmer, hewed log house and round log barn, very old; Grim, Jacob, tavern-keeper, hewed log house, grist and saw-mill; Gray, George, tenant, log cabin; Hyman, John, jobber, small cabin; Holmes, Jonathan, small hewed log house; Horne, Robert, shop-keeper, hewed log house and chip log stable; Housel, Jacob, farmer, log cabin; Housel, Martin, farmer, chip log house and stable; Hamilton, Francis, jobber, round log cabin; Humler, Daniel, farmer, chipped log cabin; Helman, John, jobber, chipped log cabin; Hickson, John, farmer, hewed log house; Hull, Thomas, farmer, chipped log cabin; Hoves, John, farmer, round log barn; Hendricks, Henry, sawyer, cabin; Humler, Adam, farmer, round log cabin; Iddings, James, farmer, shell of a cabin; Iddings, William, farmer, chipped log cabin; Irwin, John, shop-keeper, hewed log house and round log house; Johnson, Christopher, farmer, grist and saw-mill; Jones, Benjamin, farmer, chipped log house; Kennedy, Alexander, farmer, chipped log cabin, old stable, chipped log house and barn, shell, one hundred and forty acres; Kemple, John, farmer, hewed log house and barn; Keney, David, farmer, round log cabin; Kleckner, John, tavern-keeper, barn, stable, and spring house; Kester, Henry, farmer, log house and saw-mill; Kester, Peter, farmer, cabin; Kester, John, farmer, log cabin; Kester, John, sawyer, log house; Kester, Peter, stiller, cabin; Kleckner, Solomon, clock-maker, chipped log cabin; Lyman, Michael, carpenter, hewed log house; Langabaugh, Henry, weaver, hewed log house; Leighty, John, tanner, round log house; Lowdon, John, farmer, hewed log house, barn, spring-house, and saw-mill; Laughlin, Adam, farmer, log cabin; Lewis, Paschal, farmer, log house; Mathias, Jacob, jobber, hewed log house and barn, one hundred acres; Moor, James, hunter, hewed log cabin; Moore, Henry, cordwainer, round log cabin, log still-house; Mettlen, Patrick, farmer, round log cabin; Mizner, Adam, farmer, hewed log cabin; Midker, Conrad, farmer, round log cabin thatched; Mitchell, John, farmer, round log cabin; Miller, Bastian, farmer, round log cabin, thatched roofed barn; Mann, Philip, farmer, log house; Metzger, Henry, jobber, cabin; Means, Andrew, millwright, log cabin; Mathers, Samuel, farmer, chipped log cabin; McLain, John, cordwainer, hewed log house; McCutchen, Hugh, schoolmaster; McGrady, Alexander, farmer, round log cabin; McCaley, Alexander, farmer, round log cabin, barn shingled; McMurtrie, Hugh, farmer, cabin; Noll, Henry, cropper, cabin building; Neel, William, weaver, chipped log weaver shop; Neel, Henry, tailor, hewed log house; Owens, Abel, farmer, chipped log house; Pontius, Andrew, farmer, house and cabin, barn, one hundred and fifty acres; Pontius, Andrew, junior, farmer, round log house; Pontius, Henry, farmer, hewed log house and log cabin; Peterson, Robert, hunter, chipped log house and cabin stable; Piper, Henry, farmer, hewed shell house; Peters, Michael, round log cabin; Rockey, Jacob, does what he thinks best; Rearick, John, farmer, hewed log house, springhouse and cabin barn; Richey, Andrew, jobber, cabin; Rockey, William, farmer, hewed log house, cabin barn, grist and saw-mill; Rockey, John, tavern-keeper, hewed log house and kitchen, round log stable; Rote, George, tavern-keeper; Ray, George, tavern-keeper, hewed log house and barn; Royer, Peter, farmer, hewed log house and barn; Reed, Mary, Mifflinburg; Reedy, Nicholas, jobber, log house; Ross, Charles, jobber, scutched house; Rote, Peter, farmer, round log cabin; Ridabaugh, Michael, farmer, hewed log house and barn; Reznor, John, junior, farmer, log house; Reznor, John, senior, farmer, round log cabin; Reznor, George; Rote, John, Jacob, and George; Reznor, Hugh, Moses Caruther's miller; Rhinemacker, Baltzer, farmer, round log cabin; Spangler, Christian, farmer, log house and barn, one hundred and fifty acres; Spangler, John, jobber, one hundred and twenty-one acres; Shanke, Jacob, blacksmith, hewed log kitchen and shop; Skiles, James, jobber, chipped log house, small; Sample, Nicholas, carpenter, hewed log house; Stotan, William, farmer, chipped cabin, barn and still-house; Shrock, John, farmer, round log cabin; Smith, John, farmer, round cabin, house, and saw-mill, round log cabin; Shriner, Nicholas, cropper, hewed log cabin; Shriner, Peter, jobber, hewed log cabin; Smith, Melchior, farmer, chipped log house; Shirtz, Michael, farmer, log house, cabin; Snook, William, farmer, log house; Smith, Ludwig, farmer, log house, grist and saw-mill; Smith, David, farmer; Shriner, Henry, jobber, log cabin; Spencer, Joshua, jobber, cabin; Tate, David, farmer, cabin, house, scutched log barn; Thompson, James, farmer, hewed log house, round log cabin; Thomas, Enoch;

Tittleman, Godfrey, farmer, round log cabin; Tibbens, David, sawyer, cabin; Trippy, George, weaver; Wise, Jacob, farmer, hewed log house, spring-house, and cabin barn; Wagner, Christopher, carpenter, hewed log house; Welker, William, jobber, hewed log house and kitchen; Welker, Jacob, tailor, hewed log house; Williams, Benjamin, chipped log house; Wigdon, John, farmer, hewed log shell of a house; Wilson, Hugh, tavern-keeper, hewed log house, red log barn, on Colonel Hartley's place; Wilson, David, farmer, one slave; Wirebaugh, Catherine, house-keeper, log house; Wirebaugh, Nicholas, single man; Winkelpleck, John, farmer, log house; Ultz, Joseph, farmer, hewed log house, red log stable; Ultz, John, farmer, log cabin, round log stable; Vorgan, John, farmer, round log cabin; Youngman, George, shop-keeper, hewed log house, shop, scutched log stable; Youngman, Thomas, with his father, a shell of a scutched log house; Youngman, Elias, hatter, chipped log house; Young, Christian, potter, hewed log house, round log stable; Zellers, Peter, farmer, hewed log house, round log barn; Zipperneck, Frederick, farmer, round log house and barn; Metzgar, Jacob, farmer, round log cabin.

Single Freemen—Barnes, Aaron; Chambers, Joseph; Caruthers, Moses; Crotzer, John; Duncan, James; Emery, Joseph; Hunter, John; Love, Alexander; Moore, Jacob; Moore, John; McCalley, David; Rockey, Jacob.

A List of all the Inhabitants of White Deer Township, Dwellings, their Occupation, &c.

All whose occupations are not named were farmers. Adams, Joseph, log house and barn; Adams, James, square log house and double barn; Allen, Joseph, cabin and still-house; Allen, John, cabin, stable; Anderson, Gailand, cabin, saddletree-maker; Awl, Samuel, cabin, shoe-maker; Bennage, Simon, log house, one and a half stories, double barn; Bogender, Lemuel, Thomas Howard's place, carpenter; Bole, Samuel, log house, double barn; Bower, John, cabin and stable, shoe-maker; Boyl, William, tenant of Gideon Smith; Buchanan, David, cabin and stable, millwright; Carnahan, Robert, cabin and still-house; Chamberlin, William, frame house, log barn, oil, grist, and saw-mill, log still-house; Clark, Walter, square log house and double barn ; Clark, Robert, square log house and double barn ; Clark, William, stone house, log barn, still-house ; Clark, George ; Cleland, Arthur, cabin and stable ; Clendening, William, cabin, weaver ; Coburn, William, cabin and stable ; Connelly, William, cabin, weaver ; Coulter, Nathaniel, cabin, laborer ; Darlington, Joseph, cabin ; Davidson, Thomas, blacksmith, log house ; Dean, Samuel, cabin, no trade ; Dickey, George, saddler ; Dinning, Samuel, log house and barn ; Drielly, James, cabin, weaver ; Eaker, Joseph, cabin and stable, doctor ; Elder, Thomas, school-master, cabin, stable, and corn-crib ; Elder, James ; Farley, Caleb, cabin and stable ; Finney, Robert, log house and double barn ; Finney, Lazarus, no improvement ; Fisher, Paul, log house and double barn ; Fisher, Henry, cabin and stable ; Fisher, Michael, log house ; Fisher, George, no improvement ; Fisher, Elizabeth ; Fisher, Christian, cabin ; Fisher, John, jobber ; Freeman, Samuel, cabin, weaver ; Fruit, Robert, square log house and barn ; Fruit, Richard, log house, one and a half stories, stable ; Gilliland, Joseph, cabin, cooper ; Gillespie, Charles, cabin ; Gilman, Henry, large cabin ; Gilman, Jacob, large cabin, weaver ; Goodlander, Christian, cabin, tailor ; Gottshall, John, carpenter ; Graham, Edward, cabin, tailor ; Gray, William, Esquire, log house, one and a half stories, double barn, and still-house ; Groninger, Jacob, lived on William Wilson's place, cabin, weaver ; Heckle, Andrew, log house and double barn ; Henderson, William, cabin, carpenter, on William Wilson's ; Heriot, Samuel, carpenter ; Hies, George, cabin, blacksmith ; High, Peter, carpenter and tavern-keeper ; Hill, John, cabin, shoe-maker ; Hill, James, small cabin, shoe-maker ; Hilliard, Guy, cabin, shoe-maker ; Howard, Thomas, square log house and barn ; Hudson, William, cabin, mason ; Huffman, George, log house ; Huffman, John, log house and double barn ; Hunt, John, cabin, blacksmith ; Hunter, Agnes, cabin ; Hutchinson, Thomas, square log house, (Patterson's place ;) Iddings, William, cabin, blacksmith ; Iddings, Henry, log house ; Iddings, Jonathan, small cabin ; Iddings, Isaac, small cabin ; Irwin, Richard, log house and barn, weaver ; Irwin, William, cabin ; Johnson, Jean, cabin, and stable ; Jordon, Jean, cabin and barn, clapboard roof ; Jordon, William, cabin, boatman ; Keller George, small cabin, wheelright ; Kelly, John, Esquire, log house and double barn , Kiles, James, cabin, laborer ;

Laird, Matthew, log house and barn; Lantz, Arthur, log house and kitchen; Linn, John, log house, one and a half stories, double barn, and still-house; Linn, Isaiah, cabin and stable; Lukey, John, log house; Luther, Andrew, cabin and stable, tailor; McBeth, Robert, lóg house, blacksmith; McClenachan, Finney, small cabin; McClenachan, William, cabin and stable, carpenter; McClenachan, Andrew, square log house; McClure, Roan, cabin and double barn; McCorley, Widow, log house, still-house; McCorley, James, small cabin, laborer; McGaughey, Andrew, small cabin, school-master; McGinnes, James, weaver; McKinley, Hugh, small cabin, laborer; McLaughlin, James, small cabin, laborer; McLaughlin, William, small cabin; McWilliams, James, small cabin, laborer; Marshall, William, still-house, distiller; Marshall, Stephen, small cabin, laborer; Martin, George, log house, old stable, shoemaker; Martin, James, log house; Miller, Samuel, cabin and stable, carpenter; Mool, Nicholas, weaver, (John Huffman's;) Moore, James, cabin and stable; Moore, Joseph, log house and double barn; Moore, George, cabin; Nevius, Christian, log house and double barn; Nickles, Thomas, cabin, William Wilson's place; Nogel, Charles, log house, carpenter; Norcross, Abraham, laborer, cabin; Norcross, John, frame house, hatter, shop, ferry, and tavern; Painter, Jacob; Pollock, Adam, stone house and double barn; Pollock, Joseph, log house and double barn; Rank, John, log house and stable; Reed William, stepson of C. Gillespie; Reninger, George, grist, saw-mill, cabin, and stable; Riddle, George, square log house; Rodman, Hugh, carpenter; Shannon, William, weaver; Shaw, Hamilton, large cabin, stable; Shaw, James, cabin; Sherer, Richard, cabin, still-house, and barn; Smith, Gideon, log house, double barn, and still-house, joiner; Smith, Catherine, grist and saw-mill; Smith, Peter, cabin; Smith, John, cabin; Smith, Ludwig; Snook, Philip, double cabin; Steel, John, log house; Steel, Alexander, small cabin; Steel, William, tanner, log house, stable, tan-yard; Stillwell, Daniel, square log house; Sweesy, Daniel, cabin; Thompson, William, carpenter, cabin; Thompson, William, school-master, cabin; Vandyke, John, cabin, barn; Vandyke, Huston, shoe-maker; Vartz, Dietrick, large cabin; Vogen, Robert, small cabin, cooper; Ward, Thomas, Robert Clarke's place, old cabin, weaver; Ward, John, cabin, jobber; Ward, George, cabin, jobber; Walles, John, weaver, cabin; Watts, John, carpenter, cabin; Welsh, Nicholas, stable and cabin; Welsh, Ludwig; Wheeland, Michael, carpenter, cabin; Whittemore, Peter, cabin, stable, and blacksmith shop; Wilson, William, stone house, bank barn, and apple-mill, tailor; Woods, John, cabin and still-house, reed-maker; Woodside, David, large cabin, stable, and blacksmith shop.

Single Men—Adams, James; Adams, John; Chamberlin, Enoch, miller; Clark, Charles; Clark, George; Foster, Hugh, weaver; Fisher, William, miller; Huffman, George; Hawthorne, Archibald; Iddings, Samuel; Irwin, John, distiller; Irwin, Samuel, weaver; Johnston, William; Lukey, William, joiner; Lukey, James; McCluskey, Patrick, distiller; Nicholas, John; Painter, Henry; Pollock, James; Pollock, Thomas; Ray, William; Russell, Alexander, distiller; Wheeland, Samuel.

Penn's—Brause, Adam; Deal, John; Deitz, Jacob; Filman, John; Gaughler, Nicholas; Gehr, Jacob; Hughes, Garret; Jarret, Jacob; Kern, Widow; Kratzer, Daniel; Leckington, Abraham; Musselman, Jacob; Price, Thomas; Schuyler, Nicholas; Weirick, John.

List of Residents, &c., of Mahantango Township made in 1796— Territory, Chapman, Perry, West Perry, now in Snyder County.

Albright, Frederick, senior and junior; Albright, John; Ault, George; Anderson, William; Arnold, Casper, saw-mill; Barnhart, Henry; Bay, John; Bickart, John; Birchfield, Charles; Blasser, John; Bower, Daniel; Bower, Peter; Bowman, Jacob; Bright, Michael; Brumbach, George; Burget or Burkhart, Philip, Esquire; Eckhart, Jacob; Forrey, Christian; Garman, Henry, saw-mill; Garman, John and Peter; Gaughler, George; Geltnitz, Casper; Getherd, Henry, cooper; Goy, Frederick; Graybill, Jacob; Graybill, Christian; Graybill, John; Gunckel, Jacob; Haflig, Jacob; Hagerman, John; Hamilton, James; Hawn, Michael, saw-mill; Hawn, Michael, junior; Heem, Paul; Heffer, Jacob; Heimback, Peter; Heintz, Doctor Christian; Heisler, Henry; Herrold, Simon, grist and saw-mill; Herrold, George; Hershey, John; Hershey, John, junior; Hetzel, Mathias; Hoff, James, tailor; Hosterman, Peter; Imhoff, Charles, two stills; Johnston, John, saw-mill; Jordon,

John ; Keiser, Jacob ; Kerstetter, John ; Kerstetter, George ; Kerstetter, Leonard ; Kerstetter, Martin ; Kerstetter, John, junior ; Kerstetter, Widow; Leiter, John; Livengood, Jacob; Livengood, John, Livengood, Jacob, saw-mill ; McClintock, Samuel ; Martin, Jacob ; Meiser, George ; Meiser, Adam ; Meiser, Henry, junior ; Meiser, Henry, senior, saw mill ; Meiser, Michael; Meiser, Philip ; Metterling, Baltzer ; Nieman, Wiant, saw-mill ; Nitz, Jacob and Philip ; Patterson, Robert ; Pfeill, Henry ; Reber, John ; Reed, Frederick ; Reed, Casper ; Reichenbach, John ; Reichenbach, Jacob ; Reinerd, George ; Richter, Christian ; Richter, John ; Rine Henry, two stills ; Roush, Jacob ; Roush, Jacob, junior ; Saddler, Stephen ; Seecrist, Christian, saw-mill and distillery ; Shaffer, John ; Shaffer, Michael, saw-mill ; Shaffer, Peter ; Shedde, Henry, saw-mill ; Shetterly, John, saw-mill ; Shetterly, Henry ; Shetterly, Catherine ; Shetterly, Andrew ; Shower, Adam and Michael ; Shreiber, Philip ; Smith, David, oil-mill ; Snyder, Herman ; Snyder, John, senior ; Snyder, Thomas ; Snyder, Herman, senior ; Snyder, George, shoe-maker ; Snyder, John, tanner ; Speese, Herman ; Stahl, Frederick ; Stahl, John ; Stees, Frederick, grist and saw-mill and shopkeeper ; Stephenson, Earnest, weaver ; Stephy, Adam and Leonard ; Straub, Charles ; Straub, Charles, junior ; Straub, Peter ; Strausser, Nicholas, horse jockey ; Swartz, Martin ; Swartz, John and Peter ; Thornton, John ; Thorsby, William ; Troub, John ; Vance, Robert ; Whitmer, Widow ; Whitmore, Jacob ; Whitmore, Samuel, distillery ; Wiant, Jacob ; Wiant, John , Witmer, Abraham ; Witmer, Peter, saw-mill ; Woodrow, Simon ; Woomer, Adam and Godfrey ; Zellers, John ; Zimmerman, Stophel and William ; Zually, John, weaver.

*Single Freemen—*Goy, Frederick ; Haak, Jacob ; Meiser, George, joiner ; Nitz, Jacob ; Shaffer, Andrew ; Stephy, Frederick, carpenter ; Whitmore, Samuel ; Wiant, Michael ; Zimmerman, Jacob.

Married.

Sunday evening, June 12, Simon Snyder, Esquire, of Selinsgrove, to Catherine, daughter of Colonel Frederick Antes, of Northumberland.

Deaths.

Henry Peters, East Buffalo. Children : Anna, Maria, Mary, and Barbara.

Joseph Taveler, East Buffalo.

Abraham Piatt, of Haines. Children: Jane, Eleanor, John, and James.

March 14, George Riddle, son-in-law of General James Potter, deceased.

1797.

WHITE DEER ELECTION DISTRICT—BOOKS', FISHER'S, AND BARBER'S MILLS BUILT—GREENVILLE LAID OUT.

EMBERS of Assembly, Simon Snyder and Samuel Maclay. County Commissioners, Henry Vanderslice, Nathan Stockman, and Charles Irwin. Justices of the Peace appointed: Thomas Shipton, January 6; John Hayes, February 2; James Parks, March 30; Thomas McCormick, Washington township, March 30; Frederick Evans, April 18; and Christian Espick, November 27.

March 21, by act of Assembly, all that part of Washington that belongs to Northumberland county, and of White Deer to Little Spruce run; thence down the same to Matthew Laird's; and thence to the river, where Peter Swartz formerly lived, (now Mr. Miller's place;) thence down the river to the mouth of Buffalo creek, was included in the eighth election district, which held its election at William Gallagher's in Milton; and, by the apportionment of this year, Northumberland county became entitled to two members.

Additional Taxables of White Deer—Adams, John; Adams, William; Busser, Jacob; Chamberlin, William, junior; Kelly, John, junior; Shrock, Aaron;. Spotts, Jacob. Henry Gray, Thomas Fredericks, and Michael Greenhoe, had saw-mills, and George Books erected the Books' saw-mill, in West Buffalo. He was a powerful man. In a fight at Rockey's mill, he caught two men, Bogenreif and Iddings, and butted their heads together. Books removed to Ohio, and died there.

Peter Fisher built the grist-mill, lately Samuel Weidensaul's, on Penn's creek, at the mouth of Laurel run. Fisher's successor at the mill was John Williams, his son-in-law. George, Henry, and John Weirick built Robert Barber's grist-mill, on White Spring run. William Weirick, who was the head of the firm of Weiricks, millwrights, lost his life about this time, at a mill on the Juniata. He slept in the mill, arose in sleep, and fell through an opening to the bottom of the mill.

Store-keepers in Lewisburg—James Black, who had William Hayes for his clerk, William McQuhae, and Henry Spyker. Christian Read built the barn of the latter. He charges him with sixteen gallons of whisky, used at the work from June 29 to September.

April 3, George Derr sold Tobias Lehman his Lewisburg mill property and two hundred and eight acres of land.

May 18, Frederick Evans laid out the property, late of George Rote, in lots, and called it Greenville. It adjoined Youngmanstown, and is now within the limits of Mifflinburg.

At the election in October, Robert Irwin had eighteen hundred and forty-six votes; Robert Brady, the next highest, ten hundred and fifty-three. The majority for Irwin was so large, he could not be safely set aside, and was accordingly commissioned, October 18.

Married.

February 9, Thomas Howard married to Elizabeth, daughter of Widow Mary Harris.

Deaths.

January 8, Mary, wife of Robert Chambers, aged sixty-one years.

George Rote. Children: Peter, Jacob, George, Abraham, and John. Sons-in-law, John Kessler, Michael Shirtz, Adam Colpetzer, Joseph Ultz, Frederick Bartges, and James Ben. The latter married the daughter who was a prisoner with the Indians. They last resided on Spring creek, Centre county, where she died, and he married a Widow Murphy.

1798.

THE PRESBYTERIAN GRAVE-YARD AT LEWISBURG—FERRY LANDING DISPUTE—POLITICS—DEATH OF CAPTAIN JOHN LOWDON.

AMUEL DALE and Samuel Maclay, Senators. Members of Assembly, Simon Snyder and Jacob Fulmer. Sheriff, Robert Irwin. Register and Recorder, Jeremiah Simpson, commissioned July 24. Justice of the Peace, Simon Snyder, junior, March 13. John Lawson, May 3. Seventh division, Major General William Montgomery. Second brigade, Brigadier General William Wilson, commissioned March 24. Brigade Inspector, Bernard Hubley, commissioned June 8.

Buffalo : Supervisors, Peter Frederick and John Beatty. Collector, Hugh Beatty.

West Buffalo: Supervisors, David Smith and John Reznor. On the 4th of April West Buffalo was erected into the fourth district, and the election directed to be held at the house of James Forster.

January 10, James Sherer appointed the first postmaster at Lewisburg.

In February, Walter Clark, William Gray, and William Wilson, trustees of the Presbyterian grave-yard at Lewisburg, presented a petition to the Legislature, setting forth that many had buried their friends in lot No. 48, (next Weidensaul's hotel lot,) and there were no persons buried in No. 42, (C. D. Cox's hotel lot,) and asking authority to sell No. 42, (which, with 44 and 46, were, on the 26th of March, 1785, conveyed to them for the use and benefit of the Presbyterian congregation of Buffalo, for the purpose of a burying-ground, by Ludwig Derr, the proprietor,) and to buy No. 48. An act passed accordingly.—3 *Smith's Laws*, 304.

Additional Taxables in Penn's township—John Binkomer, storekeeper; Joseph Barger, saw-mill; Adam Brause, saw, grist-mill, and distillery; John Dusing, shoe-maker and fiddler; Frederick Dreone, surgeon and fiddler; Michael Galer, saw-mill; Adam Fisher, storehouse and ferry; Henry Haus, saw-mill; George Kessler, tanner; Valentine Laudenslager, grist-mill and store; Francis Rhoades, tavern, ferry, and store-house; John Swineford, tavern; Neal St. Clair, taxed with a negro; A. Swineford, two mulattoes.

During this year James Black, owner of lot No. 341, on which Nesbit & Brother's store and house now stand, brought an ejectment to maintain their landing privilege on the river opposite that lot. William Stedman and John Smith had a store in the stone building opposite, owned by Cowden & Hepburn, and the writ was served upon them as tenants.

Francis Guise had bought No. 341 of George Derr, on the 5th of October, 1785, and on his deed was recited the privilege of a landing on the bank of the river, opposite to and of the same breadth of No. 341. The claim was for the ground between the eastern boundary of said lot and low water-mark, on part of which the stone building was erected, but the landing was unobstructed. Black was defeated on the ground that an ejectment will not lie for a mere privilege or an incorporeal hereditament.—2 *Yeates*, 331. Hugh Wilson bought No. 341 at the sheriff's sale of James Black's property, in 1800, and sold it 4th May, 1810, to Adam Grove, who sold it on the 8th of May, 1822, to the late Thomas Nesbit, deceased.

During the summer, politics ran high; the Republicans attacking the alien and sedition laws, and elevating to the rank of martyrs those who had been prosecuted under the sedition laws. At a meeting held in Lewisburg, for the purpose of addressing the President, John Adams, Reverend Hugh Morrison was one of the principal speakers, and in his public speech, indulged in abuse of Samuel Maclay and his family.

Deaths.

Robert Clark, leaving a widow, Jane. Children: Eleanor Fruit,

Margaret Ayres, Robert, George, Charles, and John. His brother, Walter, and his son, John, executors.

John Murphy, Lewisburg. Children: Benjamin, John, Henry, Mary, Nancy, and Sally.

John Wales, New Berlin. Widow, Ann M. Children: James, John, Joseph, Jacob, and Sarah.

Christian Miller, distiller, New Berlin.

Captain John Lowdon died at his residence, near Mifflinburg, in February. His parents were Richard Lowdon and Patience Wright, (married by Friends' ceremony, June 5, 1728,) of Hempfield, (now Columbia, Pennsylvania.) He was born July 5, 1730; married March 27, 1760, by Thomas Barton, missionary, at Lancaster. As early as 1756, Mr. Shippen recommends him for a commission as ensign. He was an inn-keeper at Lancaster in June, 1770, and during this year took up a great deal of land in Buffalo Valley. The land on which Northumberland now stands was patented to his wife, Sarah, in 1770, and, in connection with William Patterson, he laid out that town. Reuben Haines made an addition to it, January 19, 1781, of land sold him by Lowdon in 1775. In the spring of 1772, he moved into Buffalo Valley, residing at a place he called Silver Spring, afterward sold by his executors to Roush, now owned by Levi Shoemaker. His wife died previous to the year 1775, as during this year he signed deeds alone, and it appears by a letter dated the 18th of July, 1775, to Captain Lowdon, at that time in the field, that his five children were with his mother's family, at Hempfield. His prominence in political agitations prior to the Revolution, will be seen by the correspondence of that period, published under those years, and what he said in the cabinet he was not afraid to make good on the field of battle. As soon as the news of the battle of Bunker Hill reached the county, he enlisted a company of ninety-seven men and set off for Cambridge. After his return, on November 7, 1776, he was elected a member of the Supreme Executive Council of Northumberland county, serving for one year. He owned an immense body of land during his life, embracing nearly the whole of West Buffalo township, besides large quantities now lying in Centre and Northumberland. Philip Pontius told me he often visited at his father's, Lieutenant Henry Pontius, and he recollects his appearance distinctly. He was a large, well-proportioned man, with a very pleasant expression of countenance. Doctor W. I. Wilson (of Potter's Mills) told me, when a boy he often saw Captain Lowdon at the Buffalo Cross-Roads church. He wore a cocked hat, blue coat, buff vest and breeches, silver knee and shoe buckles. He was married the second time. His will, dated November 10, 1797, named his wife, Ann, and two daughters, Susanna, married to Samuel Wright, (grandfather of Samuel Wright, of Columbia, Pennsylvania,) Catherine, unmarried, and three grandchildren, John Lowdon Stake, Charlotte and Catherine Stake. He left an annuity to his brother, Richard, who died unmarried. Captain Lowdon's children by his first wife were, Margaret, Susan, James, Patience, and Catherine. Margaret married J. Stake; Susan, Samuel Wright, above named; their child, the late John L. Wright. Margaret's children were Charlotte and Catherine. Charlotte married J. Quest; Catherine, A. Chenowith. Lowdon Stake never married, and that name became extinct. Captain Lowdon's remains were conveyed down the river to Columbia, and buried there in the old burying-ground. Mrs. Wright, mother of William Wright, of Harlem, Stephenson county, Illinois, and daughter of the late Paschal Lewis, of Buffalo Valley, now in her eighty-first year, says her father and mother went part of the way, the day of the funeral, from Lowdon's house to the river, or possibly to Penn's creek; that after Captain Lowdon's death, his slaves were brought over from his farm and left, part of them at Robert Barber's and part at her father's, to stay until such time as Robert Barber was ready to start down with a raft or ark. He took them to Columbia in that way. They had been slaves previous to 1780, and the young ones were still in their apprenticeship, and as his estate was bound to take care of the older ones, Samuel Wright, his son-in-law, set apart forty acres for their habitation and maintenance, on the east side of Columbia, back of the river. Among these were Chloe and Phillis. Chloe was a regular Congo. Phillis died a few years ago, aged one hundred and five. This was the beginning of the famous Tow Hill, so well known to Maryland and Virginia slave hunters as the refuge of their slaves. [William Wright's letter, 1871.] John C. Watson said, the day of Captain Lowdon's funeral the creek rose very high, and they could not get over with the coffin, when "Mel," Colonel Clarke's slave, shouldered the coffin and went over the foot-log with it.

1799.

HARTLETON—SKETCH OF COLONEL THOMAS HARTLEY—LISTS OF TAXABLES —MARTIN DREISBACH—THOMAS WILSON.

NDREW GREGG, Member of Congress. Samuel Dale and Samuel Maclay, Senators. Jacob Fulmer and Simon Snyder, members of the House. Henry Spyker, commissioned Justice of the Peace for East Buffalo, March 9; John Cummings, Beaver, December 6.

Hartleton was laid out by Colonel Thomas Hartley, who owned the site and a considerable body of land around it. His first deed for a lot is dated March 28, 1799. There is no plan of the place on record. Colonel Hartley was a distinguished lawyer, born near Reading, September 7, 1748, admitted at York, July 25, 1769. He was lieutenant colonel of sixth Pennsylvania battalion, Colonel William Irvine, and commanded the battalion after Colonel Irvine's capture at Three Rivers. The anonymous letters published in *Force's Archives*, describing this campaign, were written by Colonel Hartley. This battalion served one year. There were two additional regiments to the Pennsylvania line raised in the State in 1777, whose officers were to be appointed by General Washington. Colonel Hartley was appointed to one, and commanded, temporarily, a brigade at Brandywine. In 1778, his regiment was ordered into the West Branch valley. On the 13th of January, 1779, it was combined with the other additional regiment, Colonel John Patton's, under the name of eleventh, the old eleventh having been broken up; whereupon, February 13, Colonel Hartley retired from service, and Lieutenant Colonel Adam Hubley succeeded to the command of the eleventh. In 1783 he was a member of the Council of Censors; in 1787, of the State Convention. In 1788, he was elected to Congress, and continued a member until his death, December 21, 1800. He died at York, aged fifty-three, and is buried in St. John's church-yard there. He left two children, Charles William Hartley, some time prothonotary of York county, and Eleanor, married to Doctor James Hall, afterward physician to the lazaretto, at Philadelphia.

Among Taxables in White Deer—Awl, John; Bennage, George; Baughner, William; Bellman, George; Bennage, John; Bower, Moses; Covert, Isaac; Covert, John; Gottshall, Michael; Linn, Charles; Nees, Henry; Orr, John; Oliphant, Andrew; Rauthraff, Henry; Sheetz, Jacob.

Single men—Chamberlin, Tenbrooke; Davis, Stephen; Luther, John; Stahl, George; and Rank, Adam.

In West Buffalo—Christopher Johnston is taxed with grist and saw-mill; Peter Rote, grist and saw-mill; Burrows, Aaron; Betz, Adam, tavern-keeper; McClelland, James, miller at Barber's White Springs. He was a great joker, and his fun was still current among the old people when I began these Annals. Saunders, Henry; Shively, Christian, son of John; Webb, George, hatter; Wilt, Adam; Wilt, George.

In East Buffalo—Auple, Conrad; Baker, Wendell, two mills; Barber, Joseph, blacksmith; Beatty, Ann, widow; Betzer, Conrad, cordwainer; Betting, Joseph; Boyles, William; Breyvogel, Jacob; Christie, James; Collin, John; Cook, John, cabin; Cornelius, John; Coser, Andrew; Ewing, Joshua; Eyer, John; Frederick, George, inn-keeper; Gross, Jacob; Hudson, William, mason; Kinney, Martin; Lehman, Tobias, two mills; McKinley, Hugh; Ness, Jonathan; Nevel, Nicholas; Oldt, John; Poeth, Joseph; Sherer, William, weaver; Shout, Adam, shoe-maker; Strayhorn, Nathaniel; St. Clair, John; Taylor, James Graham; Taylor, William, tailor; Truitt, Andrew; Watkins, Joseph, weaver; Wetzel, Jacob; Whitmer, Peter, blacksmith; Wigton, John; Wilson, Hugh, (Ridge;) Wright, John; Wolfe, Michael; Young, Jacob; Zeihrung, John.

Philip Callahan was one of the principal school-teachers in the

Valley. He had a large account at Henry Spyker's store for whisky and tobacco.

The difficulty between Reverend Hugh Morrison and Honorable Samuel Maclay terminated in a suit for slander. Morrison *vs.* Maclay, 101 August term; Evan R. Evans for plaintiff, Messrs. Moore, Cooper, and Roberts for defendant. It was regularly continued until 1817, when the clients and most of the lawyers had appeared before another bar.

George Frederick started the first hotel at Buffalo Cross-Roads.

In 1799, Mifflinburg was the largest town in the Valley. Its residents were Ayers, James, shoe-maker; Bartges, Michael, nailor; Barton, Kimber, tavern-keeper; Black, William, shoe-maker; Carmony, John, shoe-maker; Carothers, Moses; Clark, Daniel, tanner; Clark, Adam, jobber; Collins, Michael, jobber; Crotzer, John, carpenter; Crotzer, Jacob, tailor; Derr Christian, joiner; Dreisbach, John, gunsmith; Earnhart, John, blacksmith; Eilert, Christopher, farmer; Ely, John, clock-maker; Evans, Nathan, saddler; Forster, James, tavern-keeper; George, Simon, laborer; Getgen, Ludwig, mason; Gibbons, John, joiner; Hassenplug, Henry, brewer; Herring, Adam; Herrington, Nathan, cooper; Holmes, Robert, store-keeper; Holmes, Jonathan, jobber; Irvine, John, store-keeper; Layman, Michael, joiner; Lighty, John, tanner; Longabaugh, Henry, laborer; Moss, Patrick, jobber; Neel, Henry, tailor; Paget, George, school-teacher; Patterson, John; Patton, Andrew, wheelwright; Peters, Philip, carter; Rockey, Jacob; Rote, Widow; Rudy, Nicholas, tailor; Russ, Charles; Russ, George, tailor; Sampsel, Nicholas, wheelwright; Shock, Michael, carpenter; Shock, Jacob, blacksmith; Skiles, James; Van Buskirk, Richard, tavern-keeper; Wagner, Christopher, farmer; Webb, John, hatter; Welker, Jacob, tailor; Welker, William, jobber; Young, Peter, shoemaker; Youngman, Elias; Youngman, George, post-master; Youngman, Thomas, store-keeper.

Additional Taxables in Penn's—Adams, John, weaver; Anderson, Jacob, inn-keeper; Auple, Peter, inn-keeper; Balliet, Nicholas, tanner; Bard, Jacob, skin-dresser; Berger, Bostian, weaver; Berry, John, potter; Beyer, Christian, carpenter; Bleiler, David, millwright; Bloom, Henry, weaver; Bowersox, George A., mason; Bower, Philip, inn-keeper; Boyer, John, blacksmith; Bryan, George, tailor; Bucher, John, blacksmith; Bull, Nicholas, tailor; Bum, Peter, saw-mill; Clymer, Isaac, shoemaker; Cooper, Martin, cooper; Dauberman, John, carpenter; Deitz, Jacob, blacksmith; Engel, George, weaver; Epler, John, nailor; Esterlin, Frederick, carpenter; Etzweiler, George, potter; Filman, John, weaver; Fisher, Peter, weaver; Frey, David, shoe-maker; Fuehrer, Joseph, tobacconist; Gaughler, Nicholas, gunsmith; Gemberling, Jacob, nailor; Gemberling, George, carpenter; Giltner, Christian, carpenter; Grove, Richard, saddler; Grub, John, carpenter; Hackenberg, John, carpenter; Hager, John, died; Haines, John and George, wheelwrights; Harland, Thomas, miller; Holtzapple, Henry, miller; Hummel, Jacob, distiller; Hummel, Frederick, shoe-maker; Kelly, John, carpenter; Kratzer, Benjamin, shoe-maker; Kreider, Isaac, carpenter; Kuhn, Jacob, weaver; Leist, Andrew, mason; Long, Peter, shoe-maker; Maurer, John, nailor; Merkel, George, turner; Meyer, John, son of Stephen, shoe-maker; Meyer, Jacob, son of Stephen, tailor; Miller, George, tailor; Neaman, Peter, fiddler; Nelson, John, tailor; Oberdorf, Henry, mason; Oswald, John, tailor; Row, John and Frederick, masons; Rupp, George, carpenter; Shearer, Andrew, blacksmith; Shock, Jacob, blacksmith; Snyder, John, tailor; Snyder, George, shoe-maker; Snyder, George, inn-keeper; Snyder, Simon, junior, inn-keeper; Spade, George, mason; Straw, Andrew, hatter; Stump, Jacob, shoe-maker; Wales, James, millwright; Weiser, Benjamin, tailor; Weikel, Christian, tailor; Werlin, Michael, ferry and saw-mill; Westman, Jacob, carpenter; Wittenmoyer, Michael, clock-maker; Wolf, Philip, millwright; Yoder, Henry, carpenter; Yoder, Jacob, potter.

Beaver, additional Residents, &c.—Aurand, Daniel; Barlet, Jacob; Blompon, Conrad, mill; Cummings, John; Fry, Jacob and Abraham; Gilman, Henry; Grosscope, Samuel; Heil, Daniel; Howell, John, fulling-mill; Lehr, William; Manning, Richard; Middlesworth, John; Miller, John; Peters, Jacob; Reigeldorf, Adam; Romig, Joseph, mills; Rote, Jacob and John; Smith, Adam; Steele, Adam; Sterninger, Dewalt; Wise, John, miller; Zerns, Jacob, paper mill.

Single Men—Hoyn, Henry, in a store with Henry Aurand; Kern, Adam; Kern, Peter; Mussina, Zacharias; Weber, John.

At the October election, Thomas McKean received, in Northumberland county, 2,997 votes; James Ross, of Pittsburgh, 637 for Governor. Jacob Fulmer and Simon Snyder were the two highest candidates for Assembly, Fulmer having 3,569; Snyder, 3,047.

Deaths.

On the 18th of February, Martin Dreisbach, senior, aged eighty-two. He emigrated from Germany in 1752, and came into Buffalo Valley in 1773, having purchased from Doctor William Plunket the tract still owned by the Dreisbachs. He left four sons, Henry, Jacob, John, and Martin, junior. Henry went to Ohio in the year 1804, and laid out the town of Circleville. Jacob died on John Dunkle's farm. John lived and died at Mifflinburg. George, Ellis, and John were his sons. Martin, junior, died at his place, near the church. Martin, senior, was of the German Reformed faith, and donated seven acres of his place for church and grave-yard purposes. "The Dreisbach Church" will be his memorial in all future time. One of his daughters married Henry Aurand; another, Peter Fisher. Honorable Martin Dreisbach, (third,) and Honorable John Dreisbach, formerly of the State Legislature, are of his grandchildren.

Philip Stahl, of White Deer. (He was a brother of Jacob.) His children were John, Jacob, Philip, and Peter.

Thomas Wilson.

February 23, Thomas Wilson, of East Buffalo. He lived on the Meixell place, (fair ground.) His grandfather was the first to pass the Boyne, when William of Orange defeated the Irish Papists. For his services he drew two hundred and sixty acres of land. He resided within a mile of Coats' Hill, county town of Cavan, in the north of Ireland. He owned a large body of land there, having sixty tenants. His son Thomas had but one child, Hugh, to whom his estates descended. The latter disliked living among the Papists so much, that he sold his estates, and came to America, and finally settled in the forks of the Delaware. Hugh bought twelve hundred acres of land of the Allens, but lost six hundred, a superior title intervening. His farm in Northampton was owned, in 1844, by a man named Levan, had mills upon it, and is very valuable. In 1737, he, with Colonel

Martin, laid out the town of Easton, and, with Judge Craig, organized and held the first court held in Northampton county, in 1752. He left a large family.

1. William Wilson, a merchant, in Philadelphia. He went to the West Indies, and died there. 2. Ann, married to Reverend McReynolds, of Deep Run, Presbyterian preacher. 3. Elizabeth, married to Captain William Craig. 4. Charles, father of Judge Hugh Wilson, of the Ridge, some of whose grandchildren are still in the Valley : Robert, a merchant at Mifflinburg ; Charles, a grandson, is baggage-master on the Pennsylvania road, at Altoona. 5. Samuel. 6. Margaret, married to McNair. 7. Francis, went back to the old country, and returned an Episcopal minister ; settled near Mount Vernon, taught in General Lee's family, and was intimate in General Washington's family. His family called him "Aun Boyne," to remind him that he had made too great concessions in becoming an Episcopalian. 8. Thomas Wilson, whose death we are recording. He was twelve or thirteen years of age, when his father, Hugh, moved his family to America, making their emigration about 1730. He spent a great deal of his means purchasing flour, and forwarding it to the revolutionary army. He was paid in Continental money, and his loss on its depreciation was about seven thousand dollars, which reduced his circumstances very materially. He sold out his place in Northampton, moved to the Susquehanna, and bought the place now owned (1877) by Joseph Meixell's heirs, about one half mile from Lewisburg, where he died. His grave is under the steps of the Presbyterian church. It was not disturbed by the building, but the tombstones of himself and his son Francis, were removed to the Wilson lot, in the Lewisburg cemetery. His widow, whose name before marriage was Elizabeth Hayes, moved, in 1803, with her sons, William and Thomas, to Beaver county, where she died in 1818. Their children were Hugh, father of Francis Wilson ; Sarah, married to Richard Fruit, moved to Mercer county, died in the spring of 1844 ; Eliazbeth, married to James Duncan, of Aaronsburg ; she died in 1797 ; Mary, married to Jonathan Coulter, sheriff of Beaver county ; William Wilson, died in Beaver, 1841 ; James Wilson, attorney-at-law, died in New Orleans, 1800 ; Margaret Wilson, married John Thomas, storekeeper, at Hartley, moved to Beaver ; Thomas Wilson, of Beaver, who died 6th July, 1860, aged eighty-

21

five years; Colonel Joseph H. Wilson, of the one hundred and first Pennsylvania, who died near White House, Virginia, July 11, 1862, was his son. He had been district attorney of Beaver county, and a member of the Legislature. Thomas Wilson left ten children, residing in Beaver county.

1800.

INHABITANTS OF NEW BERLIN AND LEWISBURG—SKETCHES OF THE NORTHUMBERLAND COUNTY BAR—DANIEL SMITH, EVAN RICE EVANS, CHARLES HALL, &c.

OVERNOR, Thomas McKean. Members, Simon Snyder, Jacob Fulmer. September 24, Daniel Levy, Esquire, commissioned Prothonotary, &c., *vice* Jasper Ewing, deceased. October 23, Henry Vanderslice commissioned Sheriff. Brigade Inspector, Frederick Lazarus.

List of Inhabitants of New Berlin in 1800.

Beatty, William; Beatty, Hugh; Berger, Philip, potter; Clark, John; Cook, James; Gill, Isaac; Grove, George, saddler; Herman, Philip, carpenter; Myer, George, weaver; Myer, George, tailor; Overmyer, Philip; Parks, James, Esquire, store-keeper; Rearick, William; Rothrow, Jacob; Seebold, Christopher; Smith, Peter, sailor; Spaight, Adam; Trester, Martin, carpenter; Wagoner, Andrew, inn-keeper.

List of Inhabitants of Lewisburg in 1800.

Albright, Andrew, inn-keeper; Beatty, John; Black, James; Bole, Samuel, weaver; Byers, Charles; Clark, George, store-keeper; Dreisbach Jacob; Endsworth, Andrew, saddler; Evans, Joseph, joiner; Fairchild, Caleb, blacksmith; Grove, Adam; Kemmel, Lawrence, tinsmith; Knox, George, tanner; Lawshe, John, tavern; Leisenring, John, potter; McLaughlin, Hugh, tailor; Metzgar, Daniel, saddler; Metzgar, George, hatter; Metzgar, John, storekeeper; Miller, Valentine; Park, Thomas, tanner; Pollock, John, store-keeper; Pollock, William, tailor; Reed, Christian, joiner; Shaffer, Mathias, carpenter; Shearer, Richard, store-keeper; Spyker, Henry, store-keeper; Stedman, William, inn-keeper, Strickland, Timothy, carpenter; Troxel, Abraham; Wilson, Hugh, store-keeper.

List of Single Freemen in East Buffalo, in 1800.

Anderson, Samuel; Baker, Jacob, fuller; Betzer, Peter, weaver; Bolender, George; Bracken, James; Callahan, Patrick; Callahan, Philip; Dale, Samuel; Deratt, Daniel; Dreisbach, Martin; Finess, John; Forster John; Forster, William; Frantz, John, cordwainer; Frantz, Jacob, weaver; Frederick, George; Hafer, Lewis; Hartley, Thomas, carpenter; Hays, Philip, junior; Hayes, William; Hayes, Patrick; Keeth, Andrew; McClay, William; McClosky, William; McQuhae, William; Markle, John, blacksmith; Morton, John; Nickle, John; Pollock, Edward; Price, John, store-keeper; Reedy, Conrad; Russell, Alexander; Slater, Peter; Smith, Benjamin; Spyker, Peter; Stahl, John, wheelwright; Thompson, James; Ward, Thomas; Ward, William; Wise, John; Wise, Daniel; Wolf, John; Yentzer, Christian.

Sketches of the Northumberland Bar, by Charles Miner.

" Daniel Smith, Esquire, a tall, delicate looking gentleman, always elegantly dressed. He turns pale and actually trembles as he rises to speak. You are interested by such exceeding modesty, and half fear he will not be able to go on. His voice breaks sweetly on the ear, and words of persuasive wisdom begin to flow, and now pour along in a rapid torrent. Ah! that is eloquence." He graduated at Princeton in 1787.

" Evan Rice Evans, a heavy, stout gentleman, with a large head and florid complexion. His delivery rapid; his words crowd upon each other as sometimes to choke utterance. He talks good sense. Why should he not? His head has more law in it than half a modern library. He is a powerful advocate, with a good fee and an intricate case." He died in 1811. His daughter married Hugh Brady, Esquire, son of William P., of Indiana county.

"Charles Hall, Esquire. A very handsome man. His dress is rich, ruffles neatly plaited. Slow, distinct, and very pleasant in speaking. He prepares with care, and argues his cause with excellent skill." He came from Lancaster county. His wife was a Coleman, owning a great estate, still called the Hall farms, above Muncy.

"Honorable Thomas Cooper. Short round figure, stooping forward; has a florid, high, English countenance and complexion. His *forte* is to seize two or three strong points, and present them forcibly to the court and jury. He never wearies by long speeches; never uses a word, or an illustration, or an argument that is not to the purpose; a man of extraordinary endowments and of most distinguished genius." From John Binns' Autobiography I take some notices: When I came first to Northumberland, September 1, 1802, there then resided Doctor Joseph Priestly, son, and family, and Thomas Cooper, Esquire, afterwards president judge in that district, and also president of the State College of South Carolina. He was fined and imprisoned for libel on President John Adams. The fine, with interest, was, on a petition of Doctor Cooper, refunded by a vote of Congress, many years afterwards, I think when General Jackson was President. The doctor wielded a powerful pen in favor of the general's election, and he was a man who rarely forgot to repay both partisans and opponents. Before Judge Cooper came to this country, he accompanied Mr. Watt, of steam engine memory, to Paris, and they took their seats in the French convention as representatives of the Manchester Philosophical Society. In 1820, Doctor Cooper resided in Philadelphia, as professor of chemistry in the University of Pennsylvania, and was a member of a club, with John Binns, which met every Monday evening at each other's houses. While here, he published his "Jurisprudence," and his edition of the "Institutes of Justinian." Binns says the first breach in their club was made by the removal of Doctor Cooper to South Carolina. His extensive knowledge, wit, and good humor were sufficient to instruct and enliven any society. His literary and scientific knowledge were of world-wide fame. His reply to "Burke's Invective" was inferior to no answer that was published.

It took rank with those of Paine and Mackintosh. At the time he was printing that book, William Y. Birch was apprentice to the publisher. He said, when Cooper stepped in to correct the proof, the printer would say, "We want more copy, sir," and Cooper would set down and write two or three sheets, and hand it to the printer without reading, much less correcting. He had a heart as warm and capacious as his mind was richly stored. He was my ardent and faithful friend for a period of nearly half a century. I have his portrait, taken when ninety years of age. He was a chemist of no common caliber; admirable in compounding sauces and gravies, and enjoyed them very much. He was somewhat of a gourmand, yet he was never idle, and lived to the very advanced age of ninety-eight or ninety-nine, cheerful and polite to his last days.

Miner mentions Daniel Levy, Thomas Duncan, and Charles Huston, but makes no particular note of them. Daniel Levy was the survivor of these old-style lawyers, who always dressed in broadcloth, wore queues, gold watch seals, and were eminently dignified and respectful.

October 14. Bishop Newcomer again visits the Valley. "Crossed the West Branch at Northumberland with a great deal of trouble, and reached the house of Abraham Eyerly after dark. Next day he went to Brother Aurand's, where a great many people had collected and he and Brother David Snyder addressed them. On 16th, preached at John Rank's, in White Deer. 17th, at John Baer's. 18th, sacrament at Martin Dreisbach's; rode twenty miles through the rain to get there. Held class meeting, and had a happy time. Text on Sunday, 19th, "For the time is come when judgment must begin at the house of God." Preached at Mr. Dreisbach's in the evening; next day, at Mr. Walter's, and at night at a poor man's house, on Middle creek."

At the presidential election in 1800, parties were clearly defined under the names of Federalists and Democrats.

Kimber Barton, who lived at Mifflinburg, was assessor of United States taxes. The tax on window glass was very unpopular. The assessor had to go to each house and count the panes. Before he arrived, some people went to the trouble of taking out their glass and putting in paper. John Bower, father of Thomas Bower, of Middleburg, was married to a sister of Kimber Barton.

Deaths.

Jasper Ewing, attorney-at-law, and late prothonotary of the county, died. He was from Lancaster county. His library he left to his four nieces, daughters of General Edward Hand, of Lancaster; his fees to his nephews, John and Jesse Hand, together with his gun, fishing rod, and gold watch; his cane to Charles Hall, Esquire.

He was adjutant of the first Pennsylvania, Colonel Hand, in July, 1776. In April, 1777, when Hand was promoted brigadier, and appointed to the command of the Western department, Ewing went with him to Fort Pitt, as brigade major, and served as such during the years 1777-1778.

1801.

REJOICING AT JEFFERSON'S ELECTION—CONDITION OF THE REFORMED CHURCH IN THE VALLEY.

MEMBERS of Congress, Andrew Gregg and John A. Hanna. Senators, Samuel Maclay and James Harris. Act of February 27, reduced the number to one. Members, Jacob Fulmer, Jesse Moore, Samuel Dale, and Simon Snyder. July 18; William Montgomery appointed Associate, *vice* Thomas Strawbridge, resigned. County Commissioners, John Metzgar, John Frick, and Abram McKinney.

February 27, Apportionment bill allows Northumberland one Senator and four members. Taxables, four thousand seven hundred and forty-four.

Additional Residents of East Buffalo—Robinson, William, John Lawshe, keeping the "Pennsylvania Arms," at Lewisburg.

Additions to White Deer Township—Clingan, William, Esquire;

Cornelius, James; Espy, John, shoe-maker; Hafer, Lewis; Iredell, Seth, miller at White Deer mills; Linn, David; Long, Joseph; Lutz, Jacob; Lutz, Samuel; McGinnes, John; McGinnes, James; Marr, David; Sarvey, Christian; Shuck, Andrew; Stillwell, Joseph; Weikel, George.

George Wilt, of Cumberland county, bought the Narrows property of Michael Shirtz. His sons, Adam and George, came up and built a new mill, and jointly kept the hotel, afterwards kept by Roushs, Stitzers, &c. Adam Wilt and John Fisher, who formerly lived on Esquire Lincoln's place, ran arks out of Penn's creek, from 1810 to 1818. Adam was the first man that ran Conewago falls with an ark, successfully. Products of the Valley then went down in the shape of whisky, linseed oil, &c.

March 4, a meeting was held at Bethuel Vincent's, in Milton, to celebrate the inauguration of Thomas Jefferson. Colonel Kelly's toast was: "May this be the happy day to unite the hearts of all true Americans in their duty to God and our illustrious President." This year the road from Jenkins' mill to where it joins the Mifflinburg and Lewisburg road, was laid out by Abraham Eyerly and Daniel Rees.

Richard Sherer, postmaster at Lewisburg, advertises that the Philadelphia mail arrived at Northumberland every Saturday at two, P. M., and returned on Sunday at six, A. M.

The following sketch, taken from Doctor Harbaugh's Fathers, relates, of course, to the Reformed portion of Dreisbach church:

The Buffalo church, now called Dreisbach, had, for some time, been in a very distracted condition, having the irregular attention of the irregular Pfruemer, called Frömmer, but was, for the most part, closed entirely. The young men were growing up without adequate spiritual instruction, and the old members having passed through scenes of strife, had grown, to a great degree, indifferent. Seeing, however, at length, that religious matters were tending in a bad way, they awoke and saw that something must be done. Reformed ministers being at that time few, and difficult to be secured, they thought they saw in Deitrich Aurand, who was still on his farm, a man who could be useful among them as a Reformed minister. About the beginning of the year 1801 they came together, and unanimously and very cordially agreed to call upon him to preach a sermon in that church, which he consented to do. The appointment was made. The day arrived. The people assembled in great numbers. The pews, the galleries, the isles, the doors, the lower windows, and even the grove in front of the church were crowded with listeners, anxious to hear the new preacher. Some, no doubt, came from motives of curiosity, but the greater portion were there with a true desire to hear the Gospel. " Never," says an eye witness, "have I seen a multitude so eager to hear the words of life." The sermon ended, he came down from the pulpit, and standing in the altar, he was soon surrounded by the "ancient men" of the church, who earnestly desired him to make another appointment. The congregation, having, in the meantime, stood still, he announced that he would preach again as desired, appointing the time.

The second sermon was attended by a still greater multitude of people, some coming from a distance of ten and fifteen miles. The day was pleasant. The organ, long silent, had been repaired by the skillful hands of Mr. John Betz, the school-master, and was made to accompany the hymns by Stophel Aupel. The theme of the preacher was the astonishing love of Jesus Christ, in condescending to come into the world to save sinners. The absolute necessity of timely preparation to meet death was earnestly and pathetically urged upon all present. Towards the conclusion, different classes were separately addressed and exhorted. The young were asked how the hope for a blissful eternity stood with them? and they were entreated to seek the Lord early, and remember their Creator in the days of their youth. Then the preacher turned to those in middle life, and in words of melting tenderness and burning zeal, were they warned against delay, and urged to flee from the wrath to come. Finally he turned to the aged, among whom sat his own venerable father, crying with the deepest feeling, Oh ! you who are hoary-headed, how stands the matter between you and your God? You stand already with one foot in the grave, and in a few more days will sink into it, and have no more any portion forever in all that is done under the sun. You have, through a long life, enjoyed the mercies and favors of your kind Heavenly Father. Have you served Him with full submission to His will, and loved Him supremely? and have you the assurance that you are reconciled to Him, through His dear Son

Jesus Christ? If so, oh! then it will be well with you. But, if this has not been done, oh! then, I now entreat you, as you value the everlasting rest and peace of your souls, do not delay, but accept the offers of mercy in Christ, our dear Redeemer. "Such," says one who was present, "was the spirit and substance, and such, as near as I can recollect, even the closing words of this never-to-be-forgotten sermon. It made a deep impression upon me as a youth, and I remember distinctly of having seen his own father, and such men as the Dreisbachs, the Dunkels, the Barnharts, the Betzs, the Goodmans, and others, bathed in tears."

He was unanimously elected pastor, and the congregation of New Berlin joined with them in the call, which he agreed to accept. He had been licensed by the "Brethren," but was not yet ordained or even licensed by the Synod. He began, however, to catechise in the Dreisbach church, and large numbers attended, whom he confirmed, baptizing such as had not been. "Never since that day," says an aged eye-witness, "have I witnessed such solemnity and strong feeling as on that day of the consecration of those youth, and the next day at communion."

On the 3d of May the Synod met at York, and a request was made by the congregations of Buffalo Valley and New Berlin for the examination and ordination of Mr. Aurand. The matter, however, was deferred, principally at his own request, until he might improve himself. He, however, continued to preach to the congregations of Buffalo Valley and New Berlin, until his removal to Huntingdon county, in October, 1804, where he founded the congregation of Water street. He died near there, on the 24th of April, 1831, aged seventy years five months and sixteen days, and is buried in front of Zion's church, at Water street.

November 11, Reverend Hugh Morrison regularly dismissed from the Presbyterian congregation at Buffalo Cross-Roads.

Marriages.

September 27, by William Irwin, Esquire, Jacob D. Breyvogel, printer, of Sunbury, to Susanna Baldy, daughter of Colonel Christopher Baldy, of Buffalo.

November 19, by Reverend Bryson, William Kirk, of Turbut, to

Miss Jane Knox, of Lewisburg, and Daniel Dreisbach, merchant, to Katy Dreisbach, both of Lewisburg. "Whosoever findeth a good wife findeth a good thing, and obtaineth favor of the Lord."

Deaths.

Sunday, September 20, Colonel Frederick Antes, of Northumberland, died at Lancaster, buried in the German Reformed churchyard. John Thompson, of Buffalo, died. His children, James, Benjamin, Rachel Lincoln, Susanna Patterson, and Sarah Piper. John Reznor, West Buffalo, leaving a widow, Rebecca, and children, John, George, Agnes, &c.

November 4, Mrs. Jean McClure, buried on the 5th, in the Presbyterian yard, Lewisburg. She left fourteen children, one hundred and ten grandchildren, one hundred and forty-eight great-grandchildren, and four great-great-grandchildren; total, two hundred and seventy-six. Thirty-six of them attended the funeral. She was of an amiable, benevolent, and friendly disposition, and might be called a true christian.—*Kennedy's Gazette.*

1802.

Residents in Freeburg, Middleburg, &c.—St. Peter's Church, in Kelly, and Ray's Church Built—Tabular Statement of Election Returns—Death of Joseph Green.

ENATOR, SAMUEL MACLAY ; elected Speaker of the Senate, December 7. On the 14th of December he was elected United States Senator. Members, Jesse Moore, Jacob Fulmer, Daniel Montgomery, and Simon Snyder. County Treasurer, Christopher Dering. County Commissioner elect, Flavel Roan. Andrew Albright, Postmaster, Lewisburg.

Hotels: Adam Wilt, Narrows ; Richard Van Buskirk, Youngmanstown ; C. Baldy, Cross-Roads ; Isaac Latshaw, Lewisburg ; John Metzgar, Andrew Albright, at the ferry.

Residents in Straubstown, or Freeburg.

Alspice, Doctor Henry ; Felmly, Jacob ; Hackenberg, Michael, joiner ; Long, Peter ; Moore, Andrew ; Moore, Philip ; Myer, Michael ; Myer, Jacob, son of Stephen ; Myer, George ; Nagle, John ; Reigert, Paul ; Roush, John, tan-yard ; Rupert, John ; Schock, Jacob ; Smith, John, weaver ; Straub, George, son of Peter ; Stump, Abraham ; Weaver, Michael.

Swinefordstown—Aurand, John, joiner ; Epler, John ; Fry, David, shoe-maker ; Fry, Jacob, senior ; Kennel, Mark ; Lechner, Jacob, inn-keeper ; Leist, David ; Mertz, Isaac ; Mussina, Zacharias ; Nelson, John ; Smith, Martin, cooper ; Smith, Robert ; Spade,

George; Spade, David; Swineford, George; Weller, John; Wiant, Michael; Wittemyer, Michael, clock-maker.

Selinsgrove and Weisertown—Clymer, Isaac; Drum, Charles; Dusing, John; Etzweiler, George; Fisher, Peter; Four, Joseph, weaver; Gaughler, Nicholas; Gemberling, Charles; Gettig, Frederick; Good, Adam; Hegins, Charles, tavern; Hughes, Widow; Kemerer, Christian; Krider, Isaac; Laudenslager, Valentine, tavern; Meyer, Widow; Mewhorter, Henry, tanner; Myer, Jacob; Newmauer, Michael; Oberdorf, Henry; Price, Thomas; Rhoads, Francis; Rhoads, Henry; Rhoads, Daniel; Reim, Nicholas; Robins, Alexander, tailor; Roop, George; Silverwood, James; Snyder, Simon; Tryon, Frederick; Ulrick, George.

Mahantango Township—Bergstresser, John, millwright; Christ, Valentine; Derstein, Michael; Gordon, Willis; Hagerty, Robert; Heimback, George and Jacob; Holtzapple, Widow; Light, Adam; Richter, Widow; Richter, John; Stees, Frederick, adds fulling-mill and smith shop; Walter, Conrad.

Additional Residents in East Buffalo—Barbin, Joseph; Bellman, Henry; Benner, John; Bickle, Leonard; Billmyer, Jacob; Billmyer, George; Brouse, Peter; Cummings, James; Coser, Andrew; Dale, James; Dale, Samuel, junior; Dreisbach, John, gunsmith; Dreisbach, John, carpenter; Elder, Robert, on John Kelly's place; Freeman, Widow, on John Wiggin's place; Hull, Thomas, on Conrad Reedy's place; Irwin, Andrew; Jodon, James, on Andrew Struble's place; Maclay, William P.; Maclay, Charles; Markley, John, junior; Messinger, John; Reedy, Andrew; Shoemaker, Jacob; Slough, Christian; Tietsworth, Jacob, on Simington's place; Wolfe, George Wendell; Winegarden, Peter; Young, Abraham.

Lewisburg—Brice, John; Donachy, John, weaver; Franklin, Daniel; Hartley, Thomas, carpenter; McKinty, Barney; Russell, David, mason.

New Berlin—Himmelreich, Peter; Mussina, Zacharias; Reminger, Peter, shoe-maker; Speddy, Jeremiah, shoe-maker.

White Deer—Armstrong, John, on Margaret Blythe's place; Bayard, Benjamin; Blackeney, John; Bowers, John; Bowers, Barbara, widow; Criswell, Joseph; Espy, John, shoe-maker; Lawshe, John, still-house, on George Derr's place; Marr, David, on Riddle's place; Servey, Christian; Weikel, George.

Improvements—John Hoffman, saw-mill; Seth Iredell, three-story stone grist-mill, Anthony Morris having recovered the property of the Widow Smith. The mill had two pair of overshot wheels. A new saw-mill was added, stone dwelling-house and barn were on the premises, and an excellent shad fishery.

West Buffalo—Baxter, Robert; Blunbaum, Conrad; Boop, John; Boop, Davidson, George; William; Deal, Henry; Deering, Christopher; Englehart, George; Gill, Isaac, on Robert Barber's place; Gutelius, Frederick, cooper; Heise, Solomon; Imhoof, John; Leberick, George, tanner; Shultz, Daniel; Smith, Melchior, saw and hemp-mill on Laurel run; Spigelmoyer, John. The stone house on Mather's place, in Limestone township, built.

St. Peter's Church.

The church known as St. Peter's Lutheran church, in Kelly, was built upon land donated by Philip Stahl. Jacob Lotz, his executor, by deed, dated August 13, 1802, recorded at Sunbury, in deed book L, pages 712–713, conveys to Christian Zerbe and George Reininger seven acres and ninety-one perches, in Kelly township, in trust to and for the use of building or erecting a school-house and a German Lutheran church on the same, and for a burying-ground, by the following bounds and measures: beginning at a line of Henry Neese; thence S. 88° W. 78, to a post; thence S. 2° E. 22, to a post; thence N. 80° W. 80 perches, to a post; thence N. 2° W. 11, to beginning.

Ray's Church.

Ray's church, in Lewis, was founded by a gift of one acre of land by Mr. Ray. The first church was never finished. The timbers furnished seats in the gallery up to the time of the building of the new church.

September 24, Bishop Newcomer again visits the Valley, preached in Youngmanstown and at Aurand's. 25th, quarterly meeting commenced at Martin Dreisbach's. Brother Kempt preached the first discourse, and Brother Farley, a Methodist, spoke in English.

Republican standing committee, General William Montgomery,

Henry Vanderslice, Simon Snyder, Robert Giffen, and Christopher Baldy. April 2, Northumberland, Lycoming, and Centre made a congressional district. September 16, meeting of delegates at John Metzgar's, in Lewisburg, John Barber, chairman. Nominated Andrew Gregg for Congress.

Saturday, 18th. The following delegates met in convention at Lewisburg, at Metzgar's hotel: Augusta, Charles Maus; Shamokin, Jesse Simpson; Point, Robert Irwin; Chillisquaque, James Strawbridge; Mahoning, Mathew Collum; Penn's, Charles Drum; Derry, George Langs; Turbut, Bethuel Vincent; West Buffalo, John Dreisbach; East Buffalo, Andrew Albright; White Deer, Andrew McLanachan. Thomas McKean nominated for Governor; Samuel Maclay, for Senator; Jesse Moore, Jacob Fulmer, John Bull, and Daniel Montgomery, junior, for Assembly; Solomon Markley and John Wilson for Commissioners.

ELECTION RETURNS, 1802.

DISTRICTS.	GOV'NR.		CON	SEN	ASSEMBLY.				
	Thomas McKean.	James Ross.	Andrew Gregg.	Samuel Maclay.	Jesse Moore.	Jacob Fulmer.	D. Montgomery.	Simon Snyder.	Samuel Dale.	John Bull.
Sunbury,	180	26	189	194	200	199	180	133	12	87
Northumberland,	133	35	152	153	140	138	65	32	36	112
Buffalo,	201	14	211	209	205	156	97	143	191	5
West Buffalo,	194	17	210	210	206	203	11	74	79	9
Berlin,	136	1	136	139	137	137	1	136	138	1
Swineford,	119		121	129	112	121	1	111	118	
Bloom and Brier,	95	20	114	112	112	20	108	102		111
Milton,	347	21	356	352	366	323	356	53	36	175
Selinsgrove,	231	9	232	234	234	227	59	217	152	41
Mahanoy,	139	2	140	140	134	140	74	45	101	52
Washington,	340	8	337	342	341	335	343	164	20	159
Catawissa,	66	63	100	111	118	125	125	4		121
Mifflinburg,	63		65	65	65	65	65	3		62
Beaver,	130		130	130	130	130		130	129	
Shamokin,	173	9	150	159	172	127	179	134		72
Fishing Creek and Greenwood,	96	4	99	96	106	101	106	55	42	
Total,	2674	221	2746	2766	2778	2556	1749	1536	1054	1007

For this schedule, and other political statistics, I am indebted to the papers of Flavel Roan, carefully preserved by the late Flavel Clingan, of Kelly, his nephew. Flavel Roan was general scribe for the Valley, clerked at the election meetings of return judges, wrote the obituary and marriage notices, &c.

On settlement, Frederick Antes, late treasurer, allowed a credit of $15 36, paid for hanging Edward Jones.

December 22, Samuel Maclay presides at the trial of Judge Alexander Addison.

23d-24th, a fire in the night occurred at Nesbit's, on the east side of the river. It was noticed by Andrew Albright. The night was fearfully cold, and, observing no one stirring at the house, he mounted his horse and swam him, through the floating ice, across the river, awakened the family, and thus saved them from destruction. Barnaby McMaster, the weaver, lost his loom and all he had, barely escaping with his life and family.

In November, Reverends Messrs. Graham and Moody preached as supplies at Buffalo Cross-Roads church.

At November sessions, a road was laid out from Milton, by way of the ferry at Orr's or John Boal's, (Miller's place now;) thence through Boal's and Heckle's land, crossing Little Buffalo at William Clingan's, Buffalo creek, near Chamberlin's mill; thence to the Derrstown and Mifflinburg road.

Deaths.

George Frederick. His daughter, Catherine, was Tobias Sheckler's wife.

George Ray, of West Buffalo. Children: the late John Ray, first sheriff of Union county, George, William, Barbara, Margaret, Sarah, Nancy, and Catherine.

Phœbe Jenkins, widow of James, the elder.

William Jordon, White Deer. Left widow, Jane, and twelve children: Thomas, Mary, married to James Hill, Margaret, Daniel, Andrew, William, Samuel, James, John, Elizabeth, George, Jane.

Edward Tate, of West Buffalo. Children: Edward and Thomas. Hugh Beatty took the land at the appraisement.

Joseph Green died in the spring of this year. He was a prominent citizen of the Valley, and one of its first settlers. He resided first where Benjamin Thompson, junior, lives, east of Mifflinburg, then built the mill of late known as Bellas', which was sold from him. He then removed some distance up Penn's creek, and built a saw-mill, where he died. He was buried in the Lewis grave-yard. His first wife's name was Margaret, and his second, Mary. He was a surveyor, and dealt largely in lands. Was prominent in the revolutionary struggle. His first wife died in 1783, and in 1784 he married a widow, Mary Irvin. His children were: Elizabeth, married to Henry Shively; her daughters, Margaret, married Jesse Matthews; Elizabeth, Ephraim McMullan; Sarah, Eli Landis; and one was married to Robert Barber. Alice Green married James McCoy. Joseph Green's sons were: John, Timothy, Joseph, William, Thomas, George, and General Abbot. The sons all went West, except General Abbot. John went to Louisiana, and one of his sons was in Congress from that State, some years ago. Joseph Green's widow had a son, James Irvin.

1803.

JENKINS' MILL ROAD—ADDITIONAL RESIDENTS—FLAVEL ROAN'S JOURNAL.

AMUEL MACLAY, Speaker of the Senate. Simon Snyder, of the House. March 16, Honorable Samuel Maclay resigned the office of Speaker of the Senate. County Commissioners, Flavel Roan, David Taggert, and Solomon Markley. John Frick, Clerk. Sheriff, Andrew Albright, commissioned October 24. Thomas Youngman, Postmaster, Mifflinburg.

January 8. Andrew McClenachan, justice for White Deer and Washington.

Road from Jenkins' mill to Michael Smith's, (first house east of Farley's now,) in East Buffalo, laid out.

Additional Residents of White Deer—Anderson, Samuel, (miller;) Baker, Michael; Candor, Josiah; Hayes, John, justice; Mole, Christopher; Musser, Joseph, from Strasburg, Lancaster county, in place of Walter Clark, who moved to the western part of the State; Spotts, Peter; Steens, Ephraim; Wallace, William.

West Buffalo—Bliler, Michael; Brown, Christian; Clark, Aaron; Gable, Jacob; Getgen, Adam; Larrabee, Doctor John; Roush, George; Rudy, Abraham; Withington, Peter, junior.

Additional Residents, East Buffalo—Cooper, Daniel; Epler, John, (miller;) Grier, David, on Reverend H. Morrison's land; Hinely, John; Housel, Joshua; Kaufman, John; Kessler, George; Musser, Jacob, on Thomas Wilson's farm; Nyhart, David; Reber John; Ritter, Philip; Simington, Thomas; Slear, Charles; Stearns, John.

Lewisburg—Ely, John ; Gucker, George ; Moore, John, blacksmith.

New Berlin—Hackenberg, Peter ; Haughawaut, Leffard ; Lucas, Robert ; Solomon, John ; Spyker, Daniel.

Candidates for Assembly—Simon Snyder, Robert Giffen, Leonard Rupert, Jacob Fulmer, John Bull, M. Withington, James Forster, Jacob Haller, Joseph Hutchinson, William Stedman, James Laird, Richard Sherer. Simon Snyder, (who received 3,187 votes, nearly every vote polled,) Robert Giffen, Leonard Rupert, and Colonel John Bull were elected.

Flavel Roan's Journal.

In order to have a picture of the social enjoyments and domestic events, I will quote from Flavel Roan's diary, still extant, at Mr. Flavel Clingan's. It is complete for the year 1803, commences again with 1807, and extends to the close of 1813. It is as beautiful as copper-plate engraving, and the letters are so small it requires a magnifying glass to read. He made accurate observations of the weather three times a day. It is said he wrote with a crow-quill.

Monday, 3d. I taught school in Derrstown. Eighteen scholars. Went in the evening with William Hayes and William Wallace to Mrs. Williams', where we had a social hop. 4th. Spent the evening at Andrew Albright's, where upwards of sixty children held a ball. About forty spectators. Some of the parents well pleased with the acting of their children. 6th. Spent the evening at widow Mary Harris' with the Wilson and Hayes families, and had a social hop. 7th. Posting books for John Dreisbach's lottery. 11th. Attended a social hop at Hugh McLaughlin's. William Hayes, Miss Mussers, and Mr. Black there. January 13. Ball at Colonel Baldy's, Cross-Roads. 26th. Spent evening at Musser's. Fifteen persons present.

February 1. John Foster came down from Penn's valley, and wanted a ball gotten up at the stone house ; spoke to Edward Morton to be manager. 3d. The ball came off ; over one hundred persons attended. 6th, Sunday. Mr. Graham preached : text, Luke xviii : 1. N. B.—I make it an established rule to put up at Baldy's. 8th. Met Mr. Graham, Billy Maclay, and others at Hugh Wilson's. 14th. Spent the evening socially, at Mrs. Harris', with twenty others.

18th. Shearer, McClure, and Fruit returned with their wagons from Philadelphia; away above three weeks. 21st. Mrs. Stedman died. Sun eclipsed. Harris and Wilson's families had a social hop at Hugh Wilson's. 25th. Ball at Colonel Baldy's. 28th. Frolic at Billy Poak's to-night.

Tuesday, 1. March comes in like a lion. Thinking about Billy Poak's. 3d. Breakfasted at George Clark's, with McCord, Dale, James Dunlap, and Mrs. Young. Taggart called with a petition to sell the old jail. 6th. Mrs. McLanachan buried. 8th. At L's in the evening; about twenty playing cards there. 9th. With Squire Kelly, Hayes, Gray, Clarke, and Colonel Baldy, at Billy Poak's. 10th. Quit school-keeping, and moved my things to Caleb Fairchild's. 11th. William Brady's barn burned; seven horses and two cows burned. Spent the evening with Foster's girls, at Dunlap's. James Thompson came there in the evening. 13th. Richard Sherer's wife had another daughter. Mr. Jackson preached at Buffalo Cross-Roads. 15th. John W. Clark very sick. I went down for the doctor; not at home; he and Mr. Jackson at Stedman's. Stayed until all was blue; good company.

Deaths.

James Jenkins, of East Buffalo, aged forty, buried at Northumberland, father of Miss Harriet, still living at Northumberland. He left a widow, Sarah. Children: Thomas S., Mary, Sarah, Harriet, and Elizabeth.

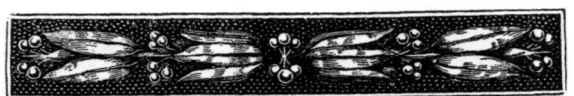

1804.

CONTEMPORARY NOTICES OF THE PEOPLE OF THE VALLEY—HENRY SPYKER'S FORM OF WRITING THEIR WILLS—DOCTOR JOSEPH PRIESTLY—COLONEL WILLIAM COOKE.

JACOB FULMER, Senator; Speaker of the House, Simon Snyder. Sheriff, Andrew Albright. County Commissioner, George Bright.

East Buffalo, Additional Residents—Brown, John; Bucher, John, ferry; Dimpsey, James; Frederick, Jacob; Gibbons, William; Hill, Daniel; Kremer, Frederick; Lloyd, John; Pancoast, William; Reichly, Conrad; Renner, Frederick; Shock, Peter; Swinehart, Henry; Wormly, George. Single men: Lincoln, John; Machamer, Daniel; Morton, Edward.

White Deer—Gillespie, Edward; High, Jacob; Laird, William; Robb, Eleanor; Robb, James, blacksmith; Smith, Boyd.

West Buffalo—Gable, Jacob; Glasgow, William; Glover, John, taxed with a slave; Jones, Ezekiel; Miller, John; Mingle, Andrew; Reeser, William; Roush, Jacob; Roush, George; Royer, John, smith; Spiegelmyer, John, junior; Thomas, William. The David Smith mill passed into the hands of Robert Barber, Esquire. Thomas Frederick, who had been of the rangers, in the Revolution, and whose name appears on the tax-list in 1782, settled originally on the Thomas Paschall tract, (on Laurel run, lately owned by George Fees,) where he built a saw-mill, and made considerable money farming and rafting down Penn's creek. He sold out to Ezekiel Jones, and moved to Ohio this year, where he founded the town of Fredericksburg, Wayne county, Ohio, and built the first mill there.

Michael Brown's Recollections, &c.

John Brown, father of Abraham, Michael, &c., came to the Valley this spring from Pine Grove township, Berks county. He bought the Andrew Edge warrantee, (late Michael and Christian Brown, Getz, &c.,) of Henry Spyker, for £8 per acre. There was then an old log cabin on it, in which Peter Spyker, son of Henry, lived. Michael Brown, late county commissioner, who was then seven years old, stated that he had eight children when he came, John, who went to Ohio; Elizabeth, married to Simon Christ, moved to Ohio; Christena, married to Philip Frederick; Peter, who went to Ohio; Abraham, lately deceased; William, Christian, Michael, and Jacob. Their mother died in 1806, the father, 1838, and both are buried in the Dreisbach grave-yard. He was born in Pennsylvania, served in the Revolution, was in the battle of Brandywine. His father came from Germany. Our neighbors were Lorentz Barnhart, who lived where Peter Getz lives; Kreighbaum, at David Schrack's; Christopher Weiser had a fulling-mill where Peter Wolfe now lives; Henry Poeth, father of old Henry, late of Lewisburg, was the sole inhabitant of Smoketown, which was a part of Spyker's land. He made there all the brick that were used in Lewisburg. Edward Morton lived where A. Frederick's barn now is; Bailey on R. Laird's place; John Zellers, where Samuel lately lived; John Aurand, on the Aurand place, now owned by John Zellers; Christian Gundy lived where John W. Brown now lives. From our place to Derrstown only ten acres were cleared where George Wolfe now lives. The road commenced at Spyker's, (now James S. Marsh's,) at the river, passed through part of the cemetery, the lane at Chamberlin's, came out at George Wolfe's, passed through Smoketown, skirted the ridge at Ellis Brown's and along by Morton's, (Schrack's now,) crossed the present pike above Beale's tavern; that, with the road to the cross-roads and the one up along the river, were the only three roads I recollect of. Jacob Musser lived on Meixell's place. The streets in Lewisburg were laid out, but the lots not fenced in. Black had a ferry near the dam. Valentine Miller was the undertaker of that day. John Beeber, lately living at Lewisburg, told me he came with his father this year to get a wagon at Jacob Stahl's, near the Union church. He was the wagon-maker of the day. People came from Muncy and all around the country to get wagons made by him. He said, also, the locusts were so plenty, that while riding along with his father above Milton, they made so much noise he could not hear what his father said. At Miller's place they crossed the ferry; were polled over by two of George Hoffman's daughters. Ernhart, at Mifflinburg, ironed their wagon. John Stahl had one son, Enos, and a daughter, Salome, married David Herbst. Charles Hall, Esquire, built the stone house and barn now owned by Martin Rishel's heirs. Daniel Shappell moved into the house as tenant.

June 22, fast day. Mr. Bryson lectured in the morning. Mr. Dunham preached in the evening.

On 26th of July, Mr. Hood arrived. He introduced Watts' version of the Psalms. Members were offended on that account, and whether he would accept the call or not was doubtful. Reverend Mr. Morrison died September 13, and in December Mr. Hood again visited the congregation, and it was understood that he would accept the call.

In December there was great rejoicing over the election of President Jefferson. Maclay's boys went to Derrstown, where they had large bonfires, fired cannon, and burned up their hats. Old Judge Wilson and Nathan Stockdon took the back road home by Baldy's, at the cross-roads. Their dearborn was loaded with china and crockery. Getting a little too much cider oil on, they upset at the little bridge, a few rods east of the hotel. The broken china and crockery laid there for years after.

Abel Owen lived near Rengler's. He was a lame man, but could whip any man in the Valley, so it was said.

John Betz kept school at the Dreisbach church school-house. He and wife were celebrated as a very handsome couple.

Marriages.

March 27, by Reverend John Patterson, William Thompson to Susan, daughter of John Linn.

Deaths.

Knowing something by tradition of the prominent characters of these times, the highly pious strains in their dying testimonies somewhat startled me. On examination, however, I found they were all written by Henry Spyker, Esquire, and from the mouths of all, saints and sinners, flowed his churchly rhetoric: "I commend my soul into the hands of God, hoping, through the merits of my Saviour's sacrifice, for the remission of my sins and a happy admission into heaven."

February 6, Doctor Joseph Priestly, aged seventy-one. Epitaph: "Return unto thy rest, oh my soul, for the Lord hath dealt bountifully with thee. I will lay me down in peace, and sleep until I awake in the morning of the resurrection." His remains were removed to the new cemetery, near Northumberland, a few years since. Binns, in his Autobiography, says Doctor Priestly published nearly one hundred moderate sized octavo volumes, on a great variety of subjects. He had an extensive library and chemical laboratory. He rose early, retired at ten, P. M. He slept on a cot in his library. (His wife died September 11, 1796, aged fifty-five.) He played chess and back-gammon, a few games nearly every day. Some time before his death, when he was very ill, I occasionally sat with him during the night, in a large arm chair by his cot. He was then writing and I was publishing his "History of the Christian Church," in six volumes. The fourth or fifth volume was printed. "I should," said he, "have been gratified if it had pleased God to spare me to finish my History of the Church. I should have nothing more on earth to do or regret at leaving undone." He recovered so far as to finish and correct the proof of his history. Some months after, when very feeble, at the dead hour of the night, he asked me if I had recollected what he said about the history. I said I did. He said I wished to remind you of it, and to say that I have now nothing unfinished—nothing that I feel uneasy about, and I am ready to depart when I am called hence. Some hours after, surrounded by his family, he departed. On his death bed he expressed himself to me, in substance, as follows: "Reflecting on the Divine love of the Creator, and the felicities of a future state, I have thought that when the immortal portion of the human frame should be called hence, that it would be conveyed to a region of blissful enjoyment, proportioned to its capacity and preparation, there to remain until, from its superior opportunities and acquirements, it should become better prepared and more capable of yet sublimer and more spiritual enjoyments; whence, through Divine mercy and love, it would, from time to time, be removed from one region of bliss to a higher, and yet a higher, until it should attain the most sublime and perfect state of felicity, of which our most improved nature should be made susceptible; enjoyments becoming more and more blissful without end." It will be noticed that Binns wrote his Autobiography in 1854, and asks for reasonable allowance for the errors of an octogenarian. He continues: "Doctor Priestly told me he had written four volumes of commentaries on the laws of England, which were burned by the "church-and-king" mob in Birmingham, 1791 and 1792."

February, Daniel Rees of Buffalo.

April 16. Died on Monday last, (April 16,) at his country seat, adjoining Harrisburg, in the sixty-eighth year of his age, William Maclay, Esquire, a member of the Legislature of this State.

April ——. Colonel William Cooke, twelfth Pennsylvania. His children were John, (father of Jacob Cooke, of Muncy, Robert, of Howard, Centre county;) Rebecca Stedman; Jane, married to William P. Brady, son of Captain John; Mary, married to Robert Brady, brother of the former; Sarah McClelland, and William, father of William L. Cooke, of Northumberland.

May 8, Margaret, wife of Mathias Alsbaugh, born May 27, 1759.

June 5, Thomas Forster, aged fifty-eight. (Major in the Revolution.)

September 13, Reverend Hugh Morrison, aged forty-eight. His wife died in April, aged forty-nine. They are both buried in the old yard at Sunbury. They left five children: Mary Ann, who afterwards married Andrew Hutchinson, and who died in Lewisburg, October 18, 1868, aged eighty-two; Isabella, married to Isaac B. Jones; Eliza, John, and Jane. In 1822, these heirs sold their father's place in Buffalo to Conrad Dunkle, whose descendants still own it. Eliza willed her all to the Presbyterian church, at Lewisburg. (I saw her broken tombstone lying about the church not long since.)

September 27, Honorable Samuel Dale, aged sixty-three, and left a widow, Eliza, who died April 23, 1835. Children: Judge Samuel Dale, of Lancaster; William Dale, Chillisquaque; James Dale,

Esquire, late of Lewisburg; Ann, afterwards married to John Maclay; Elizabeth, afterwards married to Aaron Chamberlin; Margaret Simonton, late of Lewisburg, deceased. In his will, he speaks of the black girl, "Dinah," belonging to his wife. Dinah was living within our recollection.

October 16, Esther Laughlin, wife of Adam Laughlin, of West Buffalo.

Michael Buttorf, of White Deer.

Peter Swartz, of White Deer.

Eve Iddings, wife of William.

John Simpson, former register and recorder. His handwriting looks like copper-plate engraving. He was succeeded by his son, Jeremiah, in 1798.

Jacob Dreisbach, of Buffalo.

Jacob Brunner, of West Buffalo, (now Limestone.)

Deitrich Wertz, of White Deer.

1805.

Sudden Adjournment of the House of Representatives—Ordination of Reverend Thomas Hood—First Acadamy built at Lewisburg—Duel between John Binns and Samuel Stewart—Political Parties in 1805.

NITED States Senator, Samuel Maclay. Member of Congress, Andrew Gregg. Speaker of the House, Simon Snyder. Members elected in October, Robert Smith, Leonard Rupert, John Bull, and Abraham McKinney. Register and Recorder, John Boyd, commissioned December 20.

Christopher Seebold, commissioned Justice of the Peace for East Buffalo, January 7.

Prices, February 18, flour, $11 50 to $12 per barrel; wheat, 13*s.* 6*d.*, and will keep up, as a war between England and Spain is almost certain; Rye is 5*s.* 6*d.* to 6*s.*; flax seed, 9 to 9¼.—Thomas Stubbs, Middletown. May 28, flour very dull, selling from wagons on the streets at $10 50, at $11 on credit; but price is $11 50 to $11 75.— G. & W. G. Latimer, Philadelphia.

A road was laid out in April, from the west line of Andrew Billmyer's, by Mary Harris', to intersect the road from Derrstown to Japhet Morton's. This is the road from Kephart's to the turnpike, past W. L. Harris.' Hugh Wilson, Daniel Rees, and John Brice were the viewers.

For a singular freak of a Buffalo Valley boy, I quote from Binns' Autobiography: "During the session of 1804–5 I was in the House of Representatives of Pennsylvania, at Lancaster, when a well-dressed young man, of a respectable family from Northumberland county, about the dusk of the evening, threw open the inner door, and entered the body of the House. In a loud, clear and distinct voice he said: 'Mr. Speaker, I am charged by the Lord God with a message to this House, to direct them forthwith to pass a law for the removal of the seat of government from Lancaster to the top of the Blue Hill.' Many of the members called out, 'Turn him out.' Instantly the door-keeper and sergeant-at-arms, both elderly men, one at each side, seized the intruder by the collar of his coat to eject him from the House, upon which he tripped up their heels, and left them both sprawling on the floor. A motion to adjourn was promptly made and carried. The young man, who was laboring under insanity, remained three days about Lancaster, then started for home on horseback. It is said and believed that he never drew bit until he arrived home, a distance of one hundred and fifteen miles. In a few minutes after he arrived, the horse dropped dead."—*See Roan's Journal, May* 20, 1809.

Mr. Hood at Buffalo.

Mr. Hood preached at Buffalo from the 1st of April. He was ordained on the 2d of October. Mr. Stewart preached the ordination sermon from 1 Corinthians ix: 16: "For though I preach the Gospel, I have nothing to glory of," &c. Mr. Bryson gave the charge to the people. Mr. Hood's first sermon after was from Romans v, 5: "And hope maketh not ashamed." In which he showed the nature and advantages of evangelical hope, and the amazing difference between the life of the believer and that of the hypocrite. His salary was fixed at $220 per year. In May, a resolution was passed to raise it to $300, but not carried out, as in 1809–10–11–12 he was still paid but $220.

September 5, trustees elect of Buffalo—George Knox, Gideon Smith, Andrew McClanachan, James McClellan, Christopher Johnston, Robert Forster, Adam Laughlin, and Hugh Wilson.

Removals out of the bounds—Tenbrooke Chamberlin, John Clarke, junior, Joseph Gilliland, Thomas Sutherland, and William Thompson, junior.

In 1805, among the names of members of Dreisbach's congregation, occur: Barnhart, Lorentz; Heinly, John; Reber, John; Reedy, Andrew; Ream, George; Spyker, Peter; Wormley, George; Zeller, Benjamin; Zeller, John.

The log cabin academy built by subscription. It occupied the present site of the parsonage of the Presbyterian church in Lewisburg.

Doctor Charles Byers was the principal physician of Lewisburg and vicinity.

Binns and Stewart Duel.

The duel between John Binns and Samuel Stewart is noteworthy as being one of the last fought upon the soil of Pennsylvania, and on account of the prominence of the actors, having special influence in causing the passage of the act of 31st March, 1806. The duel was fought on Sunday, the 16th of December. Tradition says Stewart spent the night before at Andrew Albright's tavern, in Lewisburg. I extract a circumstantial account of it from John Binns' Autobiography:

On Saturday, November 5, 1805, while I was in the public ball alley, at Sunbury, with a bat in my hand, tossing a ball against the wall, waiting for Major Charles Maclay to play a game, a very tall, stout stranger came to me, and said, "My name is Sam Stewart, of Lycoming county; your name, I understand, is John Binns, and you are editor of the *Republican Argus*." I replied, "I was." "I wish to know who is the author of the letters published in that paper signed 'one of the people.'" "For what purpose," said I. He replied, "There are remarks in one of them which reflect on my character, and I must know the author." I declined to tell him, but said if there was anything untrue it should be corrected. He was standing on my left, and instantly threw his left arm across my breast, and with it held both my arms tight above the elbows, and, at the same time, threw his right arm across the back of my head, violently pushing his forefinger into the corner of my right eye, evidently with the intent to tear it out of my head. I struck him with the bat with all my strength, when he left go his hold, seized me about the waist, and endeavored to throw me down. We were separated by Major Maclay and others, who came into the alley. In his effort to gouge out my eye, he left a scar which will accompany me to my grave. The ball alley was attached to Henry Shaffer's hotel. I went into the hotel and wrote a note:

SUNBURY, *November* 2, 1805.

After threatening me like a bravo, you have attacked me like a ruffian. Some satisfaction ought to be rendered for such conduct.

If you have the spirit and courage to meet me as a gentleman, and will appoint time and place, and meet me with pistols, accompanied by a friend, what has passed shall be overlooked by

JOHN BINNS.

SAMUEL STEWART, Esquire.

To this note Mr. Stewart returned a verbal answer, "that he was going to the city, but would be back in two or three weeks."

On the 13th of December, a note was handed me by Mr. Andrew Kennedy, printer of the *Northumberland Gazette*:

NORTHUMBERLAND, *December* 13, 1805.

When I received your challenge I was on my way to the city, and had it not in my power to meet you; but now I am here, ready to see you. You will, therefore, mention the time and place, and you will have it in your power to try my spirits, that you so much doubted. It must be immediately. Let me hear from you.

SAMUEL STEWART.

I replied that as soon as I could get Major Maclay here I would be ready. That I had sent for him, expected him that evening, and the meeting could be the next morning. On the evening of the

13th, a friend informed me that application had been made to a magistrate for a warrant of arrest, to bind me over to keep the peace. I immediately wrote a note :

SATURDAY MORNING.

SIR :—I have just heard that application has been made to a magistrate to prevent our meeting. I write to request that you will instantly appoint some other place, say Derrstown, Milton, or any other place more convenient to you, where my friend and myself will attend.

I then wrapped a pair of pistols in my overcoat pocket, walked about half a mile to the house of William Bonham, where I directed my horse, and any note that came, should be forwarded. Major Maclay soon arrived, and, after giving him a full statement of the occurrences, he went to Northumberland to settle the time and place. While we talked in the back room, the constable rapped and inquired if I was in the house. He was told I had gone up the road. On Mr. Maclay's return, he told me the meeting was to be at seven o'clock the next morning, at the end of a fence behind Lawshe's house, opposite Derrstown, where we agreed to sleep that night.

We were on the ground at seven o'clock, just in the gray of the morning. In a few minutes we saw Mr. Stewart and Mr. Kennedy coming down the lane. After mutual salutations, Mr. Maclay proposed that we should cross the swamp, and retire to a more private place, where the ground was perfectly clear. Mr. Kennedy proposed that the parties should settle the distance. I objected, that being the duty of the seconds. Mr. Maclay and Kennedy then retired, and, after some conversation, stepped eight paces, and placed Mr. Stewart and myself at the extreme ends of the line. Mr. Maclay then said, "It is agreed between Mr. Kennedy and myself that if either of the parties shall leave his ground before the affair is entirely settled, such party shall be regarded as disgraced." The seconds then retired to load the pistols. Mr. Maclay told me afterwards that he at this time suggested to Mr. Kennedy the propriety of an effort at reconciliation. Mr. Kennedy said " that was impossible, unless Mr. Binns would apologize for the language used in his message to Mr. Stewart. For my part, I think nothing should be attempted until the parties have at least interchanged a shot." Maclay and Kennedy drew near to us, and Maclay said : "When the word 'fire' is given you are to fire soon as you can. If either delay while one of us count three, and say 'stop,' that one shall, for that time, lose his fire. A snap to be considered a fire."

The seconds tossed up to determine which should give the word. Maclay won. The pistols were handed us, and discharged so simultaneously that but one report was heard. Neither balls took effect. The pistols were again handed to the seconds. They retired a few paces, and Mr. Maclay assured me afterwards that he used every honorable argument to move Mr. Kennedy to present a proposition for settlement. This he did without effect. Maclay then raised his voice and said, you had better consult your principal, and I will do the same. Maclay's first words to me were: "Kennedy is a scoundrel; he is determined to have you shot." I said: "you know the terms we agreed upon, and we will carry them out." The pistols were again handed to us. After a short pause, Mr. Maclay came between us and said: "Gentlemen, I think this business has gone far enough, and may be amicably and honorably adjusted." He proposed that Mr. Stewart should apologize for his attack, and that then Mr. Binns should declare that the publication was not made to wound the feelings of Mr. Stewart, or affect his character; but because Mr. Binns believed it to be true, and that it was matter proper for public information. Mr. Stewart then said: "If God has given me more strength than other men, I do not think I ought to abuse it. I never struck a man in my life that I was not sorry for it." This was not held sufficient apology. After a pause Mr. Stewart made the required apology, and I made the declaration my friend proposed. The parties shook hands, and at a tavern in the neighborhood, they and their friends breakfasted together. Mr. Stewart and I continued friends until his death, many years afterward. When he was elected to the Assembly from Lycoming, some years after, he voted for me, then editor of the *Democratic Press*, as a director of the Pennsylvania Bank. Major Maclay was then about twenty-eight years of age, and a man of much promise. Son of Honorable Samuel Maclay, at that time a United States Senator. He returned to Buffalo Valley; I to Northumberland. He died soon after this.

I found, on my return, that it was Joseph Priestly that had the warrant issued for my arrest. He saw me leave with a small mahogany case, in which he knew Judge Cooper kept his pistols, and suspected what was about to take place. The termination of this business put an end to anything like personal rudeness by any member of the Federal party, so long as I remained in Northumberland, and doubtless had its effect after my removal to Philadelphia.

This duel was fought beyond the marsh, near what was then called Allen's. Andrew Kennedy was the father of the late Andrew Kennedy, of Lewisburg. Lawshe's hotel was below the dam, nearly opposite Strohecker's, kept by John Lawshe, grandfather of A. M. Lawshe. Flavel Roan, in his journal, carefully notes the fact, that he always took a drink there before crossing the ferry to Derrstown. The house was burned down some years ago. Sam Stewart, as he was called, was sheriff and treasurer of Lycoming county, and the Federal candidate for Senator, in 1808, against General John Burrows, the Democratic candidate.

Political.

July 10. Extract from a letter of James Cochran, of Mead township, Crawford county, to Robert Irwin: "On the call for a convention to amend the constitution and on our new candidate for Governor, the people are much divided; but there will be a majority in favor of the convention and Simon Snyder in this county and many of the neighboring counties. From every appearance the majority will be considerable. From the insolent behavior of old Tom, (Governor Thomas McKean,) in my opinion, he merits no longer the approbation of the people, not only from his impertinent language, but for the last three years he has an undoubted right to be charged with wasting his Lord's goods; therefore, agreeably to St. Luke, xvi: 3 v., he has a right to either dig or beg, whichever he thinks he can do best, for he will be no longer steward. The "Feds" and "Quids" are squealing like fell-hyenas about it, and fear of being drowned before they see the water; but it will turn out like all the rest of their hot-water injections—they will burst like the bubble, with the weight of their own air, and leave them a blank in society, or rather, a vestige of contempt by all the true friends of the principles of seventy-six." A mingle of metaphors not often found in so short a composition.

October 4, the Governor, by his secretary, William Thompson, writes from Lancaster to Robert Irwin: " The friends of Mr. Snyder have circulated in the counties of Northampton and Berks, that Governor McKean has promised, after his re-election, to appoint Mr. James Ross, of Pittsburg, Chief Justice of the Supreme court. I am authorized to assure you that the tale is wholly a falsehood, fabricated on the eve of the approaching political contest, for base electioneering purposes, an idea of the kind having never been suggested to the Governor by any friend of Mr. Ross, or by the Governor to any person whatever; nor, indeed, is it believed Mr. Ross would accept the appointment if offered to him."

In order that my readers may understand the allusions in the Cochran letter, I will state, as part of the history of the time, that Governor McKean had vetoed an act substituting referees for jury trials, and prohibiting the employment of counsel in reference cases; also, the act extending the jurisdiction of justices of the peace, which, however, was passed over his veto. This, with the acquittal of the judges who were impeached, incensed the ultra Democrats, and they immediately started the project of remodeling the Constitution. The moderate Democrats took the name of Constitutionalists, and organized a constitutional society, and the other section of Democrats a club called "The Friends of the People," the Federalists looking on, and enjoying the strife. The *ultra* Democrats nominated Snyder for Governor, and the friends of the Constitution, McKean, who was elected Governor, and entered upon his third term on the 17th of December.

Marriages, by Henry Spyker, Esquire.

Peter Epler to Eve Christ. Witnesses, Henry Fulmer, Christian Van Gundy, John Smith and wife, &c., (April 4.)

September 8, John Lawshe with Polly Sites. Witnesses, Nancy Robb, John Dreisbach, &c.

Deaths.

George Martin, White Deer. Children: Jane, Elizabeth, John, Robert, and Matthew. January 15, John Swineford, of Middleburg; born April 16, 1755. Martin Housel, West Buffalo. Children: Jaçob, Joshua, Catherine, Mary and Elizabeth. September 22, Catherine, wife of Abraham Eyer; born, October 15, 1752; married, May, 1776. Peter Jodon, of West Buffalo. Captain George Overmeier. Children: George, Peter, Philip, John, David, Jacob, Catherine, (Margaret, then dead,) Elizabeth, Eve, Esther, Magdalena, and Barbara. To Jacob he left his rifle and shot-pouch carried in the Revolution. Adam Shewel, of Centre. Jabel Frederick, of Buffalo. George Motz, Penn's. Children: John, Lorentz. December 19, Catherine Dunkle. She was born February 13, 1769; married October 24, 1784.

1806.

Additional Residents of East Buffalo, Lewisburg, White Deer, and West Buffalo—First Methodist Camp-Meeting.

THOMAS COOPER, President Judge, commissioned March 1. Members, Simon Snyder, Leonard Rupert, Abraham McKinney, and Major Robert Smith, of Turbut. David Taggert, Charles Maclay, and Samuel Awl, County Commissioners. John Frick, Clerk. April 1, John Thompson, junior, commissioned Justice of the Peace. July 4, William Poak. John Lynn, of Erie, was the principal School-Teacher of the Valley.

Additional Residents, East Buffalo—Ammon, Andreas; Badorf, Michael, blacksmith; Bostian, Andrew; Brown, John, miller; Culp, Peter, shoe-maker; Daugherty, James; Geddes, James, single; Graham, Alexander, merchant; Haverling, Jacob, weaver; Hafer, Ludwig; Holmes, Jonathan, tanner; McClure, Richard, chair-maker; Marriner, James; Mettlin, Patrick; Morrow, Alexander; Reem,

George, carpenter; Reish, Daniel; Renner, Jacob; Renner, Frederick; Strayhorn, Nathaniel; Vaness, John; Winter, Daniel, carpenter.

Lewisburg—Conser, John; Crosgrove, Samuel; Kremer, George; Renfrew, Jacob; Wolfe, Christian, hatter.

Additional Residents of White Deer—Clark, John, William's son; Dersham, Jacob; Farris, Dennis; Lushbaugh, John; Madden, Neal, tailor; Marshall, James; Monpeck, Nicholas; Reznor, David; Rorabaugh, Philip; Schock, Andrew, wagon-maker.

West Buffalo—Aikey, Lewis; Betzer, Peter; Bohr, Michael, miller; Eilert, John; Green, Abbot; Hildebrand, Levi; Kaufman, David; Kimple, Jacob, potter; Kleckner, John, tavern and stillhouse; Maize, Jacob, tavern; Mitchell, George, blacksmith; Shriner, Jacob; Zeller, John; Zeller, Henry.

In August, the first Methodist camp-meeting in this part of the State was held on Chillisquaque creek, one and one half miles from the river.

Marriages.

January 2, Ludwig Coasin with Susanna Olifant, in presence of both their parents, Joseph Stillwell, Thomas Nesbit, &c.

April 7, Frederick Renner with Magdalena Krause, daughter of Christian Krause, deceased, in presence of his father, and stepmother, and brothers, Jacob Renner and wife, Benjamin Renner, Daniel Sheckler and wife.

May 15, George Troxel with Mary Hoffman, in presence of William Clark and wife, Doctor James Dougal, Andrew Heckle and wife, George Derr and wife, John Betz and wife, Andrew Ensworth and wife, Abraham Troxell and wife.

June 12, John Sergeant with Catharine Beyer, in presence of her parents, brother James, Peggy Evans, &c.

November 16, Michael Straub to Sarah Grove.

Deaths.

John Pollock, Lewisburg. Michael Smith. John Graybill, Mahantango. William Steele, Buffalo. Henry Richard, East Buffalo. James Adams, White Deer, left a widow, Margaret; children: Agnes, Joseph, Sarah. James was his grandson, and son of Joseph. Mary Green, widow of Captain Joseph Green. Henry Myer, West Buffalo.

1807.

PENN'S CREEK IMPROVEMENT LOTTERY—EXTRACTS FROM BINNS' ARGUS—COUNTY CONVENTION—GERMAN HIGH SCHOOL IN BUFFALO TOWNSHIP—ROAN'S JOURNAL—JOHN AURAND—CHARACTER OF THE LEGAL BUSINESS AND SKETCHES OF LEADING CIRCUIT LAWYERS, BY LATE GEORGE A. SNYDER, ESQUIRE.

NITED STATES SENATORS, Samuel Maclay and Andrew Gregg, the latter elected January 13. Member of Congress, Daniel Montgomery, junior. Senator, James Laird. Speaker House of Representatives, Simon Snyder. Members elected in October, Simon Snyder, Leonard Rupert, Abraham McKinney, and John Murray.

Commissioner elect, Samuel Bond. Total expenditures of the county last year, $5,716. Sheriff, Jared Irwin. Treasurer, Simon Snyder. Postmaster at Lewisburg, C. Baldy.

Additional Residents of West Buffalo—Harris, Amos, shoemaker; Lytle, Charles; Peters, Philip, tinner; Reed, Robert and William; Ruhl, Philip; Stitzer, John, junior; Stover, John and Samuel; Wilkert, Jacob.

Mifflinburg—Keener, William, tailor; Lemon, Thomas, schoolmaster; Miller, Doctor; Smith, Doctor; Swentzell, Jacob; Yearick, Simon. Andrew Ensworth sold his property and removed from the Valley; also, William Irwin, junior, Robert Harris, and Alexander Steel.

In White Deer new Names on the Assessment List—Anthony, Henry; Anthony, Nicholas, shoe-maker; Billman, John and Josiah; Chamberlin, Uriah; Clingan, Thomas; Heckle, George; Huntingdon, Simon; McCorley, Robert; Shaffer, John; Shamp, Jesse; Pancoast, William, blacksmith; Yocum, Jesse.

Additional Residents in East Buffalo—Beidleman, Valentine,

Daniel, and Jacob; Cochran, John; Eagler, Conrad, shoe-maker; Forsythe, Samuel; Hight, Henry, shoe-maker; Hummel, Christian, shoe-maker; Jamison, John; Linn, Daniel, miller; Noll, Henry; Trester, George; Wagner and Kline, grist-mill; Wallace, William; Wilson, Charles; Wommer, Jacob.

Lewisburg—Bellman, George, clock-maker.

New Berlin—Berger, Jacob, millwright; Miller, Philip; Shrefler, Henry; Stain or Stem, Doctor Jacob.

By act of March 31, Samuel Templeton, George Long, Robert Barber, Peter Fisher, and James Duncan, commissioners, were authorized to raise by lottery $4,000, for the improvement of Penn's creek, from the mouth of Green's saw-mill. Robert Barber was appointed treasurer, and in October, they advertised a scheme of cash prizes, amounting to $30,000; nothing came of it.

April 10, the middle district of the supreme court was created, and Sunbury fixed for the place of holding the court, on the first Monday of July.

The Political Situation.

Argus, July 27, "appointments by the Governor: William Wilson, major general of the ninth division; William Hepburn, of the tenth. Both these gentlemen are associate judges, and thorough-paced Federalists. Elections by the people: Christopher Baldy, brigadier general first brigade, a Democrat, by a large majority. Colonel John Jones, Alexander Moore, George Weirick, and Thomas Youngman, all Democrats, by decided majorities. For brigade inspector, Frederick Evans, 435 to 80 for Charles Drum, Quid."

February 4, Binns' *Argus* has the message relative to Burr's conspiracy. The lot of ground on which the old jail stood, offered for sale. Binns says, at the court of quarter sessions of Centre county, held last week, there was no business for the grand jury, save one bill for keeping a tippling-house. So much for the peaceable demeanor of one of the most Democratic counties in Pennsylvania. He thinks Rankin's vote for Gregg for United States Senator will prevent his return as representative of that county. "Hugh White and other Federalists" contested the election of Isaac Smith, member for Lycoming; but Smith was declared the sitting member.

In his valedictory he says he has sold his type, fixtures, and rented his house and office, in Northumberland, to Mathew Huston, by whom the *Argus* will be conducted. Mr. Huston is clerk of the House of Representatives, which will detain him at Lancaster, until the 1st of April. Mr. Huston is a man of good understanding, and will be an independent editor. In politics, he is a decided Democratic Republican. Has been a soldier in the Revolution, and served in the Legislature. In bidding farewell to John Binns' paper, I quote one of his saucy items: "I do not know whether Rudolph Spangler was or was not, as the *Lancaster Journal* says, at a cock-fight, for a whole day. If he was, to the neglect of his public duty, he was to blame; but I do know most certainly that Timothy Matlack, the master of rolls of this State, was at a common cock-fight, the cheek-by-jowl companion of negroes, vagabonds, and spoilsmen."

June 3, Mathew Huston issued the first number of his *Argus*, and in his second number attacks Governor McKean for appointing a number of Senators to lucrative offices before their terms expired. Says it is morally certain he had no relatives in Pennsylvania or any quarter of the globe, who might be imported to fill those offices.

The attack of the Leopard, on the Chespeake, on the 22d of June, brings forth a fearful editorial, in which Great Britian is styled an "incurable old bawd," &c. I quote some of the toasts at the 4th of July celebration, to show the drift of politics. At Selinsgrove: "Thomas McKean—alas, how art thou fallen." "2d Tuesday of October, 1808—may it give us a farmer for Governor, who will care more for the people than for the dust under his feet, and not a student of morality, whose only care is for his family, lawyers, and sharpers." "The besotted, card-playing general and the golden calf—may they ever be haunted with trout visions." "The Democratic presses—the nurses of political virtue."

At Milton, Captain Thomas Pollock, president, Doctor James Dougal, vice president: "Thomas McKean—political damnation to all political hypocrites." "Aaron Burr, the treacherous apostate Whig—may the portion of eternal infamy be the fate of every traitor to virtue, liberty, and independence." "The American fair—may Columbia boast of a race of daughters, amiable and beautiful, and may Hymen join them to Republican merit." Kennedy's paper,

May 19, attacks an article in Binns' paper, as smelling strongly of the committee-room at Derrstown, and says Esquire Laird, the State Senator, is a favorite pupil of the professors at the political college of Derrstown, and hints that Tilghman might be got out to run against Simon Snyder for Governor. The Quids, he says, talk of Judge Spade, who knows no more of politics than of Arabic, and who may possess qualifications for the place, but nobody knows it.

Huston on Burr: "Burr is to the body-politic like an emetic to the physical body. Since he has got into operation, the body-politic has discharged and brought into view a huge mass of swindlers, speculators, sharpers, jugglers, jockies, pettifoggers. These followers of our Cataline, whom he collected from the harlot's stew, the gaming table, and the wine-bibber's shop, must appear truly pitiful when they slink home with their golden prospects blasted, and their leader the subject of scorn and contempt."

James Boyd's toast at the Danville celebration is unique: "The Quids—a jackass apiece to them, and a snail's horn for a spur, so that each mule may ride his own ass." Daniel Montgomery presided at this meeting. James Laird was vice, and Andrew Russell was secretary. The names are given, so that we may know on what side in politics our antecedents were.

July 13, Governor McKean issued a general order for a draft of the militia of the State, in prospect of a war with Great Britain, to be divided into two grand divisions, of which Major General Thomas Craig and General Joseph Heister were appointed commanders. The quota for Northumberland division was ten hundred and forty. The delegates from the different townships to the meeting held at Sunbury, on the 18th of August, to express the sentiments of the county, in reference to the attack upon the Chesapeake, were: Sunbury, Andrew Albright and John Boyd; Buffalo, Samuel Maclay and Christopher Baldy; West Buffalo, George Youngman and Henry Gray; Centre, George Weirick and Michael Wittenmyer; Penn's, Jacob Lechner and Daniel Rhoads; Point, Matthew Huston and Andrew Kennedy; White Deer, Seth Iredell and William Clark; Washington, William Pollock, &c. Colonel Robert Clark, of Derry, was chosen president. They resolved unanimously to support the Government in such measures as may be necessary and proper to obtain satisfaction for former injuries and insults committed by the British Government, and security against such aggressions in time to come. The meeting at Selinsgrove to appoint delegates to this meeting, was presided over by George Holstein. Committee on resolutions, Frederick Evans, Christian Welker, and Daniel Rohrer.

By an order of Frederick Evans, it appears that the thirty-ninth regiment (district Buffalo Valley) was to furnish one hundred and thirty-seven men, to rendezvous at General Baldy's, on the 24th of September. Seventy-seventh regiment draft, one hundred and twenty-seven men, to meet at Swinefordstown, on the 23d.

At a meeting of the Society of the Friends of the people of Sunbury, held at the public buildings, on Saturday, September 26, and at a meeting of the same society of Point township, held at the house of David Taggert, on Monday, September 29, resolutions were passed arraigning Michael Leib at the tribunal of public opinion, for secretly and hypocritically laboring to defeat Simon Snyder in 1805; for intriguing with the Quids to bring forward Joseph Hiester for Governor. These proceedings are signed by Andrew Albright, president of the society of Sunbury; David Taggert, at Point.

June 27. John Sierer and wife, Susanna, Christopher Baldy and wife, Susanna, conveyed two acres and one hundred and ten perches of the Henry Sees tract to John Kaufman and John Rengler, trustees elect of a German high school, in Buffalo township, to be erected on said premises, and kept for that purpose forever.

Domestic Incidents taken chiefly from Flavel Roan's Journal.

He was teaching school at this time at Jimmy Wilson's schoolhouse, near where Adam Stahl now lives.

January 1. Citizen Kremer (afterward Honorable George) called at Clingan's, (William Clingan, Esquire's.) A very great talker. Brought sweetmeats for the ladies. 5th. Roan McClure's youngsters and Richards', from Derrstown, at Clingan's. Amusements, selling pawns, shaving, &c., until after twelve. 10th. Citizen Kremer again at Clingan's. Has a great memory, and likes to hear himself discourse. 13th. Clingan's young people down at Roan McClure's until after twelve. 24th. Went to Sunbury, crossing on the ice. Got a hard fall. Stopped at James Black's. Agreeably entertained by Esquire Buyers' daughters and Mr. Black's young people. 29th.

Young people at Derrstown singing-school. Thirty young people at Baldy's singing.

February 8, Sunday. The ladies would not sing, because Tommy raised an old tune, "Isle of Wright." 9th. Six degrees colder than it has been for two years, by Doctor Dougal's thermometer. 11th. Visitors at Clingan's, Doctor Dougal and lady, Mrs. Linn and relatives, Sister Clark, &c. 13th. Ice broke in Buffalo creek, and carried off the bridge. 17th. Youngsters went to Esquire Kelly's. 22d. Youngsters at Dale's. Returned at three, A. M. 25th. Charles Hall, Esquire, and lady at Clingan's, and Mrs. David Linn, Esquire Kelly's youngsters, J. Thompson's youngsters, Charlotte Candor, and Thomas Howard came. All went over to Aunt Dale's, to spend the evening. Kelly's lads very sociable. 26th. Esquire McLanahan and lady at C's. I think the Squire will run for Assembly. 27th. Thompson's, Dale's, Chamberlin's youngsters, Boyd Smith, Bella Kelly, Charlotte Candor, spent an agreeable evening at C's. Went away at one, A. M.

March 5. Clingan's youngsters, with Gideon Smith and J. Thompson, went to visit at Chamberlin's. Returned at three A. M. Citizen Kremer here again. 7th. Roan Clarke at C's. He is making great progress at knowledge with citizen K. Has a learned book with him, puzzling Tommy and George. Roan's route to Sunbury—cross at Nesbit's ferry, drink at Lawshe's, stop to see Judge Wilson at Chillisquaque, leave his horse at D. Taggert's, and walk over to Sunbury. Return—stops at Dentler's, Lawshe's, Metzgar's, Derrstown, call at Roan McClure's, sleeps at Giddy Smith's. 17th. Wilson Smith calls to request Clingans to spend to-morrow evening at Doctor Vanvalzah's. 21st. Called at Poak's, Metzgar's, and went to see the rope-dancing at Rees'. 23d. Rope-dancing at Baldy's. 27th. Went to Hoffman's. Had a talk with Tom Iddings about Steel being an officer. 31st. Snowed all day. Snow eighteen inches deep.

April 4. View on the bridge at Derrstown. Slept at Kremer's. Called at Metzgar's. Went down to Franklin's. Saw some boats start down the river. Called at Doctor Byers'. Saw Franklin's leg ; an ugly sight. 8th. Snow five feet deep in Jimmy Wilson's lane. 10th. Left Clingan's, stopped at Baldy's, then to Youngmanstown, where I stopped at Van Buskirk's. Met Esquire Robert Barber and Abbot Green, with whom I had business. Slept at Smelcher's, in a bed at the fire, and saw sparking going on. 13th. Came to Baldy's; drank too much whisky; spent the evening with Sheriff Jared Irwin there. 15th. Crossed at Black's, went to Lawshe's, spent the evening there, and slept with old Sam Brady.[1]

May 2. Went with Mrs. Hood to White Deer valley. They sing new tunes and Watts' Psalms here. 4th. Went to Newbury, where I met Billy Dougan, and went home with him. 5th. Heard Mr. Siers preach from the text "Come, for all things are ready." He said the man should have brought his wife with him to the wedding. [He was no doubt the ancestor of the sensational preachers of our day.] Sunday, 10th. Heard Mr. Smilie, Baptist, preach at Jaysburg, on the fruitful vine. Crossed from Jaysburg to David Russel's, where Doctor Davidson prescribed for me. 13th. Crossed the mountain with Mr. Smilie. Stopped at Week's, [now Uniontown.] He went to preach, and I to Esquire Brown's. His route home is marked by stops at G. Anderson's, Graham's, Hugh Donnelly's, [Uniontown,] Iredell's fishery, and John Hoffman's.

June 7. Hoffman's son and daughter went to the consecration of the new church at Youngmanstown. 9th. The boys went fishing with Mr. Hood. 14th. Reuben Davis, a student full of self-importance, dined at Clingan's. 24th. At George Clark's, took tea with the amiable Miss Becca, who displayed a gold ring on her finger.

Wednesday, July 1. Election at Baldy's for militia field-officers. Cider oil plenty, which occasioned words and blows. 5th. Mr. Hood preached at Buffalo, Psalm xxvii: 4. He gave me a rub, in the last part of his sermon, for not attending church. 19th. A great thunder storm, with hail. 20th. Reverend Mr. Hood with us, cutting wheat. He is a great cradler. 24th. Mr. Clingan has seven hundred dozen, and not two bottles of whisky drank at the cutting. Sunday, 26th. Mr. Grier and Mr. Hood exchange. Buffalo people not used to such long sermons. He is not so able an orator as Mr. Hood. 27th. Election at Derrstown. Fighting going on in the evening. Citizen Kremer got marked. Miss Wilson and Miss Craig, of Northampton, at Mr. Hayes'. They are great belles. 28th. Election for rifle company officers, at Clingan's. 29th. Election for company officers, at Richard Irwin's, [White Deer.] Ed-

---

[1] Uncle of Captain Samuel Brady.—*Linn*.

ward Morton and I attended and clerked. We had plenty of talk and whisky. 30th. Went down to John Reber's. Clerked here, too. Another election of officers. Plenty of drink here, also. 31st. Went to Michael Fought's, [near Chappell hollow.] Clerked at another election.

August —. Captain Fought went along. Got to Baldy's before breakfast. Another election. Plenty of cider royal. 8th. At Milton. The Flemings and Vincents there, raising a troop. 13th. At Mr. Huston's, his daughter, though small, a great belle, [afterwards wife of John Taggert, Esquire, of Northumberland. She is recently deceased, 1871.]

September 6. Mr. Clingan and George went to John Cornelius' funeral. Mathew Laird says he will be very much missed in his family, as he was a very shifty man. Saturday, 19th. Over at the camp-meeting beyond Milton. Went to town. Called at Dan Smith's, William Pollock's, and drank wine at Calhoun's, with the Barrs. Sunday night at camp. Sermon from Revelations, iii : 18. The moon shining through the trees, the fire, candles in the camp, the large, quiet crowd of people, made the scene romantic and solemn. 20th. Great carrying on at camp. Criswell's boys got happy. 26th. Mr. Bryson preached on Psalm cxxxiii. Billy Poak's wife fainted in meeting.

October 3. Drank a morning dram with Mr. ———, the Methodist minister from Lycoming, and went home with Robert Lyon. He is very poor, but hospitable. 6th. At Franklin's. Albright and wife there. Took dinner at Doctor Byer's. Called at Poak's. Much diverted with the girls and Donaldson's wife and daughter. Then called at Hayes' and Cramer's and went to George Clark's. 9th. Clingan brought home Mr. Hood and Reverend H. R. Wilson, Bellefonte ; the latter a very facetious man. Comet still in view. 13th. Clerked at the election at Billmyer's. Tommy stole a bag string to cure Trimmer's ancle. 20th. Review at Derrstown. Several bottles in the evening. George stole a bag string for another horse. 31st. My horse broke his bridle at Robert's tavern, Milton. Staid and slept with old Peter Vincent.

Sunday, November 1. Mr. Hood got a letter, stating that the horse had ran away with his wife and Ann Dale, broke the chair, and Mrs. Hood's leg. [This accident happened near Harrisburg.

They were going to Chester county on a visit. Mrs. Hood was a Haslet, from that county.] 2d. Tommy took sixty-eight bushels corn to deGruchy's, at Northumberland. 7th. Mr. Hood and James Dale set off in a boat to bring Mrs. Hood home. 11th. Mrs. Hood arrived at Derrstown. Mr. Wilson brought her home on a sled. Annie Dale much hurt, too. [My uncle, Doctor W. I. Wilson, says he recollects well of riding the horses attached to the sled which brought Mrs. Hood to her home from the river.] 15th. Clingan's youngsters, Aunt Dale's youngsters went with Mr. Haslet to visit at Senator Maclay's. December 9. Clingan butchering. George Weikel assisting Beau Barber here. Mr. Haslet and Mr. Hood helping butcher. 10th. George at a tramping frolic at Uncle Clark's. 11th. Beaux Kremer, Haslet, Barber here. "Where the carcase is, thither will the eagles gather together." 12th. Billy Thompson died. 20th. Mr. Hood preached from II Timothy, i : 10. The people seemed too lazy to leave the meeting-house. *There is a stove in it now.* 21st. Girls up at Mrs. Linn's last night. George, Nancy, Haslet, Sam Maclay, Dale, &c. 24th. Shooting match at Zerbe's, [now John Grove's.] 31st. Billy Forster and citizen Kremer at Clingan's. George fired off guns at midnight.

The Leading Circuit Lawyers, by George A. Snyder.

At this time, the courts of Northumberland, Lycoming, and Luzerne were attended by the lawyers of Lancaster, York, Harrisburg, and Carlisle. From Lancaster came Charles Smith, one of the ablest jurists of Pennsylvania. Mr. Hopkins also came, but seldom. Bowie[1] was the only one I can remember from York. Thomas Duncan and David Watts, from Carlisle. From Harrisburg came George Fisher, Thomas Elder, William Irwin, and others. Each lawyer kept his saddle-horse. The Lancaster, York, and Carlisle lawyers met at Harrisburg; when that court terminated, they came to Sunbury; then to Williamsport and Wilkesbarre. As their numbers were recruited at each county town, they formed a considerable troop of cavalry on entering the two last places.

The nature and character of the law business were then different from what they are at present. Almost all the important actions

[1] Ralph Bowie, Esquire, died at York, Pennsylvania, October 22, 1816. He is said to have been an elegant lawyer.—*Linn.*

were ejectments upon disputed original titles. The number of witnesses was very great, the means of traveling scanty, the district large, so that much allowance had to be made for failure of attendance. The causes were, therefore, frequently continued, so that they usually stood upon the trial list several years before they could be acted upon. This, added to the dilatory habits always prevalent in frontier settlements, produced that leisurely, time-wasting habit of doing business which, until lately, characterized our county courts. The lawyers of this district seldom undertook an important cause without calling in the aid of Duncan, Watts, Fisher, or some other able practitioner.

Duncan was a small man, with keen looking gray eyes, and a sharp, unmusical voice. His knowledge of law was more extensive and accurate than that of any of his compeers, and he possessed great tact in the trial of a cause, almost always managing to put his opponents, though they were plaintiffs, on the defensive—an immense advantage in law as well as in war. My father placed him upon the Supreme Bench, where he was considered an important acquisition.

Mr. Watts was a large man, with a powerful voice. His self-reliance was great, and of great advantage to him, for his abilities were considerable. He contemned authorities, preferring to argue his case from first principles, and this he did with much power. He was apt to be violent and overbearing, and was in the habit of heaping abuse upon his opponents. He was a good classical scholar, and on that score was susceptible to flattery. He maintained that squinting was an infallible mark of dishonesty. He himself squinted, though he was not aware of it, and could not be convinced of it by others. He spent his money with careless profusion. He died of cancer, about the year 1821. He was the father of Judge Frederick Watts, a man of talent and industry, and greatly esteemed for his many excellent qualities.

George Fisher was a large man, of imposing exterior. Inferior in ability either to Duncan or Watts, he was still able to make a good figure at the bar. His practice was mostly confined to the defensive side, as it was dangerous to allow him to collect money. He lived to a great age—eighty-four, I believe.

Charles Hall, of Sunbury, was a good lawyer, and highly esteemed as a man. He was shrewd, laborious, and very attentive to the interests of his clients. He had not, however, the gift of a ready speaker, being rather tedious.

Daniel Smith was the only lawyer of the district who could be called eloquent in a high sense.

Daniel Levy, of Sunbury, outlived all the old lawyers, as they were popularly called, except Mr. Bellas. He was a conceited man, active as a cat, an insatiable dancer, and a hard fighter. He had considerable science as a boxer, and although not large or strong, his skill joined to his prodigious activity made him quite formidable. His vanity and fondness for dress made him a capital butt, and subject of jokes for his fellow-members of the bar. He lived to the age of seventy, and a fop to the last.

[I have dropped Mr. Snyder's strictures on the morals of these old legal giants. But that the truth may be told in a general way, drinking habits got the better of some of them.]

Hugh Bellas was the last survivor of the old lawyers. A man of singular energy, and the most elastic spirit, I ever knew. He came to this country from Ireland, when he was about ten years of age. George Bellas, his father, was poor, and unable to educate his children. Hugh was bound to Robert Irwin, of Northumberland, to learn the mercantile business. Here he found a congenial spirit in Robert Christie, the senior clerk. Robert was the son of an English teacher, and had been well educated. Store-keeping was not then conducted on the go-ahead style of the present, and our clerks, having considerable leisure at certain periods, devoted themselves to reading and study. Mr. Bellas' father was a strict Presbyterian, and had brought up his family in the faith of that Church; but the active and independent mind of Hugh, let him into inquiries, which caused him to reject Calvanism, and even to doubt seriously the entire christian faith. About this time (1799) he heard much said of three remarkable sermons of Doctor Priestly, on "habitual devotion," the "danger of bad habits," and the "duty of not living to ourselves." Meeting the doctor one day, he expressed a desire to read these sermons. "My young friend," replied the doctor, "I judge from your opinions on the subject of revelation, that you would not be able to appreciate these discourses. Before you undertake them, I will, if you please, put a tract into your hands, the reading of which will, I hope, prepare you for the doctrine of my sermons." The seed fell into good ground and brought forth an hundred fold.

While at Irwin's, Mr. Bellas commenced studying law with Jonathan Walker, afterward Judge Walker. It was about the year 1803, Mr. Bellas applied for admission, but he met a most formidable opposition. Every lawyer then at the bar in this district was a decided Federalist, and as Mr. Bellas was not only an active and influential Democrat, but of the plebeian stock, the aristocratic gentlemen objected to his admission, on the ground of his not having studied actually *in the office* of Mr. Walker, but in a store, and while conducting a business of another character.

Whether the court decided against him, or he was induced by the clamor of his opponents to suspend application, I am unable to say. This happened during the session of the court at Bellefonte. Returning to Northumberland, and stating the case to Mr. Walker, the latter advised him to employ counsel in his behalf, and renew his application at Sunbury. Mr. Bellas accordingly retained Daniel Smith, who brought his case before the court, and advocated it so ably that an examination was ordered, and Charles Hall, the most determined of his opponents, appointed one of his examiners. The examination was held in open court, and was most rigorous. Mr. Hall came prepared with a sheet of written questions; many of them mere trials of memory. Such as the date of certain statutes of Queen Elizabeth. Mr. Bellas' memory was, however, never at fault. The judge perceiving that he had no ordinary candidate before him, was highly gratified. At one stage the judge asked him what is criminal law? Mr. Bellas, after a moment's hesitation, commenced: Law is a rule of action. Here the judge interrupted him in his quick, nervous way, with "I don't want a general definition of law, but of criminal law." Criminal law, resumed Mr. Bellas, is a rule of action defining and prohibiting crime, and prescribing due punishment. That will do, remarked the judge, I only asked the question in order to try your judgment. There is no definition of criminal law in the books. The three hours' ordeal passed. Mr. Hall most grudgingly admitted that the young man had passed a satisfactory examination, and recommended his admission to the bar.

My father, [afterward Governor Snyder,] who was at the time county treasurer, witnessed the whole proceedings, and resolved to patronize the young lawyer. He accordingly employed him in the memorable Isle of Que case, which terminated in his favor, after more than twenty years litigation.

Hugh Bellas, Esquire, died October 26, 1863, aged eighty-three and a half years.

Marriages.

May 11, Peter Kreechbaum with Elizabeth Davis, in presence of his father Peter, and brother George.

June 21, Martin Billmyer with Margaret Himmelrich, in presence of her parents, George Billmyer and wife, Stephen Frantz and wife, George Withington, &c.

November 13, George Kreechbaum with Polly Keller, daughter of George Keller, now in Sciota.

December 10, By Reverend Henry R. Wilson, Thomas Burnside, Esquire, to Miss Mary Fleming, of Bellefonte.

December 26, John Brobst with Lydia Marriner. Witnesses, Sophia Nixon, Thomas Poak, John Conser, &c.

Deaths.

February 15, Adam Young.

March 30, John Aurand, of East Buffalo. He was born in Dillenberg, Germany, February 5, 1725; was, therefore, eighty-two years six months three weeks and four days old. His grave, in the Dreisbach yard, is unmarked, and possibly cannot be identified. His wife, Mary Elizabeth, died before him. His children were: Henry, who lived and died in Snyder county; Peter and Jacob, lived in Reading; Daniel, in Sunbury; Reverend Dietrich, who died in Huntingdon county; George Aurand, Esquire, died July 18, 1850, buried in the Hassinger grave-yard, near Middleburg, (father of Jacob Aurand, Esquire, of Middleburg;) Elizabeth, intermarried with Francis Zeller; John, who died soon after, (his widow Catherine married Henry Rhiem;) Abraham; Mary, married to John Wolfe. His descendants are, like the sands of the sea, innumerable, scattered all through New York, Ohio, Illinois; and the family Bible, written for by the agent in New York, which will secure a large fortune to the family, can be produced by Jacob Aurand, Esquire, of Middleburg.

September 16, Florence, wife of Colonel John Clarke, aged seventy-six.

William Thompson, of White Deer township, in the seventieth year of his age. His remains were interred in the Presbyterian burial ground, in Derrstown, followed by a numerous assemblage of friends and relations. He left a widow, Jane, who died in Lewisburg. Daughter, Ruth; granddaughter, Nancy T. Reznor; son, James.[1]

George Wilt, of West Buffalo, died in the spring. Widow, Catherine. Children: Elizabeth, Adam, George, Barbara, and Mary.

Daniel Franklin, inn-keeper, died in September.

William McKim, of Buffalo. Robert McKim.

Reverend John Hoge. Children: Ebenezer, Samuel, David, Jonathan D., Elizabeth Brice, Mary Redrick, Priscilla Bennett.

David Katherman, West Buffalo. Children: Barbara, George, Jacob.

Lewis Frantz. Children: Stephen, John, Jacob, Philip, Catherine, George, Margaret.

William Steele, of Buffalo.

[1] Reverend James Thompson studied theology under Mr. Hood. Licensed, 1817. April 17, 1819, installed pastor of Shaver's Creek and Alexandria churches. Died October 8, 1830. Left a widow, Eliza, (Stewart,) one son, and two daughters.—*See Gibson's History of the Huntingdon Presbytery.*

1808.

The First Baptist Church Organized—Political Affairs—Simon Snyder Elected Governor—Death of John Brady, (Sheriff,) and Notices of his Family.

EMBER of Congress, George Smith. Members of Assembly, elected in October, John Murray, Leonard Rupert, Frederick Evans, and Andrew Albright. Clerk of the Middle District of the Supreme Court, John L. Finney. County Commissioner elect, Andrew McClenachan. Amos Ellmaker, Deputy Attorney General for Dauphin and Northumberland. By the act of 21st March, Northumberland county was entitled to four members of the House, and, with Luzerne, to two members of the Senate.

January 23, the congressional caucus nominated James Madison for President and George Clinton for Vice.

Under date March 16, the *Argus* notices a meeting of the Republican members of the Legislature, which declared unanimously for Simon Snyder, for Governor. The Federalists, it says, favor James Ross. The Quids, John Spayd. Democratic Presidential electors: William Wilson, Robert Giffen, Jacob Hostetter.

29th March, Adam Wilt commissioned justice. May 15, Reverend John Dietrich Adams, of the Reformed Church, called to the Middle Creek, Beaver Dam, &c., churches. He accepted, and seems to have served until 1812, when he was excommunicated. Tradition says love for strong drink was his ruin. Postmaster at Mifflinburg, Thomas Youngman. During this year and the next, the Reverend Jacob Diffenbach, of the Reformed Church, lived in

Mifflinburg, preached there, and at times in Brush valley and Selinsgrove. He married a Miss Lydia Hughes, of Selinsgrove, subsequently removed to Espytown, and died there in 1825. One of his children, Samuel Dieffenbach, resides near Selinsgrove, Snyder county. 30th September, George Clark commissioned justice, White Deer. James McClellan, Esquire, taught school at Chamberlin's mill.

Additional Residents in East Buffalo.—Baldy, Benjamin ; Beard, Christian, blacksmith ; Brewer, John ; Bossler, John ; Christ, Adam, junior; Christ, Henry ; Dentler, John ; Deratt, Daniel, both on Mathias Macpherson's place; George, John; Heiser, Frederick ; Jackson, Robert, (colored ;) Kitchen, John ; Kline, Jacob ; McCurdy, Daniel, at James Dale's; Searfoss, George ; Shields, William ; Snook, Martin, (Jenkins ;) Snook, Peter, (Jenkins ;) Snyder, Daniel, blacksmith ; Taylor, Robert.

Lewisburg—Billman, Henry ; Clark, George; Friedly, John ; Guy, Thomas ; Horning, Conrad ; Kremer, George, store in Chamberlin's building ; Martin, John, carpenter ; Myers, Peter ; Rees, Daniel, inn-keeper; Sergeant, John, nailor ; Sitgreaves, Charles, saddler ; Stillwell, Joseph, school-teacher ; Stroub, Michael, weaver ; Wagner, Henry.

New Berlin—Estrich, Christian, merchant ; Feather, Jacob, hatter ; Frantz, William ; Fought, George ; Lehman, Thomas, schoolteacher ; McCullough, William ; Maurer, Adam ; Pontius, Henry, junior, carpenter ; Smith, Peter, gunsmith ; Springer, Henry, chairmaker ; Winter, Daniel, inn-keeper.

White Deer—Awl, Samuel and John, junior ; Ferris, Joseph, on William Clingan's place ; Heckle, George ; Heckle, Simon ; Huntingdon, Abraham ; Kline, Charles, on Ranck's place ; Thomas, Arthur, miller.

West Buffalo—Charles, John ; Elert, Widow ; Elder, John ; Geddes, Samuel ; Jodon, James ; Komp, Adam ; Kline, Jacob ; Miller, Peter ; Shaup, Henry.

Mifflinburg—Clark, Widow Sarah ; Cronmiller, Martin, blacksmith ; Grove, Andrew, blacksmith ; Hofferd, John, taxed with grist and saw-mill, late Christopher Johnson's, on Rapid run, after whose death it passed into the hands of John Reish ; Lane, William, hatter ; Yearick, Henry.

Enumeration of the Taxable Inhabitants of the different Townships of Buffalo Valley—Buffalo East, four hundred and forty-seven, and one slave ; Buffalo West, three hundred and seventy-four ; White Deer, two hundred and five, and one slave ; Washington, eighty-one, and one slave.

First Baptist Church.

The first regular Baptist church in what is now Union county, was raised under the labors of Thomas Smiley, in Washington (now Gregg) township, and was recognized by sister churches October 23, 1808. Elder Smiley remained its pastor until his death, in 1832. He was succeeded by George Spratt, M. D., 1833-1834; his son, George M. Spratt, D. D., 1835-1839; William S. Hall, 1840-1843; John Edminster, 1843-1847; William T. Bunker, 1849-1853; Professor Robert Lowry, 1854; George Frear, D. D., 1855; Joshua Kelly, 1857-1858; W. R. McNeal, 1859 ; Samuel W. Ziegler, 1860; J. Green Miles, 1861-1865 ; George W. Snyder, 1867; and J. Green Miles since 1869.—*O. N. Worden.*

Political.

Northumberland and Luzerne composed the senatorial district. Centre, Lycoming and Northumberland composed the congressional district. General Daniel Montgomery declined a re-election. At the Democratic-Republican convention, held at Sunbury, on the 28th of June, the delegates from Buffalo were Samuel Maclay and General C. Baldy; West Buffalo, John Wilson and Thomas Youngman ; Penn's, Frederick Evans and Philip Moore; White Deer, Andrew McClenachan and William Chamberlin.

The nominating convention was held at Derrstown, on the 20th of August. Thirty-seven delegates from twenty townships. General Robert Giffen was elected president; Matthew Huston, secretary. Simon Snyder was unanimously nominated for Governor ; George Smith, of Lycoming, for Congress ; Nathan Palmer, of Luzerne, for State Senator; John Murray, Andrew Albright, Leonard Rupert, and Frederick Evans, for Assembly.

The Federal leaders of that day were General William Wilson,

Charles Hall, Esquire, Captain Christian Brobst, William Mears, Samuel Miles, Esquire, John Buyers, &c. The canvass for Governor this year was exceedingly bitter. Among other stories, was that the Honorable Samuel Maclay had expressed himself in favor of James Ross for Governor, at William McAllister's, in Juniata county, when he and the Honorable Daniel Montgomery were on their return from Congress ; that Simon Snyder had said in the presence of one George Church, who made affidavit to that effect, that no poor man ought to have the right of voting at an election ; that he had voted for a bill to fine Mennonists and Quakers $10 for not attending militia trainings ; that he intended, or favored, dividing the property of the rich among the poor. The Snyder men were accused of suing the Rossites for debts. Jared Irwin, the sheriff, certifies that Simon Snyder has not issued an execution for twelve months ; Judge Cooper, that Simon Snyder did not behave improperly in handing a paper to the judge, &c. James Ross was declared to be a man of mercenary and avaricious disposition ; accused of blasphemy and mockery of religion ; said to be "the candidate of the nabobs and lawyers ; that while member of the United States Senate, he advocated the wresting of New Orleans from the Spaniards by force, instead of acquiring it by treaty. During the reign of terror, (Adams' administration,) his violence for its measures secured him the Federal patronage." All manner of tricks were resorted to.

Andrew Albright and Robert Smith were nominated by the Federal meeting, at Milton, for Assembly, although known to be Democrats, in favor of Jefferson and his embargo. Both came out in the *Argus*, disclaiming the nomination.

As early as this year, Andrew C. Huston, with John Frick and others, issue an address, as representatives of the young men of Northumberland county, in favor of Simon Snyder. Judge Thomas Cooper, in a communication, vindicates the private character of Simon Snyder, although he did not feel at liberty to vote for either Simon Snyder or James Ross.

OCTOBER ELECTION.

	SNYDER.	ROSS.	SPAYD.
Buffalo,	311	68	
West Buffalo,	300	70	8
Berlin,	209	10	1
Swineford's,	166	8	
Milton,	467	127	
Selinsgrove,	237	28	
Mifflinburg,	49	32	6
Beaver,	138	3	9

Snyder's majority in the county, over both, was 2,927. Colonel John Bull was the Federal candidate against Colonel George Smith, for Congress. Colonel John Kelly, against Nathan Palmer, for Senate. For Assembly, the Federal candidates were Sol Markley, Robert Barber, Esquire, Abraham Miller, and Thomas Wallace. Henry Musser was elected commissioner, over Theodore Kiehl and James Smith. For presidential electors on the Democratic-Republican and Whig side—for the party recognize all three names—were William Montgomery and Robert Giffen. The Federalists are called the Tories. John Boyd was the Federal candidate for elector. Vote, 2,793 to 221.

Marriages.

March 22, John Freedly with Elizabeth Lehman, by H. Spyker, in presence of Daniel Nyhart, her brother-in-law, &c.

May 4, Peter Myers to Sophia Nixon, by same, in the presence of her step-father, James Marriner, and her mother, Peter Spyker, George Graham, Thomas Poak, Margaret Graham, Betsy Smith, Lydia Pross, &c.

May 17, by the same, Henry Zerbe with Susanna Heckel. Witnesses: Adam Wertz, Peter Leonard, John Snyder, &c.

July 5, Peter Brown with Catherine Kantz, in presence of her brother, Peter Kantz, brother-in-law, John Hartman.

March 24, by Reverend T. Hood, William Nesbit, of Chillisquaque, to Nancy Musser, of East Buffalo.

November 29, George Freedly with Catherine Frantz, by H. Spyker, Esquire, in presence of Andrew Billmyer and wife, George Billmyer and wife, John Frantz, Jacob Frantz, Peggy Librunen, &c.

Deaths.

Samuel Dunning and James McCorley, White Deer.

Neal Madden, father of the late James Madden, Esquire, West Buffalo.

17th May, Adam Christ, aged sixty-six. Left widow, Elizabeth. Children: Henry, Elizabeth, Eve, married to John Snook.

Elizabeth Earne, Buffalo. (Her daughter married Jacob Moore.) Children: John, Anna M., Balisa, and Susanna.

Joseph Ultz, of West Buffalo.

John Aurand, junior, East Buffalo.

James Boveard, East Buffalo, soldier of the Revolution. Enlisted, 1776, as private in Captain David Kilgore's company, eighth Pennsylvania, and served three years. His family as follows: Children: Hannah, Robert, Alexander, Mary, married to Robert McBride, Jane, to Doctor James Charleton, ——, to John Steans.

Daniel Metzgar, hotel-keeper at Lewisburg. His widow, Eve, afterwards married to Colonel Christopher Baldy.

Saturday, 30th January, Mrs. Annie McBeth, of White Deer, formerly of Cumberland county, buried at Buffalo Cross-Roads. Her ancestors fled from Scotland on account of religious persecution. They were of the first settlers at Brandywine, in Chester county. She was twice married, first to John Fleming, and afterwards to Andrew McBeth; had four children by her first, and five by her last husband. One of her sons fell at Long Island.—*Argus.*

27th July, Susanna Baldy, consort of General C. Baldy, aged fifty-two. A faithful observance of all the relative duties of wife, mother, and friend, marked the conduct of this truly excellent woman.—*Argus, 3d August.*

December 10, at Milton, John Brady, inn-keeper, and former sheriff of Northumberland county, aged forty-eight. He is buried in the cemetery at Lewisburg. His wife, Jane, survived him twenty years, and is buried in the same grave. A mural monument, covered with a heavy marble slab, marks their grave and that of Mary Brady, widow of Captain John Brady.

John Brady's children were: Lieutenant Samuel Brady, born 22d February, 1793. At the commencement of the war of 1812, he served as a volunteer, under Governor Edwards, in a campaign against the Indians. They had one battle, defeating the Indians. Shortly afterwards, he received a commission as ensign in the twenty-second United States regiment, commanded by his uncle, General Hugh Brady, and served in the unfortunate campaign under General Wilkinson. In the summer of 1814 he was attached to General Brown's army, on the Niagara frontier. He was in the bloody battle of Lundy's Lane; a second lieutenant in the sortie from Fort Erie. He was the only platoon officer of his regiment that was not either killed or wounded in the former battle, and Major Arrowsmith was the only field-officer of General Scott's brigade that was left on horseback. See his letter to Captain B. Vincent, under date of 1814.

After peace was proclaimed, Lieutenant Brady entered into an arrangement with Captain John Culbertson, a brother officer, to go on a trading expedition to the Rocky Mountains, supposing that, upon the reduction of the army, he would not be retained in the service. He was retained, however; but thinking he could not, in honor, break his engagement with the captain, he resigned. The Government declined to accept his resignation, and sent him an unlimited furlough. His health, however, failed him, and he was advised to winter in the South. He went to New Orleans, accompanied by his friend, Lieutenant Colonel Trimble, of Ohio, and died there on the 17th of February, 1816, not quite twenty-three years of age. He was six feet five, and a remarkably fine looking man. His disease was hurried on by exposure in the Niagara campaigns, when he should have been in the hospital, instead of the field. In the *Sunbury Times* of that year, there is an eloquent obituary, by his friend, Colonel Trimble, in which he says: "In Lieutenant Brady's death, the country has lost an intelligent and gallant officer, and myself a firm and distinterested friend."

William Perry Brady, his brother, was born 16th February, 1795. He worked for a while at his trade—cabinet making— in Aaronsburg. In 1813 he entered the army as private. His regiment was at Erie when Perry was fitting out his fleet. The commodore, not having a sufficient number of regular marines, called for volunteers. William was the first who volunteered. Before Perry sailed, Colonel Hugh Brady came to Erie, and through his influence, Perry appointed him a purser's steward. He was attached to one of the small vessels, and was in the battle of the 10th of September. His vessel had to be abandoned, and he was the last man to leave his gun. His shirt sleeves were shot away. He took great pride in the old shirt, and often showed it to his friends in after years. After the battle, and the return of the fleet to Erie, William and two of his Centre county friends, waited on the commodore. He granted them their discharges, and advised them to return home and settle in civil life, remarking that they had already rendered important service to their country. William took his advice, returned to Aaronsburg, and in a short time married Rachel Mussina, of that place. In 1846, he was elected assistant sergeant-at-arms of the Pennsylvania Senate, which place he retained until his death, at Harrisburg, on the 4th of April, 1864. Every one having business in Harrisburg in the last twenty years, will recollect the genial companionship of William P. Brady. He survived all his children, except one son, who died about one year after his father.

Jasper Ewing Brady, Esquire, the fourth son, was born March 4, 1797. He first learned the trade of hatter, and, after traveling from place to place for two or three years, he settled in Franklin county, Pennsylvania. He there abandoned his trade, and taught school several years, meanwhile studying law. He was admitted at Chambersburg in 1826 or 1827, and there commenced practice. In 1843 he was elected to the Assembly, and re-elected in 1844. During the first session, although he represented an anti-improvement county, he offered an amendment to the bill to reduce the State tax providing for the assessment of a three-mill tax, which redeemed the credit of the State. He was treasurer of Franklin county for three years. In 1846 he was elected to Congress, beating Honorable Samuel Hepburn some eight hundred votes. He was, however, defeated in 1848, by Honorable James X. McLanahan. The Whig loss in the Carlisle district was some two hundred votes. Mr. Brady was beaten only one hundred and sixty-seven votes. In September, 1849, he removed to Pittsburgh, and practiced law very successfully until 1861, when he was appointed to a responsible position in the paymasters' department at Washington. He was removed in July, 1869, by General Rawlings, then Secretary of War. He then resumed the practice of law at Washington, where he died.

John Brady, the third, died several years ago. James, the youngest, died in Franklin county, in 1829. He was a man of fine intellect, and was thought to be the most talented of the family.

Of the daughters of Sheriff John Brady, Mary married William Piatt, uncle of Judge Piatt, of Brady township, Lycoming county; Hannah married Judge Piatt; Charlotte married H. C. Piatt; Jane married Roland Stoughton; her descendants, Mrs. Lyndall's children, still live in Lewisburg; Nancy married George B. Eckert, of Lewisburg.

I am indebted to O. N. Worden, late of the Lewisburg *Chronicle*, for the following narrative he took down at the time. He says: In June, 1857, I took the following notes of a conversation I had with Mrs. Mary Brady Piatt, aged seventy-two, born in 1785:

"My father was a brother of Sam Brady, the Indian fighter. I saw him once. He was then on a visit to my father's, at Sunbury. I went with them over to Northumberland. On the way over, my father asked Sam if he could jump as well as ever? He said he could not, but coming to a high fence in a few minutes, he sprung clear over it, with but little effort. 'I never could do that,' said my father. 'You could, if obliged to,' said Sam.

"Sam killed three Indians after peace was declared, and a reward of $300 was offered for his apprehension. Shortly after, he was sitting with a tavern-keeper, in West Virginia, when two strangers, Virginians, rode up, alighted, and asked for horse feed and dinner. They laid their pistols upon a table, near which sat Sam, rolling his rifle upon his knees. In the course of conversation with the landlord, they found out that he knew Brady, and that he lived in that region, and was very popular. They told the landlord that they had come to arrest him, and if he gave them assistance, they would share the reward with him. The landlord said they could never take him, nor could any one take him alive. They declared they could. 'I am Sam Brady,' said the man at the table. They were startled. They looked at him for a minute, and, estimating his power, waived the attempt. After dinner, they went to the table to get their pistols. Brady said they could not have those pistols, nor could the landlord's entreaty or their threats prevail. 'Go back to your homes, and tell them Sam Brady took your pistols,' was all the answer he made. He afterwards gave their pistols to his sons.

"After awhile he delivered himself up for trial at Pittsburgh. He was defended by James Ross. Brady laid the scalps on the bar. ' There they are ; I killed them.' A great many women attended this trial, or rather men in women's clothes, ready to rescue him, if convicted ; but there was no occasion for their intervention."

Mrs. Piatt, like her brother, the late William Perry Brady, remained a Federalist to the last. She said when Washington was burned, through the inefficiency of a granny President, her blood boiled, and she longed to go, that she might shoot at least one British invader.

1809.

OFFICIALS—RESIDENTS—ROAN'S JOURNAL—ELECTION RETURN—MARRIAGES AND DEATHS.

OVERNOR, Simon Snyder. Surveyor General, Andrew Porter, appointed April 4, *vice* Samuel Cochran. Deputy Attorney General, E. G. Bradford, appointed January 19. Prothonotary, &c., Hugh Bellas, commissioned January 3. Register and Recorder, John Frick, commissioned January 18. Sheriff, Daniel Lebo, commissioned October 24. Coroner, Joseph Lorentz, re-commissioned October 24. County Commissioner elect, Henry Masser. Justices commissioned: Penn's, Joseph Führer, February 28 ; Mahantango, Michael Rathfon and Philip Burchart, the same day. Postmaster at Lewisburg, William Hayes.

James Moore, senior, built the bridge at the mouth of Buffalo creek.

Tobias Lehman's property divided. His children were : Henry, Barbara, married to George Baily, Elizabeth, married to John Freedly, Margaret Spidler, Catherine, married to Daniel Nyhart,

Mary, married to John Brown, Freedly took the mills and four acres; John Brown. one hundred and thirty-two acres one hundred and one perches; and Nyhart the tract next Derr's, fifty-five acres one hundred and twenty-six perches.

Reverend John G. Heim became pastor of the Lutherans, at Dreisbach's church, where he remained until 1831.

East Buffalo Additional Residents—Aurand, Abraham; Badger, Joseph, tailor; Boveard, Robert; Brown, Peter, stiller; Clinger, Adam; Gross, Mathias; Hauck, Andrew; Herbst, Henry; Jarman, Jacob; Johnston, John, colored; Knittle, Adam, shoe-maker; Shamp, Jesse; Sheckler, Martin, miller; Thompson, Samuel; Thompson, Moses; Updyke, Isaac; Wise, Henry, shoe-maker; Zeluff, David.

Lewisburg—Baldwin, Doctor Ethan; Espy, John; Nyhart, Daniel; Smith, Robert.

White Deer—Bellas, James; Davis, John, school-teacher; Landis, Jacob, shoe-maker; Smith, William Walker; Sypher, Jacob.

West Buffalo—Anthony, Henry; Bergstresser, John; Bruner, John; Caldwell, William; Hayes, John; Keeply, John; Koons, Peter; Linn, Isaac; Yerger, John.

Mifflinburg—Auple, Conrad; Haslet, John; Larabee, Widow; Manly, John; Millhouse, Nicholas; Smelker, Godfrey, tavern; Staple, Conrad; Wolf, Andrew; Young, Christian.

Roan's Journal.

14th January. Scholars at Mr. Hood's had a public exhibition of their speaking abilities. Elder Brown, Honorable George Kremer, and others attended. Sunday 29th. Mr. Hood's text, John xiv: 6 v. Thirty-six sleds and sleighs at meeting.

February 9. Roan, Sally, Becky, and Bob Clark, and John Eaker came and staid all night. Sunday, 12th. Saw a woman putting a hippen to her child during church. Read twenty-two chapters, verse about, to-night. 15th. Maclays and their connections spent the day at Clingan's. 16th. George and Davy Reznor went to Easton, with grain, in sleds. They returned on the 22d. 27th. Billy Clark, Uncle Giddy, Wilson's, &c., at Aunt Dale's, in all seventeen, for supper. Had two turkeys.

March 1. The young folks at Roan McClure's. Turkey for supper, and plenty of cider and apples. 3d. Debate at Mr. Hood's school-house. Question: "Is a lawyer a promoter of justice?" 12th, Sunday. No singing at meeting, as people cannot agree about the psalms and music. 13th. Black Grace free to-day, and left us. Seven Methodists dined at Clingan's to-day. 15th. Met Doctor Baldwin at Lewisburg to-day. He is a Democrat, full of ostentation. 18th. Mr. McClure's family, Richard Fruit and wife, Judge Wilson and wife, came to my school to-day to hear the boys speak. Wednesday, 22d. John Linn died last night. 23d. Went to John Linn's funeral. Stopped at Baldy's, and wrote a piece on his death for both papers at Northumberland.

April 8. Saw a clegyman, a Congressman, six esquires, and a constable at Billy Poak's to-day. River very high. Congressman Smith bought a silk shawl at Kremer's for Betsey Smith. 18th. Planted the locusts at Clingan's; got them down at Billy Clark's. Eight ministers here, Mr. Wilson of Bellefonte, Mr. Bard, &c. 19th. Planted some Lombardys. Presbytery in session. 22d. At Northumberland; called at Seidel's, Jones', Taggart's, Priestly's, Welker's, Irwin's, Huston's, and Bonham's. Spent the evening at Reverend Isaac Grier's. He is a very friendly man. I heard Isaiah Linn was buried to-day.

May 7th. Clingan came home from Lancaster. He had news of General Bright's trial, Snyder's ignorance, foreign decrees revoked. He brought the girls fashionable ear-rings. Tommy got fifty shad, at Hoffman's, sent down from Lawson's. 11th. Went to the review at Voneida's, [near Samuel Maclay's.] Five hundred and fifty men in line, and a great many spectators. Any number of studs. 13th. A good foot-way made over the creek, at my instigation. Got the slabs in Derrstown. Doctor Beyer and Dan Rees each gave a bottle of whisky. 17th. Jimmy Thompson building a barn on the Hafer place, for Clingan. 20th. Josiah Cander called, with proposals for an astronomical wheel. I called at Esquire Clark's, Captain Gray's; then went to Derrstown, at Rees', Hayes', Poak's, Black's, and Stillwell's. Saw crazy John Maclay at Metzgar's. I and Sam Awl went to look after him. Called at Baldy's, then at Captain Robinson's for shirting, and at Anderson's for lasts. 25th. John Cochran, [surveyor general,] wife, and two sons at Clingan's, with Mrs. Thompson. 29th. Violent storm last night; blew down trees, and took the roof off several barns and houses.

3d June. Went to Centre county, for balm of Gilead for Roan Clark, who is sick. Fed at Wilt's, [Narrows.] Aaronsburg, at three. Left with Evans Miles, and came to George Wood's. Had psalm-singing, the old way, and prayers. He is a very religious man. 4th. Called at Kern's. Stopped at Benner's, (old fort.) Then to Ludwig Reily's, on Hasting's place, where I got some leaves and branches. Stopped at Barber's tavern, and back to Eaker's—twenty-four miles—a good Sabbath-day's journey. 5th. Left Aaronsburg with John Forster. At eleven fed at Wilt's, and at Youngman's at five. Stopped at Baldy's, with Holmes and Kimmell. 7th. Raising at Hafer's; sixty-eight feet by thirty wide, forty-two rounds high. There were seventy people there. Finished before night, and then had a sumptuous entertainment. 12th. Called to see General Baldy and lady, (married last night to Eve Metzgar.) 13th. Long John Maclay called. He is from Genessee. 20th. Anne Roan Laird here to-night, getting a dress for her name. 23d. William Patterson here from Lewistown. A social man and great talker. 28th. Called at Lawyer Hall's, with Billmyer. Dined at Lebo's, with Lawshe. Snyder lost his suit with Voneida. Judge Yeates called to-night. Asked me how I could live honest, and be single.

July 1. Called at Grier's, Shannon's, and Irwin's. Sent a snuff-box to Mrs. Robert Lyon. Had business at Priestly's with Rees and Bonham. Met John Hayes at Jones'. 6th. Flavel bit by a snake. Indigo extracted the poison. 13th. Jacob Zerbe married to Miss Ferris. Mr. Hood called on the way home, and craddled all afternoon. He is very jocose, and good company. 22d. Went to Giddy Smith's, and read a play; then crossed the creek to Hudson's. [Cameron's place now.] 30th. Ensign Seeley and others, from Sunbury, at meeting to-day. Clingan came home by Derrstown, to attend christening of Graham's children. 31st. I am forty-nine years old to-day.

August 1. Clingan had six hundred dozen on the Hafer place, one thousand at home, and not a quart of whisky drank in all haying and harvesting. 2d. James Dougal commenced at the Latin school. 3d. Fishing with Mr. Hood. 8th. Mrs. Nevius had a young son. 9th. Mr. Potter's son came to the Latin school at Mr. Hood's.

[W. W. Potter, Esquire.] 14th. Mr. Hood gave us Caul Kail pet, II Peter, i : 5, 6, 7. Commenced to rain as the sermon closed, and we were kept there two hours. 15th. Stahl had his barn burned with lightning, yesterday. Two horses killed. 16th. At Derrstown. Went with Cremer to Methodist meeting. Hamer squeezing Nancy McDonald behind the stove. Returned and slept with Kremer. 23d. Jamy Wilson hauled the stuff for the fence at my schoolhouse, and Cherry put it up. Sent Joseph Wallis for another bottle of whisky for him. 27th. Tommy and sister, James McClellan, Ruth Thompson, and others, went to church. At the river, men rode over and the women were ferried at Milton. Met a great company, and went on to Warrior Run. Mr. Bryson preached in the forenoon. Two hundred and thirty-seven communicants. Mr. Hood gave us C. K. p., II Peter, i : 5, 6, and 7. Mr. Nesbit asked my advice about marrying. 30th. Referees sitting at Sunbury, on suit Snyder and Drum. Sat up until midnight, talking with Esquire Maus. 31st. Rode out to see John Cooke. Drank cider royal at Shriner's. Dined at Reverend Grier's. Gave Eliza a copy of an enigma. Carried widow Allison on behind me part of the way home. Took a drink at Lawshe's.

September 2. Rode with McEwen to Alexander Griffey's, on electioneering business. Went over the Muncy hills with Umbrella Hayes, whom I met at Shannon's. Stopped at Frederick's, in Pennsboro'. Met with Mrs. Pott's son-in-law, Fiester, and carried him home with me on the horse, three miles. 3d. Went to Shoemaker's mills. Called on Robert Robb. He is eighty two; his wife, seventy. Went to Williamsport. Fed at Mrs. Moore's, then to Jaysburg, to Mrs. Dunlap's. Called to see John Davis and wife. She is a great Baptist. 4th. Went to James Stewart's, from that to Esquire Salmon's ; then to Larry's creek, at John Thomas' ; to Sherer's, at Jersey Shore. Called to see Lawshe, and then to Morrison's, at Pine creek. 5th. Drank tea at Boyd Smith's. Great ball at Wilson's. Judge Cooper and Mrs. deGruchy led off the dance. Doctor Baldwin and wife there. 21st. The Governor's carriage in Derrstown, with Fred Evans. They brought citizen Kremer home in great pomp. 30th. Called on D. Smith, Esquire. He promised to attend to my business, but got into company, and soon got past business.

October 19. The Governor's son, Prince John of the Isle of Que, commenced school with me. 29th. Colonel Chamberlin's wife had a young son, his twenty-third. He is above seventy-three years, I believe.

November 3. Clerked at Mrs. Hutchinson's vendue all day. Continued over until to-morrow. Went to bed with the cryer and Derrickson. Four ladies and a child slept in a bed in the same room. 7th. D. Reasoner married to Miss Hamil. 16th. Clerked at Lawshe's vendue. Spent a high old night. Four from Milton, three from Northumberland, and the sheriff full of mischief, not drunk. Markley cried the sale. 21st. Sunbury court. Peter Smith's wife fined one dollar for flogging Miss Adams. Esquire Youngman one cent for whipping Doctor Smith. 23d. At Shaffer's for breakfast this morning. Billy Covert and two other shoe-makers working at Clingan's. [By the custom of that day, shoe-makers and tailors went to the houses of their employers.] The shoe-makers made thirteen pairs shoes, at 4s. 6d. per pair. 30th. At Dale's. Met Colonel S. Dale on his way to the Assembly. [He was a son of Samuel Dale, deceased, and represented Mercer and Venango.]

2d December. Went with Roan Clark and James Forster's son, John, to Billy Forster's. Met Captain John Wilson there. Had eleven sorts of diet for supper. 5th. Got my shoes mended at Mr. Espy's, in Derrstown. A dose of salts at Doctor Beyers'. 10th. Mr. Hood's text, Ecclesiastes, xi : 19–20. 13th. I gave one Meloner a certificate that he was taken prisoner with me on shipboard. 17th. At Derrstown, heard Kremer tell of arresting Langs for passing counterfeit money at four taverns and two stores. 18th. Eight strangers at supper. 19th. George, Tommy Scott, and Allison went to Colonel Kelly's. A quilting party there. Plenty of rye there. Mr. Allison, a spark of Betsey Kelly's. 25th. Christmas—very quiet. Met some Penn's valley folks, Billy Clark, and gentry, going to George's to spend the evening. 27th. Walter Clark called, and took George along to a "kicking frolic". [Old settlers well know what that means.] 28th. Party at Mr. Hood's. McClures, Howards, &c., there. Two turkeys and twelve sorts of diet. 30th. At Milton. Called at D. Smith's, McKisson's, Donaldson's, McCann's, Calhoun's, on Hannah Rees. Dined at Doctor Dougal's, with Sam Hood. 31st. General Baldy's wife has a young son.

Marriages.

January 4, Henry Grove with Hannah Leisenring, of Lewisburg, (by Henry Spyker, Esquire,) in presence of his three brothers, John, Samuel, and Frank, two sisters, Betsey and Sarah, &c.

January 8, by same, Philip Frederick with Christena Brown, in presence of John Brown and wife, T. Sheckler and wife, Peter Brown and wife, Abraham Brown, George Frederick.

April 11, by A. McLanachan, Esquire, John Vandyke to Miss Margaret Adams, both of White Deer.

April 13, by same, John Ranck to Miss Nancy Luther.

June 11, by Henry Spyker, Esquire, General Christopher Baldy with Eve Metzgar.

June 28, by Henry Spyker, Esquire, Joseph Bower with Susanna Machamer.

July 25, by Henry Spyker, Esquire, Lawrence Martin with Polly Juge.

August 31, Robert Montgomery with Nancy Knox, in presence of her father, George Knox, her brother, James, and sister, Bell, (by Henry Spyker, Esquire.)

On Tuesday, the 12th October, by the Reverend Mr. Deffenbaugh, Mr. John Sierer, aged sixty-five, to the amiable Miss Louisa McMillan, aged nineteen, both of Buffalo; and on Thursday, the 21st ultimo, by Esquire Hamilton, Mr. George Knox, of Derrstown, to Miss Jane McIlroy, near Pine Creek.

Deaths.

Tuesday, 21st March, in the fifty-seventh year of his age, John Linn, of White Deer township, of pleurisy, on the tenth day of his sickness. He was buried at Buffalo Cross-Roads, on the Thursday following. The funeral was attended by a large concourse of people. He was an inhabitant of this county upwards of thirty-six years, and twenty-one years an elder of Buffalo church, and principal clerk, conducting the music. He came into the Valley in 1772, and endured the hardships incident to the early settlement of the country, frequently sleeping on his cabin floor, with a bag of grain for a pillow, and his rifle by his side. During the year 1779, while off on a tour of service, his cabin was spoiled by the Indians. He was married by his brother, Reverend Doctor William Linn, to Ann Fleming, of Middleton township, near Carlisle. She was of the Fleming family, of Chester county. Her ancestor, William Fleming, came over before 1714, and settled in Caln township, in Chester county. From there, his descendants moved up to Cumberland and Northumberland counties. John Linn's children were: Susan, married to William Thompson, (son of Captain James,) in 1804, and shortly after removed to Venango county; Ann, married to Andrew McBeth, a son of John McBeth, of Aaronsburg, died at Greencastle, Indiana, October 1873, aged eighty-six; William Linn, who moved to Miami county, Ohio, died there, October 26, 1834. John Linn, married to Mary F., daughter of Colonel William Chamberlin. He resides at Mount Vernon, Ohio. Margaret Linn, married to Joseph McCalmont, of Venango county, died February 7, 1873. The late James F. Linn, Esquire, of Lewisburg, who died October 8, 1869, aged sixty-seven, and Jemima Linn, who died April 17, 1873.

Doctor William Kent Lathy, of Northumberland, July 28.

August 10, Mathew Huston, editor of *Argus*, aged fifty-one years. He was an officer in the Revolution, participated in the battles of White Plains, Trenton, Princeton, Brandywine, and Germantown. Afterwards representative of the county of Philadelphia, and was six times elected clerk of the House. Father of the late Mrs. Hannah Taggert, of Northumberland, and of Andrew C. Huston, Esquire.

Albright Swineford died. His children were: Catherine Cummings, (wife of John, senior, and mother of John J.,) George, Michael, Peter, and Jacob.

Adam Ranck, of White Deer. Children: Rachel, John, Daniel, Noah, Mary, and Adam, junior.

Conrad Reedy, of Buffalo. Children: John and Jacob.

John Beatty.

October 22, Colonel John Clarke, aged seventy-three. He is buried in the Lewis grave-yard. His children were: Jane, wife of David Watson, (mother of John C., William, and David Watson;) Joseph Clarke, who had two children, William and Grace.

October 6, Mary Hutchinson, of White Deer township, aged sixty-seven, thirty-six years a resident of the Valley. Children: Sarah, wife of James Cornelius; Mrs. Elizabeth Criswell, (mother of James, of Lewisburg.)

John Swineford. Children: John, Mary, married to Jacob Foltz; Margaret, with George Snyder; Susanna, with Jacob Fryer; Elizabeth, with John Smith; Catherine, with John Aurand; Jacob, and Albright.

1810.

COUNTERFEITERS ARRESTED—LANGS' SUICIDE—DANIEL DOUDLE—ROAN'S JOURNAL—NOTICE OF NATHAN EVANS.

ENATOR, James Laird. Representatives, John Murray, Jared Irwin, Leonard Rupert, Frederick Evans, elected in October. Treasurer, David Taggert. Commissioner elect, Joseph Gaston. Commissioners' Clerk, Nathan Patton. Postmaster at Mifflinburg, Thomas Youngman. Henry Yearick commissioned Justice of the Peace, June 4.

Passing counterfeit money seems a very prevalent offense. Doctor Thomas Barrett, of Danville, convicted. George Langs and Jared Langs also. Barrett made his escape from jail at Sunbury. Sheriff Lebo was complained of for his negligence with prisoners. At April term (20th) George Langs received his sentence. He bowed to the court, and retired. The next morning his daughter called on him. He asked her to withdraw a little while, and about one hour afterwards he was found hanging on an iron bed, near the door of his room. He was convicted of passing a counterfeit $20 note upon John Sargent, of Lewisburg.

Additional Residents East Buffalo—Bird, John and William; Brewer, Matthew; Brewer, Thomas; Clements, Michael; Gross, Jacob, carpenter; Hahn, Andrew; Kreisher, Henry; Lilly, Peter; Slear, Charles; Zellers, George.

Lewisburg—Bower, Joseph ; Gordon, John B., dyer ; Hutchinson, Alexander; McClure, Matthew; Pross, John. November 10, McQuhae and Hepburn opened a new store.

New Berlin—Kessler, William ; Shout, John; Sproul, James, merchant.

White Deer—Caldwell, Daniel; Dieffenbach, Adam; Eyer, Daniel ; Guyer, John ; Haas, Peter ; Huff, Thomas ; McKisson, James, single ; Reed, Robert.

West Buffalo—Beidelman, Valentine ; Bilman, Dewalt; Braucher, Christian ; Deal, John, carpenter ; Wright, John.

Mifflinburg—Montelius, John. John Bergstresser bought Henry Snyder's mill on Rapid run. The latter probably died this year.

Daniel Doudle.

Daniel Doudle was an acquaintance of Governor Snyder in his boyhood, and in maturer years he would sometimes pay the Governor a visit, at Selinsgrove, and thus formed acquaintance with George Kremer. After George moved to Derrstown, and established himself in business and a bachelor's hall there, Daniel extended his visits thither, and became so much pleased that he resolved to forsake York altogether, and remain with George. Accordingly, he sent for his money, a considerable stock of dollars, and took up his abode in Derrstown. He and George agreed very well, for George humored him in all his whims, but he quarreled sadly with old Peggy Miller, the housekeeper. Sometimes he would come in a towering passion to George, with "Now, George, I can't live with the old devil any longer. Just send me off to Selinsgrove, to Simon, and he will send me to York." "Well, well," said George, "Roan (Clark) or John shall take you and your money in the cart to Selinsgrove as soon as you like." "Do you think," Daniel would reply, "I would trust myself with the damned rascals? They would murder me for my money before we got half way to Selinsgrove." Then an argument would commence on the honesty of Roan and John, which generally lasted until Daniel, in his rage against these two, had forgotten his wrath toward old Peggy. At length, Daniel fell into the hands of an old Methodist woman, who, by her exhortations, made considerable impression on him. After spending an evening at Mother

Grove's, Daniel came home with a face so solemn and important that the whole family noticed it, and, knowing where he had been, the clerks followed him on his retreat to bed, and peeped and listened at his door. Daniel locked his door, looked carefully around, undressed, (taking off his hat the last of all, as was his custom,) kneeled by the bedside, and commenced thus: "O, Lord God;" then ensued a long pause. Up rose Daniel, exclaiming "It is too damned cold to pray here!" and jumped into bed. Whether Daniel made another effort to pray is uncertain. He once acted godfather for one of his friend's children. The clergyman asked the name of the child. Daniel, understanding him to ask *his* name, promptly replied: "Daniel Doudle, to be sure. Don't you know me any more?" Daniel, at this time eighty years of age, usually dressed himself once a day in state, in a blue silk-velvet coat, white vest, ruffled shirt, brown silk-velvet small-clothes, and turned-up shoes, and paraded himself down to the river bank and back, to exhibit himself to the ladies. He lived to be one hundred and one or one hundred and two years of age, dying in August, 1828, at Mr. Kremer's, near Middleburg, where his bones rest with those of his friends, Frederick Evans and George Kremer. Certainly three more singular men were never so intimately associated in life and rest so close together in the solemn silence of death.

Among other characters of this date, were Billy Nicholas, a carpenter of White Deer, and old Mr. Mook, the revolutionary soldier. Saturday was the usual day to assemble in Lewisburg, and getting pretty drunk, old Mook asserted he could "hex a bullet" at an hundred yards. Mook held a silver bullet in his hand and began powwowing. Billy shot from the porch of Metzgar's tavern, knocked the bullet out of Mook's finger, skinning the latter considerably, thus disabusing Mook's mind of the idea that he could "hex."

Roan's Journal.

January 23. T. Clingan had a water-smeller, to find where he should put the well on his place. Grand ball at Baldy's. Poaks and a number from Milton there. 24th. Rees' vendue at Derrstown.

April 8. T. Clingan, Wilson Smith, and I went to Daniel Smith's funeral; eighteen chairs and carriages; one hundred and twenty on horseback. 14th. Planted two Lombardys at the school-house. Met Mr. Coryell at Poak's. He brought his family from Williamsport in a canoe. 17th. Review day. Seven hundred on parade at Derrstown.

June 2. Hoffman sold his place to one Boal. 3d. At Chillisquaque grave-yard. Saw Dan Smith's grave. 4th. I dreamed Dan Smith came to life, and exhorted us to "remember our Creator in the days of our youth." Hail storm broke a great quantity of glass at Derrstown. 5th. George Clark left for the State of Ohio. 11th. John Clark died. 12th. Fair at Sunbury. 18th. General Baldy's flitting in town. Moving to Cayuga lake. 22d. Fast day. Clerked at the election of elders. 23d. Mr. Grier ordained four elders.

July 3. Rode with Adam Smith to Centre county. Stopped at Wilt's and fed at Miles', at Aaronsburg. 4th. Met Esquire Woods, Barbers, and a great company at Gregg's. 5th. At Mrs. Van Horn's, a very fashionable old lady. Dined at James Potter's, with Doctor Dobbins. 6th. Saw the grave Nuby was stolen from. 27th. Fair at Derrstown. 29th. Buffalo creek higher than it has been for twenty years. Mr. Hood could not attend church. Hudson's surrounded.

August 2d. Esquires Hall, Evans, Albright, and Maclay at an audit, in Derrstown. 9th. Black Judy came to wash. 24th. Met John Hayes and his brother, Patrick, at Esquire Gray's. 31st. Thirty bills for bastardy before the grand jury.

September 6th. Robert Boveard married to Hugh Wilson's daughter, the amiable Miss Peggy.

October 4th. Mr. Priestly got Clingan's carriage to carry his family to Philadelphia, on their way to England. 9th. Clerked at the election, at Derrstown. One hundred and forty-eight votes polled. George Smith candidate for Congress; no opposition. James Laird *vs*. A. McKinney for Senate; Laird elected. Candidates for Assembly, John Murray, Fred Evans, Jarad Irwin, Leonard Rupert, D. Montgomery, and Samuel Maclay. Commissioners, George Holstein and Flavel Roan. 13th. I have seven hundred and eighty-six majority for commissioner. 14th. Hugh McLaughlin's wife buried. 16th. Battalion at Derrstown. Sergeant and James Patterson had a box. Great dinner at Billmyer's.

November 11th. Esquire Harding here, on his way from Luzerne county to Kentucky. His horse got lame; they killed a cat and put it to his foot.

December 3d. Doctor Dougal dissected black Tom, and made an anatomy of him. 18th. Went to Esquire Gray's to see Samuel Hutchinson married to Jenny Wallace. Groom did not come. I went up to Hoffman's to see what was the matter. He could not cross for ice. Came down in a sleigh to Nesbit's, and crossed there.

Marriages.

March 13, Moses Bower with Catherine Moyer, daughter of Philip, in presence of her brother, Peter, John Fulmer and wife. March 15, Joel Ranck with Sarah Long, daughter of Joseph, in presence of his father, John Ranck. May 27, George Bower with Polly Smith, daughter of Michael, deceased. August 26, Sunday, Anthony Selin, of Selinsgrove, to Miss Catherine Yoner, of Sunbury. Same day, Conrad Weiser to Elizabeth Snyder, both of Penn township. October 7, Philip Stahl with Susanna Spotz. October 9, William Highland with Mary Gann, widow of Christian. November 11, Michael Meyer with Sarah Kelley. December 13, by Reverend T. Hood, Washington Dunn, of Lycoming county, to Miss Betsy Musser, of White Deer. December 18, by Reverend Mr. Patterson, Samuel Hutchinson, of Derry, to Mrs. Jenny Wallace, daughter of Captain William Gray, White Deer.

Deaths.

April 6, at his seat, at Milton, aged forty-five, Daniel Smith, Esquire, attorney-at-law. Left a widow, Cassandra. Children: Samuel, Jasper, and Grace. He was buried at Chillisquaque graveyard. July 7, Alexander Hunter, former treasurer of the county. Joseph J. Wallis, deputy surveyor. Peter Getz, East Buffalo. July 4, John Weirick. Children: William, Sarah, and John. October 15, Albright Swineford, born February 16, 1728. Henry Myers, West Buffalo. Children: Henry, Daniel, Valentine, William, John, Elizabeth, wife of Royer, Mary, and Eve Maria. Joseph Ultz, West Buffalo. November —, Thomas Forster, of West Buffalo. Left widow, Jane. Children: John, William, Thomas, Mary, and Elizabeth Jane.

Nathan Evans died this year, and his widow removed to Bucks county with his family. He was an active christian, and he and his wife were Baptists. He was in the habit of preaching at Baptist meetings, although not a clergyman. His granddaughter, Mrs. Professor C. S. James, of Lewisburg, has in her possession many abstracts of his sermons, preached in the Valley.

1811.

HARTLEY TOWNSHIP ERECTED—PRESBYTERY OF NORTHUMBERLAND FORMED—IMPEACHMENT OF JUDGE COOPER—REVEREND YOST HENRY FRIES—DEATH OF HONORABLE SAMUEL MACLAY, AND NOTICE OF HIS FAMILY.

MEMBER of Congress, George Smith. Senator, James Laird. Members elected in October, Samuel Bond, Jared Irwin, Andrew McClenachan, and Frederick Evans. President Judge, Seth Chapman, commissioned July 11. Register and Recorder, John L. Finney, commissioned April 3. County Commissioner elect, Flavel Roan.

April sessions, Robert Barber, John Wilson, and Peter Fisher reported favorably to the erection of a new township, to be called Hartley, by the following boundaries: Beginning on the line between West Buffalo and Washington townships; thence along the same to the four-mile tree, on Reuben Haines' road, on the line of Centre county; thence south along said line, across Penn's creek, to the top of Jack's mountain; thence along the summit, to a point south of where Adam Laughlin formerly lived; thence north across Penn's creek, and by a line of marked trees, to the beginning.

By a resolution of the Synod of Philadelphia, May 16, the Presbytery of Northumberland was set off from that of Huntingdon by the following line: Beginning at the mouth of Mahantango creek, a north-west course to the west branch of the Centre and Lycoming county lines, leaving eastward Reverends Asa Dunham, John Bryson, Isaac Grier, John B. Patterson, Thomas Hood, and their respective charges, and the vacant charges of Great Island, Pine Creek, and Lycoming.

Additional Residents of West Buffalo—Aikey, Lewis; Beaucher, Jacob; Orwig, Jacob; Schnure, Christian; John Bergstresser, taxed with oil and fulling-mills.

Mifflinburg—Clark, Roan, merchant; Wallis, Doctor Thomas.

White Deer—Boal, John; Covert, Isaac, ferry at Caldwell's; Davis, Stephen, miller at Dan Caldwell's; DeHaven, Jacob, shoemaker, on Roan McClure's place; Heitzman, Jacob; Leiser, Jacob; Mervine, Samuel, brick-maker; Sypher, Peter; Williman, Thomas.

Additional Residents in East Buffalo—Albertson, John, Jenkins' place; Betz, John; Beaver, Peter; Brown, Abraham; Dieffenbach, John; Hafer, Michael, at Hugh Wilson's; Hamilton, Francis; Hentzleman, George; Highlands, William; Howard, George; Kreechbaum, Peter, junior; Kremer, Charles; Leiby, Jacob; Lytle, Samuel; McCrea, Robert, shoe-maker; McDonnel, John, weaver at Jenkins'; McFadden, John, tailor; Newman, Michael; Newman, John; Phillips, George; Shannon, Joseph; Shirtz, William, weaver; Smalley, Abraham.

Lewisburg—Collins, Joseph, tailor; Donaldson, Robert; Evans & Kremer, store; Kemerer, Charles, tailor; Langs, Widow; McQuhae, William; Miller, Andrew; Wilson, William, store-keeper.

New Berlin—Charleton, James; Dennis, Jacob, blacksmith; Dennis, John, junior, cordwainer; Hubler, Abraham, weaver; Yost, Casper.

Improvements—Daniel Clarke, tan-yard in White Deer.

Domestic Incidents.

Uriah Silsby commenced singing schools in the Valley.

January 16. An article appears in the *Argus* in favor of the division of the county. The distance the people have to travel, the expense of ferriage over the river, then an appeal to the pocket on account of the expense of ornamenting the town of Sunbury. Appropriation for a fire engine there. An appropriation that was urged for the building of fire-proof buildings for the records. This was the entering wedge of the erection of Union county. In the succeeding paper was a strong argument, founded on increase of the value of property in the new county. Nearer market for purchase. Facility of reaching the county seat. Saving of expense of court trials.

From Diary of James McClellan, Esquire.

April 9. Had my house and barn consumed by fire. Lost grain, meat, and everything but a little flour. Happened between ten and eleven, A. M. Received the same evening, of John Rangler, two loaves of bread, a shoulder, potatoes, cabbage, &c. James Thompson, a bag of corn and hay; Joshua Ewing, bag of corn, &c. Next day, of William Irwin, Esquire, bag corn, two bushels wheat, load of hay. Matthew Irwin, dry peaches, wheat, &c. William Clingan, wheat and rye, and other articles from John Frantz, Jacob Reedy, Jacob Dunkle, Martin Dreisbach, Jacob Hinely, John Stahl, John Kelly, William Dunkle, Samuel Templeton, Mrs. Linn, Samuel Sterret, John Baker, Jacob Baber, David Watson, Peter Dunkle, John Kaufman, Thomas Howard, Hugh Wilson, William Hayes, James Magee. Reverend Isaac Grier, Academy at Northumberland, the educational point. Latin and Greek languages taught for $24 per annum.

The Impeachment of Judge Cooper.

The first charge against him was fining persons and immuring then in prison for whispering in court. Cooper's reply was, one Hollister, a constable, was merely given in custody of the sheriff one hour, until the disposal of a case, and then fined $2. This was at Wilkesbarre, in 1807.

Second charge. Imprisoning a respectable citizen for wearing a hat, in conformity with a religious habit. Cooper replies that he did not recollect the circumstances exactly, and presented the affidavit of Doctor James Dougal, who says he was present in court, and on account of the confusion and deafening noise there was formerly in court, he recollected the circumstances vividly. John Hanna was standing close to the bar, with his hat on. A young looking man stood behind him, with his hat on also. Judge Cooper arose and said: I will thank you, Mr. Hanna, to tell that young man to take his hat off. The young man walked away. Judge Cooper waited a little while, and then said to Mr. Hanna: I will thank you to pull off your own. Hanna made no reply. The judge repeated the request. Hanna replied in a coarse, low voice, which I could not hear distinctly, but I thought he said, if you want it off, take it off yourself. The judge then said, this is not a worshiping assembly, nor a play-house, nor a dance-house. Is a court of justice entitled to less respect than any of these places? And then requested him again. On Hanna making the same reply, I believe, as above, the judge said: Sheriff, take this man to jail. The sheriff took Mr. Hanna by the hand and they both walked off. Judge Cooper then states that Hanna lived at Northumberland, and was an old neighbor. He had never heard or suspected that he had any scruples on the point; that he asked him when he came to fine him, whether he was a Quaker, and he said not; then whether he had any religious scruples on the subject, he said yes. I then said, if he had said so, that would have been sufficient to entitle him to keep his hat on.[1]

Third charge. After sentencing a felon, calling him from prison, and pronouncing a second sentence, increasing the penalty. This referred to the case of young Gough, a horse-thief, convicted at Wilkesbarre. The court sentenced him to twelve months, he having plead guilty. The next morning, Judges Hollenbach and Fell informed Judge Cooper they had understood he was an old offender. I gave it as my opinion, says Judge Cooper, that during the sessions, the judgments were in the power of the court, and subject to revisal. He was re-sentenced to three years.

Fourth charge. That he has decided important causes in which

---

[1] It is not many years since the courts in Clearfield county were also hard to keep in hand. The folks stood around, as Judge G. W. Woodward said, like people in an auction-room. When the Honorable James Burnside held his first court there, the people crowded in among the lawyers, and in front of the bench. An indictment was brought against one Pennington. The judge called out: "Is Pennington in court?" A stalwart man standing in front of the crowd, said: "Jedge, you better call out the whole damn grist of the Penningtons." The judge put on a severe look, and commenced a lecture to the man for disturbing the court. After he proceeded awhile, the man said: "Hush up, jedge, you are making a damned sight more disturbance than I did."

he was interested. Judge Cooper's contradiction is too long for insertion.

Fifth. Setting aside the verdict of the jury in an intemperate and passionate manner. In the case of Albright and Cowden, Judge Cooper and his associates, Wilson and Macpherson, agreed in opinoin. Judge General Montgomery differed. Judge Cooper charged the jury, and General Montgomery also, and the jury went with the latter. The verdict was set aside by Judge Cooper. The latter denied intemperance of language.

Sixth. Browbeating counsel and witnesses. Judge Cooper admits reprimanding members of the bar, for unprofessional conduct, in managing a cause; for making statements not supported; for persevering in objections, after the court had decided; for want of silence, and keeping order; but denied anything further contained in the charge.

Seventh. That he appeared armed. Judge Cooper says he never carried arms but once, and then on the road from Northumberland to Williamsport, as he had been warned that he would be attacked. After calling the jury at Williamsport, Judge Cooper went off the bench, and made information against the party who had threatened him. The party, a professional gentleman in the neighborhood, of good character, came forward, and, finding himself mistaken, the complaint was dropped.

Eighth charge. That he refused to hear persons in their own defense. This denied in *toto*.

Ninth. That he had issued a proclamation against horse-racing, and then ordered a suppression of the proclamation. Judge Cooper says: This is true. Some of my friends, engaged in the said horse-race, applied to me, and stated that horses were expected from Philadelphia; that the county was generally notified, and that there would be a great assemblage of people; that the tavern-keepers had made expensive preparations, and that it was too late to put a stop to the meeting. They said if I insisted in my opposition to the race, they would submit to the law; but this should be the last race, and they would be individually responsible for keeping order, suppressing gambling, riot, &c. This was acceded to, and there has been no horse-racing since in Sunbury or in the county, that I know of.

Tenth charge. Fining and imprisoning a constable for neglecting to execute a process issued contrary to the Constitution and laws. This referred to the case of Conner, who so misused the warrant Judge Cooper had issued for arresting Jacob Langs, a counterfeiter, that the latter escaped. Judge William Montgomery, of Danville, although he frequently differed with Judge Cooper, came out in a strong affidavit, in which he said Judge Cooper was a good lawyer, earnest in preparing public business, prompt in his decisions, and clear of partialities, and that he had, with manly firmness, opposed further and unnecessary litigation, and disposed of the charges as far as they referred to Judge Cooper's practice in Northumberland county.

The committee to investigate the charges met on the 7th of March, (at Lancaster.) John B. Gibson, Samuel Dale, and Jared Irwin were of the committee. Mr. Duncan, of Carlisle, appeared for Judge Cooper; Mr. Greenough, for the petitioners. Jared Irwin complained to the committee that Daniel Levy, Esquire, was interfering outside in favor of Judge Cooper; whereupon, Mr. Duncan disclaimed having any connection with Mr. Levy, and added, that it was this young man's folly that caused Judge Cooper to be here. After an examination of Charles Hall, Esquire, Frederick Evans, and many other witnesses, the committee reported that the Judge's conduct had been arbitrary, unjust, and precipitate, and in favor of an address to the Governor for his removal. "More than two thirds of the Legislature voted for his removal," says the *Argus*, of April 3. The witnesses called on his side were Doctor Dougal, Joseph Priestly, George Kremer, Colonel D. Montgomery, Charles Hegins, John Cowden, E. G. Bradford, &c. "Judge Cooper spoke four and a half hours, in a very eloquent and impressive manner."—*Ibid.* In the *Argus* of the 17th, the testimony of the witnesses is printed in full. Judge William Wilson (of Chillisquaque) says: "The court was very disorderly before Judge Cooper's time. I have seen Judge Rush leave the bench. It is now very orderly. Judge Cooper cannot see very well. John Dreisbach, of Mifflinburg, was one of the parties Judge Cooper fined for talking to a witness. Dreisbach said he was merely telling the witness that court had adjourned, as the man was hard of hearing. Esquire Youngman came forward to speak in my favor, and the judge told him he would fine him a dollar if he did not keep still." The courts in May were held by

Judges Wilson, Montgomery, and Macpherson. A queer rule was adopted: "No bills on the return of a constable, unless at the request of the mother of the child, or the overseers of the poor, or by special direction of the court, should be returned."

September 17, convention met at Derrstown, and made the following nominations: Simon Snyder for Governor; Jared Irwin, Frederick Evans, Samuel Bond, and Andrew McClenachan for members; Commissioner, Henry Vanderslice; Auditors, Hugh Wilson, (ridge,) Charles Gale, and Andrew Albright.

The election returns gave Simon Snyder all the votes, except twelve, polled in Buffalo for Jacob Bumberger. Bond, Irwin, McClenachan, and F. Evans were elected to the Assembly, with Henry Vanderslice for county commissioner. Auditors as above.

Argus, of November 13, says: "William Hayes, of Derrstown, raised five pumpkins on one vine, largest weighing one hundred and sixty pounds; least, fifty-four pounds."

Roan's Journal.

February 1. Judge Cooper a good deal annoyed about the petitions to remove him. 2d. Stopped at Irely's, (Winfield.) 4th. Scurrilous poetry circulating among the neighbors about last hallow-een night. [The family feuds in the Valley may be traced to this practice. It will be all understood by the old residents.] Entry of the 7th. James Dale and James McClure had a bout at Derrstown about hallow-een night stories. 14th. Mr. Barber married to Polly Vanvalzah. 19th. Thomas Proctor and Polly Musser married.

March 5. At Jimmy Wilson's: three Moores, of Lycoming, two Vanvalzahs, Bob Fruit and Nancy, two of the Nevius girls, and Polly Darragh, at the spinning. March 8. Tailor McFadden working at Clingan's. James McClellan had his house and barn burned. 13th. R. Mc—— and Aaron C—— would have fought at Rees' tonight, but Long John Maclay prevented them. All about hallow-een night. 20th. Concert of the singing-school at Derrstown. Eat cakes and drank cider with a number of young ladies and gentlemen at Granny Phillips'. 29th. Firing of cannon and rejoicing at Northumberland, on account of the removal of Judge Cooper.

April 5. Citizen Kremer has lost popularity by taking Judge Cooper's part.

May 18. Great horse-race at Derrstown.

August 19. The new Judge, Chapman, took his seat.

September 8. A blazing star, like a comet, appeared in the north for some time. 17th. Nominating convention met at Derrstown. McLanachan put on the legislative ticket, with Evans. 18th. Comet still visible, going around the north star like the pointers in the bear. 19th. Quilting at Mr. Laird's. Thirty ladies there. Hayes says Fred Evans is a Burrite. 29th. Graham had a child baptized Caroline.

October 8. Election at Derrstown. Two hundred and forty-six votes polled. People pretty quiet. 15th. William McQuhae married to John Cowden's daughter. 22d. Review at Derrstown. Fiddles going all day at the tavern. 26th. John Musser, with Thomas, at Philadelphia. He had a horse stolen there. It takes two weeks to make the trip.

November 9. Called at Giddy Smith's, to get signers to the petition for a new county. Giddy says there are too many Federalists on the petition. 11th. Esquire Vincent, Esquire Brown, and Mr. Iredell here on a road view. They are very jocose, sociable, and funny men.

December 11. James Clark took Flavel home with him to a kicking frolic. 17. T. Woodside here, surveying Mr. Lyons' land, sold to Frantz.

Governor Snyder's message, of December 3, is worthy of remark, as containing an emphatic protest against slavery, and also a strong recommendation of the canal system.

That noted divine, Yost Henry Fries, now enters the Valley, and his wide-spread influence takes its start. The Reformed congregations had become vacant, by the resignation of the Reverend Jacob Dieffenbach, in 1810, and Mr. Fries was induced to make a visit to Buffalo Valley from his congregation in York county. He was born in Westphalia, town of Gusterhain, 24th April, 1777. He landed in Baltimore, 20th August, 1803. From early childhood he had a strong inclination to the ministry, and, being poor, saw little hope of entering the ministry at home, where so many strict formalities were observed. He could not pay his passage, and was forced to become a "redemptioner;" that is, he was bound to serve out a certain length of time, generally three years, for the benefit of the man who paid his passage. When a ship arrived, farmers and others, needing laborers, would go to the port, and buy the time for which they were to serve from the captain. Mr. Fries had his certificate of church membership, and also a recommendation to a wealthy man named Hinckel, at Philadelphia. It seems he never presented the latter, as Doctor Harbaugh found it among his papers, long preserved after his death by a daughter, near Mifflinburg. Mr. Fries fell into the hands of a kind German farmer, in York county. He was honest, industrious, and trusty, and soon won the full confidence of his employer. He was fond of improving his mind in spare hours, and his desire to be a minister stirred him strongly. He spoke in small assemblies, when he got the opportunity. There was, however, nothing fanatical about him, yet he went so far once as to preach a sermon, in a school-house, on the words, "Much study is a weariness to the flesh," Ecclesiastes, xii : 1. A singular text certainly to begin with. He commenced his preparatory studies with Reverend Daniel Wagner, in Frederick, Maryland, April 3, 1809, and, after being with him a year, was licensed at Harrisburg, and on the 20th of June, 1810, took charge of eight congregations in York county.

In June, 1811, he came up on a visit to Buffalo Valley, and on the 22d preached in the Dreisbach church, on Acts, v : 31 ; on the 23d in Mifflinburg, Acts, xxvi : 28 ; in the afternoon of the same day, at New Berlin, on II Peter, i : 19, and in the evening again at Mifflinburg, on I Corinthians, xvi : 13. In October, 1811, he made a second visit to Buffalo Valley, from 17th to the 24th. He preached at Anspach's school-house, Dieffenbach's, White Deer school-house, Dreisbach church, Mifflinburg, New Berlin, Aaronsburg, and in Brush valley, and on the 28th was home again in his charge. A strong effort was now made by the churches in Buffalo Valley and neighborhood to secure his services.—*Harbaugh.*

The first meeting of the Northumberland Presbytery was held in the Presbyterian church of Northumberland, on the first Tuesday of October. Reverend Asa Dunning opened it with a sermon from Ephesians, ii : 14. The members composing it were Reverends Dunham, Bryson, Grier, Patterson, and Hood, with Elders James Sheddan, James Hepburn, William Montgomery, and Thomas Howard.

Marriages.

Evan Rice Evans was married, last Thursday evening, to Mrs. Forrest. She was a widow of five months. (Roan's Diary, 12th January.) September 8, Elijah Updike to Elizabeth Snook, daughter of Martin. Witnesses: John Brown, (miller,) Peter Snook, Sarah Smith. October 7, William Davis to Catherine Derr, daughter of George Derr. December 25, by Reverend Slater Clay, Samuel Hepburn, Esquire, to Miss Ann Clay, of Montgomery county. December 26, John Cochran, junior, with Anna M., daughter of Adam Grove. James Kelly, George Kremer, John and Sarah Montgomery, and Catharine Gordon.

Deaths.

George Holstein, of Penn's, father of George, of Lewisburg.

Joseph Evans, Lewisburg.

Evan Rice Evans, Esquire, in December.

Henry Myer, of West Buffalo, left wife, Elizabeth. Children: Henry, Daniel, Valentine, William, John, Elizabeth, Margaret, Eve, and Maria. Daniel took his land at the appraisement, and in 1813 sold it to William Forster.

William Douglass, West Buffalo. John, James, Elizabeth.

George Cramer, (of now Union.) Children: Matthew, Howard, Chatam.

Jacob Albright, Beaver. Children: Rachel, married to James Moore; Stephen, Peter, Jacob, Juliana, Catherine.

February 23, Mrs. Mary Bull, wife of General John Bull, of Northumberland, in her eightieth year. She was buried in the Quaker grave-yard. Previous to the grave being closed, General Bull, although much reduced by sickness and old age, addressed the audience as follows: "The Lord gave and the Lord hath taken away, blessed be the name of the Lord. May we, who are soon to follow her, be as well prepared as she was."

At Sunbury, on Sunday, March 11, John Frick, Esquire, Register and Recorder, aged fifty-one. Left widow and eleven children.

Honorable Samuel Maclay

Died at his residence, in Buffalo Valley, October 5, 1811. He was born June 17, 1741, in Lurgan township, Franklin county. Of his early education I can learn nothing. His field-note books, as assistant deputy surveyor to William Maclay, in 1767 and 1768, are before me, and indicate a cultivated hand. He next appears in 1769, as assistant to his brother on the surveys of the officers' tract, in Buffalo Valley. He surveyed largely in what is now Mifflin county, and took up a good deal of land there. R. P. Maclay, his son, still living, related an anecdote which he had from the late Judge Brown, of Mifflin county, which is worth transcribing. He said: "I was wandering out in the Valley, in search of good locations. I was traveling, looking about on the rising ground for a bear, I had started, when I came suddenly upon the Big spring. [This spring is four miles west from Reedsville, in the rear of a blacksmith shop. Still called Logan's spring.] Being thirsty, I set my rifle against a bush, and rushing down the bank, laid down to drink. Upon putting my head down, I saw reflected in the water, on the opposite side, the shadow of a tall Indian. I sprang to my rifle, when the Indian gave a yell—whether for peace or war, I was not, just then, sufficiently master of my faculties to tell; but upon my seizing my rifle and facing him, he knocked up the pan of his gun, threw out the priming, and extended his open hand toward me in token of friendship. After putting down our guns, we again met at the spring and shook hands. This was Logan, the best specimen of humanity I ever met with, either white or red. He could speak a little English, and told me there was another white hunter a little way down the stream, and offered to guide me to his camp. There I first met Samuel Maclay. We remained together in the Valley for a week, looking for springs and selecting lands, and laid the foundation of a friendship which never has had the slightest interruption.

"We visited Logan at the camp, at Logan's spring, and he and Mr. Maclay shot at a mark for a dollar a shot. Logan lost four or five rounds, and acknowledged himself beaten. When we were about to leave him, he went into his hut and brought out as many deer skins as he had lost dollars, and handed them to Mr. Maclay, who refused to take them, alleging that we had been his guests, and did not come to rob him; that the shooting had been only a trial of skill, and the bet merely nominal. Logan drew himself up with great dignity, and said: 'Me bet to make you shoot your best; me gentleman, and me take your dollar if me beat.' So he was obliged to take the skins, or affront our friend, whose nice sense of honor would not permit him to receive a horn of powder in return, even."

Mr. Maclay was lieutenant colonel of a battalion of associators, and as such, delegate with McLanachan, Geddes, and Brady, to the convention at Lancaster, July 4, 1776, which elected two brigadiers and organized the associators, the then militia of the State.

In 1792, he was appointed one of the associate judges of the county, and resigned December 17, 1795. In October, 1794, he was a candidate for Congress, and carried the county by eleven hundred majority; vote only two thousand eight hundred and fifty. In Buffalo, he had four hundred and sixty-four, to fourteen for his opponent, John Andre Hanna. Served for the year 1795–96.

On the 2d of December, 1801, Mr. Maclay was elected Speaker of the Senate, and re-elected December 7, 1802. On the 14th, he was elected United States Senator, and, being Speaker, had to sign his own certificate. In January, 1803, he presided at the impeachment trial of Judge Addison, and continued acting as Speaker (against the protest of the opposition, however, after March 3) until March 16, when he resigned that position, and, on the 2d of September, his position as State Senator.

He resigned his seat in the United States Senate on the 4th of January, 1809.

Mr. Maclay was very popular in his manners, a good scholar, and efficient writer. He had an extensive library, containing many valuable books. He was always of the people and for the people, plain and simple in his manner, disliking ostentation. On one occasion he brought a handsome coach home from Lancaster, and the family took it to Buffalo church the next Sabbath. Mr. Maclay noticed the impression, and that coach never left the carriage-house afterward; it rotted down where it was left that Sunday evening. He stopped once at the late Hugh Wilson's about tea time. They had mush only, and Mrs. Wilson commenced getting something better, as she thought. "No," said he, "mush is good enough for a king's dinner." He was a large man, resembling Henry Clay very much, though much stouter in his latter years. Honorable Martin Dreisbach, who still recollects him well, says his return home was always indicated by the hogs being driven out of the fields, the repairing of the fences, and general activity over the whole place. He was a good mechanic also, and often amused himself working in the blacksmith shop. His servant, Titus, was a character. His hair was white as the snow; always dressed in a ruffled shirt. He walked with a long staff, and on public days he came out in a many-colored coat, looking like the king of Africa. He lectured the boys somewhat after this style: "Massa Dave a damn fool; he no shoot a pheasant, he no shoot a coo; cuss a damn fool; he go into the meadow and shoot a blackbo, (bird.)

Mr. Maclay's wife was Elizabeth Plunket, an account of whose family appears *ante* year 1791. Their children were:

1. William Plunket Maclay, born in Buffalo Valley, 23d August, 1774. Married, in 1802, to Sally Brown, daughter of Judge William Brown, of Mifflin county, and was, therefore, brother-in-law to General James Potter, second, and John Norris, many years cashier of the old bank at Bellefonte. Mrs. Maclay died in 1810, leaving three sons, Doctor Samuel, of Milroy, William P., and Charles J., and in 1812, William P. married Jane Holmes, of Carlisle, who died in 1844, leaving four sons, Holmes, David, Robert P., and Joseph H. William P. Maclay died in Millroy, September 2, 1842.

2. Charles Maclay (John Binns' second in his duel with Sam Stewart) died, unmarried, while on a visit in Wayne county, New York, aged twenty-eight.

3. John Maclay, register and recorder of Union county, also prothonotary for two terms. Married to Annie Dale, daughter of Honorable Samuel Dale, and sister of the late James Dale, Esquire, of Buffalo township. In 1833, John moved to Vandalia, Illinois, and soon after died, leaving two sons and two daughters, Charles, William P., Elizabeth, (afterwards Mrs. Armstrong,) Anne, all since deceased. His eldest son, Samuel, died in Buffalo Valley.

4. Samuel Maclay, married first to Margaret and afterwards to Elizabeth, daughters of Reverend James Johnston, of Mifflin county. Samuel died February 17, 1836, leaving seven sons and three daugh-

ters, of whom only three are living, Robert P., in Louisiana, and Elizabeth and Jane, in Galesburg, Illinois.

5. David Maclay, married to Isabella, daughter of Galbraith Patterson, Esquire, died in 1818, leaving no issue. David was a ripe scholar, and would have made his mark in public life, if his health had not failed. His widow married Honorable A. L. Hayes, late and for many years associate law judge of Lancaster county, Pennsylvania.

6. Robert Plunket Maclay, born in April, 1799. Senator from Union, in 1842. Still living in Kishacoquillas valley, Mifflin county. His wife was a Lashells, of Union county.

Samuel Maclay's daughters were:

1. Eleanor, the eldest, married to her cousin, David Maclay, of Franklin county, Pennsylvania. Herself and children dead.

2. Hester, who accompained Charles to Wayne county, New York, and died there about the same time.

3. Jane E., married to Doctor Joseph Henderson, died without issue, January, 1848. Doctor Henderson was a captain in the war of 1812, and in Congress four years, during General Jackson's administration. He was a brother-in-law of Reverend James Linn, D. D., of Bellefonte, now deceased.

Mr. Maclay is buried on the farm now owned by Joseph Green. The brick wall inclosing the grave is within sight from the turnpike, after passing the New Berlin road. It is immediately in front of his old stone mansion. How few now know that within it rest the remains of one of Pennsylvania's ablest statesmen. The *disjecta membra* of a fine monument, intended to be placed at the head of his grave, still lie in one corner of the inclosure, as they were unloaded forty years ago.

1812.

DIVISION OF THE COUNTY AGITATED—LEWISBURG INCORPORATED—ROAN'S JOURNAL—ROLLS OF CAPTAINS JOHN DONALDSON'S AND NER MIDDLESWARTH'S COMPANIES—REVEREND JUST HENRY FRIES, PASTOR AT MIFFLINBURG.

MEMBERS of the House of Representatives elected in October, Samuel Bond, Andrew McClenachan, Leonard Rupert, and George Kremer. Treasurer, Andrew Albright. Commissioner elect, Henry Vanderslice.

February 9, Frederick Evans writes to George Kremer: "Musser gave me petitions amounting, in signatures, to seven hundred and eighty-nine. Get the next sent forward as early as possible. I think John Swineford and Seebold would interest themselves to get signatures, as Buffalo has agreed to their proposals; that is, to have the seat of justice fixed not more than three miles from the center of the inhabitable part. By the time you receive this, no doubt you will hear that a resolution recommending the petitioners in the Forks to the early attention of the next Legislature, on the subject. If it should dishearten the favorers of a division, you can inform them that if the west side only sends down five hundred signers more, the Forks petition will be re-considered, and things will go on fortunately yet. Had the west side petitions came in as early as the Forks, the county would, by this time, have been divided. However, there are still hopes. If five hundred more signatures cannot be obtained, send on as many as can be got. Four hundred and fifty-one would be a majority of the taxables. I am glad you are willing to clear out of Derrstown. I will leave the place before long, at all events."

May 25, Methodist church organized in Lewisburg. Sermon at Gordon's house; text: 1 John, iii : 1.

June 18, President Madison's proclamation declaring war. The first bridge was erected over the North Branch to Northumberland, during this and the following year, by aid of a State appropriation. The division question was the all-absorbing one. By combining with Derry people, and others in favor of the erection of Columbia county, the division ticket, Bond, Kemer, &c., was elected. It was, however, bitterly opposed, and an able paper against the division presented, which, among other things, urged that if the soldiers' vote at Meadville had been counted, that ticket would not have been elected.

Borough of Lewisburg.

March 31, the act incorporating the directors of streets, &c., of Lewisburg was passed. The first election held under this act for directors of streets, lanes, and alleys of the town of Lewisburg was held at the house of Andrew Billmeyer, on Saturday, the 17th day of October. Henry Spyker, John Martin, John Lawshe, John Gordon, and William McQuhae were elected.

October 23, the directors elected John Lawshe president, and Henry Spyker secretary. James Geddes was appointed supervisor, Andrew Sherrard constable, George Knox overseer of the poor. The first ordinance passed was one requiring the opening of the streets, the most of which were fenced in and cultivated at that time. They were finally opened in 1813, except in the case of Doctor Charles Beyer, who, May 5, 1813, represented that he had not rails to fence with, and if he opened the streets he had inclosed in his lots, it would be to the great damage of his grain ; and the directors agreeing that this was so, let him off, upon his agreement to pay two bushels of wheat and two of rye, immediately after harvest, for the use of the corporation, after which they were to be opened.

Simon Wehr purchased his tavern stand, in Limestone township now, and William Pancoast erected his blacksmith shop in Buffalo, so long known as Ritter's.

Incidents from Roan's Journal.

April 25. Christopher Johnson *vs.* Mathew Irvine, tried. Verdict for plaintiff, $150. 29th. Beyers for Sarah Wister *vs.* Clark tried. *Duncan* squealed a long time for Sarah. 30th. Dance in the courthouse to-night.

May 19. George Clingan went to Mr. Hood's to see Mr. Wright married to Miss Lewis. Mr. Hood got $2 for the job. [Mrs. Wright was a few years since living in Stevenson county, Illinois. She was a daughter of Paschal Lewis.] 21st. Billmyer executed a deed for his land to Gebhart.

June 4, Thursday. This is Nimrod Hughes' day, but he is mistaken about the dissolution of the world. Went to the meeting of the regiment, at Reedy's, about drafting men for the war. 9th. Captain Patrick Hayes called. Went with him to Billy Clark's, and then to Esquire Gray's. Met John and Robert Hayes there, and Judge Macpherson. Thursday, 11th. James Sanderson married, on Tuesday, to Miss Griffen. He gave Mr. Hood $20. 12th. Libby Robinson married to John Bell, of Chester.

July 7. Visited my father's grave, in Derry church-yard, Dauphin county, with Captain P. Hayes. Tomb-stones are still good. 23d. Set off to James Moore's funeral, but was too late. 30th. Continental fast-day. Mr. Hood's text, Jeremiah, xiv: 7. Old Captain Kearsley spent the evening here. [Captain Kearsley, of the Revolution, died March 22, 1830, aged eighty-one, at Middle Spring, Cumberland county.] 31st. Went with Captain K. Called at Roan McClure's, at Derrstown; Judge Wilson's; then at Jones' tavern, Northumberland. Went to see the new bridge building over the river.

August 20. President Madison's fast-day. Jared Irwin's rifle company paraded, and went to the German church. Drank wine at Enoch Smith's, with Judge Cooper, Mr. Bradford, Gray, Brady, *et al.* Took tea at Mr. Finney's.

September 7. Three hundred enlisted troops left Milton, to join General Dearborn's volunteers and drafted men. Have orders to march to Meadville. 8th. Great consternation in the Valley about the volunteers going away. 9th. Volunteers from our neighborhood went as far as Derrstown to-night. 10th. Volunteers on their march. A number of our neighbors among them. 16th. Delegates met at

Derrstown, and formed two tickets. 20th. Three hundred soldiers passed through Milton.

October 10. Rob. Smith came from Meadville. Troops had reached that place, and were in high spirits. 13th. Went to Derrstown. Left my horse at James Geddes', and clerked the election. Three, A. M., before we got through. 17th. Borough officers elected in Derrstown. 25th. Five doctors tapping Davy Reasoner. 26th. D. R. died. 30th. Clerked at presidential election at Derrstown. Governor Snyder's daughter visiting at Kremer's.

November 1. A big bear made his appearance near Billy Clark's to-day. 3d. Andy Steel shot at a bear in the meadow at Tommy's place. 5th. Tommy returned from Philadelphia. Made trip in eleven days. 6th. Clerked at Esquire Gray's vendue. 8th. Mrs. Colonel Chamberlin had a young son. This is his twenty-third child. Fourth wife. 19th. Young Doctor Kennedy fined $4, for assaulting Doctor Martin. 22d. Roan Clarke came for Kremer. His wife has a young daughter. 27th. Biddle & Dougal *vs.* Cochran, about some land, below Milton. Cochran argued his own case, and spoke nearly all day. [Surveyor General Cochran.] Hall, Duncan, and Watts against him; Fisher and Hepburn for him. Cochran got a verdict. 30th. Betsy Myers and Hetty Shaffer came here to spin.

December 8. Bill Morton went to hustling match at Myers'. Flavel at Mr. Hood's chopping frolic. 13th. Three volunteers went past, probably deserters from Canada. 14th. More volunteers went by. John Forster, the widow's son, a volunteer from Canada, here to-night. He says, General Smythe being a traitor, is the reason of volunteers returning. 16th. Sam Lytle, another volunteer, breakfasted here. 21st. Twenty volunteers passed Green's house. 25th. Great quilting and ball at William Wilson's to-night. 31st. At Shaffer's tavern, at Sunbury. Got little sleep. They were shooting away the old year all night.

Roll of Captain John Donaldson's Company, Pennsylvania Militia, Colonel Snyder's Regiment, September 25 to November 24.

Captain—Donaldson, John.
Lieutenants—Chamberlin, Aaron; Hall, John.

Sergeants—McFadden, John; Johnston, Abel; Eilert, Jacob; Cimfort, Henry.
Corporals—Alsbach, Jacob; Jones, Samuel.
Fifer—Dennis, Michael.
Drummer—Parks, Robert.
Privates—Auple, Christopher; Barbin, James; Barklow, Francis; Black, Robert; Bower, Joseph; Chamberlin, Uriah; Clements, Uriah; Cornelius, William; Cosier, Jonathan; Culbertson, Jacob; Curtis, Thomas; Frederick, Samuel; Frederick, Peter; Frederick, Jacob; Frock, Jacob; Forster, John; Forster, William; Forster, William, junior; Gibson, John; Gile, John; Glover, John; Gray, Robert H.; Harman, Benjamin; Hoff, James; Hollinshead, Francis; Jodon, George; Johnston, William; Jones, Benjamin; Kelly, John; Kimple, Philip; Kline Daniel; Klingaman, Jacob; Klingaman, John; Klingaman, George; Klingaman, Peter; Linn, David; Lytle, Samuel; Lytle, William; McGinnes, John; McKinley, John; McKinley, James; Magee, John; Martin, Peter; Meekert, Daniel; Mies, Jonathan; Miller, Thomas; Miller, Henry; Nelson, Daniel; Norman, William; Parks, John; Pearson, John; Rearick, John; Reeder, Henry; Reininger, Henry; Renner, Michael; Renner, Henry; Seebold, Christopher; Shaw, Samuel; Slear, John; Snook, Peter; Stine, Frederick; Struble, Peter; Struble, Henry; Stuttlebach, Jacob; Thompson, Samuel; Turner, John; Vanhorn, William; Walker, John; Wartz, George; Weaver, Benjamin; Weikel, Henry; Wise, John; Wright, John; Zimmerman, David.

It was to this company that Reverend J. H. Fries preached, September 10, in Elias church, from Joshua, xxiii : 6, 11. It marched to Meadville and Erie; thence to Black Rock. "You will think strange to hear that all of our volunteers are returned home. They give different accounts of the proceedings at Black Rock, but all say that they came off without being discharged, and all agree that General Smythe has acted the part of a traitor."—*Roan Clark's Letter to George Kremer, December* 14.

Roll of Captain Ner Middleswarth's Company, Eighth Riflemen, Colonel James Irwin's Regiment, September 25 to November 24, 1812.

Captain—Middleswarth, Ner.
Lieutenants—Youngman, Thomas, and Kline, John.
Sergeants—Wise, George; Zigler, George; Devore, Daniel, and Schwartz, Daniel.
Corporals—Nerhood, Adam; Bremenger, Henry; Heater, Adam, and McNade, John.
Bugler—Huick, George.
Privates—Baker, George; Bong, John; Bristol, Peter; Brunner, Henry; Clements, John; Devore, Andrew; Devore, George; Doebler, Daniel; Etzler, Benjamin; Fete, Simon; Frock, Henry; Frock, Jacob; Frock, Benjamin; Harbster, David; Hassinger, David; Hassinger, Jacob; Heter, John; Hammer, Andrew; Hummel, George; Kaler, John; Krebs, Samuel; Layer, Peter; Layer, David; Love, William; Lowder, Peter; Lowder, Michael; Mook, Henry; Moyer, George; Nerhood, Jacob; Peter, Leonard; Shay, Timothy; Stewart, Thomas; Stock, Peter; Stock, Melchoir.

Reverend J. H. Fries was called, 27 April, 1812, to Buffalo Valley. Early in June, Mr. John Reber an elder[1] in the Dreisbach church, left home with his team, and proceeded to York county to bring up the new minister. Often have we seen this worthy man in his old age, renew his youth, while he related, in the most circumstantial manner, the varied events of this eventful journey down into a strange country, with much anxiety, and back again, with a precious load and a glad heart. Having arrived safely in Mifflinburg, Mr. Fries entered upon his duties in his new field on the 17th of June, 1812. His field extended east and west from Brush valley, and the lower end of Penn's valley, to Bloomsburg, and up and down the Susquehanna from Muncy to Selinsgrove. His first regular charge was composed of Mifflinburg, Dreisbach's, New Berlin, Aaronsburg, and Brush Valley. Besides these, he preached at many

---

[1] John Reber was a warm and staunch friend of the church and her ministers, whose house was always open to God's servants; and who for his generous hospitality and piety, is held in grateful rememberance by all who knew him.

other points, in school-houses, gradually laying the foundations of future congregations.—*Harbaugh.*

Marriages.

February 2, David Black with Catherine Berrey. February 11, John Maclay to Annie Dale. February 11, Aaron Chamberlin to Betsy Dale. February 12, Michael Engleman with Barbara Gilman, daughter of Jacob. February 25, by Mr. Hood, Robert Fruit to Maria Nevius. He was the youngest of eleven children, and Maria the oldest of eleven. March 1, James Kelly with Hannah Seitz, daughter of George. "March 19, James Lawson to Nancy Clingan. Calf and two turkeys killed. Twenty-six strangers at the wedding. March 26, Thomas Barber to Betsy Clingan. Groom came with fourteen attendants; thirty-seven strangers, altogether. 27th, twenty strangers, beside the bride and groom, breakfasted at Clingan's; twenty-two of us left Clingan's with the bride and groom; four joined us at Doctor Vanvalzah's; went to Esquire Barber's, where there was a very large party and much dancing, although Quakers."[1] November 1, John Grove with Sarah Montgomery, daughter of John.

Deaths.

January 5, Colonel Thomas Youngman, aged forty. Left wife and seven children. March 9, John Steel, of White Deer. July 7, John Walter, born January 6, 1749. Charles Sechler, East Buffalo. Children: Jacob, John, George, Daniel, Catherine, wife of C. Reichly. Alexander McGrady, second, shoe-maker, of White Deer township. His widow, Elizabeth, died in Ohio, in 1861, aged ninety-six. Children: Polly, Margaret, Thomas, William, Elizabeth, Nancy, and Isaac. They all moved to Ohio in 1819. Thomas was in Lewisburg in 1863. Isaac was in the army, near Corinth, then.

[1] From Flavel Roan's Journal.

1813.

Union County Erected—Officials—Efforts for a Union of the Albright Brethren with the United Brethren—School-House Lot in Union—Lewisburg in 1813—Re-survey of the Town.

EMBER of Congress, Jared Irwin. Members elected in October, Samuel Bond, Leonard Rupert, Thomas Murray, junior, and George Kremer. President Judge, Seth Chapman. Associate, Hugh Wilson, appointed October 11. First sheriff of Union county elected, John Ray. Prothonotary, Clerk of the several Courts, Register and Recorder, Simon Snyder, junior, commissioned October 14, 1813. Deputy, John Lashells, Esquire. District Attorney, William Irwin, Esquire. November 11, County Commissioners sworn, Daniel Caldwell, Frederick Gutelius, and Philip Moore. Clerk, Flavel Roan. Coroner, John Dreisbach.

March 22, the act erecting Union county out of Northumberland passed. The territory was that part of Northumberland west of the river; the act to go into effect after the first of November. Courts to be held at Mifflinburg until the commissioners appointed by the Governor should determine the locality of the county seat. The commissioners were directed in the act to select the most central point.

March 23, Governor Snyder appointed James Banks and Henry Haines commissioners to fix the site of the court-house, &c.

March 29, election place for Buffalo, &c., changed to Andrew Reedy's, at Cross-Roads. Washington and White Deer, north of a line from Spruce run, at Matthew Laird's, to John Boal's, at the river, to hold their election at Dan Caldwell's. As the tax-books are at Lewisburg, it is unimportant to take further account of them in these Annals.

April 21, Bishop Newcomer reaches Martin Dreisbach's again. The Albright brethren had their conference here. Eighteen preachers in attendance. He stayed with them until the 24th. They discussed the practicability and propriety of a union between the two societies. He laid the discipline of the United Brethren before them for examination. They made no objection, but, on the contrary, appeared to cordially approve of it. They delivered to him a written communication on the subject, addressed to the conference of the United Brethren. On the 10th of November, he was again in the Valley, held a meeting at John Walters', and preached at Mr. Mack's, near New Berlin, from Psalm xxxiv, last four verses. On the forenoon of the 11th, Christian Crum, Joseph Hoffman, Jacob Bowlus, and himself appeared for the United Brethren, and Messrs. Miller, Walter, Dreisbach, and Mebel for the Albright Brethren. The consultation continued until the 13th, but they were not able to effect a union. The greatest stumbling-block appeared to be this: According to the United Brethren's discipline, their local preachers have a vote in the conference as well as the traveling preachers. This was a *sine qua non* which the United Brethren could or would not accede to, so we parted and came to Youngmanstown.—*Newcomer's Journal.*

October 25, John Snook and wife conveyed the school-house lot in Union township to Christian Gundy, *et al.*, trustees, bounded by Macpherson, Jenkins, Epler, &c.

November 12, the county commissioners met at Mifflinburg and elected Flavel Roan clerk, at $1 33 per day while on duty. Hired a room of George Roush for the prothonotary. Standard of valuation of first-rate land: East Buffalo, $40 ; West Buffalo, $40 ; Beaver, $30 ; Centre, $30 ; Hartley, $40 ; Penn's, $40 ; Mahantango, $40 ; White Deer, $40 ; Washington, $30.

March 30, Henry Beck came to Lewisburg from Earl township, Berks county. Then Frederick Freedley owned Brown's mill; George Knox had Hull's tan-yard ; Henry Spyker lived in the brick house at the river ; Robert Smith, a boatman, where James S. Marsh lives ;

Mathias Shaffer, in a two-story house, where M. Halfpenny now lives; Richard McClure, where his grandchildren do now; William Evans, where Joseph Housel now lives; on the opposite side lived Evans' sister. These were all on Front street. Garman kept ferry at the stone house, now Martin Hahn's; John Sargent had a nail factory, where F. Davis now lives; Andrew Shearer kept at Weidensaul's; William McQuhae had a store, where C. S. Wolfe now lives. George Kremer's was the only store-house on the river; James Black had a distillery, and kept store just above the latter, and where Norton's coal-yard now is; White Roost, now M. Halfpenny's, was occupied by Billman; the old Albright tavern by William Poak. At the mouth of Buffalo creek there were three houses, owned and occupied by John Pross, Valentine Miller, &c. Leisenring, a potter, lived opposite John A. Mertz's; Mrs. Nicely's lot was occupied by John Lawshe, senior; J. B. Linn's, by John Metzgar; Esquire Cameron's, the Black Horse, was kept by John Lawshe, junior; George Kremer had a store, where Jonathan Wolfe now lives. Second street was then vacant down to Joseph Glass' lots, lying in common, and pine trees growing on them. The brick house of Joseph Glass was built by Henry Beck in 1823; Joseph Bennett lived where the Union National Bank now is; on part of Peter Beaver's lot, Henry Burget kept a tavern; George Metzgar lived where Captain Brooke has his jewelry store, and had a hatter shop; an old log house, in from the street, next Jonathan Wolfe's, was occupied by John Montgomery; old Mr. Kimmell kept store in the next house; William Hayes kept store where Peter Nevius' widow now lives. Doctor Beyers lived on the corner of Third and St. Catherine. No house from there to Market. Alexander Graham lived and kept store on Doctor Harrison's corner. There were no houses on Third street north. On the Billmyer lot, depot lot, &c., was a large pond, where they often shot ducks. On Fourth and St. Louis, Betsy Ammon's house was built this year. There was an old house at the race at St. George, and one at the east end of Fourth, occupied by Strickland; Doctor Wilson's lot was occupied by Mr. Espy, who kept tavern; on William Moore's, Thomas Poak kept bachelor's hall, and a brewery; William Shearer lived in the old house, lately standing on Cherry alley, and followed weaving; opposite C. Gemberling's, Caleb Fairchild had a blacksmith shop; north was a stone house, occupied by Daniel

Rees as a tavern; C. Beyers' was occupied by a family named Seydel; next was Sam Grove, a boatman; Adam Grove lived on Thomas Nesbit's, deceased, lot; he was the youngest of the Grove brothers, Indian fighters, and followed boating; James Geddes lived on the corner of Fourth and St. Anthony, and had a saddler shop; next, north, John Norton, and the next Burgets' house, which Henry Beck moved into. On the opposite side lived John Moore, famous many years as a blacksmith; George Snider, father of widow Strohecker, lived where John Bieber lately resided; there was an old tan-yard on the property.

The streets were re-surveyed in the spring of 1813, and a slight angle made to suit the buildings. James Geddes and Thomas Fisher carried on a tannery. Peter Nevius, Joseph McCool, and Andrew Best were their apprentices. John Musser lived at the Slifer mansion farm. High's mill, at the fording, was then abandoned. George Derr had built another mill, where Joseph W. Shriner's now is. In repairing it, some years ago, Mr. Shriner found an old stone, with date of 1778 carved upon it, no doubt the date of Gundy's mill, a few rods above it. On Derr's farm lived Abram Troxell and William C. Davis; John Guyer, on the Shuck place; Thomas McGuire kept tavern at the old ferry, now George F. Miller, Esquire's; Jonas Butterfield kept school in the Market street school-house, now Presbyterian parsonage; Breyvogel kept where the Lutheran parsonage now stands; Charles Cameron lived on Front and St. Mary's. Among those who enlisted in the regular army, Doctor Beck recollects of Valentine Miller, George Christ, Dennis O. Boyle, John Buck, and Alexander Hutchinson. Abram Fry lived at the boatyard; Granny Phillips kept cakes and beer next the Revere House, on late Judge Schnable's lot; John McFadden kept tavern where Charles Penny now lives. John Rees, John Beyers, and James Forrest succeeded Jonas Butterfield, as school-teachers.

May 16, Justice Spyker fines Henry Burket, Edward Morton, and William Keller each $20, for horse-racing on Market street, Lewisburg, on oath of Andrew Shearer, John McFadden, and Thomas Fisher.

June 1, The inhabitants of the town met and resolved that the president, secretary, and directors should serve free gratis, and this agreement was to remain in full force for ever. The same day, John

Hayes' account for surveying the town was examined and allowed.
One item was a gallon of Geneva whisky, one dollar.

The duplicate for 1813 and 1814 amounted to $96 88. Expenditures on streets and survey, in full, $103 06.

November 2. George Sweeny commenced the publication of the *Columbia Gazette*, at Northumberland, a strong war paper, and the *Sunbury and Northumberland Gazette* of A. Kennedy was suspended. Kennedy was a Federalist, and the war feeling was too strong for that paper. Chillisquaque and Northumberland county up to the Lycoming line had been erected into Columbia county, accounting for the new name. In 1815 this territory was put back to Northumberland.

Marriages.

January 24, Jacob Billman to Charity ———, daughter of Caleb. February 4, Paul Goodlander with Rachael Heckel, daughter of Andrew. February 11, Jesse Dickson to Polly Merkel, daughter of Christian. April 1, Philip Lesher to Polly Billmyer, daughter of Andrew. April 4, Alexander Donarchy with Fanny Seitz, daughter of George. April 6, Daniel Keenly with Maria Richter, daughter of John. May 16, Samuel Dersham with Susanna Shadel. August 1, Levi Burd with Eve Winegarden, daughter of Henry. August 12, Francis Jodon with Elizabeth Cherry, daughter of Charles. August 26, Hugh McLaughlin with Elizabeth McClister.

Deaths.

February 1, John Sierrer, leaving a widow, Lucy, and the following children: Jacob, Catherine, married to Jacob Reedy, John, Elizabeth, married to John Frantz, and Sarah to George Smith.

William Irwin, Esquire, member of Assembly during the Revolution. He left all his property to William, son of John.

William Clark, an original settler, leaving widow, Elizabeth. Children: George, Mary, (who married James Forster, and was dead, leaving Jane, married to Thomas Smith, John, William, and Ann, married to George Monroe,) Rebecca, Roan, Sarah, William, Walter, Flavel, and James.

February 21, David Watson, father of late David, John C., and William Watson, aged sixty-one.

March 27, Henry Deal. Family: Henry, junior, Elizabeth, married to Jacob Maize; Mary, to John Grossman; Nancy, to Jonathan Waters; and three grand-daughters, children of John: Nancy William, and Elizabeth.

Nicholas Egbert, West Buffalo.

May 18, John Bishop, aged seventy, buried at New Berlin.

Christopher Seebold.

September 13, Honorable Thomas Strawbridge, aged eighty-two.

John Walter, of Buffalo. Children: John, Benjamin, William, George, Jonathan, Elizabeth, married to Focht; Catherine, with George Reed; Margaret, with Adam Witmer; and Mary, with John Rodman. His widow, Margaret.

1814.

LEWISBURG BRIDGE CHARTERED—FIRST COURTS HELD AT MIFFLINBURG—BATTLE OF CHIPPEWA—CAPTAIN EVANS AT FORT MCHENRY—ROSTER OF LIEUTENANT COLONEL GEORGE WEIRICK'S REGIMENT—ROLLS OF CAPTAINS HENRY MILLER, JACOB HUMMEL, VALENTINE HAAS, JOHN BERGSTRESSER, AND NER MIDDLESWARTH'S COMPANIES.

SENATOR, Thomas Murray, junior, elected in October. Members, David E. Owen, Robert Willett, Joseph Hutchinson, and Henry Shaeffer.

On the 21st of March, the Houses passed, over Governor Snyder's veto, the act regulating banks. One was allowed for Northumberland, Union, and Columbia, to be called the Northumberland, Union, and Columbia Bank. It was located at Milton. John Dreisbach was one of the commissioners for this bank.

On the 26th of March, the charter of the bridge over the Susquehanna at Lewisburg, was granted by the Assembly, under the corporate name of "The President, Managers, and Company for erecting a Bridge over the West Branch of Susquehanna, at the Town of Lewisburg," and John Dreisbach, Jacob Brobst, William Hayes, William McQuhae, James Geddes, and Andrew Reedy, appointed commissioners to open subscription books. On the 28th, the act transfering all suits, and all unsettled estates where the defendant or decedent resided in the territory of Union to its courts, was passed.

Roads laid out—From Mortonsville, by Hugh Wilson's and Derr's mill, &c., two and one half miles; from Rockey's mill to Reznor's saw-mill, five miles; from Reznor's saw-mill to the Brush Valley and Mifflinburg road, four miles one hundred and forty-one perches.

The first court was held at Mifflinburg, on the 14th of February. First grand jurors, John Boal, Adam Regar, Arthur Thomas, Jacob Musser, John Fisher, James Madden, Robert Chambers, Valentine Haas, Jacob Houseworth, John Nogel, James McClure, John Williams, Aaron Chamberlin, Levi Zimmerman, Philip Gemberling, Frederick Wurtz, James Caldwell, Andrew Grove, David Simmons, Abraham Tenbrooke, Henry Ramstone, John Aurand, John Seidel, and John German. The commissions of Judges Chapman and Wilson were read.

On motion of Enoch Smith, for himself, E. G. Bradford, Samuel Hepburn, Ebenezer Greenough, Charles Maus, William Irwin, and John Lashells, were sworn in as attorneys. On motion of Mr. Lashells, John Johnston, and Ethan Baldwin. William Irwin sworn as deputy attorney general. On motion of Mr. Bradford, Charles Hall, George A. Frick, Alem Marr, and Hugh Bellas were qualified as attorneys. The survivor of this bar, George A. Frick, Esquire, of Danville, died at Danville, June 10, 1872, aged eighty-five.

April 21, Gideon Smith sold his farm on Buffalo creek to William Young. Andrew Kennedy, junior, commenced a paper at Mifflinburg. He sold out to Henry Shaup, in 1815, and the latter removed the press to New Berlin. The month of May was remarkable for the appearance in the Valley of locusts in vast numbers.

June 28, James Banks, of Mifflin county, Henry Haines, of Lancaster, (Edward Darlington not acting,) commissioners appointed by Governor Snyder, met at Selinsgrove, and explored the county, generally, and viewed a number of different situations which had been in contemplation. After considering advantages of each, and having due regard to territory and population, they reported the village of New Berlin, *alias* Longstown, the most eligible and proper situation in the county of Union for the seat of justice therein, and fixed the site of buildings, of court-house and public offices, on a lot belonging to C. Seebold, Esquire, and the site for a prison on a lot belonging to John Solomon.

Battle of Chippewa.

CAMP AT FORT ERIE, WEST CANADA, *July* 28, 1814.

DEAR SIR: Blood, carnage, death, and destruction of men are the contents of this painful letter. On the 22d, we had orders to reduce our baggage, allowing one tent to ten men, and two shirts to each officer. The surplus was sent across the Niagara, at Queenstown, where we then laid, to be sent to Buffalo. On the 24th, we marched to Chippewa. On the 25th, the enemy appeared on the heights, near the Falls of Niagara, two miles distant from our camp. At three o'clock, we were ordered to parade. At five, our brigade, under General Scott, marched out. At six, the action commenced, when, great God! to tell the details from that time till ten o'clock at night, is impossible. Could I converse with you for the length of time we were engaged, I could give some idea of it, but to make an attempt will, doubtless, not be unsatisfactory to you. Our brigade fought a much superior force, under great disadvantages, for one hour and a half, and we were completely cut up, more than half the officers and men being killed and wounded, when the second brigade, commanded by General Ripley, came to our assistance. The enemy, at the same time, received reinforcements, which made the action again severe. General Ryall and a number of prisoners were, previous to this, taken by our brigade. Colonel Brady was wounded before we were fifteen minutes engaged, and commanded the regiment till the action was nearly closed. I assisted him off and on his horse during the engagement, when he was like to faint from loss of blood. We got possession of the heights, and kept them till we got off our wounded. The British made three different charges to gain them, but they were as often beat back. Our brigade made three charges, in the last of which we lost three officers of our (the twenty-second) regiment, our brave General Scott heading each charge. He was severely wounded in the shoulder near the close of the action. General Brown was also wounded. When we returned from the ground, there were, of our regiment, Major Arrowsmith, myself, and thirty privates, that marched into camp. The balance were killed, wounded, missing, and in camp. Colonel Brady can inform you that I was the only platoon officer of our regiment that kept the ground to the last, and marched in with the men. For the satisfaction of your friends and yourself, I inclose you a copy of our report of the killed, wounded, and missing; likewise, the officers' names who were in the action. Our wounded are at Buffalo, in good quarters. Let me hear from you.

I am yours, sincerely,

SAMUEL BRADY,
Twenty-second Infantry.

Captain BETHUEL VINCENT.

N. B. Our total loss in killed, wounded, and missing on that day must have been eight hundred. The British loss no doubt exceeded that, as General Ryall acknowledged that they were whipped when he was taken, and we fought two hours after that, and took nineteen British officers.

You shall see the report in my next. I wish you to show it to my friends, but it must not be published.

13th September, occurred the bombardment of Fort McHenry, Baltimore. Frederick Evans was then a captain in the second regiment of artillery. His commission is dated 23d July, 1812, to rank from the 6th. Mrs. George Kremer told me he assisted in building the fort, and was one of its noble defenders. He often described the scene inside as terrific. Three bomb-shells struck and exploded inside of the fort, and he remarked one man shaking as if he had a chill. He asked to sit under one of the cannon. Evans gave him permission, when shortly another shell struck inside and killed him instantly. Another man was killed within three feet of him. Their coffee ran out, and they had very little to eat for three days. He spoke of a woman who brought water for them. A bomb-shell hitting her, exploded, and she was blown to atoms. He brought a small piece of her dress home with him, the largest part of her remains that he could find. The fourth shell that came in was marked "a present from the King of England." This did not explode. It weighed within two pounds as much as an ordinary barrel of flour. This he brought home with him, and it may still be seen at Evans' mill, in Juniata county. He said only four shells fell inside.

Muster Roll of the Field and Staff Officers belonging to the Regiment, or Detachment, commanded by Lieutenant Colonel George Weirick, Brigadier General H. Spearing, First Brigade, Second Division, in the service of the United States.

Lieutenant Colonel—George Weirick, September 24, 1814.
Majors—William Taggert and Jacob Lechner, September 24, 1814.
Adjutant—George Coryell, September 24, 1814.
Surgeon—John Y. Kennedy, September 24, 1814.
Surgeon's Mate—Thomas Vanvalzah, September 24, 1814.
Quartermaster—George Clingan, October 31, 1814; Quartermaster Sergeant, John Reehl, November 5.
Sergeant Major—Daniel Rohrer, October 5.
Aid-de-camp to General Spearing—Hugh Maxwell.
Camp Marcus Hook, November 14, 1814.

Roll of Captain Henry Miller's Company.

Pay-roll of the company of infantry from Union county, under the command of Captain Henry Miller, attached to the regiment commanded by Lieutenant Colonel George Weirick, Marcus Hook, November 10, 1814:
Captain—Miller, Henry.
Lieutenant—McMillan, John.
Sergeants—Williams, Benjamin; Rearick, John; Ruhle, Philip; Francis, William.
Corporals—Specht, Adam; Wilson, Foster; Spangler, George; Robinson, Richard.
Privates—Baker, George; Baker, Peter; Barber, John; Bitting, Charles; Bobb, Conrad; Bobb, John; Black, Robert; Bossler, George; Cooke, Andrew; Coryell, George, appointed sergeant major, September 26, 1814; Crossgrove, Samuel; Dar, Elias; Dreis-

bach, John; Dreisbach, Thomas; Dunsipe, Daniel; Egbert, Cyrus;
Eilert, William; Farres, Garrett; Forster, William; Fought, George;
Fought, Jacob; Fox, Conrad; Fry, John; Gearig, Jacob; Gear-
hart, Samuel; Gill, John; Gill, William, discharged October 26,
1814, died at Bellefonte, November 21, 1876, aged eighty-nine;
Hanius, Peter, (called Panier;) Herger, Henry; Hasenplugh,
Henry; Hasenplugh, Samuel; Kleckner, Abraham; Kleckner,
Anthony; Kleckner, Isaac; Maclay, John, appointed assistant quar-
termaster general, October 9, 1814; Mangel, David; Mayer, John;
Moyer, John; Moyer, William; Myer, William; Norman, John;
Phelps, Francis; Rearick, John; Reichly, William; Ritter, Henry;
Rote, John; Royer, Henry; Saunders, Michael; Shaffer, William;
Shaffer, Jacob; Smith, John; Snyder, Michael; Sleer, George;
Shaw, Samuel; Slough, Benjamin; Stitzer, David; Spangler, Chris-
tian; Speer, David; Spiegelmeyer, Daniel; Solomon, Abraham;
Thompson, James; Weight, John; Zimmerman, Jacob.

Roll of Captain Jacob Hummel's Company.

Pay-roll of the company of infantry under the command of Captain Jacob Hummel, attached to the regiment commanded by Lieutenant Colonel George Weirick, Marcus Hook, November 10, 1814.

Captain—Hummel, Jacob.
Lieutenant—Brady, Walter.
Ensign—Swartz, Francis B.
Sergeants—Baldy, Stephen; Eisely, John; Hammer, John; James, John S.
Corporals—Gordon, John B.; Petery, John; Leisenring, Jacob; Martin, James.
Privates—App, John; Applegate, John; Armstrong, John; Barn-
hart, John; Bear, William; Bestler, Henry; Born, John; Buck-
ner, John; Burn, Henry; Buyers, John; Campbell, John; Ca-
ruthers, Andrew; Conor, Daniel; Crutchley, John; Delany, Dan-
iel; Espy, George; Forly, George; Furman, Jona; Gearhart,
Daniel; Haupt, Henry; Hedrick, Jacob'; Housel, John; Hoy,
Lockwood G.; Huff, Benjamin; Hull, Isaac; Lowdon, Zachariah;
McCloughen, Joseph; Mahoney, William; Marsh, Griggs; Mettler,
William; Mirely, Balser; More, David; Morgan, Joseph; Morgan,

James; Masteller, John; Newcomer, Abraham; Overdurf, Peter; Redline, John; Renn, John W.; Rinehart, Frederick; Ringler, Daniel; Roadarmel, John; Sterner, Henry; Stroh, Jonathan; Wagner, Christian; Warner, James; Weaver, Frederick; Willet, William; Willet, Samuel; Woodruff, Elias; Woldigan, William; Zeluff, David.

Roll of Captain Valentine Haas' Company.

Roll of the company of infantry from Union county, under the command of Captain Valentine Haas, seventy-seventh regiment Pennsylvania militia, commanded by Lieutenant Colonel George Weirick, Marcus Hook, November 10, 1814.

Captain—Haas, Valentine.

Lieutenant—Shedle, Samuel.

Sergeants—Eckhart, Jacob C.; Hosterman, George; Boyer, Henry; Hendricks, Andrew.

Corporals—Johnston, John; Kleckner, Jacob; Richter, Frederick; Overmyer, David.

Privates—Alter, Joseph, discharged October 5; Bachman, Lorenzo; Bear, Isaac; Berger, Joseph; Berman, Anthony; Benfer, George; Binckly, Jacob; Bous, Frederick; Bosler, Jacob; Brous, Henry; Buttenstine, Philip; Clendinin, John; Doebler, Ludwig; Derk, Jonathan; Doffe, John; Duke, Jacob; Duke, George; Everhard, Barnes; Everhard, Philip; Fetter, Benjamin; Folk, John; Foltz, Joseph; Gordon, Willis; Gaugher, Jonas; Grim, Henry; Haas, Henry; Haas, Daniel; Hentricks, E.; Herrold, Philip; Hobb, Frederick; Hummel, John H.; Jarrett, Jacob; Karstetter, George; Keely, John, discharged October 22; Kesler, Michael; Kreisher, Henry; Kreitzer, Frederick; Kuns, John; Miller, Daniel; Mowrer, Jacob; Moyer, Philip; Neitz, Jacob; Pontius, Henry; Rettig, William; Richenbach, John; Rusher, John; Shedler, Jacob; Shoemaker, Peter; Smith, Abraham; Smith, John; Smith, Joseph; Sold, Philip; Spaid, Henry; Stahl, Henry; Stimeling, George; Stock, Peter; Swartz, Peter; Swartzlender, George; Trester, John; Wagner, George; Weaver, John; Weller, Isaac; Witmer, Samuel; Woodling, Henry; Wool, Daniel; Yeager, John; Yeager, Adam; Yeisly, Henry: Yerger, Philip; Yordon, John; Young, Ludwig.

Roll of Captain John Bergstresser's Company.

Pay-roll Union county company of militia, attached to the regiment commanded by Lieutenant Colonel George Weirick, Marcus Hook, November 18, 1814.

Captain—Bergstresser, John.
Lieutenant—Fisher, Thomas.
Ensign—Noll, Henry.
Sergeants—Silsby, Uriah; Reedy, Philip; Gilláspy, John; Rengler, Daniel; Merwine, Samuel; Sargint, John; Clingan, George.
Corporals—Nevyus, William; Vartz, John; McCorley, Jacob; Lutz, John.
Privates—Aikey, Lewis; Anderson, James H.; Baldy, Benjamin; Bellman, George; Bennage, Samuel; Bennett, John; Bidleman, Abraham; Bower, William; Bower, George; Bower, John; Campbell, William; Campbell, John; Campbell, Joseph; Clarke, Joseph; Clark, Flavel; Clark, Francis; Clark, William; Darraugh, John; Dempsey, Jonathan; Darsham, Ludwig; Diefenderfer, Philip; Egburd, Jesse; Flickingner, Charles; Frederick, Peter; Frederick, Jacob; Frederick, Samuel; Gilman, Jacob; Goodlander, Paul; Hufford, John; Heiser, Frederick, discharged October 2; Herrendon, William; Housel, Joshua; Hubler, Jacob; Irwin, John; Irvin, William; Jamison, John; Jodun, William; Jodun, Benjamin; Johnston, Thomas; Jones, John; Kaufman, Jacob; Kelly, Andrew, discharged October 28; Kimmell, Adam; Kunts, Daniel; Kline, Abram; Kline, George; Lilley, Peter, discharged October 3; Lutz, Samuel; McClure, Richard; McGuire, Richard; McKinley, Hugh; McLaughlin, James; Maughamer, Daniel; Magee, James; Mizener, John; Mengel, George; Mowry, Peter; Myers, Peter; Moyer, Henry; Quinn, Michael; Rees, John; Ranck, Jonathan; Rorabough, Christopher; Rorabough, Philip; Rose, Adam; Shaffer, Daniel; Shaffer, Henry, substitute for John Hummel; Sheckler, Jonas; Sheckler, Simon; Smith, Jonathan; Smith, Adam; Steel, Richard; Steel, David; Stoner, Daniel; Strickland, Samuel; Struble, Peter; Sypher, Jacob; Vanderhoof, Henry; Vanderhoof, William; Vanhorn, William; Vanhorn, Abram; Wallace, James; Walters, John; Welch, Nicholas; Williamson, Gideon; Wilson, Thomas; Wilson, Samuel; Young, Abraham; Zearphus, George, (Sarphus.)

In Captain Robert McGuigan's company, November 12 to 24, we find the names of—Egbert, John ; Hafer, James ; Haslet, Joseph ; Ranck, Adam ; Stadden, William ; Vanlew, Peter ; Whitacre, John ; Wurtz, Daniel.

Roll of Captain William F. Buyers' Company.

Roll of the Northumberland County Blues, volunteer company, attached to the regiment, under the command of Lieutenant Colonel George Weirick, Marcus Hook, November 10, 1814.

Captain—Buyers, William F.
Lieutenants—Jenkins, Thomas S.; Scott, Samuel H.
Ensign—Hepburn, John.
Sergeants—Wilson, Samuel H.; Wallis, Joseph T.; Sweeney, A. M.
Corporal—Reehl, John.
Fifer—Armor, William.
Drummer—DeLong, Samuel.
Privates—Armstrong, Jacob ; Black, David ; Bonham, Thomas ; Buyers, George P. ; Cameron, William ; Campbell, Robert ; Chapman, Edward ; Cooke, William ; Cook, Adam ; Cramer, Joseph B.; Cramer, Abram ; Dale, Henry ; Dieus, William ; Dougal, James S.; Frazier, Charles ; Gale, William ; Grant, Mact ; Grant, Thomas, junior, discharged October 23 ; Grant, William M. ; Gray, William ; Harris, Thomas ; Hendershot, Isaac ; Hopfer, Jacob ; Huffman, Joseph ; Jones, William ; Jones, Jeremiah ; Latherland, William ; Layton, William ; Lebo, Daniel ; Lyon, Robert ; Lyon, Jeremiah ; McCord, Isaac ; McPherson, John ; Martin, John ; Maus, Charles ; Oliphant, James ; Prune, George ; Quinn, John ; Reininger, Henry ; Rockele, Theodore J. ; Ross, John ; Watson, William ; Weisner, John ; Weitzel, George ; Wilson, Samuel.

Jacob Armstrong, John Martin, Robert Campbell, and William Dieus, drafts in Captain Hummel's company, joined my company on 29th. They have been in service the same time our company has.

WILLIAM F. BUYERS,
Captain Northumberland County Blues.

The following memoranda are from Lieutenant Colonel Weirick's order-book, now in possession of M. L. Schoch, Esquire, of New Berlin :

General Order, dated at Headquarters, Fourth Militia District, Philadelphia, October 19, 1814.

The advance corps will consist of the light brigade, under Brigadier General Cadwalader, who will report directly to the commanding general, and act alone under his orders, and those of the War Department. Colonel Irvine's regiment of regulars will support the advance. The army of the center will consist of Brigadier General Spearing's, Smith's, and Snyder's brigades, forming Major General Worrell's division. The volunteers and recruits at Bush Hill will form the reserve. The New Jersey troops, under General Elmer, form the left wing. The officers and men of the fifth United States infantry, at camp near New Castle, will form a detachment, under the immediate command of the senior officer, and act under Colonel Irvine.

By order of

Major General EDWARD P. GAINES.

Major General Isaac Worrell's headquarters were transferred to Marcus Hook, on the 20th of October. Henry Sheets, major general, second division; Brigadier General Henry Spearing commanding first brigade, second division,—drafted militia, Northampton, Montgomery, Lehigh, Pike, Northumberland, &c.; Hugh Maxwell, aid-de-camp; Thomas J. Rodgers and W. C. Rodgers, brigade majors.

November 13, Ensign Farnsworth transferred to Captain Miller's company. November 15, Lieutenant Colonels Heister and Weirick, and the field officers of their respective commands, ordered to report, at twelve o'clock, at General's quarters, to decide their precedence of rank by lot.

John Campbell, Griggs Marsh, and David Moore, who have been absent without leave, have come this day, and joined their companies. I, therefore, order the same to be entered on the regimental book.

GEORGE WEIRICK,
Lieutenant Colonel Commanding.

November 16. The above, who have been reported as deserters, are to be tried as absentees.

GEORGE WEIRICK,
Lieutenant Colonel.

November 16, lot determined in favor of Lieutenant Colonel Weirick, who is hereby announced first lieutenant colonel in first brigade, second division, Pennsylvania militia, under the command of Brigadier General Henry Spearing, and is to be obeyed and respected accordingly. It was determined to mutual satisfaction that Major Taggert was properly entitled to the first rank and Major Lechner to the second rank in Colonel Weirick's regiment, and will hereafter take precedence accordingly.

November 17, the lot for rank of captain resulted: first captain, Miller; second, Hummel; third, Haas; fourth, Bergstresser. The court-martial held at Adjutant Coryell's marquee, John Bergstresser, president, Lieutenants John McMillan and Samuel Shedle members, Thomas Jenkins, judge advocate, sentenced John Campbell, Griggs Marsh, and David Moore to stand camp guard every other day, and to be within the limits of the camp during the remainder of their tour.

November 23. The German troops in Major General Sheetz's division will be formed upon the parade to-morrow, at ten o'clock, with their side arms, for divine worship in German.

The last orders in the book are dated at Marcus Hook, December 1 : The sick troops are to be discharged on furlough to their respective homes until further orders. Adjutant of the day, Coryell.

The discharge of Peter Myers, signed by Captain John Bergstresser, is dated Philadelphia, December 20, 1814, and I presume that is the date of the muster out of the regiment.

Pay-roll of the Union Rifle Volunteers, commanded by Captain Ner Middleswarth, attached to the Rifle Battalion, commanded by Captain John Uhle, in the Light Brigade, commanded by General Thomas Cadwalader, in actual service at Camp Dupont, October 27, 1814.

Captain—Middleswarth, Ner.
Lieutenants—Mertz, Isaac; Aurand, John.
Ensign—Devore, Daniel.
Sergeants—Fryer, Jacob; Weiser, Daniel; Stees, Frederick, junior; Weikel, George.
Corporals—Frederick, Abraham; Layer, Daniel; Swineford, Albright; Long, Jacob.

Privates—Beitler, Jacob; Bird, John; Bowersox, Daniel; Boyer, Samuel; Campbell, Elias; Carroll, Henry W.; Clemence, George; Dreese, Henry; Ely, Asher; Freedley, Ludwig; Gilbert, Jacob; Gill, Jacob; Gilmore, Robert; Grubb, Jacob; Kaley, Abraham; Katherman, John; Kratzer, Henry; Kuhns, John; Loehr, Joseph; Loehr, Peter; Martz, Samuel; Miller, Daniel; Miller, Jacob; Mitchell, John; Moyer, George; Moyer, Jacob; Shneb, Henry; Smith, James; Stock, Melchior; Troxell, Jacob; Thurston, Israel; Wakey, John; Wales, John; Weirick, Henry; Wient, George.

Marriages.

22d February, John Beeber married to Miss Anna Baker, by H. Spyker, Esquire.

Deaths.

At Lewisburg, January 16, Charles Cameron, father of the late John Cameron, William Cameron, Esquire, General Simon Cameron, Mrs. A. B. Warford, of Harrisburg, Mrs. Boggs, of Indiana, Colonel James Cameron, who was killed at Bull Run, and of Daniel, who died in the naval service.

August 23, Reverend Isaac Grier, died at Northumberland. Born 1763; graduated at Dickinson college in 1788; licensed December 21, 1791. He taught the academy, and was father of Honorable R. C. Grier, Isaac Grier, D. D., &c.

John Turner, tailor, of Lewisburg. He left a widow, Elizabeth, and daughters, Christena and Matilda.

Jacob Wolfe, of Buffalo, leaving a widow, Catherine, and children, Catherine, Elizabeth, Jacob, John, Jonathan, and Samuel.

August 29, Adam Laughlin, of Hartley township, aged sixty-six.

Wendell Baker, of East Buffalo. Children: John, Jacob, Mrs. Mathias Alsbach. Grandchildren: John and Ann Mizener.

October 14, Paul Collins, of West Buffalo, aged seventy-nine.

Adam Struble, of West Buffalo.

1815.

Courts held in New Berlin—Union Township Erected—St. Peter's Church, Kelly—Death of Captain William Gray, of Buffalo.

CT 8th March provided that after the first Monday of May, the courts should be held at New Berlin, in the court-house, provided a full and sufficient deed be made, for the consideration of sixty-seven cents, to the commissioners, before the first Monday in April, for the court-house and lot. The original receipt for sixty-seven cents may be seen in the commissioner's office, at Lewisburg. 11th March, Washington township annexed to Lycoming.—P. L., 119. April 1, Hugh McLaughlin's land, in Kelly, was sold to John Gotshall for $36 per acre, and the Japhet Martin place, East Buffalo, now Frederick's, appraised at $48. 15th April, Reverend C. Newcomer arrived at Michael Maize's. "On 16th preached at Martin Dreisbach's, 17th at George Miller's, and on the 18th had a long conversation with Messrs. Miller and Niebel on the union of our respective societies, but we could not bring it about."

Union Township Erected.

September sessions, upon the report of Andrew McLenachan, John Hayes, and Adam Wilt, Union township was erected, with the following boundary: Beginning at a double walnut, on the West Branch, (below Jenkins' mill,) S. 73° W. 3 miles 100 perches to stones on the top of Shamokin ridge; along same, S. 75° W. 3 miles 10 perches, to chestnut oak; N. 150 W. 1 mile 200 perches to top of

Limestone ridge; S. 75° W. 2 miles 100 perches to line between Buffalo and West Buffalo; along same, S. 150 perches to head of John Stees' spring; thence down same and Switzer run to Penn's creek; down Penn's creek to the line between Buffalo and Penn's; thence along the same to the river; thence up the river to the mouth of West Branch; thence up West Branch to beginning.

St. Peter's Lutheran Church, in Kelly.

On the 4th of November, Christian Zerbe and George Reininger, trustees in the conveyance made by Jacob Lotz, executor of Philip Stahl, granted, permitted, allowed, and confirmed the full right, liberty, and privilege unto the members of the Presbyterian congregation (German Reformed) of White Deer township, in common with the members of the Lutheran congregation of, in, and to the aforesaid premises and church, when built, in consideration of the German Reformed congregation contributing to the purchase of the lot and building of the house, &c.

Marriages.

Daniel Shannon with Christena Pross, February 23. March 23, Samuel Strickland with Elizabeth Turner. April 2, Jonathan Ranck with Catherine Long, daughter of Joseph. May 30, Jacob Wehr with Margaret Sassaman. June 25, Jacob Rees and Elizabeth Williamson, in presence of her brother, Gideon. September 3, Elisha Barry with Elizabeth Herbst, daughter of Henry. October 12, George Mook with Julia Fastnock, daughter of Adam. All by Henry Spyker, Esquire.

Deaths.

4th April, Catherine, wife of John Dreisbach, born 11th March, 1785. Married 18th April, 1811. 11th April, Elizabeth, wife of William Wilson, aged fifty-seven. June 27, John Freedly, (miller,) "found this morning lying in a water sluice, in his meadow, dead. George Knox, George Schnable, John Lawshe, senior, George Metzgar, Henry Colway, Philip Lesher, Alexander Graham, George

Kremer, Robert Smith, Alexander Morton, Jonathan Spyker, and James Knox, a jury empaneled, found he came to his death by accident, and not by violence." (He was the owner of Ludwig Derr's mill.)

Captain William Gray, one of the first settlers in the Valley, died. His children were: Sally, Mrs. Mary Dunlap; Susanna, married first to William Hudson, after his death, to Andrew Forster; Eleanor, to John Robinson; Margaret, to John Hayes, Esquire; Nancy, widow of Hudson Williams; Jane, widow of William Wallace, married to Samuel Hutchinson.

Hugh McLaughlin, White Deer. He lived, adjoining William Clingan's, owning a farm of seventy acres. His children: James Eleanor, wife of William Cameron, Esquire; Hugh, who recently (1871) died at Lewisburg, and Margaret, who died unmarried.

Japhet Morton, East Buffalo. Children: Edward, William, John, Alexander, Isabella, married to Thomas McGuire, and Rachel and four grandchildren, sons of Thomas, deceased: Martha, Betsey, Polly, and Japhet.

November 1, Christian Nevius, aged fifty-six. He left a widow, Lucretia, who died January 19, 1841, aged seventy-five. Children: Peter, John, Ann, Ralph, Aaron, Elizabeth, Phoebe, and Sarah.

1816.

HENRY SHAUP'S NEWSPAPER—SUSQUEHANNA BIBLE SOCIETY FORMED—LEWISBURG BRIDGE BUILT—A NEW CHURCH AT CROSS-ROADS—PRESIDENTIAL ELECTION—SIMON SNYDER'S LETTER TO GEORGE KREMER—JUDGE COOPER TRANSFERRED TO THE UNIVERSITY OF PENNSYLVANIA.

ITEMS taken from Henry Shaup's *Union Newspaper*—Markets in Philadelphia: wheat, $2.20; rye, $1.45; corn, $1.50; butter, 14 cents pound. Proposals are published by Frederick Gutelius, James Dale, and John Bower, county commissioners, for building the jail. Israel Inman was the principal store-keeper in New Berlin. George Spring notifies all persons having lots in the town of Springfield, to come forward on the 1st of April, and lift their deeds or give up their tickets. James Merrill, practicing law at Mr. Maurer's, opposite the New Berlin hotel. William Poak kept hotel at Hartleton. John Grove's vendue at New Berlin. James Monroe and Daniel D. Tompkins nominated for President and Vice President, by the Republican members of Congress. Simon Snyder had thirty votes in caucus for Vice President. Aaron Chamberlin elected colonel, *vice* George Weirick, resigned. Philip Franck, watch-maker, New Berlin. George Eisenhuth, merchant. William Dale and John Leany, executors of Samuel Fisher, of White Deer, advertise his land on White Deer creek for sale. A public market held in New Berlin on the 20th of June, continuing three days, for the purpose of selling horses, horned cattle. "Here the weary peddler was invited to repose a few days, with his pack, and at the same time vend jewelry to his advantage; the lovers of music and dancing, to spend the careless hours in pleasure. Boxers and gamblers are not invited, but may attend at their own risk." A bear beat is also advertised as one of the attractions. An association formed to suppress horse-racing, Abbot Green, treasurer. John Sargeant and Robert Smith were brought before Henry Spyker, Esquire, who fined them $20 each. He notes in his docket that "the judges of Union county say this is wrong, and have reversed my proceeding. After this, the judges may fine the horse-racers themselves."

July 23, Ann Smith, *alias* Carson, arrested above Harrisburg, with two companions, who called themselves Owen Jones and Nathaniel B. Bard. She had formed plains to abduct the Governor, and extort by violence a pardon of Richard Smith, convicted of the murder of Captain Carson, or, failing in this, to seize some member of his family.

Susquehanna Bible Society formed at Milton, John B. Patterson, president; vice presidents, Reverend Thomas Hood and Judge Andrew Albright. Shaup thus notices the demise of the *The Advocate of the Union*, Hugh Maxwell's paper: "Union county has lost an *Advocate*, Saturday, 27th September, after a lingering illness of one year and seven months. The remains, we understand, have been removed to Bellefonte."

August 24. Adam Wilt made a plan of New Berlin, showing the original as laid out by George Long, and the additions made by Christopher Seebold, Christian Miller, Henry Gross, Alexander and James Beatty. This plan was signed by the lot owners of New Berlin, and recorded as the proper plan of the place. Deed book "C," page 198.

Improvements.

15th March, supplement to the Lewisburg bridge charter passed, authorizing the Governor to subscribe four hundred shares for the State. June 19, the company organized. July 4, contract made with Reuben Fields for the erection of the bridge for $52,600. $2,400 was afterwards allowed, in addition to the contract price. The jail at New Berlin was erected this year by Frederick Hipple, of Centre township. Contract price, $4,000. The stone furnished by Henry Gross, at twelve and a half cents per perch, measured in the wall. 23d February, Buffalo Cross-Roads congregation met, William Clingan called to the chair, James McClellan, secretary, and resolved to build a stone meeting-house, sixty by thirty-five. The trustees altered it to fifty-two by forty; four rows of seats, and pulpit in the end. Jacob Hartman contracted to do all the carpenter work and painting for $625. William McLaughlin to do the mason work at seventy-five cents per perch. This stone church stood within the limits of the present grave-yard, north-west corner. The corner-stone was laid on the 23d day of July. It was completed by the 29th of December, when Mr. Dunham preached the first sermon in the new church, from Nehemiah, iv : 6 : "For the people had a mind to build." 19th March, 1817, Mr. Hood preached the first sermon in the new pulpit. Text, John, vi : 38 and 39, showing the reasonableness of the doctrine of predestination. 27th April, Peter Burg conveyed to Conrad Philips and John Walters, a lot on Walnut street and Apple Tree alley, in New Berlin, for a grave-yard for the use of the Union County Evangelical Association.

At the October election, the candidates for Congress were George Kremer, William Wilson, David Scott, Charles Maus, and Captain William F. Buyers. William Wilson and David Scott were elected. At this election, one thousand six hundred and twelve votes were polled. Democratic majority nearly seven hundred and fifty. At the November election, Monroe and Tompkins received six hundred and one votes, against one hundred and two for the opposition or Independent Republican ticket, on which were the the names of Andrew Gregg, Christian Brobst, Daniel Montgomery, and others, as electors.

October 11, Reverend C. Newcomer arrived again in the Valley; preached at old Mr. Eyers'. 12th, at Mr. Dreisbach. Sunday, 13th, had meeting in the forenoon and at night. 14th, conference of the Albright brethren commenced. 15th, attended a funeral at Mr. Gilmore's; at night preached at Solomon Betz's. 16th, preached at Youngmanstown and lodged at Mr. Corl's. Mail arrives at New Berlin once a week.

Extracts from a letter from Governor Snyder to George Kremer, 24th November : "I should like much to see you pitted against that arch fiend, Lieb, in the House of Representatives; but unless Brobst resigns, I cannot see how the Speaker could constitutionally issue a writ for the election of another. A writ of lunacy could be awarded by the court of Union county, and thereupon a writ might issue for a new election. The people might memorialize the House, that, through mental derangement, the act of God, one of their Representatives is disqualified to represent the *wisdom of the county.* This, accompanied by certificates from regular-bred physicians— Doctors Dougal, Vanvalzah, &c.—would undoubtedly bring the question fairly before the House, and a precedent established in his case, if there is not one already, in this country or in England. But, if he has any interval of sanity, this might be embraced to procure his resignation. Thus all difficulty would be removed, and make room for your election, which, I suppose, would be certain, if the Longstown interest does not oppose you. Whatever may be done, it will be all-important to keep out of view his having been mad before his election, or that the people were so who elected him."

The letter refers to Jacob Brobst, who became insane. He lived just above Mifflinburg, where he died. The path the poor old man tramped in his fearful spells and struggles was visible many years after his death.

December 6. Judge Thomas Cooper, late professor at Dickinson College, Carlisle, was elected professor in the University of Pennsylvania.

Marriages.

17th January, Daniel Shriner with Catherine Funston, daughter of William. June 6, John Hayes with Jane McFadden, daughter of John. June 23, Titus Kemp with Betsey Huntingdon, in presence of her cousin, Gabriel. *Eo die,* William Francis, widower, with Catherine Gettig, widow. November 7, Henry Moyer with Polly Strickland. December 19, John Walters with Susanna Moyer, daughter of John, in presence of her brother, Peter. December 31, by Reverend J. H. Fries, Jacob Strayer to Rachel Harmony, of New Berlin. In August, John Johnston, (painter,) of New Berlin, to Elizabeth Kress, by H. Yearick, Esquire.

Deaths.

9th March, Mrs. Elizabeth Weirick, wife of Colonel George Weirick, aged thirty-six.

Peter Bower, East Buffalo, aged sixty-eight.
Killian Dunkle, East Buffalo.
John Hoover, of West Buffalo. Children: George, Jacob, Ann, Mary, Elizabeth, Catherine, Susan, and Christena.
Philip Gebhart. Widow: Mary. Children: Jonathan, George, John, Henry, Michael, Elizabeth, Sally, and Mary.
Daniel Rees, of Buffalo, left widow, Catherine, and children, Catherine and George W.
October 15, Thomas Sutherland, father of Mrs. Doctor Thomas Vanvalzah, aged eighty-four. (His widow, Jane, died July 9, 1819, aged eighty-two.)

1817.

POLITICAL—ELECTION RETURNS—LEWISBURG BRIDGE—HENRY SPYKER, ESQUIRE—COLONEL WILLIAM CHAMBERLIN.

JOHN SNYDER, United States Collector Internal Revenue. Postmasters: Lewisburg, A. Graham; New Berlin, James Merrill; Mifflinburg, John Orwig; Hartleton, James Madden. Republican Standing Committee, Henry Yearick, James Geddes, and P. F. Deering. 19th February, Democratic Republican Convention held at New Berlin. John Gross, president; Henry Yearick, secretary. Ner Middleswarth and James Dale appointed delegates to the State Convention, and William Findlay, of Franklin, recommended for Governor. 4th March, William Findlay nominated at Harrisburg, and Joseph Hiester by the Independent Republicans, at Carlisle. June 19, Stephen Hughes, chairman, John Mauck and Lewis Bertram secretaries of the Hiester meeting, held at the house of John Solomon, in New Berlin. July 12, Findlay meeting held at New Berlin; John Wilson, president; James Geddes and Christopher Seebold secretaries. Vigilance committees: Hartley, Adam Wilt and Henry

Roush; West Buffalo, Michael Schoch, John Dreisbach, Christopher Johnston, John Ray, and Robert Forster; East Buffalo, James Dale, John Reber, Andrew Reedy, and George Knox; White Deer, Colonel Aaron Chamberlin, A. McClenachan, Major John Ranck, and Dan Caldwell; Union, Alexander Boveard, Michael Waggoner, Jacob Kline, and William Kessler. 10th September, convention at New Berlin; John Orwig, chairman; Isaac Mertz, secretary. Joseph Hiester nominated for Governor. Assembly, Fred Stees and Joseph Stillwell; commissioner, Mishael Lincoln; auditor, Samuel Baum.* Delegates: Union, George Eisenhuth; Hartley, Abbot Green and William Reed; West Buffalo, John Orwig and Daniel Reeser; East Buffalo, Christian Sterner and William Hayes. 20th September, General Adam Light nominated by the Independents for Congress.

ELECTION RETURNS.

DISTRICTS.	GOV'NR.		CONG'SS.		ASSEMBLY.				COMM'R.	
	J. Hiester.	W. Findlay.	A. Light.	J. Murray.	F. Stees.	J. Stilwell.	J. Ray.	N. Middleswarth.	M. Lincoln.	A. McClenachan.
Union,	192	145	192	141	167	184	165	152	134	141
East Buffalo,	116	222	96	229	102	98	236	228	111	219
West Buffalo,	173	115	173	114	173	167	123	116	172	113
White Deer,	45	200	23	218	43	202	201	37	204	
Hartley,	103	108	99	111	101	87	110	113	102	109
Beaver,	171	70		71	162	159	79	79	167	68
Centre,	204	35	3	232	192	186	47	46	104	35
Perry,	92	39	48	48	70	67	59	68	87	45
Freeburg,	163	49	156	55	157	157	51	53	160	50
Penn's,	248	35	182	49	238	242	44	40	246	33
Total,	1507	1018	972	1268	1405	1390	1116	1096	1320	1011

February 6, prices in Philadelphia: Wheat, $3 per bushel; rye, $1.60; corn, $1.70. February 13, Methodist church, at New Berlin, dedicated. A great assemblage of people. Over two hundred sleds and sleighs. March 13, ice broke on the river, and obstructed the stages. 9th August, Limestone Run bridge, in the town of Milton, swept out, with large portions of the road, by a sudden freshet in that stream.

Lewisburg Bridge.

November 1, superstructure up, and teams cross the Lewisburg bridge. James Lee, the old tavern-keeper, at Northumberland, in a suit, Burr *vs.* McCay, 6 Barr, 149, about the " Burr bridge patent," testified to the following facts, in regard to the building of this bridge and others on the Susquehanna:

"In May, 1816, Theodore Burr was at my house, in Northumberland, and I asked him whether he proposed attending the letting of the Lewisburg bridge. He said he had enough bridges on hand, and recommended Reuben Fields as a first-rate builder, who worked with him on the Harrisburg bridge. I went to Harrisburg, got an introduction to Mr. Fields, who came to Lewisburg the week following, to look at the points for material, contiguous to the site. A few days before the letting, he brought up a plan and draft for the bridge. Theodore Burr advised Fields and myself to build on that plan. We presented the plan to the company on the 3d of July, 1816, together with our proposals. The day following, Mr. Hepburn drew the contract between the Lewisburg Bridge Company, Fields, and myself, and on the 7th we commenced excavating the foundation for stone-work. In September we had got up two piers, and the two abutments half way. Mr. Fields came up that fall, and commenced the wood-work. Early the next spring one of the reaches was up, and another part raised on the east side," &c.

Theodore Burr commenced building the Northumberland bridge in 1812. Finished it in two years. In 1814 he commenced the Harrisburg bridge, and finished it in two or three years.

Marriages.

February 20, by Henry Spyker, Esquire, Peter Long to Sarah, daughter of Jacob Moore. June 19, by Reverend J. H. Fries, Samuel Roush, Esquire, to Miss Elizabeth Dunkle. September 9, by Reverend Peter Kessler, Jacob Alter to Miss Ann Kessler. October 24, George Mitchel to Eliza Anderson. May 22, by Reverend John Patterson, Andrew McBeth to Ann Linn.

Deaths.

February 6, Enoch Smith, Esquire, attorney-at-law, Sunbury, Pennsylvania. February 19, Flavel Roan, Esquire, born July 31, 1760. Son of the Reverend John Roan, and brother of Mrs. Clingan. He was buried in the Presbyterian grave-yard, at Lewisburg, near the pavement, a little east of the present church. The grave being unmarked, it was lost sight of when the church was built. March 17, Elizabeth, wife of Reverend J. G. Heim, born April 17, 1776. April 17, Elias Youngman, born August 15, 1738. Married, January 11, 1763, to Catherine Nagle. His children were: George, father of Elias, of Jersey Shore; Thomas, who died, (Thomas' widow married Robert Forster,) and Catherine, married to John Dreisbach. Elias Youngman was a hatter, in Sunbury, in 1775. Moved into the Valley in 1783. April 27, Jacob Dunkle, who bought the Heberling mill at sheriff's sale, as the property of Captain John Bergstresser, was killed near Bear Gap, as he was coming home with the team from Philadelphia. His horses ran off, and the wagon wheels passed over his head, killing him instantly. He was the grandfather of Charles C., of Lewisburg. He left a family of seven sons and five daughters. He was married, November 24, 1789, to Ann C. Shoemaker.

July 1, Henry Spyker, Esquire. His children were: Mrs. Alexander Graham, Jonathan Spyker, &c. He was a son of Peter Spyker, who was president of the courts of Berks county in 1780. The Spykers, Christs, Kadermans, &c., came over with Conrad Weiser to New York, in 1710, from a place called Herrenburg, in Wurtemberg, Germany. In 1729, they all removed together to Tulpehocken, where Henry Spyker was born, 29th August, 1753. He was adjutant, in 1776, of a militia regiment on duty at Amboy, New Jersey, where he heard the thunder of the battle on the 25th, 26th, and 27th. His manuscript journal is yet in the possession of his granddaughter, Mary Spyker, at Lewisburg, together with many valuable papers, a complete file of almanacs from 1756 down. He was paymaster of the militia from October 1, 1777, to July 27, 1785, during which he disbursed £122,847 7s. 6d., and accounted satisfactorily for every cent. He was afterwards member of Assembly for Berks, 1788-90. In 1797, when Jonathan was twelve years old, just the age of Lewisburg, he removed to Lewisburg, where he engaged in store-keeping for a few years; was then appointed a justice, which office he exercised until within a few days of his death. He used to tell of two Germans of the Valley, who came to his office to make some sale, and have a note written, and when through, the party who was to have the note told the other to keep it, and he could then know when it was due, and come and pay him.

August 21, Colonel William Chamberlin. He came from Hunterdon county, New Jersey, where he was born, September 25, 1736. He served as lieutenant colonel in second regiment, Colonel David Chambers, his commission bearing date 9th September, 1777, in November of which year, by order of Governor Livingston, he was directed to call on Messrs. Penn and Chew, at the Union ironworks, to conduct them to Worcester, Massachusetts, and deliver them to the Council of that State. He was also directed to purchase, in Connecticut or Massachusetts Bay, twenty thousand flints for the Council of New Jersey. He participated in the battle of Monmouth, 28th June, 1778, where his eldest son Lewis was killed by a cannon ball. He moved into our Valley in 1793, and on the 16th of August, 1794, married his fourth wife, Mary Kemble. He was the father of twenty-three children, fifteen of whom were born in New Jersey. Of his children, Nelly married John Lawshe, senior; Ann, John Ross; Lucretia, Christian Nevius; William, Enoch, Tenbrooke; Sarah, married to James Wilson; Uriah; Elizabeth, married to William McCreery; Aaron, came with him. His fourth wife's children were: John, James, Lewis, Mary Frances, married to John Linn; Joseph P., James D., and Moses, the latter still residing at Milton.

James Marshall, of White Deer.

1818.

DELAWARES AND SHAWANESE REMOVE WEST OF THE MISSISSIPPI.

WILLIAM FINDLAY, Governor.

February 8, prices current in Philadelphia: flour, $10 per barrel; wheat, $1 80; rye, 95 cents. 9th, the first toll was taken on the Lewisburg bridge. On the 5th and 6th of May, David Yoder had the town of New Columbia surveyed and laid out in streets and lots. During this summer, the Christian chapel, a frame building on Fourth street, between St. John and St. Anthony, in Lewisburg, was erected.

I note, September 17, the treaty by which the Delawares and Shawanese cede their lands in Ohio and Indiana, and agree to take locations on the Arkansas river. The Delawares resided principally on Stony creek, a branch of the Maumee; the Shawanese on the Auglaize river, where it empties into the Maumee, in north-western Ohio.

The election this fall did not manifest any material change in the political situation of the State. Ex-Governor Simon Snyder was elected Senator from Northumberland, Union, &c., without any opposition.

Marriages.

Among marriages are: February 24, James Dale to Eliza Bell, of Hanover, Dauphin county. June 11, John Snyder, Esquire, to Miss Mary Kittera, daughter of late Honorable John Wilkes Kittera, deceased. November 4, Lieutenant R. H. Hammond, fifth U. S. infantry, to Miss Eliza C. Gloninger, of Lebanon.

Deaths.

Among deaths: March 30, Christopher Weiser, East Buffalo, aged sixty-one. May 25, Sarah Barber, wife of Robert, aged sixty-five.

1819.

DIFFICULTY IN MR. FRIES' CHURCH—BANK SUSPENSIONS.

THIS year is noted in our religious history for Mr. Fries' difficulty in his Mifflinburg congregation. It assumed such proportions that the Synod recommended that he should withdraw from Mifflinburg and take charge of the eight congregations at Middle creek. He came home from Synod, called a meeting of the elders of Penn's, Brush Valley, New Berlin, Dreisbach's and Mifflinburg, before whom he invited his accusers to appear. It appears they had circulated a story that, on Easter Sunday, he had conducted himself as if he were intoxicated. The elders pronounced him innocent. Their report is signed, Adam Harper, president; Adam Neidig, secretary; John Brown, Henry Herbst, John Zeigler, John Philip Meyer, Frederick Gutelius, John Ray, Sebastian Whitmer, Elias Youngman, and John Dreisbach, elders.

In August, the Northumberland, Union, and Columbia Bank, at Milton, stopped payment. Its notes in circulation were $55,000, and the debts due to the institution amounted to $190,000. Manufactures having broken down in the country, bank notes necessarily flowed in large quantities to Philadelphia and Baltimore for the purchase of goods and the payment of debts. City banks had plenty of their own paper, and, therefore, would not take them; or, if they did, forwarded them forthwith for redemption. The result followed, the country banks had to suspend. This was the case with the Reading Bank, Northampton Bank, &c.

Among the deaths this year were: Henry Iddings, aged ninety-two, leaving ten children. John Boal, of White Deer; his family were Elizabeth, married to Matthew Laird; Mary, to John Reznor; Sophia, to Samuel Woods; Margaret; Nancy, to J. Foster Wilson, of Hartleton.

Domestic.

The use of the tomato, as an edible, is noted. Prior to this, the plant was cultivated for ornament.

The large stone house in Lewisburg, now occupied by Mark Halfpenny, was built by William Hayes.

Governor Simon Snyder.

Governor Simon Snyder died at Selinsgrove, November 9, at three, A. M., aged seventy years and four days. His remains rest in the old grave-yard, at Selinsgrove, under a marble slab, without any inscription. His father was a mechanic, who had emigrated from Germany to Lancaster, where the Governor was born. In July, 1784, he removed to Northumberland county, and settled at Selinsgrove, where he opened a store, and became the owner of a mill. He soon became useful as a scrivener, and as a friend of the poor and distressed. He was soon elected justice of the peace, in which capacity he officiated for twelve years. (Justices then presided in the county court.) So universally were his decisions respected, that there never was any appeal from any judgment of his to the court, and but one writ of *certiorari* was served upon him during that time. His political record is spread forth on the foregoing pages of these Annals. Mention will, therefore, be made here of only a few incidents of his public life. With him originated the arbitration principle, first incorporated, with other wholesome provisions, for the adjustment of controversies brought before justices of the peace, called the hundred-dollar act. After a few years' experience, this salutary principle was ingrafted upon our judiciary system. General Abner Lacock was his coadjutor in these measures. His conduct during the war of 1812 was patriotic, and worthy of a Governor of Pennsylvania. His son John, afterwards the Honorable John Snyder, of the thirteenth district, then a boy of nineteen, raised a company, and marched with them as captain to Baltimore. They arrived at Harrisburg before daylight, and were halted before the Governor's door. He arose from his bed, and welcomed them, and with stirring words complimented their bravery. He always said, in speaking of the circumstance, he never before had felt so proud of his son John.

During the session of 1813-14, a very large majority of both Houses passed the bill to charter *forty banks*. The candidate for Governor was at that time nominated by the members of the Legislature. When they came into caucus, it was remarked that the bank bill was then before the Governor, and that it would be prudent to make no nomination till it was seen whether he would sanction it. Within three days, Governor Snyder returned the bill, with his objections, and it did not pass that session. His independence was the theme of universal praise, and he was that year re-elected by an immense majority. Having served out the constitutional term, he returned to Selinsgrove, and at the next general election was made State Senator, and served one session.

The crowning glory of Governor Snyder's career was his christianity. In religious culture he was a Moravian, and in public station he never forgot his vows or neglected his religious duties. His heart went out at all times in deeds of kindness to the poor and unfortunate. He was long mourned with sincere grief by them, and the few old people still surviving, tell how tenderly it was manifested when he was buried out of their sight.

His letters to his children are very affectionate, and full of good advice. I quote from one to his daughter, Amelia, afterwards Mrs. Jenks, dated the 30th of January, 1813 :

"I hope the practice I recommended, of reading by the boys in the evening, has been adopted, and the reading of a chapter in the New Testament or one of Blair's sermons on a Sunday, when there is no worship in our church. When there is, and the weather is tolerable, I trust you and all the boys attend. Your ensample may influence them. I would advise you to set apart, say two hours each day, for reading, and endeavor to store in your mind all that is worth recollecting. Write to me when you have an opportunity, or rather write when anything occurs to your mind worth communicating, and then you will be ready, and not hurried, when an opportunity offers. This is my method, or I never could get through half my business."

His parental tenderness and his earnest desire for the conversion of his children is the burden of many of his letters. From one, dated Harrisburg, 19th January, 1813, I make the following extracts:

"DEAR CHILD: I have but a few moments time, before the mail starts, to acknowledge the receipt of your letter of the 17th. I feel much distressed by your relation of John's state of health. I hope that no pains or expense will be spared to restore him. God grant that he may recover, and become sensible of the necessity to alter his mind, and prove thankful and grateful to God for his mercies. His God, from whose hand the thread of his life is suspended, will hear him, if, with a contrite heart he calls for mercy and forgiveness. I write under strong emotions of pain. God have him and you all in His holy keeping, is the prayer of your father,
S. S."

The Governor's long residence at the seat of government, during which he had not the leisure necessary for managing his extensive estates, and his liberality to his relatives and friends, had greatly embarrassed his affairs. The death of his son Frederick taking place at this time, broke his spirit. The powers of the other world soon claimed him for its silent fellowship. He is now united with the apostles and martyrs, the great and good of all ages, with those he so tenderly loved in life, and more than all, with his Saviour.

Governor Snyder's first wife was Elizabeth Michael, of Lancaster, by whom he had two children: Amelia, born 21st June, 1791. She was married March 28, 1820, by Doctor Dewitt to Doctor Phineas Jenks, member of the House from Bucks county, at Harrisburg. Mrs. Elsegood, wife of Reverend J. I. Elsegood, of East New York, is the only daughter of Amelia. The Honorable John Snyder, who married June 11, 1818, Mary Louisa Kittera, daughter of Honorable John Wilkes Kittera, of Lancaster, Congressman during the administration of General Washington, and until the election of

Thomas Jefferson, in 1801, when he died. John Snyder's children by his first wife are Miss Mary K. Snyder, postmistress at Selinsgrove, Mrs. Vandyke, who now lives in Lewisburg, widow of James C. Vandyke, Esquire, late United States district attorney for the eastern district of Pennsylvania. Among his children by subsequent marriage, is Mrs. G. W. Walls, of Lewisburg. Honorable John Snyder died at Selinsgrove, August 15, 1850. The children by his second marriage were Henry W. Snyder, born 20th July, 1797. He was a paymaster in the late war, and died at Fort Leavenworth, Kansas. Of his children, are Mrs. Joseph Musser, of Lewisburg, who has a portrait of her grandmother, which is certainly complimentary to the Governor's appreciation of beauty. George A. Snyder, a man of unmistakable genius, was the second son. His artist aspirations were early developed, and he desired his father to send him to Italy ; but he insisted upon making a lawyer of him. He never practiced, I believe. Taught school for the most part, and died in Williamsport on the 6th of July, 1865. During the war, being old and feeble, he still insisted upon doing something, and gathered all the newspapers that came in his way, cut out the interesting articles, and pasting them into small scrap-books, sent them to the hospitals to help the sick soldiers while away the tedious hours of sickness. His children are Mrs. Mathias App, now of Michigan ; Mrs. Kate Crane; Henry and George S., foundrymen of Williamsport, Pennsylvania; Mrs. Riley, Antes and Jesse D., of the same place.

Antes Snyder,[1] who died at Pottstown in December, 1861, where his widow, Mrs. Mary B., still resides, (1871,) was the child Mrs. Carson wished to kidnap, in order to obtain from the Governor the pardon of Smith. He well remembered how carefully he was guarded in door until after the execution of Smith. Antes was educated at West Point, graduated with high honors, and was soon afterwards sent by the Government to England on business connected with the railway system, then in its infancy here.

The Governor said, should Mrs. Carson succeed in the abduction of his child, the law should, nevertheless, have its course. He was spared the trial, but all who knew his stern integrity, felt assured

---

[1] Antes Snyder was the engineer who designed and built the large stone bridges over the Schuylkill, at the falls and Peacock's lock, above Reading, and one at Schuylkill Haven, and a number of small ones along the line of the Philadelphia and Reading railroad.

that the law would have been honored, even had he been put to so severe a test.

Governor Snyder was married the third time to Mary Slough Scott, a widow lady of Harrisburg, 16th October, 1814. She survived him, and died at Harrisburg October 8, 1823. She was a member of the Episcopal church, and was the first person who commenced a Sabbath-school in Selinsgrove. She is spoken of as a brilliant woman in society.

I quote from her letter to Amelia, dated Philadelphia, June 11, 1818, anticipating Honorable John Snyder's wedding. The garlands have faded this many a day ; their perfume may still linger in some households :

"MY DEAR AMELIA : At length I have a moment to devote to you, on the morning of the important day which is to connect us with Mary. At nine o'clock this evening Doctor Wilson will tie the knot. Mr. Peacock has stayed for the wedding. The fair bridesmaids are Mary Smith, Miss Houston, Hannah L. Orme. The groomsmen, Shunk, T. Conrad, Thomas and John Kittera. All the relatives will be here. The company will consist of about thirty persons. To-morrow, early, we set out, and will rest at Lancaster on Sunday, go to Harrisburg on Monday, and leave that on Thursday or Friday for Selinsgrove. I am very anxious about your father. Henry writes Mr. Peacock that he was unwell after I left him. I hope in God he is now well. Mr. Hemphill gave a dinner for me Tuesday. I had twelve of my particular friends to meet me last evening. I took tea with Mrs. Watson. She sends much love. It is so warm, I am obliged to ride everywhere, and Anthony is very accommodating. I long to get home again, and shall enjoy our old house more than ever, for this place is intolerably hot. Shunk [afterwards Governor Shunk] goes by his father's house, so we shall have no beaux. John Kittera cannot go home with us, but will be up in a few weeks. Mrs. Hall is still here, but goes home with Mrs. Humphrey and her daughter next week. Their new carriage is not yet done, and she is almost homesick. Shunk has just come in, and desires me to tell you he has tried to behave pretty, and is as polite as possible."

1820.

PHILIP MILLER was appointed court crier. He held this office thirty-three years, and was succeeded by Benjamin Shell, in 1853.

16th March, the division line of Mifflin and Union directed by act of Assembly, to be run by a surveyor appointed by the commissioners of each county; otherwise the line run by Peter Hackenberg made the line.—*P. L.* 1820, *page* 82.

28th March, James Dale, of Union, Jacob Cryder, of Centre, and John Hanna, of Lycoming, appointed to run the division line between Union and Centre counties.

In 1819 or 1820, Doctor Grier says, the Associate Reformed church, of Mifflinburg, was organized of Buffalo Cross-Roads members, a dissatisfaction having arisen on account of giving up Rouse's version, and adopting Watt's version, of the Psalms. James McClellan, Esquire, and Samuel Templeton were of the elders. James McClellan gave up his pew in Buffalo in April, 1820. So it was probably in this year. This church was served by the late Doctors George Junkin and David Kirkpatrick. In October, 1827, on application of Mr. Kirkpatrick and his congregation, they were received into and taken under the care of the Northumberland Presbytery. (This congregation is still served by Doctor Grier, although there is another Presbyterian church organized at Mifflinburg.)

Political.

At the October election for Governor, General Joseph Hiester received 1,621 votes, and William Findlay, 1,040 in Union county.

For Congress, Thomas Murray ran against William Cox Ellis. 4,341 tickets had the name of Thomas Murray on; 3,074 had Thomas Murray, junior. Mr. Ellis' vote in the district was 6,526, and he received the certificate, but not considering it fair, Mr. Ellis resigned in June, 1821, and another election was held that fall. At the November election James Monroe carried every State, John Quincy Adams receiving only one electoral vote, (in New Hampshire.)

Census 1820.

Penn's,	2,099	Hartley,		1,239
Centre,	2,094	New Berlin,		515
Beaver,	2,036	Union,		1,369
Perry,	1,330	White Deer,		1,677
Washington,	1,427	Lewisburg,		579
Mifflinburg,	620	Buffalo,		2,376
West Buffalo,	1,183			
Hartleton,	75	Total,		13,619

Value of leather manufactures, $19,200; linseed oil, $2,790; pottery, $1,050; whisky; corn and rye, used for, 16,000 bushels, value, twenty-five to thirty-one cents per gallon. Twenty-two stillhouses. Wheat manufactured into flour, 23,300 bushels. Fourteen mills in operation. For cotton yarn, one hundred and twenty spindles, one carding machine, one spinning machine. "The whole establishment gone to ruin for want of a market. It formerly employed four men and three boys."

Notices of Revolutionary Soldiers Residing in the County in 1820.

Brown, Jonathan, had served three years as a private in Captain Elijah Humphrey's company, Colonel William Douglas' regiment, and was sixty-two years old.

Britton, Joseph, enlisted at John Stetler's tavern, in Limerick township, Montgomery county, in the spring of 1776, in Captain Caleb North's company, of Colonel Anthony Wayne's regiment. Captain Frederick Evans testified in his behalf, that he had lived forty-three years before with David Evans, whose land joined his father's, in Montgomery county; that he recollected of hearing Britton had enlisted, and about a year afterwards he came back very much emaciated; that forty-four years had elapsed since he had seen Britton, and he was so much altered he had no recollection of his person; but from conversation with him, he had no doubt he was the same Joseph that had enlisted with Captain Caleb North's company, and marched to Ticonderoga. Britton was, in 1820, seventy-one years old, a farmer, and had a wife and two daughters.

Billman, Dewalt, aged sixty-seven, enlisted at Reading, in Captain Jacob Bowers' company.

Burd, Daniel, seventy-five years old, enlisted at Amboy, Colonel James Treddle's regiment; served five years nine months, except three months, when he was at home sick. He was wounded in the left thigh at Battle Hill, with two musket balls. He had two sons and four daughters, youngest named Anne.

Bower, George, of White Deer. Pressed in the fall of 1777 as teamster; had charge of an ammunition wagon at Valley Forge. Drafted in June, 1778; arrived on the field of Monmouth as the battle was closing. He received a sword cut on the knee from a British soldier who lay in ambush by the road. Recollected of seeing Lafayette at Monmouth.

Campbell, McDonald, served in Captain John Conway's company, Colonel William Wind's New Jersey regiment, thirteen months. Re-enlisted in Colonel John Conway's regiment and served nine months, and then was detailed by General Green as his express rider, and remained such during the war. Was a fifer in Captains Conway's and Furman's companies. He married a widow Valentine, who had two children, Jesse, aged thirteen, Jane, aged ten. His children by her were, Isaac Wilson Campbell, Sally Walls, Almeda, Eleanor, and Elizabeth; latter aged eight months.

Carney, Anthony, blacksmith, Hartley, enlisted in Orange county, North Carolina, served three years. He was sixty-seven in 1820, and had no family except his wife, Catherine.

Clemmens, Peter, private in Captain Stake's company, Colonel Butler's regiment, and served two years. He left a daughter, Elizabeth. His wife, Elizabeth, died in 1820.

Campbell, John, (still living in West Buffalo, 1838, and then eighty-three years old,) was drafted into the militia from Derry township, Lancaster county, in 1776, served under Captain Robert McKee, arrived at Trenton the day after the capture of the Hessians, and went thence to Morristown. Took oath of allegiance before Jacob Cooke, Esquire, 2d August, 1777. In the latter part of 1777, he was again drafted, and went to Trenton. Saw British horses and wagons brought into camp and sold at auction. His third tour was at the close of the war, in a company commanded by Lieutenant James Laird. They lay at Chestnut Hill awhile. General Potter and Major Stewart had a quarrel there about the treatment of the militia, and were on the point of fighting it out with their swords. Campbell moved to Buffalo Valley in 1777, lived on Captain Gray's farm one year, then moved to another farm of the captain's near James Dale's. He lived there seven years, then moved near Buffalo mountain, then into West Buffalo, where he died.

Cook, John, private in Captain Herbert's company, from Womelsdorf, who was taken prisoner at the surrender of Fort Washington, exchanged, and appointed ensign in the twelfth, Colonel Cooke's. He was unmarried and childless in 1820, seventy-eight years old.

Coryell, George, was a native of Hunterdon county, New Jersey, was born at Coryell's ferry, on the Delaware river, now Lambertville, on the 28th of April, 1761. He entered the army in Captain Craig's company of dragoons, in 1776, just after the taking of the Hessians, and before the cannonade at Trenton, on the 2d of January, 1777. His company marched up the creek, and was in the battle at Princeton. He was a year with Captain Craig. He was afterwards drafted into a company of dragoons, under Lieutenant Reading, in which he served one year. He was afterwards drafted into the company of Captain Palmer, in which he continued until the fall of 1780. He was only sixteen years of age when he enlisted, and while in Captain Craig's company, he was sent, as an express, to Boston, leaving orders at Danbury and other places on the route. He said there were gray-headed men and minors in Craig's company. At one time General Washington had his headquarters at his father's house, at the ferry, while the army encamped partly in his orchard. The British and Hessians got possession of his father's premises at one time, and cut the bedding, threw the feathers into the street, and burned all the fences on the farm, which lay in common a long time. George Coryell was married, in 1790, to a sister of Richard Van

Buskirk, of Mifflinburg, and moved, in 1793, to the premises of
Samuel Maclay, in Buffalo township. He was a carpenter by trade,
and built many houses in Buffalo Valley, among others, the old
"Black Horse tavern," at Lewisburg; of barns, he built the one
on Maclay's place, now owned by Joseph Green. In 1799 he was
captain of the Buffalo Valley Republican troop, and always rode on
parade days a sorrel horse that had been wounded at St. Clair's defeat. John Webb, a hatter, father of Colonel Webb, who, some
years ago, kept hotel in Philadelphia, was first lieutenant of the company. Webb lived in Mifflinburg, and moved to Ohio many years
ago. Coryell was adjutant of Colonel George Weirick's regiment, at
Marcus Hook, in 1814. He removed to Lycoming county once;
then back to Buffalo valley; then to White Deer valley; thence to
Butler county, near Hamilton, where he died, 1837–38. His wife
soon followed him to the grave. He had four sons, Tunison, John,
Joseph R., and Abraham, of whom Tunison, the eldest, and Abraham, the youngest, alone survive. There were several daughters,
most of whom ended their days in Ohio and Indiana. Tunison resides in Williamsport, and occupies the house in which he was married, in 1815, and where his golden wedding was celebrated.

Derr, Christian, West Buffalo, aged, in 1820, seventy-two. Enlisted at Reading, in Captain Nagle's company, Colonel Thompson's
regiment, and served one year; re-enlisted in November, 1776, in
Captain Moore's company, Colonel Humpton's regiment, and served
in the battle of King's Bridge, 11th January, 1777, Brandywine, and
Germantown. In the last action he was wounded, had several ribs
broken, and was, therefore, discharged. He was a carpenter, and had
eleven children. He had three balls in his body, which he carried
to his grave. His children were Ellis Derr, Mifflinburg; Samuel,
Uniontown; Henry, Schellsburg, Bedford county; Susan, married to
Jesse Egbert, afterwards David Kline, of Hartley; Polly, to ——
Jones, of Sugar valley; Elizabeth, to William Kepner, moved to
Venango; John, Oley township, Berks; Catherine, to Henry Barrich; Christian, junior, who died in Spring township, Centre county,
in 1852. His children live in and about Bellefonte: Daniel, Rachel,
married to William Young; William, in Benezet; Christian and
Solomon, in Bellefonte.

Ewig, Christian, aged sixty, enlisted at Sunbury, in Captain Weitzel's company, Colonel Miles' regiment, in April, 1776, served one year, nine months, then re-enlisted at Sunbury, in Captain James Wilson's First Pennsylvania, Colonel James Chambers, in which he served until the close of the war. A wheelwright by trade.

Kerstetter, George, blacksmith, Washington township, aged sixty-four. Served four years in Captain Burkhart's company, Colonel Hunsecker's regiment. Children: Jacob and Dorothy. Wife's name was Elizabeth.

Linn, John, aged sixty-five, enlisted in the winter of 1778, at Lancaster, in third troop, Captain Erasmus Gill, fourth regiment Pennsylvania cavalry, Colonel Stephen Moylan. Discharged in October, 1783. Had five children; Robert Bruce, born May 21, 1806: Altha, January 15, 1808; James Smith, October 20, 1811; Eliza, June 4, 1814; Mary Jane, November 23, 1816. Weaver by trade.

Lennox, George, private, Captain Bankson's company, Colonel Stewart's regiment.

Reger, Elias, enlisted in May, 1775, Captain George Nagle's company, Colonel Thompson, first rifle regiment. In the siege of Boston. Discharged at Long Island, in June, 1776. Cooper by trade. Seventy-seven years old.

Rorabaugh, Philip, Buffalo township, served three months in Pennsylvania line, Captain Slaymaker's company, Colonel Bull's regiment, while the army lay at Valley Forge. Served also in the campaign of 1794, known as the whisky insurrection, and three months in Captain John Bergstresser's company, at Marcus Hook, in 1814. This hero of three wars died February 3, 1837, aged eighty-six, and is buried in Lewisburg German grave-yard.

Swesey, Daniel, died in White Deer, 31st January, 1836, leaving a widow, Mary.

Strickland, Timothy, carpenter, Lewisburg, enlisted in 1776, in Berkshire county, Massachusetts, Captain Bacon's company, Colonel Porter's regiment, and served therein one year. Re-enlisted in September, 1777, in Captain Mill's company, New York State line, and was honorably discharged after three years' service. Aged in May, 1824, seventy-three, but very much crippled. He had four sons, (Samuel was a soldier of 1814.) His grandchildren reside still in Lewisburg; Cyrus, a grandson, in Bellefonte.

Smith, Adam, was a teamster during the Revolution. He settled upon the place now owned by Jacob Kunkle, above Henry Mertz's. He died there and was buried at the Dreisbach grave-yard. His sons were: Adam, George, Michael, and John, and a daughter, married to Michael Maize, another to Steffy Touchman. Adam, junior, moved to Beaver township, Snyder county. His descendants are about Beaver town yet. George died in Union county, John at Beaver town, and Michael in Union county, in 1841. He had a blacksmith shop above Henry Mertz's, and that is the point so often spoken of in old road views. Michael's children were Michael, who moved to Michigan; Daniel, who moved to Ohio; Benjamin, to Illinois; David, now, 1869, living near the old place. His daughters married, one to Jonas Nyhart, one to John Wolfe, one to David Oldt, near New Berlin. Michael had three wives: first was a Bower, of Dry valley; second, Susanna Bartges, of Mifflinburg; third, Sophia Bickle, whose father, Henry Bickle, was killed by the Indians. Michael had also a son Jonathan, father of A. W. Smith, Esquire, late jury commissioner, who died in Hartley township, in 1870.

Yiesely, Michael, aged sixty-seven, enlisted in August, 1776, in Captain B. Weiser's company, in Colonel Haussegger's regiment. Served during the war, and was discharged in 1783. He had a wife and five children, Henry, Catherine, George, Elizabeth, and Maria.

Deaths.

June 17, Paschal Lewis, aged sixty. His family: Elizabeth, widow, who died August 26, 1828, aged seventy-one. Margaret, married to Thomas Clingan; Mary, married to Samuel Wright, (she is still living in Stephenson county, Illinois;) Sarah, married to James Merrill, Esquire; Elizabeth L., wife of Robert Candor, Esquire; Amelia B., married to Samuel Heise, of Columbia.

1821.

Governor Hiester's Appointments—General Items.

PPOINTMENTS — Secretary of the Commonwealth. Andrew Gregg. Auditor General, James Duncan, of Carlisle. Samuel Cochran, Chester county, Surveyor General. (He held office nine years, under Governor Snyder.) James Brady, of Westmoreland, Secretary of the Land Office.

Prices current at Philadelphia, in April: wheat, seventy cents, rye thirty-seven, corn thirty-two, butter ten cents per pound, bacon seven per pound, whiskey twenty cents per gallon. In July wheat advanced to eighty cents; in October to ninety, and in November to $1 50. The other grains proportionably. February 19, "a comet made its appearance in the western horizon. It was seen last evening between seven and eight o'clock, considerably elevated, and could be found by drawing a line due north from the planet Saturn. It was but a few degrees from it." On June 8th the locusts made their appearance in great numbers in Buffalo Valley.

The Union county Democratic nominations were Ner Middleswarth and James Dale, for Assembly; commissioner, Joseph Fuehrer; auditor, John Maclay; all opposed to Hiester. The Federal party had really gone under, and politics was now confined to factions in the Democratic ranks. Binns and Buchanan appear among the Hiester men, who are called bank men, and aristocrats, and "Feds." The Findlay papers style themselves indifferently Democrats, Democratic-Republicans, and Republicans.

In Union county, Thomas Murray, (Findlay,) for Congress, had ten hundred and forty-five; William Cox Ellis, opposition, eight hundred and thirty-six; and Murray was elected in the district by a small majority. The fall election resulted in the choice of a Legislature in opposition to Governor Hiester, which elected William Findlay United States Senator.

Deaths.

Among deaths this year were, June 27, Captain William F. Buyers, former editor of the *Times*, Sunbury, aged forty; and December 7, John Baker, of Buffalo, aged sixty-five.

1822.

CERTAIN LAWS—NEWSPAPERS NOTICED—DEATH OF WILLIAM CLINGAN, ESQUIRE, HONORABLE ANDREW ALBRIGHT, AND HENRY PONTIUS.

HE act of February 18, Pamphlet Laws, 29, required all the original lists of assessments for land situate in Union county, to be transmitted to the commissioners of Union county, and were made evidence in suits.

March 21, Lewisburg incorporated as a borough.—(*Pamphlet Laws*, 68.) The election place was fixed at Randall Wilcox's, who kept the Black Horse, and John Nesbit and Alexander Graham were appointed to superintend the first election.

March 25, Northumberland and Union placed in the ninth senatorial district, and entitled to two members.

April 2, Union, Northumberland, Columbia, Luzerne, Susquehanna, Bradford, Lycoming, Tioga, Potter, and McKean placed in one congressional district, and entitled to three members, and on the same day the borough of Lewisburg was erected into a separate election district.

In January, the prices current in Philadelphia for wheat was $1.12; rye, 60 cents; corn, 62: oats, 30. In April wheat rose to $1.20, and in May it stood at $1.48.

Nathaniel Henrie bought out the New Berlin *Gazette*, of Frederick Wise, and started the Union *Times*. May 31, Simon Cameron became the junior editor of the *Intelligencer* at Harrisburg. Hugh Maxwell was editing the opposition paper at Lancaster.

In December, a special election, occasioned by the death of Andrew Albright, resulted in the election of Lewis Dewart, Federal, as he was called, over Ner Middleswarth and E. G. Bradford, Democrats, to the State Senate. The vote was light, and stood in the district: Dewart, 1192; Middleswarth, 1059; Bradford, 606.

Marriages.

At Selinsgrove, March 28, George A. Snyder, Esquire, to Miss Ann Ellen, daughter of the late Stephen Duncan. June 11, at Lewisburg, by John Nesbit, Esquire, Lewis Moore to Dorothy Smith.

Deaths.

January 23, Catherine, widow of Elias Youngman. She was born in 1745, and was a daughter of George Nagel, sheriff of Berks county in 1772. May 24, William Clingan, Esquire, of White Deer, aged sixty-six. He left a widow, Jane. Children: Margaret, wife of Thomas Scott; Ann, wife of Joseph Lawson; Thomas; Elizabeth, married to Thomas Barber; George, and Flavel. His wife was a daughter of Reverend John Roan. They were married June 11, 1778, and resided on a farm, which is now within the borough of Mount Joy, Lancaster county, until their removal to Buffalo Valley, in 1800. William Clingan, member of Congress from Chester county, during the Revolution, was his uncle. August 9, Mary, wife of Peter Himmelreich, and daughter of Captain Peter Withington, deceased. Born July 18, 1765. Buried in the Dreisbach church-yard.

Tuesday, November 26, Honorable Andrew Albright died at Sunbury, after an illness of three months, in his fifty-third year. He was born at Litiz, February 28, 1770. His father's name was Andrew; his mother, Elizabeth Orth, of Lebanon. His first wife was a daughter of Melchoir Rahm, a very prominent man in Dauphin county. Mr. Albright came to Lewisburg in 1798 and opened a tavern where Halfpenny's factory now stands, where he resided until he was elected sheriff, when he removed to Sunbury. He was member of Assembly in 1808. His wife died March 9, 1810, and he subsequently married the mother of Mrs. John G. Youngman, of Sunbury. He was appointed associate judge in 1813, in place of General Wilson, deceased, and had just been elected to the State Senate when he died. He was noted for his integrity, and was very popular throughout our Valley. He owned Colonel Slifer's upper farm on Buffalo creek when he died. He left no children, but brothers, Henry, Jacob, Godfrey, and a sister, Susanna, married to Philip Backman. An obituary in the *Sunbury Enquirer* of that date concludes: "Society has been deprived of a valuable member, and a wife of an amiable husband. In private life he sustained the character of an honest man and christian, and was universally beloved. He has held various public and responsible offices, with honor to himself and advantage to his fellow-citizens."

December 13, Henry Pontius. He was born on the 25th of February, 1744, came into the Valley as a pioneer at the close of the French war, and permanently in 1770. He was a son of John, and his brothers were Andrew, Peter, Nicholas, John, junior, George, and Frederick. Henry Pontius left a large family: Andrew, born June 17, 1770; Frederick, June, 1772; Henry, December 22, 1773; Nicholas, 19th April, 1775; Catherine, (King,) 19th May, 1777; John, October 8, 1778; George, 13th December, 1780; Peter, 20th March, 1783; Christena, 12th June, 1785; Barbara, June 13, 1787; Philip, August 15, 1789. The latter died upon the old place on Cedar run, a mile east of Mifflinburg, in 1872. He was a fine old gentleman, and his excellent memory preserved many incidents related in these Annals. His remains now moulder with their ancestral dust, in the old burying-ground upon the place.

1823.

GENERAL ITEMS—ELECTION RETURNS—CHRISTIAN CHAPEL AT LEWISBURG—KELLY TOWNSHIP.

ARKET quotations in Philadelphia: Wheat, $1 35; rye, 75 cents; butter, 18 cents; whisky, 28 cents. David Ramsay carried on a fulling and carding-mill in White Deer; Daniel Moyer at Weiser's old mill in East Buffalo. Thomas R. Lewis kept hotel at the sign of "The Lewisburg Stage," on Market, above A. Graham's store.

14th March, first election held under the borough charter of Lewisburg: John Nesbit, burgess; James Geddes, Alexander Graham, George Knox, Henry Beck, and William Hayes, council. 3d May, meeting of the stockholders of the Lewisburg bridge; George Kremer elected president, and the first dividend of $1 50 per share of $50 was declared. 15th May, the Lewistown convention held; Dan Caldwell and John Stees delegates from Union; Andrew Gregg nominated for Governor. 9th August, a Republican meeting held at New Berlin; Frederick Evans, president; Andrew McClenachan and George A. Snyder, secretaries; in favor of J. A. Shulze for Governor. October 4, Simon Snyder, junior, and James Dale, candidates on the Shulze ticket for Assembly; William Hayes and Francis A. Boyer on the Gregg ticket; Uriah Silsby for commissioner on the Shulze ticket, against John Rank. October 5, Andrew Reedy, in pursuance of a banter from Major John C. Coverly, attended at his house and counted down $1,000, which he offered to bet on Shulze's election, and could get no takers.

ELECTION RETURNS—October, 1823.

DISTRICTS.	GOVERNOR.		ASSEMBLY.				COMM'RS.	
	Gregg.	Shulze.	Boyer.	Hayes.	Dale.	Snyder.	Rank.	Silsby.
Centre, ...	106	106	112	111	98	94	108	100
Weirick's, . . .	26	74	29	30	72	70	26	74
Chapman, . . .	61	73	70	70	62	62	43	69
Perry, ...	29	94	30	23	97	95	27	97
Beaver, ...	102	183	98	98	186	185	97	188
Washington, . .	82	79	10	83	73	65	84	76
Penn's, ...	132	183	135	145	175	165	134	179
Lewisburg, . . .	51	62	51	64	59	52	37	76
Hartley, ...	90	153	88	96	152	149	89	148
White Deer, . . .	77	210	66	83	223	211	41	250
East Buffalo, . .	62	209	60	71	209	102	55	215
West Buffalo, . .	144	164	141	45	168	151	136	171
Union, ...	141	181	137	139	178	171	126	178
	1103	1765	1117	1058	1752	1572	1003	1821

November 15, the stockholders in the German school-house in Lewisburg met, and elected Henry Hursh, Charles Beyers, and John Martin, trustees, and decided by vote that the trustees should select the school-master, instead of the stockholders. This school-house was situated on the lot now occupied by the Lutheran parsonage, and was erected before 1812, and kept in repair by subscription.

14th September, Sabbath, the Christian chapel in Lewisburg was opened for worship. Reverend James Kay delivered a sermon on the occasion. It will be gratifying to the friends of religious liberty and free inquiry to learn that this church has been built upon the most liberal principles, and is intended to accommodate all those who acknowledge the divine mission of our Lord Jesus Christ.—*Miltonian.* Elijah Bacon commenced a series of meetings in 1822, which resulted in the formation of this congregation. There were to be no pews in the church, but Elder Badger, who succeeded him before the church was completed, had them put in. George Richmond became the preacher in 1825. Bacon's points were mainly against the discipline of the orthodox, and the church was open to all persons for free discussion of religious tenets.

The *Times* of Saturday, November 1, says: "On Friday morning last, as Mr. Jacob Yutten, son-in-law of Mr. Royer, of East Buffalo township, in this county, was engaged, with several others, in tearing down a log house, to move it a short distance, he fell, and, distressing to relate, hit his head again a joist, and mangled it in such a manner that he expired immediately after."

Friday, December 4, the first snow of the season fell.

Kelly Township first called Pike.

At December sessions, 1823, Adam Wilt, Christian Miller, and George Aurand reported a new township, to be erected from White Deer, and called Pike. This report was set aside, at the instance of Dan Caldwell, so Flavel Clingan informed me, and new viewers appointed, of whom Frederick Evans was one, who finally reported a township, to be called Kelly, after Colonel Kelly.

Marriages.

18th March, John P. Gutelius, of Mifflinburg, to Miss Maria Aurand, of Lebanon. 10th April, Conrad Grove, merchant, of New Berlin, to Miss Mary Gingerich, of Juniata county. 31st July, by Reverend Samuel Gutelius, Michael Hoffman to Lydia Wagner, both of White Deer. September 25, by Reverend John Thomas, Jacob Wagoner to Rachel, daughter of Thomas McGuire, of White Deer.

1824.

KELLY TOWNSHIP ERECTED—STATE ROAD FROM BELLEFONTE TO THE MOUTH OF WHITE DEER CREEK—POLITICAL—THE CLOWN AND ROPE DANCER AT NEW BERLIN—SNYDER'S HEIRS VS. SIMON SNYDER—SHOW OF WAX FIGURES—TRIAL OF SAMUEL JOHNSTON.

REDERICK EVANS to George Kremer, at Washington, D. C.—"3d January. Duncan's wife, of Penn's valley, died lately, and Thomas R. Lewis died about the same time. Sick since November 8. Solomon Betz and Wormly's trial came on last court. Verdict for Wormly, $195. Betz cut scollops until he had the judges and jurors angry. [This is an allusion to the celebrated trial between Betz and Wormly, about a piece of stove-pipe, that lasted many years, and broke up Wormly.] 8th February. Yesterday I was over at court, and find we shall send delegates to Harrisburg, with instructions to vote for General Jackson. If we cannot succeed, then to use a sound discretion. My opinion would be, to say, if we cannot get Jackson nominated, our delegates should withdraw. [He, with others, was getting the grist ready for the county convention.] But I do not believe such a motion would carry, if made. I spoke with Middleswarth. He says he is for Jackson, but will support the congressional caucus man. I think if a caucus cannot be prevented, the friends of Jackson should attend, but not pledge themselves to a foul nomination. I saw Dan Caldwell. He says McClenachan is opposed to Jackson, and one Reed, and they are all the opponents he has in the township, [White Deer,] if Caldwell tells the truth."

Kelly township was erected during this year. After careful search, I could not find the record. The first constable, however, was Albright Bower, who attended at May sessions, 1825.

On the 29th of March, an act was passed to lay out the State road from Bellefonte, by way of Sugar valley, to the river, at the mouth of White Deer creek.

Political.

September 17, the Democratic-Republican convention met at New Berlin, John Snyder, president; William Linn, secretary. Kremer, Montgomery, and McKean nominated for Congress; Aaron Chamberlin and F. P. Deering for Assembly.

5th October, Independent-Republican meeting, Joseph Musser, chairman; Mathew Brewer, secretary. Peter Hackenburg and James McClellan nominated for Assembly; George Weirick for commissioner. At the conferee meeting, on the 21st of September, McKean, Kremer, and Espy Van Horne were nominated.

In November, Union county gave seven hundred majority for Andrew Jackson, twenty-six votes for Crawford, two for Clay.

Social.

The following are the names of a dancing party at Mrs. Grossman's tavern, in New Berlin, on the evening of February 12: John Lashells, Esquire, and wife, James Merrill, Robert Forster, John Mumma, Nathaniel Henrie, Henry M. W. Kirke, Elias P. Youngman, Robert P. Maclay, Conrad Grove, John Maize, George Shock, John Seebold, John Lotz, James F. Linn, Mrs. Henrie, Elizabeth Jones, Sarah Messimer, Catherine Jones, Mrs. Grove, Elizabeth Brooke, Margaret Kessler, Mary L. Duncan, Sarah Weikert, Margaret C. Lashells, Eleanor C. Lashells, Elizabeth S. Stillwell, Elizabeth Winters, Sarah A. Ingram. John Mumma and James F. Linn were managers.

It was a Buffalo Valley custom, on wedding occasions, to welcome the bride with a party composed of elderly folks. Here is a list, Wednesday night, October 20: Colonel John Kelly, Elizabeth Kelly, Doctor Robert Vanvalzah, Elizabeth Vanvalzah, William Poak, Esquire, and wife, James Dale, Esquire, Mrs. Eliza Dale,

Colonel Aaron Chamberlin and wife, Andrew McBeth and wife, John Campbell, Maria Campbell, Thomas Sawyer, Elizabeth Sawyer, William Linn and wife, Charles Maclay, Elizabeth Vanvalzah. The next evening, October 21st, at the same place, the festivities were taken up by the young people, of whom were: William Kelly, Andrew Kelly, Joseph Kelly, Robert P. Maclay, Samuel Gamble, James Mathers, F. F. Linn, James Sawyer, Joseph Candor, John Young, John Vanvalzah, Robert Forster, John Chamberlin, Mrs. S. Kelly, Miss Sarah Dorrough, Sarah McClellan, Margaret and Catherine McClellan, Sarah Forster, Hetty Forster, Catherine Hood, Mary Hood, Frances Chamberlin, Elizabeth Vanvalzah, Margaret Vanvalzah, Harriet Candor, Matilda Sawyer, Eleanor Young, Jane Davidson.

A Rope Dancer at New Berlin.

"This summer a rope-dancer and his clown visited New Berlin, and put up at Seebold's, where he proposed to display his agility for the amusement of the people and the replenishment of his pockets. Before he mounted the slack rope, however, he must needs make an equestrian display, in order to attract the attention of the public. He applied to me for my horse, but I declined giving it. Nat Henrie, a waggish printer, happened to be present, volunteered to lend him his, a handsome, young gray mare. The offer was accepted, and Nat went away to bridle her. He soon came back to my office, and notified me that there would be some fun presently. He said he had put on the mare a broken bit, which he had mended with twine. He said the mare was as wild as the devil, and if the clown attempts to hold her in with that bridle, there will be a ride worth seeing. Nat then walked over to Seebold's, and engaged the clown in conversation, while the showman, dressed in red jacket, white pants, white kid boots, and with his hair put up like a lady's, with side combs and in puffs, mounted and set out. When Nat judged that the showman had made sufficient headway, he let loose his hold of the clown's stirrup. The clown followed his master at a full gallop, with a whoop and halloo; the mare quickened her speed at the sound. The showman drew bridle with all his strength, the bit gave way, the rider fell on his back, with his heels in the air, and then, rolling off, alighted on hands and knees upon the ground.

Nat ran to his stable, whither the affrighted mare had fled, put on another bridle, and, returning, condoled with the showman on his misfortune, and offered him the chance of another ride. This he declined. The show was not good that night, on account of the want of agility of the rope-dancer."

4th December, the first snow of the winter fell. 24th and 25th December, show of wax figures at Christopher Seebold's, in New Berlin: Macbeth Consulting the Witch; General Butler and the Indian; Two Chinese Dwarfs; An American Dwarf; Harriet Newell presenting Tracts to Heathen Children; Seven Boys Chiming Bells; hand organ. Admittance, twelve and a half cents.

If a man had a lion or leopard, a porcupine or the skin of a huge snake, he wandered about the country, collecting the odd change of idlers, children, and curiosity hunters. These were usually exhibited in a stable or out-house. Theaters and rope dancing in the ball-rooms of the tavern, rooms communicating with folding-doors, of which the hotels of the olden times were never without. There was exhibited a cat's skin, which excited considerable attention, and was, indeed, a great curiosity. The skin was white, except a black spot in the middle of the back, resembling the bust of a man in profile. So perfect was the resemblance, that it required close examination to satisfy the beholder that the picture was not a work of art. The owner, on one occasion, refused three thousand dollars for it. I cannot tell what has become of it, but believe the owner took it to Europe, and disposed of it. This fact should induce us to be less skeptical as to some of the stories of the ancient historians about the *lusus naturæ*, which so often alarmed the superstitious Greeks and Romans. The outline of the head was as perfect and complete in all its parts as if it had come from the hands of the most skillful profile cutter.—*G. A. S.*

John Snyder's Heirs vs. Simon Snyder.

This hardly-contested case deserves especial mention from the great interest it excited in the minds of our people at that time. It was originally brought at Sunbury, and the claim was for ninety-three acres of land on the Isle of Que. George A. Snyder's narrative of it is as follows:

John Snyder, brother of my father, purchased the property of Peter Weiser, in 1785. John died from a fall from his horse, and his widow removed to Lancaster, with her children. She afterwards married Jacob Kendig, who lived a mile from Selinsgrove, up the road to Sunbury.

Simon Snyder, John Miller, and Martin Kendig were appointed administrators of John Snyder. The estate was incumbered largely, and an order of sale was obtained. The property was offered for sale at Selinsgrove, and adjourned, for want of bidders, to Sunbury, and, on the 12th of November, 1790, was struck off to Anthony Selin, who married my father's sister. My father advised Selin not to buy, thinking he would have trouble in paying for it. Just as it was about being struck down, Jacob Kendig put in a bid, for what reason he never explained, but as he and the whole party were somewhat fuddled, he probably bid to vex Selin. The purchaser, after some swearing at Kendig, treated all hands, and they got into the ferry scow with unsteady steps and heated brains. On the water Selin took occasion to call Kendig a damned rascal, and then to lick him for not acknowledging the truth of the charge.

Selin entered into possession, and commenced farming the land. He was then in partnership with my father in a mill, erected on a tract of forty-two acres, part of the tract originally owned by John Snyder, and which they had purchased of John, in 1787. Selin died in 1792, leaving two children, Anthony and Agnes. The latter married James K. Davis, about the year 1808. My father was nominated for Governor, and, among other slanderous reports started against him, was one that he had been in league with Selin, and cheated his brother's orphan children out of the land. Daniel Smith, a lawyer and active politician, is supposed to have been the originator of the story. At all events, he was active in spreading it, and persuaded the guardians of John Snyder's children to bring an ejectment for the land.

The plaintiff on the trial, before Judge Chapman, claimed on three grounds: 1. That the orphans' court proceedings were irregular. 2. That Selin's violent conduct at the sale prevented others from bidding. 3. That Simon Snyder was in partnership with Selin in the purchase, had come into possession after Selin's death, and had spoken of the property as his own. The first ground, being matter of record, was decided by the court to be insufficent. The second and third grounds, if proved to the satisfaction of the jury, were sufficent to justify a verdict for the plaintiff. The jury, however, without much hesitation, gave a verdict for the defendant. The judgment was reversed on some exceptions to the admission of testimony being such as lawyers are wont to make in order to have the chance of another trial.

Soon after the decision, Anthony Snyder (John's son) removed to the Genessee country, (New York.) He became a pettifogger, and met with great success in his vocation. Union county was erected in 1813, and the cause removed thither. Anthony Snyder and Daniel Rhoads came to Pennsylvania, as the representatives of the plaintiffs, to attend to the trial. There being much delay in coming to trial, on account of the difficulty of collecting the witnesses, who were numerous and much scattered, and on account of the indolence and dilatory temper of Judge Chapman, Anthony and Daniel traversed the county, visiting the taverns and all kinds of gatherings, and holding forth in piteous style on the subject of the frauds, whereby the defendant had cheated his orphan nephews and neices out of their inheritance. A general prejudice was thus excited, and an impartial trial became impossible. Had the judge been a man of courage and firmness, in whose legal qualifications the bar and the public had confidence, he might have secured a righteous verdict. But the clamor terrified him. He continued the cause from term to term, and from year to year, on almost any pretext; his fears and indolence making him unwilling to face the long and wearisome case.

The second trial came off, I think, in 1816. The judge saw clearly where justice was, but, weak and timid, he shuffled in his decisions and in his charge, and there was a verdict for the plaintiffs. The partnership they endeavored to prove by general repute. Their only witnesses were illiterate, and sometimes dishonest, laborers, who had, more than twenty years before, worked for Selin and my father; while Kremer, Evans, Simon Snyder, junior, well acquainted with the parties, testified to the real extent of the partnership.

The amount of perjury on the plaintiff's side was surprisingly great. The main witness to the allegation that Selin's threats had frightened off bidders was a man named Bower, from Dauphin county, who swore that but for Selin's threats he would have given £400 or £500 more. The defendant proved that Bower said on his way home that the land went too high, and no sane man would give so much for it.

The oldest land-holders of the vicinity, Boyd, DeGruchy, Leisenring, Taggert, Dentler, and others, unanimously testified the land sold above its value, it being island land.

The defendant's counsel, apprehending the result from the violence of the prejudice, presented numerous points, and upon a writ of error, the judgment was reversed. Soon after this my father died, and Anthony Selin, the younger, and James K. Davis, were substituted as defendants. An attempt was made to put the costs, thus far accrued, upon Simon Snyder's estate ; but the court decided that Selin's heirs had all the time been the real defendants, and that Simon Snyder had only been nominally defendant.

The cause was tried again in 1823 ; Lashells and Hepburn for plaintiffs ; Bellas and Greenough for defendants. The clamors of the plaintiffs and the weakness of the judge made it more than ever a hopeless task for the defendants. A verdict was again had against them, followed by a reversal by the Supreme Court. Another verdict must have been, under our judicial system, final, provided it should be for the plaintiffs, and this was almost certain to be the case. The defendants resolved to refer the case to arbitrators. I was prothonotary, and, on account of my consanguinity to defendants, liable to be objected to. Mr. Maclay, the register, acted in my place. He was an upright man, and performed his duty faithfully. The number of referees was five. Joseph Rathfon was the only one that was not objected to of the five nominated by each party. Mr. Maclay made then a list of twenty names, and each party struck eight names. The board thus formed, Dan Caldwell, Michael Rathfon, Valentine Haas, John Reifsnyder, and Joseph Spotts, gave an award for the defendants. Plaintiffs then resolved to appeal, and Doctor Atlee, of Philadelphia, came with Mr. Lashells, the leading counsel on his side, to enter the appeal. I was desired to take the necessary affidavit and bond, and lay them aside for the present, until the costs, which were necessary to be paid, should be forwarded, and then I was to file the affidavit and enter the appeal. The taxation of costs was difficult and tedious. Many of the subpœnas had been lost, and as no account had been kept of time, the defendants had to make their bill very low to avoid exceptions. The amount, however, after all allowances, was upwards of $1,500. The twenty days elapsed, and no costs were paid ; the defendants demanded judgment, which I entered with good-will. So ended the Isle of Que case.

The reason why the costs were not forthcoming, we learned afterwards. When Doctor Atlee got back to Philadelphia, he took counsel of David Paul Brown, his attorney, who advised him not to pay over the costs, as the mere taking of the affidavit and bond for future costs constituted an appeal—that I would be liable to the defendants for costs. When Mr. Lashells wrote to inquire why the costs were not forthcoming, and was informed of Mr. Brown's advice, he refused to be a party to any such unfair dealing, and added that he felt sure the court would not allow an appeal to be entered ; that it was ungenerous to throw Mr. Snyder into the costs for an act of kindness to Doctor Atlee, to save him a journey from Philadelphia, by taking the affidavit and bond while he was at New Berlin.

The plaintiffs then brought a suit in the United States court, at Philadelphia, for that part which lay west of Penn's creek, and on which Selinsgrove was built. The first attempts to bring on the suit to trial failed, for the absence of witnesses, who were too old and infirm to go so far. A rule to take depositions was then entered. Here David Paul once more proved their evil genius. The rule of court required the depositions to be forwarded under the seal of the justice or commissioner, to the clerk of the court, to be by him opened. The justice did his part correctly, but the bearer, who was a friend of the plaintiffs, handed them first to Mr. Brown, who ignorantly, or regardless of the rule, broke them open and perused them. He then took them to the clerk, but the latter refused either to receive or file them. A few days afterward the case was called up, the depositions were rejected by the court, and the plaintiffs suffered a non-suit.

December 25, Samuel Johnston, aged twelve, tried for setting fire to his uncle Jacob Johnston's barn, in West Buffalo. He was convicted, but obtaining a new trial, was acquitted at May sessions, 1825. Mumma, district attorney, and C. A. Bradford for Commonwealth ; Horning, Van Horne, Packer, and W. Cox Ellis for defendant.

Deaths.

April 9, William Wilson, of Kelly township, aged eighty-two. He came into the Valley in 1772, and his eldest daughter, Martha, was born in 1774. His children were: Thomas, born August 18, 1776, died May 23, 1831; James, born August 3, 1778, died December 26, 1831; Mary, born April 14, 1783, married William Hayes, died December 10, 1827; William, junior, many years a merchant at Lewisburg, born August 10, 1787, died June 12, 1783; Samuel, died January 16, 1843; Effie, married to William Murray, died January 23, 1853; Eliza, who married Peter Nevius, alone survives.

David Soult, born March 18, 1752, enlisted in Northampton county, in Captain Marien Lamar's company, and served in Canada in 1776, and afterwards enlisted in the second Pennsylvania. His captain, who was major of the second, was killed at Paoli. Soult was in the battles of Brandywine, Germantown, Monmouth, and at the storming of the block-house. He left five children: John, Jacob, Philip, George, and Michael.

October 4, at New Berlin, Adam Specht, shoe-maker; enlisted as a private, (in Colonel Nicholas Haussegger's German regiment,) at Shafferstown, May, 1776; discharged at Northumberland by Lieutenant Colonel Lewis Wiltner, in 1779.

Marriages.

22d July, Nathan Jordan, merchant, to Miss Hannah Smith, both of White Deer. 24th August, by Reverend Heim, Conrad Pontius, of Ohio, to Miss Mary Seebold, of New Berlin. 26th, by Reverend Thomas Hood, Captain James Magee to Miss Elizabeth Strayhorn, of West Buffalo. 14th October, William Linn, of Kelly, to Miss Jane Morrow, of Franklin county. 14th October, by Reverend Jacob W. Smith, Martin Dreisbach, junior, to Miss Elizabeth, daughter of Solomon Kleckner. 31st October, by Reverend Martin Dreisbach, Isaac Peters to Miss Susan Miller, of New Berlin. December 16, William C. Stedman to Elizabeth, daughter of Hugh Wilson.

1825.

GEORGE KREMER'S ARTICLE IN THE "COLUMBIAN OBSERVER," AND HENRY CLAY'S CARD—RECEPTION OF MR. KREMER AT LEWISBURG—WEATHER RECORD—PECULIARITIES OF THE BAR—THE SHOWMAN AT NEW BERLIN—WITCHCRAFT FARCE IN BEAVER TOWNSHIP.

[From the Columbian Observer.]

WASHINGTON, *January* 25, 1825.

EAR SIR: I take up my pen to inform you of one of the most disgraceful transactions that ever covered with infamy the Republican ranks. Would you believe that men professing *Democracy* could be found base enough to lay the axe at the very root of the tree of Liberty? Yet, strange as it is, it is not less true. To give you a full history of the transaction would far exceed the limits of a letter. I shall, therefore, at once proceed to give you a brief account of such a bargain as can only be equalled by the *Famous Burr Conspiracy* of 1801. For some time past, the friends of Clay have hinted that they, like the Swiss, would fight for those who would pay best. Overtures were said to have been made by the friends of Adams to the friends of Clay, offering him the appointment of Secretary of State for his aid to elect Adams. And the friends of Clay gave this information to the friends of Jackson, and hinted that if the friends of Jackson would offer the same price, they would close with them. But none of the friends of Jackson would descend to such mean barter and sale. It was not believed by any of the friends of Jackson that this contract would be ratified by the members from the States who had voted for Mr. Clay.

I was of opinion, when I first heard of this transaction, that men, professing any honorable principles, could not, nor would not, be

transferred like the planter does his negroes, or the farmer his team
and horses. No alarm was excited—we believed the Republic was
safe. The nation, having delivered Jackson into the hands of Congress, backed by a large majority of their votes, there was on my
mind no doubt that Congress would respond to the will of the nation,
by electing the individual they had declared to be their choice. Contrary to this expectation, it is now ascertained to a certainty that
Henry Clay has transferred his interest to John Quincy Adams. As
a consideration for this abandonment of duty to his constituents, it
is said and believed, should this unholy coalition prevail, Clay is to
be appointed Secretary of State. I have no fears on my mind—I
am clearly of opinion we shall defeat every combination. The force
of public opinion must prevail, or there is an end of liberty.

[From the National Intelligencer.]

A CARD.—I have seen, without any other emotion than that of
ineffable contempt, the abuse which has been poured upon me by a
scurrilous paper, issued in this city, and by other kindred prints and
persons, in regard to the presidential election. The editor of one
of those prints, ushered forth in Philadelphia, called the *Columbian
Observer*, for which I do not subscribe, and which I have not ordered, has had the *impudence* to transmit to me his *vile paper* of the
28th instant. In that number is inserted a letter, purporting to have
been written from this city, on the 25th instant, by a member of the
House of Representatives, belonging to the Pennsylvania delegation.
I believe it to be a *forgery;* but, if it be genuine, I pronounce the
member, whoever he may be, *a base and infamous calumniator*, A
DASTARD, and A LIAR, and if he dare unveil himself and avow his
name, I will hold him RESPONSIBLE, as I here admit myself to be, to
all THE LAWS which govern and regulate the conduct of MEN OF
HONOR.

H. CLAY.

31st *January*, 1825.

ANOTHER CARD.—George Kremer, of the House of Representatives, tenders his respects to the Honorable "H. Clay," and informs
him that, by reference to the editor of the *Columbian Observer*, he
may ascertain the name of the writer of a letter of the 25th ultimo,
which it seems has afforded so much concern to "H. Clay." In the
meantime, George Kremer holds himself responsible to prove, to the

satisfaction of unprejudiced minds, enough to satisfy them of the accuracy of the statements which are contained in that letter, to the extent that they concern the course and conduct of "H. Clay." Being a representative of the people, he will not fear to "cry aloud and spare not," when their rights and privileges are at stake.

On the return of Mr. Kremer, the citizens of Lewisburg assembled at the house of Thomas R. Lewis. Alexander Graham was chosen chairman, and John Sargeant, secretary. The object of the meeting being stated from the chair, the following resolutions were unanimously adopted, viz:

Resolved, That James Geddes, Doctor Thomas Vanvalzah, Daniel C. Ambler, Jacob Bogar, and Doctor William Joyce, be a committee of arrangement to carry the object of the meeting into effect, and that they draft an address to the Honorable George Kremer, inviting him to a public dinner, at thé house of T. R. Lewis, on Saturday, the 26th instant.

Resolved, That a general invitation be given to the friends of the Honorable George Kremer.

Committee's Invitation.

DEAR SIR: We, the undersigned, appointed a committee of arrangement, present our compliments to you, and respectfully request the honor of your company, at the house of Thomas R. Lewis, on Saturday, the 26th instant, to partake of a public dinner, with your fellow-citizens of the borough of Lewisburg and its vicinity, to be given as a manifestation of their respect and gratitude for your firm, dignified, and patriotic conduct, as a member of the House of Representatives of the United States; but more especially for your unremitted and vigorous efforts to stem the torrent of corruption, which threatened to inundate the national Legislature.

With sentiments of esteem, we remain yours, dear sir, very respectfully,

                     WILLIAM JOYCE,
                     JAMES GEDDES,
                     T. VANVALZAH,
                     D. C. AMBLER,
                     JACOB BOGAR.

The Honorable GEORGE KREMER.

To which Mr. Kremer returned the following answer:

LEWISBURG, *March* 23, 1825.

GENTLEMEN: Your friendly invitation to me, to partake of a public dinner at the house of T. R. Lewis, on the 26th instant, has just been received. This new testimonial of regard and kindness towards me is a sure pledge that the representative who discharges his duty with good faith, will always be supported and sustained by a virtuous and patriotic people. I need not say to you, that however averse I should feel on ordinary occasions, on the present I shall waive all objections, and do myself the pleasure to dine with my fellow-citizens. Accept the assurance of my sincere respect and regard.

GEORGE KREMER.

Messrs. JAMES GEDDES, Doctor THOMAS VANVALZAH, D. C. AMBLER, Doctor WILLIAM JOYCE, JACOB BOGAR.

On Saturday, the 26th, pursuant to previous arrangement, the long room of Mr. Lewis was crowded to overflowing. Colonel James Dale was called to the chair, and John Sargent appointed Secretary.

The company sat down to a splendid entertainment provided for the occasion. After the cloth was removed, the following toasts were drunk with much hilarity and good glee. * * * *

9. Honorable George Kremer, our worthy guest, the intrepid and watchful guardian of the people's rights—When corruption reared its hydra head, he "cried aloud, and spared not." [Here Mr. Kremer rose, and delivered a short and very appropriate address.]

Volunteers.

By Jonathan Smith: The intrepid Kremer—Like David of old, he slew the modern Goliah, the giant of intrigue, made of Clay, daubed with corruption.

William Kelly: The apostate BRECK—a member of Congress, belonging to the Pennsylvania delegation; he was surely a bastard, not a legitimate son of Pennsylvania.

John Sargent: Our worthy fellow-citizen and guest, George

Kremer—His patriotism and manly firmness, in exposing the corrupt intrigues of a political gambler, claim our best plaudits and gratitude.

Henry Beck: Greece—The ancient seat of the muses, of science and philosophy; she was great; she will be great again.

Alexander Morton: The government of the Union, like a pure stream, may it have no foul Clay to pollute it.

John Machemer: The hero of New Orleans—the firm patriot and statesman; the second savior of his country; the protector of beauty and booty; if he is one of the "MILITARY CHIEFTANS," may the genius of liberty send us a great many of them.

Doctor Samuel Strohecker: The press—the grand engine of liberty and civilization; destined to illuminate, emancipate, and exalt the world.

John Musser: The editors of the *National Intelligencer*, who declined publishing the patriotic letter of Mr. Kremer, addressed to his constituents—Fit tools, indeed, to execute the purposes of the Holy Alliance.

Daniel Beyers: May Pennsylvania and our sister States be forever blessed with such bright members as our worthy fellow-citizen, George Kremer, who will unshield all intrigues, without respect to persons, and that, too, at the risk of his popularity.

Alexander Graham: The people of Pennsylvania, and our worthy countryman, George Kremer, Esquire.

John Reber: The press—On its freedom depends the happiness, liberty, and independence of the world.

Jacob Reedy: General Jackson—As a soldier, statesman, and patriot, unequaled; may he be our next President.

John Hummel: The Government of the United States has been seized by a Quincy, produced by the putrid exhalations of a tobacco pipe, made of Clay, drenched in corruption—It will prove fatal in less than four years.

George Schnabel: Our next Governor—A man of stern integrity and undeviating republican principles.

Andrew Reedy: Thank Providence the freemen of the United States made choice of a hero and statesman, in preference to a political gambler.

John Brown: The corruptionists in Congress—may they meet

with the same fate hereafter, as did Henry Clay in his late attempt to disgrace the Pennsylvania farmer.

Clement Beckwith : Henry Clay and John Q. Adams—From every consideration, there is nothing good they have said or can do ; may they sink in their corruption, and the friends of freedom stand up in their SHOES.

Thomas R. Lewis: Henry Clay, who smuggled J. Q. Adams into the presidential chair, as the serpent did original sin into Paradise —May the flaming sword of the people thrust them both out in the year 1829.

Jacob Musser : Adam, the first man, was made of clay—Adams was made President by Clay and corruption.

George Kremer was the nephew of Governor Snyder, and came to reside with him when a mere lad. He was very ill formed, but not the least ashamed of his ugliness, and rather inclined to feel proud of his distinction in this respect. He grew up to be stout, and soon became able to fight his own battles, in an age and a district where broils were of daily occurrence. This region, then called by the general name of Shamokin, was in those days the frontier, and looked upon by the dwellers on the sea-board, as we look upon Iowa and Kansas at the present time. It served as a place of refuge for all runaway and desperate characters from the south eastern counties. The sheriff and constable seldom ventured into the wilds on this side of the river, which acquired the significant title of *Rascal's* creek.

George was remarkable for shrewdness, no less than for courage and bodily strength, and he became, in a short time, a person of great influence among the hardy inhabitants of the new country. In addition to his other good qualities, he was strictly honest, and his word was his bond. Whatever he did, he did it with all his might. With such qualifications and endowments, it is no matter of wonder that he became a leading man so soon as he embarked in politics. After serving several terms as a member of our State Legislature, he was elected to Congress, and here acquired the distinction which he enjoyed.

In 1825, it having been ascertained that neither of the candidates for the Presidency had received the constitutional majority of votes, the matter was referred to Congress. Mr. Adams, General Jackson,

Mr. Clay, and Mr. Crawford were the candidates, and as the choice of Congress lay between the two first, there was, of course, considerable intriguing on the part of the two latter and their friends. The friends of Jackson, finding that Mr. Clay and his friends were decidedly hostile to their candidate, and, indeed, made no secret of their aversion to him, resolved, after in vain trying the arts of persuasion, to resort to intimidation. They caused a letter to be written and published in the *Columbian Observer*, of Philadelphia, which stated that a corrupt bargain had been made between Messrs. Adams and Clay, in pursuance of which, the latter was to transfer his vote, and the vote of his friends to Mr. Adams, who was to make him Secretary of State, as his reward.

On the day after the appearance of the letter, Mr. Clay, then Speaker of the House of Representatives, moved that a committee be appointed to inquire into the truth of this charge. Mr. Kremer seconded the motion, stating that he was ready with the proofs, and willing to meet the inquiry. The motion was opposed by Mr. McDuffie and some others, friends to Jackson, on the ground that there was not sufficient reason to consume the time of the House in investigating a frivolous newspaper charge—a charge which no one acquainted with the parties concerned would believe. Mr. Clay had even insisted on his right to clear his character from the stain thus publicly attempted to be fixed on it, and Mr. Kremer eagerly seconded him, exulting in the anticipated certain confounding of the Clay and Adams party.

Not one, however, of those who had put him upon writing the letter, supported him, or manifested any anxiety for the proposed inquiry. The committee was appointed. On the evening of the same day, Kremer discovered that his friends could furnish him with no evidence to support his charge, and that he must get out of the scrape as well as he could. On the succeeding day, the committee notified him they were ready to proceed. In answer to which, he wrote a long letter to the chairman, declining to appear, alleging that as he had made no formal charges, the committee could have no jurisdiction—that his charge was made for the public, &c. This special pleading was so nearly identified with the argument of Mr. McDuffie on the preceding day, in the motion for inquiry, as to lead some to suspect that he, (Mr. McDuffie,) was its author; but the character of Mr. McDuffie forbids us to harbor any such suspicion. It was probably the production of Mr. Ingham, who, as afterwards appeared, was Kremer's chief prompter in this business. It was natural for him to adopt Mr. McDuffie's arguments, being the best and, indeed, only mode of getting clear of the difficulty.

One might have supposed that this disgraceful retreat would have convinced the whole public of the falsehood of Kremer's charge, but political faith covers mountains, and the charge was eagerly entertained and reiterated by the partisans of Jackson. Kremer himself, as appears from the testimony of Mr. Crowninshield, doubted, at the last, and had a letter of apology ready for Mr. Clay, which Mr. Ingham found means to suppress.

Such was the eagerness with which the Pennsylvanians received the corruption story, and such the cloud of incense with which Kremer was fumigated, that it is no wonder that his brain was affected, and he really believed himself the savior of his country's liberty. His vanity became excessive, and as Cicero of old continually rung the charges in his later orations, on the names of Lentulus and Cataline, so Kremer made corruption, and his famous letter, the eternal burden of his song.

Finding that the corruption story was unsparingly used against him by the Jacksonians, notwithstanding the way in which they had backed out of the charge, and that even General Jackson had condescended to lend the authority of his name to this shameless calumny, Mr. Clay took the trouble to collect the letters, certificates, and affidavits of almost every one who could have any knowledge of the matter in agitation, and published them in a pamphlet. These testimonials, coming from upwards of fifty persons of *all* parties, formed a most triumphant refutation of the corruption story. But it was all in vain for Messrs. Adams and Clay. The popular mind had been roused to phrensy, and was utterly inaccessible to all reason. Jackson was elected, in 1828, by a decided majority, and Kremer, having answered the purpose of his party, was forgotten at once. Too honest to take a part in the intrigues of his fellow-partisans at Washington, he could not make himself of any further use to them, and was pushed aside to make room for those who knew how to make the best use, for selfish purposes, of his services. For some years after he was left out of Congress, he continued to make speeches at public meetings, the burden of which was "corruption" and "*My letter to the Columbia Observer.*" His action, in speaking, was vehement and ungraceful, his voice loud, and his accentuation false and ranting, such as school-boys are apt to acquire under the tuition of an injudicious teacher. His honesty and zeal no one doubted ; but designing demagogues contrived, by dexterous management, to keep him back, as he was too straightforward for them, and if admitted to their councils, would mar the harmony of their best laid plans by denouncing their selfishness and unfair dealing. There was neither selfishness nor meanness about him, and had he condescended to cringe to the party leaders in 1828–1829, when his name was in the mouth of every one, or had he intimated that his influence might possibly be turned against Jackson, there is no donbt but that he could have obtained highest reward in the form of political preferment. Indeed, it was a matter of wonder and remark, among his unsophisticated constituents, that he remained without office. They little thought that their favorite was altogether thrust aside by the throng of hungry office-hunters, who assailed the President with their importunate cries for the spoils of victory. He was not blind to the intrigues and foul play going on at the seat of Government, for on his way home once, he met an acquaintance whom he mistook for one of his own political caste, and to whom he said : "Adams and Clay were *corrupt*, but their corruption was child's play to what is going on at Washington now."—*G. A. S.*

Weather Record.

The spring was early; peach trees in bloom on the 10th of April; plum trees on the 18th ; flowers in the garden on the 16th ; rye in head on the 8th of May. July 13, the thermometer stood at ninety-six degrees. Many springs in the Valley gave out, and the pasture burned up. July 16, the crops in Union county were most extraordinary. It was generally acknowledged that the yield was one fourth more upon the same quantity of ground than ever has been raised before. Jonathan Spyker, of Lewisburg, cut twenty-three dozen of wheat off thirty-eight perches. October 4, a comet visible. December 4, the first snow fell.

Various Items.

March 29, a dinner at Jacob Maize's, in Mifflinburg, to Honorable George Kremer. The latter sold out his stock of store goods at Lewisburg to Samuel Roush, Esquire, who removed it to Mifflinburg. William Taggert kept the hotel at the Cross-Roads; Valentine Hahn and Roland Stoughton at Lewisburg; John Hoffman, "The Rising Sun," at New Berlin; and Thomas Crotzer, "The Bull's Head," at Mifflinburg. May 18, George Kremer, James Merrill, and Ner Middleswarth, appointed delegates to the internal improvement convention, at Harrisburg. July 2, John Cummings, junior, took charge of the *Union Times*, succeeded on the 1st of October by John A. Sterrett, Esquire. The candidates on the Democratic ticket for Assembly were Ner Middleswarth and William Forster, junior. On the Independent ticket, James Madden and J. Reifsnyder. For a convention, 1,715; against, 717. November 1, Camp Calhoun held at McEwensville. The Lewisburg Guards, commanded by Captain Jackson McFaddin, numbering forty-five men, were in camp. David and James Templeton left New Berlin to establish a store at Canonsburg. James to study divinity there. David C. Ambler left Lewisburg. He finally landed in Florida, where he died in 1867 or 1868. November 10, Mr. Stillwell commenced a survey of the turnpike, from Mifflinburg to Bellefonte, at Mifflinburg. James Wilson purchased Captain William Gray's place.

In July, James Magee commenced boring for salt in West Buffalo, at the place still known as the salt works. A stock company was formed, Samuel Roush, Esquire, treasurer, and an assessment of one dollar per share of "The Union Salt Works" called in. The operators humbugged the share-holders until their patience was exhausted. In December, according to the *Times*, "they had reached the depth of one hundred and fifty feet, striking on two veins of salt water of considerable magnitude. Should the anticipations be realized, Union county will, ere long, be able to supply its inhabitants and those of the neighboring counties with the indispensable article of salt." [A barrel of salt conveyed in the night to the well saturated it well enough to raise an assessment from the stockholders assembled the next day.] One good result, however, was a stream of cold sulphur water, which has refreshed and invigorated thousands of people.

"A man by the name of Ephraim Stephens, of White Deer township, was brought to the jail of this county. One report says that he had formed the resolution of killing some part of his family, and then putting an end to his own existence, and that he loaded his gun for the purpose of putting this resolution in execution. Fortunately, one of his sons caught him, and wrested the gun from his hands; but in the struggle, the gun accidently went off, and its contents lodged in the barn, which was filled with grain and hay, and which was totally consumed."—*Times.*

July 22, James Young, of Kelly township, (near Ephraim Stean's,) was found dead, his body in such a state of putrefaction, he was buried where he was found. He had gone to the mountain with some of his neighbors to cut cooper poles, and, complaining of being sick, started home and, no doubt, died from excessive heat. His neighbors searched for him all night and the succeeding day, before finding his body. "The German Reformed and Lutheran church, known as 'Emanuel Church,' at New Berlin, was dedicated on Sunday, July 31, agreeably to the German ritual, in the presence of a vast concourse of people. The Reverend Mr. Hendel, of Berks county, officiated, assisted by Reverend Messrs. Shindel, Smith, and Fries. The concourse of people was numerous, beyond all conception. The building is a handsome piece of architecture. Christopher Seebold, Esquire, was the contractor, and deserves much credit for the superb manner in which this building is finished, particularly the pulpit, which is said to be a correct model of the one in the German Reformed church at Harrisburg, and which has been pronounced to be inferior to none in the State. On the subsequent Sunday, dedicatory services were held in the English language, by Reverend Martin Bruner, of Sunbury, assisted by Reverend Thomas Hood."—*Times.*

Peculiarities of the Bar, from the Manuscript of the late James F. Linn, Esquire.

"I do think, and I do say, gentlemen of the jury."—*Lashells.*
"According to the perpendicular line of justice."—*Bellas.*

"It is not in the power of mortal man to have a particle of doubt about it."—*Greenough.*

"But this is of no earthly consequence, if the Court please."—*S. Hepburn.*

"Under the statoot of hoo and cry."—*Bancraft.*

"The gentle, humane, and mild spirit which is diffused through the penal code of Pennsylvania."—*William Cox Ellis.*

"Humph! the gentlemen are marvelous witty."—*R. C. Grier.*

"Yes, stop—well, let us see—stop there—come, let us have it down in writing."—*Frick.*

"There is no evidence in the wide world to support it."—*Van Horn.*

"It is no such matter."—*Donnel.*

"I fancy."—*Jordan.*

"Hum! the big man gets up, and the little man gets up, and they try to carry their cause by a kind of mechanical operation."—*Marr.*

"The creditors of the time of this transaction had no existence."—*H. D. Ellis.*

Showman at New Berlin again.

The evil star of last year's showman brought him to New Berlin again. The place seemed charged to the full with ill-luck for him. My young friend, B——, having ascertained that he was to perform in a room on the ground-floor of Grier's tavern, went to a window of the room, soon after the performance commenced, and having silently raised the sash about one inch, introduced the nose of a large syringe filled with a most abominable compound of filth. He had not waited long before the performer, standing upon the rope, presented a full front, within point blank distance; then the fragrant liquid was squirted over his magnificent person. Grier, who sat, in the capacity of fiddler, in a line with the discharge, had his hair perfumed by the falling of divers odoriferous drops from the hissing current. Down leaped the rope-dancer, and up leaped Grier; the former ran out to plunge his head and body into a rain-barrel; the latter, foaming with wrath, to wreak his vengeance on the offender, whom, however, he could not find. The showman swore he never would set foot in New Berlin again, and he kept his oath.

A very remarkable meteor appeared during this summer. I was standing in the prothonotary's office in New Berlin, when I heard, as I imagined, some one fall heavily upon the floor of the room above me. Knowing that the room was unoccupied, I had the curiosity to go and look in, but found no one there. On my return to my house, I mentioned the matter to my wife, who said she had heard a similar sound, and I soon discovered that all my neighbors had been deceived in a similar manner. Those who were in the open air when they heard the sound, said the ground trembled under their feet, and horses were observed to start and crouch as when a bridge cracks under their feet. It appeared afterwards that the explosion had accompanied the appearance of a meteor, and had been heard at Bellefonte and Lewistown, on the Juniata, and at Sunbury and Liverpool, on the Susquehanna. The flight of the fiery ball was distinctly seen by the workmen on the Juniata, and at Liverpool. I was told a fiery body was seen to fall apparently on the north side of Peter's mountain.

Temperance associations began to be formed in the Valley in this year. Those connected therewith bound themselves to use no intoxicating liquor, except in such cases as required their use as medicines, and to discontinue the custom of offering strong drink to visitors. The latter practice had been so common that to omit it was considered a breach of politeness. Every one knows with what a whirlwind force public opinion in America, when once excited, bears down everything before it, and here was an illustration of its power.

After three or four years, it became rare to offer liquors to visitors, and common to hear a person refuse to drink, on the ground that he was a temperance man. A respectable inn-keeper in Sunbury told me, about three years after this, that the sale of liquor at his bar, to travelers, had been diminished by not less than one half, under the influence of the temperance societies. The first temperance societies allowed the use of wines, on the ground that those who limited themselves to these would not get drunk on so expensive an article.

Witchcraft Farce.

During this year a remarkable farce of witchcraft was played in the family of a man named Kern, in Beaver township. He had a wife and two daughters, and followed the occupation of farming. In his immediate vicinity lived a man named Romig, who, from some unknown cause, became a hypochondriac, and the impression got abroad that he was bewitched. Soon after this the milk in Kern's spring-house became sour, within a few hours after it was placed there. This occurred daily, until the farce was concluded, which was in two or three weeks. The next act played was of a more remarkable character. Kern's tables and kitchen furniture were to be seen flying in all directions, thrown, it was SUPPOSED, by supernatural means. Knives, forks, spoons, ladles, &c., never remained more than five minutes on the dresser, after having been placed there, but were thrown in various directions about the house ; and, as the more BELIEVING portion of the neighbors asserted, it was no uncommon thing to see them thrown through the solid wall of the house, without leaving any mark of their passage in the wall ! A peddler, who stopped for the purpose of trading some of his notions to Kern, asserted that he had not been in the house ten minutes before his hat and dog were thrown through the wall of the kitchen, into the adjoining yard. It is not to be presumed that he was influenced in propagating this story by the hope of assembling a crowd around his wagon.

During these transactions, Kern had a numerous crowd daily at his house, and on Sundays there was a gathering at his door, such as the most eloquent divine would have failed to assemble. Of these, the major part came prepared to believe ALL they saw, and ALL they might hear. Of course, there was no lack of TRUE stories. The unbelieving portion of the visitors—a very SMALL number, for men of SENSE generally staid at home—kept their eyes open, and readily discovered that the old woman and the daughters were the witches, and threw the knives, forks, &c. A witch doctor was called, who proceeded, with great solemnity, to expel the evil spirit. Divers magical and mysterious rites were performed, exorcisms were chanted, and texts of Scripture nailed to every door and window in the house. The witches, however, set the doctor at naught, and baffled all his schemes. At length a party of young men, residing in New Berlin, resolved to try their skill at taking evil spirits. One of them, having procured a mask, a huge flaxen-wig, a pair of furred gloves, and other necessary apparatus, set out with the rest, in the afternoon, and arrived at Kern's early in the evening. At their request, the witches performed, to their great satisfaction, until a late hour. At length, when all the visitors, except the young witch doctors, had left the house, it was resolved to commence operations. They desired to see how the witches acted above stairs, and were accordingly conducted up the ladder, accompanied by the whole family. In the meantime, one of the party, who had a remarkably hoarse and deep-toned voice, and who was to act the part of the devil, was notified by a preconcerted signal—for he had not entered the house—to prepare for action. He accordingly put on his wig and mask, which he rubbed with phosphorus, and wrapped himself in a buffalo-skin. The party up stairs were well provided with squibs. One of them had a piece of phosphorus, with which he wrote on the wall such words as "devil," "hell," &c., in a number of places. The signal being given, the candle was extinguished, the squibs distributed most copiously, and the horrid words on the wall shone out in liquid fire. The barrels and furniture in the room were trundled about the floor, and an astounding uproar was kept up for some minutes. Presently a terrific roar was heard from below. All parties ran to the stair-door, and saw, at the foot of the ladder, HIS GRIM MAJESTY, in all the terrors of flames, flax, fur, and horns. Satan made an appropriate speech on the occasion, and then retired. His address was followed by a most edifying exhortation, by the wag of the party, on the sin of deceiving, and the danger of another visit from old Nick, if the present practices should be persisted in. The terrified witches made a full confession, and so ended the enchantment.—*G. A. Snyder*.

Marriages.

January 18, by Reverend J. W. Smith, Hezekiah Amberg, of New Berlin, to Miss Elizabeth Brooks. February 10, by Reverend T. Hood, David Nesbit to Miss Mary, daughter of Jacob Musser. February 24, by Reverend Patterson, Thomas Candor, of Kelly, to Margaret, daughter of John Montgomery. March 15, James Duncan, of Aaronsburg, to Mrs. Sophia Maxwell, of New Berlin. April

7, by Reverend Fries, John Orwig, of Mifflinburg, to Miss Maria Bright. April 28, by Reverend T. Hood, John Linn to Mary F. Chamberlin. May 5, by Reverend Heim, Daniel Ludwig to Miss Sarah Hoffman. May 6, by Reverend John Dreisbach, Robert P. Maclay, of East Buffalo, to Miss Margaret C. Lashells, of New Berlin. May 20, Henry B. Mussena to Miss Elizabeth Winter, of New Berlin. June 5, by Reverend Fries, Mathias Benner to Elizabeth Overmyer, of New Berlin. October 6, by Reverend Fries, Daniel Apple to Miss Susan Orwig, of Mifflinburg. October 9, John Maize to Miss Elizabeth Jones, of Mifflinburg. October 13, Mr. Strawbridge, of Columbia county, to Miss Louisa, daughter of Charles Maus, Esquire. November 2, by Reverend Heim, Jonathan Wetzel to Miss Hettie Hoff, of Union. November 3, by Reverend J. H. Fries, Jacob G. Chestney, of Mifflinburg, to Juliana, daughter of John Cummings, Esquire, of Hartley. November 3, by James McClellan, Esquire, Daniel Mook to Miss Mary Dieffenbach. November 20, David Mauck to Miss Nancy Shriner. December 22, by Reverend Stewart, William Kelly, of Union, to Miss Margaret Allison, of Centre. December 26, John Row to Miss Rachel Kunkle, of Dry Valley.

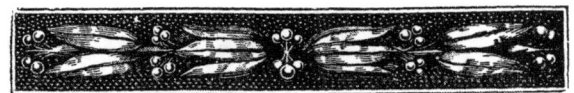

1826.

LOTTERY ADVERTISEMENTS—FOURTH OF JULY CELEBRATION—MURDER OF JACOB SWINEFORD—WEATHER RECORD—BISHOP NEWCOMER'S DEATH—POLITICAL—OBITUARY.

ANUARY 7, prices current in Philadelphia: Wheat, ninety cents; rye, fifty-eight; corn, sixty-two; whisky, twenty-six. Samuel Baum, postmaster at New Berlin, in April; Alexander Graham, at Lewisburg; Jacob Maize, at Mifflinburg. February 13, the coldest day of the year. The Democratic-Republican convention met at New Berlin. Robert Taylor, president; John Bossler, secretary; William Forster and Henry C. Eyer were appointed delegates to the State convention, with instructions to support the re-nomination of Governor Shulze. February 18, Judge Seth Chapman, who was impeached for misdemeanors in office, was acquitted by the Senate, twenty-six Senators voting not guilty, five voting guilty. March 13, James F. Linn admitted to the bar. April 10, the turnpike company incorporated to make a road from the end of the Lewisburg bridge to Mifflinburg. Commissioners, William Hayes, James Geddes, Jacob Maize, Henry Roush, and James Duncan.

Lottery advertisements fill the county papers this year. John A. Sterrett was agent for the Union Canal lottery, at New Berlin, and James Appleton, at Mifflinburg. New Berlin lottery, by Peter Smith. In Mifflinburg, one by John and Henry Orwig; James Cummings, Samuel Roush, John Ray, James Appleton, George Bogar, and Conrad Grove, managers. William Wolfinger advertises the Selinsgrove lottery. Andrew Reedy, one at William Taggert's, Buffalo

Cross-Roads. Two prizes of $3,000, one of $2,000. Severe drouth
which continued until the 23d of June, when it rained so excessively
as to spoil much hay.[1] 28th, a great freshet on the river. The old
market house, on Market street, in Lewisburg, taken down. 4th of
July celebrated at New Berlin. Reverend J. H. Fries delivered a
discourse from Psalm lxxxv: 10 and 11 verses; Charles A. Bradford, Esquire, an oration. The singing was under the direction of
Mr. Hickok. After which the company repaired to Gross' spring,
where Mr. Eilert had prepared a dinner. Abbot Green was then
made chairman, George A. Snyder, secretary, and a number of
toasts were read.

Murder of Jacob Swineford.

Jacob Swineford, Esquire, of Middleburg, in this county, was
murdered on the night of the 4th of July, in Lebanon. The facts,
as far as we can learn from a German paper published in that place,
are as follows: Swineford and his son had been, for some days previous to the 4th, in the vicinity of Lebanon, with a drove of sheep,
consisting of about three hundred and eighty, which he had disposed
of, except about fifty, with which he arrived in Lebanon on the
morning of the 4th, where he spent the day. In the evening he
met with a Mr. Greenawalt, an old acquaintance, at the tavern of a
Mr. Williams, where they drank together, after which Swineford
asked Greenawalt to walk with him. They went, and when they
came to an alley in Hill street, they were suddenly attacked by three
men, by one of whom Greenawalt was knocked down twice, but
succeeded in making a retreat, calling to Swineford to run also.
Immediately afterwards, some boys, while passing, discovered some
one lying on the ground. Light was immediately brought, and it
was found to be Swineford, who was then in the agonies of death,
and expired immediately afterwards. He had received two blows
on his head, which occasioned his death. The deceased is supposed

[1] At this time a farmer in West Buffalo made several attempts to haul in his hay,
only to be disappointed by sudden showers. Finally he had a load within a short
distance of his barn, when a terrible storm came on. In his wrath, he swore he would
have *some* hay in dry at any rate, and grabbing from the wagon as much as he could
carry in his arms, he ran for the barn. Unfortunately for him, the creek intervened,
and as he was running with all his might, his foot slipped at the middle of the foot
log, and he plunged, with his hay, into the stream.

to have had between $400 and $500, in a large pocket-book, which was missing. About $80 in a small pocket-book was found about his person. Two men were arrested on suspicion of having committed the crime, but were afterwards discharged. The deceased has left a wife and six children to mourn his untimely end.—*Times, July* 14.

In August it became very sultry, with no rain. Dust followed the plow, and a great deal of sickness prevailed in the Valley. In September, fever and ague prevailed extensively. In December, there was a great deal of snow and good sleighing, and the river was frozen, and crossed by sleds. The first snow fell on the 4th of November.

September 28, Bishop Newcomer visited the Valley for the last time, on his return from a trip into Canada, staying at Martin and John Dreisbach's. He died at his own home, in Hagerstown, on 12th March, 1830, aged eighty-one. "Long will he be remembered by thousands. Many, very many, souls will, at the great day, own him as the instrument, in the hand of God, by which they have been turned from the error of their ways, and have been brought from darkness to light."

Utica for girl's name having become quite common, it is, perhaps, proper to state its origin. In this year, Captain John Snyder went on a visit to New York, taking with his newly-married wife, Margaret. Having a race-horse with him, he was lucky enough to win a match at Utica, in memory of which he named his daughter, born within the year, Utica, and the name, through mere fancy or personal liking, became quite the rage.

Political.

September, Democratic convention at New Berlin, Michael Rathfon, chairman; Samuel Aurand, secretary. William Forster, junior, and George Aurand nominated for Assembly; Elias P. Youngman for commissioner; Andrew McClenachan and William Kessler, senatorial conferees, with instructions to support Ner Middleswarth for Senator, and indorsed the nomination of Governor Shulze.

At a county meeting, held on the 20th, Frederick Gutelius, chairman, Dan Caldwell and John Montelius, secretaries, John Ray was nominated for Senator; James Madden and Robert Willet for Assembly: John Montelius, commissioner; Conrad Grove, James K. Davis, and Simon Shaffer, standing committee.

The congressional conference met at the house of William A. Petriken, in Pennsborough. Henry Yearick and Jacob Hummel, conferees. George Kremer, Samuel McKean, and Espy Van Horn nominated for Congress.

25th September, a senatorial conference met at Randall Wilcox's, in Lewisburg, and John Ray was nominated as a canal man.

Governor Shulze had no opposition in the county, receiving 1062 votes, nor had Van Horn, McKean, and Kremer. For Senate, John Ray received 929 votes; Middleswarth, 785.

Marriages.

2d February, by Reverend T. Hood, John Chamberlin to Elizabeth, daughter of William Hayes, of Lewisburg. 21st February, James Caldwell, of Lewisburg, to Isabella, daughter of James Duncan, of Centre county. 11th April, Jonathan Reedy to Miss Amelia Buchner. July 20, by Reverend T. Hood, James F. Linn, Esquire, of Lewisburg, to Miss Margaret, daughter of Hugh Wilson, of Buffalo township. 17th August, by Reverend T. Hood, Thomas Grier to Mrs. Rachel Stratton, of New Berlin. In New York, by Reverend Doctor Roberts, John Snyder to Miss Margaret Hammond. 31st October, John Devling to Mary Wilson, daughter of Judge Hugh Wilson. 19th October, by Reverend T. Hood, James Merrill, Esquire, of New Berlin, to Miss Sarah Hepburn, of Northumberland. 22d October, by Reverend J. H. Fries, Jesse Mauck, of New Berlin, to Miss Catherine Crotzer, of Mifflinburg. November 14, by John Nesbit, Esquire, William Alsbach to Catherine Shively. December 26, by Reverend John Dreisbach, John Yost, of New Berlin, to Miss Sarah Shaffer, of Buffalo.

Obituary.

Samuel Templeton died at his residence, near New Berlin, on Saturday, February 18, aged seventy-two. He was born in Ireland, and came to this country at the age of nineteen, and has since then resided in this neighborhood. He has been for many years an elder in the Presbyterian church, and, by an exemplary life, gave evidence that his profession of religion was sincere. He departed, after a long and distressing illness, in full possession of his mental faculties, and relying on the mercy of God, through the merits of our Redeemer, for salvation. His children were: Alexander, David, Reverend James, Ann, and Nancy, married to Doctor Charlton.

On Monday morning, February 20, after a lingering illness of several months, John Mumma, Esquire, aged twenty-eight. His remains were interred with masonic honors on Tuesday last.

At her residence, in Centre township, February 20, Mrs. Mary Wales, consort of James Wales.—*Times, February* 25.

1827.

CANAL MEETING—DEBATING SOCIETIES—MIFFLINBURG ACADEMY ESTABLISHED—BOROUGH OF MIFFLINBURG INCORPORATED.

FLOUR in Philadelphia, in January, $6 per barrel. The newspapers note the winter of 1826-27 as the coldest since 1782. February 16, a public debate between the Lewisburg Debating Society and the Mifflinburg Debating Society took place at William Taggert's tavern, at the Cross-Roads. George A. Snyder, the president, awarded the victory to the Mifflinburg society. A little newspaper war between the societies resulted. William Cameron, Esquire, president of the Lewisburg society, and Doctor William Joyce, secretary, cudgel the Mifflinburg society in a pretty lively way, in the *Times*.

February 20, a meeting in favor of canals was held at Lewisburg, president, Andrew McClenachan; secretary, James Dale; committee on resolutions, Dan Caldwell, Doctor Thomas Vanvalzah, and William Hayes.

April 2, Honorable George Kremer moved from Lewisburg to the Stees place, adjoining Middleburg, and Joseph Hutchinson opened store in the Kremer building. Under the act erecting circuit courts, Judge Molton C. Rogers held the first circuit court in New Berlin, on the 9th of April. On the 10th, Peter Gearhart was put on trial for murder; Bellas and Bradford for the Commonwealth, Lashells and Maus for the defendant. (May 16, George A. Snyder remarks: "Took Judge Chapman two and one half days to try Henry Frock for stealing walnuts, while Judge Rogers, in April, tried a murder case, two fornication and adultery cases, in three days.")

14th April, act establishing the Mifflinburg academy.—*Pamphlet Laws*, 322. Henry Yearick, James Appleton, Jacob Maize, James Merrill, John Forster, Joseph Musser, Michael Roush, Thomas Vanvalzah, and John F. Wilson, trustees. Three trustees to be elected annually by the people of the county.

April 13, the borough of Selinsgrove incorporated.—*Pamphlet Laws*, 278. 14th April, the borough of Mifflinburg incorporated, by the following boundaries: Beginning at a post on line of the heirs of Jacob Brobst, N. 2° W. 362; thence along line of the heirs of George Rote, deceased, N. 76° E. 118; by the same, S. 2° E. 145; thence, N. 88° E. 120, to a post in the center of the road leading from George Rockey's to Mifflinburg; thence along the center thereof, S. 2° E., in a line between Michael Bartges, John Charles, Conrad Mull, *et al.*, 210; thence along the north side of Limestone hill, S. 88° W. 240, to beginning.—*Pamphlet Laws*, 305. These boundaries embrace the whole of Ensign Meen's, the south half of Ensign Forster's, and part of the Elias Younkman warrantees.

July 30, John Musser's (Kelly township) still bursted, and scalded himself, James Wilson, and the stiller. They applied to Jonathan Spyker to "hex" the fire out of them.

August 2, William Hayes' store robbed of $100. The taker confessed, and Mr. Hayes let him off. Some few years since a person from Lewisburg stopped over night at a farm-house in Ohio, and recognized in the owner of the fine farm the penitent subject of Mr. Hayes' clemency.

August 25, Lafayette Lodge, New Berlin, appropriated $40 to the Greek fund, "to be applied in accelerating the cause of liberty in

Greece," and James Aiken returned to Lewisburg, after an absence of two years. Doctor E. Appleton, of New Berlin, made a great sensation about a recipe he had made for curing drunkenness. It had a great run for awhile, but proved of no account.

10th September, Peter Nevius, constable, took charge of a party of town boys convicted of an affray at Poak's, to convey them to jail at New Berlin. On the Shamokin hill he pretended something was wrong with the harness, and got out to fix it. The boys saw their opportunity, and ran off. As some of them became prominent citizens, remarkable for good works, it is not worth while to say who they were.

9th October, John Dreisbach, Ner Middleswarth, Jackson men, elected to the Assembly, over James Madden and R. P. Maclay. 14th, masonic procession at New Berlin. Sixty-seven appeared in regalia. Reverend Fries and James Merrill, Esquire, addressed them. 11th November, John Sheckler's barn burned ; fired by his aunt, who is deranged. 21st November, snow storm, ground covered. December 4, Ner Middleswarth chosen Speaker of the House.

Marriages.

February 13, John Yarger to Miss Margaret Kelly, of Hartley, by Samuel Haupt, Esquire. April 19, Thomas Wilson, of Kelly, to Mrs. Drake. May 10, John Housel to Margaret Musser, daughter of Jacob, Esquire. June 5, Saul McCormick to Catherine, daughter of Reverend Thomas Hood. August 30, John Magee to Susan Struble.

Deaths.

Thomas Shipton, Esquire, died in Middleburg, February 4, aged seventy-four years. He officiated as justice of the peace for upwards of thirty years, and was very highly esteemed.

Honorable John Macpherson died on the 2d of August, at his residence, near Winfield. He served in the navy of the Revolution, was badly wounded, and, on that account, received a pension from the State. He was associate judge of Northumberland county for twenty-three years.

September 26, Mrs. Conrad Foutz, aged eighty-eight, mother of Mrs. Charles Cameron, was buried at Lewisburg. Her husband was one of the rangers who, with the Groves and Samuel Brady, were a great terror to the Indians. Conrad Foutz's grandson, General Simon Cameron, was Secretary of War under Abraham Lincoln, and his great-grandson, J. D. Cameron, Secretary of War under General Grant.

1828.

LIST OF ATTORNEYS—CANAL LOCATED—LEWISBURG AND MIFFLINBURG TURNPIKE LOCATED.

JANUARY 5, Frederick Evans and Robert P. Maclay, delegates to the State convention which nominated Andrew Jackson for President.

List of attorneys attending February court, Union county: James Merrill, John Lashells, John A. Sterrett, John Wyeth, Charles Maus, Jacob H. Horning, and James F. Linn; from Northumberland county, Hugh Bellas, Ebenezer Greenough, Alexander Jordan, Charles G. Donnel, Samuel J. Packer, and Samuel Hepburn; Lycoming, William Cox Ellis, James Armstrong, and Robert Fleming; Schuylkill, Charles A. Bradford, Esquire.

There was not snow sufficient for sleighing during the entire winter, and arks passed down the river as early as the 10th of February.

22d March, public debate at Lewisburg on the question: "Will the present Government of the United States decline and fall?" Affirmative, Isaac Slenker, J. F. Linn, and Jackson McFadden; negative, James Aiken, Doctor William Joyce, and William Nesbit, Esquire; presiding judge, Reverend George Richmond; associates, Doctor Thomas Vanvalzah, John Vandyke, Frederick Pontius, T. R. Lewis, John Machemer, and John H. Hickok. People from

New Berlin, Milton, and all the Valley attended. A majority of the judges decided for the negative, Vanvalzah and Lewis dissenting. The debate was continued all the afternoon and evening. 26th, news arrived that grain had fallen rapidly at Baltimore. All the merchants lost heavily. Worth only sixty-five cents. Hayes settled with his customers at seventy-two cents per bushel.

Sunday, 13th April, north-east snow storm prevailed. Laird Howard, Francis Wilson, and James F. Linn, only, put in appearance at Buffalo church. Mr. Hood thought it not worth while to preach to three men. This snow storm did a great deal of damage to fruit. 30th, Judge Rawle, Robert Faries, and William Wilson, engineers to locate the canal, arrived at Lewisburg; Rothrock, draftsman; Paul Geddes and Joseph Green, chain-carriers.

[1]May 13, Isaac Slenker admitted to the bar. Judge Chapman remarked that he passed the best examination had before him in five years.

July 13, Elijah Bacon made his appearance, and preached in the Union church.

August 28, Messrs. Hayes, Caldwell, Cameron, Joyce, and Vanvalzah, who were representing the interests of the west side, returned from Harrisburg, and reported that the canal would be located on the east side; Rawle estimating that the west side would cost $340,000 more. Our people, however, believed it the result of intrigue and good management.

September 11, James F. Linn surveyed a route for the turnpike between Lewisburg and Mifflinburg. Alexander Graham, James Geddes, William Wilson, William and Daniel Cameron, Jackson McFaddin, Robert Hayes, John Reber and, Thomas McGuire, went along all the way. Started at eight, and reached Mifflinburg half-past four, where Joseph Musser and John Machemer met the party with wagons, and took them back. Straight course between the two places, S. 71° 39' W., distance, eight miles thirty-four perches. 12th, the mill, house, and barn, late Adam Wagoner's, on Rapid run, (now Cowan,) belonging to Jacob Baker's heirs, burned at one o'clock last night. Family escaped with difficulty. This was the

---

[1] Honorable Isaac Slenker studied law with the late James F. Linn, Esquire. In 1862 he was elected Auditor General, and served from May 4, 1863, to May 1, 1866. He died at New Berlin, April 17, 1873, aged seventy-three years.

second time the mill was burned in Wagoner's time, having been burned once fourteen or fifteen years ago. Supposed to be the work of an incendiary.

October 1, West Branch division of the canal let at Milton; and a horse-race between Petriken's gray and Doctor Getz's mare. The gray led three or four lengths; stakes, $400.

September 28, Isaac Bockener, who lived on Colonel Ruhl's place, died from the effects of an injury received at David Linn's clover-mill. The water-wheel caught his leg, stripped the flesh off, and gangrene set in. This mill was erected during this summer.

October 31, presidential election. Jackson electors had eighty-seven, Adams six votes, in Lewisburg.

November 4, Subscription to the turnpike completed. Wheat rose to $1 25. 29th, the committee met to draft a petition for a cross-cut canal to Lewisburg: William Hayes, James Geddes, William Wilson, Doctor Joyce, and James F. Linn.

December 22, James F. Linn commenced surveying the turnpike. 29th, he commenced locating, and got as far as James Harris'. Finished on the 30th.

Marriages.

3d January, William Miller, of New Berlin, to Miss Elizabeth Myers. January 16, by Mr. Hood, Jacob Derr to Isabella Hunter. 13th March, John Haus, late deputy sheriff, to Margaret Roush, of Mifflinburg. April 8, Mrs. Abigail Iddings, widow of Isaac, married to old Mr. Mackey, by James McClellan, Esquire. 28th May, by Reverend Richmond, Abner Metzgar to Eleanor Lawshe. November 6, by Reverend T. Hood, Hugh McLaughlin to Frances, daughter of George Derr. 11th, by same, John Forster, to Margaret, youngest daughter of Doctor Robert Vanvalzah. 20th, Joseph Chamberlin to Nancy Deal. December 9, by Mr. Hood, David Duncan, of Centre county, to Miss Susan Hayes, of New Berlin.

1829.

Union Hickory Newspaper—Supreme Court Personnel—An Unpublished Opinion.

THE winter of 1828-29 particularly unpleasant; rain fell daily for seventy days, and spring was fifteen days later than usual, when the weather became suddenly warm.

June 17, most of the farmers commenced mowing. Market price of wheat in May, $1 40.

January 27, the turnpike let to John Maclay for $3 90 per perch, the whole distance from Lewisburg to Mifflinburg.

February 17, a large meeting held at New Berlin to appoint delegates to 4th of March convention. George Weirick and William Kessler, Esquire, appointed delegates, with instructions to support, first, for Governor, George Kremer; second, Ner Middleswarth; third, Samuel D. Ingham; and, if neither succeeded, to unite in nominating a Jackson man, no way connected with the present Administration, by blood or otherwise.

3d March, an appropriation made by the Legislature for the improvement of Penn's creek.

May 5, William Carothers moved the *Union Hickory* newspaper press from New Berlin to Lewisburg, and continued its publication till April 13, 1830. In May, James F. Linn surveyed and laid out the river road from Lewisburg to Selinsgrove. Jacob K. Boyer, of Reading, who had done a large mercantile business, and bought a great deal of wheat through Buffalo Valley, was convicted of passing counterfeit money. He was said, by the district attorney, to be guilty of the most expert, extensive, and wholesale counterfeiting ever known within the United States.

June 26, Supreme Court *personnel:* Gibson is a large, portly man, somewhat corpulent, small eyes, black hair, clean shaven, noble countenance. Rogers, small, thin-faced man, dark hair, no whiskers, very intelligent countenance. Huston, tall, awkward, prominent eyebrows, eyes deep set, large nose, iron gray hair, and short whiskers. Tod, short, corpulent, red complexion, light hair, very little of it, and that frizzled. Smith, short, fat, white headed, large nose, large rolling eyes, stooping a little as he walks.

An Unpublished Opinion.

Sunbury, June 27, the news arrived of the nomination of Joseph Ritner for Governor, by the Anti-Masonic convention, at Harrisburg, yesterday. Justice Frederick Smith took his seat in the court-house some time before the meeting of the court. Justice Rogers next appeared, to whom Smith said : " Well, Mr. Rogers, whom think you the Anti-Masons have nominated?" Rogers: "I have not heard; have you?" Smith: "Yes, they have fixed on Joseph Ritner." "Why, the damned fools, what do they think they can do with him. He wont get ten thousand votes. Oh, the damned fools, ha! ha! ha!" Justice Tod came in next, when Smith went on : " Well, Mr. Tod, have you heard whom the Anti-Masons have nominated for Governor?" Tod: "No; have you?" Smith: "Joseph Ritner." Tod: " Joseph Ritner! Joseph Ritner! Joseph Ritner! Well, I'll vote for any Anti-Mason, any Anti-Jackson, Anti-canal candidate ; but Joseph Ritner, I won't vote for him, by God ! " Then in sauntered Chief Justice Gibson, and Smith began again : " Mr. Chief Justice, have you heard whom the Anti-Masons have nominated for Governor?" Gibson: "No; who is it?" Smith: "Joseph Ritner." Gibson : " Oh, hell ! " The chief justice whistled a slow march, and took his seat without further remark. Justice Huston did not enter until the court had proceeded to business, so that he delivered no opinion on this momentous subject.—*G. A. S.*

This year is noted for its tremendous Anti-Masonic excitement. September 15, Reverend J. H. Fries delivered an address before the Masonic Wolf meeting, in New Berlin, when George Kremer and

John Dreisbach were nominated for Assembly. August 29, the Anti-Masonic convention nominated Ner Middleswarth and Philip Ruhl. George Bogar, president. Delegates were, Union, Charles Maus and George Bogar; East Buffalo, William L. Harris and Peter Voneida; Hartley, Michael Peters and Daniel Speigelmyer; White Deer, Jacob Sypher and Christian Reichly; Kelly, Joseph Spotts and George Moyer; Mifflinburg, John Montelius and John Van Buskirk; West Buffalo, Henry and David Jordan. Joseph Ritner recommended for Governor; county commissioner, William Betz. In October, the Ritner vote in Union county was 2,068; Wolf, for Governor, had 764; Middleswarth and Ruhl had each 1,914; Kremer, 810; Driesbach, 971. For Governor, Ritner had 61 votes in Lewisburg, Wolf had 58 votes.

Horse races very common this year in and about Lewisburg. August 20, occurred the one between Sargent's sorrel and "Tamany," of Milton. The Milton people came down and bet all the money they had on their favorite; watches, knives, and, in fact, everything they had about them. Sargent's horse won by five to six lengths. J. P. Ross used to relate the scenes of this day, and laugh until the tears ran down his cheeks. He said the Lewisburg fellows had to lend the Milton men money to pay their toll going home. October 3, race between John Forster's horse and Silverwood's.

Thomas Sawyer and family left the Valley for Ohio. Road from Chamberlin's mill to Kelly's saw-mill laid out. Farm of Benjamin Schrack, deceased, appraised at $15 per acre. General Green bought the Stedman farm, opposite Lewisburg, one hundred and forty-seven acres, at $36 per acre, cash. December 4, the first snow fell. December 28, turnpike managers met, and the commissioners appointed by the Governor reported it completed.

Marriages.

17th January, William Wilson (son of Judge Hugh) to Ruth Waddell, of Centre county, by Reverend Mr. Todd, at Mifflinburg. 20th, Walter Devling to Eliza, daughter of Judge Hugh Wilson, by Mr. Hood. February 17, Doctor Joseph F. Grier to Margaret, daughter of A. Graham. February —, Peter Strayhorn to a daughter of James Cornelius. Robert Forster to Miss Jane Rutherford, of

Harrisburg. February 27, Abraham Amberg to Charlotte Brookes, of Chillicothe, Ohio, formerly of New Berlin. 28th April, Simon Grove to Miss Mary Miller, of Reading. 20th May, C. H. Charles, of Hartley, to Juliette Mann, of Tioga. 28th May, by Reverend T. Hood, Robert Hayes to Emily Fields, (daughter of the bridge-builder.) 31st, by Samuel Wilson, Esquire, Henry Benner to Miss Moyer, of Union. 11th June, George Aurand, Esquire, to Mrs. Mary Royer. 23d, by J. F. Linn, Esquire, John Shaw to Margaret Baker, at Jacob Musser's hotel. July 2, Daniel K. Hill to Barbara A. Musser, Lewisburg. By Reverend James Kay, Christopher Woods, junior, to Miss Maria Little, of Lewisburg. July 14, Israel Zentmyer to Eve Snook, daughter of John, of West Buffalo. 4th August, by James F. Linn, Esquire, Henry Myers to Hannah Walter. 11th August, L. B. Christ, Esquire, to Esther Bogar. September 22, by Reverend Nathaniel Todd, John A. Vanvalzah to Miss Rebecca Chambers.

1830.

WEATHER RECORD—JOHNNY MORTON—CENSUS OF 1830.

N the 16th of May, oak leaves made their appearance— a very early spring—blossoms all off the trees by the 30th of April, except apple, which were in bloom two or three weeks since. The month of July was excessively hot. The 18th, 20th, and 22d, were the warmest days. Saturday morning, in shade, ninety-three degrees; Monday, ninety-five degrees; Wednesday, ninety-five degrees.

Officers of Lafayette Lodge: H. W. Snyder, W. M.; George A. Snyder, S. W.; John Seebold, J. W.; Doctor John Baskins, secretary; Henry C. Eyer, treasurer.

January 11, the New Berlin Anti-Horse-Race Association formed.

Peter Beaver, president, John Mauck, secretary. February 22, James Sargent fell off Kremer's boat, at the mouth of Brown's run, and was drowned. March 2, a union agricultural association formed at R. H. Hammond's, in Milton, embracing Columbia, Lycoming, and Union counties. Dan Caldwell chosen president. March 12, Samuel Reber opened hotel at Lochiel now. May 1, Daniel Gottshall issued the first number of the *Lewisburg Journal*. May 28, the Mifflinburg Anti-Horse-Racing Association formed; Henry Yearick, president, Frederick Gutelius, secretary. The road between Lewisburg and Mortonsville vacated, and the Turtle Creek road, at the latter place, extended to the turnpike. June 12, William Linn sold his farm in Kelly to Adam Stahl, for $34 per acre. October 15, farm of C. Nevius, deceased, sold to his son-in-law, Samuel Wilson, at $40 per acre. October 21, George Ritter's farm, in Buffalo, sold to Roan McClure for $36 25 per acre. August 10, Anti-Masonic ticket formed at New Berlin: E. Greenough for Congress, S. J. Packer for Senator, Ner Middleswarth and Philip Ruhl for Assembly, Peter Hackenburg for commissioner. Democratic ticket: Lewis Dewart for Congress, Samuel Bloom for Senator, John Dreisbach and Jacob Wittenmeyer for Assembly. October 26, the first agricultural fair was held at Milton. December 16, Abner C. Harding, a student at law with James F. Linn, Esquire, was admitted to the bar.[1]

Johnny Morton.

Johnny is now dead. I wonder that he lasted so long. Although everybody called him "Johnny," he never suffered himself to be so called, without displaying a sense of offended dignity. "My name is John," he used to say; "Johnny is a boy's name." He disliked also the name of beer; beer was trash, only fit for hogs; "a bier was a thing for the dead."

[1] General Abner C. Harding was born in East Hampton, Connecticut, educated at Hamilton, New York, studied law at Lewisburg, and settled finally in the State of Illinois. He was a member of the Illinois Constitutional Convention of 1848, and served in the State Legislature in 1848–9–50; and was for ten years engaged in managing railroads. In 1862 he enlisted as a private in the eighty-third Illinois, and having been appointed colonel, served at Fort Donelson; was made a brigadier general, and had command at Murfreesboro' in 1863. In 1864 he was elected to the Thirty-Ninth Congress, serving with Honorable George F. Miller, another student of Mr. Linn, in that Congress. He died at Monmouth, Warren county, Illinois July 19, 1874, worth, it is said, over $1,000,000.

Johnny's love of whisky and his hatred of beer afforded abundance of amusement to the idle boys of New Berlin and Mifflinburg, who flocked around him as soon as he made his appearance in the streets, as did the small birds around the owl, who happens to be overtaken in the daylight. "Johnny! Johnny! do you want any beer?" was shouted by the blackguards; to which Johnny replied with curses, and sometimes with stones. Johnny came to New Berlin one day, and having drank, and run the gauntlet of the boys, laid himself down upon the door-steps of the jail. The sheriff found him here, and, with the assistance of two or three others, carried him into the dungeon,[1] and made all fast. A few hours afterward one of the sheriff's family went to the door to make observations, and heard Johnny beginning to stir, probably just waking. After muttering something to himself, he was heard to say, "I wonder where I am?" and after a brief pause, "Well, I guess I am in hell," and, seemingly satisfied with this conjecture, quietly laid himself to rest until the sheriff came to release him.—*G. A. S.*

Census, 1830.

White Deer,	1,295	Lewisburg,	924
Kelly,	739	Buffalo,	2,130
Mifflinburg,	663	Centre,	1,952
West Buffalo,	1,404	Beaver,	2,280
Hartley township,	1,730	Union,	2,085
Washington,	1,097	Penn's,	2,304
Perry,	1,050		
Chapman,	1,094	Total,	20,747

One male and two female slaves.

[1] In all old jails was a room from which the light was altogether excluded, called the dungeon, a relic of barbarism or popery now, happily abolished.

1831.

CROSS-CUT CANAL—FIRST TEMPERANCE SOCIETY FORMED IN THE VALLEY—
BETHEL CHURCH ORGANIZED.

ARCH 22, news of the passage of the improvement act, and its signature by the Governor, which includes the Lewisburg cross-cut, reached Lewisburg. The town was illuminated, cannon fired, and toasts drank. Northumberland Bank incorporated.—*Pamphlet Laws*, 298.

April 12, A. Reedy's, deceased, stone house at Buffalo Cross-Roads sold by his administrators to John A. Vanvalzah, for $586.

May 10, price of grain in Philadelphia, $1 25. May 12, Messrs. Cameron, Vanvalzah, and Joyce returned from Harrisburg, having succeeded in getting the cross-cut canal under contract.

"*A Penny saved is a Penny made—Old Adage.*—Canal boat 'Merchant's Choice,' Captain Blair, arrived here on Monday last, in nine days from Philadelphia, with merchandize for Messrs. Comly and Cadwallader. Her cargo was twenty tons.

12 for C. Comly, at $10, ...	$120
8 do. S. Cadwallader, ...	80
	$200

"These twenty tons by wagons would come to 600 dollars, at 30 dollars per ton, or $1 50 per cwt., the usual price. Now, what is saved to us, the consumers, in this single trip? Why, only $400. Sugars we used to pay 12½ cts. per lb. is now sold for 10 cents. This is what we call canal politics."—*Frick's Miltonian, May* 14, 1831.

Mowing commenced in the Valley as early as the 8th of June.

4th July celebrated by the Lewisburg Guards and citizens, at Brown's spring, below Lewisburg. James Aiken made an address.

28th September, the first temperance society formed at Lewisburg. Reverend Seiwers delivered an address. Only seven persons, John Nesbit, Esquire, James Aiken, James F. Linn, Caroline Graham, Mary Irwin, Elizabeth Irwin, and Abner C. Harding joined.

During this year, the Bethel church in White Deer was organized from members of the Buffalo Cross-Roads church; elders, Andrew McClenachan and Matthew Laird.

Deaths.

Mrs. Sarah Kelly, wife of Colonel John Kelly, 2d January. She went to bed in her usual health the night before; got up in the night and made herself a cup of tea; was heard to groan, and complained of pain in her stomach. By the time the family were awakened she was dead. She was a daughter of James Poak, sister of Mrs. Darraugh.

23d May, Thomas Wilson, of Kelly, died. He was injured on Thursday, 19th, by a log falling from the top of a wagon-wheel upon him.

1832.

LEWISBURG PRESBYTERIAN CHURCH BUILT—LAURELTON CHURCH ORGANIZED—SKETCH OF COLONEL JOHN KELLY.

ARCH 4, General Abbot Green, delegate to the State convention to form an electoral ticket. 5th, A. C. Harding addressed the temperance society and sixty-eight names were added. 17th March, over $3,000 subscribed to build a Presbyterian church in Lewisburg, and General Green, Alexander Graham, James Geddes, Thomas Clingan, William L. Harris, Doctor Thomas Vanvalzah, and William Nesbit directed, as trustees, to go on with the building.

4th May, Samuel Oaks, Colonel Thomas Smith, and Abraham Straub appointed to run the county line of Lycoming and Union: Beginning at a marked red oak, 58 perches above Lafferty's run, S. 89° W., until it intersects the original division line between Northumberland and Lycoming; thence along the same to the Centre county line.—*Pamphlet Laws*, 458.

July 4, thirty-seven survivors of the Revolution still living in Union county. Twenty-six joined in the procession at the celebration in New Berlin to-day; among them were John Linn, Frederick Bingaman, Hugh Wilson, George Engle, Christopher Seebold, and John Wilson. Isaac Slenker, Esquire, delivered an oration, and afterwards entertained the old soldiers at his house. Ice was then just coming into use, and one old gentleman was observed picking the pieces out of his brandy. He thought it was glass.

August 9 was observed as a day of fasting and prayer to avert the cholera. On the 16th Doctor Ezra Styles Ely preached at Lewisburg. His delivery was rapid, but his discourse he seemed to make very plain to every one. The Laurelton church was organized—an offshoot of the Buffalo Cross-Roads Presbyterian church.

Colonel John Kelly.

Colonel Kelly died on the 18th of February, aged eighty-eight. The following sketch of him is taken from an address made by James Merrill, Esquire, on the 8th of April, 1835, when the monument, purchased by his relatives, was put in position with public ceremony.

Colonel John Kelly was born in Lancaster county, in this State, in February, 1744. After the purchase from the Indians of 1768, and before the opening of the land office in 1769, he came to Buffalo Valley, then a part of Berks county. Here he suffered all the hardships and privations, which are inseparable upon the first settlement of a new country. He was tall, about six feet two inches in height, vigorous and muscular, with his body so inured to labor as to be almost insensible to fatigue, and a mind so accustomed to dangers, that dangers ceased to alarm. In the prime of manhood, and in the vigor of health, with intelligence to understand correct principles, and with firmness to adhere to them, it may well be supposed that he took a commanding position among his fellows. He was a captain, and a major at twenty-seven years of age, and when his country called on her sons to save her from the fangs of a tyrant, he was ready. At the very darkest period of the revolutionary war, when all was lost, but honor and hope, and when hope was almost buried in despair, in the fall of 1776, he volunteered to assist in the protection of New Jersey. He was present at Trenton, when the Hessians surrendered, and assisted in that most masterly movement on Princeton, by which the chain of communications of the enemy was broken, all their plans deranged, and their army compelled to return to New York and its neighborhorhood, and to leave New Jersey free to avenge her wrongs. When we consider the depression of public spirit, how public confidence in the final success of our cause was shaken by the battle of Long Island, and the losses of Fort Washington and Lee, with most of our military stores ; when we consider that at one time the American army numbered less than two thousand men, we would not think it wonderful if all should have been given up for lost—and so it would, if the stake had been less. But our people believed that they had no right to abandon their cause of liberty. They were bound to protect it for themselves, and upon their success depended the freedom of their posterity. They must decide, whether or not, their children should be slaves. They must decide whether all people must bow their necks to the iron yoke of despotism, or whether they might anticipate a time when free institutions should prevail through the world. Our friend and his confederates of that day might have retired into an ignoble and contemptible security. They might have said, what is New Jersey to us? We have homes and firesides, which may be endangered. But they argued better: if we refuse to come to the rescue, we cannot expect security. We cannot propitiate the monster tyranny, by shrinking from our duty. Influenced by these considerations, our friends went to the rescue of our sister State.

Our friend joined the army fully resolved to do his duty. Then was the time to test his vigor of body, as well as the firmness of his mind. For three days at one time, there was no regular service of provisions, and for more than thirty-six hours, at another time, they were constantly on the march, or in action, without a moment's sleep or giving up their arms. In the course of one of their retreats, the commander-in-chief, through Colonel Potter, sent an order to Major Kelly to have a certain bridge cut down to prevent the advance of the British, who were then in sight. The major sent for an axe; but represented that the enterprise would be very hazardous. Still the British advance must be stopped, and the order was not withdrawn. He said he could not order another to do what some might say he was afraid to do himself; he would cut down the bridge.

Before all the logs on which the bridge lay were cut off, he was completely within the range of the British fire, and several balls struck the log on which he stood. The last log broke down sooner than he expected, and he fell with it into the swollen stream. Our soldiers moved on, not believing it possible for him to escape. He, however, by great exertions, reached the shore through the high water and the floating timber, and followed the troops. Incumbered, as he must have been, with his wet and frozen clothes, he, on his road, made a prisoner of a British scout, an armed soldier, and took him into camp. What did Curtius do more than this? If such an instance of devoted heroism had happened in Greece or Rome, the day would have been distinguished from all other days. A medal would have been struck, and every means used to secure the everlasting remembrance of such a deed. In England such a man would have been made a knight or a lord, with the thanks of Parliament. In our poor devoted land such instances were too common to receive especial notice. History mentions that our army was preserved by the destruction of that bridge; but the manner in which it was done, or the name of the person who did it, is not mentioned. It was but one of a series of heroic acts, which happened every day, and our soldiers then were more familiar with the sword than with the pen. As we have met to erect a marble tomb over the remains of that individual, it is right for us to bring out this act into more bold relief.

Let it be borne in mind, that at this time no arrangement had been made respecting prisoners; that the British commanders only admitted that they arrested rebels, and not that they took prisoners of war. Thus all who fought on our side, in addition to the common dangers of war, might expect, if taken, to suffer an ignominious death. After his discharge, Major Kelly returned to his farm and his family, and during the three succeeding years the Indians were troublesome neighbors to this then frontier settlement. He became colonel of the regiment, and it was his duty to keep watch and ward against the incursions of hostile Indians, through our mountain passes. At one time our people were too weak to resist, and our whole beautiful country was abandoned. Colonel Kelly was among the first to return—for at least two harvests reapers took their rifles to the fields, and some of the company watched while others wrought. Colonel Kelly had the principal command of the scouting parties in this Valley, and very often he was out in person. Many and many nights has he lain among the limbs of a fallen tree to keep himself out of the mud, without a fire, because a fire would indicate his position to the enemy. He had become well skilled in their mode of warfare. One circumstance deserves particular notice. The Indians seem to have resolved on his death, without choosing to attack him openly. One night he had reason to apprehend that they were near. He rose in the morning, and, by looking through the crevices of his log-house, he ascertained that two, at least, if not more, were laying with their arms, so as to shoot him when he should open his door. He fixed his own rifle, and took his position, so that by a string he could open the door, and watch the Indians. The moment he pulled the door open, two balls came into the house, and the Indians rose to advance. He fired and wounded one, and both retreated. After waiting to satisfy himself that no others remained, he followed them by the blood; but they escaped.

For many years Colonel Kelly held the office of a magistrate of the county. In the administration of justice, he exhibited the same anxiety to do right, and the same disregard of self gain, which had characterized him in the military service of the country. He would at any time forgive his own fees, and if the parties were poor, pay the constable's costs, to procure a compromise. While, by industry and economy, his own pecuniary circumstances were comfortable and easy, he seemed to desire the prosperity of all men, and most anxiously to desire, that all neighbors should be friends. No man ever in vain sought his interposition to reconcile conflicting interests, to soothe angry passions, to stand, as the defender and protector of the poor man, the widow, and the orphan.

He obeyed the injunction, "be given to hospitality." There are few middle aged men in this country, who have not experienced the cordial welcome, which every friend received at his house. It is true, that so general is the hospitality of his neighborhood that the want of it would be considered a great vice; but in him it was a part of the same character, indicating a freedom from selfishness, an inability to enjoy fully God's bounties alone; a feeling that a good thing is rendered far more valuable by participation; and a conviction that the diffusion of happiness is not merely right in itself, but the source of great joy to every well-regulated mind.

Colonel Kelly was an affectionate husband, and a kind and judicious father, as well as a friendly and hospitable neighbor.

Thus have we seen our venerable friend performed his domestic, social, military, and political duties in such a manner as to entitle himself to the love and esteem of his neighbors, and to the thanks and honors of his countrymen and of posterity. It may be asked, could a man so punctiliously perform all those duties, and leave out of his regard his obligations to his Maker? No, indeed, my friends, he did not lack that crowning virtue. He was a sincere and an exemplary Christian, and he adorned all his other virtues by exhibiting a pattern of humility well worthy of imitation. Having no anxieties who should be greatest in the kingdom of Heaven, he had no striving who should be greatest in the Church on earth, his profession of religion was well sustained by his practice.

Towards the end of a long and active life, Colonel Kelly became, by disease, incapable of much motion, and seldom left his home. He seemed to be retiring from public view, and preparing to leave this world when he should be called. He had that true characteristic of bravery, an indisposition to fight his battles over again, and that feeling of humility, that where a man has only done his duty, boasting has no place. It is in some measure owing to this reserve that our notice of his life must be so brief and so imperfect. He seemed not to know, that other men would have done differently from him; but to believe that whatever distinguished him from others, arose mainly from the circumstances under which he acted. We are of another generation, and his contemporaries have either gone down to the grave, or through lapse of time and failing faculties, are unable to give particular details. From himself, but a few gleanings from a life long and full of incidents, have been obtained.

His last end proved his character to be consistent. He met the grim messenger calmly; "for he knew in whom he had trusted;" and he could "walk through the valley and shadow of death, fearing no evil." Age brought its weakness, no doubt. The frame was bent, and the muscles relaxed; but the mind—the immortal mind—could not be obscured. It brightened more and more "unto the perfect day." He has passed beyond "that bourne, whence no traveler returns." He has gone, we humbly trust, to that Heaven where "there remaineth a rest for the righteous, and where the wicked cease from troubling." Emphatically may it be said, that after a life well spent, and in firm hope of a resurrection to immortal glory, at the age of eighty-eight years, he departed, leaving his memory to our care and his virtues for our imitation—*James Merrill, Esquire's, Address.*

Colonel Kelly's children were: James, who moved to Penn's valley, and died there. He was the father of Honorable James K. Kelly, United States Senator, of Portland, Oregon; John, who also moved to Penn's valley; William, who married a daughter of Archibald Allison, of Centre county, and died, January 27, 1830; Andrew, a bachelor, who was born 1783, and died on the old place, September 24, 1867, aged eighty-four; Samuel Kelly, of Armstrong county, Pennsylvania; Elizabeth, married to Simeon Howe; Maria, married to John Campbell, of Lewisburg; Robert, who died April 12, 1865, aged seventy-seven; Joseph, died March 2, 1860, aged sixty-six; David H. Kelly, Esquire, deceased, late county commissioner of Union county.

I note, also, the death of Reverend Thomas Smiley, aged seventy-three, born (in Dauphin county now) in 1759, of Scotch-Irish parentage. Served in Colonel Curtis Grubb's battalion of militia. Ordained in December, 1802. Settled in White Deer in 1808, where he established the first regular Baptist church within the bounds of Union county.

1833.

Methodist Church in Lewisburg Dedicated—The Presbyterian Church Completed, and the German Church Commenced—Rain of Fire—Court and Lawyers.

ANUARY 5, the new Methodist church, on Third street, Lewisburg, consecrated. The weather was so warm that the windows had to be opened. Sunday, 6th, Reverend Mr. Steele preached in A. M., in the new church. Mr. Hood in P. M. Weather still very warm. The 11th of January was probably the coldest day of the year.

January 30, David Myers, of East Buffalo, who was kicked in the abdomen by a horse, on Monday, 28th, died to-day.

March 21, J. F. Quay, J. F. Murray, and David Rockefeller appointed to run the division line between Lycoming and Union counties.

May 31, Jesse Cornelius, miller, at Trester's old mill, on Turtle creek, was caught in the machinery. Ribs, breast bone, &c., broken. He died immediately.

July 26, Ephraim Darraugh's widow buried at Lewisburg. 31, Presbyterian church building completed, and on the 4th of August Mr. Hood preached the first sermon therein, on the text, "Remember the Sabbath day, to keep it holy." August 31, Thomas Clingan, William Nesbit, Esquire, Robert H. Laird, and James F. Linn were elected elders.

September 30, Reverend Mathew Laird married, at Mr. Hood's, to Miss Harriet Myer, school-teacher at Lewisburg. They sailed, on 15th October, as missionaries to Africa.

October 15, Thomas Jones, inn-keeper, died. 18, Roan McClure, after fifteen minutes' sickness.

November 4, a subscription was started, for the purpose of building a Union German Reformed and Lutheran church, on Third and St. Lewis streets, in Lewisburg, to be called St. Lewis church, "in honor of the original proprietor of the borough, and the benefactor, (Ludwig Derr,) who gave three lots for religious use."

On 19th May, 1834, John Reber, John Snook, and Henry Noll, elders; Henry Noll and Ludwig Long, deacons of the German Presbyterian congregation, entered into an agreement with Jonathan Spyker and John Gundy, trustees of the German Lutheran congregation, giving the latter "the same privilege of the German burying-ground, which Ludwig Derr, in his liftetime, gave to the German Presbyterian congregation, being on lots Nos. 121, 123, and 125, as well as an equal privilege of the church built or building on said ground, to be tenants in common," &c. See deed book K, pages 173 and 174, (at Lewisburg.) In the year 1851, the Lutheran congregation bought out the interest of the German Reformed, the latter having built on the corner of St. John and Third streets.

November 13, from two o'clock until daylight occurred a firestorm, or the fall of small particles of fire, which appeared to extinguish a few feet from the ground. It was observed all through Buffalo Valley.

December 7, the first boats passed through the Lewisburg crosscut. December 29, Lorenzo Dow preached at Lewisburg. 30th, John Clark, Esquire, of Beaver, a member of the Legislature, from that county, visited Lewisburg. He is is a son of Walter Clark, deceased, one of the first settlers on Buffalo creek. 31st, Mrs. Hayes, mother of William, (merchant formerly,) died suddenly.

Court and Lawyers.

At September term the grand jury of the county, William Forster, foreman, petitioned the Governor for the appointment of William W. Potter, Esquire, of Bellefonte, as president judge, *vice* Seth Chapman, resigned. On the 16th of December Judge Ellis Lewis' commission as president judge was read, who, with Hugh Wilson and General Adam Light, associates, comprised the court. George F. Miller and Samuel Weirick, Esquires, were admitted to the bar on the 15th of May.

1834.

ECLIPSE OF THE SUN—ANTI-SCHOOL MEETINGS—ELECTION RETURNS.

RICE of wheat in Philadelphia, in May, $1 10; in September, $1 04; corn, 64; rye, 65. There was no snow during the month of February, and the weather was as mild as it usually is in April. On the nights of the 31st of May and the 1st of June occurred a black frost so severe as to kill the leaves of almost every species of plants in this part of the country. Even the locust, a hardy tree, did not escape. Cherries, apples, peaches, and all orchard and garden fruits, except currants and gooseberries, perished. Bears, missing their summer supply of whortleberries, came down from the hills to feed upon the green corn, and were killed in unusual numbers. It was interesting to see robins, woodpeckers, and other birds now searching among the limbs of the trees for caterpillars and other insects; fortunately the caterpillars were prodigiously numerous. During the summer, bituminous coal was received at Lewisburg from the western part of the State, by the canal, and sold at twenty-five cents per bushel. At Hartleton, R. H. Kerr was postmaster ; and J. H. Seiwers was principal of the academy at Lewisburg.

February 2, Lorenzo Dow died at Georgetown, D. C. March 18, Charles Sargent (son of John, inn-keeper,) found drowned below Brown's mill. Has been missing since the 16th. He was dederanged. 30th, Mr. Hood preached his last sermon as pastor. April 10, John Moore, merchant, of Lewisburg, died. Reverends Henry Tarring and Oliver Ega, Methodist ministers for this circuit this year. April 21, Joseph Evans, of Lewisburg, found drowned in the canal at Selinsgrove. Job Harvey, a young preacher of the Christian church, preached his funeral sermon. May 19, corner-stone of German church in Lewisburg laid. J. H. Fries, pastor. June 19, Howard Vanvalzah, son of Doctor Thomas, fell from the steeple of the new German church to the ground, striking the timbers as he fell, his thigh and leg broken. He fell forty-five feet. (He is still living at Lewistown.) June 30, news arrived of the death of Reverend Matthew Laird and his wife, missionaries in Africa. He died on the 4th of May, his wife on the 3d. Wednesday, 9th July, thermometer at ninety-nine degrees in shade. July 28, John Geary, an apprentice of David Ginter, drowned at the upper landing in Lewisburg, last night. November 13, Presbytery met at Lewisburg, and ordained and installed Reverend P. B. Marr, pastor of that church. Sunday, 30th November, eclipse of the sun. Began quarter before one, went off twenty-five minutes past three. During its greatest obscuration it became very cold, and it seemed like a bright, moonlight night, and one star was visible.

Anti-School Meeting.

Agreeably to public notice, the citizens of Union county opposed to the school law passed at the last session of the Legislature, met at the court-house, in New Berlin, on Thursday, the 18th September, when Henry Yearick, Esquire, was called to the chair; Robert Taylor, Esquire, was appointed vice president ; and John Montelius and John Snyder were appointed secretaries. On motion of the Honorable George Kremer, a committee of fifteen were appointed to draft a preamble and resolutions expressive of the sense of the meeting; whereupon, the following persons were appointed, viz:

George Kremer, Peter Richter, Doctor John G. Piper, Frederick Pontius, Abbot Green, John Boyer, Frederick Kremer, John S. Ingram, George Schnable, John Zigler, James Madden, Henry Roush, Henry C. Eyer, John Snyder, John Reber, junior.

After retiring a short time, returned and reported the following, which were unanimously adopted:

WHEREAS, The Legislature of Pennsylvania, at their late session, passed a law known as the common school law, the principles of which we consider dangerous to our rights and destructive of our interests; therefore, be it

Resolved, That, in the opinion of this meeting, it behooves us to use every honorable means in our power to procure a prompt repeal of the law in question.

Resolved, That the chair appoint two persons from each township or borough in the county, as the case may be, whose duty it shall be to act as delegates for their respective districts, and bring with them the election returns, which will take place to-morrow, for the adoption or rejection of the school law, and report the same to this meeting.

Resolved, That should a school man, by mistake, be selected by the chair, he shall be rejected by the anti-school delegate of that district, &c., who shall have full power to supply his place with a man opposed to the school law.

Resolved, That this meeting adjourn to meet again at the courthouse, in New Berlin, on Tuesday next, at one o'clock in the afternoon, and that the present officers are again requested to preside, to adopt further measures in relation to this oppressive law.

The following persons were appointed by the chair, as delegates from the several townships, to meet in New Berlin, on Tuesday, the 23d instant, viz:

East Buffalo—Philip Ruhl, Peter Voneida.
Lewisburg—William Hayes, Jacob Zentmire.
Kelly—Laird Howard, George Meixell.
White Deer—John Rank, Jacob Sypher.
Union—John S. Ingram, Michael Benfer.

Chapman—Frederick Kremer, John Snyder.
Washington—John Boyer, Henry Hilbish.
Penn's—Peter Richter, George Miller.
Perry—George Shetterly, senior, Joseph Schnee.
Centre—George Kremer, Henry Bolender.
Beaver—John Highley, John Shipton.
Centreville—Stephen Bruce, George Weirick.
Hartleton—James Madden, George Ruhl.
West Buffalo—Robert Taylor, John Reber, junior.
Mifflinburg—Henry Yearick, John Montelius.—*Times, September* 19, 1834.

Anti-School Delegate Meeting.

At a meeting of the delegates appointed by the anti-school meeting of the 18th instant, held at the court-house, in New Berlin, on Tuesday last, Henry Yearick, Esquire, presided; assisted by John Montelius and Captain John Snyder, as secretaries.

The names of the delegates having been called, the following gentlemen were present, representing the different townships, as follows:

Union—John S. Ingram, Michael Benfer.
Hartley—James Madden, Esquire, George Ruhl.
West Buffalo—Robert Taylor, John Stees, junior.
Mifflinburg—Henry Yearick, John Montelius.
East Buffalo—Philip Ruhl, Peter Voneida.
Lewisburg—George Schnabel, Jacob Zentmire.
White Deer—Jacob Sypher, Samuel Baker.
Kelly—John Hummel, Joseph Spotts.
Chapman—John Snyder, Frederick Kremer.
Penn's—Peter Richter, George Miller.
Perry—George Shetterly, Joseph Schnee.
Centre—George Kremer, Henry Bolender.
Beaver—John Highley, John Shipton.
Washington—John Boyer, Henry Hilbish.

On motion of James Madden, Esquire, a committee of nine delegates were appointed by the chair to draft a preamble and resolutions, expressive of the sentiments of the delegation.

Whereupon, the chair appointed George Kremer, John S. Ingram,

Peter Richter, Henry Hilbish, George Schnabel, James Madden, Jacob Sypher, Philip Ruhl, and John Reber, junior.

The committee retired a short time and reported the following, which were unanimously adopted:

Preamble and Resolutions.

FELLOW-CITIZENS: Your committee view with deep interest the law of our last Legislature, creating a system of education by common schools. They consider it as affecting the interests and encroaching upon the rights of the honest and industrious citizens of the Commonwealth. They view the system as unwarranted by the Constitution, and at war with the interests of every useful member of the community; as a system of *education* was only asked, and not one of unjust and unequal *taxation*. For these reasons, and others, we oppose the bill, urging our constitutional objections, and will merely here state its local effects upon the county of Union.

The $75,000 appropriated for common school purposes, of which Union county will be entitled to about $1,100, is a fund arising from the unpatented lands in this Commonwealth. Owing to the scarcity of money, the law has, from year to year, been extended; but as this amount is now appropriated, and will be drawn out of the treasury, consequently, all those whose lands are unpatented, will now be compelled to pay, as the finances of the Commonwealth will not warrant a longer credit. All men know its enormous debt and embarrassed condition.

By the law in question, Union county must raise $2,200, double the amount of the appropriation, to entitle them to the proffer made by the Legislature. To this add our already exhorbitant State tax, of about $3,000, and we have upwards of $5,000 to pay by taxation, for merely receiving the bill.

Agreeable to the law, the six directors are to divide each township into as many school districts, and build as many school-houses as they may think proper; and this additional debt you will be bound to pay by taxation, which will amount to at least $800 for every township in the county, making a sum total of $17,000, adding the other taxes imposed by this bill.

To this may be added the teachers. Suppose each township have six teachers, who cannot be engaged at a less expense than $250 per annum, each, making a gross amount of $1,500 per annum for each township, the whole cost for this purpose in the county would be $22,500. Deduct from this the $1,100 proffered by the Legislature, and the people have $21,400 to pay for teachers, $17,000 for buildings, $2,200 for accepting the proffer—making a sum total of $40,600, all to be paid by the people by various taxations.

Resolved, That five persons be appointed a committee to draw petitions to be signed by the citizens of this county, praying the Legislature to repeal the school law for Union county.

Resolved, That the chair appoint two persons in each township, who shall have authority to appoint as many more as may be necessary in each township to solicit subscribers to said petition.

Resolved, That the chair appoint a committee of five persons, a corresponding committee to correspond with other committees in this Commonwealth to procure a repeal of the school law in this Commonwealth.

On motion George Kremer, John S. Ingram, and Philip Ruhl were appointed a committee to prepare and publish a petition for a repeal of the law in question.

The chair then appointed Peter Richter, John S. Ingram, George Kremer, George Schnabel, and John Reber, junior, a committee of correspondence, in accordance with a resolution of the committee of nine.

On motion, it was then *Resolved*, That the delegates of this convention act as township committees to circulate and procure signers to the petitions praying for a repeal of the school law.

On motion of John S. Ingram, the secretary was called upon to report the votes at the different township elections held on Friday, the 19th instant; which was carried, and the following result exhibited, viz:

Townships.	Against School.	For School.	Townships.	Against School.	For School.
Union,	205	—	Perry,	63	—
Hartley,	144	30	Centre,	170	—
West Buffalo,	187	7	Beaver,	192	—
Mifflinburg,	67	41	Washington,	85	—
East Buffalo,	87	3			
Lewisburg,	55	71		1620	267
White Deer,	26	52		267	
Kelly,	70	7			
Chapman,	71	1	Balance vs. school, 1353 votes.		
Penn's,	198	55			

Political.

Delegates to the 4th of March convention, "to oppose executive usurpation," Simon Shaffer, William Cameron, Ner Middleswarth, William L. Harris, George Weirick, and R. P. Maclay.

Delegate Meeting.—On Tuesday last the delegates from the different townships of Union county, representing the Anti-Masons, assembled at the court-house, in New Berlin. Samuel Paulding, of Penn's, was called to the chair, and Solomon Engle, Esquire, of Centre, appointed secretary.

As soon as the meeting was thus organized, George Aurand, Esquire, of Centre, rose, and moved that no delegate be received in this convention, unless he be a *pure* Anti-Mason. This motion, however, was postponed until after the credentials had been presented.

The credentials were then presented, in regular order, which comprised the following delegation:

Centre—George Aurand, Solomon Engle.
Union—Henry Frock, George Schnee.
Mifflinburg—Jacob Haus, David Eckstein.
Lewisburg—Doctor I. S. Vorse, G. F. Miller.
East Buffalo—Peter Wise, Robert Laird.
West Buffalo—Samuel B. Barber, John Kutz.
Hartley—William Glover, Jacob Snyder.
Kelly—John Hummel, Joseph Lawson.
Penn's—Samuel Paulding, Philip Gemberling.
Beaver—Archibald Thomas, John Reger.
Washington—J. P. Hackenberg, Jacob Garman.
Perry—Michael Gougler, John Weimen.
Centreville—Jonathan Farnsworth, S. Bruce.

The credentials being thus presented in due order, when Lewisburg came in turn, Doctor Vorse rose and stated that a motion had been made to expel any member of the convention who was not an avowed Anti-Mason. He said he did not wish to act the hypocrite, and consequently he would inform the convention that he was *not* an Anti-Mason—that he was an anti-Jackson man—that he came here to represent that portion of the borough of Lewisburg who were opposed to Jackson, and that while he would perform such incumbent duty, he wished it to be distinctly understood that he had no claims to the character of an Anti-Mason.

Mr. Aurand then stated that as he was not a political Anti-mason, he would move that he be not permitted to occupy a seat in the convention.

Mr. Miller, his colleague, then rose, and hoped that the convention would not act rashly on this subject; that Doctor Vorse was not in an individual capacity, but serving as the representative of the party in Lewisburg; that he had his instructions and would conform to them. He hoped such a vote would not be taken.

Mr. Aurand, however, persisted in the vote, which was taken, and resulted as follows :

  For rejection, ... 23 votes.
  For retention, ... 2 votes.

Doctor Vorse was, therefore, ejected from the convention. He rose, and returned his thanks to the meeting for their kind treatment; and while he expressed his regret at having put the gentlemen to so much trouble, he retired from any participation in the proceedings, considering the decision a very curious one.

Mr. Miller then moved that Lewisburg be entitled to a full representation, by suffering the remaining delegate to have two votes; but on the question, "Shall Lewisburg have a full representation?" it was decided in the negative.

The convention then proceeded to make nominations, which resulted in the following ticket:

For Congress—Samuel J. Packer.
For Senate—Robert P. Maclay.
For Assembly—Simon Shaffer and Ner Middleswarth.
For Coroner—Jacob Aurand and Daniel Winter.
For Commissioner—James Harrison.
For Auditor—Jacob H. Hummel.
For Trustees—Israel Gutelius, John Kutz, and Samuel Wright.

Mr. Aurand then offered the following resolution; which was adopted:

Resolved, That a committee be appointed to address James Merrill, Esquire, on the subject of Masonry, and to request an explanation on that subject, in terms which he may think most proper.

Whereupon the chair appointed George Aurand, J. P. Hackenberg, and J. H. Horning, Esquires.

On motion, William Glover and George F. Miller were appointed conferees, to meet other congressional conferees at Milton.

On motion, David Eckstein and Solomon Engle, Esquire, were appointed senatorial conferees, to meet similar conferees at Lewisburg.

The following persons were then appointed a standing committee for the ensuing year, viz : Jacob Fryer, Jacob Haus, Joseph Lawson, Matthew Brewer, S. Weirick, George Schnee, and Jacob Snyder.

It was then

Resolved, That the convention adjourn, and that the proceedings be published in all the papers.—*Times, August* 8.

Democratic Convention.

On Tuesday last, the following delegates, from the different townships of Union county, met at the court-house, in New Berlin, to form a ticket for support at the next general election, viz:

Union—Jacob Spangler, Jesse Beaver.

Buffalo—Hugh Wilson, junior, Samuel Reber.

West Buffalo—Robert Taylor, Thomas Forster.

Penn's—C. M. Straub, Isaac Hottenstein.

Chapman—John Snyder, Philip Herold.

Mifflinburg—Michael Schoch, Thomas McCurdy.

Lewisburg—John Nesbit, Joseph Hutchinson.

Centre—George Kremer, John Bower.

Hartley—George Roush, Andrew Cook.

Beaver—George Swartz, Thomas Youngman.

Perry—Philip Benner, George Shetterly.

Kelly—Alexander McClure, John Young.

White Deer—Samuel Baker, William Mackey.

The convention was organized by electing Captain Alexander McClure, president; Robert Taylor, Esquire, vice president, and Joseph Hutchinson, secretary.

On motion, it was unanimously

Resolved, That no candidate, for any office, should be considered nominated, who had not a majority of all the votes of the delegates present.

The following nominations of candidates were then made, and resulted as follows: Senator, Isaac Slenker. Assembly, Captain Jacob Hummel and James McClure. Commissioner, Peter Beaver. Auditor, Martin Dreisbach. Coroner, Jacob McCorley. Trustees of the Mifflinburg Academy, Philip Pontius, Samuel Barber, and William Irwin.—*Times, August* 15.

OFFICIAL ELECTION RETURNS.

DISTRICTS.	CONG'SS.		SENATE.		ASSEMBLY.				SHERI'F	
	Anthony.	Packer.	Slenker.	Maclay.	McClure.	Hummel.	Middleswarth.	Shaffer.	Cummings, jr.	Barbin.
Union,	216	120	241	88	150	220	188	101	207	142
White Deer,	93	47	105	31	55	79	79	55	95	47
Kelly,	45	43	64	24	21	56	74	34	61	22
Lewisburg,	105	55	134	17	100	85	73	45	125	27
East Buffalo,	158	137	148	123	186	122	174	96	123	148
West Buffalo,	117	86	114	78	101	90	106	104	135	66
Mifflinburg,	86	48	75	56	88	78	41	58	84	34
Hartley,	192	112	191	99	153	169	138	132	230	80
Centreville,	6	73	5	73	12	7	71	66	25	60
Penn's,	254	124	233	141	148	233	216	143	281	133
Centre,	76	171	55	189	61	77	181	173	69	187
Beaver,	61	242	49	253	33	76	249	247	99	230
Washington,	109	68	100	76	95	102	82	78	122	73
Chapman,	115	31	102	32	108	120	31	24	122	29
Perry,	82	41	84	40	78	85	42	40	88	46
Total,	1716	1398	1700	1320	1389	1599	1745	1396	1866	1324

Honorable Joseph B. Anthony was elected to Congress in the district composed of Union, Northumberland, and Lycoming, by a majority of 2,218, and Mr. Slenker in the district composed of Union and Northumberland, by a majority of 1602. September 12, John S. Ingram retires from the *Times*, and James M. Kuester took charge. He retired December 19, and Gabriel Yearick became editor.

1835.

DEBATE IN THE LEWISBURG TEMPERANCE SOCIETY—COLONEL KELLY'S MONUMENT ERECTED WITH IMPOSING CEREMONIES—FOURTH OF JULY CELEBRATIONS.

THE winter of 1834 and 1835 was very severe. On Shade mountain, a pack of twenty wolves were found frozen after the melting of the snow. They appeared to have huddled together, perhaps exhausted with a long march, and perished of cold and hunger.

On Friday evening, the 13th of February, the Lewisburg Temperence society again met, and resumed the discussion of the propriety of adopting the resolution, "that the distillation and vendition of ardent spirits, *as a drink*, is morally wrong," which, it must be known, had been discussed before by the society, and adopted by a majority of four votes; but the opponents of the resolution, not being satisfied with the proceedings, on account of illegal votes having been taken, as they alleged, it was, therefore, agreed by both parties to re-consider the resolution.

The debate was held in the Methodist church. Mr. Merrill, Mr. Marr, and Mr. Aiken for affirmative. General Green, Doctor Joyce, Mr. Barber, and James P. Ross in the negative.

The first resolution: *Resolved*, That the distilling and vending of ardent spirits, as a drink, is morally wrong. Second, that it is expedient that the temperance societies of Pennsylvania adopt the above resolution.

The vote on the first, yeas, 70; nays, 36. Second, yeas, 58; nays, 30.

February 24, Isaac G. Jones admitted to the bar.[1] April 8, the monument to the memory of Colonel John Kelly was erected with impressive ceremonies, in the Presbyterian burial-ground, in the borough of Lewisburg. A company of cavalry from Northumberland county, one from Union, with three infantry companies, participated. Abbot Green was grand marshal, with Michael Brobst, General R. H. Hammond, Colonel Philip Ruhl, and Doctor J. S. Dougal as aids. The procession was formed by the adjutant, Colonel Jackson McFadden, with the military, in front, followed by the revolutionary soldiers and citizens; after whom came the monument, drawn by four gray horses, flanked by cavalry; then the marshal and aids, preceding the orator, clergy, and relatives; lastly, the ladies, and a section of cavalry brought up the rear. On its arrival at the ground, the cavalry were stationed outside the burial-ground, and the infantry formed a square about the grave, inclosing the relatives, clergy, &c. The monument was set by the architects, William Hubbard, F. Stoughton, Samuel Hursh, and Charles Penny; after which the grand marshal performed the rites of dedication, and James Merrill, Esquire, delivered an oration.

On the 12th of April, Mr. Hood preached his farewell sermon to the Milton congregation, and on the 19th, to the Buffalo congregation, thus closing with the latter a pastorate of thirty-one years. On the 3d of May, Reverend Isaac Grier succeeded him at Buffalo Cross-Roads. On the 31st of May, the German church in Lewisburg was dedicated. A great number of people in attendance.

The 4th of July was celebrated at Buffalo Cross-Roads by a meeting, at which Colonel Philip Ruhl presided and James D. Chamberlin acted as secretary. Colonel Henry Noll delivered an oration, and James C. McCreight read the Declaration of Independence. The citizens of New Berlin and Hartleton united in a celebration at Mifflinburg. James A. Cummings was grand marshal, and there was a grand parade, in which Captain Forster's infantry, the Jackson guards, and the Lafayette troop, under the command of Captain Eilert, took part.

A fourth of July sentiment, of a partisan character, appeared in the proceedings of the Mifflinburg celebration, contrary to an under-

---

Isaac G. Jones, Esquire, moved to Beaver, Pennsylvania, where he practiced law until his death, March 30, 1853.

standing that all political toasts should be suppressed. It appeared among the proceedings, and was published accordingly. The following is the toast:

By J. H. Fries: Democrats, Jackson, and Anti-Bank men of Pennsylvania, will you, or can you, suffer to be beaten after such a glorious victory as you achieved in 1834? Lay all personal and family desires aside, and think on the true and faithful saying: "United we stand, divided we fall."

Military Election.

Abbot Green, Esquire, of Lewisburg, in this county, was, a few days ago, elected to the honorable station of major general of this division. We believe this selection has given general satisfaction. Henry Noll was elected colonel; Samuel Reber, lieutenant colonel; John Gundy and George Roush, junior, majors of the forty-third regiment.—*Times, July* 6.

At September court, politics were lively in New Berlin. A Wolf meeting was held on Monday, a Muhlenburg meeting on Tuesday, and a Ritner meeting on Wednesday. September 24, John Sargent and family left Lewisburg, moving eight miles west of Meadville. November 27, an explosion occurred in Charles F. Schaffle's drug store at Lewisburg, in which he was badly burned. December 24, Beck's tannery burned down.

1836.

Political Appointments—Accident on the Fourth of July.

INTER of 1835-6 was very severe; snow frequently over twelve inches deep, and the river frozen to the depth of two or three feet. Joseph Ritner having been elected Governor, appoints his friends to office. Robert P. Maclay succeeding Joseph Stillwell as prothonotary, and George Aurand succeeding Samuel Roush as register and recorder. Ner Middleswarth was elected Speaker of the House of Representatives. On the 1st of April, the Lewisburg, Penn's Valley, and Hollidaysburg railroad was incorporated, and on the 16th of June an act was passed re-districting the State. Juniata, Mifflin, and Union a district, entitled to three members.

May 23, James Reasoner died. He had hitched his horse to a post in Hartleton; the horse frightened and pulled out the post, and Mr. Reasoner, in trying to catch the horse, was struck with the swinging post, and died from the effects. James McClune commenced his classical school in Lewisburg.

16th June, Charles de Haas, engineer, commenced surveying the Lewisburg, Penn's Valley, and Hollidaysburg railroad. He ran his line up Cherry alley, Lewisburg.

4th of July celebration terminated unfortunately. Towards evening, a party were firing a cannon at the foot of St. John street. They had fired twice, when, in the act of ramming the third charge, it exploded. Joseph McCool had his right hand blown off, and his arm had to be amputated below the elbow. John Bower lost his two forefingers. Peter Bower had his thumb torn off.

August 24, Kirkham, the grammarian, delivered a lecture in Lewisburg.

October 5, heavy snow-storm; one and a half feet deep in Penn's valley and on Buffalo and White Deer mountains.

November 4, James Merrill, Esquire, and William P. Maclay, elected Senatorial delegates, and William L. Harris, Ephraim Banks, and John Cummin, Representative delegates to the Convention to propose amendments to the Constitution of the State.

1837.

First Abolition Lecture in the Valley—Shows—Report of the Union County Agricultural Society.

FEBRUARY 5th, Philip Rorabaugh buried in the German grave-yard, at Lewisburg, with military honors, aged eighty-five. He was a hero of three wars, the Revolution, the whisky insurrection, and the war of 1812.

March 15, Mrs. Dunlap's house, on Buffalo creek, a mile below Chamberlin's mill, was burned last night; Sally Gray and her son, (both deranged,) John Young, about seventeen years old, and a son of Joseph G. Wallace, eight years old, burned. There were eight in the house; four escaped.

April 17, Doctor Thomas Vanvalzah, and others, left the Valley to settle in Illinois. This was the start of an emigration which has made Stephenson county, Illinois, a counterpart of Buffalo Valley.

November 10, Miller McKim delivered his first lecture in Lewisburg on the abolition of slavery. On the 14th there was a meeting which, upon a motion made to determine whether McKim should be allowed to speak, ended suddenly in a small riot.

Shows.

Shows have changed in character with the increase of population. Welsh & Purdy's came through the county. They have collected upwards of one hundred beasts, birds, and reptiles, in a great caravan of wagons; have an excellent band of musicians, and held their exhibition under a huge pavilion, capable of containing five thousand people. It is quite a grand spectacle to see them entering New Berlin. In front marches the elephant, clad in red housings, with a lofty saddle, on which are mounted two musicians; next, came a band of musicians, mounted upon gray horses, gaily caparisoned, followed by a train of wagons, containing the animals. The whole establishment embraced one hundred horses, all grays, and eighty men. The hotels were open before daylight, and people gathered in from the country as soon as it was light. The largest room in the house was thrown open for dancing, and the fiddles only ceased with the news of the entrance of the procession, to be resumed after the procession, and continued until the call for dinner.

Union County Agricultural Society.

It is with regret that we notice so late the reports of three committees of this society, made on the 20th of October. They were the reports of the committee on grain, on hogs, and on butter and cheese. The way in which these reports came to be omitted in the report published in the *Union Times*, of the 4th instant, was, that they were handed to the former treasurer, who supposed that they would be called for, and the present treasurer, not knowing that such reports existed, they were omitted to be laid before the committee on premiums. Consequently, the articles recommended in those reports as worthy of premiums had no premiums awarded them out of the funds appropriated for that purpose. These reports are now noticed, because it is due to the producers of the articles noticed in them. It is only to be regretted, that the funds of the society will not afford them the premiums they merited. The following is an abstract of the reports:

The committee on grain reported, that John Wilt, of Hartley township, produced evidence of the best yield of wheat per acre, according to the quality of the soil, having raised *thirty-five* bushels off an acre, selected out of a field of about eight acres, the wheat having been cultivated alike. They report the soil as being of second-rate land—a gravel shale—adjacent to limestone soil.

That Colonel Samuel Barber, of West Buffalo township, exhibited evidence of the next best specimen of wheat, having raised forty bushels off an acre, selected out of a field containing eleven acres, all cultivated alike. That the soil is of first rate limestone. Considering the quality of the soil, the committee awarded the first premium to Mr. Wilt, and to Colonel Barber the second. The committee also considered Colonel Barber worthy of a premium for the best specimen of summer wheat. Francis Wilson's corn, being seventy bushels of shelled corn to an acre, was also deemed worthy of a premium. The committee also notice in terms of commendation Mr. Wilt's yield of corn ; as also Philip Seebold's grapes; Samuel Templeton's potatoes, having yielded eighty bushels per quarter of an acre, (one single potato weighing four and three quarter pounds;) Mrs. Merrill's sugar-beet, and Mrs. Shroyer's red-beet, and Mrs. Schoch's cabbage. To some of these small premiums are recommended, especially Mr. Seebold's grapes.

The committee on hogs awarded to John Clemmens a premium for the best breed of hogs, considering their size and age.

The committee on butter and cheese recommended a specimen of butter exhibited by Mrs. Margaret Pontius, as of a superior quality, both in color and taste.

JOSEPH STILWELL, *Recording Secretary.*

Philadelphia Prices Current, October 21, 1837—Grain: Wheat, Pennsylvania, bushel, $1 55 ; Rye, 80 ; Corn, yellow, 93 ; Barley, inferior, 83 ; Oats, 35 to 38. Spirits: Whisky, rye, 33 ; hogsheads, 31. Wool: American, full blood, lb. 50 to 63.

At the October election, Yearick, for Assembly, received 1,381 votes in Union county; Boyer, opposition, 1,666.

1838.

Locust Year—Buckshot War.

HIS is the "locust year." I saw and heard them for the first time this year on the 17th of June, and the last of them were heard in the last week of July. They were very numerous, and most of the oak trees in this neighborhood bear witness of their labors; the present year's shoots of the branches being killed by the punctures this creature makes in laying its eggs. The common opinion is that they re-appear every fourteen years, (some say seventeen,) but I incline to think they are by no means regular in their visits. The first time I saw them was in 1804, when they were very numerous about Selinsgrove. In the year 1817, I saw them at Princeton, N. J.; in 1821, at Sunbury; at Selinsgrove, in 1832; and, lastly, here, (Milton.) A gentleman who had a contract on the canal in 1827-28-29, informed me that the laborers frequently dug up this insect in the aurelia state, in the flats. Their size diminished according to the depth beneath the surface. Some were found at the depth of four feet, and were small, soft, and entirely white. They do not make their appearance in all parts of the country at the same period.—*G. A. S.*

To the Electors of the District composed of the counties of Union, Juniata, and Mifflin :[1]

FELLOW-CITIZENS : I have been in a deplorable situation for eight or ten days past. I was elected your representative. As such, I am

[1] This communication was published as an extra of the *Union Times*, Wednesday, December, 19, and gives Mr. Montelius' reasons for withdrawing from his party organization at that interesting epoch in Pennsylvania political history, known as the "Buckshot War," causing a collapse of Thaddeus Stevens' "Rump Legislature," as it was called. Mr. Montelius was commissioned associate judge of Union county, February 27, 1845, by Governor Shunk, and died at Mifflinburg, March 31, 1864, aged eighty years two months and twenty-three days.

bound faithfully to discharge my duty to you, to myself, to God, and my country. You are already informed that there were two Speakers elected on the 4th instant, in the House of Representatives. With the information I had, and the advice of the friends in whom I confided, I was induced to act here with the party who profess the same principles with those of my constituents who nominated and elected me. But full information, cool and deliberate reflection, and warnings of my conscience, have convinced me that my party friends here have mistaken their course, and that, as a faithful representative, and an honest man, I was bound to retrace my steps, do what I conscientiously believed to be right, and trust to the impartiality of your judgment, upon a full and fair examination of all the facts. Finding my political friends had done wrong, according to my judgment, I withdrew from them immediately, and have waited for several days to give them time to retrace their steps, and to allow all concerned to arrange, peaceably and justly, the unhappy difference that had arisen ; but finding this has not been accomplished, I have nothing left for me but to do that which I believe to be right, and leave to those who would destroy our beloved State the consequence of their rashness. Do not think I have acted rashly. The step I have taken was taken deliberately and coolly, and in obedience to my understanding of the constitution and laws of our dear country. I am for peace. "*Es wird meiner seele bange zu wohnen bey denen die den frieden hassen.*" And I hope the course I have taken may help to save our beloved Pennsylvania from bloodshed and the horrors of civil war. The great question is whether the majority shall rule, and upon this question I know you all think with me. Now, all I have done has been done with an honest desire to carry out this great principle in our free government, that the minority must yield to the majority. And I am certain not one of you, however strong a party man he may be, will blame me for maintaining this principle. My constituents, particularly in Union county, all know me, and I beg of them all, before they condemn me, fully and coolly to examine the facts. I have not, in this instance, acted as a party man, but I have acted honestly, and according to my conscience.

In joining with my party friends in organizing the House of Representatives, with the eight Philadelphia county members of the

Whig party, I thought these had been elected by the majority of the votes of the county, and had been returned by a majority of the judges, but I soon found that this was not true, and that the eight members of the opposition party in the county of Philadelphia, had been elected by a majority of about five hundred votes in the whole county, and had been returned elected by a majority of the judges.

I am sorry to say that the Secretary of the State kept back these returns, which I think was wrong. Under these circumstances, I could not continue to act with men who had no right to their seats, no more than my opponent had to mine. You would not, as honest men, ask me to sanction so bad a principle, and it is that I know your honesty that I have joined those who have been fairly elected by the majority. My party opinions and principles have not changed, and my future course will show that I am true to those principles. On your calm judgment I rely. What I have done has been done for what I believe to be your interest, and is approved by my conscience.

I remain your friend,

JOHN MONTELIUS.

HALL OF THE HOUSE OF REPRESENTATIVES, *December* 17, 1838.

On the 17th of December, Messrs. Butler and Sturdevant, of Luzerne, and Mr. Montelius, of Union, appeared in the House, over which Mr. Hopkins was presiding, and, after some remarks by Mr. Butler, explanatory of their course, were duly sworn as members, thus ending the contest.

1839.

AURAND'S HOTEL BURNED—POLITICS—OBITUARY NOTICE OF REVEREND J. H. FRIES.

ANUARY 15, David R. Porter proclaimed Governor. February 19, Samuel Aurand's hotel, at New Berlin, burned. It was court week, and the house full of lawyers, jurors, suitors, and witnesses. Some made narrow escapes, with the loss of their clothing, as the fire broke out in the night, when all were abed. April 5, John Egbert's stable, at Lewisburg, burned, with his horse and cow. This was followed by the burning of Alexander Graham's and a number of others, caused by incendiaries.

The *Times*, August 21, publishes the following as the "Democratic-Republican Anti-Bank ticket: Assembly, Doctor Isaac Hottenstine; Prothonotary, Samuel Roush; Register and Recorder, Robert Forster; Commissioner, George A. Snyder; Auditor, Jacob Wittenmyer; Trustees of the Mifflinburg Academy, Colonel Samuel Barber, John Hilbish, and Charles Pellman; and the following as the "Abolition United States Bank ticket:" Assembly, John A. Vanvalzah; Prothonotary, Jacob H. Horning; Register and Recorder, John Glover; Commissioner, Henry Hilbish; Auditor, Samuel Pawling; Trustees, Samuel B. Barber, James Simington, and David Watson. Anti-Masonic candidate for Register and Recorder, David Schwenck. At the October election, Vanvalzah's vote was 1,577. Average majority of his colleagues on the ticket in Union county, 277.

In October, the banks in Philadelphia and Baltimore suspended specie payment, and the Northumberland bank was compelled to follow. The directors of the latter bank, John Walls, Alexander Jordan, John Taggert, &c., however, published a card, in which they pledged their individual responsibility that all its issues should ultimately be made good.

October 3, grew on the farm of Samuel Zellers, in East Buffalo township, two pumpkins on one vine, one measuring two feet three inches in diameter, and two feet five inches in length, and weighs one hundred and twenty pounds; the other measures six feet eleven inches in circumference, and weighs one hundred and seventeen pounds.

November 19, Absalom Swineford, Esquire, admitted to the bar. On the 8th of December, the new Lutheran and Reformed church, at the place of the old Dreisbach church, in Buffalo township, was dedicated. The building committee were John Sheckler, Samuel Reber, Peter Engel, and Jacob Ritter.

Obituary.

Just Henry Fries died on Wednesday evening, the 9th of October, aged sixty-two years five months and sixteen days. For some years before his death, he was deprived of his sight, but his astonishing memory enabled him to give out the hymns in full, and preach with a precision for which he was always noted. He refused to take medicine in his last illness, saying he wished to die in the full possession of his senses. His disease was of a very singular character. In July he cut a corn on his toe, mortification took place, spreading gradually, with intense pain, to his knee. Here it remained seated in his knee, the pain having nearly ceased, when suddenly it commenced spreading, and affected his whole body. He is buried in the Mifflinburg grave-yard. The grave-yard lies along a slope, somewhat elevated above the town, which lies immediately in front; beyond it, west and east, extends one of the finest valleys in Pennsylvania. To the west, in the distance, are the jutting knobs; and to the north, the broad, blue side of the mountains, with quiet nooks between; and as far as the eye can reach, in the north-east, are the breaks in the mountains, with the broad levels between, which indicate the course of the noble Susquehanna. Thus does his quiet grave still overlook the wide scene of his labors, while he has gone to await the final issues of his care, as they shall gather around him in the resurrection of the just.

Mr. Fries was remarkably open, honest, and true. His word could be depended upon. He hated all sham and hypocrisy to such a degree that he was constantly in danger of falling into a blunt frankness, without giving due attention to that suavity of manner, which is to an open heart what the fragrance is to an open flower. He was fearless in preaching.[1]

He was unnecessarily open and free with his political views. He not only argued readily on this subject in private circles, but often introduced political matters, with more or less plainness, into the pulpit, referring even to candidates and parties. He also wrote numerous articles for the papers during the heat of contests, anonymously, it is true, yet still so that their parentage was recognized by many. This was one of his weaknesses, which his friends always regretted, but which he was never able to see in its true light. He was very kind hearted, which he manifested in great affection towards his family and in kindnesses to his friends. His labors in the ministry were very extensive, and the complete statistics of his services show an astonishing result, &c.—*Harbaugh's Fathers.*

He was twice married, first to Catherine Groff, by whom he had two children; second, to Susanna Groff, by whom he had eleven. Judge Henry W. Fries, late of Lewisburg, now of Iowa, is his son.

[1] I have often heard quoted a remark he made in a sermon in Brush Valley: "Money rules the world, but ignorance rules Brush valley."—*Linn.*

1840.

WEATHER RECORD—STATE ROAD FROM HEBERLING'S TO ELK CREEK, CENTRE COUNTY, LOCATED—CENSUS OF 1840.

ANUARY —, the deep snows of this winter, followed by intensely cold weather, drove the wolves down from Shade and Jack's mountain. A pack of thirteen attacked and destroyed an ox near Beavertown. Friday, January 16, was called the "cold Friday," thermometer being seventeen degrees below zero. On the 10th of February the ice broke in the river, and passed off, and on the 4th of December the first snow of the succeeding winter fell.

The following is the result of the elections held on the 5th March, in the borough and township, for and against the common school:

Borough of New Berlin.

For the school,	64
Against the school,	31
Majority in favor of the school,	33

Union Township.

Against the school,	154
For the school,	12
Majority against the school,	142

May 26, the commissioners, Anthony Wolfe, of Centre county, Henry Noll, of Union, and Jacob Stitzel of Northumberland, commenced locating the State road from Heberling's mill, in West Buffalo township, to Elk creek, in Miles township, Centre county, through the Brush Valley narrows. James F. Linn was the surveyor, David Wolfe and Henry Peters, chain carriers, and Colonel Samuel Reber, axeman. July 4, a monument to the memory of Captain Samuel M. Patterson was erected in the Presbyterian grave-yard at Lewisburg, with appropriate ceremonies, by the "Union Hornets." On the 19th of October, Reverend Thomas P. Hunt commenced his series of temperance lectures, at Lewisburg, which gave a very remarkable impetus to the cause through Buffalo valley. On the 29th, Reverend Hugh Pollock, from Belfast, Ireland, arrived and took charge of the Lewisburg academy, made vacant by the removal of James McClune to Mifflinburg.

United States Pensioners Residing in Union County in 1840.

Centre, Conrad Swartzlander, aged 85. Union, George Miller, 81; Jacob Bickel, 85; John Derr, 86. Mifflinburg, Peter Lenhart, 85; John Linn, 84. West Buffalo, Robert Barber, 89. East Buffalo, Jacob Mook, 86; Adam Schout, 86. White Deer, Joseph Bitting, 83. Hartley, Peter Klingaman, 85.

Census of 1840.

Mifflinburg,	704	Penn's,		2,280
Kelly,	788	Middle Creek,		562
Buffalo,	1,348	Chapman,		1,297
White Deer,	1,252	Perry,		1,254
Hartley,	1,866	Union,		1,630
Centre,	1,891	Washington,		1,135
New Berlin,	679	Beaver,		2,609
Lewisburg,	1,220			
West Buffalo,	1,460	Total,		22,787
East Buffalo,	812			

Samuel Roush, Esquire, was the deputy marshal, who took the census of the south side of the county. Captain John Forster, deputy marshal for the north side.

1841 to 1855.

DEATH OF JAMES MERRILL, ESQUIRE—DEVELOPMENT OF IRON ORE IN THE VALLEY—NEWSPAPERS—POLITICS—DANVILLE ENCAMPMENT—NOTICE OF WILLIAM HAYES—MILLERISM—CAMP POTTER—LIBERTY PARTY FORMED—FURNACES BUILT—DEATH OF WILLIAM L. HARRIS—DAGUERREOTYPES INTRODUCED—RAILROAD MEETING—ACCIDENT AT TURTLE CREEK—LIST OF VALLEY SOLDIERS IN THE MEXICAN WAR—VOTE ON LICENSE—DEATH OF JOHN LASHELLS, ESQUIRE, AND GENERAL R. H. HAMMOND—LEWISBURG UNIVERSITY CHARTERED—HIGH'S MILL BURNED—THE LAST BATTALION—TAXABLES AND VALUATION—CENSUS OF 1850—SUSQUEHANNA RAILROAD COMMENCED—FIRST COMMENCEMENT AT LEWISBURG—RAILROAD EXCITEMENT—UNION COUNTY AGRICULTURAL SOCIETY FORMED—LEWISBURG, CENTRE, AND SPRUCE CREEK RAILROAD COMPANY CHARTERED—GREAT FIRE AT LEWISBURG—DEATH OF HONORABLE GEORGE KREMER—UNION FURNACE AT WINFIELD ERECTED—ERECTION OF SNYDER COUNTY—VOTE IN FAVOR OF DIVISION—VOTE ON THE LOCATION OF THE COUNTY SEAT.

[1841.] In the spring, J. & M. Halfpenny started the Laurel woolen factory, at the mouth of Laurel run, in Hartley township. They built the Winfield woolen factory, near Laurelton, and removed thither in 1851. The Presbyterian church, at New Berlin, was organized. Elders, John Lashells, James Merrill, and Joseph Stillwell. Mr. Hugh Pollock published his pamphlet, entitled "The Present State of America compared with England and Ireland." April 12, the *People's Advocate*, at Lewisburg, suspended publication. September 4, S. K. Sweetman and D. O. E. Maize commenced the publication of the *Independent Press* at Lewisburg. In October, the vote for Governor, in Union county, was: For David R. Porter, 1,568; for John Banks, 2,132. October 29, James Merrill, Esquire, died at New Berlin, after a lingering illness, from cancer of the face. He was born at Peacham, Vermont, May 8, 1790. Eldest son of Jesse and Priscilla (Kimbell) Merrill. Graduated at Dartmouth College in

1812, in the same class with Honorable John Blanchard, and came with him to Pennsylvania. He studied law with David Cassat, Esquire, at York, and settled in New Berlin in 1816. As a jurist, he soon became prominent in every department of legal science. He was always upright and candid in all his professional intercourse, and was a faithful and efficient advocate. He was a member of the Constitutional Convention of 1837–1838. In the fall, the iron ore below the mouth of Turtle creek was found to be of a superior quality, and its development was commenced by Napoleon Hughes, of Franklin county, a short distance above the site of the present furnace of Beaver, Marsh & Co., a few hundred yards from the river bank. On the 25th of December, Nathan Mitchell and James S. Marsh commenced the manufacture of the "Hathaway Cooking Stove," at the Lewisburg foundry. Current prices of grain at Lewisburg, September 18: Wheat, $1.20; rye, 50 cents; corn, 56 cents; oats, 33 cents; butter, 10 cents.

[1842.] Current prices at Lewisburg, June 11, wheat, $1.00. August 20, wheat, 80 cents. The military spirit of the Valley may be inferred from the number of volunteer companies: Lafayette Troop, Union Troop, Patriotic Blues, Union Rifle Rangers, Mifflinburg Greens, and the Lewisburg Infantry. The *Union Times*, at New Berlin, was published by Jacob Reichly & Co., John M. Baum, editor. The *Independent Press*, at Lewisburg, by S. K. Sweetman and J. F. Busch. February 10, twelve, P. M., distillery of R. M. Musser, in Kelly township, burned down. March 2, the Northern temperance convention met in the Methodist church at Lewisburg. March 14, Elder William Lane commenced his labors at Lewisburg. March 21, Jonas Kelchner, editor of the *People's Advocate*, at Lewisburg, died, aged thirty-five. June 1, the encampment at Danville was held. General Winfield Scott was the distinguished guest. Lewisburg Infantry, Captain McFadden, and the Union Troop, Captain Vanvalzah, were in attendance. June 6, the election for field officers of the forty-third regiment resulted as follows: Colonel, Levi B. Christ; Lieutenant Colonel, Jacob Ritter; Major, Robert B. Green. Independent Battalion—Lieutenant Colonel, S. H. Laird; Major, S. F. Lyndall. July 4, General Abbot Green was elected major general of the eighth division.

Union County Democratic Standing Committee—James Dale, Honorable George Schnable, Jacob Reichly, Honorable John Baskins, Thomas Bower, Colonel Samuel Reber, Captain John Forster, Major George Roush, Major John Gundy, Valentine Haas, Esquire. Democratic convention at New Berlin, August 29, was composed of the following delegates: New Berlin, Samuel Wilson and Sem Schoch; Union, Adam Miller and Jacob Wetzel; West Buffalo, Elias Kleckner and William Forster; Mifflinburg, J. G. Chestney and Joseph Eilert; Buffalo, Jacob Ritter and Martin Dreisbach; Kelly, David Kelly and David Howard; East Buffalo, James Reber and David Herbst; Lewisburg, John Walls and C. D. Kline; White Deer, Samuel Henderson and J. W. Drum; Hartley, Henry Charles and Charles D. Smith. Henry C. Eyer was nominated for Senator, and Samuel Reber for Assembly. Samuel Wilson, president; Thomas Bower, secretary. The Whig convention also met in August, and nominated the following ticket: Congress, William L. Harris; Senate, Ner Middleswarth; Assembly, John A. Vanvalzah; Register and Recorder, Michael H. Weaver; Commissioner, Solomon Engel; Auditor, S. H. Laird; Trustees, Robert Chambers, William A. Piper, Charles Montelius. This ticket is called, in the choice language of the *Union Times*, The Anti-Masonic, Anti-Suffrage, Peg Beatty, Blue Light, Federal Whig ticket of Union county. Vote in October: For John A. Vanvalzah, for Assembly, 1,562; for Samuel Reber, 1,405.

October 29, the church at Laurel run, in Hartley township, dedicated. December term, George W. Graham, Esquire, admitted to the bar. December 13, Reverend S. H. Reed installed pastor of the German Reformed church at Lewisburg. December 23, New Berlin Artillerists organized by Colonel Jackson McFadden, brigade inspector. Officers: Captain, J. J. Maclay; first lieutenant, Michael Kleckner; second lieutenant, Charles D. Roush, and the event celebrated by a dinner at Michael Kleckner's hotel.

[**1843.**] In January, Honorable John Baskins resigned the office of associate judge of Union county, preparatory to moving to Mercer county, and on the 24th,[1] B. F. Baskins was admitted to the bar. February 17, William Hayes, merchant of Lewisburg, died, aged sixty-one. His ancestors, John Hayes and Jane, his wife, with four children, emigrated from Londonderry about the year 1730—settled in Chester county, where his house burned. He then moved to

Northampton county, where he kept public house and store. During the Indian troubles, he used to beat a drum on the hill-top, near his house, to warn the settlers of approaching danger. He died in 1788, aged eighty-three. His widow died at Derry, Northumberland county, aged ninety-four, in 1806. Of the four children born in Ireland : 1, William, moved to the State of Virginia at an early period ; 2, Isabella, married to Patton, whose descendants live near Bellefonte ; 3, John, died near Meadville, Pennsylvania ; 4, Mary, married a Gray, afterwards a Steele. Of those born in Pennsylvania : 5, Elizabeth, married Thomas Wilson, (grandfather of Francis Wilson, of Buffalo ;) 6, James ;[1] 7, Robert, born in Northampton county, in 1742; 8, Francis, who moved to Tennessee ; 9, Jane, married a Brown, settled first in Virginia and afterwards moved back to Pennsylvania. Robert married Mary Allison, and moved to Northumberland county in 1790. He lived nine years on a farm near Warrior Run church, seven years at Derry, and in 1806 moved to the farm in Delaware township, where his son Joseph lately lived. He was a school-master, and at that time there were seven or eight acres of the place cleared and two indifferent huts on the premises, which he used as a dwelling and school-house. He died in 1819, and his children were : 1, John, whose descendants live at Waterford, Erie county, Pennsylvania; 2, Jane, married to Moses Laird, (father of Robert H. Laird, Esquire, of Lewisburg ;) 3, William Hayes, born in 1776 ; 4, James Hayes; 5, Joseph Hayes, who was living a few years since, at the age of ninety ; 6, Mary Walker, who died at eighty-four years of age ; 7, Sarah Shipman, descendants residing in Michigan; 8, Elizabeth, married her cousin Brown, living near Franklin, Pennsylvania. William Hayes' wife was Mary, daughter of William Wilson, of White Deer, now Kelly township. Children : Robert and Thomas of Philadelphia, Mrs. Doctor Seiler of Harrisburg, Mrs. John Chamberlin, Mrs. Doctor Thomas Murray, James Hayes, late of the Auditor General's office, at Harrisburg, Doctor William Hayes of Muncy. Mr. Hayes was the second postmaster of Lewisburg, and held the office a long time, in con-

[1] Lieutenant James Hayes served under Colonel Bouquet in the French and Indian war, and received for his services a tract of land at the mouth of Beech creek, in Clinton county, on which he settled, raised a large family, and died. He is buried in the Hayes grave-yard, so called from him, at Beech creek. He is the only one of his brother officers who fulfilled to the letter his contract with the Proprietaries by settling upon his allotment.

nection with his store, which was the principal one in the Valley for many years. The late George A. Snyder relates the following incident of Mr. Hayes' early life in Lewisburg :

"Soon after I commenced business in Lewisburg, said my old friend William Hayes, I was so unfortunate as to lose an entire cargo of wheat at Conewago falls. I was indebted to several persons for money borrowed, and much of the wheat had been purchased from the farmers on credit, who, being in easy circumstances, were content to leave the money in my hands, receiving interest after six months. So heavy a loss to so new a dealer created alarm. It was feared I should not be able to answer my liabilities, and every creditor discovered that he had just then need of his money. I paid out to every one who came, though with each payment my heart grew heavy, for it felt that I must be crippled, if not ruined, before all were paid. One of my creditors, however, on the day after I had paid him $400, came to my store and returned me the money, saying, 'by taking the money, I have been only making sure to you the ruin which I apprehended; take it back, I can trust it to your honesty, and it will help you get afloat again.' From that time I took courage and worked with a good heart, and was enabled to become what you see."

In April, 1843, Isaac G. Gordon,[1] a student-at-law with James F. Linn, Esq., was admitted to the bar.

Millerism.

The grand delusion of this year was Millerism. A clergyman named Miller undertook the task of ascertaining when that hour should come "whereof no man knoweth; no, not the angels of God, neither the Son." Relying on the chronology of Rollin, and seemingly not aware of the impossibility of verifying the dates of the Old Testament writers, he confidently predicted that the visible and personal reign of Christ would commence in the year 1843. His preaching, vehement and fanatical in its tone, and the seeming accuracy of his calculations, quickly gained him hearers and prose-

[1] In 1860-61 Honorable Isaac G. Gordon was elected member of the House from Jefferson, &c., April 12, 1866, commissioned president judge of the twenty-eighth judicial district, and in October, 1873, elected one of the justices of the Supreme Court of Pennsylvania.

lytes. Miller was content to take the whole year for the fulfillment of his prophecy, but some of his disciples had undertaken to fix the precise day and hour. One preacher fixed on twelve, 'P. M., 14th February. He and his little flock provided themselves with ascension robes, and repaired to the church-yard to await the resurrection of their departed friends, and join them in their ascent. The clock struck twelve, one, and two, but the graves gave not up their dead, and the company gradually dispersed to their homes.

September 23, William B. Shriner commenced publishing the *Lewisburg Chronicle*. October 28, some little boys collected some shavings at the new Presbyterian church, in New Berlin, and kindled a fire, which burned M. Kleckner's barn, with his poultry, hay, and oats, and almost set the whole town on fire. John Robinson, principal of the Lewisburg Academy. In Union county, in October, the vote on the State ticket for Canal Commissioner was, Whig, 2,034; Democratic, 1,393. General Henry Frick, Whig, was elected Congressman in the district by a majority of 249 over Honorable John Snyder. Lewisburg market prices in November: wheat, 75 cents; buckwheat, 40 cents; rye, 44 cents; corn, 37½ cents; oats, 25 cents; butter, 10 cents. December 20, the revival services under the charge of Reverend William D. Grant, were crowned with success, in the baptism of a number of persons this day, which culminated in the formation of the first Baptist meeting at Lewisburg. December 31, Reverend Henry Harbaugh preaching in Lewisburg.

[**1844.**] January 3, the Baptist church at Lewisburg was recognized as such, with Reverend C. A. Hewitt as temporary pastor. January 8, the new Lutheran church at Selinsgrove was dedicated. February 29, the Presbyterian church at New Berlin was dedicated. March 1, General Henry Frick, member of Congress from this district, died at Washington, D. C., aged forty-eight. He was interred at Milton on Monday, 4th. He established the *Miltonian* September 21, 1816. March 18, Charles G. Donnel, president judge of the eighth district, died at Sunbury, of paralysis, and on the 1st of April, Joseph B. Anthony, of Williamsport, held his first court at Sunbury. On the 5th, a special election for Congressman, *vice* General Frick, deceased, was held. In Union county, James Pollock received 2,086; Honorable John Snyder, 1,289. Pollock had

5 majority in Northumberland county, and 154 in Lycoming. Snyder had 89 in Clinton. May 16, John Hayes, deputy surveyor of Union county, died. Of his children were R. G. H. Hayes, Nancy, William, David, Esquire, and James Hayes. July 4 was celebrated in Brown's woods, at Lewisburg, four schools from the town and two from the country joining. There were seven hundred Sabbath-school scholars in procession, who were addressed by Reverends Crever, Harbaugh, Zeller, and Sutton. August 27, Camp Potter, on the farm of James F. Linn, in East Buffalo township, organized, by the arrival of two troops and three foot companies, General James Potter in command. September 2, Methodist camp-meeting on the farm of Jacob Ziebach. September 14, large Democratic meeting on the island, at Milton. Honorable James Buchanan spoke, and assured his auditors that James K. Polk was as good a tariff man as Henry Clay. The summer was noted for great efforts in the temperance cause—the burden of the speeches an appeal to the ballot-box. Reverend W. H. H. Barnes, who afterwards became a backslider, and was murdered by guerrillas during the Mexican war, canvassed the county and made a fine impression from his eloquence in advocating that appeal. General Reily, of Rochester, New York, also lectured frequently during this period. October 8, at the gubernatorial election, Francis R. Shunk and General Joseph Markle were the opposing candidates. Markle (Whig) received 2,721 votes in Union county; Shunk (Democrat) received 1,777. For the sale of the main line of canals, 1,289 votes were cast, against 2,113. F. J. Lemoyne was voted for by the Liberty party for Governor. November 1, presidential election. Henry Clay had 1,024 majority. James G. Birney (Liberty party) had 8 votes in Lewisburg. The names of those who voted for the latter were John K. Housel, H. R. Noll, ——— Augstadt, ——— Poeth, Samuel Evans, Dennis Phillips, and James F. Linn. December 18, a Native American meeting was held in the court-house, at New Berlin, which was addressed by Absalom Swineford, Esquire.

[1845.] Market prices at Lewisburg, March: Wheat, 75 to 80 cents; rye, 50 cents; corn, 37 cents. In June, wheat, 80 cents. In October, 85 to 95 cents. J. M. Kuester editing the Pittsburgh *Daily* in January. February 4, occurred the first deep snow of the winter. It was over twelve inches in depth. April 30, James Kelly, senior, opened a temperance house, on Market street, in Lewisburg. July 7, the first metal made at the Berlin iron-works, operated by Wilson, Green & Mitchell, was brought to Lewisburg. The Baptist church at Lewisburg, that stood on the corner of Pine alley and Third street, now the site of Music Hall, was built during the summer by L. B. Christ, Esquire, contractor. August 9, John Wolfe's barn, in East Buffalo township, was struck by lightning, and burned. August 13, Honorable Hugh Wilson, late associate judge of Union county, died, at three, P. M., aged eighty-four. His wife, Sarah Craig, was a daughter of Colonel Thomas Craig, of the third regiment, Pennsylvania Line, afterward General Thomas Craig, of Northampton county. August 29, West Branch Division, No. 53, Sons of Temperance, organized at Lewisburg. September 3, barn of George F. Miller, Esquire, in East Buffalo, burned by an incendiary. September 28, Reverend Joel E. Bradley preached the first sermon in the lecture room of the Baptist church at Lewisburg. September 13, first frost. October 9, Hugh Wilson, of Buffalo township, died. He moved to this Valley from Northampton county, and got here a few days before Christmas, 1790. Lived the winter of 1790–91 in an old cabin, on his father-in-law's, William Irvine, (Irish,) place, in Buffalo; then kept tavern for two years, one mile above Mifflinburg, (late John Kleckner's.) In the latter part of March, 1793, moved to a place owned by Colonel Hartley, one fourth of a mile east of Hartleton, on the old road, (late Yerger's,) where he lived five years, and in the spring of 1798 moved to Lewisburg, where he kept store in a log building, formerly Thomas Caldwell's, (which stood where Doctor F. C. Harrison's house now is,) until 1804, when he was succeeded by William Hayes, and then moved on to his farm, one mile west of Lewisburg, where he died, lacking twelve days of eighty-five years of age. His children were, Doctor William I. Wilson, of Potter's Mills, still living; Mrs. William C. Steadman, Francis Wilson, and Mrs. James F. Linn. At the October election, S. D. Karns, Whig candidate for Canal Commissioner, received 2,015 votes in Union county; James Burns, Democrat, 1,416. October 30, Frederick Bingaman died in Beaver township, aged ninety years. He was in the militia, under General James Potter, at Brandywine. In November, Green, Howard & Green commenced erecting the Forest iron-works, in White Deer township. November 11, Honorable William L. Harris died at four, P. M., from the effect of an operation, performed between twelve and one, P. M., for the removal of a tumor. He was highly respected, and as it was not known that he was the subject of a disease, his death caused a great shock to the people of the Valley. He was a member of the House in 1833, and of the Constitutional Convention of 1837-1838. In December, an artist named Felch took the first daguerreotypes in the Valley. He charged $6 50 for a group of five in a small four-inch glass case. December 16, Charles Merrill, Esquire, admitted to the bar.

[1846.] January 8, a large railroad meeting was held at Mifflinburg, Henry Yearick, president, to urge the incorporation of a company to make a railroad through the Valley. February 5, the act to establish the University at Lewisburg was passed, (Pamphlet Laws, 32,) and on the 5th of October, Professor Stephen W. Taylor opened its high school in the lecture room of the Baptist church. Friday evening, March 13, Thomas Follmer and his son Henry and William Gundy, son of Major John Gundy, who were managing the Farmers' company store at Turtle creek, were drowned at the mouth of that creek. They were going in a boat, about ten, P. M., to visit the store-house on the opposite side of the creek, and were on their return, when the mill dam gave way, and the boat struck a timber raft. William Gundy's body was found in the boat under the raft, the next day; the others were carried down the river, and their bodies were found three weeks afterward, some miles below. The flood in the river at this time exceeded that of 1810, being six and one half inches above the mark of that date on Kremer's store-house. The canal was broken, mails stopped, the Milton bridge badly injured, the bridge on the North Branch, at Northumberland, carried away, as well as the one at Duncan's island, and the Harrisburg bridge in part. March 21, price of wheat at Lewisburg, eighty-five to ninety cents. April 1, the last sermon preached in the old stone church, at Buffalo Cross-Roads, by Reverend Isaac Grier, from Matthew, xxviii: v. 5. The congregation worshipped twenty nine years and three months in that building. In August, Reverend Samuel Shaeffer had charge of the Lewisburg academy. At the October election, in Union county, James M. Power received 1,976 votes, and William B. Foster, 905, for canal commissioner. November 15, Baptist meeting-house at Lewisburg dedicated. November 27, John

Derr, a revolutionary soldier, died in Centre township, aged ninety-three years. Monday, December 28, the Columbia Guards, afterwards company C, second regiment, Captain John S. Wilson, passed through Lewisburg on their way to the seat of war in Mexico. They were provided with dinner by the citizens. Charles H. Shriner delivered an address, and Colonel Jackson McFadden presented them with a flag.

List of Soldiers in the Mexican War from Union county.

App, Jacob, Selinsgrove, company C, second regiment, died at San Francisco, California, in October, 1849, aged twenty-four; Best, Francis R., Mifflinburg, company C, second regiment, died at Perote, June 30, 1847; Bower, Doctor Charles, surgeon; Bruner, William, Hartleton; Cronmiller, Henry, Mifflinburg, Independent rocket and howitzer battery; Forster, R. H., Mifflinburg, company C, second regiment; Leopard, Joseph, Kelly, company I, first regiment; Miller, George; McFadden, Hugh, Lewisburg, company C, second regiment, died at Perote, September 14, 1847; McLaughlin, William, Lewisburg, fifth United States infantry, died in service; Montgomery, John C., company M, second regiment; Nyhart, Peter, died January 14, 1849; Oliphant George; Quiddington, Thomas; Yarnell, Peter; Zentmyer, Enos, first regiment. The survivors of company C returned to Danville in August, 1848, and shortly after Lieutenant Clarence G. Frick returned the flag, tattered by the storms of war, and little left beside the staff, to Colonel McFadden, at Lewisburg.

[1847.] March 19, vote in Lewisburg against licensing taverns, 210; in favor of, 75. In April, price of wheat in Lewisburg was $1 30 to $1 35. May 7, corner-stone of the German Reformed church in Lewisburg laid. Reverend Doctor John W. Nevin preached and performed the services. In April, the extreme distress in Ireland and Scotland, on account of failure of crops, caused meetings to be held for their relief, and large contributions of money and provisions were made by the people of Buffalo Valley. May 18, John Lashells, Esquire, died at New Berlin. He came to this county from Adams county, and his legal experience was contemporary with the county. He was buried at Buffalo Cross-Roads, on

the 20th, the following members of the court and bar attending:
A. S. Wilson, president judge; Joseph Stillwell and John Montelius,
associates; Hugh Bellas, Ebenezer Grenough, Alexander Jordan,
James F. Linn, Isaac Slenker, George F. Miller, Joseph Casey,
Samuel Weirick, D. W. Woods, R. B. Barber, William Van Gezer,
and Henry C. Hickok. June 2, General R. H. Hammond, who
was a paymaster in the United States army, died on board of a
vessel, between Vera Cruz and New Orleans, aged fifty-seven. He
served in Congress two terms. His body was interred with military
honors at Milton, on Monday, August 2. Independent Grays, of
Selinsgrove, Lewisburg Infantry, Danville Rifles, Lycoming and
Northumberland troops, Masonic fraternity, in full regalia, were
in procession; General Green commanding the military. In all,
over six thousand people in attendance upon the ceremonies. In
August, Alexander McClure was appointed postmaster at Lewisburg,
vice William Murray. On Saturday, August 21, a meeting favoring the nomination of General Zachary Taylor for President, was
held at New Berlin. Honorable George Kremer presided; General
Abbot Green, William Cameron, Jacob Reedy, Henry Yearick,
vice presidents; John Walls, Thomas Bower, and John M. Baum, secretaries. The meeting was addressed by Henry C. Hickok, Esquire,
and Charles H. Shriner. September 15, a Democratic meeting, presided over by John Cummings, junior, recommended General Taylor
for President. In October, the vote in Union county for Governor
was, for James Irvin, 2,463; Francis R. Shunk, 1,479. October 9,
river rose very high, and the west half of the Buffalo creek bridge
was carried away, and lodged upon the river bridge. The river is
said to have been one foot higher at Lewisburg than it was in the
spring of 1846. October 20, Philadelphia synod met at Lewisburg, and was opened by a sermon by Doctor Yeomans, of Danville.
December 25, O. N. Worden became editor and publisher of the
Lewisburg Chronicle.

[**1848.**] January 8, the German Reformed church at Lewisburg, was dedicated; the exercises were conducted by Reverend
H. Harbaugh, pastor, assisted by Reverend Messrs. Fishers and
Reverend Mr. Funk. It is situated on Third street, below Market, and is sixty feet by forty—H. R. Noll, architect. In February ground was broken for the academy building of the Univer-

sity. Noll and Crites had the carpenter work, L. B. Christ the brick and plastering; brick-work was let to Reed & Baker, painting to Metzgar & Munson. March 2, a meeting was held to secure a suitable place for a cemetery at Lewisburg. The company was incorporated April 10, (Pamphlet Laws, 446,) and in July they purchased six acres from John Chamberlin, adjoining the western limit of the borough. March 17, Reverend Thomas Hood died, aged sixty-eight. He was born in Chester county, in July, 1781, graduated at Dickinson college at the age of seventeen, studied theology under Reverend Nathan Grier, of Brandywine, was licensed in 1802, and was married April 16, 1803, to Miss Mary Haslet, of Chester county. Mrs. Hood died November 10, 1840, and he married Miss Hannah McClure, March 4, 1845. His children were Mrs. Catherine McCormick, of Mill Hall, Clinton county, Mrs. Mary Rutter, Mrs. Margaret Harvey, and Wilson Hood. June 6, Charles L. Shoemaker, of West Buffalo, was kicked by a horse, and died on the 7th, aged thirty-five years. June 14, J. S. Hawke sold the *Union Star* to D. W. Woods, Esquire. The *Union Democrat*, published at New Berlin, by J. Young. June 9, Lewisburg market: wheat, $1 06; rye, 60 cents; corn, 35 cents; butter, 12 cents. October 10, Ner Middleswarth's vote for Canal Commissioner was 2,941; Israel Painter, 1,580. Joseph Casey had 1,333 majority for Congress in Union county, and 223 in the district. In November General Taylor had 1,473 majority in Union county. In Lewisburg, Taylor had 205; Cass, 124; Van Buren, 10. In New Berlin Taylor, 79; Cass, 57; Van Buren, 5.

[1849.] January —, A. Kennedy appointed postmaster at Lewisburg, and R. P. Maclay appointed associate judge of Clarion county. Doctor Thomas A. H. Thornton commenced the practice of medicine at Lewisburg. The Berlin iron-works were blown out, and Forest iron-works in the hands of the sheriff. The California gold fever reached the Valley, and on the 26th of February, R. B. Green, David Howard, Cyrus Fox, W. H. Chamberlin, Frederick Schaffle and John D. Musser, set out for California, by the overland route. James K. Kelly, James M. Duncan, and others, left Lewistown for the same destination. March 5, Peter Struble, of West Buffalo, aged about fifty-eight, was found dead on the public road near Buffalo Cross-Roads. He had accompanied a newly married daughter to her home in Lycoming county, and was returning on foot, when death met him with a paralytic stroke. April 25, High's flouring-mill, at White Deer, burned. Over $5,000 worth of grain destroyed. Kaufman & Reber bought the Forest ironworks for $7,000. May 21 was the last of the battalions, one company only, the Lewisburg infantry, paraded. A great crowd of boys and people from the townships had come to Lewisburg. "The meanest battalion I ever seed," was the general expression. October 9, H. M. Fuller, candidate for Canal Commissioner, received 2,431 votes in Union county; John A. Gamble, 1,820. Colonel Eli Slifer's majority over John Cummings, junior, for Assembly, was 617. Against a poor-house, 2,537 votes were cast; for, 910. November 5, James McClellan, Esquire, died, aged eighty-two. He had lived over fifty years in the Valley, and was nearly the last of those worthies who settled our Valley. He came from Chester county, and married Mary Irvine, daughter of Captain William Irvine, of the Valley. He was a school-master and justice of the peace for many years. He was considered by many, who could not appreciate his worth, as an obstinate man, the true reason of which was, that he was firm in his opinions, and in nine cases out of ten right. I never knew a man who was more willing to acknowledge his error when he discovered it. Among his last expressions was, "when a man came to die, this world and all its interests were of little account." He was a living encyclopedia of church history, and with him passed away forever many interesting incidents of the early history of the Presbyterian church in Pennsylvania.—*J. F. Linn's Diary.*

[**1850.**] January 2, H. C. Hickok, Esquire, takes the editorial chair of the *Lewisburg Chronicle*, O. N. Worden, publisher, and Reverend Henry Harbaugh issues the first number of *The Guardian.* February 26, report of James Marshall, John App, and Leonard Wolfe confirmed, erecting a new township, which the court direct shall be called *Limestone.*

	Taxables.	Valuation of Real Estate.
Buffalo,	251	$573,260
Buffalo, East,	198	282,842
Buffalo, West,	294	391,144
Hartley,	384	403,495
Kelly,	209	299,007
Union,	346	441,105
White Deer,	315	233,575
Lewisburg,	428	168,782
Mifflinburg,	207	57,147
New Berlin,	153	86,922

In April, Frick & Slifer removed their boat-yard to Lewisburg, a pecuniary advantage both to the borough and the Valley, which should be specially noted. April 18, Doctor Robert Vanvalzah died at Buffalo Cross-Roads, aged eighty-five. He was born near Croton river, New York, April 17, 1764, and when a boy of sixteen, he served two tours in the militia with the Continental army. He came to Buffalo Valley in 1786, so poor, that one of the Beattys gave him a shilling to pay his ferriage over the river at Sunbury, a favor he never forgot, and repaid with much interest in providing for one of the family for many years. He settled on Penn's creek, and in connection with his father-in-law, Colonel Sutherland, built the mills, two miles below New Berlin, lately owned by the Maurers. He located at Buffalo Cross-Roads, about the year 1796, and his history is intimately associated with that of the Valley for sixty-four years. His practice extended into the present counties of Mifflin, Centre, and Juniata. Two of his sons, Doctors Thomas and Robert, became eminent practitioners in the Valley, and his grandsons, in the same profession, have been and are numerous and skillful. In May, Reverend D. Y. Heisler was installed pastor of the German Reformed church at Lewisburg, and a post-office was established at Forest Hill in West Buffalo township, on the Brush Valley road, A. H. Lutz, postmaster. In April, wheat at Lewisburg was at 95 cents to $1 00, and in June, $1 05 to $1 10. June 7, Captain William Housel died in Lewisburg, aged sixty-one. He served five years in the regular army, was captured in 1813, taken to Quebec, and there was exchanged, and rejoined his regiment. He was in the engagements at Chippewa and Lundy's Lane, and was in Fort Erie when the magazine exploded. He was buried with military honors by the Lewisburg infantry and the Cameron guards. Thursday and Friday, July 18 and 19, a north-east storm raged for thirty-two hours. Limestone run higher than ever known, and Chillisquaque creek higher than known before in fifty-seven years. In October, Henry W. Snyder had 2,172 votes for Auditor General; Ephraim Banks, 1,443. For the judicial amendment, 1,451 votes were cast; against, 1,424.

Census of 1850.

Buffalo,	1,346	Mifflinburg,		783
Buffalo, East,	970	New Berlin,		741
Buffalo, West,	1,007	Union,		1,452
Hartley,	2,142	White Deer,		1,537
Kelly,	834			
Lewisburg,	2,042	Total,		13,631
Limestone,	807			

[1851.] Honorable Ner Middleswarth was the Whig caucus nominee for State Treasurer. The following post-offices were established in January: Chestnut Ridge, Samuel R. Baum, postmaster; Dry Valley, J. Mitman; Winfield, M. H. Taggert; Crotzerville, H. Heiser. In April, the old bridge at the mouth of Buffalo creek was removed, and a new one commenced. The Sugar Valley and White Deer turnpike received an appropriation from the State, and was completed. *Volksfreund*, started at New Berlin, by F. & E. Smith. April 26, Thomas Howard, in digging a ditch, near his residence, in Kelly, dug up a tusk of a mammoth, ten feet long and nine inches in diameter. It was found in a layer of blue clay, two feet below the surface. In May wheat was 80 to 85 cents; rye, 50 cents; corn, 50 cents. May 26, the telegraphic wire was brought to Lewisburg, and before night a message dispatched to Philadelphia, and an answer received; and a meeting was held favoring the construction of the Susquehanna railroad, on the west side of the river, from Sunbury to Williamsport. August 20, the first commencement of the University at Lewisburg was held, and its first class graduated as follows: Salutatory, J. M. Linn, Washington Barnhurst of Philadelphia, R. M. Fish of Beaver, George O. Ide of Philadelphia, J. M.

Lyons of Chester county, Henry Pomerene of Pittsburgh. Valedictorian: J. H. Castle. The degrees were conferred by Professor Taylor, and Professor George R. Bliss delivered his inaugural address. Professor S. W. Taylor then took formal leave of the institution, having accepted the presidency of Madison university at Hamilton, New York; and Doctor Howard Malcolm was formally installed president of the University by Thomas Watson, Esquire, president of the board of trustees. October 14, vote in Union county: For Governor, William F. Johnston, 2,817; William Bigler, 1,949. For president judge, Joseph Casey received 2,379, and A. S. Wilson, 2,283.

[1852.] March 13, a railroad convention was held at Baltimore, attended largely by delegates from the Valley. April 15, Daniel L. Miller, junior, Esquire, president of the Sunbury and Erie railroad, visited Lewisburg and endeavored to interest the people in favor of that road, but public sympathy was with the Susquehanna or Baltimore company, and the railroad controversy was inaugurated, which ended in 1855 with a division of Union county by a proposition that the county commissioners should subscribe $200,000 to the stock of the road. This was done by Captain John Wilt and George Heimbach, county commissioners, on the 28th of April. The borough authorities of Lewisburg subsequently subscribed $75,000. In May the Union County mutual fire insurance company was organized; John Gundy, president, J. A. Mertz, Esquire, secretary. June 10, weather as cold as in December, a heavy frost on the morning of the 11th. August 31, the largest meeting ever witnessed in New Berlin assembled to take action on the railroad question. The court-house being too small, the meeting convened in front of the public buildings. John Swineford nominated R. B. Barber for president, and took the ayes, but not the nays. He then read a list of vice presidents and secretaries. The nays were again demanded, and when put the whole organization was voted down. C. H. Shriner attempted to offer a resolution, and Mr. Barber proceeded to state the object of the meeting, but his voice was drowned by a shout that compelled him to desist. Mr. Casey then nominated Honorable Ner Middleswarth for president, which motion was carried. He was helped into the wagon, and proceeded to state the object of the meeting. The repudiators of the bonds had retreated to the steps of the jail to make another stand, when a delegation of them sallied forth, seized the wagon, and carried off president Middleswarth and his fellow officers around the corner towards Penn's creek. The audience, however, kept its place, and the president returned and mounted another wagon, when the meeting was addressed by Messrs. Casey, S. C. Wilt, G. F. Miller, and resolutions passed approving of the $200,000 subscription to the Susquehanna railroad.

The watchword of the Democratic party this fall in the county, "no more hay for Breyman's cow," arose from the fact that C. Breyman farmed and pastured the public lots. October 12, for Canal Commissioner, Jacob Hoffman received 2,555; William Hopkins, 1,807. Ner Middleswarth, for Congress, had 706 majority; Adam Sheckler, for county commissioner, had 718 majority over Philip Ruhl.

The Union County agricultural society was formed at the courthouse at New Berlin, Saturday, November 13; the East Buffalo society, which had been in existence for a year, passed a resolution calling the meeting for such organization. Martin Dreisbach presided at this meeting, Samuel Weirick acting as secretary, and Jacob Gundy presented a form of constitution, which, after several amendments, was adopted. Jacob Gundy was elected president of the society; Samuel Shedle, of Perry, and others, vice presidents; R. H. Laird, treasurer; R. V. B. Lincoln, assistant secretary; O. N. Worden, recording secretary; Samuel Weirick, librarian; executive committee, James P. Ross, Isaac Slenker, and Henry W. Snyder. In November, Nesbit Hayes and Fichthorn commenced erecting the first steam flouring-mill, upon Water street, in Lewisburg. December 14, at a meeting held at New Berlin the Crawford county system of voting directly for candidates was proposed. Joseph Casey, Esquire, Israel Gutelius, and John Wilt favoring its introduction. Ner Middleswarth, D. A. Woods, Samuel Weirick, and James Marshall, opposing. It was finally agreed to try the system for one year.

[**1853.**] February 11, a meeting was held at Potter's Fort tavern favorable to building a railroad from Lewisburg to Spruce creek, and on the 12th of April, the Lewisburg, Centre, and Spruce Creek railroad company was incorporated, and on the 16th of May Thomas A. Emmett, with a corps of engineers, commenced the survey. April 20, the Lewisburg saving institution was incorporated; books were opened on the 23d of June, and two hundred shares taken. It commenced business September 19, with William Cameron as president, H. P. Sheller, cashier. In October, the vote in Union county was, for Thomas A. Budd, judge of the Supreme Court, 2,616; John C. Knox, 1,521. On 13th and 14th of October, "The Union County agricultural society" held its fair at New Berlin; two hundred and seventy-five articles were entered for competition, and a plowing match came off. October 15, Frick, Slifer & Co.'s steam saw-mill burned down, with the newly erected county bridge, three boats, &c. Captain John Forster appointed postmaster at Mifflinburg, and Henry W. Crotzer, at Lewisburg. December 9, the workmen on the Susquehanna railroad, about two and a half miles below Lewisburg, on Major John Gundy's farm, came upon the skeleton of a full grown person covered with stones. The bones crumbled on exposure. The site was on the side of a steep and almost impassible hill, and the body must have been deposited there with considerable effort.

[1854.] In April, price of wheat was $1 50; rye, 75 cents; corn, 55 cents. In June, wheat advanced to $1 87. At February term Jackson township was formed, out of parts of Penn's, Middle Creek, Limestone, and Union townships. In June, Professor J. S. Whitman was elected the first superintendent of public schools for Union county, with a salary of $300, and one hundred and fifty schools to oversee. July 15, W. A. Patterson, of Kelly, died, in his eighty-third year. He held a pen in his hand, preparatory to signing a note, when the "grim messenger" came, and he died before making a mark. Honorable George Kremer died, near Middleburg, on Sunday, September 10, aged seventy-nine. His last public appearance was in July, 1847, when he presided over a public meeting, held at New Berlin, to advocate the election of General Taylor to the presidency. He was buried in the family burying-ground, on his own farm, on Wednesday, attended by a large concourse of people. The new Christian chapel, on Third street, below Market, in Lewisburg, was built this year. At the election, in October, James Pollock had 2,881, and William Bigler, 1,913, for Governor in Union county. The vote in the county for a prohibitory liquor law was 1,440; against, 2,614. In October, the Union furnace at Winfield was built by Beaver, Marsh & Co. The University extension of the town plan of Lewisburg laid out by Reverend A. K. Bell, treasurer of the University, and James F. Linn, surveyor.

[1855.] Wheat, in March, $2 00; rye, $1 00; corn, 75 cents; butter, 16 cents; eggs, 12 cents. *Chronicle* published by O. N. Worden and J. R. Cornelius, Henry C. Hickok having been appointed Deputy Superintendent of Public Schools. Thursday evening, January 18, Clinton Welch, Esquire, a lawyer from Lewisburg, was drowned in the Delaware, at Philadelphia. March 2, the act creating a new county, to be called Snyder, out of Union, was approved. The election provided for therein was held on the 14th of March. The vote was as follows:

	For.	Against.
Buffalo,	189	84
Buffalo, East,	175	4
Buffalo, West,	114	62
Hartley,	152	191
Kelly,	143	22
Lewisburg,	485	1
Limestone,	3	60
Mifflinburg,	69	92
White Deer,	254	21

In the county the vote stood, for division, 1,688; against, 1,643. In May, Union seminary at New Berlin was established. Reverend W. W. Orwig, president; Reverend F. C. Hendricks and Hoffman, professors. October 9, the election was held to determine the site of the county seat, Lewisburg and Mifflinburg were the competing towns, having each furnished a guarantied subscription, that the county buildings should be erected by the successful town, without any cost to the taxpayers. The vote was as follows:

	For Lewisburg.	For Mifflinburg.
Lewisburg, North Ward,	286	—
" South Ward,	233	—
East Buffalo,	174	8
Union,	79	26
Kelly,	145	21
White Deer,	255	26
Buffalo,	157	121
West Buffalo,	13	200
Hartley,	78	321
New Berlin,	7	139
Jackson,	4	39
Limestone,	5	129
Mifflinburg,	1	196
	1,436	1,226

For Canal Commissioner, Nicholson's majority was 607.

Census Returns for 1860 and 1870.

	1860.	1870.
Buffalo,	1,560	1,521
Buffalo, East,	968	1,011
Buffalo, West,	1,075	1,046
Hartley,	1,530	1,143
Hartleton, (incorporated 1858,)	288	292
Kelly,	779	942
Lewisburg,	2,666	3,121
Lewis, (taken from Hartley 1856,)	658	1,007
Limestone,	913	880
Mifflinburg,	865	911
New Berlin,	672	646
Union,	820	840
White Deer,	1,639	1,676
	14,433	15,036

LIST OF OFFICIALS.

MEMBERS OF THE SENATE.

District composed of the Counties of Northumberland, Union, Columbia, Susquehanna and Luzerne.

1814-15, Thomas Murray, junior.
1816-17, Charles Fraser.
1818-19, Simon Snyder.
1820-21, Redmond Conyngham.

Northumberland and Union.

1822, Andrew Albright.
1823-26, Lewis Dewart.
1826-30, John Ray.
1830-34, Samuel J. Packer.
1834-38, Isaac Slenker.

Perry, Mifflin, Juniata, Union, and Huntingdon.

1837-38, Isaac Slenker.
1838-39, Robert P. Maclay.
1841-42, Robert P. Maclay.
1843, Henry C. Eyer.

Mifflin, Union, and Juniata.

1844, Henry C. Eyer.
1845-48, Jacob Wagenseller.*

1848, Ner Middleswarth.†
1849-51, Jonathan J. Cunningham.
1852-54, Eli Slifer.
1855-57, James M. Sellers.‡

Clinton, Lycoming, Centre, and Union.

1858, Andrew Gregg.
1859-61, Andrew Gregg.
1862-64, Henry Johnson.

Lycoming, Union, and Snyder.

1865-67, John Walls.
1868-70, John B. Beck.
1871-73, Andrew H. Dill.

Snyder, Perry, Northumberland, and Union.

1872-73, Andrew H. Dill.
1873-76, Andrew H. Dill.

Union, Snyder, and Northumberland.

1875-76, Andrew H. Dill.

* Died, 1847.   † *Vice* Wagenseller.   ‡ Died in Philadelphia, June 21, 1877.

MEMBERS OF ASSEMBLY.

District composed of the Counties of Northumberland, Union, and Columbia.

1814-15, David E. Owen.
         Robert Willett.
         Joseph Hutchinson.
         Henry Shaffer.

Union County.

1815-16, Ner Middleswarth.

1815-16, Jacob Brobst.
1816-17, Ner Middleswarth.
         Jacob Brobst.
1817-18, Frederick Stees.
         Joseph Stillwell.
1818-19, John Ray.
         Ner Middleswarth.
1819-20, John Ray.
         Ner Middleswarth.
1820-21, Frederick Wise.
         Dan Caldwell.

1821-22,	Ner Middleswarth.	1847,	John McMinn.
	James Dale.	1848,	John McMinn.
1822-23,	Simon Snyder.		Samuel Weirick.
	James Dale.	1849,	Samuel Weirick.
1823-24,	James Dale.		John McLaughlin.
	Simon Snyder.	1850,	Eli Slifer.
1824-25,	Ner Middleswarth.		John McLaughlin.
	William Forster.	1851,	Eli Slifer.
1825-26,	Ner Middleswarth.	1852,	William Sharon.
	James Madden.	1853,	John Beale.
1826-27,	James Madden.	1854,	John W. Simonton.
	William Forster, junior.	1855,	J. W. Crawford.
1827-28,	Ner Middleswarth.		
	John Dreisbach.		

Union, Juniata, and Snyder.

1828-29,	John Dreisbach.	1856,	George W. Strouse.
	Ner Middleswarth.	1857,	Thomas Bower.
1829-30,	Ner Middleswarth.	1858,	Thomas Hayes.
	Philip Ruhl.		Daniel Witmer.
1830-31,	Ner Middleswarth.	1859,	John J. Patterson.
	Philip Ruhl.		William F. Wagenseller.
1831-32,	Henry Roush.	1860,	Thomas Hayes.
	Philip Ruhl.		William F. Wagenseller.
1832-33,	William L. Harris.	1861,	Thomas Hayes.
	George Weirick.		John J. Patterson.
1833-34,	Robert P. Maclay.	1862,	H. K. Ritter.
	Simon Shaffer.		J. Beaver.
1834-35,	Ner Middleswarth,	1863,	H. K. Ritter.
	Jacob Hummel.		George W. Strouse.
1835-36,	Ner Middleswarth.	1864,	John Balsbach.
	John Montelius.		Samuel H. Orwig.

Union, Juniata, and Mifflin.

Lycoming, Union, and Snyder.

1836-37,	Henry Yearick.	1865,	S. H. Orwig.
	Enoch Beale.		Samuel Alleman.
	James Hughes.		Charles Wilson.
1837-38,	Abraham S. Wilson.	1866,	S. C. Wingard.
	James Hughes.		D. A. Irwin.
	Henry Yearick.		Isaac Rothrock.
1838-39,	John Funk.	1867,	S. C. Wingard.
	William Ramsey.		Charles D. Roush.
	John Montelius.		J. H. Wright.
1840,	Abraham S. Wilson.	1868,	R. H. Lawshe.
	Isaac Hottenstein.		C. D. Roush.
	William Cox, senior.		George G. Glass.
1841,	Ner Middleswarth.	1869,	W. P. I. Painter.
	John Funk.		Thomas Church.
	Joseph A. Bell.		William G. Herrold.
1842,	John H. McCrum.	1870,	Theodore Hill.
	William Ross.		Thomas Church.
	John A. Vanvalzah.		Andrew H. Dill.
1843,	Thomas J. Postlethwaite.	1871,	Samuel Wilson.
	David Glenn.		John Cummings.
	Samuel Reber.		William Young.

Union and Juniata.

Snyder and Union.

1844,	John Hall,	1872,	William G. Herrold.
	John Adams.	1873,	Charles S. Wolfe.
1845,	John Hall.	1874,	Charles S. Wolfe.
	John Adams.		

Union.

1846,	John McCrum.	1875-76,	Charles S. Wolfe.
	Jacob McCorley.	1877-78,	Alfred Hayes.
1847,	Jacob McCorley.		

PRESIDENT JUDGES.

Seth Chapman*,	July 11, 1811	S. S. Woods,	Nov. 20, 1861
Ellis Lewis,	Oct. 14, 1833	Joseph C. Bucher,	Nov. 7, 1871
Abraham S. Wilson,	Mar. 30, 1842		

ASSOCIATE JUDGES.

Hugh Wilson,	Oct. 11, 1813	Philip Ruhl,	Nov. 17, 1855
John Bolender,†	Aug. 26, 1815	John W. Simonton,	Nov. 12, 1856
Adam Light,	Dec. 11, 1820	John Walls,	Nov. 20, 1860
George Schnable,	Mar. 26, 1840	John W. Simonton,	Nov. 23, 1861
John Baskin,	Mar. 15, 1841	Martin Dreisbach,	Feb. 3, 1865
Joseph Stillwell,	Jan. 21, 1843	Martin Dreisbach,	Nov. 6, 1865
John Montelius,	Feb. 27, 1845	John W. Simonton,	Nov. 9, 1866
Jacob Wittenmyer,	Feb. 28, 1848	Jacob Hummel,	Nov. 9, 1870
James Harrison,	Mar. 7, 1850	Cyrus Hoffa,	Nov. 17, 1871
James Marshall,	Nov. 10, 1851	Jacob Hummel,	Dec. 3, 1875
Jacob Wittenmyer,‡	Nov. 10, 1851	William F. Wilson,	Dec. 8, 1876

* Resigned, October 10, 1833.   † Resigned, December 11, 1820.   ‡ Legislated out.

DEPUTY ATTORNEYS GENERAL.

William Irwin,	1814	Isaac Slenker,	1830
John Lashells,	1815	Samuel Weirick,	1836
M. McKinney, junior,	1818	Robert B. Barber,	1839
James Merrill,	1821	John Porter,	1842
John Mumma,	1824	George W. Graham,	1843
C. A. Bradford,	1826	Robert B. Barber,	1846
John A. Sterrett,	Feb. 1828	William Van Gezer,	1848
John Wyeth,	Sept. 1828		

DISTRICT ATTORNEYS.

George Hill,	Dec. 1850	Joseph C. Bucher,	Dec. 1859
William Van Gezer,	Dec. 1853	Alfred Hayes,	Dec. 1862
James B. Hamlin,	Dec. 1856	Andrew A. Leiser,	Sept. 1876

PROTHONOTARIES.

Simon Snyder, jr.,*	Oct. 14, 1813	John P. Gutelius,	Oct. 13, 1840
Joseph Stillwell,	Feb. 7, 1821	William Roshong,	Nov. 12, 1841
George A. Snyder,	Jan. 22, 1824	Jacob Haus,	Nov. 11, 1847
Joseph Stillwell,	Jan. 28, 1830	Joseph Eyster,	Nov. 25, 1850
Robert P. Maclay,	Jan. 6, 1836	Samuel Roush,	Nov. 22, 1853
Samuel Roush,	Jan. 31, 1839	James W. Sands,	Nov. —, 1862
Jacob H. Horning,	Nov. 14, 1839	C. H. Hassenplug,	Nov. 18, 1865

* Simon Snyder, junior, Esquire, was born at Lancaster, November 9, 1763, and died at Harrisburg, May 10, 1839.

REGISTERS AND RECORDERS.

Simon Snyder, junior,	Oct. 14, 1813	Henry Aurand, junior,	Aug. 25, 1845
Peter Hackenberg,	Feb. 7, 1821	Daniel Bellman,	Nov. 17, 1845
John Maclay,	Jan. 22, 1824	Christian Breyman,	Nov. 22, 1851
Samuel Roush,	Jan. 28, 1830	J. W. Pennington,	Nov. 29, 1854
George Aurand,	Jan. 6, 1836	George Merrill,	Nov. 27, 1857
Robert Forster,	Jan. 31, 1839	Elisha H. Weikel,	Nov. 28, 1863
John Glover,	Nov. 14, 1839	Reuben Kline,	Nov. 22, 1869
Samuel Aurand,	Nov. 12, 1842		

SHERIFFS.

John Ray,	. . . . .	Dec. 13, 1813
Frederick Wise,	. .	Oct. 30, 1816
Isaac Mertz,	. . . .	Oct. 30, 1819
Jacob Rhoads,	. . .	Oct. 21, 1822
Philip Seebold,	. . .	Oct. 20, 1825
John Haas,	. . . .	Oct. 24, 1828
John Cummings,	. .	Oct. 18, 1831
John Cummings, jr.,	.	Nov. 3, 1834
William Glover,	. .	Oct. 17, 1837
Israel Gutelius,	. .	Oct. 24, 1840
John M. Benfer,	. .	Oct. 17, 1843
Henry S. Boyer,	. .	Oct. 24, 1846
Archibald Thomas,	.	Oct. 24, 1849
John Kessler,	. . .	Oct. 27, 1852
Daniel D. Guldin,	. .	Oct. 24, 1855
Lafayette Albright,	.	Dec. 16, 1861
Thomas Church,	. .	Dec. 16, 1864
Lafayette Albright,	.	Dec. 17, 1867
Michael Kleckner,	.	Dec. 10, 1870
Lafayette Albright,	.	Nov. 31, 1873
Thomas P. Wagner,	.	Dec. 26, 1876

COUNTY COMMISSIONERS.

1813, Dan Caldwell, Frederick Gutelius, and Philip Moore.
1814, James Dale.
1815, John Bower.
1816, Henry Roush.
1817, Mishael Lincoln.
1818, Jacob German.
1819, William Kessler.
1820, Sebastian Witmer.
1821, Joseph Fuehrer.
1822, Christian Miller.
1823, Uriah Silsby.
1824, George Weirick.
1825, Samuel Aurand.
1826, John Montelius.
1827, Thomas Youngman.
1828, John Ziegler.
1829, William Betz.
1830, Peter Hackenburg.
1831, Philip Franck.
1832, J. F. Wilson.
1833, John Keller.
1834, James Harrison.
1835, Samuel B. Barber.
1836, John K. Snyder.
1837, Archibald Thomas.
1838, Jacob Hummel.
1839, Henry Hilbish.
1840, Samuel Boop.
1841, Jacob McCorley.
1842, Solomon Engel.
1843, Michael Clemens.
1844, Henry Saunders, junior.
1845, Jacob Martin.
1846, R. H. Laird.
1847, Joseph Winters.
1848, James Barbin.
1849, John Wilt.
1850, George Heimbach.
1851, S. K. Herrold.
1852, Adam Sheckler.
1853, Sem Leitzel.
1854, John D. Romig.
1855, R. V. B. Lincoln, Jacob Hummel, George Schoch.
1856, William Rule.
1857, R. V. B. Lincoln.
1858, James Pross.
1859, D. H. Kelly.
1860, F. Bolender.
1861, J. M. Walters.
1862, Robert Reed.
1863, Samuel Marshall.
1864, Michael Kleckner.
1865, Michael Brown.
1866, T. V. Harbeson.
1867, S. B. Hoffman.
1868, E. S. Gudykunst.
1869, T. V. Harbeson.
1870, S. B. Hoffman.
1871, Willam Steans.
1872, J. W. Kauffman.
1873, Joseph Boop.
1874, George Schoch.
1875, Joseph Boop, George Schoch and John Yarger.

COMMISSIONERS' CLERKS.

1813, Flavel Roan.
1817, Frederick Gutelius.
1821, John Mauch.
1831, J. H. Horning.
1834, S. Weirich.
1836, M. H. Weaver.
1841, J. J. Maclay.
1843, J. S. Dubois.
1851, C. Breyman.
1851, (Nov.,) David Schwenck.
1853, A. J. Peters.
1855, Andrew Kennedy.
1869, Peter Hursh.

COUNTY TREASURERS.

1814, Michael Schoch.
1817, Joseph Stillwell.
1818, Thomas Shipton.
1820, Christopher Seebold.
1823, William Kessler.
1826, Samuel Wilson.
1829, Samuel Aurand.
1831, Jacob Mauck.
1835, Isaac Peters.
1838, John P. Seebold.
1841, Michael Kleckner.
1843, Philip Gross.
1845, Archibald Thomas.
1847, Charles Seebold.
1849, Daniel Horlacher.
1851, Jacob Mauck.
1853, Henry Solomon.
1855, R. H. Laird.
1857, H. P. Sheller.
1859, R. H. Laird.
1861, John A. Mertz.
1863, William Jones.
1865, John Hayes.
1867, William Jones.
1869, William Hauck.
1871, John Hertz, deceased. William Jones appointed to fill vacancy.
1873, James Pross.
1875, B. F. Eaton.

DEPUTY SURVEYORS.

1813, Simon Snyder, junior.
1818, Adam Wilt.
1821, John Hayes.
1833, Robert G. H. Hayes.
1836, Solomon Engle.
1836, Michael H. Weaver.
1839, Robert G. H. Hayes.
1846, James Madden.
1846, Philip Hilbish.
1850, Robert G. H. Hayes.
1854, J. Henry Motz.
1858, Wilson I. Linn.
1859, Conrad Sheckler.
1868, Reuben F. Brown.
1874, Conrad Sheckler.

CORONERS.

1816, Isaac Mertz.
1819, Daniel Winter.
1822, Jacob Swineford.
1825, Christian Shroyer.
1828, Robert Vanvalzah, junior.
1831, John Bower.
1834, Jacob Aurand.
1837, Joseph Long.
1841, Matthew Brewer.
1842, Jacob Reichley.
1845, John D. Smith.
1858, William L. Harris.

NOTARIES PUBLIC.

Christian Miller, . . Jan. 6, 1820
Henry C. Hickok, . April 12, 1853
George A. Frick, . . Dec. 28, 1854
O. Norton Worden, . May 14, 1855
John B. Miller, . . Aug. 12, 1856
Samuel Slifer, . . . Dec. 9, 1857
William Jones, .· . Jan. 12, 1858
Andrew Kennedy, . Jan. 15, 1858
George A. Frick, . . Jan. 2, 1861
Samuel Slifer, . . . Jan. 12, 1861
Andrew Kennedy, . June 24, 1861
Joseph J. R. Orwig, . Jan. 14, 1864
Samuel Slifer, . . . Jan. 14, 1864
Andrew Kennedy, . June 29, 1864
S. P. Myers, ... April 7, 1865
Samuel Slifer, . . . Jan. 11, 1867
Andrew Kennedy, . Oct. 30, 1867
Simon P. Myers, . . April 7, 1868
Paul Geddes, . . . July 15, 1869
John Stitzer, . . . Nov. 12, 1869
Samuel Slifer, . . . Jan. 6, 1870
Mellville Reese Dill, May 5, 1870
John S. Stitzer, . . Nov. 15, 1872
Samuel Slifer, . . . Jan. 9, 1873
William Rule, . . . April 30, 1873
D. B. Miller, . . . May 6, 1873
Samuel Slifer, . . . Jan. 12, 1876
John Stitzer, . . . Jan. 22, 1876
William Rule, . . . Mar. 20, 1876
D. B. Miller, . . . May 3, 1876
G. N. LeFevre, . . Mar. 29, 1877

ANNALS OF BUFFALO VALLEY.

JUSTICES OF THE PEACE BY APPOINTMENT.

Name	Date	Name	Date
John Bolender,	Mar. 20, 1813	Henry Strubel,	Apr. 14, 1828
George Weirick,	Mar. 20, 1813	Henry Herold,	Apr. 14, 1828
Thomas Shipton,	Aug. 27, 1813	Hottenstine, Dr. Isaac,	Mar. 12, 1828
Thomas Youngman,	Nov. 10, 1813	Michael Wittenmoyer,	Apr. 20, 1829
John Cummings,	Dec. 10, 1813	Isaac Smith,	Apr. 20, 1829
Christopher Seebold,	Mar. 26, 1813,	James Fleming Linn,	Jan. 2, 1829
Henry Spyker,	Mar. 30, 1813	John Maclay,	Dec. 7, 1829
Adam Wilt,	Mar. 26, 1813	Robert G. H. Hayes,	Mar. 12, 1829
Henry Yearick,	Mar. 26, 1813	Simon Snyder,	Feb. 3, 1829
John Wilson,	Nov. 1, 1813	John Rank,	Feb. 3, 1829
Philip Burchart,	Mar. 26, 1813	Jacob McCorley,	Feb. 3, 1829
Joseph Fuehrer,	Mar. 26, 1813	George Clingan,	Dec. 15, 1829
Peter Hackenberg, jr.,	Mar. 26, 1813	Amos Stroh,	May 5, 1830
Dan Caldwell,	Mar. 26, 1813	James Madden,	Feb. 24, 1831
Christian Miller,	Jan. 25, 1814	Samuel Geddes,	Aug. 2, 1831
Frederick Gutelius,	Nov. 11, 1814	John Reifsnyder,	Apr. 25, 1831
Abraham Aurand,	June 23, 1814	Jacob J. Marr,	May 31, 1831
William Kessler,*	June 24, 1816	Jacob Musser,	May 17, 1832
John Schnee,	May 13, 1816	William Kessler,	Jan. 11, 1833
George Schnable,	July 14, 1817	William Roshong,	Sept. 3, 1834
Jacob German,†	May 9, 1817	Jonathan Farnswarth,	Feb. 2, 1835
Robert Willett,	Oct. 20, 1817	John Highly,	Nov. 18, 1835
Andrew McClenahan,	May 30, 1817	Isaac Jones,	Mar. 27, 1835
Samuel Wilson,	June 3, 1819	Samuel Roush,	Dec. 1, 1835
Michael Rathfon,	Mar. 16, 1819	Henry Noll,	Dec. 9, 1835
John Reifsnyder,	June 3, 1819	Peter H. Hawk,	Nov. 4, 1835
John Bassler,	May 17, 1819	John Lenig,	Apr. 20, 1835
George Aurand,	Jan. 4, 1820	John Emmit,	Mar. 14, 1835
John Nesbit,	Mar. 26, 1821	David Schwenck,	June 7, 1836
James McClellan,	June 4, 1821	James Harrison,	Feb. 3, 1836
Samuel Haupt,	Oct. 4, 1821	Samuel B. Barber,	June 7, 1836
John Glover, junior,	Mar. 21, 1822	Peter Hackenberg, sr.,	June 8, 1836
Jacob German,	Mar. 29, 1822	Philip Ruhl,	Mar. 27, 1837
Valentine Haas,	Sept. 23, 1822	Joseph McCool,	Nov. 6, 1837
Samuel Ludwig,	Mar. 29, 1822	Daniel Bellman,	Mar. 3, 1837
Charles Weirman,	Dec. 11, 1823	Andrew Glover,	Mar. 27, 1837
Joseph Stillwell,	Nov. 18, 1823	John Courtney,	Oct. 24, 1838
Joseph Musser,	Dec. 8, 1823	Lewis Bertram,	Dec. 25, 1838
Mathew Brewer,‡	Dec. 10, 1823	Levi B. Christ,	Jan. 3, 1838
John Mauck,	June 22, 1825	Jacob F. Hummel,	Nov. 14, 1838
Solomon Engle,	Apr. 17, 1827	Jacob Riblet,	Dec. 26, 1838
William Cameron,	Feb. 19, 1827	Conrad Stock,	Jan. 11, 1839
Thomas R. Lewis,	Nov. 23, 1827	George N. Youngman,	Apr. 16, 1839

* Resigned, April 30, 1819.   † Resigned, December 14, 1821.
‡ Resigned, September 27, 1838.

NECROLOGY,

COMMENCED BY JAMES F. LINN, Esquire, in 1826.

	Date of Death.	Age.		Date of Death.	Age.
Ackerman, Mrs. C.,	Jan. 16, 1874	76	Badger, Robert,	Oct. 16, 837	
Adams, Joseph,	Jan. —, 1825		Baker, John,	—— —, 1821	
Adams, William,	Oct. 18, 1868	50	Baker, Peter,	—— —, 1823	
Adams, Mrs. Mary,	Oct. 6, 1872	85	Baker, Mrs. Sarah,	Oct. 25, 1853	34
Aikey, Lewis,	Apr. 22, 1862	73	Baker, Jacob,	Oct. 11, 1855	42
Albert, Jacob,	July 6, 1848	80	Baker, Mrs. Ann S.,	Apr. 9, 1862	35
Albert, Benedict,	May 26, 1875	71	Baker, John,	Apr. 7, 1868	58
Alsbach, Solomon,	Jan. —, 1828		Baker, John, W. D.,	Sept. 20 1874	82
Alter, Mrs. Mary,	Feb. 5, 1817	40	Barber, Robert,	Nov. 27, 1841	91
Alter, Abraham,	July 19, 1829		Barber, Mrs. Mary,	Feb. —, 1846	
Ambers, Mrs. M.,	Sept. 3, 1861		Barber, Col. Sam'l,	Mar. 2, 1846	
Ammon, Andrew,	Mar. 14, 1842		Barber, Thomas,	Apr. 14, 1856	
Ammon, Samuel,	Sept. 14, 1852	38	Barber, Mrs. S. A.,	Dec. 26, 1860	56
Ammon, Beyer,	Feb. 21, 1862	52	Barber, Rev. D. M.,	Oct. 30, 1865	66
Ammon, Elizabeth,	Feb. 14, 1868	82	Barber, Mrs. A. B.,	Dec. 17, 1871	30
Anderson, James,	May —, 1847		Barber, Mrs. Eliz.,	Apr. 5, 1872	86
Anderson, Jere.,	Jan. 28, 1864	76	Barber, Eleanor,	Aug. 25, 1873	81
Anderson Moses,	June 6, 1874	75	Barber, Mrs. Jane,	Feb. 13, 1874	60
Andrews, George,	Jan. 10, 1860	33	Barber, James W.,	May 30, 1877	82
Angle, Mrs. L. T.,	Oct. 9, 1871	26	Barkdoll, John H.,	May 3, 1868	
Angstadt, Mrs.,	Apr. 2, 1853		Barnes, Charles L.,	Jan. 21, 1862	70
Angstadt, Gideon,	—— —, 1854		Branhart, Mrs. S.,	Feb. 18, 1854	78
Angstadt, Benj.,	Feb. 15, 1863	55	Barnhart, Rev. W.,	Apr. 19, 1862	35
Anthony, Hon. J. B.	Jan. 10, 1851		Barrett, Able C.,	Sept. 10, 1849	
Arbegast, Eve,	Jan. 29, 1868	90	Barrett, Mrs. S. H.,	Jan. 8, 1872	
Ard, Dr. Joseph B.,	Feb. 24, 1861		Barton, Esq., S. S.,	Sept. 14, 1864	65
Armstrong, Mrs. S.,	Feb. 20, 1829		Baskins, Hon. J.,	Sept. 26, 1851	63
Armstrong, Wm.,	Aug. 26, 1854	60	Baum, Mrs. Eliz.,	Sept. 23, 1839	61
Armstrong, James,	Aug. 13, 1867	75	Baum, Samuel,	Oct. 3, 1842	
Armstrong, Marg't,	July 20, 1869		Baum, John M.,	June 29, 1862	39
Arnold, George,	May 12, 1848	75	Beaver, Rev. Peter,	Aug. 26, 1849	67
Atwood, Henry,	Apr. 27, 1836		Beaver, W. M.,	Nov. 13, 1854	22
Aubel, Mrs. Barb.,	July 11, 1843	82	Beaver, Mrs. E. G.,	Oct. 30, 1861	41
Aurand, Samuel,	Aug. 19, 1845		Beatty, Jane,	Mar. 4, 1829	62
Aurand, Mrs. Geo.,	Aug. 18, 1848	71	Becher, Capt. D. L.,	Mar. 17, 1858	84
Aurand, Abram,	Jan. 25, 1855		Bechtel, Peter,	Feb. 3, 1852	
Aurand, Henry,	Mar. 1, 1844	62	Bechtel, Samuel,	Apr. 9, 1870	58
Anspach, Susan'h.,	Sept. 19, 1842	29	Beck, Henry,	Jan. 2, 1846	
Backhouse, Dr. S. T.	Dec. 28, 1848	44	Beck, Isaac L.,	May 21, 1856	45

	Date of Death.	Age.		Date of Death.	Age.
Beck, Adam,	Dec. 21, 1867	91	Bowes, John,	——, 1832	
Beck, Mrs. Susan'h,	Mar. 11, 1870	89	Boyd, John B.,	Aug. 1, 1845	
Beckly, sr., Daniel,	July 22, 1831		Boyer, Mrs. Barb'ra	Mar. 1, 1868	93
Becker, John,	Sept. 18, 1843	84	Boyer, Mrs. Sarah,	Jan. 3, 1872	68
Beckly, Benjamin,	May 29, 1856		Boyer, Samuel,	Apr. 10, 1874	69
Beeber, John,	May 11, 1872	83	Bradford, E. G.,	May 17, 1836	
Beisel, Mrs. Susan,	Feb. 28, 1862	45	Brady, Charlotte,	June 6, 1848	
Beiler, sr., John,	Mar. 3, 1868	84	Braucher, Jacob,	July 7, 1870	86
Bell, Berryhill,	Nov. 15, 1861	62	Braucher, George,	May 11, 1874	80
Bell, W. G.,	June 27, 1875	69	Brautigam, Daniel,	Mar. 10, 1863	75
Bell, Mrs. M. R.,	July 28, 1876	65	Brause, Jonathan,	Jan. 12, 1876	73
Benner, John,	Mar. 8, 1854	73	Breyman, Christ'n,	May 26, 1862	67
Benner, George,	Nov. 10, 1854	78	Brice, Thomas,	Oct. 20, 1858	53
Benner, Elizabeth,	Dec. 29, 1834	79	Bridge, Mrs. Eliz.,	Nov. 22, 1873	62
Benner, John B.,	Sept. 1, 1875	70	Bright, Schreyer,	Nov. 15, 1854	16
Bennett, Elizabeth,	Mar. 2, 1872	80	Bright, George,	May 18, 1862	62
Bennett, Charles,	Aug. 5, 1874	85	Bright, Jacob,	Feb. 13, 1865	75
Berkley, Joseph,	Oct. 7, 1850	42	Bright, Joseph,	Mar. 6, 1872	67
Bertolette, Jona.,	Jan. 1, 1874	60	Brobst, Jacob,	Mar. 22, 1825	73
Betz, Solomon,	Oct. 23, 1837	81	Brooks, Enos,	Feb. 23, 1872	66
Beyer, Daniel,	Oct. 31, 1826		Brown, John, Esq	July 27, 1831	65
Beyer, Charles,	July 19, 1866	73	Brown, John,	Dec. 13, 1838	82
Boyer, Dr. Charles,	Sept. 13, 1830		Brown, John,	Aug. 7, 1845	62
Bibighaus, Dr. Jno.,	July 2, 1860	53	Brown, John,	Dec. 30, 1846	61
Bibighaus, Mrs. J.,	Mar. 1, 1861	55	Brown, Christ. G.,	July 29, 1850	
Biddle, John,	Aug. 29, 1867	66	Brown, William,	July 15, 1855	59
Billington, Thomas,	Mar. 10, 1856	41	Brown, Mrs. Susan,	Sept. 28, 1858	30
Billmyer, Clara,	June 25, 1844		Brown, Christian,	July 29, 1860	
Billmyer, Martin,	Apr. 3, 1862	40	Brown, Matthew,	Aug. —, 1860	67
Billmyer, Mrs. S.,	Nov. 14, 1874	53	Brown, Mrs. Han'h,	Jan. 7, 1865	62
Binns, John,	June 16, 1860	88	Brown, Lt. Hogan,	May 10, 1861	
Bird, Jonathan,	Feb. 13, 1873	64	Brown, Abraham,	Nov. 11, 1869	81
Bishop, John,	Nov. 21, 1854		Brown, Jacob,	Dec. 28, 1870	71
Black, James,	Mar. 9, 1837		Brown, Christian,	Oct. 28, 1873	80
Black, Mrs., Isa'la,	Apr. 25, 1847	76	Brown, George,	Apr. 4, 1875	80
Black, Hannah,	Aug. 11, 1858	59	Brown, William,	Sept. 29, 1875	84
Black, Mary,	Apr. 18, 1862	67	Brown, Michael,	Mar. 9, 1876	79
Black, Thomas S.,	Nov. 29, 1870	61	Bryson, Robert,	Oct. 30, 1832	
Black, Mrs. M. B.,	Feb. 7, 1872	79	Bryson, Rev. John,	Aug. 3, 1855	98
Blackwell, Mrs.	Nov. 23, 1849		Bucher, Maggie, G.,	Mar. 23, 1869	7
Blair, Jane,	Nov. 17, 1861	56	Buckner, Isaac,	Sept. 28, 1828	
Blythe, Esq., Cal.,	June 27, 1849	57	Buckner, William,	——, 1849	
Boal, Capt. David,	Oct. 11, 1824		Buckner, Amelia,	Aug. 18, 1858	57
Boal, Esq., Geo. F.,	Jan. 18, 1856	45	Buckner, Sarah,	May 18, 1864	
Bobst, Michael,	May 1, 1841		Budd, Mrs. Anna,	Aug. 4, 1866	71
Bockener, Isaac,	Sept. 28, 1828		Buoy, Edward,	Feb. 20, 1874	75
Bogar, Jacob,	Aug. 15, 1826		Burn, Sarah,	Dec. 5, 1842	77
Bogar, John D.,	Apr. 15, 1862	44	Burr, Henry H.,	Nov. 21, 1853	58
Bogar, Hester,	Aug. 16, 1863		Burrell, Joseph,	Oct. 15, 1827	
Boggs, Rose G.,	Aug. 4, 1872	49	Burris, John L.	Mar. 5, 1869	83
Boop, Peter,	Aug. 14, 1872	70	Bussler, Mrs.,	Fall of 1825.	
Bergstresser, Geo.,	May 3, 1856	72	Butterfield, Jonas,	Oct. 3, 1826	
Bossler, John,	June 4, 1859	82	Byler, Samuel,	May 28, 1868	43
Boveard, Mrs.,	Nov. 20, 1847	91	Cadwallader, Seth,	Aug. 26, 1863	67
Bower, Mrs. Sarah,	Mar. 1, 1846		Caldwell John,	May —, 1834	
Bower, Jacob,	Sept. 22, 1847	86	Caldwell, Mary,	Aug. —, 1834	
Bower, William,	Dec. 21, 1851		Caldwell, Dan,	Dec. 16, 1836	60
Bower, George,	Aug. 13, 1854	65	Caldwell, James D.,	Mar. 14, 1847	48

ANNALS OF BUFFALO VALLEY.

	Date of Death.	Age.
Caldwell, Jane M.,	Dec. 11, 1868	40
Calvin, Miss Mary,	Apr. —, 1863	
Cameron, Martha,	Nov. 10, 1830	
Cameron, Daniel,	June 30, 1832	
Cameron, Col. Jas.,	July 21, 1861	
Cameron, jr., Wm.,	Nov. 29, 1861	24
Campbell, John,	Oct. 27, 1838	
Campbell, Maria,	Jan. —, 1861	
Campbell, Rebecca,	Jan. 25, 1861	83
Campbell, Wm.,	Sept. —, 1861	
Campbell, F. C.,	Apr. 21, 1867	80
Candor, Harriet,	May —, 1836	
Candor, Mrs. Eliz.,	Dec. 14, 1836	
Candor, J. Howard,	Sept. 23, 1839	
Candor, Josiah,	June 26, 1840	70
Candor, Joseph,	Apr. 18, 1849	57
Candor, John M.,	Nov. 13, 1849	23
Candor, Miss Lydia,	Mar. —, 1862	61
Candor, Franklin,	Mar. 12, 1862	67
Candor, Elizabeth,	Apr. 12, 1862	38
Carson, John B.,	Mar. 25, 1849	
Carothers, William,	Jan. 7, 1861	75
Carothers, Annie M.	Jan. 10, 1861	36
Caul, John,	Jan. 9, 1861	83
Cawley, James,	Sept. 25, 1840	
Cawley, Miss Eliz.,	July 11, 1862	38
Cawley, Charles,	May 16, 1871	45
Chamberlin, Ann,	Apr. 2, 1832	
Chamberlin, Uriah,	Feb. 1, 1853	
Chamberlin, Col. A.	Jan. 12, 1856	68
Chamberlin, John,	Apr. 15, 1858	61
Chamberlin, Mrs M.	Mar. —, 1859	89
Chamberlin, G. A.,	Apr. 13, 1860	32
Chamberlin, Mary,	Apr. 3, 1865	61
Chamberlin, M. E.,	July 25, 1866	17
Chambers, Robert,	—. —, 1835	
Chambers, Reb'a E.	Mar. 11, 1836	27
Chambers, Benj.	Dec. 19, 1847	64
Chambers, Mrs. M.,	Aug. 2, 1863	48
Chambers, Robert,	Oct. 15, 1864	55
Chambers, Benj.	Oct. 19, 1872	60
Chambers, Mrs. M.,	Oct. 26, 1875	49
Chappell, Lucinda,	Sept. 2, 1849	23
Chappell, Mrs. M.,	Oct. —, 1849	68
Chappell, Jason L.,	Aug. 26, 1855	78
Chappell, Mearit,	Oct. —, 1872	
Charles, Samuel,	Sept. 23, 1873	63
Charlton, Dr. Jas.,	Oct. —, 1831	
Cherry, Charles,	Sept. —, 1823	
Chesney, Jacob G.,	Mar. 9, 1858	55
Chestnut, J.,	Feb. —, 1825	
Chestnut, Rev. D.,	—— —, 1837	
Chestnut, Ann,	June 10, 1851	
Christ, Jacob,	July 27, 1832	
Christ, Mrs. Cath.,	Feb. 23, 1861	71
Christ, Mrs. Hester,	Aug. 16, 1863	64
Christ, Levi B.,	Oct. 4, 1876	70
Christie, Mrs. Mar.,	Oct. 27, 1860	64

	Date of Death.	Age.
Clark, Sarah,	Aug. 13, 1854	68
Clark, Sarah,	May 10, 1857	67
Clark, Flavel,	Mar. 6, 1858	44
Clark, James,	Oct. 22, 1864	
Clemmens, Mich'l,	Apr. 7, 1859	77
Clingan, Wm. Esq.,	May 24, 1822	
Clingan, Mrs.,	May 7, 1838	85
Clingan, Thomas,	Apr. 24, 1858	73
Clingan, jr., Flavel,	Apr. 21, 1859	24
Clingan, George,	Jan. 14, 1860	72
Clingan, Mrs. M.,	Dec. 31, 1861	72
Clingan, Flavel R.,	Oct. 17, 1876	82
Coburn, Dr. Chas.,	Apr. 23, 1858	72
Cole, George,	Mar. 2, 1868	69
Collins, Mrs. Mary,	Aug. 2, 1874	82
Colsher, ———,	May 26, 1857	96
Comly, Thomas,	Apr. 13, 1866	47
Conner, David,	Feb. 8, 1840	
Conner, Elizabeth,	Sept. 26, 1840	
Conner, John,	Sept. 3, 1846	
Conrad, George,	July 5, 1849	45
Cook, Adam,	Aug. 21, 1832	
Cook, Elizabeth,	Jan. 4, 1849	
Cook, James,	Feb. 21, 1873	81
Cook, Andrew,	Sept. 16, 1873	82
Cooper, Judge Jno.	June 21, 1863	79
Cornelius, William,	About 1814.	
Cornelius, Jesse,	May 31, 1833	
Cornelius, Mrs. J.,	Aug. 26, 1843	80
Cornelius, James,	Nov. 19, 1849	
Cornelius, Mrs.,	Oct. 1, 1854	
Cornelius, John,	Apr. 8, 1866	68
Cornelius, Mrs. F.,	Sept. 23, 1867	80
Cornelius, Mrs. S.,	Aug. 10, 1868	70
Cornelius, James,	Jan. 24, 1874	91
Cornelius, Thomas,	Mar. 10, 1874	65
Corry, George,	Aug. 15, 1856	70
Costenbader, Hen.,	Aug. 27, 1853	
Courtney, William,	Sept. 5, 1854	50
Coverly, Maj. J. C.,	May 18, 1856	
Covert, Mrs. Mary,	Mar. 29, 1858	47
Cowden, Esq., Jno.,	Jan. 13, 1837	70
Cox, Mrs. Sarah F.,	Oct. 13, 1868	47
Craig, Mrs. Anna,	Jan. 26, 1848	89
Crawford, Dr. J. W.,	Apr. 17, 1861	45
Cress, Conrad,	Oct. 24, 1844	
Criswell, Thomas,	Apr. 26, 1860	32
Criswell, Mrs. E.,	June 4, 1861	79
Criswell, Mrs. Sar.,	Feb. 10, 1862	46
Cronmiller, Martin,	Jan. 26, 1838	76
Crosgrove, Samuel,	Sept. 24, 1861	88
Crosgrove, James,	Feb. 27, 1876	76
Crotzer, Thomas,	Sept. 14, 1852	53
Cummings, John,	Aug. 27, 1829	
Cummings, sr., J.,	Feb. 16, 1836	
Cummings, James,	Jan. 19, 1859	72
Cummings, Alex.,	Mar. 30, 1862	58
Dale, Mrs. Eliza,	Apr. 23, 1835	80

ANNALS OF BUFFALO VALLEY. 567

	Date of Death.	Age		Date of Death.	Age
Dale, Samuel,	Aug. 9, 1848		Dreisbach, Ellis,	Oct. 29, 1860	61
Dale, William,	Sept. 12, 1857		Dreisbach, Charles,	Apr. 29, 1861	21
Dale, Mary Ellen,	May 7, 1861	39	Dreisbach, John,	Feb. 7, 1869	78
Dale, Col. James,	Sept. 11, 1862	81	Dreisbach, Rev. J.,	Aug. 19, 1871	82
Dale, Miss Agnes,	June 23, 1865		Dreisbach, Thomas,	May 4, 1872	77
Danowsky, Wm. F.,	Mar. 1, 1875	73	Dreisbach, Mrs. E.,	Oct. 2, 1875	73
Davidson, Ann,	July —, 1827		Duncan, James,	Oct. 12, 1843	85
Davis, James K.,	Mar. 10, 1847		Dubois, James S.,	June 7, 1852	56
Davis, William,	Aug. 11, 1860	57	Duncan Martha,	Feb. 13, 1847	65
Davis, Mrs. Sarah,	Sept. —, 1860		Duncan, David,	Sept. 6, 1855	58
Davis, Miss Ann,	Apr. 5, 1861	82	Duncan, Mrs. D.,	Sept. 8, 1865	
Dawson, Rev. A.,	Nov. 4, 1855	68	Duncan, Thos. F.,	July 27, 1867	
Dawson, Mrs. R.,	Jan. 27, 1863	77	Dundore, George,	Mar. 31, 1866	80
Deck, Godfrey,	June 30, 1870	65	Dunkle, Mrs.,	Sept. 29, 1842	
Dennius, Mrs. H.,	Jan. 27, 1848	66	Dunkle, Conrad,	Jan. 26, 1845	82
Deibert, Henry,	Sept. 9, 1872	70	Dunkle, John,	Jan. 2, 1846	
Dentler, Peter,	Apr. 21, 1843		Dunkle, sr., John,	Feb. 18, 1864	69
Dennis, John, W. B.	Mar. 22, 1876	82	Dunlap, Mrs. Mary,	Sept. 8, 1837	
Dennis, Mrs. Mich.,	May 18, 1876	65	Dunlap, John,	Sept. 26, 1842	
Dentler, John,	Aug. 18, 1853	76	Dunn, Josiah,	——— —, 1823	
Dentler, Hon. J. F.,	Jan. 5, 1860	54	Dunn, James,	Oct. 14, 1849	95
Dentler, Mrs.,	Mar. 6, 1866	77	Dunn, Mrs. Eliz.,	June —, 1861	
Deratt, Daniel,	Mar. 20, 1848	72	Dunn, Mrs.,	Feb. 18, 1862	64
Deratt, Nancy,	Nov. 22, 1850		Dunseif, Hironem's,	July 12, 1830	
Derr, George,	Feb. 5, 1829	67	Eartley, Mrs. Maria,	Nov. 13, 1842	45
Derr, Frances,	Oct. 9, 1832		Eaton, Cyrus,	Mar. 9, 1873	79
Derr, Mrs. Fanny,	Feb. 15, 1842	72	Eckert, George,	Jan. 25, 1850	
Derr, Elizabeth,	Nov. 17, 1848	35	Eckert, George B.,	July 21, 1868	55
Derr, John H.,	Aug. 14, 1861	21	Eckert, Mrs. N. B.,	Mar. 10, 1876	70
Derr, Lewis,	June 17, 1862	71	Egbert, jr., John,	Aug. 29, 1855	78
Derr, Benjamin,	Nov. 11, 1862	56	Eilert, Mrs. Ann,	Apr. 7, 1874	72
Derr, Joseph Y.,	July 21, 1864	54	Eilert, Christopher.	Aug. 7, 1824	64
Derr, John,	Feb. 1, 1869	72	Elder, Mrs. Eliza,	June 1, 1870	60
Derr, Mrs. Char.,	Feb. 8, 1873	77	Elliott, John W.,	Jan. 20, 1857	40
Derr, Jacob,	Aug. 2, 1873	70	Elliot, Henrietta G.,	May 9, 1872	60
Derring, Miss Eliz.,	Aug. 16, 1859	58	Ellis, Esq., H. D.,	July 21, 1851	45
Dersham, Abra. V.,	Nov. 3, 1873	84	Ellis, William,	Sept. 19, 1868	69
Dersham, Mrs. H.,	Nov. 8, 1875	86	Ely, Issac,	Apr. 11, 1843	
Dieffenderfer, F.,	Aug. 17, 1825		Ely, Richard Har.,	Oct. 15, 1849	22
Diffenderfer, Philip	Sept. 12, 1876	85	Engle, Solomon,	Nov. 19, 1852	55
Dieffenderfer, J.,	May 19, 1875	86	Engle, Samuel,	Nov. 6, 1872	63
Dieffenbach, Mrs.,	Fall of 1819.		Englehart, Mrs. H.,	Sept. 19, 1874	80
Dilcomb, George,	Dec. 13, 1842	59	Ettman, John,	Sept. 22, 1827	
Dillen, Mrs. R.,	July 15, 1867	44	Evans, Joseph,	Apr. 21, 1834	
Donaldson, Mr.,	——— —, 1823		Evans, Elizabeth,	Mar. 26, 1836	
Donaldson, Mrs. A.,	Aug. 4, 1826	67	Evans, William,	Aug. 24, 1841	
Donarchy, John,	Nov. 23, 1841		Evans, Dr. Chas. R.,	Sept. 23, 1867	28
Donarchy, Benj.,	Jan. 30, 1845		Ewing, Joshua,	July 22, 1844	80
Donarchy, Mrs.F.S.	Apr. 20, 1872	80	Ewing, Agnes,	Sept. —, 1851	25
Donnel, Esq., H.,	Jan. 17, 1826		Ewing, Mrs.,	Mar. 8, 1855	
Dorman. Peter,	Feb. 13, 1874	83	Ewing, James,	Mar. 22, 1856	45
Dorman, Mrs. C.,	Dec. 11, 1875	74	Ewing Rev. James,	Sept. 22, 1861	74
Dorough, Sarah,	Jan. 11, 1832		Ewing, Elizabeth,	Aug. 19, 1869	53
Dorough, James,	Feb. —, 1860		Eyer, Abraham,	Oct. 30, 1823	75
Dougal, Dr. John,	Oct. 28, 1830		Eyer, Jacob,	July 14, 1827	
Doudle, Daniel,	Aug. —, 1828	101	Eyer, Jacob,	Sept. 19, 1854	28
Dougal, Mrs. S. A.,	Apr. 17, 1862	36	Eyer, jr., Isaac,	July 9, 1868	45
Dreisbach, Martin,	Oct. 20, 1831	67	Eyerly, Prof. Jacob,	Aug. —, 1864	75

Name	Date of Death.	Age.
Farley, Abraham,	July 29, 1875	84
Faries, Esq., Robert,	Nov. 12, 1864	60
Fetter, Mrs. Abram,	Oct. 21, 1868	78
Fetter, Abram,	May 4, 1876	84
Fenner, Mary R.,	Aug. 13, 1865	74
Fess, David,	July 29, 1876	76
Fessler, Mrs. Mary,	Sept. 21, 1854	64
Fessler, Jacob,	Sept. 25, 1854	36
Fiedler, Fred. G.,	June 9, 1861	26
Fields, Emily,	Apr. 12, 1830	
Fillman, Jacob,	Sept. 22, 1827	
Finney, James,	Sept. 7, 1826	
Finney, Mrs. Eliz.,	Sept. 7, 1826	
Fisher, Rebecca,	—— —, 1823	
Fisher, Lieut. Thos.	Feb. 9, 1854	68
Fisher, Esq., A. C.,	May 16, 1855	35
Fisher, Rev. A.,	Jan. 27, 1857	53
Fleming, James,	July 30, 1824	
Follmer, Daniel,	Mar. 29, 1875	
Fleming, Gen. Rob.	May 31, 1874	
Follmer, Thomas,	Mar. 13, 1846	
Follmer, Mrs. M.,	Sept. 6, 1853	64
Forry, Nathan, shff.	Jan. 4, 1860	43
Forster, Robert,	Jan. 29, 1834	76
Forster, Joseph,	Mar. 11, 184–	
Forster, John,	Aug. 9, 1849	75
Forster, William,	Mar. 26, 1853	76
Forster, John,	July 2, 1864	78
Forster, Mary Lou.,	Mar. 19, 1865	
Forster, John V.,	Mar. 19, 1865	
Forster, William,	Mar. 27, 1865	71
Forster, Mrs. Jane,	Sept. 29, 1868	71
Forster, T. H. B.,	Jan. 16, 1861	26
Fowler, Mrs. A.,	Sept. 24, 1860	50
Fox, Peter,	Jan. 10, 1856	83
Frain de, Henry,	Jan. 4, 1864	70
Frank, John Philip,	Sept. 25, 1856	71
Frederick, Philip,	Feb. 19, 1852	64
Frederick, Matilda,	Sept. 6, 1866	47
Frick, Mrs. Eliz.,	Sept. 2, 1859	65
Frick, Dr. Clar. H.,	Jan. 21, 1861	26
Frick, Esq., G. A.,	June 10, 1872	85
Fries, Rev. Just H.,	Oct. 9, 1889	63
Fries, John,	May 1, 1869	54
Frock, Henry,	Nov. 25, 1861	72
Fryer, Jacob,	Feb. 13, 1864	81
Fulmer, Andrew,	Apr. 5, 1862	65
Gable, John,	Sept. 11, 1873	67
Gearhart, John L.,	Nov. 6, 1860	43
Gebhart, Jonathan,	Nov. 3, 1838	
Gebhart, George,	Dec. 13, 1876	72
Geddes, John R.,	Jan. 7, 1837	
Geddes, Miss Maria,	Oct. 1, 1854	
Gemberling, Mrs. E.	Oct. 13, 1861	63
Gemberling, Philip,	Apr. 26, 1870	75
George, Rev. John,	Dec. 13, 1867	60
George, Sarah Ann,	Feb. 18, 1864	39
German, Jacob,	Jan. 6, 1848	60
Gessner, Francis J.,	Sept. 9, 1855	36
Gessner, Mrs. F. J.,	Sept. 9, 1855	35
Getz, Mrs. Barbara,	Jan. 13, 1864	66
Geyer, Adam,	Dec. 13, 1832	
Gibbons, Hugh,	Apr. 7, 1871	78
Gibson, Henry,	Aug. 22, 1871	63
Gilfillan, Dr. Ed.,	Apr. 12, 1833	64
Ginter, Mrs. Ann,	Sept. 24, 1863	60
Ginter, Charles,	Dec. 17, 1836	
Glass, Joseph,	July 25, 1870	77
Glass, Mrs. Mary A.,	Apr. 30, 1870	61
Glover, John,	Mar. —, 1825	
Glover, Esq., Wm.,	Nov. 8, 1854	70
Glover, Esq., John,	May 17, 1862	80
Goddard, Abner S.,	Sept. 11, 1852	44
Goodlander, J. V.,	Aug. 22, 1863	50
Gordon, Mrs. Har.,	July 17, 1846	52
Gordon, Mary,	Sept. 20, 1855	
Gottshall, David,	July 14, 1849	45
Graham, Alex.	Aug, 23, 1839	
Graham, T. W.,	July 22, 1859	53
Graham, Mrs. M. M.,	Mar. 18, 1863	77
Graham, Thomas,	Aug. 20, 1864	42
Graham, Rosetta,	Aug. 4, 1872	
Graham, H. Spyker,	Aug. 28, 1868	59
Grant, Deborah,	Feb. 22, 1847	
Gray, John,	Mar. 23, 1849	84
Gray, Robert,	Oct. 17, 1854	70
Gregg, Mrs. C. H.,	Jan. 14, 1865	28
Gregg, Andrew,	May 14, 1869	78
Green, Dr. Geo. W.,	Jan. 12, 1848	
Green, Robert B.,	Dec. 29, 1849	28
Green, Abbot,	Mar. 23, 1851	68
Green, Mrs. Marg.,	Sept. 6, 1856	77
Green, Margaret,	May 7, 1858	45
Green, Thomas,	Dec. 3, 1865	52
Green, Mrs. Eliz.,	June 6, 1867	46
Green, Mrs. J. H.,	Apr. 30, 1870	61
Greenough, Esq., E.	Dec. 25, 1847	
Grier, Thomas,	Feb. 2, 1829	31
Grier, Joseph F.,	Feb. 10, 1858	56
Grier, Thomas G.,	Oct. 6, 1864	24
Grier, Maria Jane,	Dec. 7, 1865	33
Grier, Mrs. Marg.,	June 1, 1870	62
Groff, Abraham.,	Oct. 8, 1873	63
Grove, Mrs, Cath.,	Feb. 29, 1848	79
Gross, Henry,	Aug. 15, 1842	80
Grove, Mrs. Nancy,	June 12, 1853	32
Grove, Michael,	Sept. —, 1827	
Grove, David,	May 30, 1866	54
Grove, Eliza,	Nov. 3, 1869	78
Grove Samuel,	Sept. 1, 1873	75
Gudykunst, Chas..	Jan. 13, 1865	66
Gundrum, George,	Apr. 29, 1853	45
Gundy, Eliza,	May 15, 1829	
Gundy, Christain,	Sept. 30, 1836	
Gundy, George,	Nov. 6, 1843	
Gundy, William S.,	Mar. 13, 1846	

ANNALS OF BUFFALO VALLEY. 569

	Date of Death.	Age.		Date of Death.	Age.
Gundy, John,	Oct. 11, 1864	66	Hayes, R. G. H.,	May 2, 1854	59
Gutelius, Fred.,	May 30, 1839	72	Hayes, Esq., David,	June 15, 1858	49
Gutelius, Esq., I.,	Sept. 11, 1863	60	Heckel, Mrs. Mary,	Sept. 15, 1864	
Gutelius, Rev. S.,	July 17, 1866	72	Heckel, Mrs. Han'h,	Dec. 13, 1871	87
Gutelius, Andrew,	Sept. 5, 1874	66	Heckendorn, D.,	Apr. 26, 1864	41
Guyer, Adam,	July —, 1835		Heinbach, George,	Oct. 23, 1860	59
Guyer, Peter,	Sept. 2, 1843	84	Heinly, John,	Feb. 27, 1845	75
Guyer, Rev. John,	Dec. 13, 1867	60	Heiser, Catherine,	Dec. 18, 1844	72
Guyer, Israel,	Mar. 11, 1875	54	Heiser, Frederick,	Mar. 27, 1845	73
Guyer John,	Mar. 21, 1875	57	Heitzman, Jacob,	Sept. 7, 1861	
Haak, John,	Mar. 14, 1828		Hendrick, Andrew,	Feb. 15, 1868	80
Hackenberg, Peter,	Dec. 25, 1847	75	Henderson, Sam'l,	Sept. 29, 1875	84
Hafer, Mrs. Eliz.,	Jan. 22, 1873	80	Henning, John,	June 18, 1853	.
Hafer, Mrs. Eliz.,	Apr. 7, 1875	76	Hepburn, Esq., S.,	Oct. 16, 1865	84
Hafer, Jacob,	Oct. 3, 1875	79	Herbst, Henry,	Aug. 15, 1829	7
Hagenbuch, Peter,	Feb. 17, 1875	60	Herbst, Henry,	Apr. 22, 1848	82
Halfpenny, Mrs. C.,	June 2, 1877	54	Herbst, Mrs. Cath.,	Sept. 24, 1863	41
Hall, Esq., Charles,	Mar. —, 1825		Herbst, Mrs. M. M.,	Aug. 3, 1866	94
Hall, Ebenezer,	Apr. —, 1847		Herbst, Josiah,	Nov. 27, 1870	51
Hall, Rev. Wm. M.,	Aug. 28, 1849	51	Herbst, Esq., D.,	Feb. 16, 1875	60
Hall, John,	Oct. 15, 1856		Herr, David,	Feb. —, 1872	63
Hammond, Joseph,	———, 1823		Hertz, John,	June 16, 1872	46
Hammond, Marg.,	Oct. 15, 1835		Hess, Henry,	Apr. 7, 1858	62
Hammond, Oscar,	Mar. 23, 1857	35	Hess, jr., Henry,	Mar. 9, 1860	23
Hann, Jacob,	Mar. 12, 1841		Hess, Mrs. Eliz.,	May, 8, 1864	67
Hann, Jared,	Aug. 6, 1864	51	Hess, Mrs. L. C.,	Apr. 25, 1876	49
Hannah, John,	Aug. 20, 1832	83	Heverling, John,	Feb. 15, 1869	69
Harbaugh, Mrs. L.,	Sept. 26, 1847	23	Hicks, Christian,	Dec. 22, 1853	
Harkens, John,	July 15, 1870	50	Hicks, Mrs. C.,	Jan. 27, 1863	84
Harbaugh, Rev. H.,	Dec. 28, 1867		Hickok, John H.,	Jan. 14, 1841	
Harimer, Mrs. M.,	Dec. 27, 1872		Hickok, Mrs. M. L.,	Sept. 4, 1868	
Harmon, Susan,	Oct. 12, 1875	67	Higgins, Chas. W.,	Jan. 2, 1862	49
Harmony, Benj.,	———, 1833		High, John,	Sept. 20, 1855	68
Harris, Sally,	Dec. 30, 1827		High, Elizabeth M.,	Jan. 29, 1860	23
Harris, Mrs. Mary,	Dec. 13, 1842	93	Hilands, Robert,	———, 1824	
Harris, Mrs. Mary,	Oct. 21, 1863	80	Hilbourn, James,	Mar. 15, 1851	
Harris, Caroline D.,	Sept. 19, 1864	29	Himmelreich, P.,	Nov. 2, 1828	
Harris James,	July 15, 1868	88	Himmelreich, Dan.,	Jan. —, 1830	
Harris, Miss M.,	Feb. 13, 1873	89	Himmelreich, jr., P.	Sept. 2, 1866	75
Harrison, James,	July 10, 1850	19	Himmelreich, D.,	June 12, 1873	67
Harrison, Hon. Jas.,	Apr. 15, 1866	72	Hixson, Mrs. Jane,	Feb. 21, 1876	82
Hartman, George,	July 26, 1861	81	Hoffman, Mrs. L.,	Nov. 17, 1872	
Hassenplug, J. H.	Nov. 30, 1829	73	Hoffman, Mrs. C.,	Apr. 20, 1875	86
Hassenplug, ——,	Apr. 14, 1859		Hoffman, Mrs. C.,	July 28, 1876	90
Hassenplug, Wm.,	Feb. 11, 1876	80	Hogendobler, Jos.,	July 6, 1864	
Hauck, George,	Mar. 26, 1864	70	Hood, Jane,	Feb. 26, 1826	17
Haupt, jr., Sam'l,	Jan. 25, 1864	46	Hood, Julia,	Mar. 11, 1839	
Haupt, Esq., Sam'l,	Feb. 20, 1869	70	Hood, Wilson H.,	May 26, 1849	
Haus, John,	July 21, 1849	82	Hood, Catherine,	June 9, 1867	61
Haus, Susannah,	July 16, 1852	72	Hoover, George,	July 21, 1869	66
Haus, Jacob,	Oct. 25, 1855	71	Horning, Mrs. Ann,	Mar. 10, 1842	
Hawn, Mrs. Eliz.,	Sept. 20, 1865	75	Horlacher, Daniel,	July 24, 1873	72
Hawn, Daniel,	Dec. 8, 1865	84	Houghton, Mrs. S.,	Jan. 21, 1847	
Hawn, Nancy Jane,	Jan. 29, 1859	33	Houghton, M. A.,	Sept. 1, 1853	24
Hayes, Mrs. Mary,	Dec. 10, 1827		Houghton, John,	Oct. 25, 1863	57
Hayes, Mrs. Emily,	Apr. 12, 1830		Houghton, Jas. M.,	Apr. 26, 1873	40
Hayes, Sarah,	Aug. 28, 1845		Housel, William,	Aug. 9, 1829	91
Hayes, John,	Mar. 17, 1850		Housel, Mrs. Wm.,	July 7, 1835	

	Date of Death.	Age.		Date of Death.	Age.
Housel, William L.,	Aug. 3, 1849		Johnson, Abel,	Nov. 19, 1849	
Housel, Jacob,	July 26, 1850	19	Johnson, Mrs. S. J.,	Apr. 14, 1862	29
Housel, Capt. Wm.,	June 7, 1850		Jones, Thomas,	Oct. 15, 1833	
Housel, Joshua,	Sept. 17, 1852	80	Jones, Mrs. Eliz.,	June 15, 1847	84
Housel, Jacob,	Aug. 4, 1859	60	Jones, Mary A.,	May 11, 1863	
Housel, Mrs. Mary,	July 30, 1860	66	Jordan, Mrs. M. H.,	Feb. 3, 1857	62
Housel, Wm. Esq.,	Apr. 21, 1867	77	Joyce, Isabel,	July 27, 1850	
Housel, Mrs. Mary,	Dec. 14, 1868	82	Joyce, Dr. William,	Apr. 18, 1851	
Howard, Elizabeth,	Mar. 30, 1829		Kaufman, Peter,	Dec. 10, 1845	83
Howard, Thomas,	Jan. 15, 1842		Kaufman, John,	Nov. 30, 1849	86
Howard, Mrs. E.,	May 21, 1842		Kaufman, David,	Sept. 27, 1863	
Howard Thomas,	July 17, 1859	22	Kaufman, Mrs. L.,	Dec. 24, 1859	73
Howard, David,	Nov. 15, 1859		Kaufman, Mrs. D.,	May 1, 1861	25
Howard, Laird,	Mar. 19, 1870	65	Kaufman, Daniel,	Jan. 7, 1866	65
Hoy, John,	Aug. 27, 1853	86	Kaufman, Jas. B.,	July 6, 1836	30
Hubler, John,	Mar. 14, 1845	82	Kaufman, Isaac,	July 18, 1871	60
Hubler, Mrs. John,	Mar. 27, 1845	80	Kaufman, Mrs.H. B.	May 31, 1872	69
Hubler, Henry,	July 3, 1874	73	Kay, James,	Apr. 22, 1856	76
Huff, Mrs. Marg.,	Sept. 22, 1832		Keeler, Jacob,	Mar. 8, 1870	90
Humes, Samuel,	Mar. 28, 1859	57	Keeler, Mrs. Barb.,	Dec. 13, 1869	84
Hummel, Mrs. Chr.	Aug. —, 1847	61	Keiser, John,	Nov. 23, 1850	
Hummel, John,	July 11, 1853	72	Keiser, Jacob,	Feb, 12, 1867	60
Hummel, Capt. J.,	Dec. 17, 1860	80	Kelly, William,	Jan. 27, 1830	
Hummel, Daniel,	Sept. 7, 1861	76	Kelly, Mrs. S.,	Jan. 2, 1831	
Hunsicker, Cath.,	July 5, 1872	80	Kelly, James W.,	Dec. 26, 1831	
Hunter, Montg.	Aug. 18, 1860	46	Kelly, Esq., Col. J.,	Feb. 18, 1832	88
Hunter, Barbara H.	Apr. 7, 1862	69	Kelly, James S.,	May 14, 1854	39
Huntingdon, John,	Feb. 8, 1873	65	Kelly, Joseph,	Mar. 2, 1860	67
Hursh, Henry,	Aug. 15, 1829		Kelly, Robert H.,	Nov. 26, 1860	
Hursh, Mrs.	Jan. 27, 1848		Kelly, Peter M.,	Aug. 19, 1861	27
Hursh, George,	May 2, 1873	77	Kelly, James M.,	Mar. 27, 1862	23
Hursh, Samuel,	Dec. 14, 1875	70	Kelly, Rev. Joshua,	Apr. 10, 1862	40
Huston, Hon. Chas.,	Nov. 10, 1849		Kelly, Ellen,	June 16, 1862	34
Hutcheson, Mrs. P.,	June 10, 1825		Kelly, Robert,	Apr. 12, 1865	77
Hutcheson, John,	Jan. 22, 1828		Kelly, Andrew,	Sept. 24, 1867	84
Hutcheson, James,	Oct. 13, 1860	43	Kelly, Mrs. H.,	Feb. 20, 1868	77
Hutchinson, M. A.,	Oct. 8, 1868		Kelly, David H.,	Feb. 11, 1875	72
Iddings, Henry,	—— —, 1820		Kennedy, Mrs. N.,	Feb. 24, 1865	57
Iddings, Samuel,	—— —, 1820		Kennedy, Andrew,	Aug. 24, 1870	75
Iddings, Isaac,	—— —, 1823		Kerr, Hamlet A.,	Sept. 3, 1849	
Iddings, Elizabeth,	—— —, 1823		Kessler, Catherine,	Sept. 1, 1827	
Iddings, Abigail,	May 16, 1828		Kessler, Esq., W.,	Feb. 21, 1861	80
Iddings, Mrs. Isab.,	Mar. 8, 1838		Ketchum, Mrs. M.,	July 13, 1870	81
Iddings, Thomas,	Aug. 24, 1848	73	Ketner, Catherine,	July 13, 1826	54
Iddings, Lewis,	Nov. 7, 1857	37	Kiehl, George W.,	July 3, 1858	53
Iddings, Mrs. Mary,	Mar. 8, 1861	40	Kieffer, Miss Sallie,	June 11, 1873	55
Iddings, Sarah Em.	Jan. 4, 1862	19	Kieffer, Henry,	Aug. 4, 1874	66
Ingram, John S.,	Apr. 22, 1848		Kimbell, John,	May 19, 1876	74
Ireland, John W.,	Oct. 14, 1862	19	Kimple, Adam,	Dec. 17, 1831	
Irvine, Mrs. Nancy,	Jan. 25, 1830		Kimple, John,	Mar. 12, 1856	76
Irvine, Susan,	July 6, 1834		Kimple, Miss Sarah,	Jan. 11, 1876	73
Irvin, Sarah Harris,	Mar. 1, 1857	96	King, sr., James,	Dec. 15, 1870	94
Irwin, Mrs. Nancy,	Jan. 23, 1830		King, Mrs. Marg.	Apr. 5, 1874	80
James, Mrs. Marg't,	—— —, 1823		Kingan, Sarah,	July 2, 1857	90
Jenks, Mrs. A.,	Aug, 6, 1859		Kinkead, Joseph,	Dec. 17, 1845	
Jodon, Casper,	July 31, 1826		Kinkead, Eug. W.,	—— —, 1846	
Jodon, Joseph,	Feb. 5, 1863	74	Kirkpatrick,Rev.D.	Jan. 5, 1869	74
Johnson, Jacob,	June 3, 1835		Kleckner, Solomon,	Aug. 18, 1837	72

ANNALS OF BUFFALO VALLEY. 571

	Date of Death.	Age.		Date of Death.	Age.
Kleckner, John,	Aug. 23, 1839	89	Lee, James,	May —, 1853	
Kleckner, William,	Jan. 5, 1861	79	Leiby, Christena,	July —, 1852	77
Kleckner, George,	May 3, 1874	77	Leiby, Jacob,	May 21, 1856	80
Kleckner, Isaac,	May 14, 1877	84	Leiby, George,	Aug. 9, 1872	65
Kline, Jacob,	Nov. 15, 1852	55	Leiby, John,	Oct. 21, 1872	67
Kleckner, Eliz.,	July 19, 1876	67	Leinbach, Rev. T.,	Mar. 31, 1864	62
Kleckner, Miss M.,	Aug. 9, 1829	77	Leisenring, John,	Jan. 24, 1859	75
Kline, Charles,	Mar. 22, 1860	81	Leiser, Jacob,	May 28, 1862	83
Kline, John H.,	Mar. 28, 1868	50	Leonard, Peter,	Jan. —, 1862	
Kling, Jeremiah,	Jan. 20, 1861		Lepley, Jacob,	Jan. 17, 1848	66
Kling, John,	Jan. 22, 1863	19	Lepley, George,	Jan. 23, 1874	63
Kling, John,	July 17, 1872	73	Levan, Mrs. Sophia,	Aug. —, 1847	
Klingaman, Peter,	Apr. 27, 1848	92	Levy, Esq., Daniel,	May 12, 1844	77
Knarr Anna Mary,	Mar. 1, 1875	87	Lewis, Mrs. Mary,	Aug. 18, 1846	78
Knittle, Mrs.,	Sept. 12, 1860	73	Lewis, John,	May 20, 1869	91
Knight, Mrs. Rach.,	Oct. 17, 1875	50	Lewis, Thomas R.,	Aug. 17, 1872	77
Kohler, Anna,	June 7, 1868	72	Lincoln, John,	Aug. 19, 1862	80
Koser, Jonathan,	May 12, 1864	70	Linn, William,	Oct. 26, 1834	
Koser, John,	Oct. 17, 1873	75	Linn, Mrs. Ann,	Sept. 4, 1841	80
Kratzer, Daniel,	Apr. 4, 1869	72	Linn, Franklin F.,	Nov. 27, 1846	
Kreamer, Mrs.Abr.,	Dec. 13, 1842		Linn, John,	Sept. 28, 1847	91
Kreamer, Abraham,	Mar. 2. 1847		Linn, David,	July 26, 1848	71
Kremer, Hon. Geo.,	Sept. 10, 1854	79	Linn, Mrs. Marg'y,	Nov. 19, 1865	85
Kreamer, Michael,	Aug. 23, 1855	56	Linn, Mrs. Marg't I.	June 2, 1868	64
Kreider, Hon. Jac.,	May 13, 1852	77	Linn, Esq., Jas. F.,	Oct. 8, 1869	67
Kreitzer, Fred.,	Feb. 4, 1868		Locker, John,	May 5, 1860	76
Lafey, Margaret,	Apr. 22, 1855	64	Long, Jonathan,	July 8, 1824	24
Lafey, Isaac,	Mar. 1, 1860	70	Long, Jacob,	Oct. 31, 1828	
Laird, Matthew,	Oct. —, 1821		Long, Mrs.,	July 13, 1847	
Laird, Rev. Matt.	May 4, 1834		Long, Ephriam,	Jan. 13, 1856	41
Laird, Mrs, Matt.	Mar. 1, 1837		Long, Mrs. Mary,	Jan. 27, 1863	
Laird, Jane,	May 29, 1849		Longbay, Caroline,	June 30, 1862	
Laird, Mrs. Maria,	July 7, 1862	71	Longmore, Rev. D.,	Sept. 12, 1855	
Laird, Col. S. H.,	Mar. 14, 1870	66	Lotz, Mrs. Ann,	Aug. 8, 1824	
Laird, Mrs. Jane,	Apr. 4, 1863	89	Lotz, Henry,	Apr. 6, 1845	48
Laird, Matthew,	Oct. 29, 1867	80	Lotz, Dr. Joseph R.,	Jan. 18, 1875	76
Lantz, Samuel,	July 30, 1850		Ludwig, Dr. W. H.,	Nov. 28, 1848	40
Lashells, John,	Feb. 7, 1832		Ludwig, Daniel,	Aug. 17, 1855	
Lashells, Mrs. Geo.,	July 7, 1834		Ludwig, Sam'l W.,	Oct. 2, 1860	50
Lashells, George R.,	Apr. 16, 1835		Luker, John,	Jan. 2, 1850	
Lashells, Mrs. Mart.	Oct. 12, 1837		Lyndall, Henry,	Nov. 26, 1860	46
Lashells, Marg. C.,	—, 1845		Lyndall, Steph. F.,	May 12, 1856	43
Lashells, George,	May 29, 1844		McAlarney, John,	May 16, 1876	65
Lashells, jr., John,	Sept. 14, 1845		McBeth, Eliz. A.,	Dec. 20, 1850	
Lashells, Ida,	Mar. 15, 1849		McBeth, Andrew,	July 3, 1854	77
Lashells, Elean. C.,	Dec. 2, 1850		McBeth, John A. H.	Oct. 12, 1854	33
Love, William,	—, 1834		McCall, John,	May 28, 1863	60
Love, Mrs. Eliz.,	—, 1842		McCall, jr., John,	Nov. 24, 1864	30
Lawrence, George,	Dec. 30, 1863		McCarty, William,	Apr. 8, 1861	75
Lawson, Joseph,	Feb. 24, 1843		McClanachan, And.	Mar. 19, 1836	
Lawshe, sr., John,	Feb. 8, 1832	80	McClanachan, Mrs.,	Jan. 30, 1846	
Lawshe, jr., John,	Sept. 14, 1845		McCleary, John,	June 21, 1851	
Lawson, Mrs. Nan.,	Apr. 17, 1867	84	McCleary, Dr. W.,	Dec. —, 1867	65
Lebkicker, Mich.,	Jan. 28, 1848	89	McClellan, Ruth,	—, 1820	
Lebkicker, Philip,	Sept. 19, 1854	72	McClellan, Sam'l,	Feb. 7, 1854	78
Lebkicker, John,	Mar. 18, 1870	74	McClellan, Mrs. M.,	Mar. 29, 1858	87
Lee, Catherine,	Mar. —, 1853		McClellan, Marg.,	Jan. 7, 1863	61
Lehman, Mrs. Han.	Nov. 15, 1875	74	McClure, Jona.,	Nov. 10, 1825	

ANNALS OF BUFFALO VALLEY.

Name	Date of Death.	Age
McClure, Richard,	Mar. 26, 1833	
McClure, Roan,	Oct. 18, 1833	
McClure, Mrs. H.,	Aug. 20, 1838	
McClure, James,	Aug. 30, 1840	
McClure, Jane,	July 6, 1849	
McClure, Richard,	Aug. 7, 1850	
McClure, Alex.,	Sept. 25, 1853	
McClure, Nancy N.,	Sept. 24, 1854	73
McClure, Mrs. M.,	Oct. 24, 1855	
McClure, Hannah,	Oct. 21, 1859	61
McClure, William,	Nov. 20, 1859	36
McClure, Miss Jane,	Dec. 21, 1876	88
McClure, Miss Jane,	July 17, 1875	55
McClure, Robt. M.,	Jan. 2, 1876	62
McCool, Esq., Jos.,	—— —, 1844	
McCorley, Esq., R.,	Dec. 11, 1869	86
McCorley, Esq., J.,	Apr. 15, 1872	82
McCormick, W. S.,	Dec. 7, 1868	29
McCoy, William,	Dec. 1, 1846	
McCoy, Mrs. Eliz.,	Nov. 11, 1869	76
McCreight, James,	June 30, 1862	
McCreight, Mary D.	Sept. 22, 1865	22
McDowel, George,	May 26, 1864	45
McEwing, Alex.,	Nov. 26, 1850	94
McFadden, John,	Feb. 9, 1835	
McFadden, Mrs. C.,	Oct. 15, 1845	
McFadden, Mrs. N.,	Mar. 2, 1848	90
McFadden, Col. J.,	June 18, 1851	
McFadden, J. A.,	July 27, 1855	31
McGrady, Alex.,	—— —, 1830	
McGrady, Alex.,	—— —, 1812	
McGrady, William,	—— —, 1836	
McGrady, Mrs. E.,	June 3, 1861	96
McGregor, Charles,	Mar. 2, 1866	52
McGuigan, Col. R.,	Aug. 26, 1850	
McGuire, Rachel,	Aug. 22, 1834	
McGuire, Mrs.,	—— —, 1844	
McGuire, Thomas,	Mar. —, 1845	
McGuire, John,	Dec. 14, 1852	78
McKean, Hon. S.,	June 23, 1840	
McKinley, Cath.,	Oct. 17, 1862	79
McKinney, Jacob,	Feb. 5, 1861	
McKinty, John,	Feb. 24, 1856	64
McLaughlin, Wm.,	Mar. 26, 1831	68
McLaughlin, Dr. R.	Jan. 12, 1832	
McLaughlin, Wm.,	Mar. —, 1834	
McLaughlin, Jas.,	Dec. 25, 1845	
McLaughlin, Marg.,	Apr. 19, 1848	
McLaughlin, Jane,	July 9, 1862	57
McLaughlin, Mrs. E	Apr. 16, 1865	59
McLaughlin, Hugh,	Feb. 9, 1871	66
McMahon, Samuel,	June 11, 1854	75
McNeil Dr. C. J.,	Aug. —, 1864	
Mabus, Joseph,	Feb. 18, 1876	64
Machamer, Daniel,	Aug. 3, 1856	74
Mackey, Mrs. T. S.,	May 1, 1828	
Mackey, sr., Thos.,	Aug. 4, 1849	85
Mackey, jr., Thos.,	Feb. 14, 1860	68
Maclay, David,	June —, 1818	
Maclay, Ann,	July 6, 1835	
Maclay, Mrs. Ann,	May 12, 1851	
Maclay, Esq., John,	June 25, 1855	
Macpherson, John,	Aug. 2, 1827	
Macpherson, Mrs. J.	Sept. 6, 1869	88
Madden, Esq., Jas.,	Nov. 19, 1855	67
Mader, George,	Apr. 17, 1875	71
Magee, Levina,	—— —, 1822	
Magee, James,	—— —, 1823	
Magee, Levina,	Dec. 6, 1826	
Magee, Mrs. And'w,	Aug. 16, 1827	
Magee, James,	May 4, 1851	
Magee, Joseph,	Sept. 29, 1851	55
Magee, Andrew,	Sept. 23, 1853	
Magee, John T.,	Oct. 28, 1863	37
Magee, Esq., Jas.,	Mar. 17, 1866	
Magee, Mrs. Eliz.,	Aug. 25, 1873	70
Magee, Mrs. Susan,	Feb. 17, 1875	82
Magee, Mrs. Susan,	Jan. 17, 1875	72
Magee, Eleanor S.,	July 9, 1876	70
Maize, John,	Oct. 13, 1839	
Maize, Mrs. Lydia,	May 7, 1861	43
Manning, Henry,	Aug. 28, 1863	
Markle, Gideon,	Mar. —, 1851	
Marr, David,	Feb. 2, 1864	49
Marr, Rev. P. B.,	Jan. 27, 1874	66
Marsh, Fred. C.,	Jan. 25, 1858	39
Marshall, James,	May 14, 1835	52
Marshall, Judge J.,	June 28, 1873	
Martin, Hugh,	June 22, 1827	
Martin, Esq., J. M.,	Apr. 17, 1832	
Martin, Esq., J.,	Apr. 8, 1858	49
Mason, Maria D.,	Sept. 15, 1860	20
Mason, Henry,	July 4, 1874	65
Mathers, Mary,	Aug. 20, 1845	
Mathers, Mrs. Ann,	Jan. 8, 1854	80
Mathers, Mrs. El'n,	Apr. 23, 1868	55
Mathers, Peter,	Sept. 4, 1845	
Mathers, Mrs.,	May 25, 1860	78
Mathers, James,	Aug. 4, 1874	69
Mauck, Jacob,	Aug. 5, 1869	76
Maus, Esq., Chas.,	May 8, 1830	
Maus, Emily,	May 14, 1829	
Maus, Lewis,	Aug. 22, 1854	84
Maxwell, Mrs. S.,	June 10, 1837	
Maxwell, Esq., H.,	Nov. 1, 1860	82
Maxwell, Capt. J. G.	July 19, 1867	33
Meixell, George,	July 29, 1868	82
Meixell, Joseph,	Feb. 19, 1867	
Mensch, Rev. Nich.,	Oct. 14, 1854	74
Mensch, Mrs. Maria,	Mar. 12, 1863	
Mensch, Miss Sarah,	Mar. 23, 1876	64
Mensch, Mrs. S. J.,	Apr. 18, 1876	63
Mensch, Rev. A. B.,	May 19, 1876	30
Merrill, Mrs. M.,	June 3, 1825	
Merrill, Sarah,	Sept. 17, 1831	
Merrill, Esq., Jas.,	Oct. 29, 1841	

	Date of Death.	Age.
Merrill, Esq., Chas.,	Dec. 25, 1865	42
Merrill, Mrs. S. B.,	Aug. 4, 1876	82
Mertz, Catherine,	Sept. 2, 1842	52
Mertz, Jacob,	Apr. 5, 1859	78
Mertz, Mrs. Eliz.,	Mar. 8, 1870	76
Mertz, Mrs. Nancy,	June 8, 1873	56
Mervine, Mrs. M.,	Mar. 28, 1862	36
Metzgar, Marg. C.,	Jan. 28, 1846	
Metzgar, Mrs. Eliz.,	Jan. 27, 1847	74
Metzgar, Rebecca,	Jan. 24, 1852	39
Metzgar, Mrs. C. M.,	May 13, 1865	55
Middleswarth, Ner,	June 2, 1865	83
Miller, Samuel,	Mar. 1, 1826	
Mitchell, George,	Sept. 22, 1827	
Miller, Valentine,	Oct. 3, 1828	
Miller, Mrs. Sarah,	Apr. 17, 1845	65
Miller, Mrs. Isab'a,	Apr. 20, 1849	
Miller, John F.,	Aug. 2, 1851	76
Miller, George,	Oct. 9, 1851	60
Miller, Hugh,	May 28, 1856	60
Miller, George,	Jan. 23, 1859	70
Miller, Jeremiah,	Dec. —, 1861	
Miller, Mrs. J. H.,	Mar. 28, 1862	36
Miller, Mrs. Sarah,	May 31, 1862	78
Miller, Mrs. Mary,	—, 1863	
Miller, John,	Dec. 14, 1871	86
Miller, John F.,	July 25, 1870	68
Miller, Mrs. K. V.,	Feb. 22, 1874	28
Miller, Isaac,	Feb. —, 1869	
Miller, Joseph,	Dec. 1, 1873	66
Miller, Margaret,	May 28, 1877	78
Miller, Mrs. S. H.,	July 24, 1876	
Mitchell, John,	May 3, 1862	69
Millhouse, Jacob,	Apr. 22, 1870	68
Millhouse, Jno. N.,	Apr. 14, 1835	
Millhouse, Jul'a W.	—, 1845	83
Millhouse, Mrs. R.,	Apr. 8, 1872	68
Mitchell, Nathan,	Dec. 3, 1864	
Motz, John,	Nov. 22, 1849	
Moll, Mrs.	Oct. 6, 1869	90
Montague, Thomas,	Oct. 24, 1842	37
Montelius, Peter,	July 2, 1859	68
Montgomery, Eliz.,	Mar. 23, 1850	
Montgomery, John,	Apr. 29, 1853	93
Montgomery, Thos.	—, 1853	
Montgomery, D.,	Nov. 23, 1859	93
Montgomery, Mary,	Nov. 17, 1864	63
Montgomery, Jas.,	Mar. 9, 1874	52
Mook, John,	May 16, 1867	83
Mook, David,	Apr. —, 1867	
Moon, jr., John,	Mar. 11, 1829	
Moore, John,	Apr. 9, 1834	
Moore, John,	July 17, 1840	
Moore, James,	Mar. 29, 1855	76
Moore, Mrs. Mary,	Feb. 16, 1858	80
Moore, Mrs. M. A.,	Oct. 1, 1858	44
Moore, Edward W.,	Sept 14, 1861	29
Moore, Jane W.,	Apr. 25, 1863	62
Moore, E. C.,	Apr. 21, 1868	57
Moore, D., (W. B.)	Dec. 28, 1874	
Moran, Mrs. Mary,	Sept. 8, 1859	60
Morrison, Mrs. H.	Apr. —, 1804	49
Morrison, Thomas,	—, 1826	
Morrison, Gabriel,	May 21, 1830	
Morrison, Eliza,	July 19, 1832	
Morrison, Rev.W.S.	Mar. 18, 1858	
Morrow, Jane,	Mar. 15, 1848	
Morrow, Alexander,	July 7, 1862	92
Morton, William,	Aug. 11, 1825	
Morton, Alexander,	July 30, 1826	45
Morton, Polly,	Jan. 2, 1828	
Morton, John,	Feb. 2, 1830	
Morton, Nancy,	Apr. 16, 1849	69
Morton, Elizabeth,	May 5, 1860	51
Morton, Alexander,	July 30, 1876	45
Mowery, Cath.,	June 8, 1875	75
Mowrer, Mrs.	Dec. 3, 1827	
Mowrer, Andrew,	Aug. 18, 1829	
Mowrer, James,	Feb. 1, 1839	
Moyer, John,	Feb. 1, 1848	60
Moyer, William P.	Apr. 13, 1863	35
Moyer, Jacob,	May 8, 1870	79
Moyer, Daniel,	Dec. 20, 1873	74
Murphy, Griffith,	Oct. 14, 1868	57
Murray, Joseph M.,	Nov. 27, 1830	
Murray, Marg.,	Sept. 24, 1841	31
Murray, Mrs. E. N.,	July 15, 1845	
Murray, Mrs. C.,	June 21, 1850	77
Murray, Mrs. E.,	Jan. 24, 1853	
Murray, Esq., J. F.,	Mar. 17, 1869	
Musser, John,	June 3, 1830	
Musser, Esq., J.,	Oct. 22, 1837	
Musser, Margaret,	Nov. 9, 1837	
Musser, Mary,	Mar. —, 1863	
Musser, Mrs. Sarah,	Aug. 7, 1872	81
Myers, Samuel,	Oct. 16, 1825	
Myers, Amanda,	Nov. 17, 1869	76
Myer, Harriet,	May 3, 1834	
Meyers, Peter,	Apr. 2, 1854	72
Meyers, Mrs. Sarah,	July 16, 1863	57
Nees, Michael,	Nov. 1, 1856	60
Neff, Peter,	Sept. 16, 1856	
Nelson, Joseph,	—, 1823	
Nesbit, Alexander,	Nov. 8, 1823	69
Nesbit, Mrs. Isabel.	Sept. 13, 1827	
Nesbit, Mrs.	Jan. 26, 1832	
Nesbit, Sarah Ann,	Apr. 5, 1849	
Nesbit, Mary,	Feb. 23, 1856	
Nesbit, jr., John,	Mar. 7, 1858	24
Nesbit, Jonathan,	May 19, 1859	62
Nesbit, Esq., Wm.,	Jan. 22, 1860	76
Nesbit, Mrs. Sarah,	May 26, 1861	67
Nesbit, Alexander,	June 18, 1862	70
Nesbit, Mrs. Nancy,	Aug. 24, 1862	84
Nesbit, James,	—, 1863	
Nesbit, Thomas,	Mar. 15, 1863	74

Name	Date of Death	Age	Name	Date of Death	Age
Nesbit, Sarah,	Sept. 15, 1864	74	Penny, Jane E.,	Feb. 18 1869	60
Nesbit, John,	Jan. 27, 1865	80	Penny, Alexander,	Nov. 6, 1874	63
Nesbit, Elizabeth,	May 22, 1867	70	Peters, Michael,	June 12 1854	
Nesbit, Mrs. Mary,	Nov. 25, 1868	73	Phillips, Mrs. G.,	Sept. 17, 1827	
Nesbit, R. I.,	Aug. 31, 1873	47	Phillips, Dennis,	Apr. 22, 1863	52
Neuer, Henry,	Sept. 1, 1866	65	Phlegor, Ludwig,	Mar. 15, 1858	74
Neuer, Mrs. Eliza.	Feb. 1, 1872	75	Phlegor, John,	Sept. 25, 1860	71
Nevius, Ralph,	Sept. 22, 1832		Piper, Dr. F. A.,	Apr. 22, 1831	
Nevius, Mrs. Lucr.	Jan. 19, 1841	73	Piper, Mrs. M. M.	Dec. 10, 1876	74
Nevius, Aaron C.,	Oct. 2, 1857	48	Poak, William,	Aug. 13, 1830	68
Nevius, Peter,	Feb. 22, 1869	74	Poath, Mrs. Eliz.,	Oct. 18, 1863	49
Newman, Mrs. M.,	Jan. 4, 1859	65	Poath, Henry,	April 9, 1865	79
Neyhart, Daniel,	Jan. 7, 1864	47	Pollock, Mrs. I.,	Oct. 23, 1824	
Nicely, Samuel,	Sept. 5, 1832		Pollock, Mrs. Eliza,	July 3, 1833	
Noetling, Dr. Wm.,	Jan. 22, 1861	84	Pollock, Margaret,	Oct. 13, 1842	
Nogel, Jacob,	Apr. 18, 1860	64	Pollock, Thomas,	Aug. 5, 1861	
Nogel, Mrs. Mary,	Jan. 17, 1864	37	Pontius, Peter,	Dec. 24, 1862	79
Noll, Mrs. Mary E.,	June 21, 1846	86	Pontius, Elizabeth,	May 2, 1863	39
Noll, Col. Henry,	Nov. 9, 1847		Pontius, John F.,	June 17, 1869	81
Noll, William,	Mar. 12, 1851		Pontius, Rachael,	Mar. 16, 1868	63
Noll, John,	Mar. 4, 1858	77	Pontius, Philip,	Sept. 7, 1872	82
Noll, Samuel L.,	May 5, 1864	57	Pontius, Mrs. M.,	Apr. 18, 1876	72
Noll, Samuel,	Dec. 18, 1866	64	Porter, Samuel,	Jan. 10, 1825	
Noll, Peter,	Oct. 2, 1869	80	Porter, William,	Aug. 19, 1872	68
Noll, Elias,	Apr. 13, 1876	56	Potter, Mrs. Maria,	Apr. 10, 1826	
Nyhart, Michael,	June —, 1869	67	Potter, James,	Mar. 22, 1835	75
Oliphant, Charlotte,	June 13, 1862	70	Pratt, Charles,	Aug. 24, 1829	
Orwig, John,	Aug. 19, 1828		Preistly, Joseph R.,	Nov. 10, 1863	72
Orwig, George,	Dec. 2, 1841		Pross, Richard,	Jan. 26, 1874	57
Orwig, Jacob,	Jan. 23, 1859	76	Pursel, Daniel,	May 5, 1861	78
Orwig, Samuel,	Sept. 7, 1872	75	Pursel, Peter,	Aug. 11, 1867	87
Orwig, Mrs. M. A.,	June 7, 1875	39	Quiddington, Mrs.	Nov. 13, 1874	73
Osborn, Mrs. Mary,	Apr. 7, 1874	71	Quinn, Terrence,	Aug. 10 1831	93
Painter, John,	May 22, 1854	66	Quinn, Michael,	Feb. 20, 1854	69
Painter, John,	June 6, 1862	36	Ramsey, Esq., Wm.,	Oct. —, 1831	
Painter, Thomas,	Feb. 12, 1863	78	Ranck, Barbara,	Mar. 28, 1830	75
Palmer, Lewis,	May 24, 1860	46	Ranck, Daniel, H.,	Aug. 25, 1847	
Pardoe, John,	April 1, 1859	48	Ranck, Daniel,	Nov. 16, 1854	75
Pardoe, Esq., H.,	April 4, 1864	63	Ranck, Adam,	Mar. 8, 1860	79
Parks, Elizabeth,	Aug. 22, 1829	24	Ranck, Mrs. Mary,	Aug. 1, 1864	33
Parr, Mrs. Eliz.,	Mar. 27, 1828		Ranck, Joel,	Oct. 1, 1868	82
Parsons, Rebecca, J.	Aug —, 1846	56	Ranck, William,	Apr. 29, 1875	69
Patterson, Robert,	July —, 1826		Ranck, Mrs. Jane,	May 28, 1875	70
Patterson, S. M.,	Jan. 29, 1840		Raser, Thomas,	—, 1858	
Patterson, Mrs. R.,	Jan. 20, 1842	60	Rawn, Nathan,	Jan. 28, 1865	58
Patterson, J. B.,	May 8, 1843	70	Ray, Mrs. Jane,	Mar. 3, 1860	72
Patterson, Wm. A.,	July 15, 1854	83	Ray, Esq., John,	Sept. 10, 1864	86
Paul, Sampson,	May 4, 1843	41	Reedy, Philip,	—, 1822	
Paul, John,	June 6, 1870	65	Ream, Miss Elean.,	Mar. 28, 1858	66
Peifer, George,	Aug. 7, 1861	57	Ream, John N.,	Jan. —, 1835	69
Peifer, Mrs. Cath.,	Sept. 27, 1861	67	Ream, Samuel,	Oct. 2, 1874	83
Pellman, Samuel,	July 25, 1875	81	Reber, Mrs.,	June 11, 1845	
Penny, William,	Nov. 25, 1829	75	Reber, John,	June 22, 1852	82
Penny, Jane,	July 21, 1850		Reber, James,	Sept. 20, 1853	48
Penny, William,	Jan. 20, 1852		Reber, Margaret,	Sept. 24, 1863	54
Penny, Hugh,	Dec. 3, 1853		Reed, George,	Sept. 20, 1854	74
Penny, John,	Aug. 6, 1868	78	Reed, John,	Mar. 22, 1860	79
Penny, Thomas,	Aug. 28, 1868	65	Reed, Stewart,	Nov. 6, 1864	65

ANNALS OF BUFFALO VALLEY.

	Date of Death.	Age		Date of Death.	Age
Reed, Joseph,	Jan. 28, 1868	66	Robinson, William,	Dec. 1, 1852	85
Reed, Mrs. Rachel,	June 8, 1873	64	Robinson, Adeline,	July 12, 1854	26
Reed, George,	Apr. 10, 1874	69	Robinson, Mrs. M.,	Oct. 13, 1865	95
Reed, Mrs. Cath.,	Sept. 8, 1874	73	Robinson, Wilson,	Nov. 19, 1867	51
Reed, Peter,	Apr. 4, 1875	67	Rockefeller, David,	Aug. 22, 1876	76
Reedy, Andrew,	Nov. 10, 1827	45	Rockey, John,	Apr. 20, 1842	59
Reedy, John,	Nov. 18, 1845		Rockey, George,	Oct. 3, 1853	70
Reedy, Jacob,	Nov. 22, 1854	84	Rockey, Elizabeth,	Feb. 6, 1872	73
Reedy, Mrs. Cath.,	Oct. 8, 1856	84	Rodearmel, Sam'l,	Feb. 11, 1843	52
Reedy, Jacob,	Feb. 6, 1866	40	Rohland, Richard,	Mar. 20, 1850	
Rees, Miss Hannah,	Mar. 15, 1829		Roland, Charles,	July 31, 1865	
Rees, Miss Nancy,	Nov. 17, 1853	88	Roland, John,	Jan. 31, 1866	
Rees, Sema,	July 28, 1863	63	Rorabaugh, Philip,	July 3, 1837	
Rehmel, George,	Oct. 21, 1823	35	Roshong, Henry,	Dec. 29, 1850	85
Reichly, Christian,	Apr. 7, 1863	77	Rote, Mrs. Elean'a,	Apr. 20, 1875	70
Reidenbaugh, Dan.,	July 16, 1859	60	Rothermell, Mrs. C.	Aug. 4, 1876	94
Reidenbaugh, Jno.,	Aug. 30, 1861	68	Ross, James, P.,	July 31, 1860	52
Reish, Daniel,	Oct. 12, 1847	48	Roush, George,	Aug. 23, 1839	84
Reish, John,	Feb. —, 1848		Roush, Mary Ann,	Mar. 7, 1848	25
Reitmyer, George,	Sept. 23, 1860	70	Roush, Maria E.,	Oct. 11, 1857	63
Reitmyer, Mrs. S.,	Feb. 26, 1873	77	Roush, Michael,	Apr. 19, 1859	77
Rengler, John,	Feb. 20, 1825	66	Roush, Esq., Sam'l,	Feb. 5, 1873	77
Rengler, Catherine,	Dec. 11, 1844	72	Royer, Joel,	Oct. 15, 1853	75
Rengler, Mrs. M. D.	June —, 1847		Royer, Joel,	Aug. 6, 1872	53
Rengler, Jacob,	Jan. 9, 1853		Royer, Jacob,	Mar. 30, 1876	77
Rengler, George,	May 5, 1856	70	Ruhl, George P.,	Apr. 29, 1843	82
Rengler, Mrs. Susa.	Aug. 29, 1858		Ruhl, Mrs. Sarah,	Aug. 9, 1863	67
Rengler, Daniel,	June 5, 1874	83	Sanderson, Henry,	Feb. 8, 1828	
Renner, Catherine,	Sept. 20, 1863	41	Sanders, sr., Henry,	Feb. 17, 1850	82
Renner, Frederick,	Nov. 1, 1865	82	Sanders, Henry,	Jan. 11, 1870	74
Reznor, Ann,	Oct. 25, 1828		Sands, David,	Apr. 13, 1850	
Reznor, Mrs.	Nov. —, 1828		Sands, James W.,	May 10, 1877	59
Reznor, sr., John,	Oct. 31, 1835		Sawyer, Matilda,	Feb. 8, 1827	
Reznor, James,	May 22, 1836		Sayers, Ethan,	Dec. 26, 1845	
Rheem, George,	Sept. 18, 1861	90	Sayers, Mrs. A.,	Feb. 23, 1846	
Rhoads, Jacob,	July 22, 1851	77	Schaffle, Joseph,	Jan. 11, 1863	36
Rhoads, Mrs. Eliz.,	Feb. 19, 1858	72	Schaffle, Charles D.,	Feb. —, 1863	
Rhoads, John,	Feb. 2, 1876	78	Schaffle, Frank S.,	Apr. 6, 1876	34
Richart, John F.,	Aug. 17, 1869	64	Schnable, jr., Geo.,	Aug. 5, 1854	32
Richart, Mrs. Mary,	Sept. 17, 1875	69	Schnable, Hon. G.,	Dec. 13, 1863	74
Richter, Peter,	May 25, 1846	69	Schock, Mrs. H.,	Dec. 9, 1875	60
Riehl, John,	Apr. 14, 1864	33	Schrack, Benjamin,	Dec. 9, 1828	67
Rishell, Mrs.	Apr. 11, 1846		Schrack, Susanah,	June 19, 1842	70
Rishell, Martin,	Dec. —, 1849		Schrack, Esq., Jno.,	June 4, 1860	58
Rishell, John,	Sept. —, 1851	70	Schrack, Eve,	Jan. 15, 1861	86
Rishell, John,	Dec. 30, 1859	79	Schrack, Daniel,	Dec. 25, 1869	58
Rishell, Daniel,	Nov. 8, 1868	36	Schrack, Mrs. E.,	Sept. 20, 1876	60
Ritter, George,	Sept. 17, 1825	70	Schroyer, Conrad,	Sept. 1, 1825	63
Ritter, Elizabeth,	Jan. 19, 1846	35	Schroyer, jr., C.,	Mar. 7, 1855	65
Ritter, Col. Jacob,	July 28, 1849	47	Schroyer, Cath.,	Dec. 23, 1860	64
Ritter, Willam H.,	Mar. 11, 1861	26	Schwenck, Esq., D.,	Jan. 19, 1861	75
Ritter, John,	Mar. 10, 1872	72	Scudder, Esq., D.,	Jan. 27, 1829	
Robb, James,	—, 1839		Search, Elijah,	Aug. 25, 1848	76
Robb, Nancy,	Oct. 8, 1849	87	Search, Mrs. Sarah,	Mar. 21, 1854	78
Robins, Daniel,	Jan. 20, 1864	99	Search, Thomas,	Sept. 25, 1862	
Robinson, Ann,	Aug. 12, 1825		Search, Stephen,	Apr. 15, 1864	55
Robinson, Samuel,	Sept. 15, 1825		Seebold, Mrs. B.,	Aug. 22, 1825	82
Robinson, Mrs. S.,	Sept. 19, 1825		Seebold, Sarah,	Mar. 19, 1828	

ANNALS OF BUFFALO VALLEY.

	Date of Death.	Age.		Date of Death.	Age.
Seebold, Nancy,	Apr. 24, 1828		Slifer, David C.,	Aug. 18, 1864	50
Seebold, Philip,	July 24, 1874	86	Slifer, Jacob,	Mar. 3, 1868	48
Seerer, Jacob,	Dec. —, 1824		Slonaker, Mrs. A.,	Sept. 25, 1874	87
Sergeant, Mrs.	Aug. 28, 1828		Slough, Jacob,	Apr. 21, 1876	65
Shaffer, William,	June 5, 1825		Smaltzried, Gotlieb,	Sept. 6, 1863	25
Shaffer, Esq., Hen.,	Mar. 1, 1833		Smiley, Rev. Thos.,	—— —, 1832	73
Shaffer, Esq., Sim.,	Oct. 22, 1838		Smith, Elizabeth,	About 1822.	
Shaffer, Mrs.,	Nov. 10, 1853	87	Smith, Dr. Jos. L.,	Dec. 5, 1825	
Shaffer, Mathias,	Oct. 22, 1854		Smith, Dr. Jonas,	Mar. 17, 1826	
Shaffer, Mrs. Mat.,	Sept. 11, 1861	95	Smith, Catherine,	July 3, 1829	
Shaffer, David,	May 7, 1864	89	Smith, Elizabeth,	May 22, 1836	
Shamp, Jesse,	—— —, 1824		Smith, Gideon,	Apr. —, 1841	
Shamp, Ezra,	Dec. —, 1835		Smith, Michael,	July 2, 1841	
Shannon, Mrs. M.,	Mar. 3, 1845		Smith, Charles D.,	June 10, 1844	45
Shannon, Eph. P.,	Aug. 28, 1851		Smith, Susanna,	—— —, 1850	
Shearer, Maj. Jas.,	Apr. 11, 1864	77	Smith, Rev. W. R.,	Sept. 9, 1849	58
Scheckler, Mrs. E.,	Oct. 15, 1855		Smith, Rev. J. W.,	Apr. 1, 1852	
Shamory, John C.,	July 11, 1868	95	Smith, John B.,	Mar. 19, 1859	
Shamp, Mrs. J.,	Sept. 27, 1873	79	Smith, Wilson,	Mar. 1, 1862	55
Sheckler, Mrs. C.,	Oct. 25, 1832		Smith, Mrs. Mary,	Feb. 28, 1862	33
Sheckler, Mrs. M.,	Mar. 12, 1837	74	Smith, George,	Jan. 19, 1869	66
Sheckler, Daniel,	Aug. 30, 1842	80	Smith, Esq., A. W.,	Feb. 12, 1870	53
Sheckler, Tobias,	June 10, 1850	85	Smith, George,	Mar. 6, 1871	
Sheckler, Henry,	Feb. 15, 1874	80	Snook, Daniel E.,	Sept. 14, 1845	
Sheckler, Esq., A.,	Aug. 21, 1875	76	Snyder, Mrs. Mary,	Oct. 8, 1823	
Sheller, Mrs. Marg.,	Jan. 7, 1859	78	Snyder, Simon,	May 10, 1838	75
Sheller, Christian,	Sept. 13, 1862	88	Snyder, Hon. John,	Aug. 15, 1850	60
Sheller, Mrs. J. W.,	Apr. 25, 1863	62	Snyder, George A.,	June —, 1865	66
Sherard, William,	Apr. —, 1825		Snyder, Antis,	Dec. —, 1861	
Shipton, Esq., T.,	Feb. 4, 1827	74	Snyder, Mary M.,	June 14, 1865	25
Shields, William,	May 21, 1858	80	Snyder, Reuben,	Nov. 24, 1876	60
Shively, Benjamin,	June 11, 1873	61	Snyder, Henry W.,	Apr. 18, 1866	
Shoemaker, Benj.,	Jan. 18, 1856	70	Solomon John,	—— —, 1840	66
Shoemaker, Sam.,	July 16, 1862	79	Soult, David,	—— —, 1824	72
Shoemaker, Mrs. S.,	July 29, 1865		Spatz, Lewis,	Aug. 9, 1853	26
Showers, ——,	Feb. 9, 1859	80	Spatz, Joseph,	May 20, 1877	73
Shrader, Frederick,	June 5, 1873	82	Specht, Adam,	Oct. 4, 1824	69
Shriner, Mrs. M. E.,	Oct. 22, 1856	37	Spidler, Daniel,	Aug. 5, 1826	
Shriner, Esq., Jno.,	Dec. 3, 1860	70	Spidler, David,	May 30, 1862	52
Shriner, W. B.,	Sept. 26, 1862	43	Spidler, Jacob,	Apr. 21, 1873	76
Shriner, Mrs. Eliz.,	Mar. 11, 1866	33	Spigelmyer, M. E.,	July 7, 1847	84
Shriner, Samuel,	Jan. 17, 1868	39	Spotts, Samuel,	May 17, 1864	48
Shuck, Peter,	Apr. 18, 1849	78	Spotts, Michael,	Oct. 18, 1872	86
Sierer, Sarah,	Feb. 27, 1875	62	Spotts, Mary,	Oct. 23, 1865	45
Silsby, Uriah,	May 26, 1849		Spotts, Michael,	Oct. —, 1872	86
Silsby, Esther,	Dec. 10, 1871	68	Spyker, Mrs. Maria,	Oct. 12, 1829	75
Simonton, J. W.,	Sept. 10, 1853	30	Spyker, Jonathan,	Dec. 9, 1862	78
Simonton, Jane C.,	Apr. 6, 1854	30	Spyker, Solma,	Jan. 25, 1868	81
Simonton, James,	Feb. 24, 1858	75	Spyker, Mrs. E.,	Dec. 5, 1868	80
Simonton, Mrs. M.,	Nov. 4, 1861	68	Stahl, John,	Apr. —, 1832	
Sites, George,	Oct. 6, 1824	69	Stahl, Adam,	Oct. 21, 1850	
Sites, Mrs.,	Nov. 4, 1846	87	Stahl, Lewis,	Jan. 2, 1855	30
Sleer, Jacob,	June 6, 1857	67	Stahl, Jacob,	Aug. 29, 1856	70
Slear, Mrs. Eliz.,	Jan. 13, 1872	75	Stahl, Elizabeth,	Sept. 22, 1856	71
Slear, Daniel,	Jan. 22, 1874	62	Stahl, Mrs. Cath.,	May 4, 1860	28
Slear, George,	Mar. 1, 1875	82	Stahl, George,	Apr. 12, 1861	83
Slenker, Jacob,	Nov. —, 1863	60	Stahl, Mrs. Cath.,	Aug. 25, 1861	68
Slenker, Esq., J. G.,	Feb. 11, 1871	29	Stahl, Jeremiah,	Apr. 12, 1862	26

ANNALS OF BUFFALO VALLEY.

	Date of Death.	Age
Stahl Jacob,	Dec. 29, 1864	82
Stahl, Peter,	Apr. 28, 1868	81
Steans, John,	May 27, 1851	78
Stamm, John,	Mar. 11, 1875	60
St. Clair, John,	Jun. 30, 1873	
St. Clair, Mrs. R.,	Apr. 30, 1875	
Steadman, Eliz.,	Nov. 10, 1827	
Steadman, Marg.,	Feb. 3, 1832	
Steadman, Marg.,	July 27, 1834	
Steadman, Wm. C.,	Dec. 17, 1840	
Steadman, Mrs. R.,	Oct. 7, 1843	
Steadman, David,	Mar. 22, 1863	58
Steadman, H. C.,	May 22, 1876	43
Steans, Mrs. N.,	Apr. 26, 1861	83
Stees, John,	July 29, 1855	
Sterner, Nathan,	——, 1829	
Sterner, Christop'r	Jan. 4, 1841	
Sterner, Peter,	Apr. 25, 1864	67
Sterrett, John A.,	April 4, 1872	71
Stillwell, Hon. Jos.,	Aug. 22, 1851	74
Stillwell, Mrs. Ann,	Jun. 28, 1862	72
Stinemel, Mr.,	Sept. 26, 1844	
Stitzel, Jacob,	Dec. 8, 1863	68
Stock, Martin A.,	Feb. 16, 1857	70
Stoughton, Roland	Sept. 3, 1832	
Stoughton, Mrs. J.,	Sept. 28, 1842	
Stoughton, J. S.	——, 1857	
Stoughton, Fred.,	Apr. 25, 1869	69
Stover, Mrs. M. M.,	Sept. 26, 1876	71
Strahan, Peter,	Sept. 20, 1845	
Stratton, Tyler,	Mar. 5, 1825	
Stratton, Mrs. R.,	Mar. 29, 1850	
Straub, Andrew,	Oct. 23, 1824	38
Straub, Abram,	Aug. 21, 1864	60
Strawbridge, Mary,	Oct. 11, 1829	
Strawbridge, J.,	Sept. 25, 1861	87
Strawbridge, Mrs. C.	Jun. 4, 1870	80
Strayhorn, Eliza,	Dec. 11, 1867	78
Streighorn, Peter,	Sept. 20, 1845	
Streighorn, Robert,	May 8, 1863	67
Strickland, Samuel,	Apr. 23, 1858	79
Strohecker, Leah,	Feb. 19, 1853	
Strohecker, Dr. S.,	Aug. 26, 1869	75
Struble, Mrs. M.,	Aug. 15, 1868	60
Sullivan, Wm. B.,	Sept. 1, 1850	45
Sutherland, Col. T.,	Oct. 15, 1816	84
Sutherland, Jane,	Feb. 9, 1819	82
Swarm, sr., John,	Sept. 24, 1827	
Swarm, John,	Mar. 25, 1841	66
Swartz,Geo.(W.D.)	Apr. 17, 1871	65
Swineford, John,	June 24, 1867	45
Swineford, Mrs. M.,	Aug. 13, 1872	
Sypher, Jacob,	June 6, 1854	74
Tate, William,	July 19, 1859	59
Taylor, Thomas,	Sept. 19, 1868	76
Taylor, William C.,	June 9, 1874	70
Templeton, Sam.,	Feb. 18, 1826	72
Templeton, Rev. J.,	Dec. 3, 1843	

	Date of Death.	Age
Tharp, Esq., James,	Mar. 27, 1849	
Thompson, Wm.,	Apr. 1, 1823	72
Thompson, John,	Aug. 22, 1823	70
Thompson, Benj.,	Oct. —, 1830	
Thompson, Mrs. J.,	Aug. 21, 1839	
Thompson, Rev. G.,	Jun. 28, 1864	43
Thompson, Mrs. M.,	Apr. 10, 1864	
Thompson, Chas.L.,	June 29, 1865	
Thompson, Mrs. B.,	Jan. —, 1869	60
Thornton, Dr. T. A.,	Feb. 8, 1867	51
Thornton, Mrs. A.,	Apr. 24, 1873	
Thursby, Margaret,	Jan. —, 1848	91
Todd, Rev. Nath.,	July 8, 1867	88
Trester, George,	May 28, 1850	
Trout, John,	Mar. 15, 1862	
Trutt, Mrs. Eve,	Aug. 19, 1861	
Tucker, Martha G.,	Apr. 20, 1864	22
Tweed, David,	——, 1824	
Tweed, William,	Feb. 1, 1857	68
Ulsh, Andrew,	Apr. 19, 1864	79
Valentine, Bond,	Oct. —, 1862	
Van Buskirk, Thos.	Sept. 12, 1830	
Van Buskirk, Rich.	Oct. 9, 1830	66
Van Buskirk, John,	Aug. 2, 1836	
Van Buskirk, John,	Jan. 28, 1874	80
Vanhorn, Espy,	Aug. 25, 1829	
Van Gundy,Christ.,	Sept. 30, 1836	71
Vanvalzah, Mrs. E.,	Mar. 30, 1840	74
Vanvalzah,jr.,Dr.R.	Mar. 14, 1851	62
Vanvalzah, jr.,Dr.T.	May 23, 1852	31
Vanvalzah, John A.	Aug. 26, 1854	54
Vanvalzah, Mrs. N.,	Apr. 26, 1857	57
Vanvalzah, W. W.,	Oct. 13, 1857	49
Vanvalzah, Rob. H.,	July 25, 1860	36
Vanvalzah, Mrs. S.,	Nov. 16, 1862	45
Vanvalzah, Mrs. H.,	July 25, 1870	69
Voneida, Peter,	Aug. 26, 1853	73
Voneida, John,	Mar. 26, 1858	77
Voneida, Esther,	July 8, 1865	
Vornando, Mrs.,	——, 1823	
Vorse, Dr. Isaac S.,	Jan. 17, 1839	
Vorse, Mrs. Eliz.,	Aug. 17, 1873	42
Waggenseller, Dr.,	Apr. 28, 1847	
Waggenseller, Wm.	Aug. 10, 1876	
Wagner, Andrew,	Dec. 30, 1826	
Wagner, Mrs. R.,	Aug. 22, 1834	
Wagner, Michael,	Dec. 22, 1858	72
Wagner, Daniel,	Aug. 20, 1861	62
Wagner, Mrs. S.,	Apr. 13, 1872	81
Walborn, Martin,	Sept. 20, 1865	65
Waldrum, Samuel,	Aug. 25, 1858	55
Wales, Mary, N. B.	May 15, 1826	58
Wales, Mary,	Feb. 20, 1826	
Walker, John,	Sept. 18, 1827	
Walker, Francis,	June 9, 1867	50
Walker, Mrs. Mary,	July 16, 1867	85
Walker, Thomas,	Sept. 17, 1868	58
Wallace, Polly,	Mar. 17, 1829	

	Date of Death.	Age.
Wallace, Joseph G.,	Jan. 6, 1844	
Wallace, Sarah,	July 24, 1849	
Wallace, William,	July 15, 1857	77
Wallace, Elizabeth,	Nov. 26, 1860	44
Wallace, Joseph,	Mar. 22, 1862	80
Wallace, Mrs. N.,	Oct. 26, 1868	69
Walter, William,	Feb. 10, 1874	60
Waller, Abram,	Mar. 18, 1869	57
Walls, Miss S. McC.	Mar. 14, 1860	18
Walls, Johnson,	Apr. 18, 1868	50
Waters, Thomas,	Sept. 6, 1864	65
Waters, Mrs. Ellen,	Sept. 10, 1868	95
Watson, Mrs. M.,	Mar. —, 1825	
Watson, Samuel,	Jan. 17, 1841	
Watson, Robert,	Sept. —, 1846	
Watson, Mrs. S. C.,	Mar. 25, 1849	
Watson, William,	May 22, 1866	70
Watson, David,	Oct. 9, 1874	80
Weaver, Jacob,	Apr. 13, 1862	79
Weaver, M. H.,	Feb. 13, 1872	73
Weidensaul, A. J.,	Aug. 10, 1869	59
Weirick, Mrs. M.,	Mar. 4, 1861	51
Weist, Miss E.,	Aug. 17, 1875	77
Wehr, Simon,	Dec. 19, 1840	71
Weirick, Esq., D.,	Apr. 3, 1866	61
Weirick, Esq., S.,	Feb. 9, 1869	61
Welker, Mrs. L.,	Dec. 22, 1860	87
Welch, Esq., C.,	Jan. —, 1855	
Welsh, Henry,	May 16, 1862	80
Wertz, John,	July 26, 1861	73
Wetzel, Henry,	Oct. 4, 1850	90
White, James,	Jan. 15, 1862	44
Whiting, Wm. B.,	Jan. 2, 1861	33
Whitmer, Ann,	Oct. 4, 1845	70
Whitmer, Sebas'n,	July 17, 1846	73
Whitmer, Peter,	June 8, 1877	78
Whittaker, John,	July 25, 1859	64
Wikoff, Peter,	May 29, 1832	
Wildtrout, Fred.,	June 27, 1848	71
Wilhelm, Moses,	Apr. 19, 1862	72
Williamson, Rev. J.	Apr. 10, 1865	69
Wilson, Elizabeth,	—— —, 1823	
Wilson, Mary,	July 11, 1828	
Wilson, Sarah,	Apr. 8, 1829	
Wilson, Thomas,	May 23, 1831	
Wilson, James,	Dec. 26, 1831	
Wilson, Elizabeth,	Nov. 24, 1832	
Wilson, Mrs. Cath.	Aug. 21, 1835	
Wilson, John,	Jan. 22, 1842	
Wilson, Samuel,	Jan. 16, 1843	
Wilson, Samuel H.,	Mar. 14, 1850	
Wilson, Mrs. Eliz	Aug. 9, 1851	
Wilson, Thos. C.,	May 25, 1853	
Wilson, Charles,	June 21, 1853	
Wilson, Esq., Sam.,	Nov. 3, 1855	
Wilson, Mathias,	Mar. 20, 1859	50
Wilson, John F.,	Apr. 6, 1859	66
Wilson, Louisa,	July 20, 1860	32

	Date of Death.	Age.
Wilson, William,	June 12, 1863	76
Wilson, Hon. A. S.,	Dec. 19, 1864	64
Wilson, Mrs. Ann,	Sept. 21, 1865	67
Wilson, Mrs. Sarah,	June 31, 1872	84
Wilson, Hugh,	July 3, 1873	81
Wilson, Francis,	Feb. 15, 1874	73
Wilson, Mrs. S. B.,	Nov. —, 1874	40
Wilt, Adam,	Aug. 13, 1830	
Wilt, Esq., Jno. C.,	May 24, 1858	50
Winegardner, P.,	Aug. 17, 1829	
Winegardner, N.,	July 15, 1854	76
Winegardner, H.,	Jan. 1, 1872	68
Winegardner, Alb.,	Feb. 16, 1875	64
Winters, Sarah,	Apr. —, 1821	
Winters, David,	Aug. 13, 1825	
Winters, Mrs. C.,	Mar. 19, 1829	
Winters, Margaret,	June 21, 1829	
Winters, Daniel,	Jan. 5, 1837	61
Winters, Sarah,	Jan. 7, 1868	60
Winters, Mrs. Reb.,	Oct. 18, 1873	74
Wise, Mrs. Barbara,	Oct. 11, 1823	44
Wise, Mrs. Eleanor,	Aug. 17, 1875	77
Witmer, Sebastian,	Apr. 15, 1824	78
Witmer, Mrs. S.,	July 3, 1874	73
Wittenmyer, Jacob,	June 23, 1856	60
Wolfe, Jonathan,	Nov. 6, 1834	46
Wolfe, Michael,	Nov. 25, 1847	81
Wolfe, Samuel,	Sept. 15, 1850	40
Wolfe, Anthony,	Jan. 21, 1851	76
Wolfe, ——,	Mar. 17, 1851	79
Wolfe, Samuel,	Apr. 19, 1860	20
Wolfe, Mrs. Mary,	Feb. 17, 1862	30
Wolfe, Mrs. Han'h,	Apr. 7, 1866	62
Wolfe, John,	Nov. 11, 1868	20
Wolfe, Andrew,	Jan. 21, 1871	87
Wolfe, Peter,	Dec. 20, 1871	73
Wolfe, Mrs. Eve.,	Feb. 4, 1872	63
Wolfe, Leonard,	Feb. 12, 1875	78
Wolfe, Mrs. E. M.,	May 6, 1876	60
Wolsey, Henry,	Dec. 18, 1871	62
Woods, Christop'r,	Aug. 23, 1853	52
Woomer, Mrs.,	Sept. 26, 1827	
Worman, F. S.,	Sept. 24, 1876	
Wykoff, Mrs. S.,	Jan. 16, 1876	76
Yearick, Esq., H.,	June 21, 1856	76
Yarnell, George,	June 6, 1873	60
Yerger, Jacob,	Jan. 22, 1870	72
Yoder, Jacob,	Apr. 11, 1864	84
Yoder, Samuel,	Mar. 7, 1870	85
Yohn, John,	Feb. 17, 1871	85
Yost, Elizabeth,	Oct. 5, 1856	68
Young, James,	July 20, 1825	
Young, Frederick,	Aug. 29, 1825	
Young, John,	July 8, 1840	
Young, Maria,	Jan. 7, 1843	
Young, Catherine,	Aug. 6, 1853	62
Young, Daniel,	June 4, 1854	
Young, Jacob,	June 7, 1857	82

ANNALS OF BUFFALO VALLEY.

	Date of Death.	Age.		Date of Death.	Age.
Young, William,	Nov. 20, 1859	73	Zellers, Peter,	Jan. 5, 1822	37
Young, Mrs. Marg.,	May 3, 1860	62	Zellers, John,	Aug. 1, 1832	
Young, Eleanor,	Nov. 17, 1865		Zellers, sr., John,	Nov. 12, 1843	67
Young, Mrs.,	Jan. 18, 1866	76	Zellers, Mrs. Cath.,	July 22, 1850	
Young, Adam,	Oct. 8, 1872	65	Zellers, Daniel,	Nov. 30, 1853	
Young, Abra., (B.,)	Oct. 3, 1873	76	Zellers, Mrs. Han.,	Feb. 21, 1856	79
Young, Abraham,	May 13, 1875	90	Zellers, Daniel,	Oct. 13, 1865	
Young, Mrs. Eliza.,	July 22, 1866	42	Zellers, Samuel,	Feb. 3, 1874	66
Young, Mrs. Ellen,	Feb. 18, 1867	47	Zentmyer, Jacob,	Mar. 8, 1849	
Youngman, George,	May 6, 1843	79	Zentmyer, Mrs. E.,	Mar. 13, 1863	79
Zearfos, Mrs. M. A.,	Dec. 18, 1860	30	Ziebach, Mrs. Ann,	Sept. 2, 1867	70
Zeigler, Mrs.,	—— —, 1826		Zimmerman, John,	Aug. 18, 1825	

MILITARY RECORD, 1861-5.

COMPANY E, FIFTY-FIRST PENNSYLVANIA.

Captains.
G. H. Hassenplug,
William R. Forster.

First Lieutenants.
John A. Morris,
Francis R. Frey.

Second Lieutenants.
Martin L. Schoch,
James L. Seebold,
George C. Gutelius.

Sergeants.
John M. Wierman,
Thomas D. Reed,
Elbridge G. Maize,
Charles Mills,
Cornelius Edelman,
George Diehl, discharged, July 11, 1865, for wounds received in action,
Lewis G. Titus, died, January 7, 1863, of wounds received at Fredericksburg, December 13, 1862.

Corporals.
John H. Sortman,
Cyrus A. Eaton,
Peter Strubble,
Isaac Treat,
Daniel High,
Ebert Sprowles,
William Kleckner,
Isaac G. Magee,
Adam Gluse,
Thomas F. Search,
John C. Youngman,
George W. Foote,
Levi H. Ammon,
Thomas S. Mauck, died, June 20, 1864, of wounds received at Petersburg, Virginia, buried in National cemetery, Arlington, Virginia,
George M. Aurand, killed at Weldon railroad, August 19, 1864,

James Luker,
Charles D. Kline, junior.

Musician.
Joseph A. Logan.

Privates.
Aikey, Jeremiah, captured, died at Andersonville, Georgia,
Baker, Ralston,
Barklow, George E., died at Brownsville, Mississippi, July 21, 1863,
Barnes, Albert E.,
Beers, David H.,
Bell, William H.,
Benfer, Abraham,
Benner, Asher,
Benner, Lewis J.,
Black, James,
Blair, Simon S.,
Bomgardner, John,
Boop, Jacob,
Bowers, George,
Brouse, Benjamin H., killed at Camden, North Carolina, April 19, 1862,
Burk, George P.,
Burkhart, Adolph,
Burris, Samuel,
Chappel, Ezra,
Chambers, James M.,
Chambers, M. B.,
Clapham, Thomas H., died, March 13, 1864,
Cole, Luther G.,
Cornelius, James F.
Cornelius, George W.,
Curfman, Daniel,
Curtis, Jeremiah F.,
Derkes, John D.,
Dersham, Henry,
Dewire, Alexander,
Diehl, Henry C.,
Dingman, Abraham,
Dolby, Isaac,

Dolby, Abraham,
Donachy, Thomas,
Donnison, Aaron,
Dunkle, James M., killed at Cold Harbor, June 3, 1864,
Eidem, Henry,
Engle, Solomon,
Fetter, John,
Fletcher, Justice J.,
Fox, Henry D.,
Frederick, Jacob,
Galloway, George W.,
Geniger, William,
Gordon, Jacob,
Hansell, David,
Hanselman, David,
Hanselman, Adam,
Harris, Berryhill B.,
Hassenplug, John T.,
Hauley, Timothy,
Heckman, Wm. R.,
Heinbach, Elias,
Heitsman, Isaiah,
Heitsman, Jacob,
Heitsman, Henry,
Henderson, William,
Hendershot, Christ,
Hendricks, John,
Hickernell, Robert, died of wounds received at Cold Harbor, June 3, 1864,
Hilbish, Ammon,
Hoffman, William R., killed at Camden, North Carolina, April 19, 1862,
Hoffman, Edward J.,
Hummel, John,
Hutchinson, Henry,
Irwin, Robert, H.,
Kelly, James T.,
Kennedy, Barton,
Kidson, Francis,
Kline, Joel,
Kline, Reuben,
Kline, Daniel,
Kline, Charles,
Kline, Andrew T.,
Kline, Jacob L., died May 6, 1864, buried in United States general hospital cemetery, Annapolis, Maryland,
Klingler, John,
Kunkel, Samuel,
Kunkel, Jonathan,
Laird, Samuel H.,
Laudenslager, William,
Leinbach, William F. N.,
Lenhart, John,
Lenhart, David, killed near Petersburg, Virginia, June 17, 1864,
Lloyd, Charles,
Lloyd, John,
Long, Jacob,
Lotz, Galen N.,
Lytle, Charles,
McGregor, Samuel,
McFadden, Jackson,
Marsh, Charles H.,
Masterson, Ed. J.,
Meckley, Alfred, killed at Weldon railroad, August 19, 1864,
Mertz, Jacob K.,
Middaugh, John T.,
Miller, Jacob,
Miller, Henry,
Miller, James,
Millhouse, John,
Moll, Joseph A.,
Mullen, Arthur,
Myers, Daniel,
Norton, Henry M.,
Orwig, William P.,
Orwig, John W.,
Paul, Peter G.,
Post, Victor E.,
Radenbaugh, Jeremiah,
Rahback, John,
Reed, Martin G.,
Renner, Levi,
Reese, Jonathan,
Rote, Joel,
Rote, Samuel,
Rule, John V.,
Sassman, Emanuel,
Sassman, Noah W.,
Searles, Sebastian,
Seebold, George A.,
Seebold, Castor, died at Philadelphia, Pennsylvania, May 11, 1864,
Schaffle, Frank S.,
Schnure, George,
Schnure, William,
Shaffer, Anthony,
Sheckler, John W.,
Sheary, Samuel F.,
Shreffler, Joseph,
Shriner, Josiah,
Sholley, William S.,
Simmons, Thomas,
Smith, Albert E.,
Snyder, Henry,
Snyder, Jonathan,
Speese, Daniel,
Stitzer, John T.,
Toland, Robert,
Trainer, Charles H.,
Tucker, Samuel,
Watson, William S.,
Weaver, John D.,
Webb, William,
Wilson, Charles,
Wirt, Andrew G.,

Wirt, George W., died at Lexington, Kentucky, September 15, 1863,
Wolfinger, Joseph,
Woodward, C. W.,
Zechman, Melanc'n,
Zimmerman, William,

COMPANY H, FIFTY-FIRST PENNSYLVANIA.

Captains.
J. Merrill Linn,
George Shorkley.

First Lieutenants.
J. Gilbert Beaver, killed at Antietam, September 17, 1862,
Hugh McClure.

Second Lieutenants.
Aaron Smith,
Jacob H. Santo,
David C. Brewer.

First Sergeant.
Jacob Nyhart.

Sergeants.
Matthew Vandine, killed at Antietam, September 17, 1862,
George Breon,
Seth J. Housel,
Harrison Hause,
Frederick Erwine,
George W. Brown,
John Aldenderfer,
James Kincaid,
Daniel M. Wetzell,
William Allison, killed at Fredricksburg, December 13, 1862.

Corporals.
H. J. Lingerman,
John Grambling,
Alfred Durst,
George H Kauff,
Henry Fogleman,
Michael Lepley,
Andrew Knepp,
R. A. M. Harner,
H. C. McCormick,
Henry B. Wetzell,
Reuben Baker,
Peter Koser,
Nicholas Nichols,
Robert Henry,
H. Co'y McCormick,
John Q. Adams,
Charles Merrill,
James L. Schooly,
Deitrich Beckman,
J. Bachenhamer,
Henry J. Warner.

Musicians.
Jacob Moore,
Charles P. McFadden,
Andrew Bernade.

Privates.
Allshouse, Peter,
Angstadt, Jonas,
Angstadt, Mabury,
Armpriester, William,
Auchenbaugh, William,
Ayers, James,
Baldwin, Eleazer,
Bastian, Peter,
Bastian, Abraham,
Bear, Edward, killed at Antietam
Beeber, Henry,
Beehn, Henry A.,
Beck, Isaac, killed at Antietam,
Benner, Lewis J.,
Bennett, Miles,
Berkeville, Daniel,
Blunt, James,
Brensinger, Levi,
Britton, Simon,
Brown, Asa,
Brownfield, John,
Bobst, David,
Boon, Daniel,
Bower, Harrison,
Bomgardner, Daniel,
Bordmel, Daniel C.,
Boyer, John,
Boyer, William,
Buskirk, Jacob,
Carey, George W.,
Casseck, Northell,
Chriesher, William F.,
Christy, James,
Clark, David,
Corl, John,
Dawson, John L.,
Debilzon, John S.,
Dehaven, Reuben,
Dillsplains, Mahl'n,
Dopp, J. Peter,
Dougherty, John,
Dougherty, James,
Douty, William H., killed at Knoxville, Tennessee November 29, 1863,
Doyle, Matthew,
Doyle, James,
Dumheller, Abner,

Dysher, Mathias,
Dye, Richard,
Eardly, John W., killed at North Anna, May 27, 1864,
Eglof, Samuel,
Ervine, Frederick,
Espenship, David,
Everly, Andrew F.,
Everett, William,
Farley, Samuel, died at Knoxville, Tennessee, December 19, 1863,
Fewring, George,
Fies, Henry,
Fike, John,
Foote, John W.,
Fox, William H. R.,
Frederick, Ebenezer,
Frynte, George H.,
Gallagher, William,
Gardner, William,
Getty, David H.,
Goss, Simon,
Grier, Thomas G., died at Moorehead City, North Carolina, October 6, 1864,
Haas, William,
Hain, Henry,
Hain, John,
Harding, Jarrett S.,
Harris, Joseph,
Hartline, Daniel,
Hartline, David,
Hefner, Jonathan,
Hefflefinger, George,
Henry, Adam,
Hertzog, Emanuel,
Heitsman, Isaiah,
Hoffman, Thomas,
Holen, Thomas,
Holslander, George F.,
Humphrey, John,
Ingerson, Hillman,
Jones, Thomas,
Keffer, Henry J.,
Kelly, James S.,
Kelly, James A.,
Kneph, Simon,
Knode, Albion G.,
Kyseraski, Joseph,
Lattimer, William J.,
Leamon, John E.,
Leinbach, Calvin L.,
Lenig, Jacob,
Lepley, William,
Lott, John W.,
Lyon, Conrad,
McMurtrie, Isaac,
McEwen, Samuel S.,
Marks, Levi,
Marr, Thomas P.,
Mease, George,
Miller, John,
Miller, Samuel S.,
Miller, Daniel I.,
Miller, Jeremiah,
Miller, William A.,
Miller, Henry,
Mocherman, John H.,
Moll, Joseph A.,
Moore, John,
Moyer, Daniel B.,
Moyer, Daniel,
Murphy, John,
Murphy, Joseph,
Myers, William H.,
Nainan, John A.,
Oaks, William L.,
Paroby, Joseph,
Passell, Robert W.,
Phleger, Jacob,
Phillips, Abraham F. C.,
Purcell, George,
Ream, Jacob,
Rexford, Henry E.,
Rhoades, Jacob,
Search, Thomas F.,
Seales, Edwin, (N. B.,)
Serwatznes, Joseph,
Shaffer, Lewis I.,
Shappee, Dwier,
Shalley, William,
Shriner, William H.,
Shreck, John V.,
Slottman, Daniel,
Smith, John F.,
Smith, John D.,
Smith, David,
Smith, John, H.,
Smith, Jacob,
Smith, Isaiah,
Smith, Frederick,
Smith, Peter, captured August 21, 1864, absent at muster out,
Snyder, Nathaniel,
Snyder, Samuel,
Steltz William,
Steward, Charles R.,
Sullivan, Patrick,
Swab, William,
Swaverly, Adam,
Taylor, Samuel,
Turner, James,
Wagore, George,
Watkins, Benjamin,
Weisenbach, Anthony,
Weisenbach, Leo,
Wellings, William J.,
Wentzel, Jacob,
Wien, William,
Williamson, Aaron,
Williamson, James,
Williams, William,

Wittes, Isaac, killed at Antietam,
Wood, Aaron A.,
Uhl, Christian,
Umstead, John C.,
Updegraph, Lewis,
Van-Gezer, George,
Yoder, David,
Young, David I.,
Youngman, John C.,
Zechnow, Charles.

COMPANY K, FIFTY-FIRST PENNSYLVANIA.

(Including only those from Buffalo Valley and vicinity.)

Captain.
George P. Carman.

First Lieutenants.
Josiah Kelly,
John B. Linn.

Second Lieutenant.
Franklin Beale,
Frank P. Sterner, promoted captain April 16, 1864, and killed in action May 12, 1864.

Sergeants.
L. J. Crossgrove,
Thomas C. Pierce, killed in action front Petersburg, Virginia, June 17, 1864,
James Gibson, killed at Petersburg, July 30, 1864,
John Vanlew.

Corporals.
William Buoy, died of wounds received at Cold Harbor, Virginia,
Henry G. Dentler, died at Andersonville, Georgia, May 17, 1864—grave 1,161,
Edward Held,
Thomas J. Arbuckle, died in captivity,
Nathan M. Hann.

Musician.
Montgomery S. Adams.

Privates.
Aikey, Lewis,
Aikey, Zechariah,
Allen, Benjamin,
Bastian, George W.,
Babcock, Joseph,
Baldwin, Absalom, died at Andersonville, Georgia, September 24, 1864,
Barnhart, James,
Bently, Franklin,
Berryman, Richard,
Betzer, John,
Benfer, David,
Bower, William D.,
Bratton, Philip H.,
Cole, Christopher E.,
Cox, John F.,
Crites, Kremer,
Crossgrove, Samuel,
Depo, Thomas,
Doebler, Alexander, taken prisoner May 27, 1864,
Duck, Franklin F., died in captivity,
Dull, George, died at Alexandria, Virginia, September 19, 1864—grave 2,683,
Fangboner, John,
Foster, Thomas, killed at Weldon railroad, August 19, 1864,
Garrett, James, captured, died at Andersonville, Georgia, August 19, 1864—grave 6,140,
Geddes, John,
Gift, Jonathan J.,
Hanselman, Peter,
Harris, John, killed June 17, 1864,
Henry, Isaiah,
Hoover, Daniel, died June 27, 1864,
Hoover, Charles, died at New York city, November 12, 1864,
Houtz, Henry,
Huffman, John,
Ludwig, Jarad,
McBride, Paul M.,
Macpherson, John,
Mann, Philip, J.,
Marr, James,
Meylert, William S.,
Mills, David,
Moore, Joseph G.,
Ocker, David G.,
Poeth, Joseph G.,
Rank, Benjamin, wounded at Cold Harbor,
Rank, Samuel,
Rank, John, died of wounds received in battle at Spottsylvania,
Reese, John,
Reichly, David,
Reinhart, Nicholas,
Reish, Solomon, captured at Weldon railroad,
Richards, Edward, died September 10, 1864, of wounds,
Rider, Benjamin,
Riefsnyder, William,

ANNALS OF BUFFALO VALLEY. 585

Royer, Samuel,
Sarvis Joseph,
Souders, Ephraim,
Search, William,
Shaffer, Thomas,
Sherry, George H.,
Shiers, Michael,
Shilling, Alfred, wounded at Wilderness, May 6, 1864,
Shingle, David, killed at Cold Harbor, Virginia, June 3, 1864,
Showers, Henry C.,
Stees, David C.,
Stuttsman, William M.,
Summers, Oliver,
Royer, Samuel,
Roush, Benjamin,
Terry, George W.,
Treaster, Henry,
Truitt, William M.,
Turner, Lyman B.,
Watts, John,
Weidell, John, died, October 26, 1864, of wounds received at Cold Harbor,
June 3, 1864, buried in National cemetery, Arlington, Virginia,
Wertz, Robert,
Winegardner, John, wounded in action, June 6, 1864.
Yearick, Tobias.

COMPANY D, FIFTY-SECOND REGIMENT.

Captains.

James Chamberlin, resigned May 11, 1863,
Samuel Cuskaden.

First Lieutenant.

J. P. S. Weidensaul.

Second Lieutenants.

Aaron Stoughton,
William Phillips.

Sergeants.

George W. Scott, died from wounds received at James Island, South Carolina, July 3, 1864,
Edward Zechman,
Lot Trate,
Jacob Fetter,
William J. Evans,
Jacob Getter,
Joseph H. Pardoe,
Michael Flaherty,
Samuel Chalfant,
William Richardson,
William Connelly,
Joseph R. Housel,
B. F. Machamer,
John McPherson,
William A. Sober,
James McBride, died at Washington, D. C.

Corporals.

Joseph McCracken,
Thomas Mackey,
Enoch Rice,
Martin Young,
John Tambler,
James Campbell,
John Leidabeck,
Elias K. Foust,
Patrick Kearney,

Peter Sheddel,
Abraham Kauffman,
Alexander J. Sober,
Samuel Herman,
Samuel Dolby,
I. Dunkleberger, died June 4, 1862, of wounds,
Charles A. Penny, died at Craney Island, Virginia, Sept. 25, 1862,
Gotlieb Smaltzried, died at Morris Island, South Carolina, September 6, 1863.

Musicians.

Henry Gallagher, died at White House, Virginia, June 15, 1862,
Charles McGregor.

Privates.

Able, John, died at Annapolis, Maryland, December 21, 1864,
Baker, Peter,
Barker, Henry,
Balliett, John,
Bennett, William H.,
Berkhiser, Isaac,
Blake, Christopher,
Blake, James,
Bower, Wilson M.,
Bowers, James,
Brocius, Gideon,
Buck, Frederick,
Burris, Henry H.,
Callahan, Michael, died at Andersonville, Georgia, September 27, 1864—9,886,
Carey, Archibald, died at Florence, South Carolina, November 26, 1864,
Chalfant, Samuel,
Chappell, Ira,
Chappell, George,
Cogin, John,

Cornelison, John R.,
Cornelius, Jackson,
Collins, George,
Courtwright, P. W., died at Hilton Head, South Carolina, June 13, 1864,
Danner, Samuel,
Danney, William, died at Florence, South Carolina, December 10, 1864,
Dailey, John,
Donachy, John,
Doyle, John,
Doyle, Thomas,
Duck, Daniel, killed at Fair Oaks, May 31, 1862,
Duryea, James,
Emerick, Philip,
Evans, Richard,
Fadden, James,
Fenstermacher, James,
Fertig, John,
Fisher, Peter,
Foulds, Richard,
Gahring, Charles, died at Florence, South Carolina, October 18, 1864,
Geiger, Lewis,
Gordon, George,
Greiger, Jacob,
Grey, William,
Gross, Joseph, died at Washington, D. C., June 19, 1862,
Gunn, Jeremiah,
Gooden, George,
Hall, Henry,
Hankey, John,
Hankey, Frank,
Heaton, John,
Heimbach, Benjamin F.,
Heller, Jeremiah,
Helwick, Andrew,
Hensyl, Lot,
Houtz, Austin S.,
Hufford, Lewis,
Hunter, John,
Irving, Abram A.,
Jameson, Henry,
Jarrett, Franklin,
Jones, Daniel,
Kinney, John,
Kinter, Maurice,
Kirsch, Frederick,
Krider, Jacob,
Krider, Daniel,
Kauffman, Ab.,
Kearney, Patrick,
Lemereaux, O. H.,
Lenhart, Henry,
Lennard, James,
Livengood, Abraham,
Loch, Samuel,
Long, Zephaniah,
Long, Charles,
Long, John F.,
Long, Isaac,
Lupold, Jeremiah, killed at Fort Henry, Tennessee, April 2, 1862,
McGannel, Edward, killed at Fair Oaks, May 31, 1862,
Martin, William,
Martin, David,
Messersmith, Jeremiah,
Miller, William,
Miller, Amzi W., died at Andersonville, Georgia, October 1, 1864,
Minnier, Samuel,
Moran, Patrick,
Morrison, Michael,
Moyer, Benjamin F., killed at Fair Oaks, May 31, 1862,
Mussleman, John, died at Yorktown, Virginia, November 27, 1862,
Musser, John,
Nagle, Samuel,
Neifert, Henry,
O'Gara, Dominick,
Olby, William L.,
Ott, Samuel,
Owens, John H.,
Pell, Benjamin, died at Florence, South Carolina, October 21, 1864,
Poeth, Henry C.,
Poole, Josiah, died September 23, 1864, buried in Cypress Hill cemetry, Long Island,
Poole, Gilbert, captured, died in Florence, South Carolina, August 22, 1864,
Price, William,
Pifer, Elias F.,
Phillips, William,
Pardoe, Joseph H.,
Rahmer, Charles,
Ransom, Thomas D.,
Reed, Samuel, died July 1864, of wounds received at Fort Johnson, South Carolina,
Renney, James B., died at Yorktown, Virginia, December 17, 1862,
Richard, Charles,
Richley, Frederick,
Rorabach, Henry,
Rutloss, Moritz C.,
Saunders, Samuel,
Sheibelhood, Joseph,
Smith, William H.,
Specht, Michael, died at Washington, D. C., June 24, 1862, of wounds received at Fair Oaks, Virginia, May 31, 1862,
Springer, Joseph,
Sober, Salathiel, killed at Fair Oaks, May 31, 1862,

ANNALS OF BUFFALO VALLEY.

Sober, Aaron,
Staples, Nelson, captured, died at Florence, South Carolina, October 20, 1864,
Stapleton, Franklin,
Stetler, Charles,
Souder, Henry J., died at Florence, South Carolina, October 20, 1864,
Trutt, David,
Vertz, George W.,
Wagner, Josiah,
Warner, Gideon, died at Florence, South Carolina, October 1, 1864,
Wertz, Thomas,
Wheat, John,
Wheeler, Walter,
Williams, Philip,
Willis, David, died at Morris Island, South Carolina, August 31, 1864,
Wilson, John,
Womelsdorf, J.,
Woodward, G. W.,
Wright, Franklin,
Wright, Charles,
Zellers, John, died at Florence, South Carolina, October 1, 1864.

COMPANY E, FIFTY-THIRD REGIMENT.

(Including only those from Buffalo Valley and vicinity.)

Captains.
Thomas Church,
Beach C. Ammons,
Daniel Artman.

First Lieutenant.
Henry F. Menges.

Second Lieutenant.
Albert H. Hess.

First Sergeant.
John R. Smith.

Sergeants.
William Ulrich,
Joseph Hartley,
David Davis,
John Milsom.

Corporals.
William Parry,
James Harvey,
Archibald McPherson,
William Byrne,
Ezekiel Gilham,
John McCollum,
William Tovy.

Musicians.
Jacob Bingaman,
Daniel Bingaman.

Teamster.
David Kohlen.

Privates.
Bingaman, Daniel J.,
Bingaman, James, died at Annapolis, Maryland, December 20, 1864,
Buoy, Sylvester,
Cushion, John,
Davis, Thomas,
Davis, Job,
Dickison, Samuel,
Drum, William,
Getz, George,
Hancock, Richard,
Hancock, William,
Hayden, James,
Heinback, George,
Hess, Isaac,
Hess, Francis,
Kaler, Jefferson,
McCollum, William,
McPherson, John,
Marsh, Charles P.,
Oldfield, John,
Price, John,
Rearick, Oliver, P.,
Sergeant, William,
Slayman, Russel,
Snyder, Samuel,
Stevens, William,
Thomas, William H.,
Tovy, Daniel,
Ulrich, Eisle,
Walters, Henry, C.,
Wiehr, David M. L.

COMPANY A, ONE HUNDRED AND THIRTY-FIRST REGIMENT.

Captains.
Jacob Moyer,
Joseph R. Orwig.

First Lieutenant.
Joseph William Kepler.

Second Lieutenant.
William Fitchthorn.

Sergeants.
Albert Barnes,
Forster Halfpenny,

Isaac Treat,
Josiah Shriner,
Henry Rothermal.

Corporals.

George W. Fiester,
Charles Worman,
Jacob Hower,
Harrison Hafer,
Samuel S. Smith,
William H. Weirick,
Joel Kline,
Henry Phillips,
Nathaniel W. Strahan.

Musician.

James Forrest.

Privates.

Aikey, William Henry, killed at Fredericksburg, Virginia, December 13, 1862,
Burkholder, William,
Burkholder, Lewis,
Burkenstock, H.,
Brant, Henry,
Baldwin, Absalom,
Brocius, Isaac,
Bordner, William,
Cauliflower, William,
Charles, Sturger,
Collins, Peter,
Cornelius, Washington,
Crisswell, William,
Dennis, Phares,
Devine, Peter,
Diehl, Henry Calvin,
Dollard, William,
Dresher, William,
Fiester, John Uhl,
Foltz, Martin,
Foster, Andrew,
Glover, John W.,
Grove, G. Samuel,
Hanselman, David,
Harris, John,
Hartley, Elias,
Hayes, James C.,
Henry, William G.,
Huff, George,
Huff, John,
Hultsizer, Jesse, died at Washington, D. C., November 10, 1862.
Katherman, Joseph,
Katherman, Isaiah,
Kline, Charles,
Kline, George,
Kline, Henry Charles,
Laird, Samuel H.,
Lashells, George W., killed at Fredericksburg, Virginia, December 13, 1862.
Lenhart, David,
Leib, Emanuel,
Ludwig, George,
McPherson, Archibald,
Markle, John,
Maxwell, Archibald,
Meyers, Daniel B.,
Miller, Harry,
Moyer, George W.,
Newman, Lewis,
Rarer, John,
Reed, G. Thompson,
Reed, John,
Richards, Christian,
Rorabaugh, James A.,
Rossman, William,
Rote, Joseph,
Sanders, George L.,
Schnee, Peter,
Schuck, Thomas L.,
Shaffer, Milton,
Showalter, Samuel,
Smith, Sylvester,
Snyder, William A.,
Snyder, William W.,
Snyder, Emanuel, killed at Fredericksburg, Virginia, December 13, 1862,
Solomon, Henry C.,
Sommers, Jeremiah,
Sommers, Oliver,
Stees, Henry George, killed at Fredericksburg, Virginia, Dec. 13, 1862.
Swartz, John,
Taylor, William A.,
Wertz, William,
Wilson, Frank,
Winegarden, J. A.,
Wise, Charles,
Zechman, M. Calvin.

MISCELLANEOUS.

In Battery E, First Artillery—Forty-third Regiment.

Captain Thomas G. Orwig.
First Lieutenant Benj. M. Orwig.

In Company F, One Hundred and Thirteenth—Twelfth Cavalry.

First Lieutenant David A. Irwin.

Second Lieutenant Henry E. Gutelius.

Company F, Fifty-sixth Pennsylvania.

Second Lieutenant George W. Guildin.

COMPANY E, ONE HUNDRED AND FORTY-SECOND REGIMENT.

Captains.
John A. Owens,
Charles R. Evans.

First Lieutenants.
Andrew G. Tucker, died July 5, of wounds received at Gettysburg, July 1, 1863.
Isaac S. Kerstetter.

Sergeants.
Scott Clingan,
Alfred Hayes,
Samuel Brown,
John V. Miller,
Reuben B. Fessler,
Thomas P. Wagner,
Thomas R. Orwig, died at Washington, D. C., November 30, 1862.

Corporals.
Isaac J. Kerstetter,
Isaac F. Brown,
John Gellinger,
Benjamin W. Minium,
Henry C. Penny,
John H. Martin,
William Keifer,
Nathaniel Strahan,
Henry M. Specht,
Jacob H. Rank, died, June 1, of wounds received at Spottsylvania Court House, Virginia, May 12, 1864.
Samuel Moyer, killed at Fredericksburg, Virginia, December 13, 1862.

Musicians.
William Geibel,
Hunter B. Barton.

Privates.
Ammon, William L.,
Armagast, Peter, killed at Fredericksburg, Virginia, December 13, 1862,
Baker, George,
Boope, George E.,
Boyer, Solomon,
Campbell, Reuben,
Deibert, John P., killed at Catlett's Station, Virginia, November 30, 1863,
Dellinger, John S., killed at Fredericksburg, Virginia, December 13, 1862,
Donachy, William L.,
Fangboner, Theodore,
Farley, John,
Fees, David,
Fetter, David, died of wounds received at Fredericksburg, Virginia, December 13, 1862,
Fetter, Adam,
Fullmer, William H.,
Gellinger, Jackson,
Gilboney, Jacob B.,
Gundy, James P.,
Hartman, Har'n R.,
Hoffman, Noah,
Hoffman, John,
Hoffman, Henry W.,
Hoffman, Solomon B.,
Houghton, Thomas,
Jamison, David, died of wounds received at Fredericksburg, Virginia, December 13, 1862,
Kline, John, died of wounds received at Wilderness, Virginia, May 6, 1864,
Kling, John, died at Acquia creek, January 22, 1863,
Koser, William, died at Warrenton, Virginia, November, 1862,
Koser, Uriah,
LeFevre, Frank P.,
Lenhart, Jacob,
McBride, Daniel,
Marr, James,
Martin, Henry, died at Sharpsburg, Maryland, November 24, 1862, buried in National cemetery, Antietam—section 26, lot B, grave 224,
Martin, Daniel, died of wounds received at Fredericksburg, Virginia, December 13, 1862,
Minium, John A.,
Morris, A. Judson,
Moser, Jacob, killed at Cold Harbor, Virginia, June 1, 1864,
Moser, Jeremiah, died of wounds received at Fredericksburg, Virginia, December 13, 1862,
Moyer, John N.,
Moyer, Levi H., died of wounds received at Fredericksburg, Virginia, December 13, 1862,
Pontius, Henry B.,
Raboss, John,
Raboss, Henry, killed, March 24, 1865,
Rank, Samuel,
Reichley, George,
Reish, George,
Renner, William, L.,
Renner, Levi, died at Richmond, Virginia, Febuary 23, 1863, of wounds received at Fredericksburg, Virginia, December 13, 1862,

Root, David, died at Gettysburg, Pennsylvania, July 3, 1863,
Sechler, William R.,
Shaffer, Jeremiah,
Shields, William,
Showalter, John W.,
Smith, Henry M.,
Smith, Henry C.,
Smith, Michael,
Sraham, James C.,
Sortman, Daniel,
Stapleton, George, died, July 26, of wounds received at Gettysburg, Pennsylvania, July 1, 1863,
Steinmetz, Philip,
Stettler, Henry, died at Washington, D. C., October 12, 1862, burial record, October 7, 1864, buried in Military Asylum cemetery,
Stitzer, Samuel, died at Washington, D. C., May 30, of wounds received at North Anna river, Virginia, May 23, 1864, buried in National cemetery, Arlington,
Stuck, Henry, died of wounds received at Fredericksburg, Virginia, December 13, 1862,
Wilson, Robert M.,
Wolfe, Emanuel,
Wolfe, William H.,
Wynn, Thomas.

COMPANY D, ONE HUNDRED AND FIFTIETH REGIMENT.

Captains.
Henry W. Crotzer,
William P. Dougal,
Roland Stoughton, died May 27, of wounds received at Wilderness, Virginia, May 5, 1864,
John H. Harter,
S. H. Himmelwright.

First Lieutenant.
John A. Hauck.

Second Lieutenants.
Samuel G. Gutelius,
James Cummings.

Sergeants.
Samuel C. Ranson,
Samuel Kerstetter,
James W. Marshall,
Charles A. Frey,
John Stennert,
Elias B. Weidensaul, killed at Gettysburg, July 1, 1863.

Corporals.
Albert Forster,
Howard Ritter,
Samuel Ruhl,
Amos Browand,
William Eberhart,
George L. Murray,
John Donachy,
John M. Hunt,
George W. Barkdoll,
William E. Hennings, killed at Gettysburg, July 1, 1863,
Joseph B. Ruhl, killed at Gettysburg, July 1, 1863,
William Donachy, killed at Laurel Hill, Virginia, May 8, 1864,
Ephraim Campbell, died at Washington, D. C., November 10, 1864,
Joseph J. Gutelius, killed at Gettysburg, July 1, 1863.

Musician.
Abraham Kuhn, died at Washington, D. C., December 21, 1862.

Privates.
Ammon, Aaron,
Bird, John S.,
Breyman, Mahlon,
Browand, Henry,
Brian, Michael,
Boyer, Jacob,
Buoy, Charles S.,
Chambers James M.,
Deal, Adam,
Deal, Henry,
Deal, John, died of wounds received at Hatcher's Run, Virginia, February 5, 1865,
Eberhart, Abraham,
Eberhart, James,
Eisenhaur, Isaac,
Erdey, Simon,
Fees, Henry A., killed at Gettysburg, July 1, 1863.
Fillman, Jacob,
Foust, Simon E.,
Fox, John F.,
Garrett, Edward,
Grove, Peter,
Gutelius, Fisher,
Gutelius, Charles H.,
Hafer, John,
Hassenplug, S. F.,
Hauck, Ammon L.,
Hoffmaster, B.,
Hottenstein, D. R.,

ANNALS OF BUFFALO VALLEY. 591

Hursh, William,
Kaler, John,
Keifer, Henry M.,
Knittle, James,
Lashells, Wilson,
Linn, Isaac,
Linn, Abraham, died at Washington, D. C., November 10, 1862,
Lucas, James, killed at Wilderness, Virginia, May 7, 1864,
McFadden, E. A., killed at Gettysburg, Pennsylvania, July 1, 1863,
Mader, Charles E.,
Malehom, Simon,
Master, Henry,
May, John, killed at Gettysburg, July, 1, 1863,
Miller, William R., killed at Gettysburg, July 1, 1863,
Nagle, Samuel,
Neese, Jacob,
Oberdorf, George F.,
Paige, David,
Paul, Samuel W.,
Pick, Nathan,
Putzman, Jacob D.,
Reedy, Joel,
Sarba, John,
Seamen, Jonathan,
Sedam, John, died at Richmond, Virginia, January 2, 1864.
Shaffer, Edwin, died at Elmira, New York, March, 22, 1865.
Shell, Jacob,
Smith, Hiram,
Stahl, Peter S.,
Stahle, William,
Stitzer, William,
Stoutz, Milton J.,
Trout Frank F.,
Wirth, Calvin,
Wittenmyer, Henry,
Weiser, George W.,
Wolfe John,
Zellers, Isaac.

ONE HUNDRED AND EIGHTY-FOURTH REGIMENT.

Lieut. Colonel Charles Kleckner,
George W. Kleckner, Com. Sergt.,
Charles E. Haus, Sec. Lieut. Co. I,
Corporal John L. Strong,
Charles Crotzer.

TWENTY-EIGHTH REGIMENT, EMERGENCY TROOPS.

Field and Staff.

Colonel James Chamberlin,
Lieut. Colonel John McCleery,
Quatermaster Thompson G. Evans,
Surgeon George Lotz,
Quar. Sergeant Samuel H. Orwig,

Company A.

Captain Thomas R. Jones,
First Lieutenant David M. Nesbit,
Second Lieut. Charles S. James,
First Sergeant Owen P. Eaches.
Sergeant Benjamin F. Cox,
" John B. Hutton,
" Ross Ward,
" Robert A. Townsend.
Corporal John G. Blair,
" John Ritner,
" David McDermond,
" Joseph R. Frederick,
" Henry H. Witmer,
" Harrison B. Garner,
" Joseph H. Shepperd,
" Henry C. Wolf.
Musician Frederick E. Bower,
" George D. Kincade,

Privates.

Barnhart, Daniel W.,
Bobb, Peter G.,
Brensinger, George J.,
Bowman, George,
Case, William W.,
Cook, jr., Asher,
Curtis, John W.,
Colvert, Edwin,
Donachy, John A.,
Derr, Frank C.,
Fegley, George,
Gebhart, David,
Gessler, Theodore A. K.,
Giddings, Nathaniel,
Gill, Thomas A.,
Grier, Henry F.,
Hall, George C.,
Hess, Jacob W.,
Hill, Eleazer E.,
Hutson, John S.,
Henderson, Henry J.,
James, Jacob D.,
Johnson, Jesse Z.,
Krape, Antis,
Leas, David P.,
Lotz, Galen H.,

Loomis, Freeman,
Low, Clement B.,
Leinbach, James C.,
Martz, George O.,
Maul, Webster R.,
Mettler, Charles W.,
Munro, Henry C.,
Overholt, John J.,
Phillips, Thomas E.,
Probasco, John B.,
Read, David E.,
Read, Jesse J.,
Read, Oliver J.,
Ranney, Edwin H.,
Runyan, William H.,
Spratt, Orlando W.,
Stephens, Leroy,
Shanafelt, Thomas W.,
Stone, Charles A.,
Schwartz, John J. W.,
Startzle, Franklin P.,
Shaffer, Edward H.,
Straw, Robert C.,
Small, Thomas J.,
Smith, Joseph R.,
Truitt, jr., George W.,
Vanvalzah, Robert,
Winterbottom, William,
Wolf, Jacob C.,
Wolverton, William J.,
Wynn, Isaac C.,
Yeager, Peter.

Company D.

Captain Charles C. Shorkley.
First Lieutenant Josiah Kelly.
Second Lieut. Samuel D. Bates,
First Sergeant Samuel W. Murray.
Sergeant William L. Nesbit,
" Jacob Neyhart,
" Jacob K. Mertz,
" Sylvanus G. Bennett.
Corporal George W. Cornelius,
" Daniel Meyers,
" William T. Leinbach,
" Daniel Brown,
" Thomas Shoemaker,
" George B. Miller,
" William Myers,
" Isaac Wagner.
Musician Edward McGregor.

Privates.

Brooks, David,
Bay, Franklin,
Baus, Samuel,
Balliet, John W.,
Betzer, John H.,
Barton, Bright Henry,
Crites, William K.,
Cornelius, Edward,
Cornelius, Zacheus,
Chappel, Zacheus,
Collins, Peter,
Cowley, William H.,
Dull, George,
Dunkle, Charles C.,
Donachy, William O.,
Donahower, Franklin,
Eyer, John,
Frain, John A.,
Fornwalt, John H.,
Goodman, Abraham H.,
Gussler, Isaiah,
Giffin, Samuel M.,
Heitsman, Henry,
Heitsman, Jacob,
Herr, James E.,
Howard, Thomas,
Howard, John,
Hess, John R.,
Irwin, John F.,
Kelley, James W.,
Loomis, William A.,
Lokas, William,
Lilley, Alfred,
Murphy, Howard W.,
Murty, James,
Munson, Salman D.,
Mowry, Abraham,
Meixell, P.,
Meixell, Ziba,
Mench, John,
McFadden, Theodore,
Penny, Hugh H.,
Paul, George,
Pross, George,
Pierce, Amariah H.,
Reber, Samuel,
Rossell, William R.,
Reber, Edward M.,
Rearick, Oliver P.,
Reed, Howard W.,
Straub, Elisha,
Slifer, Alfred,
Stuck, Samuel,
Slear, Jonathan W.,
Stitzer, John D.,
Solomon, Charles E.,
Winegarden, John A.,
Wetzel, Conrad,
Washeliskei, William H.,
Washeliskei, George,
Williams, Benjamin H.,
Wagner, Joseph H.,
Zechman, George W.,

Company F.

Captain George W. Forrest,
First Lieutenant Andrew H. Dill,
Second Lieutenant James Hayes,
First Sergeant David B. Nesbit,

ANNALS OF BUFFALO VALLEY. 593

Sergeant William Ginter,
" Lorenzo D. Brewer,
" Adolphus A. Kaufman,
" William H. Nesbit.
Corporal J. Henry Brown,
" John W. Brown,
" Richard Dye,
" Theodore Taylor,
" Joseph M. Housel,
" Samuel F. Gundy,
" Thomas Ritner,
" Edward H. Richards.
Musician James Forrest,
" Jacob H. Worth.

Privates.

Baldwin, Absalom,
Beck, Samuel,
Bell, Allen,
Bently, Frank,
Bower, William D.,
Brown, William F.,
Cathcart, Robert M.,
Derr, George P.,
Dotts, David H.,
Dill, M. Reese,

Dolby, Abraham,
Donachy, Thompson,
Hughes, George,
Imhoff, William H.,
Kennedy, William,
Long, Jacob,
Loudenslager, William,
Marsh, Charles,
Miller, J. Howard,
Murphy, Joseph,
Nesbit, Alvin,
Pardoe, Samuel I.,
Paul, Peter G.,
Poeth, George M.,
Rank, Lemuel,
Reese, John S.,
Simonton, John W.,
Smithers, Benjamin F.,
Smith, Jacob M.,
Search, William,
Stoughton, Frank,
Vincent, John,
Walker Edward,
Wertz, C. C.,
Wallace, John D.,
Zentmeyer, Peter.

TWO HUNDRED AND SECOND REGIMENT.

Lieutenant Colonel John A. Maus,
Surgeon S. Carson McCormick.

Company I.

Captain Jacob Neyhart,
First Lieutenant Jacob H. Brown,
Sec. Lieut. George Y. McLaughlin,
First Sergeant John B. Ritner,
Sergeant William P. Allen,
" James P. Gundy,
" Samuel S. Rank,
" George H. Gressinger.
Corporal Enos Zentmeyer,
" Joseph C. Dull,
" John W. Brown,
" Samuel S. Hess,
" George Himmerdinger,
" Henry S. Dewey,
" John M. Brown,
" Zacheus Cornelius.
Musician Cameron McGregor.

Privates.

Becher, Amos G.,
Becher, William,
Bently, John,
Bogart, Hosea,
Bogart, Joseph,
Bower, Francis,
Brintzehoff, C. W.,
Brobst, John,

Brown, William W.,
Chappel, Sheller,
Chappel, Charles,
Chappel, Charles W.,
Cleaver, Jesse,
Cornelius, Jesse M.,
Cornelius, Andrew M.,
Dennis, Levi,
Dickey, Lester P.,
Diffenderfer, D. A.,
Elce, Jonathan F.,
Ellis, James S.,
Engle, Jacob,
Engleman, Elias,
Eveland, James,
Everet, John,
Fahnestock, H. M.,
Fesler, John H.,
Fetter, Cyrus,
Fisher, Jared,
Fisher, John H.,
Fisher, Paul,
Flick, Charles W.,
Gebhart, Henry G.,
Good, Hiram,
Gossness, Joseph W.,
Ginter, William,
Gussler, Isaiah,
Hann, James R.,
Hann, David,
Hawkenberry, J. D.,

38

Haynes, John,
Heister, Jacob,
Hess, Joseph,
Hester, Henry,
Hooveman, James,
Huff, Daniel,
Huff, James,
Huff, John S.,
Huff, David,
Hummel, Benjamin,
Hummel, Frederick,
Irwin, Henry,
Jamison, senior, John,
Jamison, Augustus B.,
Keener, John,
Keyser, Jacob,
Kint, George W.,
Kupp, John S.,
Landaw, William,
Leonard, William,
Leonard, Benjamin,
Long, Peter,
Lynn, Charles,
Mathias, John A.,
Miller, Joseph P.,
Mowrer, Michael S.,
Nagle, Andrew,
Newman, Daniel,
Pierce, Amariah H.,
Platner, Lemuel J.,
Powers, Edward,
Rank, Martin J.,
Rank, David,
Rahrer, John,
Reichley, Benjamin F.,
Reichley, William A.,
Reitmeyer, George E.,
Reitmeyer, D. K.,
Rohrabach, James,
Sanders, Hiram,
Sanders, Charles,
Sanders, Henry W.,
Sanders, George L.,
Search, John B.,
Shannon, James,
Shannon, William,
Slear, David G.,
Smith, Jeremiah,
Speece, David,
Swartz, John,
Taylor, Henry O.,
Trester, Martin,
Wagner, Jesse H.,
Wertz, Henry,
Williams, George,
Young, Abraham,
Young, James A.

LIST OF SOLDIERS BURIED IN THE SEVERAL CEMETERIES IN UNION COUNTY.

Mifflinburg.—Presbyterian Cemetery.

Clapham, Thomas H.,
Rissel, David H.

Old Grave-yard.

Edleman, Elias,
Mattis, Henry,
Musser, Robert,
Oberdorf, George,
Schreck, Jacob.

New Cemetery.

Durst, John H.,
Forster, Wilson,
Montelius, W. P.,
Orwig, Benjamin M.,
Reish, Daniel K.,
Smith, Levi H.,
Smith, Hiram,
Steadman, Dr. H. C.

White Deer Church Cemetery.

Deibert, John P., Co. E, 142d,
Dersham, John S., Co. A, 199th,
Follmer, William, H., Co. E, 142d.

Buffalo Cross-Roads.

Lashells, George W., Co. A, 131st,
McGee, Isaac G., Co. E, 51st.

Union Church Cemetery.

Fetter, Jacob, Co. D, 52d,
Moyer, John W., 142d,
Richard, Edward A., Co. K, 51st.

Dreisbach Church.

Bowersox, Henry, 51st,
Dunkle, James M., Co. E, 51st,
Eachus, John F.,
Wolfe, William H., Co. E, 142d.

Lewisburg Cemetery.

Arey, William R., Orderly Sergt., Co. F, 24th U. S. C. T. Died February 19, 1871.
Arey, Milton, Co. A, 43d U. S. C. T. Died October 14, 1867.
Bennett, William A., Hospital Steward, 14th U. S. Infantry. Died November 28, 1869.
Brooks, John, Co. F, 49th Pa.
Cameron, James, Col. 79th N. Y. Highlanders. Killed in battle of Bull Run, July 21, 1861.
Chappel, Zachary, Co. B, 5th Pa. Res. Cor. Died April 6, 1865.
Cornelius, Jackson, Co. D, 52d Pa. Died June 5, 1867.

ANNALS OF BUFFALO VALLEY.

Cox, William Franklin, Sergt., Bat. K, 2d Pa. Heavy Art. Died July 9, 1866, from disease contracted while a prisoner at Andersonville, Georgia.
Dewire, Alexander, Co. E, 51st.
Derr, John H., Co. G, 4th Pa. Vol. Died August 15, 1861, from disease contracted while in service.
Dickey, Lester P., Co. I, 202d Pa. Vol. Died August 29, 1870.
Dodge, Edward R., Surgeon, U. S. Navy. Promoted Surgeon, December 21, 1869. Died March 29, 1871.
Eccleston, Charles, First Lieutenant, Heavy Artillery.
Evans, Charles R., Captain, Co. E, 142d Pa. Vol. Died September 23, 1867.
Graham, Henry Spyker, Sergeant, Co. F, 2d Pa. Cav. Died August 28, 1868.
Gussler, John A., Co. C, 161st N. Y. Vol. Died July 27, 1871.
Ireland, John W., Co. D, 5th Pa. Res. Cor. Died October 18, 1862.
Kennedy, William M., Co. E, 208th Pa. Vol. Died at City Point, Va., April 15, 1865, from wounds received before Petersburg, Virginia, April 2, 1865.
Knox, John H., Captain, Co. D, 11th Pa. Vol. Died at Jersey Shore, Pa., February 28, 1862.
Lenhart, Henry, Co. D, 52d Pa. Vol. Died November 28, 1864.
Lenhart, Benjamin, Co. I, 202d.
McBride, James, Sergeant, Co. D, 52d Pa. Vol. Died at Washington, December 1, 1861.
McFadden, Theodore H., First Lieut. Co. D, 5th Pa. Res. Cor. Wounded in battle of New Market Cross-Roads, June 30, 1862. Died January 29, 1870.
McGregor, Charles, Musician, Co. D, 51st Pa. Vol. Died March 4, 1866.
Milsom, John, Sergeant, Co. E., 53d Pa. Vol. Died at Annapolis, Md., December 30, 1864.
Murphy, Edward H., with construction train, 5th N. Y. Vol. Died February 9, 1870.
Penny, Charles A., Corporal, Co. D, 52d Pa. Vol. Died at Craney Island, Va., September 25, 1862.
Phillips, William L., Lieutenant, Co. D, 52d Pa. Vol. Died at Chambersburg, Pa., January 5, 1872.
Rohrabach, James H., Co. H, 131st.

Schaffle, Joseph J., Co. H, 90th Pa. Vol. Died at Washington, D. C., January 12, 1863, from a wound received in battle of Fredericksburg, Va., December 13, 1862.
Schaffle, F. S., Co. E, 51st.
Stapleton, George, Co. E, 142d Pa. Vol. Died July 26, 1863, from a wound received at Gettysburg July 1, 1863.
Stoughton, Roland, Captain, Co. D. 150th Pa. Vol. Died May 24, 1864.
Tucker, Andrew G., First Lieut. Co. E, 142d Pa. Vol. Killed in battle at Gettysburg, July 1, 1863.
Van Gezer, George, Co. H, 51st Pa. Vol. Died November 16, 1870.
Wertz, John H., Co. G, 4th Pa. Vol. Died May 28, 1862.
Wetzel, Conrad. Died October 20, 1866, from disease contracted while in service.
Wilkes, Noall, Co. D, 5th Pa. Res. Cor. Died September 7, 1861.
Young, Peter, Co. I, 192d Pa. Vol. Died January 6, 1869.
Zimmerman, William, Co. E, 51st Pa. Vol. Died August 3, 1866.

Buried at Various Places.

Ammon, Levi H., Corporal, Co. E, 51st Pa. Vol. Killed in Wilderness battle, May 6, 1864.
Arey, Barton, Co. A, 43d U. S. C. T. Wounded before Petersburg, Va., and taken to hospital at David's Island, where he died and was buried.
Baldwin, Absalom, Co. K, 51st Pa. Vol. Captured and died at Andersonville, Ga., September 24, 1864.
Beaver, J. Gilbert, First Lieut., Co. H, 51st Pa. Vol. Buried at Millerstown, Pa.
Dentler, Henry G., Corporal, Co. K, 51st Pa. Vol. Captured and died at Andersonville, Ga., May 17, 1864—grave 1,161.
Donachy, William, Corporal, Co. D, 150th Pa. Vol. Killed in battle at Laurel Hill, Va., May 8, 1864.
Dull, George N., Co. K, 51st Pa. Vol. Died from disease, at Alexandria, Va., September 19, 1864. Buried there—grave 2,683.
Evans, Edwin A., Captain, Battery D, 3d Pa. Heavy Art. Died, in Philadelphia, April 30, 1872. Buried at New Britain, Bucks Co., Pa.

Fichthorn, James, Sergeant, Co. D, 5th Pa. Res. Cor. Mustered June 5, 1861. Died between the 11th and 16th of February, 1865, at Salisbury, North Carolina.
Gallagher, Henry, Musician, Co. D, 52d Pa. Vol. Died at White House, Va., June 15, 1862.
Gibson, James, Sergeant, Co. K, 51st. Killed in front of Petersburg, Va., July 30, 1864.
Green, William Cameron, private, Co. D, Fifth Pa. Res. Cor. Promoted Second Lieutenant in First United States Infantry, September 27, 1861. Afterward promoted to Captain in First United States Infantry. Died on board ship, October 3, 1867.
Grier, Thomas G., Co. H, 51st Pa. Vol. Died with yellow fever, at Morehead City, N. C., October 6, 1864. Buried there.
Kelly, James A., Co. H, 51st Pa. Vol. Died at Roanoke Island, N. C., March 27, 1862.
Ludwig, Jared R., Co. K, 51st Pa. Vol. Absent at muster out; supposed to have been killed in battle or captured and died while a prisoner.
McFadden, Edward A., Co. D, 150th Pa. Vol. Killed at Gettysburg, Pa., July 1, 1863.
Mensch, John, Co. F, 49th Pa. Vol. Killed at Spottsylvania Court-House, Va., May 10, 1864.
Miller, Samuel E., Co. I, 1st Pa. Killed in battle at Fredericksburg, Va., December 13, 1862.

Musser, John D., Lieutenant Colonel. Mustered as Major of 143d Pa. Vol., October 18, 1862. Promoted to Lieutenant Colonel June 2, 1863. Killed in battle of Wilderness, May 6, 1864. Buried at Muncy, Pa.
Piper, William, Co. H, 56th Pa. Vol. Killed in battle of Spottsylvania, Va., May —, 1864.
Potter, Thomas, Corporal, Battery A, 1st Pa. Art. Killed in battle at Fredericksburg, Va., Dec. 13, 1862.
Reed, Daniel M., Corporal, Co. G, 50th Pa. Vol. Killed at Chantilly, Va., September 1, 1862.
Schaffle, Charles D., Captain, Co. D, 5th Pa. Res. Cor. Wounded and taken prisoner in battle of Fredericksburg, Va., December 13, 1862, and died in Richmond, Va., January 31, 1863.
Sedam, John, Co. D, 150th Pa. Vol. Taken prisoner, and died at Richmond, Va., January 2, 1864.
Smaltzried, Gotlieb, Corporal, Co. D, 52d Pa. Died at Morris Island, S. C., September 6, 1863.
Sterner, Frank B., Captain, Co. K, 51st. Killed at Spottsylvania Court-House, Va., May 12, 1864.
Weidensaul, Elias B., Second Lieutenant, Co. D, 150th Pa. Vol. Killed in battle of Gettysburg, Pa., July 1, 1863.
Wertz, Harrison, Co. D. 5th Pa. Res. Cor. Killed in battle of Fredericksburg, Va., December 13, 1862.
Wilson, Robert M., Died August 19, 1867. Buried at Norfolk, Va.

MILITARY RECORD, 1861-65.

ADDENDA.

COMPANY D, FIFTH RESERVES.

Captains.

Thomas Chamberlin, wounded June 3, 1862. Promoted Major of One Hundred and Fiftieth.
W. H. H. McCall,
Charles D. Schaffle.

First Lieutenants.

Jonathan E. Wolfe,
Theodore H. McFadden,
Thomas B. Reed.

Sergeants.

George C. Kelly,
William Searles,
James Doran,
Richard H. Walk,
William W. Schwenk,
James Fichthorn,
James M. Essington,
George M. Slifer,
H. J. Schofield, died November 9, 1861,
John C. McMichael, killed December 13, 1862.

Corporals.

Amos Ditsworth,
John B. Haper,
George W. Schoch,
George Eicholtz,
John Babb,
Jacob K. Mertz,
George Harbeson,
Jacob Reese,
Effinger L. Reber,
Jacob Campbell, killed June 30, 1862,
William Haskins, killed December 13, 1862,
Jacob M. Barnhart.

Musicians.

James Barnhart,
John Clymer.

Privates.

Beckly, William,
Bonnell, John,
Boylan, Michael B.,
Barnhart, Joseph,
Bennett, Sylvester,
Crawford, Thomas,
Canfield, David,
Covert, Daniel,
Connell, John,
Dougherty, John,
Ennis, John F., killed April 29, 1864,
Fravel, William,
Fry, Benjamin,
Gaskill, Thomas,
Gilbert, Daniel,
Green, William C.,
Gilman, Albert,
Hartman, John,
Huth, Nathaniel,
Harper, Isaac,
Irwine, George,
Jerns, Lewis,
Joll, Joseph
Johnson, Albert E.,
Johnson, William,
Kennedy, Thomas,
Knoll, John,
Kyle, John, killed June 27, 1862,
Kessler, John, killed June 30, 1862,
Landis, Harry L.,
Moody, Charles,
Monroe, Lawrence,
Markel, Levi,
Morrison, James A.,
Moyer, Charles,

Meteer, William,
Myers, William, killed May 9, 1864,
Peeling, Charles,
Price, John D.;
Page, Elias,
Reed, Samuel A.,
Reeder, Charles W.,
Reber, John M.,
Ripple, John,
Recker, Darius L., killed June 30, 1862,
Roberts, John E., killed June 30, 1862.
Roberts, Patrick,
Reed, John,
Snyder, Charles E.,
Stroup, Joseph,
Smith, William H.,
Smith, Levi,
Smith, Peter,
Strahan, Harrison,
Saylor, George B.,
Showers, William H.,
Sticker, Andrew H., killed May 9, 1864,
Taylor, Thomas, died May 13, 1864,
Theis, Henry,
Ulrich, Henry,
Walsh, Robert,
Wheeler, Luther,
Wertz, Isaac,
Wertz, Jackson,
Wertz, Harrison, killed December 13, 1862,
Washburn, Charles,
Woodward, York A.,
Wilson, Thomas F.,
Wilkes, Newell, died September 17, 1861,
Welsh, John, died April 13, 1862,
Woodward, O, B., died December 6, 1862,
Whatmore, William.

COMPANY B, FIFTH RESERVES.

Chappell, Zachariah,
Hawk, David,

McFall, James,
McPherson, Milton.

COMPANY C, FIFTH RESERVES.

Potter, John E.,

Potter, Thos. L.

COMPANY B, SIXTH RESERVES.

Captains.
Charles D. Roush,
Levi Epler.

First Lieutenant.
William Harding.

Second Lieutenant.
E. D. Lebkicker.

Sergeants.
John Emmett,
Robert P. Calvert, died at Andersonville, May 11, 1864,
Charles S. Swineford,
James H. Bowman,
Charles S. Bowman,
Henry L. Stock.

Corporals.
George Everett,
Henry H. Bowen,
Isaac Fink,
Michael Cantwell, died at Andersonville, July 28, 1864.
Benjamin T. Parks,
John Zergey,

Samuel Ritter,
Nevin P. Gutelius,
Henry B. Mowry, mortally wounded at South Mountain,
Thomas Robinson, killed June 27, 1862.

Musician.
Daniel P. Rumberger.

Privates.
Auckey, James,
Arnold, James,
Arnold, John,
Botdorf Reuben,
Bowersox, David,
Bender Solomon,
Bobb, William, died August 8, 1861,
Boran, Jacob F., killed September 14, 1862,
Charles, William F.,
Campbell, Peter,
Campbell, Abraham,
Campbell, Adam,
Chubb, Stephen, killed May 8, 1864,
Duck, Wilson,
Decker, Isaac,

Doney, John,
Daisey, Martin, killed December 13, 1862,
Eckert, Peter, killed December 13, 1862,
Emig, George,
Finicle, Edwin W.,
Fink, Henry,
Feeney, Patrick,
Gutsleber, Adam,
Gray, Michael, died at Andersonville,
Gregory, Cyrus,
Gundrum, Samuel,
Grow, Daniel,
Haas, Levi,
Haines, George,
Hammond, Thomas,
Keeler Nathaniel,
Keifer, Martin L.,
Kohler, John, killed September 17, 1862,
Long, Samuel,
Loy, John,
Leister, Franklin,
Miller Charles,
Mooney, Jacob E., prisoner,
Mowry, David C., prisoner,
Mackey, Clinton,
McCormick, John, prisoner,
Norwood, Joseph,
Neitz, Emanuel,
Oswald, William,
Pepper, Michael,
Parker, David,
Peifer, William H.,
Portzline, Henry,
Rupp, John C.,
Ressler, Levi C.,
Reif, Franklin
Rorick, John F.
Reigle, John,
Rogers, Samuel
Rathfon, Wilson,
Rathfon, Thomas,
Reichenbach, Joel,
Smith, John,
Seesholtz, Samuel,
Salada, Cyrus,
Sampsel. John,
Seiler, William,
Snyder, John N.,
Sterick, Theodore S. F.,
Smith, Nicholas,
Shaffer, Joel,
Seachrist, John H.,
Shultzbach, Henry,
Stahl, William,
Swartz, Nathaniel, died August 10, 1861,
Spotts, Samuel, drowned July 7, 1862,
Stever, John, killed August 30, 1862,
Shell, David, died October 1, 1862,
Troup, Simon, killed September 14, 1862,
Trego, John, died October 3, 1862,
Walt, William,
Wilmore, Rudy,
Weirick, Emanuel,
Zortman, John F.,
Zimmerman, Samuel, died September 14, 1861,
Zechmen, Jacob F., died September 16, 1862.

COMPANY H, SEVENTY-SIXTH REGIMENT.

D. B. MacGreggor, James H. Pross.

COMPANY C, ONE HUNDRED AND FIRST REGIMENT.

March 18, 1865—June 25, 1865.

Captain.
William Fichthorn.

First Lieutenant.
Samuel B. Reber.

Second Lieutenant.
Hubley D. Albright.

Sergeants.
Frank C. Stoughton,
John D. L. Bear,
Jacob L. Worley,

David G. Alter,
Christian H. Kerr.

Corporals.
William H. Cawley,
William H. McCabe,
Jacob Sheaffer,
David M. Suloff,
David James,
Edward Stevens,
Jacob Machamer,
Jonathan Miller.

Musicians.

Elias Yiesley,
Benjamin O. Rudy.

Privates.

Acker, Moses,
Arnold, Enoch,
Barkey, Isaiah,
Boyle, John,
Brackbill, Thomas,
Cassalt David A.,
Childs, David,
Chalfant, Brantley,
Chronister Adam,
Chronister, Amon,
Derr, George P.,
Derr, Henry C.,
Day, George,
Dewire Thomas,
Dewire William,
Erb Peter,
Fockler, Jacob L.,
Furman, Moses R.,
Getz, Adam,
Goodman, George F.,
Gougler, Frederick,
Gibbony, William S.,
Group, William M.
Group, Howard W.,
Gardner, John A.,
Geistwite, Joseph,
Hosler, John,
Henck, Thomas J.,
Hertzler, Ephram,
Harris, Mark H.,
Heffner, Samuel,
Hoffman, John C.,
Hollinger, George,
Hildebrand, James A.,
Henck, Cyrus M.,
Jacobs, Obediah,
Jenkins, Hiram,
Koons, Lehman L.,
Klingman, William,
Logan, John E.,
Long, Joseph E.,
Mack, Edward,
Mauck, John E.,
Martz, Peter A.,
Maister, John,
Myers, Washington S.,
Myers, Peter H.,
Miller, Howard,
Makin, William,
Mussina, H. B.,
McMeen, Hugh,
McElwee, John A.,
McGhee, Charles,
McKillip, Charles A.,
Nesbit, Alvin,
Peters, Amos,
Robinson, George W.,
Raum, John C.,
Rudy, Jacob,
Renner, Elias,
Simmers, Isaac,
Sechler, John C.
Swartz, Jacob,
Stuart, Robert M.,
Spealman, Frank,
Slaybaugh, Isaac,
Snyder, Howard,
Stitzel, Jacob,
Thompson, Charles M.,
Tayler, Samuel,
Troup, Sylvester S.,
Trimmer, Gibson,
Trimmer, John H.,
Vanada, Solomon,
Wilson, James,
Whitmer, Amos,
Wilkerson, William,
Wright, Morgan,
Wolf, Samuel,
Yeager, George,
Ziegler, Elijah R.,

INDEX.

Abolition lecture, ... 527
Aborigines of the Valley, ... 6
Academy, Lewisburg, ... 546
    " building of University, ground broken for, ... 548
Accidents, ... 439,492,496,512,514,525,526
Adams, Reverend John Dietrich, ... 369
Agricultural, Union, association formed, ... 501
    " fairs, ... 501,555
    " society, Union county, ... 528,554
    " " " " awards of committees, ... 528
Albright, Honorable Andrew, sketch of, ... 457
Allen family murdered, ... 188
Allison, Archibald, narrative of, ... 173
Allummapees, King of the Delawares, ... 20
Anti-Mason ticket formed, ... 501
Anthony, Joseph B., holds court at Sunbury, ... 543
Armstrong, Colonel John, surveys of, ... 9,19
Associators, list of companies of, ... 90
    " officers chosen, ... 90,119
    " brigadier general elected, ... 99
Associate Reformed Church, ... 448
Attorneys admitted, ... 42,
             44,89,151,235,241,418,495,501,513,524,534,540,542,546
    " list of 494
Aurand, Reverend John Dietrich, ... 152,199,284
Aurand's hotel burned, ... 533
Ayers killed, ... 157
Bacon, Elijah, visits Valley, ... 460,495
Bald Eagle creek declared a highway, ... 36
Banks, act regulating, passed, ... 417
    " suspended, ... 442,534
    " card of directors of Northumberland, ... 534
Baptist settlers, ... 283
Bar, peculiarities of the 481
Barber, Robert, builds at White Spring, ... 48,269
Barnes, Reverend W. H. H., ... 544
Barton, Kimber, ... 325
Bashor, John Michael, killed, ... 157
Baskins, Honorable John, resigns and removes, ... 540
Battalion drill at Lewisburg, ... 550
Baum, Samuel R., appointed postmaster, ... 552
Bear's mills erected, ... 232
Beaver run, ... 7
    " township, residents of, ... 258,270,284,319

Bellas, Esquire, Hugh,	365
Berlin iron-works, first metal made at,	545
" " " blown out,	549
Bickle, Henry, killed,	201
Billman, Dewalt, notice of,	450
Billmyer, Andrew, tavern of,	243,252
Bingaman, Frederick, death of,	545
Black Ann, whipped,	194
Blythe, William, notice of,	25
Boatman, Mrs. Claudius, killed,	211
Boat-yard removed to Lewisburg,	551
Boone, Captain Hawkins,	52,107,123,166,178
Boude family, notice of,	258
Bower, George, notice of,	450
Boy killed near Gundy's mill,	213
Boyd family, notice of,	143
Boyer, Jacob K., convicted,	497
Brady, Captain John,	98,143,165,166
" " " killed,	168,220,225
" James, killed,	164,225
" Mrs. Mary, death of,	219
" family reminiscences of,	219
" Captain Samuel,	81,143,219
" " " kills Bald Eagle,	175
" " " adventures of,	227
" " " death of,	230
" General Hugh,	219
" John, (sheriff,)	226
" Lieutenant Samuel, at Chippewa,	419
" " " letter to Captain Vincent,	419
Brandywine, battle of,	143
Bridge, Northumberland built,	406,438
" " carried away,	546
" Lewisburg chartered,	417
" " supplement to charter,	433
" " built,	438
" Limestone run, carried away,	437
" Harrisburg,	438
" " portion of, carried away,	546
" at mouth of Buffalo creek built,	378
" " " " " " carried away,	548
" new " " " "	552
" Milton, injured by flood,	546
" at Duncan's Island, carried away,	546
Brinton, Joseph, notice of,	449
Brobst, Jacob,	435
Bockenor, Isaac, accident to,	496
Brodhead's regiment, Eighth Pennsylvania, two soldiers of, killed,	163
Brown, Jonathan,	449
" Eleanor,	246
" Matthew, death of,	142
" Michael, recollections of the people of the Valley,	341
Buchanan, Honorable James, speaks at Milton,	544
Buffalo creek,	7
" " bridge built at mouth of,	378
Buffalo township erected,	42
" " attempt to divide,	151
" " residents of,	50, 67,148,181,194,214,236,242,244,252,258,263,269
Buffalo Cross-Roads church,	51,60,270,433,524
" " " first hotel at,	318

ANNALS OF BUFFALO VALLEY.

Buffalo, East and West, townships erected, ... 274
" East, residents of, ... 278,
     283,294,317,323,326,332,337,340,353,355,370,379,386
Buffalo, West, improvements, &c., ... 279
" " stills in, ... 280
" " residents of, ... 280,
     282,294,301,317,333,337,340,354,355,370,379,387
Caderman, Jacob and Conrad, captured, ... 199
California gold fever reaches Valley, ... 549
" emigration to, ... 549
Canal meeting 491
" located, ... 495
" let, ... 496
" Lewisburg cross-cut, ... 496,503
" " " " first boats through, ... 512
" rates of freight on, ... 503
Camp Potter organized, ... 544
Camp-meeting, first Methodist, ... 354
" " 544
Campbell, Captain, killed, ... 199
" Daniel, notice of, ... 281
" McDonald, notice of, ... 450
" John, " " 450
Campleton, Captain Thomas, (Keraplin,) 165,174,179
" " " killed, ... 198
Carner, Anthony, notice of, ... 450
Celebration, Fourth of July, ... 488,504,505,524,544
" " " toasts at, ... 526
" " " partisan toasts at, ... 524
" " " accidents at, ... 526
Cemetery at Lewisburg, ... 549
Census 1820, ... 449
" 1830, ... 502
" 1840, ... 537
" 1850, ... 552
" 1860, ... 557
" 1870, ... 557
Chamberlin, Colonel William, notice of, ... 440
Chambers, James, killed, ... 185
Chapman, Seth, acquitted, ... 487
Chappel Hollow, *alias* Haverly's Gap, ... 75
Chestnut Ridge, post office established at, ... 552
Chilloway, Job, ... 141
Chippewa, battle of, ... 419
Churches, notices of, ... 93,253,448
Church, Buffalo Cross-Roads Presbyterian, ... 51,60,231,250,270
" " " " new built 433
" " " " last sermon in 546
" Methodist, organized at Lewisburg, ... 406
" " new, at Lewisburg consecrated, ... 511
" First Pastor German Reformed, ... 259
" Baptist, effort to establish, ... 283
" Dreisbach, condition of, ... 327
" St. Peter's, in Kelly, built, ... 333,430
" Ray's, built, ... 333
" first Baptist, organized, ... 371
" " " pastors of, ... 371
" Baptist, at Lewisburg, ... 543,545
" " first sermon in new, ... 546
" Emanuel's, at New Berlin, dedicated, ... 481
" Associate Reformed, of Mifflinburg, organized 448

Church, Methodist, at New Berlin, dedicated, ... 437
"   Christian Chapel at Lewisburg built, ... 441,555
"   "   "   "   opened, ... 460
"   Bethel, organized, ... 504
"   Presbyterian, at Lewisburg, built, ... 505
"   "   "   first sermon in, ... 511
"   Laurelton, organized, ... 506
"   Union, German Reformed and Lutheran, subscription for
           starting, ... 512
"   Union, German Reformed and Lutheran, dedicated, ... 524
"   Laurel run, dedicated, ... 540
"   German Reformed, Pastor of, installed, ... 540
"   Lutheran, at Selinsgrove, ... 543
"   "   and Reformed, in Buffalo township, dedicated, . . 534
"   Presbyterian, at New Berlin, ... 538,543
"   German Reformed, in Lewisburg, corner stone of, laid, . . . 547
"   "   "   "   dedicated, ... 548
"   "   "   "   pastor of, ... 551
Clark, Esquire, John, visits Lewisburg, ... 512
Clark, George, surveyor, ... 122
Clark, Walter, &c., moves to Valley, ... 39
Clarke, Captain John, roll of his company, ... 121
Clay, Henry, card of, in National Intelligencer, ... 472
Clemens, Peter, ... 450
Clingan, William, notice of, ... 457
Coal, bituminous, received, and price of, ... 514
Cochran, James, letter to Robert Irwin, ... 351
Cole, Colonel Philip, ... 51
Cold Friday, ... 526
Columbia Gazette, ... 416
Columbia guards en route to Mexico, flag presentation and return, . 547
Comet visible, ... 398,455,479
Committee of Safety, minutes of, ... 99,127
Committee men, lists of, ... 99,110,131
Condition of the Valley, ... 153
"   "   "   court business, ... 165
Conference, Albright and United Brethren 413
Connecticut claim, ... 45,53,87
Constitution of 1776, synopsis of 94
"   United States, ratified, ... 251
"   1790 adopted, ... 266
Contributions for relief of distressed in Ireland and Scotland, . . . 547
Controversy, railroad, ... 553
Convention, Carpenter's Hall, ... 56
"   1775, ... 65
"   1776, ... 93
"   of associators, ... 99
"   constitutional, delegates to, ... 94,266,527
"   1834, delegates to, ... 519
"   Anti-Masonic, ... 519
"   Democratic, ... 521,540
"   temperance, at Lewisburg, ... 539
"   Whig, ... 540
"   railroad, at Baltimore, ... 553
Cook, John, notice of, ... 451
Cooke, Colonel William, roster of regiment, ... 124,243
Cooper, Honorable Thomas, ... 324,435
Cornelius, Jesse, accident to, ... 512
Corruption story, Adams and Clay, ... 478
Coryell, George, ... 451
Counterfeiters convicted, ... 497

ANNALS OF BUFFALO VALLEY.

County lines,	448,505,511
" seat,	18
" division of, agitated,	405
" Union, erected,	412
" seat, vote for and against,	556
" division of, vote for and against,	556
Couples, David, killed,	184
Court crier appointed,	448
" business condition of,	165
" to be held at New Berlin,	429
" first circuit, at New Berlin,	492
" " in Northumberland county,	42
" " suits in,	44
" " at Mifflinburg,	418
" Supreme, middle district of, created,	356
" " *personnel* of justices of,	498
" " justices opinion of Joseph Ritner,	498
Covenhoven, Robert, describes the Great Runaway,	156
" " " also that of 1779,	176
Crawford county system introduced,	554
Creeks, early names of	7
Crooked Billet, Abraham Smith's story,	152
Crotzerville post office established,	552
Crotzer, Henry W., appointed postmaster,	555
Dam built on Penn's creek,	275
" at Selin and Snyder's mill,	275
Dancing party at New Berlin,	463
Daguerreotypes first in the Valley,	546
Day's Collections quoted,	143,193

Deaths—

Adams, James,	354	Brady, James,	164
Albright, Jacob,	400	Brady, Captain John,	169
Albright, Andrew,	457	Brady, John,	374
Allen, Samuel,	179	Brown, Mathew,	142
Allison, Archibald,	174	Brown, Eleanor,	142
Alsbaugh, Margaret,	344	Brunner, Jacob,	345
Antes, Colonel Frederick,	330	Bull, Mrs. Mary,	400
Aurand, Jacob,	256	Burns, Peter,	267
Aurand, John,	367	Buttorf, Michael,	345
Aurand, junior, John,	374	Buyers, Captain William F.,	456
Baldy, Susanna,	374	Cameron, Charles,	428
Baker, Wendell,	428	Campbell, Michael,	154
Baker, John,	456	Campbell, Daniel,	281
Barber Samuel,	276	Chambers, James,	185
Barber, Thomas,	188	Chambers, Mary,	311
Barber, Sarah,	442	Chamberlin, Colonel William,	440
Barnhart, George,	281	Christ, Adam,	374
Barnhart, Mathias,	293	Clark, Robert,	313
Bashor, John Michael,	156	Clark, William,	416
Beatty, Alexander,	243	Clarke, Florence,	368
Bickel, Henry,	201	Clarke, Colonel John,	385
Bingaman, Frederick,	545	Clemens, Elizabeth,	450
Bishop, John,	417	Clingan, William,	457
Black, John,	266	Collins, Paul,	428
Boal, John,	443	Cornelius, Jesse,	512
Bockener, Isaac,	496	Cooke, Colonel William,	344
Bolender, Henry,	296	Cook, John,	452
Bower, Casper,	293	Couples, David,	184
Bower, Peter,	436	Cramer, George,	400
Boone, Captain,	177	Dale, Honorable Samuel,	344
Boveard, James,	374	Darraugh, Widow,	512

ANNALS OF BUFFALO VALLEY.

Deaths—

Daugherty, Captain,	177
Deal, Henry,	417
Dempsey, Cornelius,	244
Derr, Catherine,	243
Derr, John,	547
Douglass, William,	401
Dow, Lorenzo,	314
Dreisbach, Anna Eve,	260
Dreisbach, Martin,	320
Dreisbach, Jacob,	345
Dreisbach, Catherine,	430
Dunkle, Catherine,	353
Dunkle, Killian,	436
Dunning, Samuel,	374
Earne, Elizabeth,	374
Egbert, Nicholas,	417
Ellenkhusen, Mathias Joseph,	277
Emerick, David,	201
Etzweiler, George,	185
Evans, Nathan,	391
Evans, Joseph,	400
Evans, Evan Rice,	400
Evans, Joseph, (Lewisburg,)	514
Ewing, Jasper,	326
Eyer, Catherine,	353
Ferguson, James,	281
Fisher John,	293
Fleming, James,	277
Follmer, Thomas,	546
Follmer, Henry,	546
Forster, junior, John,	239
Forster, Thomas,	344
Forster, Thomas,	390
Forster, Captain John,	243
Foster, John,	234
Fought, Jonas,	267
Foutz, Mrs. Conrad,	494
Fox, Andrew,	293
Franklin, Daniel,	368
Frantz, Lewis,	368
Frederick, George,	335
Frederick, Jabel, (should be Jacob,)	353
Freedly, John,	430
Freeland, Elias,	176
Freeland, junior, Jacob,	176
Freeland, senior, Jacob,	176
Frick, General Henry,	543
Fries, Rev. Just Henry,	534
Gabriel, George,	37
Geary, John,	514
Gebhart, Philip,	436
Getz, Peter,	390
Gift, Jacob,	170
Gray, Lieut. Colonel Neigal,	244
Gray, Captain William,	431
Gray, Sallie, and son,	527
Graybill, John,	354
Green, Margaret,	256
Green, Joseph,	335

Deaths—

Green, Mary,	354
Greenlee, William,	231
Grier, Reverend Isaac,	428
Grogan, Charles,	267
Groninger, Leonard,	256
Gundy, William,	546
Harris, Honorable William L.,	546
Hammond, General R. H.,	548
Haney, Christopher,	266
Hayes, John,	544
Hayes, Mrs.,	513
Hayes, William,	540
Herrold, ———,	170
Hetrick, Christian,	208
Himmelreich, Mary,	457
Himrod, Simon,	235
Hoge, Reverend John,	368
Holstein, George,	400
Hood, Reverend,	549
Hood, Mrs. Mary,	549
Hoover, John,	436
Housel, Martin,	353
Housel, Captain William,	551
Hudson, George,	276
Hunter, Colonel Samuel,	234
Hunter, Alexander,	390
Huston, Matthew,	385
Hutchinson, Mary,	385
Iddings, Eve,	345
Iddings, Henry,	443
Irvine, William,	297
Irwin, Esquire, William,	416
Jenkins, James,	244
Jenkins, James,	339
Jenkins, Phoebe,	335
Jodon, Peter,	353
Jones, Thomas,	512
Jordon, William,	335
Katherman, David,	368
Keene, Lawrence,	260
Kelchner, Jonas,	539
Kelly, Mrs. Sarah,	504
Kelly, Colonel John,	506
Kempling, Captain Thomas,	198
Kerstetter, Sebastian,	251
Kester, George,	297
Klinesmith, Baltzer,	189
Kremer, Honorable George,	555
Laird, Matthew,	256
Langs, George, (suicide,)	386
Lashells, Esquire, John,	547
Lathy, William Kent,	384
Laughlin, Samuel,	185
Laughlin, Esther,	345
Laughlin, Adam,	428
Lee, John, and wife,	210
Lepley, Michael,	170
Lewis, Paschal,	454
Linn, John,	384
Lotz, Ulrich,	266

ANNALS OF BUFFALO VALLEY.

Deaths—

Lowdon, Captain John,	314
Lukens, John, Surveyor Gen.,	262
McBeth, Mrs. Annie,	374
McCandlish, senior, William,	231
McClellan, James,	550
McClenachan, James,	235
McClenachan, David,	261
McClure, Mrs. Jean,	330
McClure, Roan,	512
McClung, John,	251
McCracken, Henry,	193
McCorley, Robert,	281
McCorley, James,	374
McGrady, Alexander,	276
McGuire, Thomas,	62
McKee, Thomas,	50
McKim, William,	368
McKim, Robert,	368
McKnight, ———,	170
McLaughlin, Samuel,	185
McLaughlin, William,	179
McLaughlin, Hugh,	431
Maclay, Esquire, William,	344
Macpherson, Honorable, John	493
Madden, Neal,	374
Marshall, James,	440
Martin, Aaron,	179
Martin, George,	352
Merrill, James,	538
Metzgar, Daniel,	374
Miller, Theobald,	296
Miller, Christian,	314
Moore, John,	514
Morrison, Reverend Hugh,	344
Morton, Japhet,	431
Motz, George,	353
Mumma, John,	491
Murphy, John,	314
Myers, Henry,	390
Myers, David,	511
Nevius, Christian,	431
Newcomer, Bishop,	489
Overmeier, Captain George,	353
Patterson, W. A.,	555
Peters, Henry,	309
Piatt, Abraham,	310
Polhemus, Albert and wife,	157
Pollock, Charles,	296
Pollock, John,	354
Pontius, Henry,	458
Potter, Major General James,	261
Priestly, Doctor Joseph,	343
Ranck, senior, John,	256
Ranck, Adam,	385
Ray, George,	335
Rearick, John,	256
Reasoner, Davy,	408
Reasoner, James,	526
Reedy, Conrad,	385
Rees, Abel,	277

Deaths—

Rees, Daniel,	344
Rees, Daniel,	436
Richard, Henry,	354
Riddle, George,	310
Rodman, William,	209
Rorabaugh, Philip,	453
Rote, George,	311
Rotten, Joseph,	62
Row, George,	193
Sample, John and wife,	170
Sargent, Charles,	514
Sargent, James,	501
Seebold, Christopher,	417
Selin, Captain Anthony,	276
Shedacre Jacob,	163
Shewel, Adam,	353
Shipton, Thomas,	493
Sierer, John,	416
Simpson, John,	345
Smiley, Reverend Thomas,	511
Smith, Peter,	50
Smith, John,	213
Smith, Adam,	261
Smith, Nicholas,	281
Smith, George,	293
Smith, Colonel Matthew,	293
Smith, Anna M.,	297
Smith, Michael,	354
Smith, Esquire, Daniel,	390
Smith, Albright,	390
Smith, Enoch,	439
Snyder, John,	251
Soult, David,	470
Specht, Adam,	470
Spyker, Esquire, Henry,	439
Stanford, Jacob,	153
Steele, William,	354
Storms, David,	208
Strawbridge, Hon. Thomas,	417
Struble, Peter,	549
Struble, Adam,	428
Sutherland, Thomas,	436
Swartz, Peter,	345
Swesey, Daniel,	453
Swineford, John,	352
Swineford, John,	386
Swineford, Jacob,	488
Taggert, Thomas,	293
Tate, Edward,	293
Taveler, Joseph,	310
Templeton, Samuel,	490
Thompson, Captain James,	198
Thompson, John,	330
Thompson, William,	368
Thom, James,	251
Thom, James,	277
Thornburg, John,	296
Trinkle, Mathias,	231
Troxell, George,	266
Turner, John,	428

Deaths—
Ultz, Joseph, ... 374
Van Doren, Thomas, ... 163
Vandyke, Henry, ... 234
Vandyke, Lambert, ... 293
Vanvalzah, Doctor Robert, . 551
Vanvolsen, Levi, child of, . . 281
Vincent, Isaac, ... 176
Wales, John, ... 314
Wales, Mrs. Mary, ... 491
Walker, John, ... 211
Wallis, Joseph J., ... 390
Walter, John, ... 417
Watson, Patrick, ... 188
Watson, David, ... 417
Weeks, Joseph, ... 179
Weirick, John, ... 390
Weirick, Mrs. Elizabeth, . . 435
Weiser, Christopher, ... 442
Weitzell, Esquire, Casper, . . 213

Deaths—
Wertz, Deitrick, ... 345
Weyland, Michael, ... 40
Wierbach, John, ... 267
Wilson, John, ... 48
Wilson, Thomas, ... 320
Wilson, Hugh, (of Buffalo,) . 545
Wilson, Elizabeth, ... 430
Wilson, Honorable Hugh, . . 545
Wilson, William, ... 470
Wilson, Thomas, (Kelly,) . . 504
Wilt, George, ... 367
Wolfe, Jacob, ... 428
Yost, Casper, ... 209
Young, Matthew, ... 251
Young, Adam, ... 367
Young, James, ... 481
Young, John, ... 527
Youngman, Elias, ... 457
Yutten, Jacob, ... 461

Debate at Lewisburg, ... 492,523
Debating societies, ... 491
Deed, copy of Hawkins Boone's, ... 52
De Haven, Peter, letter of, ... 155
Depreciation, examples of, ... 175,184
Derr, Ludwig, ... 33,48
 "   "   mill, meeting at, ... 56
 "   "   trading house, incident at, ... 96
 "   "   mention of, ... 237
Derr, Christian, notice of, ... 452
Derr, John, death of, ... 547
Derrickson, Mrs. Mary, account of capture of Fort Freeland, . . . 176
Dieffenbach, Reverend Jacob, ... 369
Disbury, Joseph, ... 231
Dixon, Sankey, ... 243
Dog run, ... 7,32
Domestic incidents, ... 392,463
Donnel, Charles G., ... 543
Doudle, Daniel, ... 387
Dougherty, Peter, ... 246
Dreisbach's church, ... 39,253
Dreisbach, Martin, ... 320
Drouth, severe, ... 488
Dry Valley, post office established at, ... 552
Dubbendorff, Reverend Samuel, ... 185
Duel, Binns-Stewart, ... 347
Duffield, George, D. D., quoted, ... 226
Duncan, Esquire, Thomas, ... 364
Eakers, Doctor Joseph, ... 26
Eclipses, ... 514
Egbert, John, stable burned, ... 533
Ejectment cases, ... 33,35,52,54,74,195,203,313
Election, certificate of first, ... 96
 "   contested, ... 148,216,239
 "   return of, 1783, ... 215
 "   returns, ... 288,334,373,437,448,457,460,463,522
 "   first, under new constitution, ... 266
 "   districts, ... 310,312,456,526
 "   of militia officers, ... 539,540
 "   presidential, ... 496
Electors, choice of first presidential, ... 257

Ellenkhusen, Mathias Joseph, ... 277
Ely, Reverend Doctor Ezra Styles, ... 506
Emerick family captured, ... 201
Emigration, sources of, ... 13
" to the West, ... 527
Encampments, ... 480,539,544,550
Etzweiler, George, killed, ... 185
Evans, Evan Rice, ... 323
" Captain Frederick, at Fort McHenry, ... 420
" " letters to George Kremer, ... 405,462
Ewing, Jasper, death of, ... 326
Ewig, Christian, notice of, ... 452
Factories, woolen, ... 538
Famine in Ireland and Scotland, ... 547
Farley, John, quoted, ... 247
Ferry at Sunbury, ... 44
" landing dispute, ... 313
" at Lewisburg, ... 274
Fires, ... 166,335,493,495,525,533,539,543,545,550,555
Fire storm, ... 512
Fisher's, Paul, statement, ... 157
Fisher, John, ... 157
Fisher's, Samuel, mill burned, ... 166
Fisher, Esquire, George, ... 364
Flag captured at Monmouth, ... 166
Floods, great, ... 232,488,513,546,548,552
Follmer, Thomas, drowned, ... 546
" Henry, drowned, ... 546
Forest iron-works, began building, ... 545
" " " in hands of sheriff, ... 549
" " " sold, ... 550
Forest Hill, post-office established at, ... 551
" " postmaster at, ... 551
Forster, John, incident related by, ... 179
" " death of, ... 239
" " killed, ... 187
" Lieutenant Thomas, ... 122
" Captain John, appointed postmaster, ... 555
Fort Augusta built, ... 13
" Freeland captured, ... 175
" Swartz, ... 193
" McHenry, bombardment of, ... 420
" " Captain Frederick Evans at, ... 420
Fought's, Jacob, mill, ... 34,38
Fought's, Mrs. Michael, narrative, ... 159
Fought and Trinkle murders, ... 206
Foutz, Mrs. Conrad, ... 494
Freeburg, residents of, ... 331
Freeman, definition of, ... 67
Frederick, Thomas, ... 340
French Jacob's, mill attack on, ... 185
" " " locality of, ... 186
Frick & Slifer's boat-yard removed to Lewisburg, . 551
Frick, Slifer & Co's steam saw-mill burned, ... 555
Frost, severe, ... 513
Frick, General Henry, death of, ... 543
Fries, Reverend, ... 398,410,442
" " obituary of, ... 534
Furnace built, ... 555
Gabriel, George, ... 9,17,37
Galbraith, Bertram, letter of, ... 156

ANNALS OF BUFFALO VALLEY.

Gazette, Sunbury, Northumberland, publication of, commenced,	269
Gazette, Columbia, publication of, commenced,	416
Geisweit, Reverend George,	285
German regiment at Sunbury,	179
German Reformed churches,	252
" " " first pastor of,	259
Gift, Aaron K., account of Lepley,	170
Gill, William, notice of,	23
Gordon, Isaac G., notice of,	542
Grant, Reverend William D., at Lewisburg,	543
Grave-yards—Dry Run,	187
Turtle Creek,	200
White Deer,	240
Presbyterian,	312
Evangelical,	434
German and Lutheran,	512
Gray, Lieutenant William,	119,224
" Captain William, death of,	431
" Lieutenant Colonel Neigal,	232
" George,	245
Green, Joseph,	66,141,151,210
" " death of,	335
" George, letter from,	287
" General Abbot, elected major general,	539
Green's mill,	75
Greenville laid out,	311
Gregg, Andrew, marriage of, &c.,	248
Grier, D. D., Reverend Isaac,	52,61,231,524,546
Grochong's, Jacob, Mill,	185,186
Grove, Peter, pursuit of Indians,	191
" Michael, kills an Indian,	192
" family notice of,	192
Guelph's mills, action near,	146
Gundy, Van Christian, recollections of,	97,171
" " " notice of,	242
Gundy, William, drowned,	546
Haines township, formerly Potter,	264
Halfpenny, J. & M., woolen factories,	538
Hall, Esquire, Charles,	324,364
Hammond, Lieutenant David,	81
" General R. H., death and burial of,	548
Harbaugh's Fathers, quoted,	199,399
Harbaugh, Reverend Henry,	543,548,550
Harding, General Abner C.,	501
Harris, Honorable William L., death of,	546
Hartley township, formerly Upper Moreland,	61
" " erected,	391
" Colonel Thomas,	163,316
" " " expedition of,	165
Hartleton,	316
Hayes, John, death of,	544
" William, store robbed,	492
" " death of, and notice of family,	540
" " incident of early life,	542
Heckewelder quoted,	201
Heim, Reverend John G.,	379
Heiser, H., appointed postmaster,	552
Heisler, Reverend D. Y., quoted,	286
" " " installed,	551
Herrold, killed,	170
Herrold tavern opened,	232

Hetrick, Christian,	66
" " killed,	208
Hickok, Henry C., appointed Deputy Superintendent Public Schools,	556
High's mill burned,	550
Himrod, Simon,	39,235
Hoffa's mills,	232
Hood, Reverend Thomas, ordination of,	346
" " " last sermon,	524
" " " death of,	549
" Mrs. Mary, death of,	549
Horse races,	496,499
" " anti association formed,	500
Hotels mentioned,	480
Housel, Captain William, death of,	551
Hucks, Captain, tory, killed,	42
Hughes, Napoleon, develops iron ore,	539
Huling, Marcus,	114,245
Hunt, Reverend Thomas P., lectures on temperance,	537
Hunter, Colonel Samuel, letters from,	143, 144,153,154,156,174,175,179,184,207
" " " pursues the Indians,	211
" " " death of,	234
Improvement act passed,	503
Improvements,	39,283,333,433
Indian tribes, localities of,	1
" paths,	6
" Muncy, leave the Valley,	20
" Delawares, withdraw,	20
" Six Nations,	97
" re-appear as enemies,	151,153,154,171,184,201,207,210
" Muncy, in Canada,	201
" married to whites,	202
" outrages,	208
Independent press of Lewisburg,	538,544
Inhabitants, 1775,	67
Insane lad in House of Representatives,	346
Insurance company, mutual fire, organized,	553
Iron ore, development of,	539
" works, Berlin, first metal at,	545
" " " blown out,	549
" " Forest, began building,	545
" " " in hands of sheriff,	549
" " " sold,	550
Irvine, William,	297
Irwin & Johnston,	35
Isle of Que,	245
Jack's mountain, name how derived,	8
Jackson township erected,	555
Jail, appropriation for,	64
Jay's treaty,	295
Jefferson's election, rejoicing over,	327,342
Jenkins' mill,	221
Johnson, Samuel, tried for firing a barn,	469
Jones, Esquire, Isaac G.,	524
Journal, Conrad Weiser's,	2
" Richard Miles',	53
" Major Ennion Williams',	63,84
" Flavel Roan's,	338,359,379,388,397,407
Jurors, grand, list of,	43,51,53,127,151
" " petition for appointment of judge,	513
" traverse, list of,	51,53,151,231

Keene, Major Lawrence, prothonotary, ... 214
Kelly, first settlers in, ... 34,53
Kelly, Colonel John, ... 35,141,144,153,179
" " " at Princeton, ... 139
" " " pursues the Indians, ... 172
" " " kills one near his cabin, ... 172
" " " toast of, ... 327
" " " sketch of, ... 506
" " " monument erected to, ... 524
Kelly, senior, James, opens temperence hotel in Lewisburg, ... 545
Kelly, Mrs. Sarah, ... 504
Kelly township reported as Pike, ... 461
" " erected, ... 462
Kempling or Kemplen, Captain—See *Campleton*.
Kennedy's Gazette suspended temporarily, [finally in 1817,] 416
Kennedy, A., appointed postmaster, ... 549
Kerstetter, George, notice of, ... 453
Kester, George, bequest of, ... 297
Kleckner, M., barn burned, ... 543
Kelchner, Jonas, death of, ... 539
Klinesmith, Baltzer, killed, ... 189
" " notice of his daughters, ... 190
Kremer, Honorable George, death of, ... 555
Lafayette lodge, officers of, ... 500
Laird, Matthew, notice of, and family, ... 255
Laird, Reverend Matthew, sails for Africa, ... 512
Lane, Elder William, ... 539
Land office, new purchase, ... 28
" locations, drawing of, ... 32
" valuation of, ... 60
Lashells, Esquire, John, death of, ... 547
Laughlin, Samuel, killed, ... 185
Lawyers, sketches of, ... 363
" peculiarities of, ... 481
Lechmere Point, skirmish at, ... 82
Lee, Major John, ... 126,204
" " " and wife killed, ... 210
" Thomas, ... 211
Lennox, George, ... 453
Lepley, Michael, killed, ... 170
Leroy, Jacob, ... 9
" John, ... 9
" Anna M., affidavit of, ... 12
Levy, Esquire, Daniel, ... 365
Lewisburg laid out, ... 237
" residents of, ... 238,
   242,253,269,279,282,301,322,332,337,354,356,370,379,387
" survey made of, ... 254
" merchants in, ... 311
" first postmaster at, ... 312
" incorporated, ... 406,456
" sketch of, in 1787, ... 254
" University, act incorporating, passed, ... 546
" Academy, ... 546
" postmaster at, ... 548,549
" cemetery at, ... 549
" Chronicle, publication of, began, ... 543
" University, extension of, ... 556
" sketch of, in 1813, ... 413
" explosion in drug store at, ... 525
" lecture at, ... 526

ANNALS OF BUFFALO VALLEY.

Lewis, Judge Ellis, commission read, ... 513
License, applications for, ... 43, 51, 167
" vote for and against, ... 547
Lieutenants of the county appointed, and subs, ... 127
Limestone township, original settlers of, ... 76
" " erected, ... 550
Lincoln, Lieutenant Hananiah, ... 124
" Mishael, ... 169
Line of Indian purchase, ... 17
Linn, John, notice of, ... 453
" J. F., diary of, ... 550
Locusts appear, ... 418, 455, 530
Logan, son of Shikellimy, ... 5
" death of, ... 5
Loskiel quoted, ... 4
Lottery, Derr's, ... 238
" for improvement of Penn's creek, ... 356
" advertisements, ... 487
Lowdon, Captain John, ... 49
" " " copy of his commission, ... 79
" " " roll of his company, ... 79
" " " letter to, from Hooper & Haines, ... 83
" " " company mustered out, ... 85
" " " letter to, from Speaker Jacobs, ... 126
" " " sketch of, ... 314
Lukens, John, death of, ... 262
Lutheran churches, ... 253, 430, 534, 543
Lutz, A. H., appointed postmaster, ... 551
McCabe, Esquire, R. B., sketches, ... 97, 168
McCandlish, George, ... 94
" William, house built, ... 74
" " 231
McClellan, Esquire, James, ... 393
" " " death of, ... 550
McClune's, James, school, ... 526
McClure, Alexander, appointed postmaster, ... 548
McCracken, Henry, killed, ... 193
McCormick, Seth, ... 246
" Thomas, ... 246
McHarge, Joseph, soldier, ... 167
McHenry, Henry, ... 211
McKim, Miller, delivers abolition lecture, ... 527
Mack and Grube, journal of, ... 5
Maclay, Honorable Samuel, sketch of, ... 401
Maclay, William, letters of, ... 155, 175
" " Native American letter, ... 184
" " elected United States Senator, ... 255
" R. P., appointed associate judge of Clarion county, ... 549
Macpherson, John, (Judge,) 166, 493
Mahantango township, inhabitants of, ... 308, 332
Mails, arrival and departure of, ... 327, 434
Manor, survey in Valley, ... 18
Manufactures, &c., review of, ... 269
Market quotations, ... 432, 441,
455, 457, 459, 497, 503, 513, 529, 539, 543, 544, 546, 547, 549, 551, 552, 555, 556
" public at New Berlin, ... 432
Marr, Reverend P. B., ordained and installed, ... 514
Marriages—
Alsbach, William, Catherine Shively, ... 490
Alter, Jacob, Ann Kessler, ... 438
Amberg, Hezekiah, Elizabeth Brooks, ... 485

39

ANNALS OF BUFFALO VALLEY.

Marriages—

Amberg Abraham, Charlotte Brooks,	500
Apple, Daniel, Susan Orwig,	486
Aurand, George, Mary Royer,	500
Baldy, General Christopher, Eve Metzgar,	384
Barber, Thomas, Betsy Clingan,	411
Barry, Elisha, Elizabeth Herbst,	430
Beeber, John, Anna Baker,	428
Benner, Mathias, Elizabeth Overmeier,	486
Benner, Henry, Mary Royer,	500
Billman, Jacob, Charity ———,	416
Billmyer, Martin, Margaret Himmelreich,	367
Black, David, Catherine Berry,	411
Bower, Joseph, Susanna Machamer,	384
Bower, Moses, Catherine Moyer,	390
Bower, George, Polly Smith,	390
Breyvogel, Jacob, Susanna Baldy,	329
Brobst, John, Lydia Marriner,	367
Brown, Peter, Catherine Kautz,	373
Burd, Levi, Eve Winegardner,	416
Burnside, Thomas, Mary Fleming,	367
Caldwell, James, Isabella Duncan,	490
Candor, Thomas, Margaret Montgomery,	485
Chamberlin, Aaron, Betsy Dale,	411
Chamberlin, John, Elizabeth Hayes,	490
Chamberlin, Joseph, Nancy Deal,	495
Charles, C. H., Juliette Mann,	500
Chestney, Jacob G., Juliana Cummings,	486
Christ, Esquire, L. B., Esther Bogar,	500
Coasin, Ludwig, Susanna Oliphant,	354
Cochran, junior, John, Anna M. Grove,	400
Dale, James, Eliza Bell,	441
Davis, William, Catherine Derr,	400
Derr, Jacob, Isabella Hunter,	495
Dersham, Samuel, Susanna Shadel,	416
Devling, John, Mary Wilson,	490
Devling Walter, Eliza Wilson,	499
Dickson, Jesse, Polly Merkle,	416
Donachy, Alexander, Fanny Seitz,	416
Dreisbach, Daniel, Katy Dreisbach,	330
Dreisbach, Martin, Elizabeth Kleckner,	470
Duncan, James, Sophia Maxwell,	485
Duncan, David, Susan Hayes,	495
Dunn, Washington, Betsy Musser,	390
Engleman, Michael, Barbara Gilman,	411
Epler, Peter, Eve Christ,	352
Evans, Evan Rice, Mrs. Forrest,	400
Forster, Robert, Jane Rutherford,	499
Forster, John, Margaret Vanvalzah,	495
Francis, William, Catherine Gettig,	435
Frederick, Philip, Christena Brown,	384
Freedly, John, Elizabeth Lehman,	373
Freedly, George, Catherine, Frantz,	373
Fruit, Robert, Maria Nevius,	411
Goodlander, Paul, Rachel Heckel,	416
Gregg, Andrew, Martha Potter,	248
Grier, Thomas, Rachel Stratton,	490
Grier, Doctor Joseph F., Margaret Graham,	499
Grove, Henry, Hannah Leisenring,	384
Grove, Simon, Mary Miller,	500
Grove, John, Sarah Montgomery,	411

ANNALS OF BUFFALO VALLEY.

Marriages—
Grove, Conrad, Mary Gingerich, ... 461
Gutelius, John P., Maria Aurand, ... 461
Hammond, Lieutenant R. H., Ann Eliza Duncan, ... 457
Haus, John, Margaret Roush, ... 495
Hayes, Robert, Emily Fields, ... 500
Hayes, John, Jane McFadden, ... 435
Hepburn, Samuel, Ann Clay, ... 400
Highland, William, Mary Gann, ... 390
Hill, Daniel K., Barbara Musser, ... 500
Hoffman, Michael, Lydia Wagner, ... 461
Housel, John, Margaret Musser, ... 493
Howard, Thomas, Elizabeth Harris, ... 311
Hutchinson, Samuel, Jennie Wallace, ... 390
Jodon, Francis, Elizabeth Cherry, ... 416
Johnston, John, Elizabeth Kress, ... 433
Jordan, Nathan, Hannah Smith, ... 470
Keenly, Daniel, Maria Richter, ... 416
Kelly, James, Hannah Seitz, ... 411
Kelly, William, Margaret Allison, ... 486
Kemp, Titus, Betsy Huntingdon, ... 435
Kirk, William, Jane Knox, ... 330
Kreechbaum, Peter, Elizabeth Davis, ... 367
Keechbaum, George, Polly Keller, ... 367
Laird, Reverend Matthew, Harriet Myer, ... 512
Lawshe, John, Polly Seitz, ... 352
Lawson, James, Nancy Clingan, ... 411
Lesher, Philip, Polly Billmyer, ... 416
Lewis, Paschall, Elizabeth Boude, ... 258
Linn, William, Jane Morrow, ... 470
Linn, John, Mary F. Chamberlin, ... 486
Linn, James F., Margaret Wilson, ... 490
Long, Peter, Sarah Moore, ... 438
Ludwig, Daniel, Sarah Hoffman, ... 486
Mackey, Mr., Abigail Iddings, ... 495
Maclay, John, Annie Dale, ... 411
Maclay, Robert P., Margaret C. Lashells, ... 486
Magee, Captain James, Elizabeth Strayhorn, ... 470
Magee, John, Susan Struble, ... 493
Maize, John, Elizabeth Jones, ... 486
Martin, David, Jane McClung, ... 208
Martin, Lawrence, Polly Juge, ... 384
Mauck, David, Nancy Shriner, ... 486
Mauck Jesse, Catherine Crotzer, ... 490
Merrill, James, Sarah Hepburn, ... 490
Metzgar, Abner, Eleanor Lawshe, ... 495
Meyer, Michael, Sarah Kelley, ... 390
Miller, William, Elizabeth Myers, ... 495
Mitchel, George, Eliza Anderson, ... 438
Mook, Daniel, Mary Dieffenbach, ... 486
Mook, George, Julia Fastnock, ... 430
Moore, Lewis, Dorothy Smith, ... 457
Montgomery, Robert, Nancy Knox, ... 384
Moyer, Henry, Polly Strickland, ... 435
Mussena, Henry B., Elizabeth Winter, ... 486
Myers, Henry, Hannah Walter, ... 500
Myers, Peter, Sophia Nixon, ... 373
McBeth, Andrew, Ann Linn, ... 438
McCormick, Saul, Catherine Hood, ... 493
McLaughlin, Hugh, Frances Derr, ... 495
McLaughlin, Hugh, Elizabeth McAllister, ... 416

Marriages—
Nesbit, William, Nancy Musser, ... 373
Nesbit, David, Mary Musser, ... 485
Orwig, John, Maria Bright, ... 486
Peters, Isaac, Susan Miller, ... 470
Pontius, Conrad, Mary Seebold, ... 470
Ranck, John, Nancy Luther, ... 384
Ranck, Joel, Sarah Long, ... 390
Ranck, Jonathan, Catherine Long, ... 430
Reedy, Jonathan, Amelia Buckner, ... 490
Rees, Jacob, Elizabeth Williamson, ... 430
Renner, Frederick, Magdalena Krause, ... 354
Roush, Samuel, Elizabeth Dunkle, ... 438
Row, John, Rachael Kunkle, ... 486
Selin, Anthony, Catherine Yoner, ... 390
Sergeant, John, Catherine Beyer, ... 354
Shannon, Daniel, Christena Pross, ... 430
Shaw, John, Margaret Baker, ... 500
Sheckler, Tobias, Catherine Fredericks, ... 296
Shriner, Daniel, Catherine Funston, ... 435
Sierer, John, Louisa McMillan, ... 384
Snyder, John, Margaret Hammond, ... 490
Snyder, John, Mary Kittera, ... 441
Snyder, George, Anna Ellen Duncan, ... 457
Snyder, Simon, Catherine Antes, ... 309
Stahl, Philip, Susanna Spotz, ... 390
Steadman, William C., Elizabeth Wilson, ... 470
Straub, Michael, Sarah Grove, ... 354
Strawbridge, Mr., Louisa Maus, ... 486
Strayer, Jacob, Rachael Harmony, ... 435
Strayhorn, Peter, —— Cornelius, ... 499
Strickland, Samuel, Elizabeth Turner, ... 430
Swartz, Peter, Magdalena Weyland, ... 49
Thompson, William, Susan Linn, ... 342
Troxell, George, Mary Hoffman, ... 354
Updike, Elijah, Elizabeth Snook, ... 400
Vandyke, John, Margaret Adams, ... 384
Vanvalzah, John A., Rebecca Chambers, ... 500
Wagner, Jacob, Rachael McGuire, ... 461
Walters, John, Susanna Moyer, ... 435
Wehr Jacob, Margaret Sassman, ... 430
Weiser, Conrad, Elizabeth Snyder, ... 390
Wetze., Jonathan, Hettie Hoff, ... 486
Wilson, Hugh, Catherine Irvine, ... 266
Wilson, Thomas, Mrs. —— Drake, ... 493
Wilson, William, Ruth Waddell, ... 499
Woods, junior, Christopher, Maria Little, ... 500
Yarger, John, Margaret Kelly, ... 493
Yost, John, Sarah Shaffer, ... 490
Zerbe, Henry, Susanna Heckel, ... 373
Zentmyer, Israel, Eve Snook, ... 500
Masonic procession, ... 493
    " Anti, excitement, ... 498
    " " delegate meeting, ... 519
Maynard's Clinton county quoted, ... 267
Meeting, anti school, ... 514
    " " " resolutions adopted, ... 515
    " " " delegates, list of, ... 516
    " " Masonic delegate, ... 519
    " native American, ... 544
    " railroad, at Mifflinburg, ... 546

ANNALS OF BUFFALO VALLEY.

Meeting, railroad, at Lewisburg,	552
" " New Berlin,	553
" " Potters's fort,	554
Meginness' West Branch quoted,	178,191,192,210,232,283
Merrill, James, address of,	506
" " death of,	538
Meteoric shower,	512
Meteor at New Berlin,	483
Mexican war, soldiers in,	547
Middleburg, residents of,	331
Middle creek, *alias* Christunn,	12
Mifflinburg laid out,	274
" residents of,	279,282,318,355,370,379,387
" first court held at,	418
" Academy, act establishing, passed,	492
" incorporated,	492
Miles, Colonel Samuel.	13
" Richard, journal,	53
Military record, 1861–5,	580
Militia officers,	90,102,104,108,241
" elections,	525,539,540
" companies of Valley,	539
Miller, Philip, appointed court-crier,	448
Miller, George F., barn burned,	545
Millerism excitement,	542
Mills built—Fought's,	38
Smith's,	60
Titzell's,	62
Barber's,	193
Weiser's fulling,	243
Farley's, John,	247
Farley's, Caleb,	258
Chillisquaque,	251
Penn's creek,	311
Barber's, Robert,	311
Wilt's,	327
steam flour,	554
Mingo, White, murder of,	24
Minutes of the Committee of Safety,	99,127
Mitman, J. M., appointed postmaster,	548
Mizener, Adam, captured,	188
Monckton, Colonel, sword of,	162
Monmouth, battle of,	159
Montelius, Honorable John, address to electors,	530
Montour, John,	169
Moore, Colonel James, quoted,	3,283
Morgan, Jacob, letter from,	153
Morrison, Reverend Hugh,	248
" " " his call,	249
" " " sermons of,	284
" " " difficulty with Maclay,	296,318
" " " dismissed,	329
Morton, Johnny, sketch of,	501
Mountains, mention of,	8
Mumma, Esquire, John, death of,	491
Musser's distillery burned,	539
Necrology of the Buffalo Valley,	564
Nesbit's, fire at,	335
Nevin, Doctor John W., preaches in Lewisburg,	547
New Berlin, residents of,	283,301,322,332,337,356,370,387
" " courts at,	429

ANNALS OF BUFFALO VALLEY.

New Berlin, plan of, made, ... 433
" " showman at, ... 482
" " meteor at, ... 483
" " incorporated, May 16, 1837.
Newcomer, Bishop, visits Valley, ... 299,325,413,429,434,489
Newspapers—Kennedy's Gazette, suspended temporarily, ... 416
            Columbia Gazette began publication, ... 416
            Andrew Kennedy's, junior, ... 418
            Union Hickory removed to Lewisburg, ... 497
            Sunbury Northumberland Gazette began publication, 269
            "   "   " suspended, ... 416
            Union Times, ... 457
            "   " editors of, ... 480,522,539
            Lewisburg Journal published, ... 501
            People's Advocate, at Lewisburg, suspended, ... 538
            Independent Press began publication, ... 538
            "   " editors of, ... 544
            Lewisburg Chronicle began publication, ... 543
            "   " editor of, ... 543,548,550,556
            Pittsburgh Daily, editor of, ... 544
            Items from Henry Shaup's Union, ... 432
            Union Star sold, ... 549
            Union Democrat, editor of, ... 549
            The Guardian, ... 550
Northumberland county erected, ... 40
"   " first officials of, ... 41
"   " " courts held in, ... 42
"   " " sheriff of, ... 44
"   " " suits in, ... 44
"   " bar, sketches of, ... 323
"   " recruiting in, ... 151
"   " divided into election districts, ... 238
Officers, application for land, ... 26
" grant of land to, ... 27
" survey of land, ... 30,37
" " meeting, reference to, ... 36
" militia, elected, ... 525,539
Officials, list of, ... 558
Orders, general, from Lieutenant Colonel Weirick's order book, . . 426
Overmeier's, Mrs., statement, ... 187
Paoli massacre, ... 143
Parr, Major James, ... 33,81
"   "   " roll of his company, ... 86
Pastors of Baptist church, ... 371
Patterson, Captain Samuel, monument erected to, ... 537
" W. A., death of, ... 555
Pealer, Captain, in Nittany valley, ... 154
Pence, Peter, ... 8
Penn, Thomas and Richard, purchase from Six Nations, ... 26
Penn's creek massacre, ... 8
" residents on, ... 10
" public highway, ... 36
" appropriations for improvements, ... 497
Penn's township, settlers of, ... 23,37,40
" bounds of, ... 42
" list of inhabitants, ... 91,150,
        182,194,209,214,237,242,245,253,263,269,280,284,294,313
Pensioners, United States, residing in Union county in 1840, ... 537
Pennsylvania convention, ... 65
Phreemer, Reverend John G., ... 275
Pickering's life, quoted, ... 242

ANNALS OF BUFFALO VALLEY.

Pickhard, John, case of, ... 137
" Nicholas, case of, ... 138
Piscataway, skirmishes at, ... 141,143
Pittsburgh Daily, editor of, ... 544
Plunket, William, expedition to Wyoming, ... 87
" " notice of, ... 271
Poak, James, family of, ... 213
Pohlhemus, Albert, family, ... 157
Pollock, John, opens store, ... 294
" Hugh, publishes pamphlet, ... 538
" Reverend Hugh, takes charge of Lewisburg Academy, ... 537
Political notes, ... 54,76,147,257,
   266,280,282,287,295,310,312,319,325,334,351,356,369,371,434,436,
   448,455,456,459,463,487,489,493,497,499,501,505,519,525,526,527,
   529, 533, 538,540,543,544,545,546,548,549,550,552,553,554,555,557
Pontius, Philip, statements, ... 187
" Henry, notice of, ... 458
Poor-house, vote for and against, ... 550
Post-offices established, ... 551,552
Potter township, erected, ... 53
" " name changed, ... 264
Potter, General James, ... 142,144,151,243
" " " letters to and from, ... 145,146,154,163,174,200
" " " death of, ... 261
Presbyterian church, Cross-Roads, ... 51,60,231,250,270,433
" " Lewisburg, ... 505,511
" " at New Berlin, ... 538,543
Presbytery of Northumberland, formed, ... 391
Prices current, ... 432,441,455,
   457,459,497,503,513,529,539,543,544,546,547,549,551,552,555,556
Price, Sergeant Thomas, ... 119
Priestly, Doctor Joseph, ... 343
Princeton, battle at, ... 139
Prohibitory liquor law, vote for and against, ... 555
Pumpkins, big, ... 534
Purchases, 1754, ... 8
   1758, ... 16
   1768, ... 26
Quinn, Esquire, David, incident related by, ... 158
" Samuel, commissioned, ... 194
Quinn's run, origin of name, ... 194
Rahauser, Reverend Jonathan, ... 259
Railroad incorporated, ... 526
" survey began, ... 526
" Sunbury and Erie, subscription to, ... 526
" Lewisburg, Centre, and Spruce Creek, incorporated, ... 554
" " " " survey began, ... 554
Read, William, case of, ... 135
Real estate, valuation of, by townships, ... 551
Reasoner, James, accident to, ... 526
Reber, Samuel, opens hotel, ... 501
Red Bank run, ... 25
Reed family, ... 25
Reger, Elias, notice of, ... 453
Reichel, Reverend W. C., notice of, ... 19
Reily, General, ... 544
Revival at Lewisburg, ... 543
Revolutionary soldiers, notices of, ... 449
" " at fourth of July celebration, ... 505
" struggle inaugurated, ... 76
Rifle battalion, notice of, ... 82

Rifle battalion, standard of, described,	85
Riflemen, ordered to be raised,	78
" enlisted at Derr's mill,	78
River, improvement of the,	260
Road—Fort Augusta to Lycoming creek,	44
Derr's to Narrows,	51,65
Great Plains to Sunbury,	51
Reuben Haines,	65
Bald Eagle to Sunbury,	86
Head of Penn's valley to J. Davidson's ferry,	251,252,259
Lewisburg, by Cross-Roads, to Mifflinburg,	252,487,495,496,497,499
Shirtz, at Narrows, to Colonel Clarke's lane,	252
Jenkins' mill to M. and L. road,	327
Milton to Derrstown and Mifflinburg road,	335
Jenkins' mill to Michael Smith's,	337
Gephart's to turnpike,	346
Brush valley to James Irwin's,	274
Wolfe's tavern to Buffalo creek,	274
Rockey's mills to Reznor's,	418
Reznor's saw-mill to Brush valley and Mifflinburg road,	418
Bellefonte to White Deer creek,	463
Lewisburg to Selinsgrove,	497
Mortonsville, by Hugh Wilson's and Derr's,	418,501
Chamberlin's mill to Kelly's saw-mill,	499
Turtle creek,	501
State, Heverling's mill to Elk creek,	537
Sugar Valley and White Deer,	552
Roan, Flavel,	243
" " poetry of,	292
" " journal of,	338,359,379,388,397,407
Robb's, Robert, case,	115,127
Robinson, John,	543
Roll of Captain John Lowdon's company,	79
" " James Parr's company,	86
" twelfth Pennsylvania,	124
" Captain John Clarke's company,	121
" soldiers captured at Fort Freeland,	179
" Captain James Thompson's company,	188
" " Casper Weitzel's company,	118
" " B. Weiser's company,	140
" " Peter Grove's company,	206
" " Samuel McGrady's company,	206
" Rangers,	207
" Captain Lowdon's company, 1784,	233
" " Donaldson's company, 1812,	408
" " Middleswarth's company, 1812,	410
" Field and staff of Lieutenant Colonel George Weirick's regiment,	421
" Captain Henry Miller's company,	421
" " Jacob Hummel's company,	422
" " Valentine Haas' company,	423
" " John Bergstresser's company,	424
" " William F. Buyers' company,	425
" " Ner Middleswarth's company,	427
Rope dancer at New Berlin,	464
Rorabaugh, Philip, notice of,	453
" " buried,	527
Rote, George, and his sister captured,	199
Row, George, killed,	193
Royal Grenadiers' flag captured,	159
Rumsey, John,	245

ANNALS OF BUFFALO VALLEY.

Runaway, the Great, 1778, ... 154,176
Rupp, I. D., quoted, ... 13
Salt-works, ... 480
Sample, John, and wife killed, ... 171
Sargent, John, removes, ... 525
Sawyer, Thomas, ... 499
Schools, ... 297,359,413,460
School, anti, meeting of, ... 514
  "   "   " resolutions adopted at, ... 515
  "   " delegate meeting, ... 516
  "   " delegates, list of, ... 516
  " vote for and against, ... 518,536
  " first county superintendent of, ... 555
  " Deputy Superintendent of Public, ... 556
Scull's map, ... 36
Seebold, Philip, ... 159
Selin, Captain Anthony, ... 276
Selinsgrove, residents of, ... 332
  " incorporated, ... 492
  " first hotel in, ... 232
Seminary, Union, at New Berlin, established, ... 556
Settlers, early, Penn township, ... 23
  "   " of Valley, ... 33,39,49,50,53,54,62
  " first Baptist, ... 283
Shamokin. now Sunbury, ... 2
  " original name of the country, ... 7
Shaeffer, Reverend Samuel, ... 546
Shikellimy, Viceroy, ... 2
  " residence of, ... 2
  " removes to Shamokin, ... 4
  " death of, ... 20
Shikellimy's old town, ... 3,32
Shikellimy, Loskiel's notice of, ... 4
Shively, Christian, statement of, ... 187,189
  " John, carried away, ... 199
Shoemaker, Charles L., ... 549
Showman at New Berlin, ... 482
Shows, character of, ... 527
Skeleton found, ... 555
Slaves, ... 74,242,299
Slenker, Honorable Isaac, ... 495
Smith, Catherine, petition of, ... 240
  " Widow, mills, ... 60,175,240
  "   " petition of, ... 240
  " Anna M., bequest of, ... 297
  " Esquire, Charles, sketch of, ... 363
  " Enoch, sketch of, ... 439
  " Ann, *alias* Carson, arrested, ... 433
  " Adam, sketch of, ... 453
  " Michael, statement of, ... 203
  " Matthew, letters of, ... 155,186
  "   " specimen record of, ... 209
  " John, of Buffalo, family of, ... 213
  " Daniel, ... 323,365
Snyder, Governor Simon, letter from, to George Kremer, ... 434
  "   "   " sketch of, ... 443
  " Antes, ... 446
  " George A., extracts from manuscript, ... 190,
                                     464,479,482,484,502,527,530,542
  " John, heirs of, law suit, *vs.* Simon Snyder, ... 465
Snyder county, erected, ... 556

ANNALS OF BUFFALO VALLEY.

Snow storms,	495,527,536,544
Social incidents,	392,463
Society, Union County agricultural,	528,554
" Susquehanna Bible, formed,	433
" debating,	491
Soldiers, revolutionary, notices of,	449
" list of, from Union county in Mexican War,	547
Soult, David,	470
Spangenberg, Reverend Cyriacus, notice of,	217
" " " executed for murder,	218
Spalding, Captain Simon, testimony,	217
Speddy, William,	46
Spyker, Henry, house built,	294
" " notice of,	439
Stanford, Jacob, killed,	153
Starret's mill burned,	175
Steam flour-mill built,	554
Straubstown, residents of,	331
Stevens, Ephraim,	481
Still bursted,	492
Stony Point captured,	175
Storms, David, killed,	208
Storm, heavy north-east,	552
Stove, Hathaway cooking, manufacture of begun,	539
Strickland, Timothy,	453
Strubble, Peter, death of,	549
Stump, Frederick, murders by,	24
Suits, act passed transferring all unsettled, to Union county,	418
Sullivan, General, letter from,	174
Sunbury laid out,	43
" Northumberland Gazette,	269
Sunderland, Daniel,	247
Supreme Court justices opinion of Ritner,	498
" *personnel* of justices of,	498
" middle district created,	356
Surveys, first,	19,28
" officers, made,	30
" early,	34,38,48,52,61,75,237
Surveyors, deputy, appointed,	257
Susquehanna declared a highway,	36
" survey of,	264
Swan, Samuel,	246
Swartz, Peter, marriage of,	49
" " house burned,	157
Swartzel, Esquire, H.,	47
Swesey, Daniel, notice of,	453
Swineford's hotel,	247
" murder of,	488
Swinefordstown, residents of,	331
Switzer run,	7
" tract,	74
Synod, Philadelphia, met at Lewisburg,	548
Taggert, M. H., appointed postmaster,	552
Tannery burned,	525
Tan-yard at Buffalo Cross-Roads,	279
Tate, Edward,	210
Taxables, enumeration of, by townships,	551
Taylor, Thomas, anecdote of,	488
Teedyuscung, king of the Delawares,	19
Telegraph brought to Lewisburg,	552
Temperance associations formed,	483

Temperance society, ... 504
" efforts, ... 544
" sons of, organized, ... 545
Templeton, Samuel, death of, ... 490
Thompson, Captain James, narrative of, ... 195
Thornton, Doctor Thomas A. H., ... 549
Times, Union, publication of, began, ... 457
" " editors of, ... 522
Titzell's mill, ... 62
Tomato, as an edible, ... 443
Treaty at Fort Greenville, ... 223
Turtle creek, ... 7
Turnpikes, ... 495,496,497,552
Tusk, mammoth, dug up, ... 552
Union township, surveys, ... 34
" " erected, ... 429
" county, " 412
" Hickory, (newspaper,) removed to Lewisburg, ... 497
" furnace built, ... 555
" seminary at New Berlin established, ... 556
" " " " " officers of, ... 556
Utica, origin of, for girl's name, ... 489
University, Lewisburg, act to establish, passed, ... 546
" " first commencement, ... 552
" " graduating class, ... 552
" " change of presidents, ... 552
" " Academy building of, ground broken for, 548
Van Campen's narrative referred to, ... 191
Van Fleet, Cornelius, ... 245
Van Gundy, Christian, licensed, ... 51
" " narratives of, ... 91,171
" " notice of, ... 242
Vanvalzah, Doctor Robert, ... 253
" " " death of, ... 551
" " Thomas, ... 527
" Howard, accident to, ... 514
Vincent, Daniel, incident of, ... 178
Wagoner, Adam, house and mill burnt, ... 495
Walker, John, sequel to his murder, ... 212
Washington township erected, ... 239
" " inhabitants of, ... 239
Watson, Patrick, killed, ... 189
Watts, Esquire, David, ... 364
Weather record, ... 479,497,500,511,513,523,526,536
Wedding, first in the Valley, ... 49
" party, ... 463
Weeks, Rachel, ... 245
" Jesse, ... 246
Weirick, Lieutenant Colonel, order book, ... 426
Weiser, Conrad, journal of, ... 2
" Captain Benjamin, roll of his company, ... 140
Weisertown, residents of, ... 332
Weisner, Thomas, ... 245
Weitzel, Captain Casper, letter of, ... 77
" " " roll of his company, ... 140
" " " death of, ... 213
Welch, Clinton, drowned, ... 556
West Buffalo, early settlers in, ... 54
Wheat, fall of, ... 405
Whisky insurrection, incidents of, ... 286
White Deer creek—Opaghtanoten, ... 7

White Deer mills built, ... 60
   "   "   " burned, ... 175
   "   " township erected, ... 89
   "   "   " inhabitants of, ... 149,182,
                     194,214,232,236,242,244,253,258,274,279,284,294,
                     305,310,317,326,332,337,340,354,355,370,379,387
   "   "   " valuation of, ... 299
   "   " distilleries in, ... 260
   "   " election district, ... 310
   "   " Hole valley, people of, ... 245
White Mingo, murder of, ... 24
Whitman, Professor, J. S., elected county superintendent, ... 555
Weirbach's, John, daughter captured, ... 206
Williams', Major Ennion, journal, ... 63,84
Wilson, John, ... 33
Wilson, Judge William, ... 81,159,162
     " William, Doctor T. H., grandfather, ... 49,188
     " Thomas, ... 320
     "   " of Kelly, death of, ... 504
     " William, of Kelly, ... 470
     " Honorable Hugh, death of, ... 545
     " Hugh, of Buffalo, notice of, ... 545
Winfield post-offce established, ... 552
Witchraft farce, ... 484
Withington, Captain Peter, ... 124
         " Martin opens hotel, ... 269
Wolfe's, John, barn burned, ... 545
Wolfinger, John F., quoted, ... 94,143,245
Wolves perish from cold, ... 523
Woolen factories, ... 538
Worden, O. N., quoted, ... 45,283,371,548
Wright, John, (erratum for Weight, read Wright,) 422
Yellow fever, ... 280
Yeomans, Doctor, preaches at Lewisburg, ... 548
Yiesely, Michael, notice of, ... 454
Young, Margaret, story of, ... 197,251
   " James, death of, ... 481

SUPPLEMENTAL NOTE.

After these Annals had gone to press, John Jordan, junior, Esquire, of Philadelphia, found in the library of the Archives of the Moravian Church, at Bethlehem, the Narrative of Anne LeRoy and Barbara Leininger, referred to upon page 12. He writes: "it is in the German language, fourteen pages, and bound in one of the five volumes entitled '*Varia*,' in that library, of which Bishop Edward de Schweintz is custodian. It purports to be taken from the lips of the parties, but does not give exact information of the precise places where the girls were captured. They lived on adjoining farms, some miles from Shamokin. They were taken in October, 1755, and reached Philadelphia May 6, 1759."

I am glad the occasion for a note enables me to acknowledge my obligations to WILLIAM H. EGLE, M. D., of Harrisburg, for many valuable suggestions, and for his intelligent and laborious supervision of the proofs; but for which, in a book containing such an abundance of names and dates, many errors other than those which may possibly be found must have occurred.

JOHN BLAIR LINN.

July 18, 1877.

www.ingramcontent.com/pod-product-compliance
Lightning Source LLC
Chambersburg PA
CBHW071429300426
44114CB00013B/1361